AF779003

UNITED STATES LEGISLATION
on
FOREIGN RELATIONS
and
INTERNATIONAL COMMERCE

Selected Texts

1987 - 1990

Compiled and Edited by
IGOR I. KAVASS

William S. Hein & Co., Inc.
Buffalo, New York
1997

Copyright © 1997 by William S. Hein & Co., Inc.
1285 Main Street, Buffalo, New York 14209

Library of Congress Card Number 76-51898
ISBN 0-930342-00-3 (The Set)
ISBN 1-57588-124-1

Printed in the United States of America.

The quality of this reprint is equivalent to the quality of the original work.

This volume is printed on acid-free paper by William S. Hein & Co., Inc.

INTRODUCTION

With this volume, *United States Legislation on Foreign Relations and International Commerce* acquires a new format. It becomes a collection of the texts of the major legislative measures and statements on international matters enacted by the United States Congress annually, beginning with the 100th Congress (1987). Depending on the content and character of the legislation, the collection includes the full texts of the relevant laws, or individual parts or sections thereof. The criteria for inclusion is based on several considerations:

- ➢ the particular law, part of a law, or a section expresses Congressional opinion on matters relating to the conduct of United States foreign policy, or expresses the view of Congress on international defense and security, economic issues of international character, international environmental and human rights issues, or other questions of international character or significance;
- ➢ the law recognizes and enables the performance of United States international obligations, especially its obligations under treaties and other international agreements to which it is a party;
- ➢ the law regulates the conduct and performance of international trade, as well as finance, investments, and other matters of economic character which include foreign or international elements;
- ➢ the law deals with international security actions and commitments; or
- ➢ the law expresses United States practice in international law.

Laws dealing with the appropriation or authorization of funds for the performance of United States international activities and commitments are not included in the collection. However, policy statements or substantive provisions of an international character, contained in appropriation or authorization laws are included.

The collection is arranged chronologically. The content is fully indexed by subjects and keywords. The index is regularly cumulated. There are several tables and lists for easier accessibility of the content, including a numerical list of treaties and international agreements referred to in the legislation contained in the volume, as well as a list of relevant United Nations resolutions and important declarations or decisions of other international organizations.

The first six volumes of *United States Legislation on Foreign Relations and International Commerce* consisted of annotated chronological lists and comprehensive subject indexes of all public laws and joint resolutions of the United States Congress which directly or indirectly related to the international activities and expectations of this country. These volumes cover United States legislation from the 1st Congress in 1789 through the 99th Congress in 1986, and they include references even to authorizations and appropriations of funds for international purposes. In the 1980s, however, such authorizations and appropriations became too numerous and too detailed to be of documentary research significance. Tracking such minutiae became counter-productive. At the same time, significant legislation of substantive nature on matters of international character or content, especially in the development of international trade, began to emerge from Congress. Increasingly there was a need for a chronologically arranged full-text collection of the major "international" laws of the United States. Hence the change in the format and scope of *United States Legislation on Foreign Relations and International Commerce*.

The collection will be updated regularly. The indexes, tables and lists will be cumulated simultaneously with each update to ensure complete accessibility of the material.

Igor Kavass
June 1997

General Table of Contents

Analytical Table of Laws in This Volume

Summary List of Laws in This Volume

Alphabetical List of Laws in This Volume

Alphabetical List of Treaties and Other International Agreements Cited in This Volume

Numerical List of Treaties and Other International Agreements Cited in This Volume

United Nations General Assembly Resolutions Cited in This Volume

United Nations Security Council Resolutions Cited in This Volume

Parallel Table of Congressional Sessions and Dates

100th Congress 1st Session:	Jan. 6, 1987 - Dec. 22, 1987
100th Congress 2nd Session:	Jan. 25, 1988 - Oct. 22, 1988
101st Congress 1st Session:	Jan. 3, 1989 - Nov. 22, 1989
101st Congress: 2nd Session:	Jan. 23, 1990 - Oct. 28, 1990

Parallel Table of Statutes and Public Laws Cited in This Volume

Statute	Public Law
100 STAT. 391	100-71
101 STAT. 711	100-96
101 STAT. 899	100-159
101 STAT. 913	100-169
101 STAT. 1019	100-180
101 STAT. 1329	100-202
101 STAT. 1331	100-204
101 STAT. 1458	100-220
101 STAT. 1484	100-222
102 STAT. 62	100-276
102 STAT. 437	100-300
102 STAT. 452	100-305
102 STAT. 591	100-330
102 STAT. 660	100-350
102 STAT. 883	100-377
102 STAT. 903	100-383
102 STAT. 1107	100-418
102 STAT. 1851	100-449
102 STAT. 1918	100-456
102 STAT. 2270	100-463
102 STAT. 2306	100-478
102 STAT. 2504	100-502
102 STAT. 2651	100-530
102 STAT. 2853	100-568
102 STAT. 2897	100-576
102 STAT. 3045	100-606
102 STAT. 3286	100-629
102 STAT. 3969	100-669
102 STAT. 4181	100-690
103 STAT. 37	101-14
103 STAT. 162	101-62
101 STAT. 988	101-162
103 STAT. 1195	101-167
103 STAT. 1298	101-179
103 STAT. 1352	101-189
103 STAT. 1853	101-216
103 STAT. 1870	101-219
103 STAT. 1892	101-222
103 STAT. 1954	101-231

Statute	Public Law
103 STAT. 2492	101-240
104 STAT. 7	101-243
104 STAT. 15	101-246
104 STAT. 201	101-298
104 STAT. 285	101-317
104 STAT. 448	101-369
104 STAT. 484	101-380
104 STAT. 629	101-382
104 STAT. 1389	101-509
104 STAT. 1485	101-510
104 STAT. 1979	101-513
104 STAT. 2240	101-519
104 STAT. 2344	101-533
104 STAT. 2380	101-541
104 STAT. 2713	101-550
104 STAT. 2863	101-580
104 STAT. 2943	101-592
104 STAT. 2975	101-594
104 STAT. 3066	101-604
104 STAT. 3096	101-606
104 STAT. 3188	101-611
104 STAT. 3340.	101-620
104 STAT. 3350	101-623
104 STAT. 4436	101-627
104 STAT. 4789	101-647

UNITED STATES LEGISLATION
on
FOREIGN RELATIONS
and
INTERNATIONAL COMMERCE

Selected Texts

1987 - 1990

CENTRAL AMERICAN PEACE RESOLUTION, 1988

Joint Resolution to provide assistance and support for peace, democracy, and reconciliation in Central America.

Date: April 1, 1988

Bill No.: H.J. Res. 523

Public Law No.: 100-276

Cite: 102 STAT. 62

Sections reprinted:

Section 1 - General policy
Section 2 - Consistency with Sapoa Agreement
Section 3 - Purpose of additional assistance for the Nicaraguan democratic resistance

Public Law 100-276
100th Congress
Joint Resolution

To provide assistance and support for peace, democracy, and reconciliation in Central America.

Resolved by the Senate and House of Representatives of the United States of America in Congress assembled,

SECTION 1. GENERAL POLICY.—It is the policy of the United States to advance peace and democracy in Central America, and to preserve and protect security interests in the region. Pursuant to that policy, it is the purpose of this joint resolution to assist in bringing peace and democracy to Central America, in a manner compatible with the Guatemala Peace Accord of August 7, 1987, the Declaration of the Presidents of the Central American Nations at San Jose, Costa Rica on January 16, 1988, the Agreement Between the Government of Nicaragua and the Nicaraguan Resistance signed March 23, 1988 at Sapoa, Nicaragua (hereinafter referred to as the "Sapoa Agreement") and consistent with the national security interests of the United States.

SEC. 2. CONSISTENCY WITH SAPOA AGREEMENT.—The assistance and support for which this joint resolution provides shall be administered consistent with the Sapoa Agreement. No authority contained in this joint resolution is intended to be exercised in any manner that might be determined by the Verification Commission established by the Sapoa Agreement to be inconsistent with that Agreement or any subsequent agreement between the Government of Nicaragua and the Nicaraguan democratic resistance.

SEC. 3. PURPOSE OF ADDITIONAL ASSISTANCE FOR THE NICARAGUAN DEMOCRATIC RESISTANCE.—(a) CONGRESSIONAL INTENT.—It is the intention of Congress in providing additional assistance to the Nicaraguan democratic resistance to reinforce the Central American peace process by supporting negotiations leading to a permanent negotiated ceasefire agreement. Such an agreement is seen by the Congress as an essential step towards the establishment of peace and democracy in Nicaragua. The Congress provides assistance under this section with the understanding and strong expectation that the Government of Nicaragua and the Nicaraguan democratic resistance will cease permanently offensive military activities against each other and engage in good faith negotiations towards a permanent ceasefire.

(b) TRANSFER AND USE.—(1) The President is authorized to transfer to the Agency for International Development $17,700,000 of unobligated funds from the appropriations accounts specified in section 6 to provide assistance for the Nicaraguan democratic resistance in accordance with this joint resolution. Funds so transferred shall remain available through September 30, 1988.

(2) The amount which is authorized to be transferred under paragraph (1) shall be reduced by the cost to the United States Government of any items or services described in subsection (c)(1) which were previously, specifically authorized by law for the Nica-

raguan democratic resistance and which are delivered to the Nicaraguan democratic resistance under subsection (e).

(c) DESCRIPTION OF ASSISTANCE ALLOWED.—(1) As used in this section, "assistance" means only food, clothing, shelter, medical services, medical supplies, and payment for such items or services.

(2) The term "assistance" under this section also includes, to the extent consistent with the Sapoa Agreement, the use of not to exceed $1,500,000 of the funds made available under subsection (b) for the purchase of communications equipment.

(d) LIMITATIONS.—The amount of funds transferred under subsection (b) which is obligated each month for purchasing items and services described in subsection (c)(1)—

(1) for April and May 1988, shall not exceed $2,900,000, of which not less than $400,000 each month shall be available only for medical supplies and medical services; and

(2) for any month thereafter, shall not exceed $2,700,000,

except that each such amount for any month shall be reduced by the cost to the United States Government of the items and services described in subsection (c)(1) (medical supplies and medical services in the case of the second amount specified in paragraph (1)) which were previously, specifically authorized by law for the Nicaraguan democratic resistance and which are delivered to the Nicaraguan democratic resistance under subsection (e) during that month.

(e) TRANSPORTATION.—(1) The President shall transfer to the Agency for International Development, from unobligated funds from the appropriations accounts specified, in section 6, such funds as may be necessary to provide, to the extent consistent with the Sapoa Agreement, transportation for the assistance authorized by subsection (b), including rental and indemnification of aircraft, trucks or other vehicles, and transportation for the items and services described in paragraph (3) of this subsection.

(2) Transportation provided under this subsection may not be used to deliver any assistance for the Nicaraguan democratic resistance other than the assistance authorized by subsection (b) and the items and services described in paragraph (3) of this subsection.

(3) Transportation may be provided under this subsection for items and services described in subsection (c)(1) which were previously, specifically authorized by law for the Nicaraguan democratic resistance.

(f) PROHIBITIONS.—(1) Funds transferred by subsections (b) or (e) may not be obligated or expended to purchase aircraft or weapons, weapons systems, or ammunition or any other item or service not permitted under subsection (c) or to provide any transportation other than transportation permitted under subsection (e).

(2) Except for items delivered under subsection (e)(3), no item authorized by "Title II—Central America" in section 101(k) of the continuing appropriations resolution for the fiscal year 1987 (Public Laws 99-500 and 99-591) or section 111 of the joint resolution making further continuing appropriations for the fiscal year 1988 (Public Law 100-202) may be provided to the Nicaragua democratic resistance.

(g) ASSISTANCE FOR YATAMA.—(1) In order to support all elements of the Nicaraguan democratic resistance, assistance authorized by subsection (b) (including the cost of the United States Government of items and services delivered under subsection (e)(3)) in the amount of $2,190,000 shall be provided only to the Indian resistance force known as Yatama.

(2) The Agency for International Development shall ensure that assistance under this subsection for Yatama is provided consistent with the Preliminary Accord signed by Yatama and the Government of Nicaragua on February 2, 1988, and any subsequent agreement based on that Accord.

INTERNATIONAL CHILD ABDUCTION REMEDIES ACT, 1988

An Act to establish procedures to implement the Convention on the Civil Aspects of International Child Abduction, done at The Hague on October 25, 1980, and for other purposes.

Date: April 29, 1988

Bill No.: H.R. 3971

Public Law No.: 100-300

Cite: 102 STAT. 437

Sections reprinted: All

Note: The Convention is published as TIAS 11670 (KAV 2312)

Public Law 100–300
100th Congress

An Act

To establish procedures to implement the Convention on the Civil Aspects of International Child Abduction, done at The Hague on October 25, 1980, and for other purposes.

Be it enacted by the Senate and House of Representatives of the United States of America in Congress assembled,

SECTION 1. SHORT TITLE.

This Act may be cited as the "International Child Abduction Remedies Act".

SEC. 2. FINDINGS AND DECLARATIONS.

(a) FINDINGS.—The Congress makes the following findings:

(1) The international abduction or wrongful retention of children is harmful to their well-being.

(2) Persons should not be permitted to obtain custody of children by virtue of their wrongful removal or retention.

(3) International abductions and retentions of children are increasing, and only concerted cooperation pursuant to an international agreement can effectively combat this problem.

(4) The Convention on the Civil Aspects of International Child Abduction, done at The Hague on October 25, 1980, establishes legal rights and procedures for the prompt return of children who have been wrongfully removed or retained, as well as for securing the exercise of visitation rights. Children who are wrongfully removed or retained within the meaning of the Convention are to be promptly returned unless one of the narrow exceptions set forth in the Convention applies. The Convention provides a sound treaty framework to help resolve the problem of international abduction and retention of children and will deter such wrongful removals and retentions.

(b) DECLARATIONS.—The Congress makes the following declarations:

(1) It is the purpose of this Act to establish procedures for the implementation of the Convention in the United States.

(2) The provisions of this Act are in addition to and not in lieu of the provisions of the Convention.

(3) In enacting this Act the Congress recognizes—

(A) the international character of the Convention; and

(B) the need for uniform international interpretation of the Convention.

(4) The Convention and this Act empower courts in the United States to determine only rights under the Convention and not the merits of any underlying child custody claims.

SEC. 3. DEFINITIONS.

For the purposes of this Act—

(1) the term "applicant" means any person who, pursuant to the Convention, files an application with the United States

Central Authority or a Central Authority of any other party to the Convention for the return of a child alleged to have been wrongfully removed or retained or for arrangements for organizing or securing the effective exercise of rights of access pursuant to the Convention;

(2) the term "Convention" means the Convention on the Civil Aspects of International Child Abduction, done at The Hague on October 25, 1980;

(3) the term "Parent Locator Service" means the service established by the Secretary of Health and Human Services under section 453 of the Social Security Act (42 U.S.C. 653);

(4) the term "petitioner" means any person who, in accordance with this Act, files a petition in court seeking relief under the Convention;

(5) the term "person" includes any individual, institution, or other legal entity or body;

(6) the term "respondent" means any person against whose interests a petition is filed in court, in accordance with this Act, which seeks relief under the Convention;

(7) the term "rights of access" means visitation rights;

(8) the term "State" means any of the several States, the District of Columbia, and any commonwealth, territory, or possession of the United States; and

(9) the term "United States Central Authority" means the agency of the Federal Government designated by the President under section 7(a).

SEC. 4. JUDICIAL REMEDIES.

(a) JURISDICTION OF THE COURTS.—The courts of the States and the United States district courts shall have concurrent original jurisdiction of actions arising under the Convention.

(b) PETITIONS.—Any person seeking to initiate judicial proceedings under the Convention for the return of a child or for arrangements for organizing or securing the effective exercise of rights of access to a child may do so by commencing a civil action by filing a petition for the relief sought in any court which has jurisdiction of such action and which is authorized to exercise its jurisdiction in the place where the child is located at the time the petition is filed.

(c) NOTICE.—Notice of an action brought under subsection (b) shall be given in accordance with the applicable law governing notice in interstate child custody proceedings.

(d) DETERMINATION OF CASE.—The court in which an action is brought under subsection (b) shall decide the case in accordance with the Convention.

(e) BURDENS OF PROOF.—(1) A petitioner in an action brought under subsection (b) shall establish by a preponderance of the evidence—

(A) in the case of an action for the return of a child, that the child has been wrongfully removed or retained within the meaning of the Convention; and

(B) in the case of an action for arrangements for organizing or securing the effective exercise of rights of access, that the petitioner has such rights.

(2) In the case of an action for the return of a child, a respondent who opposes the return of the child has the burden of establishing—

(A) by clear and convincing evidence that one of the exceptions set forth in article 13b or 20 of the Convention applies; and

(B) by a preponderance of the evidence that any other exception set forth in article 12 or 13 of the Convention applies.

(f) APPLICATION OF THE CONVENTION.—For purposes of any action brought under this Act—

(1) the term "authorities", as used in article 15 of the Convention to refer to the authorities of the state of the habitual residence of a child, includes courts and appropriate government agencies;

(2) the terms "wrongful removal or retention" and "wrongfully removed or retained", as used in the Convention, include a removal or retention of a child before the entry of a custody order regarding that child; and

(3) the term "commencement of proceedings", as used in article 12 of the Convention, means, with respect to the return of a child located in the United States, the filing of a petition in accordance with subsection (b) of this section.

(g) FULL FAITH AND CREDIT.—Full faith and credit shall be accorded by the courts of the States and the courts of the United States to the judgment of any other such court ordering or denying the return of a child, pursuant to the Convention, in an action brought under this Act.

(h) REMEDIES UNDER THE CONVENTION NOT EXCLUSIVE.—The remedies established by the Convention and this Act shall be in addition to remedies available under other laws or international agreements.

SEC. 5. PROVISIONAL REMEDIES.

(a) AUTHORITY OF COURTS.—In furtherance of the objectives of article 7(b) and other provisions of the Convention, and subject to the provisions of subsection (b) of this section, any court exercising jurisdiction of an action brought under section 4(b) of this Act may take or cause to be taken measures under Federal or State law, as appropriate, to protect the well-being of the child involved or to prevent the child's further removal or concealment before the final disposition of the petition.

(b) LIMITATION ON AUTHORITY.—No court exercising jurisdiction of an action brought under section 4(b) may, under subsection (a) of this section, order a child removed from a person having physical control of the child unless the applicable requirements of State law are satisfied.

SEC. 6. ADMISSIBILITY OF DOCUMENTS.

With respect to any application to the United States Central Authority, or any petition to a court under section 4, which seeks relief under the Convention, or any other documents or information included with such application or petition or provided after such submission which relates to the application or petition, as the case may be, no authentication of such application, petition, document, or information shall be required in order for the application, petition, document, or information to be admissible in court.

SEC. 7. UNITED STATES CENTRAL AUTHORITY.

(a) DESIGNATION.—The President shall designate a Federal agency to serve as the Central Authority for the United States under the Convention.

(b) FUNCTIONS.—The functions of the United States Central Authority are those ascribed to the Central Authority by the Convention and this Act.

(c) REGULATORY AUTHORITY.—The United States Central Authority is authorized to issue such regulations as may be necessary to carry out its functions under the Convention and this Act.

(d) OBTAINING INFORMATION FROM PARENT LOCATOR SERVICE.—The United States Central Authority may, to the extent authorized by the Social Security Act, obtain information from the Parent Locator Service.

SEC. 8. COSTS AND FEES.

(a) ADMINISTRATIVE COSTS.—No department, agency, or instrumentality of the Federal Government or of any State or local government may impose on an applicant any fee in relation to the administrative processing of applications submitted under the Convention.

(b) COSTS INCURRED IN CIVIL ACTIONS.—(1) Petitioners may be required to bear the costs of legal counsel or advisors, court costs incurred in connection with their petitions, and travel costs for the return of the child involved and any accompanying persons, except as provided in paragraphs (2) and (3).

(2) Subject to paragraph (3), legal fees or court costs incurred in connection with an action brought under section 4 shall be borne by the petitioner unless they are covered by payments from Federal, State, or local legal assistance or other programs.

(3) Any court ordering the return of a child pursuant to an action brought under section 4 shall order the respondent to pay necessary expenses incurred by or on behalf of the petitioner, including court costs, legal fees, foster home or other care during the course of proceedings in the action, and transportation costs related to the return of the child, unless the respondent establishes that such order would be clearly inappropriate.

SEC. 9. COLLECTION, MAINTENANCE, AND DISSEMINATION OF INFORMATION.

(a) IN GENERAL.—In performing its functions under the Convention, the United States Central Authority may, under such conditions as the Central Authority prescribes by regulation, but subject to subsection (c), receive from or transmit to any department, agency, or instrumentality of the Federal Government or of any State or foreign government, and receive from or transmit to any applicant, petitioner, or respondent, information necessary to locate a child or for the purpose of otherwise implementing the Convention with respect to a child, except that the United States Central Authority—

(1) may receive such information from a Federal or State department, agency, or instrumentality only pursuant to applicable Federal and State statutes; and

(2) may transmit any information received under this subsection notwithstanding any provision of law other than this Act.

(b) REQUESTS FOR INFORMATION.—Requests for information under this section shall be submitted in such manner and form as the United States Central Authority may prescribe by regulation and shall be accompanied or supported by such documents as the United States Central Authority may require.

(c) RESPONSIBILITY OF GOVERNMENT ENTITIES.—Whenever any department, agency, or instrumentality of the United States or of any State receives a request from the United States Central Authority for information authorized to be provided to such Central

Authority under subsection (a), the head of such department, agency, or instrumentality shall promptly cause a search to be made of the files and records maintained by such department, agency, or instrumentality in order to determine whether the information requested is contained in any such files or records. If such search discloses the information requested, the head of such department, agency, or instrumentality shall immediately transmit such information to the United States Central Authority, except that any such information the disclosure of which—

(1) would adversely affect the national security interests of the United States or the law enforcement interests of the United States or of any State; or

(2) would be prohibited by section 9 of title 13, United States Code;

shall not be transmitted to the Central Authority. The head of such department, agency, or instrumentality shall, immediately upon completion of the requested search, notify the Central Authority of the results of the search, and whether an exception set forth in paragraph (1) or (2) applies. In the event that the United States Central Authority receives information and the appropriate Federal or State department, agency, or instrumentality thereafter notifies the Central Authority that an exception set forth in paragraph (1) or (2) applies to that information, the Central Authority may not disclose that information under subsection (a).

(d) INFORMATION AVAILABLE FROM PARENT LOCATOR SERVICE.—To the extent that information which the United States Central Authority is authorized to obtain under the provisions of subsection (c) can be obtained through the Parent Locator Service, the United States Central Authority shall first seek to obtain such information from the Parent Locator Service, before requesting such information directly under the provisions of subsection (c) of this section.

(e) RECORDKEEPING.—The United States Central Authority shall maintain appropriate records concerning its activities and the disposition of cases brought to its attention.

SEC. 10. INTERAGENCY COORDINATING GROUP.

The Secretary of State, the Secretary of Health and Human Services, and the Attorney General shall designate Federal employees and may, from time to time, designate private citizens to serve on an interagency coordinating group to monitor the operation of the Convention and to provide advice on its implementation to the United States Central Authority and other Federal agencies. This group shall meet from time to time at the request of the United States Central Authority. The agency in which the United States Central Authority is located is authorized to reimburse such private citizens for travel and other expenses incurred in participating at meetings of the interagency coordinating group at rates not to exceed those authorized under subchapter I of chapter 57 of title 5, United States Code, for employees of agencies.

SEC. 11. AGREEMENT FOR USE OF PARENT LOCATOR SERVICE IN DETERMINING WHEREABOUTS OF PARENT OR CHILD.

Section 463 of the Social Security Act (42 U.S.C. 663) is amended—

(1) by striking "under this section" in subsection (b) and inserting "under subsection (a)";

(2) by striking "under this section" where it first appears in subsection (c) and inserting "under subsection (a), (b), or (e)"; and

(3) by adding at the end the following new subsection:

"(e) The Secretary shall enter into an agreement with the Central Authority designated by the President in accordance with section 7 of the International Child Abduction Remedies Act, under which the services of the Parent Locator Service established under section 453 shall be made available to such Central Authority upon its request for the purpose of locating any parent or child on behalf of an applicant to such Central Authority within the meaning of section 3(1) of that Act. The Parent Locator Service shall charge no fees for services requested pursuant to this subsection.".

SEC. 12. AUTHORIZATION OF APPROPRIATIONS.

There are authorized to be appropriated for each fiscal year such sums as may be necessary to carry out the purposes of the Convention and this Act.

Approved April 29, 1988.

LEGISLATIVE HISTORY—H.R. 3971:

HOUSE REPORTS: No. 100-525 (Comm. on the Judiciary).
CONGRESSIONAL RECORD, Vol. 134 (1988):
Mar. 28, considered and passed House.
Apr. 12, considered and passed Senate, amended.
Apr. 25, House concurred in Senate amendment.

SOVIET RELIGIOUS BELIEVERS PERSECUTION IN UKRAINE RESOLUTION, 1988

Joint Resolution deploring the Soviet Government's active persecution of religious believers in Ukraine.

Date: May 2, 1988

Bill No.: S. J. Res. 235

Public Law No.: 100-305

Cite: 102 STAT. 452

Sections reprinted: All

Public Law 100-305
100th Congress
Joint Resolution

Deploring the Soviet Government's active persecution of religious believers in Ukraine

Whereas 1988 marks the Millennium of the Christianity of Kievan Rus', adopted by Prince Volodymyr in a ceremony on the banks of the Dnieper River;

Whereas today freedom of religion is a fundamental right which is explicitly guaranteed by the Universal Declaration of Human Rights, the International Covenants on Human Rights, and the Final Act of the Conference on Security and Cooperation in Europe;

Whereas the Soviet Government has violated the Universal Declaration of Human Rights, the International Covenants on Human Rights, and the Final Act of the Conference on Security and Cooperation in Europe by engaging in the persecution of religious believers in the Soviet Union, including the systematic liquidation of the historic and national churches in Ukraine;

Whereas the Ukrainian Orthodox and Ukrainian Catholic churches, both forcibly liquidated in the 1930's and 1940's, respectively, have remained outlawed while their clergy and laity have been murdered, imprisoned, or exiled for their religious beliefs;

Whereas, despite decades of severe persecution, Ukrainian Orthodox and Ukrainian Catholic believers to this day continue to practice their faiths clandestinely for fear of persecution by Soviet authorities;

Whereas the Soviet Government has, in addition, sought to restrain and undermine the spiritual mission of the Evangelical Church in Ukraine, and has established restrictive legislation in direct contravention of the Biblical precepts that undergird the evangelical movement;

Whereas many members of the Ukrainian Evangelical churches, in particular unregistered Baptist and Pentecostal congregations, are currently imprisoned and harassed for their faith;

Whereas suspected clergy and lay members of the Ukrainian Orthodox, Ukrainian Catholic, Baptist, and Pentecostal churches are victimized by job discrimination, their access to religious literature is restricted, and they are subject to various forms of harassment such as house searches, interrogations, and arbitrary arrests by Soviet authorities;

Whereas, despite the Soviet government's policies of religious persecution in Ukraine, faith in God is widespread among Ukrainians as evidenced by the underground Ukrainian Catholic movement which embraces hundreds of priests headed by a number of secret bishops assisted by more than 1,000 religious women in orders; and

Whereas Ukrainian Catholic catacomb bishops, priests, and laity have placed themselves in direct danger of persecution by appealing to the Kremlin to end its prohibition of the Ukrainian Catholic Church: Now, therefore, be it

Resolved by the Senate and House of Representatives of the United States of America in Congress assembled, That the Congress of the United States deplores the Soviet Government's active persecution of religious believers in Ukraine, as well as the forcible liquidation of the Ukrainian Orthodox and Ukrainian Catholic Churches.

SEC. 2. On the occasion of the Millennium of Christianity in Kievan Rus', the Congress of the United States—

(1) discourages official participation by the Government of the United States in ceremonies of the Millennium in the Union of Soviet Socialist Republics, so long as individuals remain harassed and imprisoned for their religious beliefs, are denied access to religious literature and the opportunity to receive religious instruction, and the Ukrainian Catholic and Ukrainian Orthodox Churches remain outlawed;

(2) sends its greetings to the Ukrainian people as they mark this solemn event in the history of the Ukrainian nation;

(3) voices its concern for those Ukrainian religious believers who are persecuted for attempting to exercise their rights to religious worship;

(4) urges the President of the United States, the Secretary of State, the United States delegation to the United Nations, the United States Delegation to the Vienna Review Meeting of the Conference on Security and Cooperation in Europe to continue to speak out forcefully against violations of religious liberty throughout the Soviet Union and specifically in Ukraine during this anniversary year;

(5) calls upon the Soviet Government to abide by the Universal Declaration of Human Rights, the International Covenants on Human Rights, and the Final Act of the Conference on Security and Cooperation in Europe, and release all those imprisoned for their religious beliefs; and

(6) urges, in observance of the Christian Millennium, the Soviet Government to legalize the Ukrainian Orthodox and Ukrainian Catholic Churches.

Approved May 2, 1988.

LEGISLATIVE HISTORY—S.J. Res. 235:

CONGRESSIONAL RECORD, Vol. 134 (1988):
Mar. 4, considered and passed Senate.
Apr. 19, considered and passed House.

SOUTH PACIFIC TUNA ACT OF 1988

An Act to implement the Treaty on Fisheries between the Government of Certain Pacific Island States and the Government of the United States of America.

Date: June 7, 1988

Bill No.: S. 1989

Public Law No.: 100-330

Cite: 102 STAT. 591

Sections reprinted: All

Note 1: Amended by Section 4 of the German Democratic Republic Fishery Agreement Act, 1988 (Pub. L. No. 100-350)

Note 2: The treaty was made on April 2, 1987 (TIAS 11100)

Public Law 100–330
100th Congress

An Act

To implement the Treaty on Fisheries Between the Governments of Certain Pacific Island States and the Government of the United States of America.

Be it enacted by the Senate and House of Representatives of the United States of America in Congress assembled, That this Act may be cited as the "South Pacific Tuna Act of 1988".

SEC. 2. DEFINITIONS.

As used in this Act—

(1) The term "Administrator" means the individual or organization designated by the Pacific Island Parties to act on their behalf under the Treaty and notified to the United States Government.

(2) The term "Authorized Officer" means any officer who is authorized by the Secretary, or the Secretary of the department in which the Coast Guard is operating, or the head of any Federal or State agency which has entered into an enforcement agreement with the Secretary under section 10(a) of this Act.

(3) The term "Authorized Party Officer" means any officer authorized by a Pacific Island Party to enforce the provisions of the Treaty.

(4) The term "applicable national law" means any provision of law of a Pacific Island Party which is described in paragraph 1(a) of Annex I of the Treaty.

(5) The term "Closed Area" means any of the closed areas identified in Schedule 2 of Annex I of the Treaty.

(6) The term "fishing" means—

(A) searching for, catching, taking, or harvesting fish;

(B) attempting to search for, catch, take, or harvest fish;

(C) engaging in any other activity which can reasonably be expected to result in the locating, catching, taking, or harvesting of fish;

(D) placing, searching for, or recovering fish aggregating devices or associated electronic equipment such as radio beacons;

(E) any operations at sea directly in support of, or in preparation for, any activity described in this paragraph; or

(F) aircraft use, relating to the activities described in this paragraph except for flights in emergencies involving the health or safety of crew members or the safety of a vessel.

(7) The term "fishing vessel" or "vessel" means any boat, ship, or other craft which is used for, equipped to be used for, or of a type normally used for commercial fishing, and which is documented under the laws of the United States.

(8) The term "Licensing Area" means all waters in the Treaty Area except for—

(A) those waters subject to the jurisdiction of the United States in accordance with international law;

(B) those waters within Closed Areas; and

(C) those waters within Limited Areas closed to fishing.

(9) The term "licensing period" means the period of validity of licenses issued in accordance with the Treaty.

(10) The term "Limited Area" means any area so identified in Schedule 3 of Annex I of the Treaty.

(11) The term "operator" means any person who is in charge of, directs or controls a vessel, including the owner, charterer, and master.

(12) The term "Pacific Island Party" means a Pacific Island nation which is a party to the Treaty.

(13) The term "Party" means a nation which is a party to the Treaty.

(14) The term "person" means any individual (whether or not a citizen or national of the United States), any corporation, partnership, association, or other entity (whether or not organized or existing under the laws of any State), and any Federal, State, local, or foreign government or any entity of any such government.

(15) The term "Secretary" means the Secretary of Commerce, or the designee of the Secretary of Commerce.

(16) The term "State" means each of the several States, the District of Columbia, the Commonwealths of Puerto Rico and the Northern Mariana Islands, American Samoa, the Virgin Islands, Guam, and any other Commonwealth, territory, or possession of the United States.

(17) The term "Treaty" means the Treaty on Fisheries Between the Governments of Certain Pacific Island States and the Government of the United States of America, signed in Port Moresby, Papua New Guinea, April 2, 1987, and its Annexes, Schedules, and implementing agreements.

(18) The term "Treaty Area" means the area so described in paragraph 1(k) of Article 1 of the Treaty.

SEC. 3. APPLICATION TO OTHER LAWS.

The seizure by a Pacific Island Party of a vessel of the United States shall not be determined to be a seizure described in section 205(a)(4)(C) of the Magnuson Fishery Conservation and Management Act (16 U.S.C. 1825(a)(4)(C)) or section 2 of the Fishermen's Protective Act of 1967 (22 U.S.C. 1972) if the seizure is found by the Secretary of State to be in accordance with the provisions of the Treaty.

SEC. 4. REGULATIONS.

The Secretary of Commerce, with the concurrence of the Secretary of State and after consultation with the Secretary of the department in which the Coast Guard is operating, shall issue regulations as may be necessary to carry out the purposes and objectives of the Treaty and this Act. These regulations shall be made applicable as necessary to all persons and vessels subject to the jurisdiction of the United States, wherever located.

SEC. 5. PROHIBITED ACTS.

(a) Except as provided in section 6 of this Act, it is unlawful for any person subject to the jurisdiction of the United States—

(1) to violate any provision of this Act or any regulation or order issued pursuant to this Act;

(2) to use a vessel for fishing in violation of an applicable national law;

(3) who has entered into a fishing arrangement under paragraph 3 of Article 3 of the Treaty, to violate the terms and conditions of such fishing arrangement if the Secretary of State has decided under section 18 of this Act that Article 4 and paragraph 6 of Article 5 of the Treaty shall apply to the arrangement;

(4) to use a vessel for fishing in any Limited Area in violation of any requirement in Schedule 3 of Annex I of the Treaty;

(5) to use a vessel for fishing in any Closed Area;

(6) to falsify any information required to be reported, notified, communicated, or recorded pursuant to a requirement of this Act, or to fail to submit any required information, or to fail to report to the Secretary immediately any change in circumstances which has the effect of rendering any such information false, incomplete, or misleading;

(7) to intentionally destroy evidence which could be used to determine if a violation of this Act or the Treaty has occurred;

(8) to refuse to permit any Authorized Officer or Authorized Party Officer to board a fishing vessel for purposes of conducting a search or inspection in connection with the enforcement of this Act or the Treaty;

(9) to refuse to comply with the instructions of an Authorized Officer or Authorized Party Officer relating to fishing activities under the Treaty;

(10) to forcibly assault, resist, oppose, impede, intimidate, or interfere with—

(A) any Authorized Officer or Authorized Party Officer in the conduct of a search or inspection in connection with the enforcement of this Act or the Treaty; or

(B) an observer in the conduct of observer duties under the Treaty;

(11) to resist a lawful arrest for any act prohibited by this section;

(12) to interfere with, delay, or prevent, by any means, the apprehension or arrest of another person, knowing that such other person has committed any act prohibited by this section; or

(13) to ship, transport, offer for sale, sell, purchase, import, export, or have custody, control, or possession of, any fish taken or retained in violation of this Act or any regulation, permit, or the Treaty, with the knowledge that the fish were so taken or retained.

(b) Except as provided in section 6 of this Act, it is unlawful for any person subject to the jurisdiction of the United States when in the Licensing Area—

(1) to use a vessel to fish unless validly licensed as required by the Administrator;

(2) to use a vessel for directed fishing for southern bluefin tuna or for fishing for any kinds of fish other than tunas, except that fish may be caught as an incidental by-catch;

(3) to use a vessel for fishing by any method other than the purse-seine method;

(4) to use any vessel to engage in fishing after the revocation of its license, or during the period of suspension of an applicable license;

(5) to operate a vessel in such a way as to disrupt or in any other way adversely affect the activities of traditional and locally based fishermen and fishing vessels;

(6) to use a vessel to fish in a manner inconsistent with an order issued by the Secretary under section 11 of this Act; or

(7) except for circumstances involving force majeure and other emergencies involving the health or safety of crew members or the safety of the vessel, to use an aircraft in association with the fishing activities of a vessel unless it is identified in the license application for the vessel, or any amendment thereto.

SEC. 6. EXCEPTIONS.

(a) The prohibitions of section 5 of this Act and the licensing requirements of section 9 of this Act shall not apply to fishing for albacore tuna by vessels using the trolling method outside of the 200 nautical mile fisheries zones of the Pacific Island Parties.

(b) The prohibitions of section 5 (a)(4), (a)(5), and (b)(3) of this Act shall not apply to fishing under the terms and conditions of an arrangement which has been reached under paragraph 3 of Article 3 of the Treaty and which, pursuant to a decision by the Secretary of State under section 18 of this Act, is covered by Article 4 and paragraph 6 of Article 5 of the Treaty.

SEC. 7. CRIMINAL OFFENSES.

(a) A person is guilty of a criminal offense if he or she commits any act prohibited by section 5(a) (8), (10), (11), or (12) of this Act.

(b) Any offense described in subsection (a) of this section is punishable by a fine of not more than $50,000, or imprisonment for not more than 6 months, or both; except that if in the commission of any such offense the person uses a dangerous weapon, engages in conduct that causes bodily injury to any Authorized Officer, Authorized Party Officer, or observer under the Treaty in the conduct of their duties, or places any such Authorized Officer, Authorized Party Officer, or observer in fear of imminent bodily injury, the offense is punishable by a fine of not more than $100,000 or imprisonment for not more than 10 years, or both.

(c) The district courts of the United States shall have jurisdiction over any offense described in this section.

SEC. 8. CIVIL PENALTIES.

(a) Any person who is found by the Secretary, after notice and an opportunity for a hearing in accordance with section 554 of title 5, United States Code, to have committed an act prohibited by section 5 of this Act, shall be liable to the United States Code for a civil penalty. Before issuing a notice of violation, the Secretary shall consult with the Secretary of State. The amount of the civil penalty shall be determined in accordance with considerations set forth in the Treaty and shall take into account the nature, circumstances, extent, any gravity of the prohibited acts committed, and with respect to the violator, the degree of culpability, any history or prior offenses, ability to pay, and such other matters as justice may require. Except for those acts prohibited by section 5(a) (4), (5), (7), (8), (10), (11), and (12), and section 5(b) (1), (2), (3), and (7) of this Act, the amount of the civil penalty shall not exceed $250,000 for each violation. Upon written notice, the Secretary of State shall have the right to participate in any proceeding initiated to assess a civil penalty for violation of this Act.

(b) Any person against whom a civil penalty is assessed under subsection (a) of this section may obtain review thereof in the United States district court for the appropriate district by filing a complaint in such court within 30 days from the date of the order and by simultaneously serving a copy of the complaint by certified mail on the Secretary, the Attorney General of the United States, and the appropriate United States Attorney. The Secretary shall promptly file in the court a certified copy of the record upon which the violation was found or the penalty imposed. The findings and order of the Secretary shall be set aside or modified by the court if they are not found to be supported by substantial evidence, as provided in section 706(2) of title 5, United States Code.

(c) Except as provided in subsection (g) of this section, if any person fails to pay an assessment of a civil penalty after it has become a final and unappealable order, or after the appropriate court has entered final judgment in favor of the Secretary, the Secretary shall refer the matter to the Attorney General of the United States, who shall recover the amount assessed in any appropriate district court of the United States.

(d) Except as provided in subsection (g) of this section, a fishing vessel (including its fishing gear, furniture, appurtenances, stores, and cargo) used in the commission of an act prohibited by section 5 of this Act shall be liable in rem for any civil penalty assessed for the violation under section 8 of this Act and may be proceeded against in any district court of the United States having jurisdiction thereof. The penalty shall constitute a maritime lien on the vessel which may be recovered in an action in rem in the district court of the United States having jurisdiction over the vessel.

(e) The Secretary, after consultation with the Secretary of State, may compromise, modify, or remit, with or without conditions, any civil penalty which is subject to imposition or which has been imposed under this section.

(f) For the purposes of conducting any hearing under this section, the Secretary may issue subpoenas for the attendance and testimony of witnesses and the production of relevant papers, books, and documents, and may administer oaths. Witnesses summoned shall be paid the same fees and mileage that are paid to witnesses in the courts of the United States. In case of contempt or refusal to obey a subpoena served upon a person pursuant to this subsection, the district court of the United States for any district in which the person is found, resides, or transacts business, upon application by the United States and after notice to the person, shall have jurisdiction to issue an order requiring the person to appear and give testimony before the Secretary or to appear and produce documents before the Secretary, or both, and any failure to obey the order of the court may be punished by the court as a contempt thereof.

(g) If a vessel used in a violation of section 5(a) (1), (2), (3), (4), (5), (6), (7), (8), (9), or (13) or section 5(b) of this Act for which a civil penalty has been assessed—

(1) had a valid license under the Treasury at the time of the violation, and

(2) within 60 days after the penalty assessment has become final, leaves and remains outside of the Licensing Area, all Limited Areas closed to fishing, and all Closed Areas until the final penalty has been paid,

there shall be no referral to the Attorney General under subsection (c) of this section or in rem action under subsection (d) of this section in connection with such civil penalty.

SEC. 9. LICENSES.

(a) Licenses to fish in the Licensing Area, to be issued by the Administrator in accordance with the Treaty, may be requested from the Secretary by operators of vessels, under procedures established by the Secretary. The license application shall designate an agent for the service of legal process to be located in Port Moresby, Papua New Guinea. The applicant shall ensure that the designated agent for service of process, acting on behalf of the license holder, will receive and respond to any legal process issued in accordance with the Treaty and will, within 21 days after notification, travel if necessary for this purpose to any Pacific Island Party at no expense to that Party.

(b) Except as provided in subsections (e), (f), and (g) of this section, the Secretary shall forward a vessel license application to the Secretary of State for transmittal to the Administrator whenever such application is in accordance with application procedures established by the Secretary, includes a complete application form as required by Annex II of the Treaty, and is accompanied by the required license fee.

(c)(1) In the initial year of implementation, fees for the first 40 vessel licenses shall be at least $50,000 each, for any 10 vessel licenses in addition to the first 40 shall be $60,000 each, and for vessel licenses in addition to the first 50 shall be in accordance with Annex II of the Treaty.

(2) After such initial year, fees for vessel licenses shall be paid in accordance with fee schedules established under Annex II of the Treaty and published by the Secretary.

(d) Licenses shall be valid for the licensing period specified by the Administrator.

(e) The Secretary may establish a system of allocating licenses in the event more applications are received than there are licenses available.

(f) For the initial year of implementation, license fees totaling at least $1,750,000 must be received by the Secretary before any license applications will be forwarded to the Secretary of State for transmittal to the Administrator.

(g) The Secretary, in consultation with the Secretary of State, may determine that a license application should not be forwarded to the Administrator for one of the following reasons:

(1) where the application is not in accordance with the Treaty or the procedures established by the Secretary;

(2) where the owner or charterer is the subject of proceedings under the bankruptcy laws of the United States, unless reasonable financial assurances have been provided to the Secretary;

(3) where the owner or charterer has not established to the satisfaction of the Secretary that the fishing vessel is fully insured against all risks and liabilities normally provided in maritime liability insurance;

(4) where the owner or charterer has not paid any penalty which has become final, assessed by the Secretary in accordance with this Act.

SEC. 10. ENFORCEMENT.

(a) The provisions of this Act shall be enforced by the Secretary in cooperation with the Secretary of State. The Secretary, after consultation with the Secretary of State, may by agreement, on a reimbursable basis or otherwise, utilize the personnel, services, equipment (including aircraft and vessels), and facilities of any other Federal agency and of any State agency in the performance of these duties.

(b)(1) The Secretary shall, at the request of a Pacific Island Party made to the Secretary of State, fully investigate any alleged infringement of the Treaty involving a vessel of the United States, and report as soon as practicable, and in any case within 2 months, to that Party through the Secretary of State on any action taken or proposed by the Secretary in regard to the alleged infringement.

(2) Upon commencement of an investigation under paragraph (1) of this subsection, the Secretary shall notify the operator of any vessel concerned regarding—

(A) the nature of the investigation;

(B) the right of the operator to submit comments, information, or evidence bearing on the investigation and to receive, upon the operator's timely written request to the Secretary, an opportunity to present such comments, information, or evidence orally to the Secretary or the Secretary's representative within 30 days after receipt of such notification.

(c)(1) Prior to instituting any legal proceedings under this Act for any action which involves an alleged infringement of the Treaty in waters within the jurisdiction of a Pacific Island Party, the Secretary, through the Secretary of State, shall notify the Pacific Island Party in accordance with paragraph 8 of Article 4 of the Treaty that the proceedings will be instituted. Such notice shall include a statement of the facts believed to show an infringement of the Treaty and the nature of the proposed proceedings, including any proposed charges and any proposed penalties. The Secretary shall not institute such proceedings if the Pacific Island Party objects within 30 days after the effective date of the notice under Article 10 of the Treaty.

(2) The Pacific Island Party exercising jurisdiction over the waters involved in such a legal proceeding shall be promptly notified by the Secretary, through the Secretary of State, concerning the outcome of the proceeding.

(d)(1) Any Authorized Officer may—

(A) with or without a warrant or other process—

(i) arrest any person, if he has reasonable cause to believe that the person has committed any act subject to prosecution under section 7 of this Act;

(ii) board, and search or inspect, any fishing vessel which is subject to the provisions of this Act; or

(iii) seize samples of fish or items for evidence (other than the vessel or its fishing gear or equipment) related to any violation of any provision of this Act;

(iv) order a vessel into the most convenient port of the United States for investigation when an investigation has been requested by a Pacific Island Party in accordance with the Treaty and when such an order is necessary to gather information for such an investigation;

(B) execute any warrant or other process issued by any court of competent jurisdiction;

(C) exercise any other lawful authority; and

(D) investigate alleged violations of the Treaty to the same extent authorized to investigate alleged violations of this Act.

(2) To the extent possible, Authorized Officers shall exercise their powers under paragraph (1)(A) (ii), (iii), and (iv) of this subsection so as not to interfere unduly with the lawful operation of the vessel.

(3) Nothing in this Act shall be construed to limit the enforcement of this or other applicable Federal laws under section 89 of title 14, United States Code.

(e) The district courts of the United States shall have exclusive jurisdiction over any case or controversy arising under the provisions of this Act.

SEC. 11. FINDINGS BY THE SECRETARY.

(a) Following any investigation conducted in accordance with section 10(b) of this Act, the Secretary, with the concurrence of the Secretary of State, and upon the request of the Pacific Island Party concerned, may order a fishing vessel which has not submitted to the jurisdiction of that Pacific Island Party to leave immediately the Licensing Area, all Limited Areas, and all Closed Areas upon making a finding—

(1) that the fishing vessel—

(A) while fishing in the Licensing Area did not have a license under the Treaty to fish in the Licensing Area, and that under paragraph 2 of Article 3 of the Treaty, such fishing is not authorized to be conducted in the Licensing Area without a license;

(B) was involved in any incident in which an Authorized Officer, Authorized Party Officer, or observer was allegedly assaulted with resultant bodily harm, physically threatened, forcefully resisted, refused boarding, or subjected to physical intimidation or physical interference in the performance of duties as authorized by this Act or the Treaty;

(C) has not made full payment within 60 days of any amount due as a result of a final judgment or other final determination deriving from a violation in waters within the Treaty Area of a Pacific Island Party; or

(D) was not represented by an agent for service of process in accordance with the Treaty; or

(2) that there is probable cause to believe that the fishing vessel—

(A) was used in violation of section 5 (a)(4), (a)(5), (b)(2), or (b)(3) of this Act;

(B) used an aircraft in violation of section 5(b)(7); or

(C) was involved in an incident in which section 5(b)(7) was violated.

(b) Upon being advised by the Secretary of State that proper notification to Parties has been made under paragraph 7 of Article 5 of the Treaty that a Pacific Island Party is investigating an alleged infringement of the Treaty by a vessel in waters under the jurisdiction of such Pacific Island Party, the Secretary shall order the vessel to leave such waters until the Secretary of State notifies the Secretary that such order is no longer necessary.

(c) The Secretary shall rescind any order issued on the basis of a finding under subsection (a)(1) (C) or (D) of this section as soon as the Secretary determines that the facts underlying the finding do not apply.

(d) No order issued in accordance with this section is subject to judicial review.

(e) Upon a request by the Secretary, the Attorney General shall commence a civil action for appropriate relief, including permanent or temporary injunction, to enforce any order issued by the Secretary under this section.

SEC. 12. REPORTING.

(a) Holders of licenses shall comply with the reporting requirements of part 4 of Annex I to the Treaty.

(b) Information provided by license holders in Schedules 5 and 6 of Annex I of the Treaty shall be provided to the Secretary for transmittal to the Administrator and to an entity designated by the license holder. Such information thereafter shall not be released and shall be maintained as confidential by the Secretary, including information requested under the Freedom of Information Act, unless disclosure is required under court order or unless the information is essential for an enforcement action under section 5, 10(b), 10(c), or 11 of this Act, or any other proper law enforcement action.

SEC. 13. CLOSED AREA STOWAGE REQUIREMENTS.

At all times while a vessel is in a Closed Area, the fishing gear of the vessel shall be stowed in such a manner as not to be readily available for fishing. In particular, the boom shall be lowered as far as possible so that the vessel cannot be used for fishing, but so that the skiff is accessible for use in emergency situations; the helicopter, if any, shall be tied down; and launches shall be secured.

SEC. 14. OBSERVERS.

(a) The operator and each member of the crew of a vessel shall allow and assist any individual identified as an observer under the Treaty by the Pacific Island Parties—

(1) to board the vessel for scientific, compliance, monitoring and other functions at the point and time notified by the Pacific Island Parties to the Secretary;

(2) without interfering unduly with the lawful operation of the vessel, to have full access to and use of facilities and equipment on board the vessel which the observer may determine are necessary to carry out observer duties; have full access to the bridge, fish on board, and areas which may be used to hold, process, weigh, and store fish; remove samples; have full access to the vessel's records, including its log and documentation for the purpose of inspection and copying; and gather any other information relating to fisheries in the Licensing Area;

(3) to disembark at the point and time notified by the Pacific Island Parties to the Secretary; and

(4) to carry out observer duties safely.

(b) The operator shall provide any such observer, while on board the vessel, at no expense to the Pacific Island Parties, with food, accommodation, and medical facilities of such reasonable standard as may be acceptable to the Pacific Island Party whose representative is serving as the observer.

(c) The operator of any vessel from which any fish taken in the Licensing Area is unloaded shall allow, or arrange for, and assist any individual so authorized by the Pacific Island Parties to have full access to any place where such fish is unloaded, to remove samples, and to gather any other information relating to fisheries in the Licensing Area.

SEC. 15. TECHNICAL ASSISTANCE.

The United States tuna industry shall provide $250,000 annually in technical assistance, including provision of assistance by technicians, in response to requests coordinated through the Administrator. The Secretary of State shall designate an entity to coordinate the provision of such technical assistance as provided by the United States tuna industry and to provide an annual report to the Secretary of State regarding the provision of such technical assistance.

SEC. 16. ARBITRATION.

In the event of a dispute requiring the establishment of an arbitral tribunal under Article 6 of the Treaty, the Secretary of State, in consultation with the Secretary, shall appoint the arbitrator to be appointed by the United States under paragraph 3 of that Article, and shall represent the United States in reaching agreement under such paragraph with each Pacific Island Party involved concerning the appointment of the presiding arbitrator of the tribunal.

SEC. 17. DISPOSITION OF FEES, PENALTIES, FORFEITURES, AND OTHER MONEYS.

To the extent required by Article 4 of the Treaty, an amount equivalent to the total value of any fine, penalty, or other amount collected as a result of any action, judicial or otherwise, taken pursuant to sections 7 and 8 of this Act shall be paid by the United States through the Secretary of State to the Administrator as soon as reasonably possible following the date that such amount is collected.

SEC. 18. ADDITIONAL AGREEMENTS.

Within 30 days after the Secretary of State's receipt of notice from a Pacific Island Party that it has concluded an arrangement pursuant to paragraph 3 of Article 3 of the Treaty, the Secretary of State shall consult with the Secretary concerning whether the procedures of Article 4 and paragraph 6 of Article 5 of the Treaty should be made applicable to such arrangement. At the conclusion of the consultations the Pacific Island Party and all other persons agreeing to the arrangement shall be notified by the Secretary of State of the resulting decision.

SEC. 19. SECRETARY OF STATE TO ACT FOR THE UNITED STATES.

The Secretary of State is authorized to receive on behalf of the United States reports, requests, and other communications from the Administrator and to act thereon directly or by reference to the appropriate authorities. The Secretary of State, after consultations with the Secretary, may accept or reject, on behalf of the United States, changes or amendments to Annex I of the Treaty and its Schedules and Annex II to the Treaty and its Schedules.

SEC. 20. AUTHORIZATION OF APPROPRIATIONS.

(a) There are authorized to be appropriated for fiscal years 1988, 1989, 1990, 1991, and 1992 such sums as may be necessary for carrying out the purposes and provisions of the Treaty and this Act including—

(1) for fiscal years 1988, 1989, 1990, 1991, and 1992, an amount not to exceed $350,000 annually to the Department of Commerce for administrative expenses; and

(2) for fiscal years 1988, 1989, 1990, 1991, and 1992, an amount not to exceed $50,000 annually to the Department of State for administrative expenses.

(b) Funds appropriated for the purposes of the Treaty may be used notwithstanding any of the provisions of the Foreign Assistance Act of 1961 (22 U.S.C. 2151 et seq.) or of any appropriations Act that imposes restrictions on the maintenance or use of cash transfer assistance, which are inconsistent with the provisions of the Treaty.

SEC. 21. EFFECTIVE DATE.

(a) Except as provided in subsection (b) of this section, this Act shall be effective on the date on which the Treaty enters into force for the United States.

(b)(1) The authority to promulgate regulations pursuant to this Act shall be effective on the date of enactment of this Act.

(2) Any regulation promulgated pursuant to this Act shall not be effective before the date on which the Treaty enters into force for the United States.

Approved June 7, 1988.

LEGISLATIVE HISTORY—S. 1989 (H.R. 3767):

HOUSE REPORTS: No. 100-645, Pt. 1, accompanying H.R. 3767 (Comm. on Merchant Marine and Fisheries).
SENATE REPORTS: No. 100-316 (Comm. on Commerce, Science, and Transportation).
CONGRESSIONAL RECORD, Vol. 134 (1988):
May 13, considered and passed Senate.
May 24, considered and passed House.
WEEKLY COMPILATION OF PRESIDENTIAL DOCUMENTS, Vol. 24 (1988):
June 7, Presidential statement.

GERMAN DEMOCRATIC REPUBLIC FISHERY AGREEMENT ACT, 1988

An Act to provide Congressional approval of the Governing International Fishery Agreement between the United States and the Government of the German Democratic Republic.

Date: June 27, 1988

Bill No.: H.R. 4621

Public Law No.: 100-350

Cite: 102 STAT. 660

Sections reprinted:

Section 1 - Approval of GIFA with German Democratic Republic

Section 2 - Amendments to South Pacific Tuna Act of 1988

Note: The act refers to an agreement of May 3, 1988. It is more likely the agreement was made on January 16 and April 12, 1988 (TIAS 11579)

Public Law 100-350
100th Congress

An Act

To provide Congressional approval of the Governing International Fishery Agreement between the United States and the Government of the German Democratic Republic.

Be it enacted by the Senate and House of Representatives of the United States of America in Congress assembled,

SECTION 1. APPROVAL OF GIFA WITH GERMAN DEMOCRATIC REPUBLIC.

That notwithstanding section 203 of the Magnuson Fishery Conservation and Management Act (16 U.S.C. 1823), the extension of the governing international fishery agreement between the Government of the United States of America and the Government of the German Democratic Republic, as contained in the message to Congress from the President of the United States, dated May 3, 1988—

(1) is approved by Congress as a governing international fishery agreement for the purposes of such Act; and

(2) shall enter into force and effect with respect to the United States on the date of enactment of this Act.

SEC. 4. AMENDMENTS TO SOUTH PACIFIC TUNA ACT OF 1988.

The South Pacific Tuna Act of 1988 is amended—

(1) in section 8(a)—

(A) by striking "any gravity" and inserting in lieu thereof "and gravity"; and

(B) by striking "history or prior" and inserting in lieu thereof "history of prior";

(2) in section 8(g)(1), by striking "Treasury" and inserting in lieu thereof "Treaty"; and

(3) in section 11(a)(2)(C), by striking "5(b)(7)" and inserting in lieu thereof "5(a)(7)".

Approved June 27, 1988.

LEGISLATIVE HISTORY—H.R. 4621:

HOUSE REPORTS: No. 100-672 (Comm. on Merchant Marine and Fisheries).
CONGRESSIONAL RECORD, Vol. 134 (1988):
June 7, considered and passed House.
June 14, considered and passed Senate.

HELSINKI HUMAN RIGHTS DAY JOINT RESOLUTION

Joint Resolution to designate August 1, 1988, as "Helsinki Human Rights Day."

Date: August 1, 1988

Bill No.: S. J. Res. 338

Public Law No.: 100-377

Cite: 102 STAT. 883

Sections reprinted: All

Note: Helsinki Accord is numbered KAV 4254 in the *United States Treaty Index.*

Public Law 100-377
100th Congress

Joint Resolution

To designate August 1, 1988, as "Helsinki Human Rights Day".

Whereas August 1, 1988, will be the thirteenth anniversary of the signing of the Final Act of the Conference on Security and Cooperation in Europe (hereafter in this preamble referred to as the "Helsinki accords");

Whereas on August 1, 1975, the Helsinki accords were agreed to by the Governments of Austria, Belgium, Bulgaria, Canada, Cyprus, Czechoslovakia, Denmark, Finland, France, the German Democratic Republic, the Federal Republic of Germany, Greece, the Holy See, Hungary, Iceland, Ireland, Italy, Liechtenstein, Luxembourg, Malta, Monaco, the Netherlands, Norway, Poland, Portugal, Romania, San Marino, Spain, Sweden, Switzerland, Turkey, the Union of Soviet Socialist Republics, the United Kingdom, the United States of America, and Yugoslavia;

Whereas the participating States have committed themselves to balanced progress in all areas of the Helsinki accords;

Whereas the Helsinki accords recognize the inherent relationship between respect for human rights and fundamental freedoms and the attainment of genuine security;

Whereas the Helsinki accords express the commitment of the participating States to "recognize the universal significance of human rights and fundamental freedoms, respect for which is an essential factor for the peace, justice and well-being necessary to ensure the development of friendly relations and cooperation among themselves as among all States";

Whereas the Helsinki accords also express the commitment of the participating States to "respect human rights and fundamental freedoms, including the freedom of thought, conscience, religion or belief, for all without distinction as to race, sex, language or religion";

Whereas the Helsinki accords also express the commitment of the participating States to "promote and encourage the effective exercise of civil, political, economic, social, cultural and other rights and freedoms all of which derive from the inherent dignity of the human person and are essential for his free and full development";

Whereas the Helsinki accords also express the commitment of the participating States to "recognize and respect the freedom of the individual to profess and practice, alone or in community with others, religion or belief acting in accordance with the dictates of his own conscience";

Whereas the Helsinki accords also express the commitment of the participating States on whose territory national minorities exist to "respect the right of persons belonging to such minorities to equality before the law" and that such States "will afford them the full opportunity for the actual enjoyment of human rights and fundamental freedoms and will in this manner, protect their legitimate interests in this sphere";

Whereas the Helsinki accords also express the commitment of the participating States to "constantly respect these rights and freedoms in their mutual relations" and that such States "will endeavor jointly and separately, including in cooperation with the United Nations, to promote universal and effective respect for them";

Whereas the Helsinki accords also express the commitment of the participating States to "conform the right of the individual to know and act upon his rights and duties in this field";

Whereas the Helsinki accords also express the commitment of the participating States in the field of human rights and fundamental freedoms to "act in conformity with the purposes and principles of the Charter of the United Nations and with the Universal Declaration of Human Rights" and to "fulfill their obligations as set forth in the international declarations and agreements in this field, including inter alia the International Covenants on Human Rights, by which they may be bound";

Whereas the Helsinki accords by incorporation also express the commitment of the participating States to guarantee the right of the individual to leave his own country and return to such country;

Whereas the Helsinki accords also express the commitment of the participating States to "facilitate freer movement and contacts, individually and collectively, whether privately or officially, among persons, institutions and organizations of the participating States, and to contribute to the solution of the humanitarian problems that arise in that connection";

Whereas the Helsinki accords also express the commitment of the participating States to "favorably consider applications for travel with the purpose of allowing persons to enter or leave their territory temporarily, and on a regular basis if desired, in order to visit members of their families";

Whereas the Helsinki accords also express the commitment of the participating States to "deal in a positive and humanitarian spirit with the applications of persons who wish to be reunited with members of their family" and "to deal with applications in this field as expeditiously as possible";

Whereas the Helsinki accords also express the commitments of the participating States to "examine favorably and on the basis of humanitarian considerations requests for exit or entry permits from persons who have decided to marry a citizen from another participating State";

Whereas the Helsinki accords also express the commitment of the participating States to "facilitate wider travel by their citizens for personal or professional reasons";

Whereas the Helsinki accords also express the commitment of the participating States to "facilitate the freer and wider dissemination of information of all kinds, to encourage cooperation in the field of information and the exchange of information with other countries";

Whereas the Governments of the Union of Soviet Socialist Republics, Bulgaria, Czechoslovakia, the German Democratic Republic, Hungary, Poland, and Romania, in agreeing to the Helsinki accords, have made a commitment to adhere to the principles of human rights and fundamental freedoms as embodied in the Helsinki accords;

Whereas, despite some limited improvements, the aforementioned Governments have failed to implement their obligations under Principle VII of the Helsinki accords to respect human rights and fundamental freedoms, including the freedom of thought, conscience, religion or belief;

Whereas, despite some limited improvements, the aforementioned Governments have failed to implement their obligations under Basket III of the Helsinki accords to promote free movement of people, ideas and information;

Whereas representatives from the signatory States are convened in Vienna to review implementation and address issues of compliance with the human rights and humanitarian provisions of the Helsinki accords: Now, therefore, be it

Resolved by the Senate and House of Representatives of the United States of America in Congress assembled, That—

(1) August 1, 1988, the thirteenth anniversary of the signing of the Helsinki accords is designated as "Helsinki Human Rights Day";

(2) the President is authorized and requested to issue a proclamation reasserting the American commitment to full implementation of the human rights and humanitarian provisions of the Helsinki accords, urging all signatory nations to abide by their obligations under the Helsinki accords, and encouraging the people of the United States to join the President and Congress in observance of the Helsinki Human Rights Day with appropriate programs, ceremonies, and activities;

(3) the President is further requested to continue his efforts to achieve full implementation of the human rights and humanitarian provisions of the Helsinki accords by raising, with the Governments of the Soviet Union, Bulgaria, Czechoslovakia, the German Democratic Republic, Hungary, Poland, and Romania, the issue of their noncompliance at every available opportunity;

(4) the President is further requested to convey to all signatories of the Helsinki accords that respect for human rights and fundamental freedoms is a vital element of further progress in the ongoing Helsinki process;

(5) the President is authorized to convey to allies and friends of the United States that unity on the question of respect for human rights and fundamental freedoms is an essential means of promoting the full implementation of the human rights and humanitarian provisions of the Helsinki accords;

(6) the President is requested to continue his efforts to achieve before the end of the Vienna meeting the release of all political prisoners of the Soviet Union, including Helsinki monitors, a significant increase in Soviet emigration, the resolution of all family reunification cases, the cessation of all radio transmission jamming, and the repeal of laws, procedures, and practices which undermine human rights;

(7) the President is further requested to seek the inclusion, in any concluding document agreed to in Vienna, of a mechanism to assure that human rights progress is sustained following the conclusion of the Vienna meeting; and

(8) the President is further requested to convey to signatory States the insistence of the United States for a balanced result

at the Vienna meeting that will not favor military security at the expense of human rights.

SEC. 2. The Secretary of the Senate is directed to transmit copies of this joint resolution to the President, the Secretary of State, and the Ambassadors of the thirty-four Helsinki signatory nations.

Approved August 1, 1988.

LEGISLATIVE HISTORY—S.J. Res. 338:

CONGRESSIONAL RECORD, Vol. 134 (1988):
July 8, considered and passed Senate.
July 14, considered and passed House.

INTERNMENT OF JAPANESE CIVILIANS ACT, 1988

An Act to implement recommendations of the Commission on Wartime Relocation and Internment of Civilians.

Date: August 10, 1988

Bill No.: H.R. 442

Public Law No.: 100-383

Cite: 102 STAT. 903

Sections reprinted: All

Note: This act includes:

- Civil Liberties Act of 1988
- Aleutian and Pribilof Islands Restitution Act, 1988

Public Law 100-383
100th Congress

An Act

To implement recommendations of the Commission on Wartime Relocation and Internment of Civilians.

Be it enacted by the Senate and House of Representatives of the United States of America in Congress assembled,

SECTION 1. PURPOSES.

The purposes of this Act are to—

(1) acknowledge the fundamental injustice of the evacuation, relocation, and internment of United States citizens and permanent resident aliens of Japanese ancestry during World War II;

(2) apologize on behalf of the people of the United States for the evacuation, relocation, and internment of such citizens and permanent resident aliens;

(3) provide for a public education fund to finance efforts to inform the public about the internment of such individuals so as to prevent the recurrence of any similar event;

(4) make restitution to those individuals of Japanese ancestry who were interned;

(5) make restitution to Aleut residents of the Pribilof Islands and the Aleutian Islands west of Unimak Island, in settlement of United States obligations in equity and at law, for—

(A) injustices suffered and unreasonable hardships endured while those Aleut residents were under United States control during World War II;

(B) personal property taken or destroyed by United States forces during World War II;

(C) community property, including community church property, taken or destroyed by United States forces during World War II; and

(D) traditional village lands on Attu Island not rehabilitated after World War II for Aleut occupation or other productive use;

(6) discourage the occurrence of similar injustices and violations of civil liberties in the future; and

(7) make more credible and sincere any declaration of concern by the United States over violations of human rights committed by other nations.

SEC. 2. STATEMENT OF THE CONGRESS.

(a) WITH REGARD TO INDIVIDUALS OF JAPANESE ANCESTRY.—The Congress recognizes that, as described by the Commission on Wartime Relocation and Internment of Civilians, a grave injustice was done to both citizens and permanent resident aliens of Japanese ancestry by the evacuation, relocation, and internment of civilians during World War II. As the Commission documents, these actions were carried out without adequate security reasons and without any acts of espionage or sabotage documented by the Commission, and were motivated largely by racial prejudice, wartime hysteria, and a failure of political leadership. The excluded individuals of Japanese ancestry suffered enormous damages, both material and intangible, and there were incalculable losses in education and job training, all of which resulted in significant human suffering for which appropriate compensation has not been made. For these fundamental violations of the basic civil liberties and constitutional rights of these individuals of Japanese ancestry, the Congress apologizes on behalf of the Nation.

(b) WITH RESPECT TO THE ALEUTS.—The Congress recognizes that, as described by the Commission on Wartime Relocation and Internment of Civilians, the Aleut civilian residents of the Pribilof Islands and the Aleutian Islands west of Unimak Island were relocated during World War II to temporary camps in isolated regions of southeast Alaska where they remained, under United States control and in the care of the United States, until long after any potential danger to their home villages had passed. The United States failed to provide reasonable care for the Aleuts, and this resulted in widespread illness, disease, and death among the residents of the camps; and the United States further failed to protect Aleut personal and community property while such property was in its possession or under its control. The United States has not compensated the Aleuts adequately for the conversion or destruction of personal property, and the conversion or destruction of community property caused by the United States military occupation of Aleut villages during World War II. There is no remedy for injustices suffered by the Aleuts during World War II except an Act of Congress providing appropriate compensation for those losses which are attributable to the conduct of United States forces and other officials and employees of the United States.

TITLE I—UNITED STATES CITIZENS OF JAPANESE ANCESTRY AND RESIDENT JAPANESE ALIENS

SEC 101. SHORT TITLE.

This title may be cited as the "Civil Liberties Act of 1988".

SEC. 102. REMEDIES WITH RESPECT TO CRIMINAL CONVICTIONS.

(a) REVIEW OF CONVICTIONS.—The Attorney General is requested to review any case in which an individual living on the date of the enactment of this Act was, while a United States citizen or permanent resident alien of Japanese ancestry, convicted of a violation of—

(1) Executive Order Numbered 9066, dated February 19, 1942;

(2) the Act entitled "An Act to provide a penalty for violation of restrictions or orders with respect to persons entering, remaining in, leaving, or committing any act in military areas or zones", approved March 21, 1942 (56 Stat. 173); or

(3) any other Executive order, Presidential proclamation, law of the United States, directive of the Armed Forces of the United States, or other action taken by or on behalf of the United States or its agents, representatives, officers, or employees, respecting the evacuation, relocation, or internment of individuals solely on the basis of Japanese ancestry;

on account of the refusal by such individual, during the evacuation, relocation, and internment period, to accept treatment which discriminated against the individual on the basis of the individual's Japanese ancestry.

(b) RECOMMENDATIONS FOR PARDONS.—Based upon any review under subsection (a), the Attorney General is requested to recommend to the President for pardon consideration those convictions which the Attorney General considers appropriate.

(c) ACTION BY THE PRESIDENT.—In consideration of the statement of the Congress set forth in section 2(a), the President is requested to offer pardons to any individuals recommended by the Attorney General under subsection (b).

SEC. 103. CONSIDERATION OF COMMISSION FINDINGS BY DEPARTMENTS AND AGENCIES.

(a) REVIEW OF APPLICATIONS BY ELIGIBLE INDIVIDUALS.—Each department and agency of the United States Government shall review with liberality, giving full consideration to the findings of the Commission and the statement of the Congress set forth in section 2(a), any application by an eligible individual for the restitution of any position, status, or entitlement lost in whole or in part because of any discriminatory act of the United States Government against such individual which was based upon the individual's Japanese ancestry and which occurred during the evacuation, relocation, and internment period.

(b) NO NEW AUTHORITY CREATED.—Subsection (a) does not create any authority to grant restitution described in that subsection, or establish any eligibility to apply for such restitution.

SEC. 104. TRUST FUND.

(a) ESTABLISHMENT.—There is established in the Treasury of the United States the Civil Liberties Public Education Fund, which shall be administered by the Secretary of the Treasury.

(b) INVESTMENT OF AMOUNTS IN THE FUND.—Amounts in the Fund shall be invested in accordance with section 9702 of title 31, United States Code.

(c) USES OF THE FUND.—Amounts in the Fund shall be available only for disbursement by the Attorney General under section 105 and by the Board under section 106.

(d) TERMINATION.—The Fund shall terminate not later than the earlier of the date on which an amount has been expended from the Fund which is equal to the amount authorized to be appropriated to the Fund by subsection (e), and any income earned on such amount, or 10 years after the date of the enactment of this Act. If all of the amounts in the Fund have not been expended by the end of that 10-year period, investments of amounts in the Fund shall be liquidated and receipts thereof deposited in the Fund and all funds remaining in the Fund shall be deposited in the miscellaneous receipts account in the Treasury.

(e) AUTHORIZATION OF APPROPRIATIONS.—There are authorized to be appropriated to the Fund $1,250,000,000, of which not more than $500,000,000 may be appropriated for any fiscal year. Any amounts appropriated pursuant to this section are authorized to remain available until expended.

SEC. 105. RESTITUTION.

(a) LOCATION AND PAYMENT OF ELIGIBLE INDIVIDUALS.—

(1) IN GENERAL.—Subject to paragraph (6), the Attorney General shall, subject to the availability of funds appropriated to the Fund for such purpose, pay out of the Fund to each eligible individual the sum of $20,000, unless such individual refuses, in the manner described in paragraph (4), to accept the payment.

(2) LOCATION OF ELIGIBLE INDIVIDUALS.—The Attorney General shall identify and locate, without requiring any application for payment and using records already in the possession of the United States Government, each eligible individual. The Attorney General should use funds and resources available to the Attorney General, including those described in subsection (c), to attempt to complete such identification and location within 12 months after the date of the enactment of this Act. Any eligible individual may notify the Attorney General that such individual is an eligible individual, and may provide documentation therefor. The Attorney General shall designate an officer or employee to whom such notification and documentation may be sent, shall maintain a list of all individuals who submit such notification and documentation, and shall, subject to the availability of funds appropriated for such purpose, encourage, through a public awareness campaign, each eligible individual to submit his or her current address to such officer or employee. To the extent that resources referred to in the second sentence of this paragraph are not sufficient to complete the identification and location of all eligible individuals, there are authorized to be appropriated such sums as may be necessary for such purpose. In any case, the identification and location of all eligible individuals shall be completed within 12 months after the appropriation of funds under the preceding sentence. Failure to be identified and located by the end of the 12-month period specified in the preceding sentence shall not preclude an eligible individual from receiving payment under this section.

(3) NOTICE FROM THE ATTORNEY GENERAL.—The Attorney General shall, when funds are appropriated to the Fund for payments to an eligible individual under this section, notify that eligible individual in writing of his or her eligibility for payment under this section. Such notice shall inform the eligible individual that—

(A) acceptance of payment under this section shall be in full satisfaction of all claims against the United States arising out of acts described in section 108(2)(B), and

(B) each eligible individual who does not refuse, in the manner described in paragraph (4), to accept payment under this section within 18 months after receiving such written notice shall be deemed to have accepted payment for purposes of paragraph (5).

(4) EFFECT OF REFUSAL TO ACCEPT PAYMENT.—If an eligible individual refuses, in a written document filed with the Attorney General, to accept any payment under this section, the amount of such payment shall remain in the Fund and no payment may be made under this section to such individual at any time after such refusal.

(5) PAYMENT IN FULL SETTLEMENT OF CLAIMS AGAINST THE UNITED STATES.—The acceptance of payment by an eligible individual under this section shall be in full satisfaction of all claims against the United States arising out of acts described in section 108(2)(B). This paragraph shall apply to any eligible

individual who does not refuse, in the manner described in paragraph (4), to accept payment under this section within 18 months after receiving the notification from the Attorney General referred to in paragraph (3).

(6) EXCLUSION OF CERTAIN INDIVIDUALS.—No payment may be made under this section to any individual who, after September 1, 1987, accepts payment pursuant to an award of a final judgment or a settlement on a claim against the United States for acts described in section 108(2)(B), or to any surviving spouse, child, or parent of such individual to whom paragraph (6) applies.

(7) PAYMENTS IN THE CASE OF DECEASED PERSONS.—(A) In the case of an eligible individual who is deceased at the time of payment under this section, such payment shall be made only as follows:

(i) If the eligible individual is survived by a spouse who is living at the time of payment, such payment shall be made to such surviving spouse.

(ii) If there is no surviving spouse described in clause (i), such payment shall be made in equal shares to all children of the eligible individual who are living at the time of payment.

(iii) If there is no surviving spouse described in clause (i) and if there are no children described in clause (ii), such payment shall be made in equal shares to the parents of the eligible individual who are living at the time of payment.

If there is no surviving spouse, children, or parents described in clauses (i), (ii), and (iii), the amount of such payment shall remain in the Fund, and may be used only for the purposes set forth in section 106(b).

(B) After the death of an eligible individual, this subsection and subsections (c) and (f) shall apply to the individual or individuals specified in subparagraph (A) to whom payment under this section will be made, to the same extent as such subsections apply to the eligible individual.

(C) For purposes of this paragraph—

(i) the "spouse" of an eligible individual means a wife or husband of an eligible individual who was married to that eligible individual for at least 1 year immediately before the death of the eligible individual;

(ii) a "child" of an eligible individual includes a recognized natural child, a stepchild who lived with the eligible individual in a regular parent-child relationship, and an adopted child; and

(iii) a "parent" of an eligible individual includes fathers and mothers through adoption.

(b) ORDER OF PAYMENTS.—The Attorney General shall endeavor to make payments under this section to eligible individuals in the order of date of birth (with the oldest individual on the date of the enactment of this Act (or, if applicable, that individual's survivors under paragraph (6)) receiving full payment first), until all eligible individuals have received payment in full.

(c) RESOURCES FOR LOCATING ELIGIBLE INDIVIDUALS.—In attempting to locate any eligible individual, the Attorney General may use any facility or resource of any public or nonprofit organization or any other record, document, or information that may be made available to the Attorney General.

(d) Administrative Costs Not Paid From the Fund.—No costs incurred by the Attorney General in carrying out this section shall be paid from the Fund or set off against, or otherwise deducted from, any payment under this section to any eligible individual.

(e) Termination of Duties of Attorney General.—The duties of the Attorney General under this section shall cease when the Fund terminates.

(f) Clarification of Treatment of Payments Under Other Laws.—Amounts paid to an eligible individual under this section—

(1) shall be treated for purposes of the internal revenue laws of the United States as damages for human suffering; and

(2) shall not be included as income or resources for purposes of determining eligibility to receive benefits described in section 3803(c)(2)(C) of title 31, United States Code, or the amount of such benefits.

SEC. 106. BOARD OF DIRECTORS OF THE FUND.

(a) Establishment.—There is established the Civil Liberties Public Education Fund Board of Directors, which shall be responsible for making disbursements from the Fund in the manner provided in this section.

(b) Uses of Fund.—The Board may make disbursements from the Fund only—

(1) to sponsor research and public educational activities, and to publish and distribute the hearings, findings, and recommendations of the Commission, so that the events surrounding the evacuation, relocation, and internment of United States citizens and permanent resident aliens of Japanese ancestry will be remembered, and so that the causes and circumstances of this and similar events may be illuminated and understood; and

(2) for reasonable administrative expenses of the Board, including expenses incurred under subsections (c)(3), (d), and (e).

(c) Membership.—

(1) Appointment.—The Board shall be composed of 9 members appointed by the President, by and with the advice and consent of the Senate, from individuals who are not officers or employees of the United States Government.

(2) Terms.—(A) Except as provided in subparagraphs (B) and (C), members shall be appointed for terms of 3 years.

(B) Of the members first appointed—

(i) 5 shall be appointed for terms of 3 years, and

(ii) 4 shall be appointed for terms of 2 years,

as designated by the President at the time of appointment.

(C) Any member appointed to fill a vacancy occurring before the expiration of the term for which such member's predecessor was appointed shall be appointed only for the remainder of such term. A member may serve after the expiration of such member's term until such member's successor has taken office. No individual may be appointed as a member for more than 2 consecutive terms.

(3) Compensation.—Members of the Board shall serve without pay, except that members of the Board shall be entitled to reimbursement for travel, subsistence, and other necessary expenses incurred by them in carrying out the functions of the Board, in the same manner as persons employed intermittently

in the United States Government are allowed expenses under section 5703 of title 5, United States Code.

(4) QUORUM.—5 members of the Board shall constitute a quorum but a lesser number may hold hearings.

(5) CHAIR.—The Chair of the Board shall be elected by the members of the Board.

(d) DIRECTOR AND STAFF.—

(1) DIRECTOR.—The Board shall have a Director who shall be appointed by the Board.

(2) ADDITIONAL STAFF.—The Board may appoint and fix the pay of such additional staff as it may require.

(3) APPLICABILITY OF CIVIL SERVICE LAWS.—The Director and the additional staff of the Board may be appointed without regard to section 5311(b) of title 5, United States Code, and without regard to the provisions of such title governing appointments in the competitive service, and may be paid without regard to the provisions of chapter 51 and subchapter III of chapter 53 of such title relating to classification and General Schedule pay rates, except that the compensation of any employee of the Board may not exceed a rate equivalent to the minimum rate of basic pay payable for GS–18 of the General Schedule under section 5332(a) of such title.

(e) ADMINISTRATIVE SUPPORT SERVICES.—The Administrator of General Services shall provide to the Board on a reimbursable basis such administrative support services as the Board may request.

(f) GIFTS AND DONATIONS.—The Board may accept, use, and dispose of gifts or donations of services or property for purposes authorized under subsection (b).

(g) ANNUAL REPORTS.—Not later than 12 months after the first meeting of the Board and every 12 months thereafter, the Board shall transmit to the President and to each House of the Congress a report describing the activities of the Board.

(h) TERMINATION.—90 days after the termination of the Fund, the Board shall terminate and all obligations of the Board under this section shall cease.

SEC. 107. DOCUMENTS RELATING TO THE INTERNMENT.

(a) PRESERVATION OF DOCUMENTS IN NATIONAL ARCHIVES.—All documents, personal testimony, and other records created or received by the Commission during its inquiry shall be kept and maintained by the Archivist of the United States who shall preserve such documents, testimony, and records in the National Archives of the United States. The Archivist shall make such documents, testimony, and records available to the public for research purposes.

(b) PUBLIC AVAILABILITY OF CERTAIN RECORDS OF THE HOUSE OF REPRESENTATIVES.—(1) The Clerk of the House of Representatives is authorized to permit the Archivist of the United States to make available for use records of the House not classified for national security purposes, which have been in existence for not less than thirty years, relating to the evacuation, relocation, and internment of individuals during the evacuation, relocation, and internment period.

(2) This subsection is enacted as an exercise of the rulemaking power of the House of Representatives, but is applicable only with respect to the availability of records to which it applies, and supersedes other rules only to the extent that the time limitation established by this section with respect to such records is specifically

inconsistent with such rules, and is enacted with full recognition of the constitutional right of the House to change its rules at any time, in the same manner and to the same extent as in the case of any other rule of the House.

SEC. 108. DEFINITIONS.

For the purposes of this title—

(1) the term "evacuation, relocation, and internment period" means that period beginning on December 7, 1941, and ending on June 30, 1946;

(2) the term "eligible individual" means any individual of Japanese ancestry who is living on the date of the enactment of this Act and who, during the evacuation, relocation, and internment period—

(A) was a United States citizen or a permanent resident alien; and

(B)(i) was confined, held in custody, relocated, or otherwise deprived of liberty or property as a result of—

(I) Executive Order Numbered 9066, dated February 19, 1942;

(II) the Act entitled "An Act to provide a penalty for violation of restrictions or orders with respect to persons entering, remaining in, leaving, or committing any act in military areas or zones", approved March 21, 1942 (56 Stat. 173); or

(III) any other Executive order, Presidential proclamation, law of the United States, directive of the Armed Forces of the United States, or other action taken by or on behalf of the United States or its agents, representatives, officers, or employees, respecting the evacuation, relocation, or internment of individuals solely on the basis of Japanese ancestry; or

(ii) was enrolled on the records of the United States Government during the period beginning on December 7, 1941, and ending on June 30, 1946, as being in a prohibited military zone;

except that the term "eligible individual" does not include any individual who, during the period beginning on December 7, 1941, and ending on September 2, 1945, relocated to a country while the United States was at war with that country;

(3) the term "permanent resident alien" means an alien lawfully admitted into the United States for permanent residence;

(4) the term "Fund" means the Civil Liberties Public Education Fund established in section 104;

(5) the term "Board" means the Civil Liberties Public Education Fund Board of Directors established in section 106; and

(6) the term "Commission" means the Commission on Wartime Relocation and Internment of Civilians, established by the Commission on Wartime Relocation and Internment of Civilians Act (Public Law 96–317; 50 U.S.C. App. 1981 note).

SEC. 109. COMPLIANCE WITH BUDGET ACT.

No authority under this title to enter into contracts or to make payments shall be effective in any fiscal year except to such extent and in such amounts as are provided in advance in appropriations Acts. In any fiscal year, total benefits conferred by this title shall be limited to an amount not in excess of the appropriations for such fiscal year. Any provision of this title which, directly or indirectly, authorizes the enactment of new budget authority shall be effective only for fiscal year 1989 and thereafter.

TITLE II—ALEUTIAN AND PRIBILOF ISLANDS RESTITUTION

SEC. 201. SHORT TITLE.

This title may be cited as the "Aleutian and Pribilof Islands Restitution Act".

SEC. 202. DEFINITIONS.

As used in this title—

(1) the term "Administrator" means the person appointed by the Secretary under section 204;

(2) the term "affected Aleut villages" means the surviving Aleut villages of Akutan, Atka, Nikolski, Saint George, Saint Paul, and Unalaska, and the Aleut village of Attu, Alaska;

(3) the term "Association" means the Aleutian/Pribilof Islands Association, Inc., a nonprofit regional corporation established for the benefit of the Aleut people and organized under the laws of the State of Alaska;

(4) the term "Corporation" means the Aleut Corporation, a for-profit regional corporation for the Aleut region organized under the laws of the State of Alaska and established under section 7 of the Alaska Native Claims Settlement Act (Public Law 92-203; 43 U.S.C. 1606);

(5) the term "eligible Aleut" means any Aleut living on the date of the enactment of this Act—

(A) who, as a civilian, was relocated by authority of the United States from his or her home village on the Pribilof Islands or the Aleutian Islands west of Unimak Island to an internment camp, or other temporary facility or location, during World War II; or

(B) who was born while his or her natural mother was subject to such relocation;

(6) the term "Secretary" means the Secretary of the Interior;

(7) the term "Fund" means the Aleutian and Pribilof Islands Restitution Fund established in section 203; and

(8) the term "World War II" means the period beginning on December 7, 1941, and ending on September 2, 1945.

SEC. 203. ALEUTIAN AND PRIBILOF ISLANDS RESTITUTION FUND.

(a) Establishment.—There is established in the Treasury of the United States the Aleutian and Pribilof Islands Restitution Fund, which shall be administered by the Secretary. The Fund shall consist of amounts appropriated to it pursuant to this title.

(b) Report.—The Secretary shall report to the Congress, not later than 60 days after the end of each fiscal year, on the financial condition of the Fund, and the results of operations of the Fund, during the preceding fiscal year and on the expected financial condition and operations of the Fund during the current fiscal year.

(c) Investment.—Amounts in the Fund shall be invested in accordance with section 9702 of title 31, United States Code.

(C) One account for the independent benefit of those Aleuts who, as determined by the Secretary, upon the advice of the trustees, are deserving but will not benefit directly from the accounts established under subparagraphs (A) and (B).

The trustees shall credit to the account described in subparagraph (C) an amount equal to 5 percent of the principal amount deposited by the Secretary in the trust under this subsection. Of the remaining principal amount, an amount shall be credited to each account described in subparagraphs (A) and (B) which bears the same proportion to such remaining principal amount as the Aleut civilian population, as of June 1, 1942, of the village with respect to which such account is established bears to the total civilian Aleut population on such date of all affected Aleut villages.

(2) Uses of accounts.—The trustees may use the principal, accrued interest, and other earnings of the accounts maintained under paragraph (1) for—

(A) the benefit of elderly, disabled, or seriously ill persons on the basis of special need;

(B) the benefit of students in need of scholarship assistance;

(C) the preservation of Aleut cultural heritage and historical records;

(D) the improvement of community centers in affected Aleut villages; and

(E) other purposes to improve the condition of Aleut life, as determined by the trustees.

(3) Authorization of appropriations.—There are authorized to be appropriated $5,000,000 to the Fund to carry out this subsection.

(d) Compensation for Damaged or Destroyed Church Property.—

(1) Inventory and assessment of property.—The Administrator shall make an inventory and assessment of real and personal church property of affected Aleut villages which was damaged or destroyed during World War II. In making such inventory and assessment, the Administrator shall consult with the trustees of the trust established under subsection (b), residents of affected Aleut villages, affected church members and leaders, and the clergy of the churches involved. Within 1 year after the date of the enactment of this Act, the Administrator shall submit such inventory and assessment, together with an estimate of the present replacement value of lost or destroyed furnishings and artifacts, to the Secretary.

(2) Review by the Secretary; deposit in the trust.—The Secretary shall review the inventory and assessment provided under paragraph (1), and shall deposit in the trust established under subsection (b) an amount reasonably calculated by the Secretary to compensate affected Aleut villages for church property lost, damaged, or destroyed during World War II.

(3) Distribution of compensation.—The trustees shall distribute the amount deposited in the trust under paragraph (2) for the benefit of the churches referred to in this subsection.

(4) Authorization of appropriations.—There are authorized to be appropriated to the Fund $1,400,000 to carry out this subsection.

(d) TERMINATION.—The Secretary shall terminate the Fund 3 years after the date of the enactment of this Act, or 1 year following disbursement of all payments from the Fund, as authorized by this title, whichever occurs later. On the date the Fund is terminated, all investments of amounts in the Fund shall be liquidated by the Secretary and receipts thereof deposited in the Fund and all funds remaining in the Fund shall be deposited in the miscellaneous receipts account in the Treasury.

SEC. 204. APPOINTMENT OF ADMINISTRATOR.

As soon as practicable after the date of the enactment of this Act, the Secretary shall offer to undertake negotiations with the Association, leading to the execution of an agreement with the Association to serve as Administrator under this title. The Secretary may appoint the Association as Administrator if such agreement is reached within 90 days after the date of the enactment of this title. If no such agreement is reached within such period, the Secretary shall appoint another person as Administrator under this title, after consultation with leaders of affected Aleut villages and the Corporation.

SEC. 205. COMPENSATION FOR COMMUNITY LOSSES.

(a) IN GENERAL.—Subject to the availability of funds appropriated to the Fund, the Secretary shall make payments from the Fund, in accordance with this section, as restitution for certain Aleut losses sustained in World War II.

(b) TRUST.—

(1) ESTABLISHMENT.—The Secretary shall, subject to the availability of funds appropriated for this purpose, establish a trust for the purposes set forth in this section. Such trust shall be established pursuant to the laws of the State of Alaska, and shall be maintained and operated by not more than seven trustees, as designated by the Secretary. Each affected Aleut village may submit to the Administrator a list of three prospective trustees. The Secretary, after consultation with the Administrator, affected Aleut villages, and the Corporation, shall designate not more than seven trustees from such lists as submitted.

(2) ADMINISTRATION OF TRUST.—The trust established under this subsection shall be administered in a manner that is consistent with the laws of the State of Alaska, and as prescribed by the Secretary, after consultation with representatives of eligible Aleuts, the residents of affected Aleut villages, and the Administrator.

(c) ACCOUNTS FOR THE BENEFIT OF ALEUTS.—

(1) IN GENERAL.—The Secretary shall deposit in the trust such sums as may be appropriated for the purposes set forth in this subsection. The trustees shall maintain and operate 8 independent and separate accounts in the trust for purposes of this subsection, as follows:

(A) One account for the independent benefit of the wartime Aleut residents of Attu and their descendants.

(B) Six accounts for the benefit of the 6 surviving affected Aleut villages, one each for the independent benefit of Akutan, Atka, Nikolski, Saint George, Saint Paul, and Unalaska, respectively.

(c) ADMINISTRATIVE AND LEGAL EXPENSES.—

(1) REIMBURSEMENT FOR EXPENSES.—The Secretary shall reimburse the Administrator, not less often than annually, for reasonable and necessary administrative and legal expenses in carrying out the Administrator's responsibilities under this title.

(2) AUTHORIZATION OF APPROPRIATIONS.—There are authorized to be appropriated to the Fund such sums as are necessary to carry out this subsection.

SEC. 206. INDIVIDUAL COMPENSATION OF ELIGIBLE ALEUTS.

(a) PAYMENTS TO ELIGIBLE ALEUTS.—In addition to payments made under section 205, the Secretary shall, in accordance with this section, make per capita payments out of the Fund to eligible Aleuts. The Secretary shall pay, subject to the availability of funds appropriated to the Fund for such payments, to each eligible Aleut the sum of $12,000.

(b) ASSISTANCE OF ATTORNEY GENERAL.—The Secretary may request the Attorney General to provide reasonable assistance in locating eligible Aleuts residing outside the affected Aleut villages, and upon such request, the Attorney General shall provide such assistance. In so doing, the Attorney General may use available facilities and resources of the International Committee of the Red Cross and other organizations.

(c) ASSISTANCE OF ADMINISTRATOR.—The Secretary may request the assistance of the Administrator in identifying and locating eligible Aleuts for purposes of this section.

(d) CLARIFICATION OF TREATMENT OF PAYMENTS UNDER OTHER LAWS.—Amounts paid to an eligible Aleut under this section—

(1) shall be treated for purposes of the internal revenue laws of the United States as damages for human suffering, and

(2) shall not be included as income or resources for purposes of determining eligibility to receive benefits described in section 3803(c)(2)(C) of title 31, United States Code, or the amount of such benefits.

(e) PAYMENT IN FULL SETTLEMENT OF CLAIMS AGAINST THE UNITED STATES.—The payment to an eligible Aleut under this section shall be in full satisfaction of all claims against the United States arising out of the relocation described in section 202(5).

(f) AUTHORIZATION OF APPROPRIATIONS.—There are authorized to be appropriated to the Fund such sums as are necessary to carry out this section.

SEC. 207. ATTU ISLAND RESTITUTION PROGRAM.

(a) PURPOSE OF SECTION.—In accordance with section (3)(c) of the Wilderness Act (78 Stat. 892; 16 U.S.C. 1132(c)), the public lands on Attu Island, Alaska, within the National Wildlife Refuge System have been designated as wilderness by section 702(1) of the Alaska National Interest Lands Conservation Act (94 Stat. 2417; 16 U.S.C. 1132 note). In order to make restitution for the loss of traditional Aleut lands and village properties on Attu Island, while preserving the present designation of Attu Island lands as part of the National Wilderness Preservation System, compensation to the Aleut people, in lieu of the conveyance of Attu Island, shall be provided in accordance with this section.

(b) ACREAGE DETERMINATION.—Not later than 90 days after the date of the enactment of this Act, the Secretary shall, in accordance with this subsection, determine the total acreage of land on Attu Island, Alaska, that, at the beginning of World War II, was subject to traditional use by the Aleut villagers of that island for subsistence and other purposes. In making such acreage determination, the Secretary shall establish a base acreage of not less than 35,000 acres within that part of eastern Attu Island traditionally used by the Aleut people, and shall, from the best available information, including information that may be submitted by representatives of the Aleut people, identify any such additional acreage on Attu Island that was subject to such use. The combination of such base acreage and such additional acreage shall constitute the acreage determination upon which payment to the Corporation under this section is based. The Secretary shall promptly notify the Corporation of the results of the acreage determination made under this subsection.

(c) VALUATION.—

(1) DETERMINATION OF VALUE.—Not later than 120 days after the date of the enactment of this Act, the Secretary shall determine the value of the Attu Island acreage determined under subsection (b), except that—

(A) such acreage may not be valued at less than $350 per acre nor more than $500 per acre; and

(B) the total valuation of all such acreage may not exceed $15,000,000.

(2) FACTORS IN MAKING DETERMINATION.—In determining the value of the acreage under paragraph (1), the Secretary shall take into consideration such factors as the Secretary considers appropriate, including—

(A) fair market value;

(B) environmental and public interest value; and

(C) established precedents for valuation of comparable wilderness lands in the State of Alaska.

(3) NOTIFICATION OF DETERMINATION; APPEAL.—The Secretary shall promptly notify the Corporation of the determination of value made under this subsection, and such determination shall constitute the final determination of value unless the Corporation, within 30 days after the determination is made, appeals the determination to the Secretary. If such appeal is made, the Secretary shall, within 30 days after the appeal is made, review the determination in light of the appeal, and issue a final determination of the value of that acreage determined to be subject to traditional use under subsection (b).

(d) IN LIEU COMPENSATION PAYMENT.—

(1) PAYMENT.—The Secretary shall pay, subject to the availability of funds appropriated for such purpose, to the Corporation, as compensation for the Aleuts' loss of lands on Attu Island, the full amount of the value of the acreage determined under subsection (c), less the value (as determined under subsection (c)) of any land conveyed under subsection (e).

(2) PAYMENT IN FULL SETTLEMENT OF CLAIMS AGAINST THE UNITED STATES.—The payment made under paragraph (1) shall be in full satisfaction of any claim against the United States for the loss of traditional Aleut lands and village properties on Attu Island.

(e) VILLAGE SITE CONVEYANCE.—The Secretary may convey to the Corporation all right, title, and interest of the United States to the surface estate of the traditional Aleut village site on Attu Island, Alaska (consisting of approximately 10 acres) and to the surface estate of a parcel of land consisting of all land outside such village that is within 660 feet of any point on the boundary of such village. The conveyance may be made under the authority contained in section 14(h)(1) of the Alaska Native Claims Settlement Act (Public Law 92-203; 43 U.S.C. 1613(h)(1)), except that after the enactment of this Act, no site on Attu Island, Alaska, other than such traditional Aleut village site and such parcel of land, may be conveyed to the Corporation under such section 14(h)(1).

(f) AUTHORIZATION OF APPROPRIATIONS.—There are authorized to be appropriated $15,000,000 to the Secretary to carry out this section.

SEC. 208. COMPLIANCE WITH BUDGET ACT.

No authority under this title to enter into contracts or to make payments shall be effective in any fiscal year except to such extent and in such amounts as are provided in advance in appropriations Acts. In any fiscal year, the Secretary, with respect to—

(1) the Fund established under section 203,

(2) the trust established under section 205(b), and

(3) the provisions of sections 206 and 207,

shall limit the total benefits conferred to an amount not in excess of the appropriations for such fiscal year. Any provision of this title which, directly or indirectly, authorizes the enactment of new budget authority shall be effective only for fiscal year 1989 and thereafter.

SEC. 209. SEVERABILITY.

If any provision of this title, or the application of such provision to any person or circumstance, is held invalid, the remainder of this title and the application of such provision to other persons not similarly situated or to other circumstances shall not be affected by such invalidation.

TITLE III—TERRITORY OR PROPERTY CLAIMS AGAINST UNITED STATES

SEC. 301. EXCLUSION OF CLAIMS.

Notwithstanding any other provision of law or of this Act, nothing in this Act shall be construed as recognition of any claim of Mexico or any other country or any Indian tribe (except as expressly provided in this Act with respect to the Aleut tribe of Alaska) to any territory or other property of the United States, nor shall this Act be construed as providing any basis for compensation in connection with any such claim.

Approved August 10, 1988.

LEGISLATIVE HISTORY—H.R. 442:

HOUSE REPORTS: No. 100-278 (Comm. on the Judiciary) and No. 100-785 (Comm. of Conference).

CONGRESSIONAL RECORD:

Vol. 133 (1987): Sept. 17, considered and passed House.

Vol. 134 (1988): Apr. 20, considered and passed Senate, amended.

July 27, Senate agreed to conference report.

Aug. 4, House agreed to conference report.

WEEKLY COMPILATION OF PRESIDENTIAL DOCUMENTS, Vol. 24 (1988):

Aug. 10, Presidential remarks.

OMNIBUS TRADE AND COMPETITIVENESS ACT OF 1988

An Act to enhance the competitiveness of American industry, and for other purposes.

Date: August 23, 1988

Bill No.: H.R. 4848

Public Law No.: 100-418

Cite: 102 STAT. 1107

Sections reprinted:

Section 1 - Short title and table of contents.
Section 2 - Legislative history of H.R. 3 applicable.

TITLE I - TRADE, CUSTOMS, AND TARIFF LAWS

Section 1001 - Findings and purposes.

Subtitle A - United States Trade Agreements

Part 1 - Negotiation and Implementation of Trade Agreements

Section 1101 - Overall and principal trade negotiating objectives of the United States.
Section 1102 - Trade agreement negotiating authority.
Section 1103 - Implementation of trade agreements.
Section 1104 - Compensation authority.
Section 1105 - Termination and reservation authority; reciprocal nondiscriminatory treatment.
Section 1106 - Accession of state trading regimes to the General Agreement on Tariffs and Trade.
Section 1107 - Definitions and conforming amendments.

Part 2 - Hearings and Advice Concerning Negotiations

Section 1111 - Hearings and advice.

Part 3 - Other Trade Agreement and Negotiation Provisions

Section 1937 - Lamb meat imports.
Title II - EXPORT ENHANCEMENT
Section 2001 - Short title.
Subtitle A - Trade and Foreign Policy
Part I - Relations With Certain Countries
Section 2101 - United States-Mexico Framework Agreement on Trade and Investment.
Section 2102 - Relations with countries providing offensive weaponry to belligerent countries in the Persian Gulf region.
Part II - Fair Trade in Auto Parts
Section 2121 - Short title.
Section 2122 - Definition.
Section 2123 - Establishment of initiative on auto parts sales to Japan.
Section 2124 - Establishment of special advisory committee on auto parts sales in Japan.
Section 2125 - Expiration date.
Subtitle B - Export Enhancement
Part I - General Provisions
Section 2201 - Commercial personnel at the American Institute of Taiwan.
Section 2202 - Country reports on economic policy and trade practices.
Section 2203 - Overseas private investment corporation.
Section 2204 - Trade and development program.
Section 2205 - Barter and countertrade.
Section 2206 - Protection of United States intellectual property.
Section 2207 - Report on worker rights.
Section 2208 - Japanese importation of manufactured goods from less developed countries.
Section 2209 - Japan and the Arab boycott of Israel.
Section 2210 - Facilitation of jewelry trade.
Section 2211 - Loan guarantees.
Part II - Assistance to Poland

Section 2416 - Control list.
Section 2417 - Trade shows.
Section 2418 - Foreign availability.
Section 2419. Review of technology levels.
Section 2420 - Functions of technical advisory committees.
Section 2421 - Negotiations with COCOM.
Section 2422 - Goods containing microprocessors or certain other parts or components.
Section 2423 - Foreign policy controls.
Section 2424 - Exports of domestically produced crude oil.
Section 2425 - Procedures for license applications.
Section 2426 - Violations.
Section 2427 - Enforcement.
Section 2428 - Administrative procedure and judicial review.
Section 2429 - Responsibilities of the Under Secretary of Commerce for Export Administration.
Section 2430 - Authorization of appropriations.
Section 2431 - Termination date.
Section 2432 - Monitoring of wood exports.
Section 2433 - Study on national security export controls.

Part II - Multilateral Export Control Enhancement

Section 2441 - Short title.
Section 2442 - Findings.
Section 2443 - Mandatory sanctions against Toshiba and Kongsberg.
Section 2444 - Mandatory sanctions for future violations.
Section 2445 - Annual report of defense impact.
Section 2446 - Improved multilateral cooperation.
Section 2447 - Technical and conforming amendments.

Subtitle E - Miscellaneous Provisions

Section 4206 - Establishment of trade assistance office.

Part 2 - Foreign Agricultural Service

Section 4211 - Personnel of the service.

Section 4212 - Agricultural attache educational program.

Section 4213 - Personnel resource time.

Section 4214 - Cooperator organizations.

Section 4215 - Authorization of additional appropriations.

Subtitle C - Existing Agricultural Trade Programs

Section 4301 - Triggered marketing loans and export enhancement.

Section 4302 - Price support programs for sunflower seeds and cottonseed.

Section 4303 - Multiyear agreements under the Food for Progress Program.

Section 4304 - Targeted export assistance.

Section 4305 - Export Credit Guarantee Program.

Section 4306 - Agricultural Export Enhancement Program.

Section 4307 - Agricultural attache reports.

Section 4308 - Dairy Export Incentive Program.

Section 4309 - Barter of agricultural commodities.

Section 4310 - Minimum level of food assistance.

Section 4311 - Food aid and market development.

Subtitle D - Wood and Wood Products

Section 4401 - Developing markets for wood and wood products under Public Law 480.

Section 4402 - Developing markets for wood and wood products under the Short-Term and Intermediate-Term Export Credit Guarantee Programs.

Section 4403 - Cooperative National Forest Products Marketing Program.

Section 4404 - Use of Department of Agriculture programs.
Subtitle E - Studies and Reports
Section 4501 - Study of Canadian wheat import licensing requirements.
Section 4502 - Import inventory.
Section 4503 - Study relating to honey.
Section 4504 - Study of dairy import quotas.
Section 4505 - Report on intermediate export credit.
Section 4506 - Imported meat, poultry products, eggs, and egg products.
Section 4507 - Study of circumvention of agricultural quotas.
Section 4508 - Study of lamb meat imports.
Section 4509 - Rose study.
Subtitle F - Miscellaneous Agricultural Provisions
Section 4601 - Allocation of certain milk.
Section 4602 - Paid advertising for Florida-grown strawberries under marketing orders.
Section 4603 - Application of marketing orders to imports.
Section 4604 - Reciprocal meat inspection requirement.
Section 4605 - Study of international marketing in land grant colleges and universities.
Section 4606 - International trade in eggs and egg products.
Section 4607 - United States access to the Korean beef market.
Section 4608 - United States access to Japanese agricultural markets.
Section 4609 - Sense of Congress relating to section 22.
TITLE V - FOREIGN CORRUPT PRACTICES AMENDMENTS
Subtitle A - Foreign Corrupt Practices Act Amendments; Review of Certain Acquisitions

Part I - Foreign Corrupt Practices Act Amendments

Section 5001 - Short title.

Section 5002 - Penalties for violations of accounting standards.

Section 5003 - Foreign Corrupt Practices Act Amendments.

Part II - Review of Certain Mergers, Acquisitions, and Takeovers

Section 5021 - Authority to review certain mergers, acquisitions, and takeovers.

TITLE VIII - SMALL BUSINESS

Section 8001 - Short title.

Section 8002 - Declaration of policy.

Section 8003 - Changes in existing Small Business Administration International Trade Office.

Section 8004 - Authorization of appropriations.

Section 8005 - Export financing provided by the Administration.

Section 8006 - Small Business Development Centers.

Section 8007 - Capital formation.

Section 8008 - Small Business Innovation Research.

Section 8009 - Globalization of production.

Section 8010 - Small business trade remedy assistance.

Section 8011 - National Seminar on Small Business Exports.

Section 8012 - Trade negotiations.

Section 8013 - Promulgation of regulations.

Section 8014 - Effective date.

TITLE IX - PATENTS

Subtitle A - Process Patents

Section 9001 - Short title.

Section 9002 - Rights of owners of patented processes.

Section 9003 - Infringement for importation, use, or sale.

Section 9004 - Damages for infringement.

Public Law 100-418
100th Congress

An Act

To enhance the competitiveness of American industry, and for other purposes

Be it enacted by the Senate and House of Representatives of the United States of America in Congress assembled,

SECTION 1. SHORT TITLE AND TABLE OF CONTENTS.

(a) SHORT TITLE.—This Act may be cited as the "Omnibus Trade and Competitiveness Act of 1988".

(b) TABLE OF CONTENTS.—

TITLE IV—AGRICULTURAL TRADE

SEC. 2. LEGISLATIVE HISTORY OF H.R. 3 APPLICABLE.

(a) IN GENERAL.—Except as provided in subsection (b), the legislative history of a title, subtitle, part, subpart, chapter, subchapter, section, or other provision of the conference report to accompany H.R. 3 of the 100th Congress (H. Rept. 100–576) shall be treated (along with any other legislative history developed by reason of this Act) as being the legislative history of the provision of this Act that has the same numerical or alphabetical designation as the provision of the conference report.

(b) EXCEPTIONS.—

(1) Subsection (a) does not apply to section 2424(a) of this Act.

(2) The legislative history for subtitle F of title VI of the conference report to accompany H.R. 3 shall be treated as the legislative history for subtitle E of title VI of this Act.

TITLE I—TRADE, CUSTOMS, AND TARIFF LAWS

SEC. 1001. FINDINGS AND PURPOSES.

(a) FINDINGS.—The Congress finds that—

(1) in the last 10 years there has arisen a new global economy in which trade, technological development, investment, and services form an integrated system; and in this system these activities affect each other and the health of the United States economy;

(2) the United States is confronted with a fundamental disequilibrium in its trade and current account balances and a rapid increase in its net external debt;

(3) such disequilibrium and increase are a result of numerous factors, including—

(A) disparities between the macroeconomic policies of the major trading nations,

(B) the large United States budget deficit,

(C) instabilities and structural defects in the world monetary system,

(D) the growth of debt throughout the developing world,

(E) structural defects in the world trading system and inadequate enforcement of trade agreement obligations,

(F) governmental distortions and barriers,

(G) serious shortcomings in United States trade policy, and

(H) inadequate growth in the productivity and competitiveness of United States firms and industries relative to their overseas competition;

(4) it is essential, and should be the highest priority of the United States Government, to pursue a broad array of domestic and international policies—

(A) to prevent future declines in the United States economy and standards of living,

(B) to ensure future stability in external trade of the United States, and

(C) to guarantee the continued vitality of the technological, industrial, and agricultural base of the United States;

(5) the President should be authorized and encouraged to negotiate trade agreements and related investment, financial, intellectual property, and services agreements that meet the standards set forth in this title; and

(6) while the United States is not in a position to dictate economic policy to the rest of the world, the United States is in a position to lead the world and it is in the national interest for the United States to do so.

(b) PURPOSES.—The purposes of this title are to—

(1) authorize the negotiation of reciprocal trade agreements;

(2) strengthen United States trade laws;

(3) improve the development and management of United States trade strategy; and

(4) through these actions, improve standards of living in the world.

Subtitle A—United States Trade Agreements

PART 1—NEGOTIATION AND IMPLEMENTATION OF TRADE AGREEMENTS

SEC. 1101. OVERALL AND PRINCIPAL TRADE NEGOTIATING OBJECTIVES OF THE UNITED STATES.

(a) OVERALL TRADE NEGOTIATING OBJECTIVES.—The overall trade negotiating objectives of the United States are to obtain—

(1) more open, equitable, and reciprocal market access;

(2) the reduction or elimination of barriers and other trade-distorting policies and practices; and

(3) a more effective system of international trading disciplines and procedures.

(b) PRINCIPAL TRADE NEGOTIATING OBJECTIVES.—

(1) DISPUTE SETTLEMENT.—The principal negotiating objectives of the United States with respect to dispute settlement are—

(A) to provide for more effective and expeditious dispute settlement mechanisms and procedures; and

(B) to ensure that such mechanisms within the GATT and GATT agreements provide for more effective and expeditious resolution of disputes and enable better enforcement of United States rights.

(2) IMPROVEMENT OF THE GATT AND MULTILATERAL TRADE NEGOTIATION AGREEMENTS.—The principal negotiating objectives of the United States regarding the improvement of GATT and multilateral trade negotiation agreements are—

(A) to enhance the status of the GATT;

(B) to improve the operation and extend the coverage of the GATT and such agreements and arrangements to products, sectors, and conditions of trade not adequately covered; and

(C) to expand country participation in particular agreements or arrangements, where appropriate.

(3) TRANSPARENCY.—The principal negotiating objective of the United States regarding transparency is to obtain broader application of the principle of transparency and clarification of the costs and benefits of trade policy actions through the observance of open and equitable procedures in trade matters by Contracting Parties to the GATT.

(4) DEVELOPING COUNTRIES.—The principal negotiating objectives of the United States regarding developing countries are—

(A) to ensure that developing countries promote economic development by assuming the fullest possible measure of responsibility for achieving and maintaining an open international trading system by providing reciprocal benefits and assuming equivalent obligations with respect to their import and export practices; and

(B) to establish procedures for reducing nonreciprocal trade benefits for the more advanced developing countries.

(5) CURRENT ACCOUNT SURPLUSES.—The principal negotiating objective of the United States regarding current account surpluses is to develop rules to address large and persistent global current account imbalances of countries, including imbalances which threaten the stability of the international trading system,

by imposing greater responsibility on such countries to undertake policy changes aimed at restoring current account equilibrium, including expedited implementation of trade agreements where feasible and appropriate.

(6) TRADE AND MONETARY COORDINATION.—The principal negotiating objective of the United States regarding trade and monetary coordination is to develop mechanisms to assure greater coordination, consistency, and cooperation between international trade and monetary systems and institutions.

(7) AGRICULTURE.—The principal negotiating objectives of the United States with respect to agriculture are to achieve, on an expedited basis to the maximum extent feasible, more open and fair conditions of trade in agricultural commodities by—

(A) developing, strengthening, and clarifying rules for agricultural trade, including disciplines on restrictive or trade-distorting import and export practices;

(B) increasing United States agricultural exports by eliminating barriers to trade (including transparent and nontransparent barriers) and reducing or eliminating the subsidization of agricultural production consistent with the United States policy of agricultural stabilization in cyclical and unpredictable markets;

(C) creating a free and more open world agricultural trading system by resolving questions pertaining to export and other trade-distorting subsidies, market pricing and market access and eliminating and reducing substantially other specific constraints to fair trade and more open market access, such as tariffs, quotas, and other nontariff practices, including unjustified phytosanitary and sanitary restrictions; and

(D) seeking agreements by which the major agricultural exporting nations agree to pursue policies to reduce excessive production of agricultural commodities during periods of oversupply, with due regard for the fact that the United States already undertakes such policies, and without recourse to arbitrary schemes to divide market shares among major exporting countries.

(8) UNFAIR TRADE PRACTICES.—The principal negotiating objectives of the United States with respect to unfair trade practices are—

(A) to improve the provisions of the GATT and nontariff measure agreements in order to define, deter, discourage the persistent use of, and otherwise discipline unfair trade practices having adverse trade effects, including forms of subsidy and dumping and other practices not adequately covered such as resource input subsidies, diversionary dumping, dumped or subsidized inputs, and export targeting practices;

(B) to obtain the application of similar rules to the treatment of primary and nonprimary products in the Agreement on Interpretation and Application of Articles VI, XVI, and XXIII of the GATT (relating to subsidies and countervailing measures); and

(C) to obtain the enforcement of GATT rules against—

(i) state trading enterprises, and

(ii) the acts, practices, or policies of any foreign government which, as a practical matter, unreasonably require that—

(I) substantial direct investment in the foreign country be made,

(II) intellectual property be licensed to the foreign country or to any firm of the foreign country, or

(III) other collateral concessions be made,

as a condition for the importation of any product or service of the United States into the foreign country or as a condition for carrying on business in the foreign country.

(9) TRADE IN SERVICES.—

(A) The principal negotiating objectives of the United States regarding trade in services are—

(i) to reduce or to eliminate barriers to, or other distortions of, international trade in services, including barriers that deny national treatment and restrictions on establishment and operation in such markets; and

(ii) to develop internationally agreed rules, including dispute settlement procedures, which—

(I) are consistent with the commercial policies of the United States, and

(II) will reduce or eliminate such barriers or distortions, and help ensure fair, equitable opportunities for foreign markets.

(B) In pursuing the negotiating objectives described in subparagraph (A), United States negotiators shall take into account legitimate United States domestic objectives including, but not limited to, the protection of legitimate health or safety, essential security, environmental, consumer or employment opportunity interests and the law and regulations related thereto.

(10) INTELLECTUAL PROPERTY.—The principal negotiating objectives of the United States regarding intellectual property are—

(A) to seek the enactment and effective enforcement by foreign countries of laws which—

(i) recognize and adequately protect intellectual property, including copyrights, patents, trademarks, semiconductor chip layout designs, and trade secrets, and

(ii) provide protection against unfair competition,

(B) to establish in the GATT obligations—

(i) to implement adequate substantive standards based on—

(I) the standards in existing international agreements that provide adequate protection, and

(II) the standards in national laws if international agreement standards are inadequate or do not exist,

(ii) to establish effective procedures to enforce, both internally and at the border, the standards implemented under clause (i), and

(iii) to implement effective dispute settlement procedures that improve on existing GATT procedures;

(C) to recognize that the inclusion in the GATT of—

(i) adequate and effective substantive norms and standards for the protection and enforcement of intellectual property rights, and

(ii) dispute settlement provisions and enforcement procedures,

is without prejudice to other complementary initiatives undertaken in other international organizations; and

(D) to supplement and strengthen standards for protection and enforcement in existing international intellectual property conventions administered by other international organizations, including their expansion to cover new and emerging technologies and elimination of discrimination or unreasonable exceptions or preconditions to protection.

(11) FOREIGN DIRECT INVESTMENT.—

(A) The principal negotiating objectives of the United States regarding foreign direct investment are—

(i) to reduce or to eliminate artificial or trade-distorting barriers to foreign direct investment, to expand the principle of national treatment, and to reduce unreasonable barriers to establishment; and

(ii) to develop internationally agreed rules, including dispute settlement procedures, which—

(I) will help ensure a free flow of foreign direct investment, and

(II) will reduce or eliminate the trade distortive effects of certain trade-related investment measures.

(B) In pursuing the negotiating objectives described in subparagraph (A), United States negotiators shall take into account legitimate United States domestic objectives including, but not limited to, the protection of legitimate health or safety, essential security, environmental, consumer or employment opportunity interests and the law and regulations related thereto.

(12) SAFEGUARDS.—The principal negotiating objectives of the United States regarding safeguards are—

(A) to improve and expand rules and procedures covering safeguard measures;

(B) to ensure that safeguard measures are—

(i) transparent,

(ii) temporary,

(iii) degressive, and

(iv) subject to review and termination when no longer necessary to remedy injury and to facilitate adjustment; and

(C) to require notification of, and to monitor the use by, GATT Contracting Parties of import relief actions for their domestic industries.

(13) SPECIFIC BARRIERS.—The principal negotiating objective of the United States regarding specific barriers is to obtain competitive opportunities for United States exports in foreign markets substantially equivalent to the competitive opportunities afforded foreign exports to United States markets, including the reduction or elimination of specific tariff and nontariff trade barriers, particularly—

(A) measures identified in the annual report prepared under section 181 of the Trade Act of 1974 (19 U.S.C. 2241); and

(B) foreign tariffs and nontariff barriers on competitive United States exports when like or similar products enter the United States at low rates of duty or are duty-free, and other tariff disparities that impede access to particular export markets.

(14) WORKER RIGHTS.—The principal negotiating objectives of the United States regarding worker rights are—

(A) to promote respect for worker rights;

(B) to secure a review of the relationship of worker rights to GATT articles, objectives, and related instruments with a view to ensuring that the benefits of the trading system are available to all workers; and

(C) to adopt, as a principle of the GATT, that the denial of worker rights should not be a means for a country or its industries to gain competitive advantage in international trade.

(15) ACCESS TO HIGH TECHNOLOGY.—

(A) The principal negotiating objective of the United States regarding access to high technology is to obtain the elimination or reduction of foreign barriers to, and acts, policies, or practices by foreign governments which limit, equitable access by United States persons to foreign-developed technology, including barriers, acts, policies, or practices which have the effect of—

(i) restricting the participation of United States persons in government-supported research and development projects;

(ii) denying equitable access by United States persons to government-held patents;

(iii) requiring the approval or agreement of government entities, or imposing other forms of government interventions, as a condition for the granting of licenses to United States persons by foreign persons (except for approval or agreement which may be necessary for national security purposes to control the export of critical military technology); and

(iv) otherwise denying equitable access by United States persons to foreign-developed technology or contributing to the inequitable flow of technology between the United States and its trading partners.

(B) In pursuing the negotiating objective described in subparagraph (A), the United States negotiators shall take into account United States Government policies in licensing or otherwise making available to foreign persons technology and other information developed by United States laboratories.

(16) BORDER TAXES.—The principal negotiating objective of the United States regarding border taxes is to obtain a revision of the GATT with respect to the treatment of border adjustments for internal taxes to redress the disadvantage to countries relying primarily for revenue on direct taxes rather than indirect taxes.

SEC. 1102. TRADE AGREEMENT NEGOTIATING AUTHORITY.

(a) AGREEMENTS REGARDING TARIFF BARRIERS.—

(1) Whenever the President determines that one or more existing duties or other import restrictions of any foreign country or the United States are unduly burdening and restricting the foreign trade of the United States and that the purposes, policies, and objectives of this title will be promoted thereby, the President—

(A) before June 1, 1993, may enter into trade agreements with foreign countries; and

(B) may, subject to paragraphs (2) through (5), proclaim—

(i) such modification or continuance of any existing duty,

(ii) such continuance of existing duty-free or excise treatment, or

(iii) such additional duties;

as he determines to be required or appropriate to carry out any such trade agreement.

(2) No proclamation may be made under subsection (a) that—

(A) reduces any rate of duty (other than a rate of duty that does not exceed 5 percent ad valorem on the date of enactment of this Act) to a rate which is less than 50 percent of the rate of such duty that applies on such date of enactment; or

(B) increases any rate of duty above the rate that applies on such date of enactment.

(3)(A) Except as provided in subparagraph (B), the aggregate reduction in the rate of duty on any article which is in effect on any day pursuant to a trade agreement entered into under paragraph (1) shall not exceed the aggregate reduction which would have been in effect on such day if a reduction of 3 percent ad valorem or a reduction of one-tenth of the total reduction, whichever is greater, had taken effect on the effective date of the first reduction proclaimed in paragraph (1) to carry out such agreement with respect to such article.

(B) No staging under subparagraph (A) is required with respect to a rate reduction that is proclaimed under paragraph (1) for an article of a kind that is not produced in the United States. The United States International Trade Commission shall advise the President of the identity of articles that may be exempted from staging under this subparagraph.

(4) If the President determines that such action will simplify the computation of reductions under paragraph (3), the President may round an annual reduction by the lesser of—

(A) the difference between the reduction without regard to this paragraph and the next lower whole number; or

(B) one-half of 1 percent ad valorem.

(5) No reduction in a rate of duty under a trade agreement entered into under subsection (a) on any article may take effect more than 10 years after the effective date of the first reduction under paragraph (1) that is proclaimed to carry out the trade agreement with respect to such article.

(6) A rate of duty reduction or increase that may not be proclaimed by reason of paragraph (2) may take effect only if a provision authorizing such reduction or increase is included

102, as appropriate, of the Trade Act of 1974 (19 U.S.C. 2111 or 2112); and

(2) any proclamation or Executive order issued pursuant to a trade agreement entered into under section 1102 shall be treated as a proclamation or Executive order issued pursuant to a trade agreement entered into under section 102 of the Trade Act of 1974.

(b) RECIPROCAL NONDISCRIMINATORY TREATMENT.—

(1) The President shall determine, before June 1, 1993, whether any major industrial country has failed to make concessions under trade agreements entered into under section 1102 (a) and (b) which provide competitive opportunities for the commerce of the United States in such country substantially equivalent to the competitive opportunities, provided by concessions made by the United States under trade agreements entered into under section 1102 (a) and (b), for the commerce of such country in the United States.

(2) If the President determines under paragraph (1) that a major industrial country has not made concessions under trade agreements entered into under section 1102 (a) and (b) which provide substantially equivalent competitive opportunities for the commerce of the United States, the President shall, either generally with respect to such country or by article produced by such country, in order to restore equivalence of competitive opportunities, recommend to the Congress—

(A) legislation providing for the termination or denial of the benefits of concessions of trade agreements entered into under section 1102 (a) and (b) that have been made with respect to rates of duty or other import restrictions imposed by the United States, and

(B) legislation providing that any law necessary to carry out any trade agreement under section 1102 (a) or (b) not apply to such country.

(3) For purposes of this subsection, the term "major industrial country" means Canada, the European Communities, the individual member countries of the European Communities, Japan, and any other foreign country designated by the President for purposes of this subsection.

SEC. 1106. ACCESSION OF STATE TRADING REGIMES TO THE GENERAL AGREEMENT ON TARIFFS AND TRADE.

(a) IN GENERAL.—Before any major foreign country accedes, after the date of enactment of this Act, to the GATT the President shall determine—

(1) whether state trading enterprises account for a significant share of—

(A) the exports of such major foreign country, or

(B) the goods of such major foreign country that are subject to competition from goods imported into such foreign country; and

(2) whether such state trading enterprises—

(A) unduly burden and restrict, or adversely affect, the foreign trade of the United States or the United States economy, or

(B) are likely to result in such a burden, restriction, or effect.

within an implementing bill provided for under section 1103 and that bill is enacted into law.

(b) AGREEMENTS REGARDING NONTARIFF BARRIERS.—

(1) Whenever the President determines that any barrier to, or other distortion of, international trade—

(A) unduly burdens or restricts the foreign trade of the United States or adversely affects the United States economy; or

(B) the imposition of any such barrier or distortion is likely to result in such a burden, restriction, or effect;

and that the purposes, policies, and objectives of this title will be promoted thereby, the President may, before June 1, 1993, enter into a trade agreement with foreign countries providing for—

(i) the reduction or elimination of such barrier or other distortion; or

(ii) the prohibition of, or limitations on the imposition of, such barrier or other distortion.

(2) A trade agreement may be entered into under this subsection only if such agreement makes progress in meeting the applicable objectives described in section 1101.

(c) BILATERAL AGREEMENTS REGARDING TARIFF AND NONTARIFF BARRIERS.—

(1) Before June 1, 1993, the President may enter into bilateral trade agreements with foreign countries that provide for the elimination or reduction of any duty imposed by the United States. A trade agreement entered into under this paragraph may also provide for the reduction or elimination of barriers to, or other distortions of, the international trade of the foreign country or the United States.

(2) Notwithstanding any other provision of law, no trade benefit shall be extended to any country by reason of the extension of any trade benefit to another country under a trade agreement entered into under paragraph (1) with such other country.

(3) A trade agreement may be entered into under paragraph (1) with any foreign country only if—

(A) the agreement makes progress in meeting the applicable objectives described in section 1101;

(B) such foreign country requests the negotiation of such an agreement; and

(C) the President, at least 60 days before the date notice is provided under section 1103(a)(1)(A)—

(i) provides written notice of such negotiations to the Committee on Finance of the Senate and the Committee on Ways and Means of the House of Representatives, and

(ii) consults with such committees regarding the negotiation of such agreement.

(4) The 60-day period of time described in paragraph (3)(B) shall be computed in accordance with section 1103(f).

(5) In any case in which there is an inconsistency between any provision of this Act and any bilateral free trade area agreement that entered into force and effect with respect to the United States before January 1, 1987, the provision shall not apply with respect to the foreign country that is party to that agreement.

(d) CONSULTATION WITH CONGRESS BEFORE AGREEMENTS ENTERED INTO.—

(1) Before the President enters into any trade agreement under subsection (b) or (c), the President shall consult with—

(A) the Committee on Ways and Means of the House of Representatives and the Committee on Finance of the Senate; and

(B) each other committee of the House and the Senate, and each joint committee of the Congress, which has jurisdiction over legislation involving subject matters which would be affected by the trade agreement.

(2) The consultation under paragraph (1) shall include—

(A) the nature of the agreement;

(B) how and to what extent the agreement will achieve the applicable purposes, policies, and objectives of this title; and

(C) all matters relating to the implementation of the agreement under section 1103.

(3) If it is proposed to implement two or more trade agreements in a single implementing bill under section 1103, the consultation under paragraph (1) shall include the desirability and feasibility of such proposed implementation.

SEC. 1103. IMPLEMENTATION OF TRADE AGREEMENTS.

(a) IN GENERAL.—

(1) Any agreement entered into under section 1102 (b) or (c) shall enter into force with respect to the United States if (and only if)—

(A) the President, at least 90 calendar days before the day on which he enters into the trade agreement, notifies the House of Representatives and the Senate of his intention to enter into the agreement, and promptly thereafter publishes notice of such intention in the Federal Register;

(B) after entering into the agreement, the President submits a document to the House of Representatives and to the Senate containing a copy of the final legal text of the agreement, together with—

(i) a draft of an implementing bill,

(ii) a statement of any administrative action proposed to implement the trade agreement, and

(iii) the supporting information described in paragraph (2); and

(C) the implementing bill is enacted into law.

(2) The supporting information required under paragraph (1)(B)(iii) consists of—

(A) an explanation as to how the implementing bill and proposed administrative action will change or affect existing law; and

(B) a statement—

(i) asserting that the agreement makes progress in achieving the applicable purposes, policies, and objectives of this title,

(ii) setting forth the reasons of the President regarding—

(I) how and to what extent the agreement makes progress in achieving the applicable purposes, policies, and objectives referred to in clause (i), and why and to what extent the agreement does not achieve other applicable purposes, policies, and objectives,

(II) how the agreement serves the interests of United States commerce, and

(III) why the implementing bill and proposed administrative action is required or appropriate to carry out the agreement;

(iii) describing the efforts made by the President to obtain international exchange rate equilibrium and any effect the agreement may have regarding increased international monetary stability; and

(iv) describing the extent, if any, to which—

(I) each foreign country that is a party to the agreement maintains non-commercial state trading enterprises that may adversely affect, nullify, or impair the benefits to the United States under the agreement, and

(II) the agreement applies to or affects purchases and sales by such enterprises.

(3) To ensure that a foreign country which receives benefits under a trade agreement entered into under section 1102 (b) or (c) is subject to the obligations imposed by such agreement, the President shall recommend to Congress in the implementing bill and statement of administrative action submitted with respect to such agreement that the benefits and obligations of such agreement apply solely to the parties to such agreement, if such application is consistent with the terms of such agreement. The President may also recommend with respect to any such agreement that the benefits and obligations of such agreement not apply uniformly to all parties to such agreement, if such application is consistent with the terms of such agreement.

(b) Application of Congressional "Fast Track" Procedures to Implementing Bills.—

(1) Except as provided in subsection (c)—

(A) the provisions of section 151 of the Trade Act of 1974 (19 U.S.C. 2191) (hereinafter in this section referred to as "fast track procedures") apply to implementing bills submitted with respect to trade agreements entered into under section 1102 (b) or (c) before June 1, 1991; and

(B) such fast track procedures shall be extended to implementing bills submitted with respect to trade agreements entered into under section 1102 (b) or (c) after May 31, 1991, and before June 1, 1993, if (and only if)—

(i) the President requests such extension under paragraph (2); and

(ii) neither House of the Congress adopts an extension disapproval resolution under paragraph (5) before June 1, 1991.

(2) If the President is of the opinion that the fast track procedures should be extended to implementing bills described in paragraph (1)(B), the President must submit to the Congress, no later than March 1, 1991, a written report that contains a request for such extension, together with—

(A) a description of all trade agreements that have been negotiated under section 1102 (b) or (c) and the anticipated schedule for submitting such agreements to the Congress for approval;

(B) a description of the progress that has been made in multilateral and bilateral negotiations to achieve the purposes, policies, and objectives of this title, and a statement that such progress justifies the continuation of negotiations; and

(C) a statement of the reasons why the extension is needed to complete the negotiations.

(3) The President shall promptly inform the Advisory Committee for Trade Policy and Negotiations established under section 135 of the Trade Act of 1974 (19 U.S.C. 2155) of his decision to submit a report to Congress under paragraph (2). The Advisory Committee shall submit to the Congress as soon as practicable, but no later than March 1, 1991, a written report that contains—

(A) its views regarding the progress that has been made in multilateral and bilateral negotiations to achieve the purposes, policies, and objectives of this title; and

(B) a statement of its views, and the reasons therefor, regarding whether the extension requested under paragraph (2) should be approved or disapproved.

(4) The reports submitted to the Congress under paragraphs (2) and (3), or any portion of the reports, may be classified to the extent the President determines appropriate.

(5)(A) For purposes of this subsection, the term "extension disapproval resolution" means a resolution of either House of the Congress, the sole matter after the resolving clause of which is as follows: "That the   disapproves the request of the President for the extension, under section 1103(b)(1)(B)(i) of the Omnibus Trade and Competitiveness Act of 1988, of the provisions of section 151 of the Trade Act of 1974 to any implementing bill submitted with respect to any trade agreement entered into under section 1102 (b) or (c) of such Act after May 31, 1991, because sufficient tangible progress has not been made in trade negotiations.", with the blank space being filled with the name of the resolving House of the Congress.

(B) Extension disapproval resolutions—

(i) may be introduced in either House of the Congress by any member of such House; and

(ii) shall be jointly referred, in the House of Representatives, to the Committee on Ways and Means and the Committee on Rules.

(C) The provisions of section 152 (d) and (e) of the Trade Act of 1974 (19 U.S.C. 2192 (d) and (e)) (relating to the floor consideration of certain resolutions in the House and Senate) apply to extension disapproval resolutions.

(D) It is not in order for—

(i) the Senate to consider any extension disapproval resolution not reported by the Committee on Finance;

(ii) the House of Representatives to consider any extension disapproval resolution not reported by the Committee on Ways and Means and the Committee on Rules; or

(iii) either House of the Congress to consider an extension disapproval resolution that is reported to such House after May 15, 1991.

(c) LIMITATIONS ON USE OF "FAST TRACK" PROCEDURES.—

(1)(A) The fast track procedures shall not apply to any implementing bill submitted with respect to a trade agreement entered into under section 1102 (b) or (c) if both Houses of the Congress separately agree to procedural disapproval resolutions within any 60-day period.

(B) Procedural disapproval resolutions—

(i) in the House of Representatives—

(I) shall be introduced by the chairman or ranking minority member of the Committee on Ways and Means or the chairman or ranking minority member of the Committee on Rules,

(II) shall be jointly referred to the Committee on Ways and Means and the Committee on Rules, and

(III) may not be amended by either Committee; and

(ii) in the Senate shall be original resolutions of the Committee on Finance.

(C) The provisions of section 152 (d) and (e) of the Trade Act of 1974 (19 U.S.C. 2192 (d) and (e)) (relating to the floor consideration of certain resolutions in the House and Senate) apply to procedural disapproval resolutions.

(D) It is not in order for the House of Representatives to consider any procedural disapproval resolution not reported by the Committee on Ways and Means and the Committee on Rules.

(E) For purposes of this subsection, the term "procedural disapproval resolution" means a resolution of either House of the Congress, the sole matter after the resolving clause of which is as follows: "That the President has failed or refused to consult with Congress on trade negotiations and trade agreements in accordance with the provisions of the Omnibus Trade and Competitiveness Act of 1988, and, therefore, the provisions of section 151 of the Trade Act of 1974 shall not apply to any implementing bill submitted with respect to any trade agreement entered into under section 1102 (b) or (c) of such Act of 1988, if, during the 60-day period beginning on the date on which this resolution is agreed to by the , the agrees to a procedural disapproval resolution (within the meaning of section 1103(c)(1)(E) of such Act of 1988).", with the first blank space being filled with the name of the resolving House of the Congress and the second blank space being filled with the name of the other House of the Congress.

(2) The fast track procedures shall not apply to any implementing bill that contains a provision approving of any trade agreement which is entered into under section 1102(c) with any foreign country if either—

(A) the requirements of section 1102(c)(3) are not met with respect to the negotiation of such agreement; or

(B) the Committee on Finance of the Senate or the Committee on Ways and Means of the House of Representatives disapproves of the negotiation of such agreement before the close of the 60-day period which begins on the date notice is provided under section 1102(c)(3)(C)(i) with respect to the negotiation of such agreement.

(d) RULES OF HOUSE OF REPRESENTATIVES AND SENATE.—Subsections (b) and (c) are enacted by the Congress—

(1) as an exercise of the rulemaking power of the House of Representatives and the Senate, respectively, and as such is

deemed a part of the rules of each House, respectively, and such procedures supersede other rules only to the extent that they are inconsistent with such other rules; and

(2) with the full recognition of the constitutional right of either House to change the rules (so far as relating to the procedures of that House) at any time, in the same manner, and to the same extent as any other rule of that House.

(e) COMPUTATION OF CERTAIN PERIODS OF TIME.—Each period of time described in subsection (c)(1) (A) and (E) and (2) of this section shall be computed without regard to—

(1) the days on which either House of Congress is not in session because of an adjournment of more than 3 days to a day certain or an adjournment of the Congress sine die; and

(2) any Saturday and Sunday, not excluded under paragraph (1), when either House of the Congress is not in session.

SEC. 1104. COMPENSATION AUTHORITY.

Section 123 of the Trade Act of 1974 (19 U.S.C. 2133) is amended—

(1) by amending subsection (a) to read as follows:

"(a) Whenever—

"(1) any action taken under chapter 1 of title II or chapter 1 of title III; or

"(2) any judicial or administrative tariff reclassification that becomes final after the date of the enactment of the Omnibus Trade and Competitiveness Act of 1988;

increases or imposes any duty or other import restriction, the President—

"(A) may enter into trade agreements with foreign countries or instrumentalities for the purpose of granting new concessions as compensation in order to maintain the general level of reciprocal and mutually advantageous concessions; and

"(B) may proclaim such modification or continuance of any existing duty, or such continuance of existing duty-free or excise treatment, as he determines to be required or appropriate to carry out any such agreement.";

(2) by amending subsection (b)(2) by—

(A) striking out "section 109" and inserting "section 1102(a) of the Omnibus Trade and Competitiveness Act of 1988", and

(B) striking out "section 101" each place it appears and inserting "such section 1102(a)";

(3) by striking out "section 101" in subsection (d) and inserting "section 1102 of the Omnibus Trade and Competitiveness Act of 1988"; and

(4) by adding at the end thereof the following new subsection:

"(e) The provisions of this section shall apply by reason of action taken under chapter 1 of title III only if the President determines that action authorized under this section is necessary or appropriate to meet the international obligations of the United States.".

SEC. 1105. TERMINATION AND RESERVATION AUTHORITY; RECIPROCAL NONDISCRIMINATORY TREATMENT.

(a) IN GENERAL.—For purposes of applying sections 125, 126(a), and 127 of the Trade Act of 1974 (19 U.S.C. 2135, 2136(a), and 2137)—

(1) any trade agreement entered into under section 1102 shall be treated as an agreement entered into under section 101 or

(b) EFFECTS OF AFFIRMATIVE DETERMINATION.—If both of the determinations made under paragraphs (1) and (2) of subsection (a) with respect to a major foreign country are affirmative—

(1) the President shall reserve the right of the United States to withhold extension of the application of the GATT, between the United States and such major foreign country, and

(2) the GATT shall not apply between the United States and such major foreign country until—

(A) such foreign country enters into an agreement with the United States providing that the state trading enterprises of such foreign country—

(i) will—

(I) make purchases which are not for the use of such foreign country, and

(II) make sales in international trade,

in accordance with commercial considerations (including price, quality, availability, marketability, and transportation), and

(ii) will afford United States business firms adequate opportunity, in accordance with customary practice, to compete for participation in such purchases or sales; or

(B) a bill submitted under subsection (c) which approves of the extension of the application of the GATT between the United States and such major foreign country is enacted into law.

(c) EXPEDITED CONSIDERATION OF BILL TO APPROVE EXTENSION.—

(1) The President may submit to the Congress any draft of a bill which approves of the extension of the application of the GATT between the United States and a major foreign country.

(2) Any draft of a bill described in paragraph (1) that is submitted by the President to the Congress shall—

(A) be introduced by the majority leader of each House of the Congress (by request) on the first day on which such House is in session after the date such draft is submitted to the Congress; and

(B) shall be treated as an implementing bill for purposes of subsections (d), (e), (f), and (g) of section 151 of the Trade Act of 1974.

(d) PUBLICATION.—The President shall publish in the Federal Register each determination made under subsection (a).

SEC. 1107. DEFINITIONS AND CONFORMING AMENDMENTS.

(a) DEFINITIONS.—For purposes of this part:

(1) The term "distortion" includes, but is not limited to, a subsidy.

(2) The term "foreign country" includes any foreign instrumentality. Any territory or possession of a foreign country that is administered separately for customs purposes, shall be treated as a separate foreign country.

(3) The term "GATT" means the General Agreement on Tariffs and Trade.

(4) The term "implementing bill" has the meaning given such term in section 151(b)(1) of the Trade Act of 1974 (19 U.S.C. 2191(b)(1)).

(5) The term "international trade" includes, but is not limited to—

(A) trade in both goods and services, and

(B) foreign direct investment by United States persons, especially if such investment has implications for trade in goods and services.

(6) The term "state trading enterprise" means—

(A) any agency, instrumentality, or administrative unit of a foreign country which—

(i) purchases goods or services in international trade for any purpose other than the use of such goods or services by such agency, instrumentality, administrative unit, or foreign country, or

(ii) sells goods or services in international trade; or

(B) any business firm which—

(i) is substantially owned or controlled by a foreign country or any agency, instrumentality, or administrative unit thereof,

(ii) is granted (formally or informally) any special or exclusive privilege by such foreign country, agency, instrumentality, or administrative unit, and

(iii) purchases goods or services in international trade for any purpose other than the use of such goods or services by such foreign country, agency, instrumentality, or administrative unit, or which sells goods or services in international trade.

(b) CONFORMING AMENDMENTS.—

(1) Section 151(b)(1) of the Trade Act of 1974 (19 U.S.C. 2191(b)(1)) is amended by striking out "section 102" and inserting "section 102 of this Act or section 1103(a)(1) of the Omnibus Trade and Competitiveness Act of 1988".

(2) Section 121 of the Trade Act of 1974 (19 U.S.C. 2131) is amended by striking out subsections (a), (b), and (c).

PART 2—HEARINGS AND ADVICE CONCERNING NEGOTIATIONS

SEC. 1111. HEARINGS AND ADVICE.

(a) ADVICE FROM ITC AND OTHER FEDERAL AGENCIES CONCERNING TRADE POLICY AND NEGOTIATIONS.—Sections 131 through 134, inclusive, of the Trade Act of 1974 (19 U.S.C. 2151-2154) are amended to read as follows:

"SEC. 131. ADVICE FROM INTERNATIONAL TRADE COMMISSION.

"(a) LISTS OF ARTICLES WHICH MAY BE CONSIDERED FOR ACTION.—

"(1) In connection with any proposed trade agreement under section 123 of this Act or section 1102 (a) or (c) of the Omnibus Trade and Competitiveness Act of 1988, the President shall from time to time publish and furnish the International Trade Commission (hereafter in this section referred to as the 'Commission') with lists of articles which may be considered for modification or continuance of United States duties, continuance of United States duty-free or excise treatment, or additional duties. In the case of any article with respect to which consideration may be given to reducing or increasing the rate of duty, the list shall specify the provision of this subchapter under which such consideration may be given.

"(2) In connection with any proposed trade agreement under section 1102 (b) or (c) of the Omnibus Trade and Competitiveness Act of 1988, the President may from time to time publish and furnish the Commission with lists of nontariff matters which may be considered for modification.

"(b) ADVICE TO PRESIDENT BY COMMISSION.—Within 6 months after receipt of a list under subsection (a) or, in the case of a list submitted in connection with a trade agreement, within 90 days after receipt of such list, the Commission shall advise the President, with respect to each article or nontariff matter, of its judgment as to the probable economic effect of modification of the tariff or nontariff measure on industries producing like or directly competitive articles and on consumers, so as to assist the President in making an informed judgment as to the impact which might be caused by such modifications on United States interests, such as sectors involved in manufacturing, agriculture, mining, fishing, services, intellectual property, investment, labor, and consumers. Such advice may include in the case of any article the advice of the Commission as to whether any reduction in the rate of duty should take place over a longer period of time than the minimum period provided for in section 1102(a)(3)(A).

"(c) ADDITIONAL INVESTIGATIONS AND REPORTS REQUESTED BY THE PRESIDENT OR THE TRADE REPRESENTATIVE.—In addition, in order to assist the President in his determination whether to enter into any agreement under section 123 of this Act or section 1102 of the Omnibus Trade and Competitiveness Act of 1988, or how to develop trade policy, priorities or other matters (such as priorities for actions to improve opportunities in foreign markets), the Commission shall make such investigations and reports as may be requested by the President or the United States Trade Representative on matters such as effects of modification of any barrier to (or other distortion of) international trade on domestic workers, industries or sectors, purchasers, prices and quantities of articles in the United States.

"(d) COMMISSION STEPS IN PREPARING ITS ADVICE TO THE PRESIDENT.—In preparing its advice to the President under this section, the Commission shall to the extent practicable—

"(1) investigate conditions, causes, and effects relating to competition between the foreign industries producing the articles or services in question and the domestic industries producing the like or directly competitive articles or services;

"(2) analyze the production, trade, and consumption of each like or directly competitive article or service, taking into consideration employment, profit levels, and use of productive facilities with respect to the domestic industries concerned, and such other economic factors in such industries as it considers relevant, including prices, wages, sales, inventories, patterns of demand, capital investment, obsolescence of equipment, and diversification of production;

"(3) describe the probable nature and extent of any significant change in employment, profit levels, and use of productive facilities; the overall impact of such or other possible changes on the competitiveness of relevant domestic industries or sectors; and such other conditions as it deems relevant in the domestic industries or sectors concerned which it believes such modifications would cause; and

"(4) make special studies (including studies of real wages paid in foreign supplying countries), whenever deemed to be warranted, of particular proposed modifications affecting United States manufacturing, agriculture, mining, fishing, labor, consumers, services, intellectual property and investment, using to the fullest extent practicable United States Government facilities abroad and appropriate personnel of the United States.

"(e) PUBLIC HEARING.—In preparing its advice to the President under this section, the Commission shall, after reasonable notice, hold public hearings.

"SEC. 132. ADVICE FROM EXECUTIVE DEPARTMENTS AND OTHER SOURCES.

"Before any trade agreement is entered into under section 123 of this Act or section 1102 of the Omnibus Trade and Competitiveness Act of 1988, the President shall seek information and advice with respect to such agreement from the Departments of Agriculture, Commerce, Defense, Interior, Labor, State and the Treasury, from the United States Trade Representative, and from such other sources as he may deem appropriate. Such advice shall be prepared and presented consistent with the provisions of Reorganization Plan Number 3 of 1979, Executive Order Number 12188 and section 141(c).

"SEC. 133. PUBLIC HEARINGS.

"(a) OPPORTUNITY FOR PRESENTATION OF VIEWS.—In connection with any proposed trade agreement under section 123 of this Act or section 1102 of the Omnibus Trade and Competitiveness Act of 1988, the President shall afford an opportunity for any interested person to present his views concerning any article on a list published under section 131, any matter or article which should be so listed, any concession which should be sought by the United States, or any other matter relevant to such proposed trade agreement. For this purpose, the President shall designate an agency or an interagency committee which shall, after reasonable notice, hold public hearings and prescribe regulations governing the conduct of such hearings. When appropriate, such procedures shall apply to the development of trade policy and priorities.

"(b) SUMMARY OF HEARINGS.—The organization holding such hearing shall furnish the President with a summary thereof.

"SEC. 134. PREREQUISITES FOR OFFERS.

"(a) In any negotiation seeking an agreement under section 123 of this Act or section 1102 of the Omnibus Trade and Competitiveness Act of 1988, the President may make a formal offer for the modification or continuance of any United States duty, import restrictions, or barriers to (or other distortions of) international trade, the continuance of United States duty-free or excise treatment, or the imposition of additional duties, import restrictions, or other barrier to (or other distortion of) international trade including trade in services, foreign direct investment and intellectual property as covered by this title, with respect to any article or matter only after he has received a summary of the hearings at which an opportunity to be heard with respect to such article has been afforded under section 133. In addition, the President may make an offer for the modification or continuance of any United States duty, the continuance of United States duty-free or excise treatment, or the imposition of additional duties, with respect to any article included in a list published and furnished under section 131(a), only after he has received advice concerning such article from the Commission under section 131(b), or after the expiration of the 6-month or 90-day period provided for in that section, as appropriate, whichever first occurs.

"(b) In determining whether to make offers described in subsection (a) in the course of negotiating any trade agreement under section 1102 of the Omnibus Trade and Competitiveness Act of 1988, and in determining the nature and scope of such offers, the President shall take into account any advice or information provided, or reports submitted, by—

"(1) the Commission;

"(2) any advisory committee established under section 135; or

"(3) any organization that holds public hearings under section 133;

with respect to any article, or domestic industry, that is sensitive, or potentially sensitive, to imports.".

PART 3—OTHER TRADE AGREEMENT AND NEGOTIATION PROVISIONS

SEC. 1121. IMPLEMENTATION OF NAIROBI PROTOCOL.

(a) PURPOSE AND REFERENCE.—

(1) The purpose of this section is—

(A) to provide for the implementation by the United States of the Protocol (S. Treaty Doc. 97-2, 9; hereafter referred to in this section as the "Nairobi Protocol") to the Agreement on the Importation of Educational, Scientific, and Cultural Materials (17 UST (pt. 2) 1835; commonly known as the "Florence Agreement");

(B) to clarify or modify the duty-free treatment accorded under the Educational, Scientific, and Cultural Materials Importation Act of 1982 (Public Law 97-446, 96 Stat. 2346-2349), the Educational, Scientific, and Cultural Materials Importation Act of 1966 (Public Law 89-65, 80 Stat. 897 et seq.), and Public Law 89-634 (80 Stat. 879); and

(C) to continue the safeguard provisions concerning certain imported articles provided for in the Educational, Scientific, and Cultural Materials Importation Act of 1982.

(2) Whenever an amendment or repeal in this section is expressed in terms of an amendment to, or repeal of, an item, headnote, Appendix, or other provision, the reference shall be considered to be made to an item, headnote, Appendix, or other provision of the Tariff Schedules of the United States.

(b) REPEAL OF THE EDUCATIONAL, SCIENTIFIC, AND CULTURAL MATERIALS IMPORTATION ACT OF 1982.—The Educational, Scientific, and Cultural Materials Importation Act of 1982 is hereby repealed.

SEC. 1124. NEGOTIATIONS ON CURRENCY EXCHANGE RATES.

(a) FINDINGS.—The Congress finds that—

(1) the benefit of trade concessions can be adversely affected by misalignments in currency, and

(2) misalignments in currency caused by government policies intended to maintain an unfair trade advantage tend to nullify and impair trade concessions.

(b) NEGOTIATIONS.—Whenever, in the course of negotiating a trade agreement under this subtitle, the President is advised by the Secretary of the Treasury that a foreign country that is a party to the negotiations satisfies the criteria for initiating bilateral currency negotiations listed in section 3004(b) of this Act, the Secretary of the Treasury shall take action to initiate bilateral currency negotiations on an expedited basis with such foreign country.

SEC. 1125. REPORTS ON NEGOTIATIONS TO ELIMINATE WINE TRADE BARRIERS.

Before the close of the 13-month period beginning on the date of the enactment of this Act, the President shall update each report that the President submitted to the Committee on Ways and Means and the Committee on Finance under section 905(b) of the Wine Equity and Export Expansion Act of 1984 (19 U.S.C. 2804) and submit the updated report to both of such committees. Each updated report shall contain, with respect to the major wine trading country concerned—

(1) a description of each tariff or nontariff barrier to (or other distortion of) trade in United States wine of that country with respect to which the United States Trade Representative has carried out consultations since the report required under such section 905(b) was submitted;

(2) the status of the consultations described under paragraph (1); and

(3) information, explanations, and recommendations of the kind referred to in paragraph (1) (C), (D), and (E) of such section 905(b) that are based on developments (including the taking of relevant actions, if any, of a kind not contemplated at the time of the enactment of such 1984 Act) since the submission of the report required under such section.

Subtitle B—Implementation of the Harmonized Tariff Schedule

SEC. 1201. PURPOSES.

The purposes of this subtitle are—

(1) to approve the International Convention on the Harmonized Commodity Description and Coding System;

(2) to implement in United States law the nomenclature established internationally by the Convention; and

(3) to provide that the Convention shall be treated as a trade agreement obligation of the United States.

SEC. 1202. DEFINITIONS.

As used in this subtitle:

(1) The term "Commission" means the United States International Trade Commission.

(2) The term "Convention" means the International Convention on the Harmonized Commodity Description and Coding System, done at Brussels on June 14, 1983, and the Protocol thereto, done at Brussels on June 24, 1986, submitted to the Congress on June 15, 1987.

(3) The term "entered" means entered, or withdrawn from warehouse for consumption, in the customs territory of the United States.

(4) The term "Federal agency" means any establishment in the executive branch of the United States Government.

(5) The term "old Schedules" means title I of the Tariff Act of 1930 (19 U.S.C. 1202) as in effect on the day before the effective date of the amendment to such title under section 1204(a).

(6) The term "technical rectifications" means rectifications of an editorial character or minor technical or clerical changes which do not affect the substance or meaning of the text, such as—

(A) errors in spelling, numbering, or punctuation;

(B) errors in indentation;

(C) errors (including inadvertent omissions) in cross-references to headings or subheadings or notes; and

(D) other clerical or typographical errors.

SEC. 1203. CONGRESSIONAL APPROVAL OF UNITED STATES ACCESSION TO THE CONVENTION.

(a) CONGRESSIONAL APPROVAL.—The Congress approves the accession by the United States of America to the Convention.

(b) ACCEPTANCE OF THE FINAL LEGAL TEXT OF THE CONVENTION BY THE PRESIDENT.—The President may accept for the United States the final legal instruments embodying the Convention. The President shall submit a copy of each final instrument to the Congress on the date it becomes available.

(c) UNSPECIFIED PRIVATE REMEDIES NOT CREATED.—Neither the entry into force with respect to the United States of the Convention nor the enactment of this subtitle may be construed as creating any private right of action or remedy for which provision is not explicitly made under this subtitle or under other laws of the United States.

(d) TERMINATION.—The provisions of section 125(a) of the Trade Act of 1974 (19 U.S.C. 2135(a)) do not apply to the Convention.

SEC. 1204. ENACTMENT OF THE HARMONIZED TARIFF SCHEDULE.

(a) IN GENERAL.—The Tariff Act of 1930 is amended by striking out title I and inserting a new title I entitled "Title I—Harmonized Tariff Schedule of the United States" (hereinafter in this subtitle referred to as the "Harmonized Tariff Schedule") which—

(1) consists of—

(A) the General Notes;

(B) the General Rules of Interpretation;

(C) the Additional U.S. Rules of Interpretation;

(D) sections I to XXII, inclusive (encompassing chapters 1 to 99, and including all section and chapter notes, article provisions, and tariff and other treatment accorded thereto); and

(E) the Chemical Appendix to the Harmonized Tariff Schedule;

all conforming to the nomenclature of the Convention and as set forth in Publication No. 2030 of the Commission entitled "Harmonized Tariff Schedule of the United States Annotated for Statistical Reporting Purposes" and Supplement No. 1 thereto; but

(2) does not include the statistical annotations, notes, annexes, suffixes, check digits, units of quantity, and other matters formulated under section 484(e) of the Tariff Act of 1930 (19 U.S.C. 1484(e)), nor the table of contents, footnotes, index, and other matters inserted for ease of reference, that are included in such Publication No. 2030 or Supplement No. 1. thereto.

(b) MODIFICATIONS TO THE HARMONIZED TARIFF SCHEDULE.—At the earliest practicable date after the date of the enactment of the Onmibus Trade and Competitiveness Act of 1988, the President shall—

(1) proclaim such modifications to the Harmonized Tariff Schedule as are consistent with the standards applied in converting the old Schedules into the format of the Convention, as reflected in such Publication No. 2030 and Supplement No. 1. thereto, and as are necessary or appropriate to implement—

(A) the future outstanding staged rate reductions authorized by the Congress in—

(i) the Trade Act of 1974 (19 U.S.C. 2101 et seq.) and the Trade Agreements Act of 1979 (19 U.S.C. 2501 et seq.) to reflect the tariff reductions that resulted from the Tokyo Round of multilateral trade negotiations, and

(ii) the United States-Israel Free Trade Area Implementation Act of 1985 (19 U.S.C. 1202 note) to reflect the tariff reduction resulting from the United States-Israel Free Trade Area Agreement,

(B) the applicable provisions of—

(i) statutes enacted,

(ii) executive actions taken, and

(iii) final judicial decisions rendered,

after January 1, 1988, and before the effective date of the Harmonized Tariff Schedule, and

(C) such technical rectifications as the President considers necessary; and

(2) take such action as the President considers necessary to bring trade agreements to which the United States is a party into conformity with the Harmonized Tariff Schedule.

(c) STATUS OF THE HARMONIZED TARIFF SCHEDULE.—

(1) The following shall be considered to be statutory provisions of law for all purposes:

(A) The provisions of the Harmonized Tariff Schedule as enacted by this subtitle.

(B) Each statutory amendment to the Harmonized Tariff Schedule.

(C) Each modification or change made to the Harmonized Tariff Schedule by the President under authority of law (including section 604 of the Trade Act of 1974).

(2) Neither the enactment of this subtitle nor the subsequent enactment of any amendment to the Harmonized Tariff Schedule, unless such subsequent enactment otherwise provides, may be construed as limiting the authority of the President—

(A) to effect the import treatment necessary or appropriate to carry out, modify, withdraw, suspend, or terminate, in whole or in part, trade agreements; or

(B) to take such other actions through the modification, continuance, or imposition of any rate of duty or other import restriction as may be necessary or appropriate under the authority of the President.

(3) If a rate of duty established in column 1 by the President by proclamation or Executive order is higher than the existing rate of duty in column 2, the President may by proclamation or Executive order increase such existing rate to the higher rate.

(4) If a rate of duty is suspended or terminated by the President by proclamation or Executive order and the proclamation or Executive order does not specify the rate that is to apply in lieu of the suspended or terminated rate, the last rate of duty that applied prior to the suspended or terminated rate shall be the efffective rate of duty.

(d) INTERIM INFORMATIONAL USE OF HARMONIZED TARIFF SCHEDULE CLASSIFICATIONS.—Each—

(1) proclamation issued by the President;

(2) public notice issued by the Commission or other Federal agency; and

(3) finding, determination, order, recommendation, or other decision made by the Commission or other Federal agency;

during the period between the date of the enactment of the Omnibus Trade and Competitiveness Act of 1988 and the effective date of the Harmonized Tariff Schedule shall, if the proclamation, notice, or decision contains a reference to the tariff classification of any article, include, for informational purposes, a reference to the classification of that article under the Harmonized Tariff Schedule.

SEC. 1205. COMMISSION REVIEW OF, AND RECOMMENDATIONS REGARDING, THE HARMONIZED TARIFF SCHEDULE.

(a) IN GENERAL.—The Commission shall keep the Harmonized Tariff Schedule under continuous review and periodically, at such time as amendments to the Convention are recommended by the Customs Cooperation Council for adoption, and as other circumstances warrant, shall recommend to the President such modifications in the Harmonized Tariff Schedule as the Commission considers necessary or appropriate—

(1) to conform the Harmonized Tariff Schedule with amendments made to the Convention;

(2) to promote the uniform application of the Convention and particularly the Annex thereto;

(3) to ensure that the Harmonized Tariff Schedule is kept up-to-date in light of changes in technology or in patterns of international trade;

(4) to alleviate unnecessary administrative burdens; and

(5) to make technical rectifications.

(b) AGENCY AND PUBLIC VIEWS REGARDING RECOMMENDATIONS.—In formulating recommendations under subsection (a), the Commission shall solicit, and give consideration to, the views of interested Federal agencies and the public. For purposes of obtaining public views, the Commission—

(1) shall give notice of the proposed recommendations and afford reasonable opportunity for interested parties to present their views in writing; and

(2) may provide for a public hearing.

(c) SUBMISSION OF RECOMMENDATIONS.—The Commission shall submit recommendations under this section to the President in the form of a report that shall include a summary of the information on which the recommendations were based, together with a statement of the probable economic effect of each recommended change on any industry in the United States. The report also shall include a copy of all written views submitted by interested Federal agencies and a copy or summary, prepared by the Commission, of the views of all other interested parties.

(d) REQUIREMENTS REGARDING RECOMMENDATIONS.—The Commission may not recommend any modification to the Harmonized Tariff Schedule unless the modification meets the following requirements:

(1) The modification must—

(A) be consistent with the Convention or any amendment thereto recommended for adoption;

(B) be consistent with sound nomenclature principles; and

(C) ensure substantial rate neutrality.

(2) Any change to a rate of duty must be consequent to, or necessitated by, nomenclature modifications that are recommended under this section.

(3) The modification must not alter existing conditions of competition for the affected United States industry, labor, or trade.

SEC. 1206. PRESIDENTIAL ACTION ON COMMISSION RECOMMENDATIONS.

(a) IN GENERAL.—The President may proclaim modifications, based on the recommendations by the Commission under section 1205, to the Harmonized Tariff Schedule if the President determines that the modifications—

(1) are in conformity with United States obligations under the Convention; and

(2) do not run counter to the national economic interest of the United States.

(b) LAY-OVER PERIOD.—

(1) The President may proclaim a modification under subsection (a) only after the expiration of the 60-day period beginning on the date on which the President submits a report to the Committee on Ways and Means of the House of Representatives and the Committee on Finance of the Senate that sets forth the proposed modification and the reasons therefor.

(2) The 60-day period referred to in paragraph (1) shall be computed by excluding—

(A) the days on which either House is not in session because of an adjournment of more than 3 days to a day certain or an adjournment of the Congress sine die; and

(B) any Saturday and Sunday, not excluded under subparagraph (A), when either House is not in session.

(c) EFFECTIVE DATE OF MODIFICATIONS.—Modifications proclaimed by the President under subsection (a) may not take effect before the 15th day after the date on which the text of the proclamation is published in the Federal Register.

SEC. 1207. PUBLICATION OF THE HARMONIZED TARIFF SCHEDULE.

(a) IN GENERAL.—The Commission shall compile and publish, at appropriate intervals, and keep up to date the Harmonized Tariff Schedule and related information in the form of printed copy; and, if, in its judgment, such format would serve the public interest and convenience—

(1) in the form of microfilm images; or

(2) in the form of electronic media.

(b) CONTENT.—Publications under subsection (a), in whatever format, shall contain—

(1) the then current Harmonized Tariff Schedule;

(2) statistical annotations and related statistical information formulated under section 484(e) of the Tariff Act of 1930 (19 U.S.C. 1484(e)); and

(3) such other matters as the Commission considers to be necessary or appropriate to carry out the purposes enumerated in the Preamble to the Convention.

SEC. 1208. IMPORT AND EXPORT STATISTICS.

The Secretary of Commerce shall compile, and make publicly available, the import and export trade statistics of the United States. Such statistics shall be conformed to the nomenclature of the Convention.

SEC. 1209. COORDINATION OF TRADE POLICY AND THE CONVENTION.

The United States Trade Representative is responsible for coordination of United States trade policy in relation to the Convention. Before formulating any United States position with respect to the Convention, including any proposed amendments thereto, the United States Trade Representative shall seek, and consider, information and advice from interested parties in the private sector (including a functional advisory committee) and from interested Federal agencies.

SEC. 1210. UNITED STATES PARTICIPATION ON THE CUSTOMS COOPERATION COUNCIL REGARDING THE CONVENTION.

(a) PRINCIPAL UNITED STATES AGENCIES.—

(1) Subject to the policy direction of the Office of the United States Trade Representative under section 1209, the Department of the Treasury, the Department of Commerce, and the Commission shall, with respect to the activities of the Customs Cooperation Council relating to the Convention—

(A) be primarily responsible for formulating United States Government positions on technical and procedural issues; and

(B) represent the United States Government.

(2) The Department of Agriculture and other interested Federal agencies shall provide to the Department of the Treasury, the Department of Commerce, and the Commission technical advice and assistance relating to the functions referred to in paragraph (1).

(b) DEVELOPMENT OF TECHNICAL PROPOSALS.—

(1) In connection with responsibilities arising from the implementation of the Convention and under section 484(e) of the Tariff Act of 1930 (19 U.S.C. 1484(e)) regarding United States programs for the development of adequate and comparable statistical information on merchandise trade, the Secretary of the Treasury, the Secretary of Commerce, and the Commission shall prepare technical proposals that are appropriate or required to assure that the United States contribution to the development of the Convention recognizes the needs of the United States business community for a Convention which reflects sound principles of commodity identification, modern producing methods, and current trading patterns and practices.

(2) In carrying out this subsection, the Secretary of the Treasury, the Secretary of Commerce, and the Commission shall—

(A) solicit and consider the views of interested parties in the private sector (including a functional advisory committee) and of interested Federal agencies;

(B) establish procedures for reviewing, and developing appropriate responses to, inquiries and complaints from interested parties concerning articles produced in and exported from the United States; and

(C) where appropriate, establish procedures for—

(i) ensuring that the dispute settlement provisions and other relevant procedures available under the Convention are utilized to promote United States export interests, and

(ii) submitting classification questions to the Harmonized System Committee of the Customs Cooperation Council.

(c) AVAILABILITY OF CUSTOMS COOPERATION COUNCIL PUBLICATIONS.—As soon as practicable after the date of the enactment of the Omnibus Trade and Competitiveness Act of 1988, and periodically thereafter as appropriate, the Commission shall see to the publication of—

(1) summary records of the Harmonized System Committee of the Customs Cooperation Council; and

(2) subject to applicable copyright laws, the Explanatory Notes, Classification Opinions, and other instruments of the Customs Cooperation Council relating to the Convention.

SEC. 1216. COMMISSION REPORT ON OPERATION OF SUBTITLE.

The Commission, in consultation with other appropriate Federal agencies, shall prepare, and submit to the Congress and to the President, a report regarding the operation of this subtitle during the 12-month period commencing on the effective date of the Harmonized Tariff Schedule. The report shall be submitted to the Congress and to the President before the close of the 6-month period beginning on the day after the last day of such 12-month period.

SEC. 1217. EFFECTIVE DATES.

(a) ACCESSION TO CONVENTION AND PROVISIONS OTHER THAN THE IMPLEMENTATION OF THE HARMONIZED TARIFF SCHEDULE.—Except as provided in subsection (b), the provisions of this subtitle take effect on the date of the enactment of the Omnibus Trade and Competitiveness Act of 1988.

(b) IMPLEMENTATION OF THE HARMONIZED TARIFF SCHEDULE.—The effective date of the Harmonized Tariff Schedule is January 1, 1989. On such date—

(1) the amendments made by sections 1204(a), 1213, 1214, and 1215 take effect and apply with respect to articles entered on or after such date; and

(2) sections 1204(c), 1211, and 1212 take effect.

Subtitle C—Response to Unfair International Trade Practices

PART 1—ENFORCEMENT OF UNITED STATES RIGHTS UNDER TRADE AGREEMENTS AND RESPONSE TO CERTAIN FOREIGN TRADE PRACTICES

SEC. 1301. REVISION OF CHAPTER 1 OF TITLE III OF THE TRADE ACT OF 1974.

(a) IN GENERAL.—Chapter 1 of title III of the Trade Act of 1974 (19 U.S.C. 2411 et seq.) is amended to read as follows:

"CHAPTER 1—ENFORCEMENT OF UNITED STATES RIGHTS UNDER TRADE AGREEMENTS AND RESPONSE TO CERTAIN FOREIGN TRADE PRACTICES

"SEC. 301. ACTIONS BY UNITED STATES TRADE REPRESENTATIVE.

"(a) MANDATORY ACTION.—

"(1) If the United States Trade Representative determines under section 304(a)(1) that—

"(A) the rights of the United States under any trade agreement are being denied; or

"(B) an act, policy, or practice of a foreign country—

"(i) violates, or is inconsistent with, the provisions of, or otherwise denies benefits to the United States under, any trade agreement, or

"(ii) is unjustifiable and burdens or restricts United States commerce;

the Trade Representative shall take action authorized in subsection (c), subject to the specific direction, if any, of the President regarding any such action, and shall take all other appropriate and feasible action within the power of the President that the President may direct the Trade Representative to take under this subsection, to enforce such rights or to obtain the elimination of such act, policy, or practice.

"(2) The Trade Representative is not required to take action under paragraph (1) in any case in which—

"(A) the Contracting Parties to the General Agreement on Tariffs and Trade have determined, a panel of experts has reported to the Contracting Parties, or a ruling issued under the formal dispute settlement proceeding provided under any other trade agreement finds, that—

"(i) the rights of the United States under a trade agreement are not being denied, or

"(ii) the act, policy, or practice—

"(I) is not a violation of, or inconsistent with, the rights of the United States, or

"(II) does not deny, nullify, or impair benefits to the United States under any trade agreement; or

"(B) the Trade Representative finds that—

"(i) the foreign country is taking satisfactory measures to grant the rights of the United States under a trade agreement, "(ii) the foreign country has—

"(I) agreed to eliminate or phase out the act, policy, or practice, or

"(II) agreed to an imminent solution to the burden or restriction on United States commerce that is satisfactory to the Trade Representative,

"(iii) it is impossible for the foreign country to achieve the results described in clause (i) or (ii), as appropriate, but the foreign country agrees to provide to the United States compensatory trade benefits that are satisfactory to the Trade Representative,

"(iv) in extraordinary cases, where the taking of action under this subsection would have an adverse impact on the United States economy substantially out of proportion to the benefits of such action, taking into account the impact of not taking such action on the credibility of the provisions of this chapter, or

"(v) the taking of action under this subsection would cause serious harm to the national security of the United States.

"(3) Any action taken under paragraph (1) to eliminate an act, policy, or practice shall be devised so as to affect goods or services of the foreign country in an amount that is equivalent in value to the burden or restriction being imposed by that country on United States commerce.

"(b) DISCRETIONARY ACTION.—If the Trade Representative determines under section 304(a)(1) that—

"(1) an act, policy, or practice of a foreign country is unreasonable or discriminatory and burdens or restricts United States commerce, and

"(2) action by the United States is appropriate, the Trade Representative shall take all appropriate and feasible action authorized under subsection (c), subject to the specific direction, if any, of the President regarding any such action, and all other appropriate and feasible action within the power of the President that the President may direct the Trade Representative to take under this subsection, to obtain the elimination of that act, policy, or practice.

"(c) SCOPE OF AUTHORITY.—

"(1) For purposes of carrying out the provisions of subsection (a) or (b), the Trade Representative is authorized to—

"(A) suspend, withdraw, or prevent the application of, benefits of trade agreement concessions to carry out a trade agreement with the foreign country referred to in such subsection;

"(B) impose duties or other import restrictions on the goods of, and, notwithstanding any other provision of law, fees or restrictions on the services of, such foreign country for such time as the Trade Representative determines appropriate; or

"(C) enter into binding agreements with such foreign country that commit such foreign country to—

"(i) eliminate, or phase out, the act, policy, or practice that is the subject of the action to be taken under subsection (a) or (b), "(ii) eliminate any burden or restriction on United States commerce resulting from such act, policy, or practice, or

"(iii) provide the United States with compensatory trade benefits that—

"(I) are satisfactory to the Trade Representative, and

"(II) meet the requirements of paragraph (4).

"(2)(A) Notwithstanding any other provision of law governing any service sector access authorization, and in addition to the authority conferred in paragraph (1), the Trade Representative may, for purposes of carrying out the provisions of subsection (a) or (b)—

"(i) restrict, in the manner and to the extent the Trade Representative determines appropriate, the terms and conditions of any such authorization, or

"(ii) deny the issuance of any such authorization.

"(B) Actions described in subparagraph (A) may only be taken under this section with respect to service sector access authorizations granted, or applications therefor pending, on or after the date on which—

"(i) a petition is filed under section 302(a), or

"(ii) a determination to initiate an investigation is made by the Trade Representative under section 302(b).

"(C) Before the Trade Representative takes any action under this section involving the imposition of fees or other restrictions on the services of a foreign country, the Trade Representative shall, if the services involved are subject to regulation by any agency of the Federal Government or of any State, consult, as appropriate, with the head of the agency concerned.

"(3) The actions the Trade Representative is authorized to take under subsection (a) or (b) may be taken against any goods or economic sector—

"(A) on a nondiscriminatory basis or solely against the foreign country described in such subsection, and

"(B) without regard to whether or not such goods or economic sector were involved in the act, policy, or practice that is the subject of such action.

"(4) Any trade agreement described in paragraph (1)(C)(iii) shall provide compensatory trade benefits that benefit the economic sector which includes the domestic industry that would benefit from the elimination of the act, policy, or practice that is the subject of the action to be taken under subsection (a) or (b), or benefit the economic sector as closely related as possible to such economic sector, unless—

"(A) the provision of such trade benefits is not feasible, or

"(B) trade benefits that benefit any other economic sector would be more satisfactory than such trade benefits.

"(5) In taking actions under subsection (a) or (b), the Trade Representative shall—

"(A) give preference to the imposition of duties over the imposition of other import restrictions, and

"(B) if an import restriction other than a duty is imposed, consider substituting, on an incremental basis, an equivalent duty for such other import restriction.

"(6) Any action taken by the Trade Representative under this section with respect to export targeting shall, to the extent possible, reflect the full benefit level of the export targeting to the beneficiary over the period during which the action taken has an effect.

"(d) DEFINITIONS AND SPECIAL RULES.—For purposes of this chapter—

"(1) The term "commerce" includes, but is not limited to—

"(A) services (including transfers of information) associated with international trade, whether or not such services are related to specific goods, and

"(B) foreign direct investment by United States persons with implications for trade in goods or services.

"(2) An act, policy, or practice of a foreign country that burdens or restricts United States commerce may include the provision, directly or indirectly, by that foreign country of subsidies for the construction of vessels used in the commercial transportation by water of goods between foreign countries and the United States.

"(3)(A) An act, policy, or practice is unreasonable if the act, policy, or practice, while not necessarily in violation of, or inconsistent with, the international legal rights of the United States, is otherwise unfair and inequitable.

"(B) Acts, policies, and practices that are unreasonable include, but are not limited to, any act, policy, or practice, or any combination of acts, policies, or practices, which—

"(i) denies fair and equitable—

"(I) opportunities for the establishment of an enterprise,

"(II) provision of adequate and effective protection of intellectual property rights, or

"(III) market opportunities, including the toleration by a foreign government of systematic anticompetitive activities by private firms or among private firms in the foreign country that have the effect of restricting, on a basis that is inconsistent with commercial considerations, access of United States goods to purchasing by such firms,

"(ii) constitutes export targeting, or

"(iii) constitutes a persistent pattern of conduct that—

"(I) denies workers the right of association,

"(II) denies workers the right to organize and bargain collectively,

"(III) permits any form of forced or compulsory labor,

"(IV) fails to provide a minimum age for the employment of children, or

"(V) fails to provide standards for minimum wages, hours of work, and occupational safety and health of workers.

"(C)(i) Acts, policies, and practices of a foreign country described in subparagraph (B)(iii) shall not be treated as being unreasonable if the Trade Representative determines that—

"(I) the foreign country has taken, or is taking, actions that demonstrate a significant and tangible overall advancement in providing throughout the foreign country (including any designated zone within the foreign country) the rights and other standards described in the subclauses of subparagraph (B)(iii), or

"(II) such acts, policies, and practices are not inconsistent with the level of economic development of the foreign country.

"(ii) The Trade Representative shall publish in the Federal Register any determination made under clause (i), together with a description of the facts on which such determination is based.

"(D) For purposes of determining whether any act, policy, or practice is unreasonable, reciprocal opportunities in the United States for foreign nationals and firms shall be taken into account, to the extent appropriate.

"(E) The term 'export targeting' means any government plan or scheme consisting of a combination of coordinated actions (whether carried out severally or jointly) that are bestowed on a specific enterprise, industry, or group thereof, the effect of which is to assist the enterprise, industry, or group to become more competitive in the export of a class or kind of merchandise.

"(4)(A) An act, policy, or practice is unjustifiable if the act, policy, or practice is in violation of, or inconsistent with, the international legal rights of the United States.

"(B) Acts, policies, and practices that are unjustifiable include, but are not limited to, any act, policy, or practice described in subparagraph (A) which denies national or most-favored-nation treatment or the right of establishment or protection of intellectual property rights.

"(5) Acts, policies, and practices that are discriminatory include, when appropriate, any act, policy, and practice which denies national or most-favored-nation treatment to United States goods, services, or investment.

"(6) The term 'service sector access authorization' means any license, permit, order, or other authorization, issued under the authority of Federal law, that permits a foreign supplier of services access to the United States market in a service sector concerned.

"(7) The term 'foreign country' includes any foreign instrumentality. Any possession or territory of a foreign country that is administered separately for customs purposes shall be treated as a separate foreign country.

"(8) The term 'Trade Representative' means the United States Trade Representative.

"(9) The term 'interested persons', only for purposes of sections 302(a)(4)(B), 304(b)(1)(A), 306(c)(2), and 307(a)(2), includes, but is not limited to, domestic firms and workers, representatives of consumer interests, United States product exporters, and any industrial user of any goods or services that may be affected by actions taken under subsection (a) or (b).

"SEC. 302. INITIATION OF INVESTIGATIONS.

"(a) PETITIONS.—

"(1) Any interested person may file a petition with the Trade Representative requesting that action be taken under section 301 and setting forth the allegations in support of the request.

"(2) The Trade Representative shall review the allegations in any petition filed under paragraph (1) and, not later than 45 days after the date on which the Trade Representative received the petition, shall determine whether to initiate an investigation.

"(3) If the Trade Representative determines not to initiate an investigation with respect to a petition, the Trade Representative shall inform the petitioner of the reasons therefor and shall publish notice of the determination, together with a summary of such reasons, in the Federal Register.

"(4) If the Trade Representative makes an affirmative determination under paragraph (2) with respect to a petition, the Trade Representative shall initiate an investigation regarding the issues raised in the petition. The Trade Representative shall publish a summary of the petition in the Federal Register and shall, as soon as possible, provide opportunity for the presentation of views concerning the issues, including a public hearing—

"(A) within the 30-day period beginning on the date of the affirmative determination (or on a date after such period if agreed to by the petitioner) if a public hearing within such period is requested in the petition, or

"(B) at such other time if a timely request therefor is made by the petitioner or by any interested person.

"(b) Initiation of Investigation by Means Other Than Petition.—

"(1)(A) If the Trade Representative determines that an investigation should be initiated under this chapter with respect to any matter in order to determine whether the matter is actionable under section 301, the Trade Representative shall publish such determination in the Federal Register and shall initiate such investigation.

"(B) The Trade Representative shall, before making any determination under subparagraph (A), consult with appropriate committees established pursuant to section 135.

"(2)(A) By no later than the date that is 30 days after the date on which a country is identified under section 182(a)(2), the Trade Representative shall initiate an investigation under this chapter with respect to any act, policy, or practice of that country that—

"(i) was the basis for such identification, and

"(ii) is not at that time the subject of any other investigation or action under this chapter.

"(B) The Trade Representative is not required under subparagraph (A) to initiate an investigation under this chapter with respect to any act, policy, or practice of a foreign country if the Trade Representative determines that the initiation of the investigation would be detrimental to United States economic interests.

"(C) If the Trade Representative makes a determination under subparagraph (B) not to initiate an investigation, the Trade Representative shall submit to the Congress a written report setting forth, in detail—

"(i) the reasons for the determination, and

"(ii) the United States economic interests that would be adversely affected by the investigation.

"(D) The Trade Representative shall, from time to time, consult with the Register of Copyrights, the Commissioner of Patents and Trademarks, and other appropriate officers of the Federal Government, during any investigation initiated under this chapter by reason of subparagraph (A).

"(c) DISCRETION.—In determining whether to initiate an investigation under subsection (a) or (b) of any act, policy, or practice that is enumerated in any provision of section 301(d), the Trade Representative shall have discretion to determine whether action under section 301 would be effective in addressing such act, policy, or practice.

"SEC. 303. CONSULTATION UPON INITIATION OF INVESTIGATION.

"(a) IN GENERAL.—

"(1) On the date on which an investigation is initiated under section 302, the Trade Representative, on behalf of the United States, shall request consultations with the foreign country concerned regarding the issues involved in such investigation.

"(2) If the investigation initiated under section 302 involves a trade agreement and a mutually acceptable resolution is not reached before the earlier of—

"(A) the close of the consultation period, if any, specified in the trade agreement, or

"(B) the 150th day after the day on which consultation was commenced,

the Trade Representative shall promptly request proceedings on the matter under the formal dispute settlement procedures provided under such agreement.

"(3) The Trade Representative shall seek information and advice from the petitioner (if any) and the appropriate committees established pursuant to section 135 in preparing United States presentations for consultations and dispute settlement proceedings.

"(b) DELAY OF REQUEST FOR CONSULTATIONS.—

"(1) Notwithstanding the provisions of subsection (a)—

"(A) the United States Trade Representative may, after consulting with the petitioner (if any), delay for up to 90 days any request for consultations under subsection (a) for the purpose of verifying or improving the petition to ensure an adequate basis for consultation, and

"(B) if such consultations are delayed by reason of subparagraph (A), each time limitation under section 304 shall be extended for the period of such delay.

"(2) The Trade Representative shall—

"(A) publish notice of any delay under paragraph (1) in the Federal Register, and

"(B) report to Congress on the reasons for such delay in the report required under section 309(a)(3).

"SEC. 304. DETERMINATIONS BY THE TRADE REPRESENTATIVE.

"(a) IN GENERAL.—

"(1) On the basis of the investigation initiated under section 302 and the consultations (and the proceedings, if applicable) under section 303, the Trade Representative shall—

"(A) determine whether—

"(i) the rights to which the United States is entitled under any trade agreement are being denied, or

"(ii) any act, policy, or practice described in subsection (a)(1)(B) or (b)(1) of section 301 exists, and

"(B) if the determination made under subparagraph (A) is affirmative, determine what action, if any, the Trade Representative should take under subsection (a) or (b) of section 301.

"(A) shall provide an opportunity (after giving not less than 30 days notice thereof) for the presentation of views by interested persons, including a public hearing if requested by any interested person,

"(B) shall obtain advice from the appropriate committees established pursuant to section 135, and

"(C) may request the views of the United States International Trade Commission regarding the probable impact on the economy of the United States of the taking of action with respect to any goods or service.

"(2) If the Trade Representative does not comply with the requirements of subparagraphs (A) and (B) of paragraph (1) because expeditious action is required, the Trade Representative shall, after making the determinations under subsection (a)(1), comply with such subparagraphs.

"(c) PUBLICATION.—The Trade Representative shall publish in the Federal Register any determination made under subsection (a)(1), together with a description of the facts on which such determination is based.

"SEC. 305. IMPLEMENTATION OF ACTIONS.

"(a) ACTIONS TO BE TAKEN UNDER SECTION 301.—

"(1) Except as provided in paragraph (2), the Trade Representative shall implement the action the Trade Representative determines under section 304(a)(1)(B) to take under section 301, subject to the specific direction, if any, of the President regarding any such action, by no later than the date that is 30 days after the date on which such determination is made.

"(2)(A) Except as otherwise provided in this paragraph, the Trade Representative may delay, by not more than 180 days, the implementation of any action that is to be taken under section 301—

"(i) if—

"(I) in the case of an investigation initiated under section 302(a), the petitioner requests a delay, or

"(II) in the case of an investigation initiated under section 302(b)(1) or to which section 304(a)(3)(B) applies, a delay is requested by a majority of the representatives of the domestic industry that would benefit from the action, or

"(ii) if the Trade Representative determines that substantial progress is being made, or that a delay is necessary or desirable, to obtain United States rights or a satisfactory solution with respect to the acts, policies, or practices that are the subject of the action.

"(B) The Trade Representative may not delay under subparagraph (A) the implementation of any action that is to be taken under section 301 with respect to any investigation to which section 304(a)(3)(A) applies.

"(C) The Trade Representative may not delay under subparagraph (A) the implementation of any action that is to be taken under section 301 with respect to any investigation to which section 304(a)(3)(B) applies by more than 90 days.

"(b) ALTERNATIVE ACTIONS IN CERTAIN CASES OF EXPORT TARGETING.—

"(1) If the Trade Representative makes an affirmative determination under section 304(a)(1)(A) involving export targeting

"(2) The Trade Representative shall make the determinations required under paragraph (1) on or before—

"(A) in the case of an investigation involving a trade agreement (other than the agreement on subsidies and countervailing measures described in section 2(c)(5) of the Trade Agreements Act of 1979), the earlier of—

"(i) the date that is 30 days after the date on which the dispute settlement procedure is concluded, or

"(ii) the date that is 18 months after the date on which the investigation is initiated, or

"(B) in all cases not described in subparagraph (A) or paragraph (3), the date that is 12 months after the date on which the investigation is initiated.

"(3)(A) If an investigation is initiated under this chapter by reason of section 302(b)(2) and the Trade Representative does not make a determination described in subparagraph (B) with respect to such investigation, the Trade Representative shall make the determinations required under paragraph (1) with respect to such investigation by no later than the date that is 6 months after the date on which such investigation is initiated.

"(B) If the Trade Representative determines with respect to any investigation initiated by reason of section 302(b)(2) that—

"(i) complex or complicated issues are involved in the investigation that require additional time,

"(ii) the foreign country involved in the investigation is making substantial progress in drafting or implementing legislative or administrative measures that will provide adequate and effective protection of intellectual property rights, or

"(iii) such foreign country is undertaking enforcement measures to provide adequate and effective protection of intellectual property rights,

the Trade Representative shall publish in the Federal Register notice of such determination and shall make the determinations required under paragraph (1) with respect to such investigation by no later than the date that is 9 months after the date on which such investigation is initiated.

"(4) In any case in which a dispute is not resolved before the close of the minimum dispute settlement period provided for in a trade agreement (other than the agreement on subsidies and countervailing measures described in section 2(c)(5) of the Trade Agreements Act of 1979), the Trade Representative, within 15 days after the close of such dispute settlement period, shall submit a report to Congress setting forth the reasons why the dispute was not resolved within the minimum dispute settlement period, the status of the case at the close of the period, and the prospects for resolution. For purposes of this paragraph, the minimum dispute settlement period provided for under any such trade agreement is the total period of time that results if all stages of the formal dispute settlement procedures are carried out within the time limitations specified in the agreement, but computed without regard to any extension authorized under the agreement at any stage.

"(b) Consultation Before Determinations.—

"(1) Before making the determinations required under subsection (a)(1), the Trade Representative, unless expeditious action is required—

by a foreign country and determines to take no action under section 301 with respect to such affirmation determination, the Trade Representative—

"(A) shall establish an advisory panel to recommend measures which will promote the competitiveness of the domestic industry affected by the export targeting,

"(B) on the basis of the report of such panel submitted under paragraph (2)(B) and subject to the specific direction, if any, of the President, may take any administrative actions authorized under any other provision of law, and, if necessary, propose legislation to implement any other actions, that would restore or improve the international competitiveness of the domestic industry affected by the export targeting, and

"(C) shall, by no later than the date that is 30 days after the date on which the report of such panel is submitted under paragraph (2)(B), submit a report to the Congress on the administrative actions taken, and legislative proposals made, under subparagraph (B) with respect to the domestic industry affected by the export targeting.

"(2)(A) The advisory panels established under paragraph (1)(A) shall consist of individuals appointed by the Trade Representative who—

"(i) earn their livelihood in the private sector of the economy, including individuals who represent management and labor in the domestic industry affected by the export targeting that is the subject of the affirmative determination made under section 304(a)(1)(A), and

"(ii) by education or experience, are qualified to serve on the advisory panel.

"(B) By no later than the date that is 6 months after the date on which an advisory panel is established under paragraph (1)(A), the advisory panel shall submit to the Trade Representative and to the Congress a report on measures that the advisory panel recommends be taken by the United States to promote the competitiveness of the domestic industry affected by the export targeting that is the subject of the affirmative determination made under section 304(a)(1)(A).

"SEC. 306. MONITORING OF FOREIGN COMPLIANCE.

"(a) In General.—The Trade Representative shall monitor the implementation of each measure undertaken, or agreement of a kind described in clause (i), (ii), or (iii) of section 301(a)(2)(B) that is entered into under subsection (a) or (b) of section 301, by a foreign country—

"(1) to enforce the rights of the United States under any trade agreement, or

"(2) to eliminate any act, policy, or practice described in subsection (a)(1)(B) or (b)(1) of section 301.

"(b) Further Action.—If, on the basis of the monitoring carried out under subsection (a), the Trade Representative considers that a foreign country is not satisfactorily implementing a measure or agreement referred to in subsection (a), the Trade Representative shall determine what further action the Trade Representative shall take under section 301(a). For purposes of section 301, any such determination shall be treated as a determination made under section 304(a)(1).

"(c) CONSULTATIONS.—Before making any determination under subsection (b), the Trade Representative shall—

"(1) consult with the petitioner, if any, involved in the initial investigation under this chapter and with representatives of the domestic industry concerned; and

"(2) provide an opportunity for the presentation of views by interested persons.

"SEC. 307. MODIFICATION AND TERMINATION OF ACTIONS.

"(a) IN GENERAL.—

"(1) The Trade Representative may modify or terminate any action, subject to the specific direction, if any, of the President with respect to such action, that is being taken under section 301 if—

"(A) any of the conditions described in section 301(a)(2) exist,

"(B) the burden or restriction on United States commerce of the denial rights, or of the acts, policies, and practices, that are the subject of such action has increased or decreased, or

"(C) such action is being taken under section 301(b) and is no longer appropriate.

"(2) Before taking any action under paragraph (1) to modify or terminate any action taken under section 301, the Trade Representative shall consult with the petitioner, if any, and with representatives of the domestic industry concerned, and shall provide opportunity for the presentation of views by other interested persons affected by the proposed modification or termination concerning the effects of the modification or termination and whether any modification or termination of the action is appropriate.

"(b) NOTICE; REPORT TO CONGRESS.—The Trade Representative shall promptly publish in the Federal Register notice of, and report in writing to the Congress with respect to, any modification or termination of any action taken under section 301 and the reasons therefor.

"(c) REVIEW OF NECESSITY.—

"(1) If—

"(A) a particular action has been taken under section 301 during any 4-year period, and

"(B) neither the petitioner nor any representative of the domestic industry which benefits from such action has submitted to the Trade Representative during the last 60 days of such 4-year period a written request for the continuation of such action,

such action shall terminate at the close of such 4-year period.

"(2) The Trade Representative shall notify by mail the petitioner and representatives of the domestic industry described in paragraph (1)(B) of any termination of action by reason of paragraph (1) at least 60 days before the date of such termination.

"(3) If a request is submitted to the Trade Representative under paragraph (1)(B) to continue taking a particular action under section 301, the Trade Representative shall conduct a review of—

"(A) the effectiveness in achieving the objectives of section 301 of—

"(i) such action, and

"(ii) other actions that could be taken (including actions against other products or services), and

"(B) the effects of such actions on the United States economy, including consumers.

"SEC. 308. REQUEST FOR INFORMATION.

"(a) IN GENERAL.—Upon receipt of written request therefor from any person, the Trade Representative shall make available to that person information (other than that to which confidentiality applies) concerning—

"(1) the nature and extent of a specific trade policy or practice of a foreign country with respect to particular goods, services, investment, or intellectual property rights, to the extent that such information is available to the Trade Representative or other Federal agencies;

"(2) United States rights under any trade agreement and the remedies which may be available under that agreement and under the laws of the United States; and

"(3) past and present domestic and international proceedings or actions with respect to the policy or practice concerned.

"(b) IF INFORMATION NOT AVAILABLE.—If information that is requested by a person under subsection (a) is not available to the Trade Representative or other Federal agencies, the Trade Representative shall, within 30 days after receipt of the request—

"(1) request the information from the foreign government; or

"(2) decline to request the information and inform the person in writing of the reasons for refusal.

"(c) CERTAIN BUSINESS INFORMATION NOT MADE AVAILABLE.—

"(1) Except as provided in paragraph (2), and notwithstanding any other provision of law (including section 552 of title 5, United States Code), no information requested and received by the Trade Representative in aid of any investigation under this chapter shall be made available to any person if—

"(A) the person providing such information certifies that—

"(i) such information is business confidential,

"(ii) the disclosure of such information would endanger trade secrets or profitability, and

"(iii) such information is not generally available;

"(B) the Trade Representative determines that such certification is well-founded; and

"(C) to the extent required in regulations prescribed by the Trade Representative, the person providing such information provides an adequate nonconfidential summary of such information.

"(2) The Trade Representative may—

"(A) use such information, or make such information available (in his own discretion) to any employee of the Federal Government for use, in any investigation under this chapter, or

"(B) may make such information available to any other person in a form which cannot be associated with, or otherwise identify, the person providing the information.

"SEC. 309. ADMINISTRATION.

"The Trade Representative shall—

"(1) issue regulations concerning the filing of petitions and the conduct of investigations and hearings under this subchapter,

"(2) keep the petitioner regularly informed of all determinations and developments regarding the investigation conducted with respect to the petition under this chapter, including the reasons for any undue delays, and

"(3) submit a report to the House of Representatives and the Senate semiannually describing—

"(A) the petitions filed and the determinations made (and reasons therefor) under section 302,

"(B) developments in, and the current status of, each investigation or proceeding under this chapter,

"(C) the actions taken, or the reasons for no action, by the Trade Representative under section 301 with respect to investigations conducted under this chapter, and

"(D) the commercial effects of actions taken under section 301.".

(b) CONFORMING AMENDMENT.—The table of contents of the Trade Act of 1974 is amended by striking out the items relating to chapter 1 of title III and inserting in lieu thereof the following:

"CHAPTER 1—ENFORCEMENT OF UNITED STATES RIGHTS UNDER TRADE AGREEMENTS AND RESPONSE TO FOREIGN TRADE PRACTICES

"Sec. 301. Actions by United States Trade Representative.
"Sec. 302. Initiation of investigations.
"Sec. 303. Consultation upon initiation of investigation.
"Sec. 304. Determinations by the Trade Representative.
"Sec. 305. Implementation of actions.
"Sec. 306. Monitoring of foreign compliance.
"Sec. 307. Modification and termination of actions.
"Sec. 308. Request for information.
"Sec. 309. Administration.".

(c) EFFECTIVE DATE.—The amendments made by this section shall apply to—

(1) petitions filed, and investigations initiated, under section 302 of the Trade Act of 1974 on or after the date of the enactment of this Act; and

(2) petitions filed, and investigations initiated, before the date of enactment of this Act, if by that date no decision had been made under section 304 regarding the petition or investigation.

SEC. 1302. IDENTIFICATION OF TRADE LIBERALIZATION PRIORITIES.

(a) IN GENERAL.—Chapter 1 of title III of the Trade Act of 1974, as amended by section 1301, is further amended by adding at the end thereof the following new section:

"SEC. 310. IDENTIFICATION OF TRADE LIBERALIZATION PRIORITIES.

"(a) IDENTIFICATION.—

"(1) By no later than the date that is 30 days after the date in calendar year 1989, and also the date in calendar year 1990, on which the report required under section 181(b) is submitted to the appropriate Congressional committees, the Trade Representative shall identify United States trade liberalization priorities, including—

"(A) priority practices, including major barriers and trade distorting practices, the elimination of which are likely to have the most significant potential to increase

United States exports, either directly or through the establishment of a beneficial precedent;

"(B) priority foreign countries that, on the basis of such report, satisfy the criteria in paragraph (2);

"(C) estimate the total amount by which United States exports of goods and services to each foreign country identified under subparagraph (B) would have increased during the preceding calendar year if the priority practices of such country identified under subparagraph (A) did not exist; and

"(D) submit to the Committee on Finance of the Senate, the Committee on Ways and Means of the House of Representatives, and publish in the Federal Register, a report which lists—

"(i) the priority foreign countries identified under subparagraph (B),

"(ii) the priority practices identified under subparagraph (A) with respect to each of such priority foreign countries, and

"(iii) the amount estimated under subparagraph (C) with respect to each of such priority foreign countries.

"(2) In identifying priority foreign countries under paragraph (1)(B), the Trade Representative shall take into account—

"(A) the number and pervasiveness of the acts, policies, and practices described in section 181(a)(1)(A), and

"(B) the level of United States exports of goods and services that would be reasonably expected from full implementation of existing trade agreements to which that foreign country is a party, based on the international competitive position and export potential of such products and services.

"(3) In identifying priority practices under paragraph (1)(A), the Trade Representative shall take into account—

"(A) the international competitive position and export potential of United States products and services,

"(B) circumstances in which the sale of a small quantity of a product or service may be more significant than its value, and

"(C) the measurable medium-term and long-term implications of government procurement commitments to United States exporters.

"(b) Initiation of Investigations.—By no later than the date that is 21 days after the date on which a report is submitted to the appropriate Congressional committees under subsection (a)(1)(D), the Trade Representative shall initiate under section 302(b)(1) investigations under this chapter with respect to all of those priority practices identified in such report by reason of subsection (a)(1)(D) for each of the priority foreign countries. The Trade Representative may initiate investigations under section 302(b)(1) with respect to all other priority practices identified under subsection (a)(1)(A).

"(c) Agreements for the Elimination of Barriers.—

"(1) In the consultations with a priority foreign country identified under subsection (a)(1) that the Trade Representative is required to request under section 303(a) with respect to an investigation initiated by reason of subsection (b), the Trade Representative shall seek to negotiate an agreement which provides for—

"(A) the elimination of, or compensation for, the priority practices identified under subsection (a)(1)(A) by no later than the close of the 3-year period beginning on the date on which such investigation is initiated, and

"(B) the reduction of such practices over a 3-year period with the expectation that United States exports to the foreign country will, as a result, increase incrementally during each year within such 3-year period.

"(2) Any investigation initiated under this chapter by reason of subsection (b) shall be suspended if an agreement described in subparagraphs (A) and (B) of paragraph (1) is entered into with the foreign country before the date on which any action under section 301 with respect to such investigation may be required under section 305(a) to be implemented.

"(3) If an agreement described in paragraph (1) is entered into with a foreign country before the date on which any action under section 301 with respect to such investigation may be required under section 305(a) to be implemented and the Trade Representative determines that the foreign country is not in compliance with such agreement, the Trade Representative shall continue the investigation that was suspended by reason of such agreement as though such investigation had not been suspended.

"(d) Annual Reports.—

"(1) On the date on which the report the Trade Representative is required to submit under subsection (a)(1)(D) in calendar year 1990, and on the anniversary of such date in the succeeding calendar years, the Trade Representative shall submit a report which includes—

"(A) revised estimates of the total amount determined under subsection (a)(1)(C) for each priority foreign country that has been identified under subsection (a)(1)(B),

"(B) evidence that demonstrates, in the form of increased United States exports to each of such priority foreign countries during the previous calendar year—

"(i) in the case of a priority foreign country that has entered into an agreement described in subsection (c)(1), substantial progress during each year within the 3-year period described in subsection (c)(1)(A) toward the goal of eliminating the priority practices identified under subsection (a)(1)(A) by the close of such 3-year period, and

"(ii) in the case of a country which has not entered into (or has not complied with) an agreement described in subsection (c)(1), the elimination of such practices, and

"(C) to the extent that the evidence described in subparagraph (B) cannot be provided, any actions that have been taken by the Trade Representative under section 301 with respect to such priority practices of each of such foreign countries.

"(2) The Trade Representative may exclude from the requirements of paragraph (1) in any calendar year beginning after 1993 any foreign country that has been identified under subsection (a)(1)(A) if the evidence submitted under paragraph (1)(B) in the 2 previous reports demonstrated that all the priority practices identified under subsection (a)(1)(A) with respect to such foreign country have been eliminated.".

(b) CONFORMING AMENDMENT.—The table of contents for the Trade Act of 1974 is amended by inserting after the item relating to section 309 the following new item:

"Sec. 310. Identification of trade liberalization priorities.".

SEC. 1303. IDENTIFICATION OF COUNTRIES THAT DENY ADEQUATE AND EFFECTIVE PROTECTION OF INTELLECTUAL PROPERTY RIGHTS.

(a) FINDINGS AND PURPOSE.—

(1) The Congress finds that—

(A) international protection of intellectual property rights is vital to the international competitiveness of United States persons that rely on protection of intellectual property rights; and

(B) the absence of adequate and effective protection of United States intellectual property rights, and the denial of fair and equitable market access, seriously impede the ability of the United States persons that rely on protection of intellectual property rights to export and operate overseas, thereby harming the economic interests of the United States.

(2) The purpose of this section is to provide for the development of an overall strategy to ensure adequate and effective protection of intellectual property rights and fair and equitable market access for United States persons that rely on protection of intellectual property rights.

(b) IN GENERAL.—Chapter 8 of title I of the Trade Act of 1974 is amended by adding at the end thereof the following new section:

"SEC. 182. IDENTIFICATION OF COUNTRIES THAT DENY ADEQUATE PROTECTION, OR MARKET ACCESS, FOR INTELLECTUAL PROPERTY RIGHTS.

"(a) IN GENERAL.—By no later than the date that is 30 days after the date on which the annual report is submitted to Congressional committees under section 181(b), the United States Trade Representative (hereafter in this section referred to as the 'Trade Representative') shall identify—

"(1) those foreign countries that—

"(A) deny adequate and effective protection of intellectual property rights, or

"(B) deny fair and equitable market access to United States persons that rely upon intellectual property protection, and

"(2) those foreign countries identified under paragraph (1) that are determined by the Trade Representative to be priority foreign countries.

"(b) SPECIAL RULES FOR IDENTIFICATIONS.—

"(1) In identifying priority foreign countries under subsection (a)(2), the Trade Representative shall only identify those foreign countries—

"(A) that have the most onerous or egregious acts, policies, or practices that—

"(i) deny adequate and effective intellectual property rights, or "(ii) deny fair and equitable market access to United States persons that rely upon intellectual property protection,

"(B) whose acts, policies, or practices described in subparagraph (A) have the greatest adverse impact (actual or potential) on the relevant United States products, and

"(C) that are not—

"(i) entering into good faith negotiations, or

"(ii) making significant progress in bilateral or multilateral negotiations,

to provide adequate and effective protection of intellectual property rights.

"(2) In identifying priority foreign countries under subsection (a)(2), the Trade Representative shall—

"(A) consult with the Register of Copyrights, the Commissioner of Patents and Trademarks, other appropriate officers of the Federal Government, and

"(B) take into account information from such sources as may be available to the Trade Representative and such information as may be submitted to the Trade Representative by interested persons, including information contained in reports submitted under section 181(b) and petitions submitted under section 302.

"(3) The Trade Representative may identify a foreign country under subsection (a)(1)(B) only if the Trade Representative finds that there is a factual basis for the denial of fair and equitable market access as a result of the violation of international law or agreement, or the existence of barriers, referred to in subsection (d)(3).

"(c) Revocations and Additional Identifications.—

"(1) The Trade Representative may at any time—

"(A) revoke the identification of any foreign country as a priority foreign country under this section, or

"(B) identify any foreign country as a priority foreign country under this section,

if information available to the Trade Representative indicates that such action is appropriate.

"(2) The Trade Representative shall include in the semiannual report submitted to the Congress under section 309(3) a detailed explanation of the reasons for the revocation under paragraph (1) of the identification of any foreign country as a priority foreign country under this section.

"(d) Definitions.—For purposes of this section—

"(1) The term 'persons that rely upon intellectual property protection' means persons involved in—

"(A) the creation, production or licensing of works of authorship (within the meaning of sections 102 and 103 of title 17, United States Code) that are copyrighted, or

"(B) the manufacture of products that are patented or for which there are process patents.

"(2) A foreign country denies adequate and effective protection of intellectual property rights if the foreign country denies adequate and effective means under the laws of the foreign country for persons who are not citizens or nationals of such foreign country to secure, exercise, and enforce rights relating to patents, process patents, registered trademarks, copyrights and mask works.

"(3) A foreign country denies fair and equitable market access if the foreign country effectively denies access to a market for a product protected by a copyright, patent, or process patent through the use of laws, procedures, practices, or regulations which—

"(A) violate provisions of international law or international agreements to which both the United States and the foreign country are parties, or

"(B) constitute discriminatory nontariff trade barriers.

"(e) PUBLICATION.—The Trade Representative shall publish in the Federal Register a list of foreign countries identified under subsection (a) and shall make such revisions to the list as may be required by reason of action under subsection (c).".

(c) CONFORMING AMENDMENTS.—

(1) The heading for chapter 8 of title I of the Trade Act of 1974 is amended to read as follows:

"CHAPTER 8—IDENTIFICATION OF MARKET BARRIERS AND CERTAIN UNFAIR TRADE ACTIONS".

(2) The table of contents for the Trade Act of 1974 is amended—

(A) by striking out the item relating to chapter 8 of title I and inserting in lieu thereof the following:

"CHAPTER 8—IDENTIFICATION OF MARKET BARRIERS AND CERTAIN UNFAIR TRADE PRACTICES",

and

(B) by inserting after the item relating to section 181 the following new item:

"Sec. 182. Identification of countries that deny adequate protection, or market access, for intellectual property rights.".

SEC. 1304. AMENDMENTS TO THE NATIONAL TRADE ESTIMATES.

(a) IN GENERAL.—Section 181 of the Trade Act of 1974 (19 U.S.C. 2241) is amended—

(1) by striking out "Not later than the date on which the initial report is required under subsection (b)(1)," in subsection (a)(1) and inserting in lieu thereof "For calendar year 1988, and for each succeeding calendar year,",

(2) by inserting "of each foreign country" after "or practices" in subsection (a)(1)(A),

(3) by striking out "and" at the end of subsection (a)(1)(A)(ii),

(4) by striking out the period at the end of subsection (a)(1)(B) and inserting in lieu thereof "; and",

(5) by adding at the end of subsection (a)(1) the following new subparagraph:

"(C) make an estimate, if feasible, of—

"(i) the value of additional goods and services of the United States, and

"(ii) the value of additional foreign direct investment by United States persons,

that would have been exported to, or invested in, each foreign country during such calendar year if each of such acts, policies, and practices of such country did not exist.",

(6) by striking out "and" at the end of subsection (a)(2)(C),

(7) by striking out the period at the end of subsection (a)(2)(D) and inserting in lieu thereof "; and",

(8) by adding at the end of subsection (a)(2) the following new subparagraph:

"(E) the actual increase in—

"(i) the value of goods and services of the United States exported to, and

"(ii) the value of foreign direct investment made in, the foreign country during the calendar year for which the estimate under paragraph (1)(C) is made.",

(9) by inserting "and with the assistance of the interagency advisory committee established under section 141(d)(2)," after "Trade Expansion Act of 1962," in subsection (a)(1), and

(10) by striking out "ACTIONS CONCERNING" in the section heading and inserting in lieu thereof "ESTIMATES OF".

(b) SUBMISSION OF REPORT.—Paragraph (1) of section 181(b) of the Trade Act of 1974 (19 U.S.C. 2241(b)(1)) is amended to read as follows:

"(1) On or before April 30, 1989, and on or before March 31 of each succeeding calendar year, the Trade Representative shall submit a report on the analysis and estimates made under subsection (a) for the calendar year preceding such calendar year (which shall be known as the 'National Trade Estimate') to the President, the Committee on Finance of the Senate, and appropriate committees of the House of Representatives.".

SEC. 1305. INVESTIGATION OF BARRIERS IN JAPAN TO CERTAIN UNITED STATES SERVICES.

The United States Trade Representative shall, within 90 days after the date of enactment of this Act, initiate an investigation under section 302 of the Trade Act of 1974 regarding those acts, policies, and practices of the Government of Japan, and of entities owned, financed, or otherwise controlled by the Government of Japan, that are barriers in Japan to the offering or performance by United States persons of architectural, engineering, construction, and consulting services in Japan.

SEC. 1306. TRADE AND ECONOMIC RELATIONS WITH JAPAN.

(a) FINDINGS.—The Congress finds that—

(1) the United States is at a critical juncture in bilateral relations with Japan;

(2) the balance of trade between the United States and Japan has deteriorated steadily from an already large United States deficit of $10,400,000,000 in 1980 to an unprecedented United States deficit of $57,700,000,000 in 1987, a magnitude that is simply untenable;

(3) approximately 90 percent of the increase in total trade between the United States and Japan since 1980 has been in Japanese exports to the United States;

(4) United States exports to Japan have not significantly benefited from appreciation of the yen;

(5) the United States deficit in the balance of trade in manufactured goods is growing: in 1987 Japan exported $82,500,000,000 of manufactured goods to the United States, while the United States exported $14,600,000,000 in manufactured goods;

(6) Japan accounts for 49 percent of the worldwide deficit of the United States in the balance of trade in manufactured goods, calculated on a customs basis;

(7) our trade and economic relations with Japan are complex and cannot be effectively resolved through narrow sector-by-sector negotiations;

(8) a major problem between the United States and Japan is the absence of a political will in Japan to import; and

(9) meaningful negotiations must take place at the highest level, at a special summit of political leaders from both countries.

(b) SENSE OF THE CONGRESS.—

(1) It is the sense of the Congress that the President should propose to the Japanese Prime Minister that a special summit be held between the leaders of the United States and Japan for the purpose of—

(A) addressing trade and economic issues, and

(B) establishing—

(i) an agreement that provides objectives for improvement in trade and economic relations, and

(ii) targets for achieving these objectives.

(2) The delegation of the United States to the summit meeting described in subsection (a) should include—

(A) Members of Congress from both political parties, and

(B) appropriate officers of the executive branch of the United States Government.

(3) The delegation of Japan to the summit meeting described in subsection (a) should include—

(A) representatives of all political parties in Japan, and

(B) appropriate officers of the Government of Japan.

SEC. 1307. SUPERCOMPUTER TRADE DISPUTE.

(a) FINDINGS.—The Congress finds that—

(1) United States manufacturers of supercomputers have encountered significant obstacles in selling supercomputers in Japan, particularly to government agencies and universities;

(2) Japanese government procurement policies and pricing practices have denied United States manufacturers access to the Japanese supercomputer market;

(3) it has been reported that officials of the Ministry of International Trade and Industry of Japan have told United States Government officials that Japanese government agencies and universities do not intend to purchase supercomputers from United States manufacturers, or take steps to improve access for United States manufacturers;

(4) the United States Government in August 1987 signed an agreement with the Government of Japan establishing procedures for the procurement of United States supercomputers by the Government of Japan;

(5) concern remains as to implementation of the procurement agreement by the Government of Japan;

(6) there have been allegations that Japanese manufacturers of supercomputers have been offering supercomputers at drastically discounted prices in the markets of the United States, Japan, and other countries;

(7) deep price discounting raises the concern that Japan's large-scale vertically integrated manufacturers of

supercomputers have targeted the supercomputer industry with the objective of eventual domination of the global computer market; and

(8) the supercomputer industry plays a central role in the technological competitiveness and national security of the United States.

(b) SENSE OF CONGRESS.—It is the sense of the Congress that the United States Trade Representative and other appropriate officials of the United States Government should—

(1) give the highest priority to concluding and enforcing agreements with the Government of Japan which achieve improved market access for United States manufacturers of supercomputers and end any predatory pricing activities of Japanese companies in the United States, Japan, and other countries; and

(2) continue to monitor the efforts of United States manufacturers of supercomputers to gain access to the Japanese market, recognizing that the Government of Japan may continue to manipulate the government procurement process to maintain the market dominance of Japanese manufacturers.

PART 2—IMPROVEMENT IN THE ENFORCEMENT OF THE ANTIDUMPING AND COUNTERVAILING DUTY LAWS

SEC. 1311. REFERENCE TO TITLE VII OF THE TARIFF ACT OF 1930.

Unless otherwise provided, whenever in this part an amendment or repeal is expressed in terms of an amendment to, or repeal of, a subtitle, section, subsection, or other provision, the reference shall be considered to be made to a subtitle, section, subsection, or other provision of title VII of the Tariff Act of 1930 (19 U.S.C. 1671 et seq.).

SEC. 1312. ACTIONABLE DOMESTIC SUBSIDIES.

Paragraph (5) of section 771 (19 U.S.C. 1677(5)) is amended to read as follows:

"(5) SUBSIDY.—

"(A) IN GENERAL.—The term 'subsidy' has the same meaning as the term 'bounty or grant' as that term is used in section 303, and includes, but is not limited to, the following:

"(i) Any export subsidy described in Annex A to the Agreement (relating to illustrative list of export subsidies).

"(ii) The following domestic subsidies, if provided or required by government action to a specific enterprise or industry, or group of enterprises or industries, whether publicly or privately owned and whether paid or bestowed directly or indirectly on the manufacture, production, or export of any class or kind of merchandise:

"(I) The provision of capital, loans, or loan guarantees on terms inconsistent with commercial considerations.

"(II) The provision of goods or services at preferential rates.

"(III) The grant of funds or forgiveness of debt to cover operating losses sustained by a specific industry.

"(IV) The assumption of any costs or expenses of manufacture, production, or distribution.

"(B) SPECIAL RULE.—In applying subparagraph (A), the administering authority, in each investigation, shall determine whether the bounty, grant, or subsidy in law or in fact is provided to a specific enterprise or industry, or group of enterprises or industries. Nominal general availability, under the terms of the law, regulation, program, or rule establishing a bounty, grant, or subsidy, of the benefits thereunder is not a basis for determining that the bounty, grant, or subsidy is not, or has not been, in fact provided to a specific enterprise or industry, or group thereof.".

SEC. 1313. CALCULATION OF SUBSIDIES ON CERTAIN PROCESSED AGRICULTURAL PRODUCTS.

(a) IN GENERAL.—Title VII of the Tariff Act of 1930 is amended by inserting after section 771A (19 U.S.C. 1677-1) the following new section:

"SEC. 771B. In the case of an agricultural product processed from a raw agricultural product in which (1) the demand for the prior stage product is substantially dependent on the demand for the latter stage product, and (2) the processing operation adds only limited value to the raw commodity, subsidies found to be provided to either producers or processors of the product shall be deemed to be provided with respect to the manufacture, production, or exportation of the processed product.".

(b) CONFORMING AMENDMENT.—The table of contents for title VII of the Tariff Act of 1930 is amended by inserting after the item relating to section 771A the following:

"Sec. 771B. Calculation of subsidies on certain processed agricultural products.".

SEC. 1314. REVOCATION OF STATUS AS A COUNTRY UNDER THE AGREEMENT.

Section 701 (19 U.S.C. 1671) is amended—

(1) by redesignating subsection (c) as subsection (d); and

(2) by inserting after subsection (b) the following new subsection:

"(c) REVOCATION OF STATUS AS A COUNTRY UNDER THE AGREEMENT.—The United States Trade Representative may revoke the status of a foreign country as a country under the Agreement for purposes of this subtitle if such foreign country—

"(1) announces that such foreign country does not intend, or is not able, to honor the obligations it has assumed with respect to the United States or the Agreement for purposes of this subtitle, or

"(2) does not in fact honor such obligations.".

SEC. 1315. TREATMENT OF INTERNATIONAL CONSORTIA.

Section 701 (19 U.S.C. 1671) (as amended by section 1314) is further amended—

(1) by redesignating subsection (d) as subsection (e); and

(2) by inserting after subsection (c) the following new subsection:

"(d) TREATMENT OF INTERNATIONAL CONSORTIA.—For purposes of this subtitle, if the members (or other participating entities) of an international consortium that is engaged in the production of a class or kind of merchandise subject to a countervailing duty investigation receive subsidies from their respective home countries to assist, permit, or otherwise enable their participation in that consortium through production or manufacturing operations in their respective home countries, then the administering authority shall cumulate all such subsidies, as well as subsidies provided directly to the international consortium, in determining any countervailing duty upon such merchandise.".

SEC. 1316. DUMPING BY NONMARKET ECONOMY COUNTRIES.

(a) IN GENERAL.—Subsection (c) of section 773 (19 U.S.C. 1677b) is amended to read as follows:

"(c) NONMARKET ECONOMY COUNTRIES.—

"(1) IN GENERAL.—If—

"(A) the merchandise under investigation is exported from a nonmarket economy country, and

"(B) the administering authority finds that available information does not permit the foreign market value of the merchandise to be determined under subsection (a),

the administering authority shall determine the foreign market value of the merchandise on the basis of the value of the factors of production utilized in producing the merchandise and to which shall be added an amount for general expenses and profit plus the cost of containers, coverings, and other expenses, as required by subsection (e). Except as provided in paragraph (2), the valuation of the factors of production shall be based on the best available information regarding the values of such factors in a market economy country or countries considered to be appropriate by the administering authority.

"(2) EXCEPTION.—If the administering authority finds that the available information is inadequate for purposes of determining the foreign market value of merchandise under paragraph (1), the administering authority shall determine the foreign market value on the basis of the price at which merchandise that is—

"(A) comparable to the merchandise under investigation, and

"(B) produced in one or more market economy countries that are at a level of economic development comparable to that of the nonmarket economy country,

is sold in other countries, including the United States.

"(3) FACTORS OF PRODUCTION.—For purposes of paragraph (1), the factors of production utilized in producing merchandise include, but are not limited to—

"(A) hours of labor required,

"(B) quantities of raw materials employed,

"(C) amounts of energy and other utilities consumed, and

"(D) representative capital cost, including depreciation.

"(4) VALUATION OF FACTORS OF PRODUCTION.—The administering authority, in valuing factors of production under paragraph (1), shall utilize, to the extent possible, the prices or costs of factors of production in one or more market economy countries that are—

"(A) at a level of economic development comparable to that of the nonmarket economy country, and

"(B) significant producers of comparable merchandise.".

(b) NONMARKET ECONOMY COUNTRY DEFINED.—Section 771 (19 U.S.C. 1677) is amended by adding at the end thereof the following new paragraph:

"(18) NONMARKET ECONOMY COUNTRY.—

"(A) IN GENERAL.—The term 'nonmarket economy country' means any foreign country that the administering authority determines does not operate on market principles of cost or pricing structures, so that sales of merchandise in such country do not reflect the fair value of the merchandise.

"(B) FACTORS TO BE CONSIDERED.—In making determinations under subparagraph (A) the administering authority shall take into account—

"(i) the extent to which the currency of the foreign country is convertible into the currency of other countries;

"(ii) the extent to which wage rates in the foreign country are determined by free bargaining between labor and management,

"(iii) the extent to which joint ventures or other investments by firms of other foreign countries are permitted in the foreign country,

"(iv) the extent of government ownership or control of the means of production,

"(v) the extent of government control over the allocation of resources and over the price and output decisions of enterprises, and

"(vi) such other factors as the administering authority considers appropriate.

"(C) DETERMINATION IN EFFECT.—

"(i) Any determination that a foreign country is a nonmarket economy country shall remain in effect until revoked by the administering authority.

"(ii) The administering authority may make a determination under subparagraph (A) with respect to any foreign country at any time.

"(D) DETERMINATIONS NOT IN ISSUE.—Notwithstanding any other provision of law, any determination made by the administering authority under subparagraph (A) shall not be subject to judicial review in any investigation conducted under subtitle B.

"(E) COLLECTION OF INFORMATION.—Upon request by the administering authority, the Commissioner of Customs shall provide the administering authority a copy of all public and proprietary information submitted to, or obtained by, the Commissioner of Customs that the administering authority considers relevant to proceedings involving merchandise from nonmarket economy countries. The administering authority shall protect proprietary information obtained under this section from public disclosure in accordance with section 777.".

(c) SUSPENSION OF NONMARKET ECONOMY COUNTRY INVESTIGATIONS.—Section 734 (19 U.S.C. 1673c) is amended by adding at the end thereof the following new subsection:

"(l) SPECIAL RULE FOR NONMARKET ECONOMY COUNTRIES.—

"(1) IN GENERAL.—The administering authority may suspend an investigation under this subtitle upon acceptance of an agreement with a nonmarket economy country to restrict the volume of imports into the United States of the merchandise under investigation only if the administering authority determines that—

"(A) such agreement satisfies the requirements of subsection (d), and

"(B) will prevent the suppression or undercutting of price levels of domestic products by imports of the merchandise under investigation.

"(2) FAILURE OF AGREEMENTS.—If the administering authority determines that an agreement accepted under this subsection no longer prevents the suppression or undercutting of domestic prices of merchandise manufactured in the United States, the provisions of subsection (i) shall apply.".

SEC. 1317. THIRD-COUNTRY DUMPING.

(a) DEFINITIONS.—For purposes of this section:

(1) The term "Agreement" means the Agreement on Implementation of Article VI of the General Agreement on Tariffs and Trade (relating to antidumping measures).

(2) The term "Agreement country" means a foreign country that has accepted the Agreement.

(3) The term "Trade Representative" means the United States Trade Representative.

(b) PETITION BY DOMESTIC INDUSTRY.—

(1) A domestic industry that produces a product that is like or directly competitive with merchandise produced by a foreign country (whether or not an Agreement country) may, if it has reason to believe that—

(A) such merchandise is being dumped in an Agreement country; and

(B) such domestic industry is being materially injured, or threatened with material injury, by reason of such dumping;

submit a petition to the Trade Representative that alleges the elements referred to in subparagraphs (A) and (B) and requests the Trade Representative to take action under subsection (c) on behalf of the domestic industry.

(2) A petition submitted under paragraph (1) shall contain such detailed information as the Trade Representative may require in support of the allegations in the petition.

(c) APPLICATION FOR ANTIDUMPING ACTION ON BEHALF OF THE DOMESTIC INDUSTRY.—

(1) If the Trade Representative, on the basis of the information contained in a petition submitted under paragraph (1), determines that there is a reasonable basis for the allegations in the petition, the Trade Representative shall submit to the appropriate authority of the Agreement country where the alleged dumping is occurring an application pursuant to Article 12 of the Agreement which requests that appropriate antidumping action under the law of that country be taken, on behalf of the United States, with respect to imports into that country of the merchandise concerned.

(2) At the request of the Trade Representative, the appropriate officers of the Department of Commerce and the United

States International Trade Commission shall assist the Trade Representative in preparing the application under paragraph (1).

(d) CONSULTATION AFTER SUBMISSION OF APPLICATION.—After submitting an application under subsection (c)(1), the Trade Representative shall seek consultations with the appropriate authority of the Agreement country regarding the request for antidumping action.

(e) ACTION UPON REFUSAL OF AGREEMENT COUNTRY TO ACT.—If the appropriate authority of an Agreement country refuses to undertake antidumping measures in response to a request made therefor by the Trade Representative under subsection (c), the Trade Representative shall promptly consult with the domestic industry on whether action under any other law of the United States is appropriate.

SEC. 1318. INPUT DUMPING BY RELATED PARTIES.

Subsection (e) of section 773 (19 U.S.C. 1677b(e)) is amended—

(1) by striking out "(3)" each place it appears in paragraph (2) and inserting "(4)",

(2) by redesignating paragraph (3) as paragraph (4),

(3) by inserting after paragraph (2) the following new paragraph:

"(3) SPECIAL RULE.—If, regarding any transaction between persons specified in any one of the subparagraphs of paragraph (4) involving the production by one of such persons of a major input to the merchandise under consideration, the administering authority has reasonable grounds to believe or suspect that an amount represented as the value of such input is less than the costs of production of such input, then the administering authority may determine the value of the major input on the best evidence available regarding such costs of production, if such costs are greater than the amount that would be determined for such input under paragraph (2).", and

(4) by striking out "paragraph (2)" in paragraph (4) (as redesignated by paragraph (2)) and inserting "paragraphs (2) and (3)".

SEC. 1319. FICTITIOUS MARKETS.

Subsection (a) of section 773 of the Tariff Act of 1930 (19 U.S.C. 1677b(a)) is amended by adding at the end thereof the following new paragraph:

"(5) FICTITIOUS MARKETS.—The occurrence of different movements in the prices at which different forms of any merchandise subject to an antidumping duty order issued under this title are sold (or, in the absence of sales, offered for sale) after the issuance of such order in the principal markets of the foreign country from which the merchandise is exported may be considered by the administering authority as evidence of the establishment of a fictitious market for the merchandise if the movement in such prices appears to reduce the amount by which the foreign market value of the merchandise exceeds the United States price of the merchandise.".

SEC. 1320. DOWNSTREAM PRODUCT MONITORING.

(a) IN GENERAL.—Subtitle D (19 U.S.C. 1677 et seq.) is amended by adding at the end thereof the following:

"SEC. 780. DOWNSTREAM PRODUCT MONITORING.

"(a) PETITION REQUESTING MONITORING.—

"(1) IN GENERAL.—A domestic producer of an article that is like a component part or a downstream product may petition the administering authority to designate a downstream product for monitoring under subsection (b). The petition shall specify—

"(A) the downstream product,

"(B) the component product incorporated into such downstream product, and

"(C) the reasons for suspecting that the imposition of antidumping or countervailing duties has resulted in a diversion of exports of the component part into increased production and exportation to the United States of such downstream product.

"(2) DETERMINATION REGARDING PETITION.—Within 14 days after receiving a petition submitted under paragraph (1), the administering authority shall determine—

"(A) whether there is a reasonable likelihood that imports into the United States of the downstream product will increase as an indirect result of any diversion with respect to the component part, and

"(B) whether—

"(i) the component part is already subject to monitoring to aid in the enforcement of a bilateral arrangement (within the meaning of section 804 of the Trade and Tariff Act of 1984),

"(ii) merchandise related to the component part and manufactured in the same foreign country in which the component part is manufactured has been the subject of a significant number of investigations suspended under section 704 or 734 or countervailing or antidumping duty orders issued under this title or section 303, or

"(iii) merchandise manufactured or exported by the manufacturer or exporter of the component part that is similar in description and use to the component part has been the subject of at least 2 investigations suspended under section 704 or 734 or countervailing or antidumping duty orders issued under this title or section 303.

"(3) FACTORS TO TAKE INTO ACCOUNT.—In making a determination under paragraph (2)(A), the administering authority may, if appropriate, take into account such factors as—

"(A) the value of the component part in relation to the value of the downstream product,

"(B) the extent to which the component part has been substantially transformed as a result of its incorporation into the downstream product, and

"(C) the relationship between the producers of component parts and producers of downstream products.

"(4) PUBLICATION OF DETERMINATION.—The administering authority shall publish in the Federal Register notice of each determination made under paragraph (2) and, if the determination made under paragraph (2)(A) and a determination made under any subparagraph of paragraph (2)(B) are affirmative, shall transmit a copy of such determinations and the petition to the Commission.

"(5) DETERMINATIONS NOT SUBJECT TO JUDICIAL REVIEW.—Notwithstanding any other provision of law, any determination made by the administering authority under paragraph (2) shall not be subject to judicial review.

"(b) MONITORING BY THE COMMISSION.—

"(1) IN GENERAL.—If the determination made under subsection (a)(2)(A) and a determination made under any clause of subsection (a)(2)(B) with respect to a petition are affirmative, the Commission shall immediately commence monitoring of trade in the downstream product that is the subject of the determination made under subsection (a)(2)(A). If the Commission finds that imports of a downstream product being monitored increased during any calendar quarter by 5 percent or more over the preceding quarter, the Commission shall analyze that increase in the context of overall economic conditions in the product sector.

"(2) REPORTS.—The Commission shall make quarterly reports to the administering authority regarding the monitoring and analyses conducted under paragraph (1). The Commission shall make the reports available to the public.

"(c) ACTION ON BASIS OF MONITORING REPORTS.—The administering authority shall review the information in the reports submitted by the Commission under subsection (b)(2) and shall—

"(1) consider the information in determining whether to initiate an investigation under section 702(a), 732(a), or 303 regarding any downstream product, and

"(2) request the Commission to cease monitoring any downstream product if the information indicates that imports into the United States are not increasing and there is no reasonable likelihood of diversion with respect to component parts.

"(d) DEFINITIONS.—For purposes of this section—

"(1) The term 'component part' means any imported article that—

"(A) during the 5-year period ending on the date on which the petition is filed under subsection (a), has been subject to—

"(i) a countervailing or antidumping duty order issued under this title or section 303 that requires the deposit of estimated countervailing or antidumping duties imposed at a rate of at least 15 percent ad valorem, or

"(ii) an agreement entered into under section 704, 734, or 303 after a preliminary affirmative determination under section 703(b), 733(b)(1), or 303 was made by the administering authority which included a determination that the estimated net subsidy was at least 15 percent ad valorem or that the estimated average amount by which the foreign market value exceeded the United States price was at least 15 percent ad valorem, and

"(B) because of its inherent characteristics, is routinely used as a major part, component, assembly, subassembly, or material in a downstream product.

"(2) The term 'downstream product' means any manufactured article—

"(A) which is imported into the United States, and

"(B) into which is incorporated any component part.".

(b) CONFORMING AMENDMENT.—The table of contents for title VII of the Tariff Act of 1930 is amended by inserting after the item relating to section 779 the following:

"Sec. 780. Downstream product monitoring.".

SEC. 1321. PREVENTION OF CIRCUMVENTION OF ANTIDUMPING AND COUNTERVAILING DUTY ORDERS.

(a) IN GENERAL.—Subtitle D (19 U.S.C. 1677 et seq.) (as amended by section 1320) is further amended by adding at the end thereof the following:

"SEC. 781. PREVENTION OF CIRCUMVENTION OF ANTIDUMPING AND COUNTERVAILING DUTY ORDERS.

"(a) MERCHANDISE COMPLETED OR ASSEMBLED IN THE UNITED STATES.—

"(1) IN GENERAL.—If—

"(A) merchandise sold in the United States is of the same class or kind as any other merchandise that is the subject of—

"(i) an antidumping duty order issued under section 736,

"(ii) a finding issued under the Antidumping Act, 1921, or

"(iii) a countervailing duty order issued under section 706 or section 303,

"(B) such merchandise sold in the United States is completed or assembled in the United States from parts or components produced in the foreign country with respect to which such order or finding applies, and

"(C) the difference between the value of such merchandise sold in the United States and the value of the imported parts and components referred to in subparagraph (B) is small,

the administering authority, after taking into account any advice provided by the Commission under subsection (e), may include within the scope of such order or finding the imported parts or components referred to in subparagraph (B) that are used in the completion or assembly of the merchandise in the United States at any time such order or finding is in effect.

"(2) FACTORS TO CONSIDER.—In determining whether to include parts or components in a countervailing or antidumping duty order or finding under paragraph (1), the administering authority shall take into account such factors as—

"(A) the pattern of trade,

"(B) whether the manufacturer or exporter of the parts or components is related to the person who assembles or completes the merchandise sold in the United States from the parts or components produced in the foreign country with respect to which the order or finding described in paragraph (1) applies, and

"(C) whether imports into the United States of the parts or components produced in such foreign country have increased after the issuance of such order or finding.

"(b) MERCHANDISE COMPLETED OR ASSEMBLED IN OTHER FOREIGN COUNTRIES.—

"(1) IN GENERAL.—If—

"(A) merchandise imported into the United States is of the same class or kind as any merchandise produced in a foreign country that is the subject of—

"(i) an antidumping duty order issued under section 736,

"(ii) a finding issued under the Antidumping Act, 1921, or

"(iii) a countervailing duty order issued under section 706 or section 303,

"(B) before importation into the United States, such imported merchandise is completed or assembled in another foreign country from merchandise which—

"(i) is subject to such order or finding, or

"(ii) is produced in the foreign country with respect to which such order or finding applies,

"(C) the difference between the value of such imported merchandise and the value of the merchandise described in subparagraph (B) is small, and

"(D) the administering authority determines that action is appropriate under this paragraph to prevent evasion of such order or finding,

the administering authority, after taking into account any advice provided by the Commission under subsection (e), may include such imported merchandise within the scope of such order or finding at any time such order or finding is in effect.

"(2) FACTORS TO CONSIDER.—In determining whether to include merchandise assembled or completed in a foreign country in a countervailing or antidumping duty order or finding under paragraph (1), the administering authority shall take into account such factors as—

"(A) the pattern of trade,

"(B) whether the manufacturer or exporter of the merchandise described in paragraph (1)(B) is related to the person who uses the merchandise described in paragraph (1)(B) to assemble or complete in the foreign country the merchandise that is subsequently imported into the United States, and

"(C) whether imports into the foreign country of the merchandise described in paragraph (1)(B) have increased after the issuance of such order or finding.

"(c) MINOR ALTERATIONS OF MERCHANDISE.—

"(1) IN GENERAL.—The class or kind of merchandise subject to—

"(A) an investigation under this title,

"(B) an antidumping duty order issued under section 736,

"(C) a finding issued under the Antidumping Act, 1921, or

"(D) a countervailing duty order issued under section 706 or section 303,

shall include articles altered in form or appearance in minor respects (including raw agricultural products that have undergone minor processing), whether or not included in the same tariff classification.

"(2) EXCEPTION.—Paragraph (1) shall not apply with respect to altered merchandise if the administering authority determines that it would be unnecessary to consider the altered merchandise within the scope of the investigation, order, or finding.

"(d) LATER-DEVELOPED MERCHANDISE.—

"(1) IN GENERAL.—For purposes of determining whether merchandise developed after an investigation is initiated under this title or section 303 (hereafter in this paragraph referred to as the 'later-developed merchandise') is within the scope of an outstanding antidumping or countervailing duty order issued under this title or section 303 as a result of such investigation, the administering authority shall consider whether—

"(A) the later-developed merchandise has the same general physical characteristics as the merchandise with respect to which the order was originally issued (hereafter in this paragraph referred to as the 'earlier product'),

"(B) the expectations of the ultimate purchasers of the later-developed merchandise are the same as for the earlier product,

"(C) the ultimate use of the earlier product and the later-developed merchandise are the same,

"(D) the later-developed merchandise is sold through the same channels of trade as the earlier product, and

"(E) the later-developed merchandise is advertised and displayed in a manner similar to the earlier product.

The administering authority shall take into account any advice provided by the Commission under subsection (e) before making a determination under this subparagraph.

"(2) EXCLUSION FROM ORDERS.—The administering authority may not exclude a later-developed merchandise from a countervailing or antidumping duty order merely because the merchandise—

"(A) is classified under a tariff classification other than that identified in the petition or the administering authority's prior notices during the proceeding, or

"(B) permits the purchaser to perform additional functions, unless such additional functions constitute the primary use of the merchandise and the cost of the additional functions constitute more than a significant proportion of the total cost of production of the merchandise.

"(e) COMMISSION ADVICE.—

"(1) NOTIFICATION TO COMMISSION OF PROPOSED ACTION.—Before making a determination—

"(A) under subsection (a) with respect to merchandise completed or assembled in the United States (other than minor completion or assembly),

"(B) under subsection (b) with respect to merchandise completed or assembled in other foreign countries, or

"(C) under subsection (d) with respect to any later-developed merchandise which incorporates a significant technological advance or significant alteration of an earlier product,

with respect to an antidumping or countervailing duty order or finding as to which the Commission has made an affirmative injury determination, the administering authority shall notify the Commission of the proposed inclusion of such merchandise in such countervailing or antidumping order or finding. Notwithstanding any other provision of law, a decision by the administering authority regarding whether any merchandise is within a category for which notice is required under this paragraph is not subject to judicial review.

"(2) REQUEST FOR CONSULTATION.—After receiving notice under paragraph (1), the Commission may request consultations with the administering authority regarding the inclusion. Upon the request of the Commission, the administering authority shall consult with the Commission and any such consultation shall be completed within 15 days after the date of the request.

"(3) COMMISSION ADVICE.—If the Commission believes, after consultation under paragraph (2), that a significant injury issue is presented by the proposed inclusion, the Commission may provide written advice to the administering authority as to whether the inclusion would be inconsistent with the affirmative determination of the Commission on which the order or finding is based. If the Commission decides to provide such written advice, it shall promptly notify the administering authority of its intention to do so, and must provide such advice within 60 days after the date of notification under paragraph (1). For purposes of formulating its advice with respect to merchandise completed or assembled in the United States from parts or components produced in a foreign country, the Commission shall consider whether the inclusion of such parts or components taken as a whole would be inconsistent with its prior affirmative determination.".

(b) CONFORMING AMENDMENT.—The table of contents for title VII of the Tariff Act of 1930 is amended by inserting after the item relating to section 780 the following:

"Sec. 781. Prevention of circumvention of antidumping and countervailing duty orders.".

SEC. 1322. STEEL IMPORTS.

Section 805 of the Trade and Tariff Act of 1984 (19 U.S.C. 2253, note) is amended by adding at the end thereof the following new subsection:

"(d)(1) Any steel product that is manufactured in a country that is not party to a bilateral arrangement from steel which was melted and poured in a country that is party to a bilateral arrangement (hereafter in this subsection referred to as an 'arrangement country') may be treated for purposes of the quantitative restrictions and related terms under that arrangement as if it were a product of the arrangement country.

"(2) The President may implement such procedures as may be necessary or appropriate to carry out the purpose of paragraph (1).

"(3) The United States Trade Representative may, in a manner consistent with the purpose of any so-called 'third country equity provision' of an arrangement entered into under the President's Steel Policy, take such actions as he deems necessary with respect to steel imports of any other country or countries so as to ensure the effectiveness of any portion of such arrangement.".

SEC. 1323. SHORT LIFE CYCLE PRODUCTS.

(a) ESTABLISHMENT OF PRODUCT CATEGORIES FOR SHORT LIFE CYCLE MERCHANDISE.—Subtitle B is amended by adding at the end thereof the following new section:

"SEC. 739. ESTABLISHMENT OF PRODUCT CATEGORIES FOR SHORT LIFE CYCLE MERCHANDISE.

"(a) ESTABLISHMENT OF PRODUCT CATEGORIES.—

"(1) PETITIONS.—

"(A) IN GENERAL.—An eligible domestic entity may file a petition with the Commission requesting that a product category be established with respect to short life cycle merchandise at any time after the merchandise becomes the subject of 2 or more affirmative dumping determinations.

"(B) CONTENTS.—A petition filed under subparagraph (A) shall—

"(i) identify the short life cycle merchandise that is the subject of the affirmative dumping determinations,

"(ii) specify the short life cycle merchandise that the petitioner seeks to have included in the same product category as the merchandise that is subject to the affirmative dumping determinations,

"(iii) specify any short life cycle merchandise the petitioner particularly seeks to have excluded from the product category,

"(iv) provide reasons for the inclusions and exclusions specified under clauses (ii) and (iii), and

"(v) identify such merchandise in terms of the designations used in the Tariff Schedules of the United States.

"(2) DETERMINATIONS ON SUFFICIENCY OF PETITION.—Upon receiving a petition under paragraph (1), the Commission shall—

"(A) request the administering authority to confirm promptly the affirmative determinations on which the petition is based, and

"(B) upon receipt of such confirmation, determine whether the merchandise covered by the confirmed affirmative determinations is short life cycle merchandise and whether the petitioner is an eligible domestic entity.

"(3) NOTICE; HEARINGS.—If the determinations under paragraph (2)(B) are affirmative, the Commission shall—

"(A) publish notice in the Federal Register that the petition has been received, and

"(B) provide opportunity for the presentation of views regarding the establishment of the requested product category, including a public hearing if requested by any interested person.

"(4) DETERMINATIONS.—

"(A) IN GENERAL.—By no later than the date that is 90 days after the date on which a petition is filed under paragraph (1), the Commission shall determine the scope of the product category into which the short life cycle merchandise that is the subject of the affirmative dumping determinations identified in such petition shall be classified for purposes of this section.

"(B) MODIFICATIONS NOT REQUESTED BY PETITION.—

"(i) IN GENERAL.—The Commission may, on its own initiative, make a determination modifying the scope of any product category established under subparagraph (A) at any time.

"(ii) NOTICE AND HEARING.—Determinations may be made under clause (i) only after the Commission has—

"(I) published in the Federal Register notice of the proposed modification, and

"(II) provided interested parties an opportunity for a hearing, and a period for the submission of written comments, on the classification of merchandise into the product categories to be affected by such determination.

"(C) BASIS OF DETERMINATIONS.—In making determinations under subparagraph (A) or (B), the Commission shall ensure that each product category consists of similar short life cycle merchandise which is produced by similar processes under similar circumstances and has similar uses.

"(b) DEFINITIONS.—For purposes of this section—

"(1) ELIGIBLE DOMESTIC ENTITY.—The term 'eligible domestic entity' means a manufacturer or producer in the United States, or a certified union or recognized union or group of workers which is representative of an industry in the United States, that manufactures or produces short life cycle merchandise that is—

"(A) like or directly competitive with other merchandise that is the subject of 2 or more affirmative dumping determinations, or

"(B) is similar enough to such other merchandise as to be considered for inclusion with such merchandise in a product monitoring category established under this section.

"(2) AFFIRMATIVE DUMPING DETERMINATION.—The term 'affirmative dumping determination' means—

"(A) any affirmative final determination made by the administering authority under section 735(a) during the 8-year period preceding the filing of the petition under this section that results in the issuance of an antidumping duty order under section 736 which requires the deposit of estimated antidumping duties at a rate of not less than 15 percent ad valorem, or

"(B) any affirmative preliminary determination that—

"(i) is made by the administering authority under section 733(b) during the 8-year period preceding the filing of the petition under this section in the course of an investigation for which no final determination is made under section 735 by reason of a suspension of the investigation under section 734, and

"(ii) includes a determination that the estimated average amount by which the foreign market value of the merchandise exceeds the United States price of the merchandise is not less than 15 percent ad valorem.

"(3) SUBJECT OF AFFIRMATIVE DUMPING DETERMINATION.—

"(A) IN GENERAL.—Short life cycle merchandise of a manufacturer shall be treated as being the subject of an affirmative dumping determination only if the administering authority—

"(i) makes a separate determination of the amount by which the foreign market value of such merchandise of the manufacturer exceeds the United States price of such merchandise of the manufacturer, and

"(ii) specifically identifies the manufacturer by name with such amount in the affirmative dumping determination or in an antidumping duty order issued as a result of the affirmative dumping determination.

"(B) Exclusion.—Short life cycle merchandise of a manufacturer shall not be treated as being the subject of an affirmative dumping determination if—

"(i) such merchandise of the manufacturer is part of a group of merchandise to which the administering authority assigns (in lieu of making separate determinations described in subparagraph (A)(i)(I)) an amount determined to be the amount by which the foreign market value of the merchandise in such group exceeds the United States price of the merchandise in such group, and

"(ii) the merchandise and the manufacturer are not specified by name in the affirmative dumping determination or in any antidumping duty order issued as a result of such affirmative dumping determination.

"(4) Short life cycle merchandise.—The term 'short life cycle merchandise' means any product that the Commission determines is likely to become outmoded within 4 years, by reason of technological advances, after the product is commercially available. For purposes of this paragraph, the term 'outmoded' refers to a kind of style that is no longer state-of-the-art.

"(c) Transitional Rules.—

"(1) For purposes of this section and section 733(b)(1) (B) and (C), all affirmative dumping determinations described in subsection (b)(2)(A) that were made after December 31, 1980, and before the date of enactment of the Omnibus Trade and Competitiveness Act of 1988, and all affirmative dumping determinations described in subsection (b)(2)(B) that were made after December 31, 1984, and before the date of enactment of such Act, with respect to each category of short life cycle merchandise of the same manufacturer shall be treated as one affirmative dumping determination with respect to that category for that manufacturer which was made on the date on which the latest of such determinations was made.

"(2) No affirmative dumping determination that—

"(A) is described in subsection (b)(2)(A) and was made before January 1, 1981, or

"(B) is described in subsection (b)(2)(B) and was made before January 1, 1985,

may be taken into account under this section or section 733(b)(1) (B) and (C).".

(b) Expedited Dumping Investigations.—Section 733 (19 U.S.C. 1673) is amended as follows:

(1) Paragraph (1) of subsection (b)(1) is amended to read as follows:

"(1) Period of antidumping duty investigation.—

"(A) In general.—Except as provided in subparagraph (B), within 160 days after the date on which a petition is filed under section 732(b), or an investigation is commenced under section 732(a), but not before an affirmative determination by the Commission under subsection (a) of this section, the administering authority shall make a determination, based upon the best information available to it at the time of the determination, of whether there is a reasonable basis to believe or suspect that the merchandise is being sold, or is likely to be sold, at less than fair value. If the determination of the administering authority under this subsection is affirmative, the determination shall include the estimated average amount by which the foreign market value exceeds the United States price.

"(B) IF CERTAIN SHORT LIFE CYCLE MERCHANDISE INVOLVED.—If a petition filed under section 732(b), or an investigation commenced under section 732(a), concerns short life cycle merchandise that is included in a product category established under section 739(a), subparagraph (A) shall be applied—

"(i) by substituting '120 days' for '160 days' if manufacturers that are second offenders account for a significant proportion of the merchandise under investigation, and

"(ii) by substituting '100 days' for '160 days' if manufacturers that are multiple offenders account for a significant proportion of the merchandise under investigation.

"(C) DEFINITIONS OF OFFENDERS.—For purposes of subparagraph (B)—

"(i) The term 'second offender' means a manufacturer that is specified in 2 affirmative dumping determinations (within the meaning of section 739) as the manufacturer of short life cycle merchandise that is—

"(I) specified in both such determinations, and

"(II) within the scope of the product category referred to in subparagraph (B).

"(ii) The term 'multiple offender' means a manufacturer that is specified in 3 or more affirmative dumping determinations (within the meaning of section 739) as the manufacturer of short life cycle merchandise that is—

"(I) specified in each of such determinations, and

"(II) within the scope of the product category referred to in subparagraph (B).".

(2) Paragraph (1) of subsection (c) is amended by inserting at the end thereof the following sentence: "No extension of a determination date may be made under this paragraph for any investigation in which a determination date provided for in subsection (b)(1)(B) applies unless the petitioner submits written notice to the administering authority of its consent to the extension.".

(3) Subsection (e)(1) is amended by adding at the end thereof the following flush sentence:

"The administering authority shall be treated as having made an affirmative determination under subparagraph (A) in any investigation to which subsection (b)(1)(B) is applied.".

(c) CONFORMING AMENDMENT.—The table of contents for title VII of the Tariff Act of 1930 is amended by inserting after the item relating to section 739 the following:

"Sec. 739. Establishment of product categories for short life cycle merchandise.".

SEC. 1324. CRITICAL CIRCUMSTANCES.

(a) COUNTERVAILING DUTY INVESTIGATIONS.—

(1) Section 702 (19 U.S.C. 1671a) is amended by adding at the end thereof the following new subsection:

"(e) INFORMATION REGARDING CRITICAL CIRCUMSTANCES.—If, at any time after the initiation of an investigation under this subtitle, the administering authority finds a reasonable basis to suspect that the alleged subsidy is inconsistent with the Agreement, the administering authority may request the Commissioner of Customs to compile information on an expedited basis regarding entries of the class or kind of merchandise that is the subject of the investigation. Upon receiving such request, the Commissioner of Customs shall collect information regarding the volume and value of entries of the class or kind of merchandise that is the subject of the investigation and shall transmit such information to the administering authority at such times as the administering authority shall direct (at least once every 30 days), until a final determination is made under section 705(a), the investigation is terminated, or the administering authority withdraws the request.".

(2) Paragraph (1) of section 703(e) (19 U.S.C. 1671b(e)(1)) is amended by inserting "(at any time after the initiation of the investigation under this subtitle)" after "promptly".

(3) Subparagraph (A) of section 705(b)(4) (19 U.S.C. 1671d(b)(4)(A)) is amended to read as follows:

"(A) RETROACTIVE APPLICATION.—

"(i) IN GENERAL.—If the finding of the administering authority under subsection (a)(2) is affirmative, then the final determination of the Commission shall include a finding as to whether retroactive imposition of a countervailing duty on the merchandise appears necessary to prevent recurrence of material injury that was caused by massive imports of the merchandise over a relatively short period of time and will be difficult to repair.

"(ii) PREVENTION OF RECURRENCE.—For purposes of making its finding under clause (i), the Commission shall make an evaluation as to whether the effectiveness of the countervailing duty order would be materially impaired if such imposition did not occur.

"(iii) EVALUATION OF EFFECTIVENESS.—In making the evaluation under clause (ii), the Commission shall consider, among other factors it considers relevant—

"(I) the condition of the domestic industry,

"(II) whether massive imports of the merchandise over a relatively short period of time can be accounted for by efforts to avoid the potential imposition of countervailing duties,

"(III) whether foreign economic conditions led to the massive imports of the merchandise, and

"(IV) whether the impact of the massive imports of the merchandise is likely to continue for some period after issuance of the countervailing duty order under this subtitle.".

(b) ANTIDUMPING DUTY INVESTIGATIONS.—

(1) Section 732 (19 U.S.C. 1673a) is amended by adding at the end thereof the following new subsection:

"(e) INFORMATION REGARDING CRITICAL CIRCUMSTANCES.—If, at any time after the initiation of an investigation under this subtitle, the administering authority finds a reasonable basis to suspect that—

"(1) there is a history of dumping in the United States or elsewhere of the class or kind of the merchandise which is the subject of the investigation, or

"(2) the person by whom, or for whose account, the merchandise was imported knew, or should have known, that the exporter was selling the merchandise which is the subject of the investigation at less than its fair value,

the administering authority may request the Commissioner of Customs to compile information on an expedited basis regarding entries of the class or kind of merchandise that is the subject of the investigation. Upon receiving such request, the Commissioner of Customs shall collect information regarding the volume and value of entries of the class or kind of merchandise that is the subject of the investigation and shall transmit such information to the administering authority at such times as the administering authority shall direct (at least once every 30 days), until a final determination is made under section 735(a), the investigation is terminated, or the administering authority withdraws the request.".

(2) Paragraph (1) of section 733(e) (19 U.S.C. 1673b(e)(1)) is amended by inserting "(at any time after the initiation of the investigation under this subtitle)" after "promptly".

(3) Subparagraph (A) of section 735(b)(4) (19 U.S.C. 1673d(b)(4)(A)) is amended to read as follows:

"(A) RETROACTIVE APPLICATION.—

"(i) IN GENERAL.—If the finding of the administering authority under subsection (a)(3) is affirmative, then the final determination of the Commission shall include a finding as to whether retroactive imposition of antidumping duties on the merchandise appears necessary to prevent recurrence of material injury that was caused by massive imports of the merchandise over a relatively short period of time.

"(ii) PREVENTION OF RECURRENCE.—For purposes of making its finding under clause (i), the Commission shall make an evaluation as to whether the effectiveness of the antidumping duty order would be materially impaired if such imposition did not occur.

"(iii) EVALUATION OF EFFECTIVENESS.—In making the evaluation under clause (ii), the Commission shall consider, among other factors it considers relevant—

"(I) the condition of the domestic industry,

"(II) whether massive imports of the merchandise in a relatively short period of time can be accounted for by efforts to avoid the potential imposition of antidumping duties,

"(III) whether foreign economic conditions led to the massive imports of the merchandise, and

"(IV) whether the impact of the massive imports of the merchandise is likely to continue for some period after issuance of the antidumping duty order under this subtitle.".

SEC. 1325. EXPEDITED REVIEW AUTHORITY.

(a) IN GENERAL.—Paragraph (1) of section 736(c) (19 U.S.C. 1673e(c)(1)) is amended to read as follows:

"(1) CONDITIONS FOR WAIVER OF DEPOSIT OF ESTIMATED DUTIES.—The administering authority may permit, for not more than 90 days after the date of publication of an order under subsection (a), the posting of a bond or other security in lieu of the deposit of estimated antidumping duties required under subsection (a)(3) if—

"(A) the investigation has not been designated as extraordinarily complicated by reason of—

"(i) the number and complexity of the transactions to be investigated or adjustments to be considered,

"(ii) the novelty of the issues presented, or

"(iii) the number of firms whose activities must be investigated,

"(B) the final determination in the investigation has not been postponed under section 735(a)(2)(A);

"(C) on the basis of information presented to the administering authority by any manufacturer, producer, or exporter in such form and within such time as the administering authority may require, the administering authority is satisfied that a determination will be made, within 90 days after the date of publication of an order under subsection (a), of the foreign market value and the United States price for all merchandise of such manufacturer, producer, or exporter described in that order which was entered, or withdrawn from warehouse, for consumption on or after the date of publication of—

"(i) an affirmative preliminary determination by the administering authority under section 733(b), or

"(ii) if its determination under section 733(b) was negative, an affirmative final determination by the administering authority under section 735(a),

and before the date of publication of the affirmative final determination by the Commission under section 735(b);

"(D) the party described in subparagraph (C) provides credible evidence that the amount by which the foreign market value of the merchandise exceeds the United States price of the merchandise is significantly less than the amount of such excess specified in the antidumping duty order published under subsection (a); and

"(E) the data concerning the foreign market value and the United States price apply to sales in the usual commercial quantities and in the ordinary course of trade and the number of such sales are sufficient to form an adequate basis for comparison.".

(b) Business Proprietary Information.—Subsection (c) of section 736 (19 U.S.C. 1673e(c)) is amended by adding at the end thereof the following new paragraph:

"(4) Provision of business proprietary information; written comments.—Before determining whether to permit the posting of bond or other security under paragraph (1) in lieu of the deposit of estimated antidumping duties, the administering authority shall—

"(A) make all business proprietary information supplied to the administering authority under paragraph (1) available under a protective order in accordance with section 777(c) to all interested parties described in subparagraph (C), (D), (E), (F), or (G) of section 771(9), and

"(B) afford all interested parties an opportunity to file written comments on whether the posting of bond or other security under paragraph (1) in lieu of the deposit of estimated antidumping duties should be permitted.".

SEC. 1326. PROCESSED AGRICULTURAL PRODUCTS.

(a) DEFINITION OF INDUSTRY PRODUCING PROCESSED AGRICULTURAL PRODUCTS.—Paragraph (4) of section 771 (19 U.S.C. 1677(4)) is amended by adding at the end thereof the following new subparagraph:

"(E) INDUSTRY PRODUCING PROCESSED AGRICULTURAL PRODUCTS.—

"(i) IN GENERAL.—Subject to clause (v), in an investigation involving a processed agricultural product produced from any raw agricultural product, the producers or growers of the raw agricultural product may be considered part of the industry producing the processed product if—

"(I) the processed agricultural product is produced from the raw agricultural product through a single continuous line of production; and

"(II) there is a substantial coincidence of economic interest between the producers or growers of the raw agricultural product and the processors of the processed agricultural product based upon relevant economic factors, which may, in the discretion of the Commission, include price, added market value, or other economic interrelationships (regardless of whether such coincidence of economic interest is based upon any legal relationship).

"(ii) PROCESSING.—For purposes of this subparagraph, the processed agricultural product shall be considered to be processed from a raw agricultural product through a single continuous line of production if—

"(I) the raw agricultural product is substantially or completely devoted to the production of the processed agricultural product; and

"(II) the processed agricultural product is produced substantially or completely from the raw product.

"(iii) RELEVANT ECONOMIC FACTORS.—For purposes of clause (i)(II), in addition to such other factors it considers relevant to the question of coincidence of economic interest, the Commission shall—

"(I) if price is taken into account, consider the degree of correlation between the price of the raw agricultural product and the price of the processed agricultural product; and

"(II) if added market value is taken into account, consider whether the value of the raw agricultural product constitutes a significant percentage of the value of the processed agricultural product.

"(iv) RAW AGRICULTURAL PRODUCT.—For purposes of this subparagraph, the term 'raw agricultural product' means any farm or fishery product.

"(v) TERMINATION OF THIS SUBPARAGRAPH.—This subparagraph shall cease to have effect if the United States Trade Representative notifies the administering authority and the Commission that the application of this subparagraph is inconsistent with the international obligations of the United States.".

(b) THREAT OF MATERIAL INJURY.—Section 771(7)(F) (19 U.S.C. 1677(7)(F)) is amended—

(1) by striking out "and" at the end of subclause (VII);

(2) by striking out the period at the end of subclause (VIII) and inserting ", and"; and

(3) by adding at the end thereof the following:

"(IX) in any investigation under this title which involves imports of both a raw agricultural product (within the meaning of paragraph (4)(E)(iv)) and any product processed from such raw agricultural product, the likelihood that there will be increased imports, by reason of product shifting, if there is an affirmative determination by the Commission under section 705(b)(1) or 735(b)(1) with respect to either the raw agricultural product or the processed agricultural product (but not both).".

(c) INTERESTED PARTIES.—Section 771(9) (19 U.S.C. 1677(9)) is amended—

(1) by striking out "and" at the end of subparagraph (E);

(2) by striking out the period at the end of subparagraph (F) and inserting in lieu thereof ", and"; and

(3) by adding at the end thereof the following new subparagraph:

"(G) in any investigation under this title involving an industry engaged in producing a processed agricultural product, as defined in paragraph (4)(E), a coalition or trade association which is representative of either—

"(i) processors,

"(ii) processors and producers, or

"(iii) processors and growers,

but this subparagraph shall cease to have effect if the United States Trade Representative notifies the administering authority and the Commission that the application of this subparagraph is inconsistent with the international obligations of the United States.".

(d) CONFORMING AMENDMENTS.—

(1) Title VII of the Tariff Act of 1930 is amended by striking out "subparagraph (C), (D), (E), or (F) of section 771(9)" each place it appears and inserting in lieu thereof "subparagraph (C), (D), (E), (F), or (G) of section 771(9)".

(2) Title VII of the Tariff Act of 1930 is amended by striking out "subparagraph (C), (D), (E), and (F) of section 771(9)" each place it appears and inserting in lieu thereof "subparagraph (C), (D), (E), (F), or (G) of section 771(9)".

(3) Subsection (a) of section 516 of the Tariff Act of 1930 (19 U.S.C. 1516(a)) is amended by adding at the end thereof the following new paragraph:

"(3) Any producer of a raw agricultural product who is considered under section 771(4)(E) to be part of the industry producing a processed agricultural product of the same class or kind as the designated imported merchandise shall, for purposes of this section, be treated as an interested party producing such processed agricultural product.".

SEC. 1327. LEASES EQUIVALENT TO SALES.

Section 771 (19 U.S.C. 1677) is amended by adding at the end thereof the following new paragraph:

"(19) EQUIVALENCY OF LEASES TO SALES.—In determining whether a lease is equivalent to a sale for purposes of this title, the administering authority shall consider—

"(A) the terms of the lease,

"(B) commercial practice within the industry,

"(C) the circumstances of the transaction,

"(D) whether the product subject to the lease is integrated into the operations of the lessee or importer,

"(E) whether in practice there is a likelihood that the lease will be continued or renewed for a significant period of time, and

"(F) other relevant factors, including whether the lease transaction would permit avoidance of antidumping or countervailing duties.".

SEC. 1328. MATERIAL INJURY.

Section 771(7) (19 U.S.C. 1677(7)) is amended—

(1) by amending subparagraph (B) to read as follows:

"(B) VOLUME AND CONSEQUENT IMPACT.—In making determinations under sections 703(a), 705(b), 733(a), and 735(b), the Commission, in each case—

"(i) shall consider—

"(I) the volume of imports of the merchandise which is the subject of the investigation,

"(II) the effect of imports of that merchandise on prices in the United States for like products, and

"(III) the impact of imports of such merchandise on domestic producers of like products, but only in the context of production operations within the United States; and

"(ii) may consider such other economic factors as are relevant to the determination regarding whether there is material injury by reason of imports.

In the notification required under section 705(d) or 735(d), as the case may be, the Commission shall explain its analysis of each factor considered under clause (i), and identify each factor considered under clause (ii) and explain in full its relevance to the determination."; and

(2) by amending subparagraph (C)—

(A) by amending the heading to read as follows: "(C) EVALUATION OF RELEVANT FACTORS.—",

(B) by striking out "price undercutting" in clause (ii) and inserting "price underselling", and

(C) by amending clause (iii) to read as follows:

"(iii) IMPACT ON AFFECTED DOMESTIC INDUSTRY.—In examining the impact required to be considered under subparagraph (B)(iii), the Commission shall evaluate all relevant economic factors which have a bearing on the state of the industry in the United States, including, but not limited to—

"(I) actual and potential decline in output, sales, market share, profits, productivity, return on investments, and utilization of capacity,

"(II) factors affecting domestic prices,

"(III) actual and potential negative effects on cash flow, inventories, employment, wages, growth, ability to raise capital, and investment, and

"(IV) actual and potential negative effects on the existing development and production efforts of the domestic industry, including efforts to develop a derivative or more advanced version of the like product.

The Commission shall evaluate all relevant economic factors described in this clause within the context of the business cycle and conditions of competition that are distinctive to the affected industry.".

SEC. 1329. THREAT OF MATERIAL INJURY.

Subparagraph (F) of section 771(7) (19 U.S.C. 1677(7)(F)) (as amended by section 1326) is further amended—

(1) by striking out "and" at the end of clause (i)(VIII),

(2) by striking out the period at the end of clause (i)(IX),

(3) by adding at the end of clause (i) the following new subclause:

"(X) the actual and potential negative effects on the existing development and production efforts of the domestic industry, including efforts to develop a derivative or more advanced version of the like product.", and

(4) by adding at the end thereof the following:

"(iii) EFFECT OF DUMPING IN THIRD-COUNTRY MARKETS.—

"(I) IN GENERAL.—In investigations under subtitle B, the Commission shall consider whether dumping in the markets of foreign countries (as evidenced by dumping findings or antidumping remedies in other GATT member markets against the same class or kind of merchandise manufactured or exported by the same party as under investigation) suggests a threat of material injury to the domestic industry. In the course of its investigation, the Commission shall request information from the foreign manufacturer, exporter, or United States importer concerning this issue.

"(II) GATT MEMBER MARKET.—For purposes of this clause, the term 'GATT member market' means the market of any country which is a signatory to The Agreement on Implementation of Article VI of the General Agreement on Tariffs and Trade (relating to antidumping measures).

"(III) EUROPEAN COMMUNITIES.—For purposes of this clause, the European Communities shall be treated as a foreign country.".

SEC. 1330. CUMULATION.

(a) THREAT OF INJURY.—Subparagraph (F) of section 771(7) (19 U.S.C. 1677(7)(F)) (as amended by section 1329) is further amended by adding at the end thereof the following new clause:

"(iv) CUMULATION.—To the extent practicable and subject to subparagraph (C)(v), for purposes of clause (i) (III) and (IV) the Commission may cumulatively assess the volume and price effects of imports from two or more countries if such imports—

"(I) compete with each other, and with like products of the domestic industry, in the United States market, and

"(II) are subject to any investigation under section 303, 701, or 731.".

(b) TREATMENT OF NEGLIGIBLE IMPORTS.—Subparagraph (C) of section 771(7) (19 U.S.C. 1677(7)(C)) is amended by adding at the end thereof the following new clause:

"(v) TREATMENT OF NEGLIGIBLE IMPORTS.—The Commission is not required to apply clause (iv) or subparagraph (F)(iv) in any case in which the Commission determines that imports of the merchandise subject to investigation are negligible and have no discernable adverse impact on the domestic industry. For purposes of making such determination, the Commission shall evaluate all relevant economic factors regarding the imports, including, but not limited to, whether—

"(I) the volume and market share of the imports are negligible,

"(II) sales transactions involving the imports are isolated and sporadic, and

"(III) the domestic market for the like product is price sensitive by reason of the nature of the product, so that a small quantity of imports can result in price suppression or depression.

For purposes of this clause, the Commission may treat as negligible and having no discernable adverse impact on the domestic industry imports that are the product of any country that is a party to a free trade area agreement with the United States which entered into force and effect before January 1, 1987, if the Commission determines that the domestic industry is not being materially injured by reason of such imports.".

SEC. 1331. CERTIFICATION OF SUBMISSIONS.

Section 776 (19 U.S.C. 1677e) is amended—

(1) by redesignating subsections (a) and (b) as subsections (b) and (c), respectively,

(2) by amending the heading to subsection (b) (as so redesignated) to read as follows: "(b) VERIFICATION.—", and

(3) by inserting before such subsection (b) the following:

"(a) CERTIFICATION OF SUBMISSIONS.—Any person providing factual information to the administering authority or the Commission in connection with a proceeding under this title on behalf of the petitioner or any other interested party shall certify that such information is accurate and complete to the best of that person's knowledge.".

SEC. 1332. ACCESS TO INFORMATION.

Section 777 (19 U.S.C. 1677f) is amended—

(1) by amending subsection (b)(1)(B)(ii) to read as follows:

"(ii) a statement to the administering authority or the Commission that the business proprietary information is of a type that should not be released under administrative protective order.";

(2) by amending subsection (c)(1)—

(A) by amending subparagraph (A) to read as follows:

"(A) IN GENERAL.—Upon receipt of an application (before or after receipt of the information requested) which describes in general terms the information requested and sets forth the reasons for the request, the administering authority or the Commission shall make all business proprietary information presented to, or obtained by it, during a proceeding (except privileged information, classified information, and specific information of a type for which there is a clear and compelling need to withhold from disclosure) available to interested parties who are parties to the proceeding under a protective order described in subparagraph (B), regardless of when the information is submitted during a proceeding."; and

(B) by adding at the end thereof the following new subparagraphs:

"(C) TIME LIMITATION ON DETERMINATIONS.—The administering authority or the Commission, as the case may be, shall determine whether to make information available under this paragraph—

"(i) not later than 14 days (7 days if the submission pertains to a proceeding under section 703(a) or 733(a)) after the date on which the information is submitted, or

"(ii) if—

"(I) the person that submitted the information raises objection to its release, or

"(II) the information is unusually voluminous or complex,

not later than 30 days (10 days if the submission pertains to a proceeding under section 703(a) or 733(a)) after the date on which the information is submitted.

"(D) AVAILABILITY AFTER DETERMINATION.—If the determination under subparagraph (C) is affirmative, then—

"(i) the business proprietary information submitted to the administering authority or the Commission on or before the date of the determination shall be made available, subject to the terms and conditions of the protective order, on such date; and

"(ii) the business proprietary information submitted to the administering authority or the Commission after the date of the determination shall be served as required by subsection (d).

"(E) FAILURE TO DISCLOSE.—If a person submitting information to the administering authority refuses to disclose business proprietary information which the administering authority determines should be released under a protective order described in subparagraph (B), the administering authority shall return the information, and any nonconfidential summary thereof, to the person submitting the information and summary and shall not consider either.";

(3) by striking out "or the Commission denies a request for proprietary information submitted by the petitioner or an in-

terested party in support of the petitioner concerning the domestic price or cost of production of the like product," in subsection (c)(2); and

(4) by adding at the end thereof the following new subsections:

"(d) SERVICE.—Any party submitting written information, including business proprietary information, to the administering authority or the Commission during a proceeding shall, at the same time, serve the information upon all interested parties who are parties to the proceeding, if the information is covered by a protective order. The administering authority or the Commission shall not accept any such information that is not accompanied by a certificate of service and a copy of the protective order version of the document containing the information. Business proprietary information shall only be served upon interested parties who are parties to the proceeding that are subject to protective order; however, a nonconfidential summary thereof shall be served upon all other interested parties who are parties to the proceeding.

"(e) TIMELY SUBMISSIONS.—Information shall be submitted to the administering authority or the Commission during the course of a proceeding on a timely basis and shall be subject to comment by other parties within such reasonable time as the administering authority or the Commission shall provide. If information is submitted without an adequate opportunity for other parties to comment thereon, the administering authority or the Commission may return the information to the party submitting it and not consider it.".

SEC. 1333. CORRECTION OF MINISTERIAL ERRORS.

(a) FINAL DETERMINATIONS.—Sections 705 and 735 (19 U.S.C. 1671d and 1673d) are each amended by adding at the end thereof the following new subsection:

"(e) CORRECTION OF MINISTERIAL ERRORS.—The administering authority shall establish procedures for the correction of ministerial errors in final determinations within a reasonable time after the determinations are issued under this section. Such procedures shall ensure opportunity for interested parties to present their views regarding any such errors. As used in this subsection, the term 'ministerial error' includes errors in addition, subtraction, or other arithmetic function, clerical errors resulting from inaccurate copying, duplication, or the like, and any other type of unintentional error which the administering authority considers ministerial.".

(b) ADMINISTRATIVE REVIEW.—Section 751 (19 U.S.C. 1675) is amended by adding at the end thereof the following new subsection:

"(f) CORRECTION OF MINISTERIAL ERRORS.—The administering authority shall establish procedures for the correction of ministerial errors in final determinations within a reasonable time after the determinations are issued under this section. Such procedures shall ensure opportunity for interested parties to present their views regarding any such errors. As used in this subsection, the term 'ministerial error' includes errors in addition, subtraction, or other arithmetic function, clerical errors resulting from inaccurate copying, duplication, or the like, and any other type of unintentional error which the administering authority considers ministerial.".

SEC. 1334. DRAWBACK TREATMENT.

(a) IN GENERAL.—Section 779 (19 U.S.C. 1677h) is amended by striking out "shall be treated as any other customs duties." and inserting "shall not be treated as being regular customs duties.".

(b) CONFORMING AMENDMENTS.—

(1) The section heading for such section 779 is amended by striking out "**DRAWBACKS**" and inserting "**DRAWBACK TREATMENT**".

(2) The table of contents for title VII of the Tariff Act of 1930 is amended by striking out "Drawbacks." in the entry for section 779 and inserting "Drawback treatment.".

SEC. 1335. GOVERNMENTAL IMPORTATIONS.

Section 771 of the Tariff Act of 1930 (19 U.S.C. 1677) (as amended by section 1316(b)) is amended by adding at the end thereof the following new paragraph:

"(19) APPLICATION TO GOVERNMENTAL IMPORTATIONS.—

"(A) IN GENERAL.—Except as otherwise provided by this paragraph, merchandise imported by, or for the use of, a department or agency of the United States Government (including merchandise provided for under schedule 8 of the Tariff Schedules of the United States) is subject to the imposition of countervailing duties or antidumping duties under this title or section 303.

"(B) EXCEPTIONS.—Merchandise imported by, or for the use of, the Department of Defense shall not be subject to the imposition of countervailing or antidumping duties under this title if—

"(i) the merchandise is acquired by, or for use of, such Department—

"(I) from a country with which such Department had a Memorandum of Understanding which was in effect on January 1, 1988, and has continued to have a comparable agreement (including renewals) or superceding agreements, and

"(II) in accordance with terms of the Memorandum of Understanding in effect at the time of importation, or

"(ii) the merchandise has no substantial nonmilitary use.".

SEC. 1336. STUDIES.

(a) STUDY OF MARKET ORIENTATION OF CHINA.—The Secretary of Commerce, in consultation with the heads of other appropriate Federal agencies, shall undertake a study regarding the new market orientation of the People's Republic of China. The study shall address, but not be limited to—

(1) the effect of the new orientation on Chinese market policies and price structure, and the relationship between domestic Chinese prices and world prices;

(2) the extent to which United States trade law practices can accommodate the increased market orientation of the Chinese economy; and

(3) the possible need for changes in United States antidumping laws as they apply to foreign countries, such as China, which are in transition to a more market-oriented economy.

The Secretary of Commerce shall submit to the Congress within 1 year after the date of the enactment of this Act a report on the study required under this subsection.

(b) SUBSIDIES CODE COMMITMENTS.—Within 90 days after the date of the enactment of this Act, the United States Trade Representative shall initiate a review of all bilateral subsidy commitments that have been entered into by foreign governments with the United States. The review shall include—

(1) an evaluation of the extent to which the commitments have been complied with;

(2) with respect to those commitments found under paragraph (1) not to have been complied with, an estimate regarding when compliance is likely; and

(3) recommendations regarding how compliance can be improved.

The United States Trade Representative shall complete the review required under this subsection and submit a report thereon to the Committee on Ways and Means of the House of Representatives and the Committee on Finance of the Senate within 180 days after the date of the enactment of this Act.

SEC. 1337. EFFECTIVE DATES.

(a) IN GENERAL.—Except as otherwise provided in this section, the amendments made by this part shall take effect on the date of enactment of this Act.

(b) INVESTIGATIONS AND REVIEWS AFTER ENACTMENT.—The amendments made by sections 1312, 1315, 1316, 1318, 1325, 1326, 1327, 1328, 1329, 1331, and 1332 shall only apply with respect to—

(1) investigations initiated after the date of enactment of this Act, and

(2) reviews initiated under section 736(c) or 751 of the Tariff Act of 1930 after the date of enactment of this Act.

(c) INVESTIGATIONS AFTER ENACTMENT.—The amendments made by sections 1324 and 1330 shall only apply with respect to investigations initiated after the date of enactment of this Act.

(d) PREVENTION OF CIRCUMVENTION OF DUTIES; DRAWBACK.—The provisions of section 781 of the Tariff Act of 1930, as added by section 1321(a), and the amendments made by section 1334 shall apply with respect to articles entered, or withdrawn from warehouse for consumption, on or after the date of enactment of this Act.

(e) GOVERNMENTAL IMPORTATIONS; STEEL.—The amendments made by sections 1321(b) and 1335 shall apply with respect to entries, and withdrawals from warehouse for consumption, that are liquidated on or after the date of enactment of this Act.

(f) FICTITIOUS MARKETS.—The amendment made by section 1319 shall only apply with respect to—

(1) reviews initiated under section 736(c) or 751 of the Tariff Act of 1930 after the date of enactment of this Act, and

(2) reviews initiated under such sections—

(A) which are pending on the date of enactment of this Act, and

(B) in which a request for revocation is pending on the date of enactment of this Act.

PART 3—PROTECTION OF INTELLECTUAL PROPERTY RIGHTS

SEC. 1341. CONGRESSIONAL FINDINGS AND PURPOSES.

(a) FINDINGS.—The Congress finds that—

(1) United States persons that rely on protection of intellectual property rights are among the most advanced and competitive in the world; and

(2) the existing protection under section 337 of the Tariff Act of 1930 against unfair trade practices is cumbersome and costly and has not provided United States owners of intellectual property rights with adequate protection against foreign companies violating such rights.

(b) PURPOSE.—The purpose of this part is to amend section 337 of the Tariff Act of 1930 to make it a more effective remedy for the protection of United States intellectual property rights.

SEC. 1342. PROTECTION UNDER THE TARIFF ACT OF 1930.

(a) IN GENERAL.—Section 337 of the Tariff Act of 1930 (19 U.S.C. 1337) is amended as follows:

(1) Subsection (a) is amended to read as follows:

"(a)(1) Subject to paragraph (2), the following are unlawful, and when found by the Commission to exist shall be dealt with, in addition to any other provision of law, as provided in this section:

"(A) Unfair methods of competition and unfair acts in the importation of articles (other than articles provided for in subparagraphs (B), (C), and (D)) into the United States, or in the sale of such articles by the owner, importer, or consignee, the threat or effect of which is—

"(i) to destroy or substantially injure an industry in the United States;

"(ii) to prevent the establishment of such an industry; or

"(iii) to restrain or monopolize trade and commerce in the United States.

"(B) The importation into the United States, the sale for importation, or the sale within the United States after importation by the owner, importer, or consignee, of articles that—

"(i) infringe a valid and enforceable United States patent or a valid and enforceable United States copyright registered under title 17, United States Code; or

"(ii) are made, produced, processed, or mined under, or by means of, a process covered by the claims of a valid and enforceable United States patent.

"(C) The importation into the United States, the sale for importation, or the sale within the United States after importation by the owner, importer, or consignee, of articles that infringe a valid and enforceable United States trademark registered under the Trademark Act of 1946.

"(D) The importation into the United States, the sale for importation, or the sale within the United States after importation by the owner, importer, or consignee, of a semiconductor chip product in a manner that constitutes infringement of a mask work registered under chapter 9 of title 17, United States Code.

"(2) Subparagraphs (B), (C), and (D) of paragraph (1) apply only if an industry in the United States, relating to the articles protected by the patent, copyright, trademark, or mask work concerned, exists or is in the process of being established.

"(3) For purposes of paragraph (2), an industry in the United States shall be considered to exist if there is in the United States, with respect to the articles protected by the patent, copyright, trademark, or mask work concerned—

"(A) significant investment in plant and equipment;

"(B) significant employment of labor or capital; or

"(C) substantial investment in its exploitation, including engineering, research and development, or licensing.

"(4) For the purposes of this section, the phrase 'owner, importer, or consignee' includes any agent of the owner, importer, or consignee.".

(2) Subsection (c) is amended by inserting before the period in the first sentence the following: ", except that the Commission may, by issuing a consent order or on the basis of a settlement agreement, terminate any such investigation, in whole or in part, without making such a determination".

(3) Subsection (e) is amended—

(A) by striking out "If" in the first sentence and inserting "(1) If"; and

(B) by adding at the end thereof the following new paragraphs:

"(2) A complainant may petition the Commission for the issuance of an order under this subsection. The Commission shall make a determination with regard to such petition by no later than the 90th day after the date on which the Commission's notice of investigation is published in the Federal Register. The Commission may extend the 90-day period for an additional 60 days in a case it designates as a more complicated case. The Commission shall publish in the Federal Register its reasons why it designated the case as being more complicated. The Commission may require the complainant to post a bond as a prerequisite to the issuance of an order under this subsection.

"(3) The Commission may grant preliminary relief under this subsection or subsection (f) to the same extent as preliminary injunctions and temporary restraining orders may be granted under the Federal Rules of Civil Procedure.".

(4) Subsection (f) is amended—

(A) by striking out "In lieu of" in paragraph (1) and inserting "In addition to, or in lieu of,"; and

(B) by striking out "$10,000 or" in paragraph (2) and inserting "$100,000 or twice".

(5) Such section is further amended—

(A) by redesignating subsections (g), (h), (i), and (j) as subsections (j), (k), (l), and (m), respectively; and

(B) by inserting after subsection (f) the following new subsections:

"(g)(1) If—

"(A) a complaint is filed against a person under this section;

"(B) the complaint and a notice of investigation are served on the person;

"(C) the person fails to respond to the complaint and notice or otherwise fails to appear to answer the complaint and notice;

"(D) the person fails to show good cause why the person should not be found in default; and

"(E) the complainant seeks relief limited solely to that person; the Commission shall presume the facts alleged in the complaint to be true and shall, upon request, issue an exclusion from entry or a cease and desist order, or both, limited to that person unless, after considering the effect of such exclusion or order upon the public health and welfare, competitive conditions in the United States economy, the production of like or directly competitive articles in the United States, and United States consumers, the Commission finds that such exclusion or order should not be issued.

"(2) In addition to the authority of the Commission to issue a general exclusion from entry of articles when a respondent appears to contest an investigation concerning a violation of the provisions of this section, a general exclusion from entry of articles, regardless of the source or importer of the articles, may be issued if—

"(A) no person appears to contest an investigation concerning a violation of the provisions of this section, and

"(B) such a violation is established by substantial, reliable, and probative evidence.

"(h) The Commission may by rule prescribe sanctions for abuse of discovery and abuse of process to the extent authorized by Rule 11 and Rule 37 of the Federal Rules of Civil Procedure.

"(i) FORFEITURE.—

"(1) In addition to taking action under subsection (d), the Commission may issue an order providing that any article imported in violation of the provisions of this section be seized and forfeited to the United States if—

"(A) the owner, importer, or consignee of the article previously attempted to import the article into the United States;

"(B) the article was previously denied entry into the United States by reason of an order issued under subsection (d); and

"(C) upon such previous denial of entry, the Secretary of the Treasury provided the owner, importer, or consignee of the article written notice of—

"(i) such order, and

"(ii) the seizure and forfeiture that would result from any further attempt to import the article into the United States.

"(2) The Commission shall notify the Secretary of the Treasury of any order issued under this subsection and, upon receipt of such notice, the Secretary of the Treasury shall enforce such order in accordance with the provisions of this section.

"(3) Upon the attempted entry of articles subject to an order issued under this subsection, the Secretary of the Treasury shall immediately notify all ports of entry of the attempted importation and shall identify the persons notified under paragraph (1)(C).

"(4) The Secretary of the Treasury shall provide—

"(A) the written notice described in paragraph (1)(C) to the owner, importer, or consignee of any article that is denied entry into the United States by reason of an order issued under subsection (d); and

"(B) a copy of such written notice to the Commission.".

(6) Subsection (k) (as redesignated by paragraph (5)(B) of this section) is amended—

(A) by inserting "(1)" before the first sentence; and

(B) by adding at the end the following:

"(2) If any person who has previously been found by the Commission to be in violation of this section petitions the Commission for a determination that the petitioner is no longer in violation of this section or for a modification or rescission of an exclusion from entry or order under subsection (d), (e), (f), (g), or (i)—

"(A) the burden of proof in any proceeding before the Commission regarding such petition shall be on the petitioner; and

"(B) relief may be granted by the Commission with respect to such petition—

"(i) on the basis of new evidence or evidence that could not have been presented at the prior proceeding, or

"(ii) on grounds which would permit relief from a judgment or order under the Federal Rules of Civil Procedure.".

(7) Subsection (l) (as redesignated by paragraph (5)(B) of this section) is amended—

(A) by striking out "claims of United States letters patent" in the first sentence and inserting "a proceeding involving a patent, copyright, or mask work under subsection (a)(1)"; and

(B) by striking out "a patent owner" in the second sentence and inserting "an owner of the patent, copyright, or mask work".

(8) Such section is further amended by adding at the end the following:

"(n)(1) Information submitted to the Commission or exchanged among the parties in connection with proceedings under this section which is properly designated as confidential pursuant to Commission rules may not be disclosed (except under a protective order issued under regulations of the Commission which authorizes limited disclosure of such information) to any person (other than a person described in paragraph (2)) without the consent of the person submitting it.

"(2) Notwithstanding the prohibition contained in paragraph (1), information referred to in that paragraph may be disclosed to—

"(A) an officer or employee of the Commission who is directly concerned with carrying out the investigation in connection with which the information is submitted,

"(B) an officer or employee of the United States Government who is directly involved in the review under subsection (h), or

"(C) an officer or employee of the United States Customs Service who is directly involved in administering an exclusion from entry under this section resulting from the investigation in connection with which the information is submitted.".

(b) TECHNICAL AMENDMENTS.—Section 337 (as amended by subsection (a)) is further amended—

(1) by amending subsection (b)—

(A) by striking out "Department of Health, Education, and Welfare" in paragraph (2) and inserting "Department of Health and Human Services"; and

(B) by striking out "Secretary of the Treasury" in paragraph (3) and inserting "Secretary of Commerce";

(2) by amending subsection (c)—

(A) by striking out "or (f)" and inserting "(f), or (g)", and

(B) by striking out "and (f)" and inserting "(f), and (g)";

(3) by striking out "or (f)" each place it appears in subsection (j) and inserting "(f), (g), or (i)";

(4) by striking out "(g)" in subsection (k) and inserting "(j)"; and

(5) by striking out "or (f)" in subsection (l) and inserting "(f), (g), or (i)".

(c) CONFORMING AMENDMENT.—The Act entitled "An Act to limit the importation of products made, produced, processed, or mined under process covered by unexpired valid United States patents, and for other purposes", approved July 2, 1940 (54 Stat. 724, 19 U.S.C. 1337a), is repealed.

(d) EFFECTIVE DATE.—

(1)(A) Subject to subparagraph (B), the amendments made by this section shall take effect on the date of the enactment of this Act.

(B) The United States International Trade Commission is not required to apply the provision in section 337(e)(2) of the Tariff Act of 1930 (as amended by subsection (a)(3) of this section) relating to the posting of bonds until the earlier of—

(i) the 90th day after such date of enactment; or

(ii) the day on which the Commission issues interim regulations setting forth the procedures relating to such posting.

(2) Notwithstanding any provision of section 337 of the Tariff Act of 1930, the United States International Trade Commission may extend, by not more than 90 days, the period within which the Commission is required to make a determination in an investigation conducted under such section 337 if—

(A) the Commission would, but for this paragraph, be required to make such determination before the 180th day after the date of enactment of this Act; and

(B) the Commission finds that the investigation is complicated.

PART 4—TELECOMMUNICATIONS TRADE

SEC. 1371. SHORT TITLE.

This part may be cited as the "Telecommunications Trade Act of 1988".

SEC. 1372. FINDINGS AND PURPOSES.

(a) FINDINGS.—The Congress finds that—

(1) rapid growth in the world market for telecommunications products and services is likely to continue for several decades;

(2) the United States can improve prospects for—

(A) the growth of—

(i) United States exports of telecommunications products and services, and

(ii) export-related employment and consumer services in the United States, and

(B) the continuance of the technological leadership of the United States,

by undertaking a program to achieve an open world market for trade in telecommunications products, services, and investment;

(3) most foreign markets for telecommunications products, services, and investment are characterized by extensive government intervention (including restrictive import practices and discriminatory procurement practices) which adversely affect United States exports of telecommunications products and services and United States investment in telecommunications;

(4) the open nature of the United States telecommunications market, accruing from the liberalization and restructuring of such market, has contributed, and will continue to contribute, to an increase in imports of telecommunications products and a

growing imbalance in competitive opportunities for trade in telecommunications;

(5) unless this imbalance is corrected through the achievement of mutually advantageous market opportunities for trade in telecommunications products and services between the United States and foreign countries, the United States should avoid granting continued open access to the telecommunications products and services of such foreign countries in the United States market; and

(6) the unique business conditions in the worldwide market for telecommunications products and services caused by the combination of deregulation and divestiture in the United States, which represents a unilateral liberalization of United States trade with the rest of the world, and continuing government intervention in the domestic industries of many other countries create a need to make an exception in the case of telecommunications products and services that should not necessarily be a precedent for legislating specific sectoral priorities in combating the closed markets or unfair foreign trade practices of other countries.

(b) PURPOSES.—The purposes of this part are—

(1) to foster the economic and technological growth of, and employment in, the United States telecommunications industry;

(2) to secure a high quality telecommunications network for the benefit of the people of the United States;

(3) to develop an international consensus in favor of open trade and competition in telecommunications products and services;

(4) to ensure that countries which have made commitments to open telecommunications trade fully abide by those commitments; and

(5) to achieve a more open world trading system for telecommunications products and services through negotiation and provision of mutually advantageous market opportunities for United States telecommunications exporters and their subsidiaries in those markets in which barriers exist to free international trade.

SEC. 1373. DEFINITIONS.

For purposes of this part—

(1) The term "Trade Representative" means the United States Trade Representative.

(2) The term "telecommunications product" means—

(A) any paging devices provided for under item 685.65 of such Schedules, and

(B) any article classified under any of the following item numbers of such Schedules:

684.57	684.67	685.28	685.39
684.58	684.80	685.30	685.48
684.59	685.16	685.31	688.17
684.65	685.24	685.33	688.41
684.66	685.25	685.34	707.90.

SEC. 1374. INVESTIGATION OF FOREIGN TELECOMMUNICATIONS TRADE BARRIERS.

(a) IN GENERAL.—The Trade Representative shall conduct an investigation to identify priority foreign countries. Such investigation shall be concluded by no later than the date that is 5 months after the date of enactment of this Act.

(b) FACTORS TO BE TAKEN INTO ACCOUNT.—In identifying priority foreign countries under subsection (a), the Trade Representative shall take into account, among other relevant factors—

(1) the nature and significance of the acts, policies, and practices that deny mutually advantageous market opportunities to telecommunications products and services of United States firms;

(2) the economic benefits (actual and potential) accruing to foreign firms from open access to the United States market;

(3) the potential size of the market of a foreign country for telecommunications products and services of United States firms;

(4) the potential to increase United States exports of telecommunications products and services, either directly or through the establishment of a beneficial precedent; and

(5) measurable progress being made to eliminate the objectionable acts, policies, or practices.

(c) REVOCATIONS AND ADDITIONAL IDENTIFICATIONS.—

(1) The Trade Representative may at any time, after taking into account the factors described in subsection (b)—

(A) revoke the identification of any priority foreign country that was made under this section, or

(B) identify any foreign country as a priority foreign country under this section,

if information available to the Trade Representative indicates that such action is appropriate.

(2) The Trade Representative shall include in the semiannual report submitted to the Congress under section 309(3) of the Trade Act of 1974 a detailed explanation of the reasons for the revocation under paragraph (1) of this subsection of any identification of any foreign country as a priority foreign country.

(d) REPORT TO CONGRESS.—By no later than the date that is 30 days after the date on which the investigation conducted under subsection (a) is completed, the United States Trade Representative shall submit a report on the investigation to the President and to appropriate committees of the Congress.

SEC. 1375. NEGOTIATIONS IN RESPONSE TO INVESTIGATION.

(a) IN GENERAL.—Upon—

(1) the date that is 30 days after the date on which any foreign country is identified in the investigation conducted under section 1374(a) as a priority foreign country, and

(2) the date on which any foreign country is identified under section 1374(c)(1)(B) as a priority foreign country,

the President shall enter into negotiations with such priority foreign country for the purpose of entering into a bilateral or multilateral trade agreement under part 1 of subtitle A which meets the specific negotiating objectives established by the President under subsection (b) for such priority foreign country.

(b) ESTABLISHMENT OF SPECIFIC NEGOTIATING OBJECTIVES FOR EACH FOREIGN PRIORITY COUNTRY.—

(1) The President shall establish such relevant specific negotiating objectives on a country-by-country basis as are necessary to meet the general negotiating objectives of the United States under this section.

(2)(A) The President may refine or modify specific negotiating objectives for particular negotiations in order to respond to circumstances arising during the negotiating period, including—

(i) changed practices by the priority foreign country,

(ii) tangible substantive developments in multilateral negotiations,

(iii) changes in competitive positions, technological developments, or

(iv) other relevant factors.

(B) By no later than the date that is 30 days after the date on which the President makes any modifications or refinements to specific negotiating objectives under subparagraph (A), the President shall submit to appropriate committees of the Congress a statement describing such modifications or refinements and the reasons for such modifications or refinements.

(c) GENERAL NEGOTIATING OBJECTIVES.—The general negotiating objectives of the United States under this section are—

(1) to obtain multilateral or bilateral agreements (or the modification of existing agreements) that provide mutually advantageous market opportunities for trade in telecommunications products and services between the United States and foreign countries;

(2) to correct the imbalances in market opportunities accruing from reductions in barriers to the access of telecommunications products and services of foreign firms to the United States market; and

(3) to facilitate the increase in United States exports of telecommunications products and services to a level of exports that reflects the competitiveness of the United States telecommunications industry.

(d) SPECIFIC NEGOTIATING OBJECTIVES.—The specific negotiating objectives of the United States under this section regarding telecommunications products and services are to obtain—

(1) national treatment for telecommunications products and services that are provided by United States firms;

(2) most-favored-nation treatment for such products and services;

(3) nondiscriminatory procurement policies with respect to such products and services and the inclusion under the Agreement on Government Procurement of the procurement (by sale or lease by government-owned or controlled entities) of all telecommunications products and services;

(4) the reduction or elimination of customs duties on telecommunications products;

(5) the elimination of subsidies, violations of intellectual property rights, and other unfair trade practices that distort international trade in telecommunications products and services;

(6) the elimination of investment barriers that restrict the establishment of foreign-owned business entities which market such products and services;

(7) assurances that any requirement for the registration of telecommunications products, which are to be located on customer premises, for the purposes of—

(A) attachment to a telecommunications network in a foreign country, and

(B) the marketing of the products in a foreign country, be limited to the certification by the manufacturer that the products meet the standards established by the foreign country for preventing harm to the network or network personnel;

(8) transparency of, and open participation in, the standards-setting processes used in foreign countries with respect to telecommunications products;

(9) the ability to have telecommunications products, which are to be located on customer premises, approved and registered by type, and, if appropriate, the establishment of procedures between the United States and foreign countries for the mutual recognition of type approvals;

(10) access to the basic telecommunications network in foreign countries on reasonable and nondiscriminatory terms and conditions (including nondiscriminatory prices) for the provision of value-added services by United States suppliers;

(11) the nondiscriminatory procurement of telecommunications products and services by foreign entities that provide local exchange telecommunications services which are owned, controlled, or, if appropriate, regulated by foreign governments; and

(12) monitoring and effective dispute settlement mechanisms to facilitate compliance with matters referred to in the preceding paragraphs of this subsection.

SEC. 1376. ACTIONS TO BE TAKEN IF NO AGREEMENT OBTAINED.

(a) IN GENERAL.—

(1) If the President is unable, before the close of the negotiating period, to enter into an agreement under subtitle A with any priority foreign country identified under section 1374 which achieves the general negotiating objectives described in section 1375(b) as defined by the specific objectives established by the President for that country, the President shall take whatever actions authorized under subsection (b) that are appropriate and most likely to achieve such general negotiating objectives.

(2) In taking actions under paragraph (1), the President shall first take those actions which most directly affect trade in telecommunications products and services with the priority foreign country referred to in paragraph (1), unless the President determines that actions against other economic sectors would be more effective in achieving the general negotiating objectives referred to in paragraph (1).

(b) ACTIONS AUTHORIZED.—

(1) The President is authorized to take any of the following actions under subsection (a) with respect to any priority foreign country:

(A) termination, withdrawal, or suspension of any portion of any trade agreement entered into with such country under—

(i) the Trade Act of 1974,

(ii) section 201 of the Trade Expansion Act of 1962, or

(iii) section 350 of the Tariff Act of 1930,

with respect to any duty or import restriction imposed by the United States on any telecommunications product;

(B) actions described in section 301 of the Trade Act of 1974;

(C) prohibition of purchases by the Federal Government of telecommunications products of such country;

(D) increases in domestic preferences under title III of the Act of March 3, 1933 (41 U.S.C. 10a, et seq.) for purchases by the Federal Government of telecommunications products of such country;

(E) suspension of any waiver of domestic preferences under title III of the Act of March 3, 1933 (41 U.S.C. 10a, et seq.) which may have been extended to such country pursuant to the Trade Agreements Act of 1979 with respect to telecommunications products or any other products;

(F) issuance of orders to appropriate officers and employees of the Federal Government to deny Federal funds or Federal credits for purchases of the telecommunications products of such country; and

(G) suspension, in whole or in part, of benefits accorded articles of such country under title V of the Trade Act of 1974 (19 U.S.C. 2461, et seq.).

(2) Notwithstanding section 125 of the Trade Act of 1974 and any other provision of law, if any portion of a trade agreement described in paragraph (1)(A) is terminated, withdrawn, or suspended under paragraph (1) with respect to any duty imposed by the United States on the products of a foreign country, the rate of such duty that shall apply to such products entered, or withdrawn from warehouse for consumption, after the date on which such termination, withdrawal, or suspension takes effect shall be a rate determined by the President.

(c) NEGOTIATING PERIOD.—

(1) For purposes of this section, the term "negotiating period" means—

(A) with respect to a priority foreign country identified in the investigation conducted under section 1374(a), the 18-month period beginning on the date of the enactment of this Act, and

(B) with respect to any foreign country identified as a priority foreign country after the conclusion of such investigation, the 1-year period beginning on the date on which such identification is made.

(2)(A) The negotiating period with respect to a priority foreign country may be extended for not more than two 1-year periods.

(B) By no later than the date that is 15 days after the date on which the President extends the negotiating period with respect to any priority foreign country, the President shall submit to appropriate committees of the Congress a report on the status of negotiations with such country that includes—

(i) a finding by the President that substantial progress is being made in negotiations with such country, and

(ii) a statement detailing the reasons why an extension of such negotiating period is necessary.

(d) MODIFICATION AND TERMINATION AUTHORITY.—The President may modify or terminate any action taken under subsection (a) if, after taking into consideration the factors described in section 1374(b), the President determines that changed circumstances warrant such modification or termination.

(e) REPORT.—The President shall promptly inform the appropriate committees of the Congress of any action taken under subsection (a) or of the modification or termination of any such action under subsection (d).

SEC. 1377. REVIEW OF TRADE AGREEMENT IMPLEMENTATION BY TRADE REPRESENTATIVE.

(a) IN GENERAL.—

(1) In conducting the annual analysis under section 181(a) of the Trade Act of 1974 (19 U.S.C. 2241), the Trade Representative shall review the operation and effectiveness of—

(A) each trade agreement negotiated by reason of this part that is in force with respect to the United States; and

(B) every other trade agreement regarding telecommunications products or services that is in force with respect to the United States.

(2) In each review conducted under paragraph (1), the Trade Representative shall determine whether any act, policy, or practice of the foreign country that has entered into the agreement described in paragraph (1)—

(A) is not in compliance with the terms of such agreement, or

(B) otherwise denies, within the context of the terms of such agreement, to telecommunications products and services of United States firms mutually advantageous market opportunities in that foreign country.

(b) REVIEW FACTORS.—

(1) In conducting reviews under subsection (a), the Trade Representative shall consider any evidence of actual patterns of trade (including United States exports to a foreign country of telecommunications products and services, including sales and services related to those products) that do not reflect patterns of trade which would reasonably be anticipated to flow from the concessions or commitments of such country based on the international competitive position and export potential of such products and services.

(2) The Trade Representative shall consult with the United States International Trade Commission with regard to the actual patterns of trade described in paragraph (1).

(c) ACTION IN RESPONSE TO AFFIRMATIVE DETERMINATION.—

(1) Any affirmative determination made by the Trade Representative under subsection (a)(2) with respect to any act, policy, or practice of a foreign country shall, for purposes of chapter 1 of title III of the Trade Act of 1974, be treated as an affirmative determination under section 304(a)(1)(A) of such Act that such act, policy, or practice violates a trade agreement.

(2) In taking actions under section 301 by reason of paragraph (1), the Trade Representative shall first take those actions which most directly affect trade in telecommunications products and services with the priority foreign country referred to in paragraph (1), unless the Trade Representative determines that actions against other economic sectors would be more effective in achieving compliance by the foreign country with the trade agreement that is the subject of the affirmative determination made under subsection (a)(2).

SEC. 1378. COMPENSATION AUTHORITY.

If—

(1) the President has taken action under section 1376(a) with respect to any foreign country, and

(2) such action is found to be inconsistent with the international obligations of the United States, including the General Agreement on Tariffs and Trade,

the President may enter into trade agreements with such foreign country for the purpose of granting new concessions as compensation for such action in order to maintain the general level of reciprocal and mutually advantageous concessions.

SEC. 1379. CONSULTATIONS.

(a) ADVICE FROM DEPARTMENTS AND AGENCIES.—Prior to taking any action under this part, the President shall seek information and advice from the interagency trade organization established under section 242(a) of the Trade Expansion Act of 1962 (19 U.S.C. 1872).

(b) ADVICE FROM THE PRIVATE SECTOR.—Before—

(1) the Trade Representative concludes the investigation conducted under section 1374(a) or takes action under section 1374(c),

(2) the President establishes specific negotiating objectives under section 1375(b) with respect to any foreign country, or

(3) the President takes action under section 1376,

the Trade Representative shall provide an opportunity for the presentation of views by any interested party with respect to such investigation, objectives, or action, including appropriate committees established pursuant to section 135 of the Trade Act of 1974 (19 U.S.C. 2155).

(c) CONSULTATIONS WITH CONGRESS AND OFFICIAL ADVISORS.—For purposes of conducting negotiations under section 1375(a), the Trade Representative shall keep appropriate committees of the Congress, as well as appropriate committees established pursuant to section 135 of the Trade Act of 1974, currently informed with respect to—

(1) the negotiating priorities and objectives for each priority foreign country;

(2) the assessment of negotiating prospects, both bilateral and multilateral; and

(3) any United States concessions which might be included in negotiations to achieve the objectives described in subsections (c) and (d) of section 1375.

(d) MODIFICATION OF SPECIFIC NEGOTIATING OBJECTIVES.—Before the President takes any action under section 1375(b)(2)(A) to refine or modify specific negotiating objectives, the President shall consult with the Congress and with members of the industry, and representatives of labor, affected by the proposed refinement or modification.

SEC. 1380. SUBMISSION OF DATA; ACTION TO ENSURE COMPLIANCE.

(a) SUBMISSION OF DATA.—The Federal Communications Commission (hereafter in this section referred to as the "Commission") shall periodically submit to appropriate committees of the House of Representatives and of the Senate any data collected and otherwise made public under Report No. DC-1105, "Information Reporting Requirements Established for Common Carriers", adopted February 25, 1988, relating to FCC Docket No. 86-494, adopted December 23, 1987.

(b) ACTION TO ENSURE COMPLIANCE.—

(1)(A) Any product of a foreign country that is subject to registration or approval by the Commission may be entered only if—

(i) such product conforms with all applicable rules and regulations of the Commission, and

(ii) the information which is required on Federal Communications Commission Form 740 on the date of enactment of this Act is provided to the appropriate customs officer at the time of such entry in such form and manner as the Secretary of the Treasury may prescribe.

(B) For purposes of this paragraph, the term "entered" means entered, or withdrawn from warehouse for consumption, in the customs territory of the United States.

(2) The Commission, the Secretary of Commerce, and the Trade Representative shall provide such assistance in the enforcement of paragraph (1) as the Secretary of the Treasury may request.

(3) The Secretary of the Treasury shall compile the information collected under paragraph (1)(A)(ii) into a summary and shall annually submit such summary to the Congress until the authority to negotiate trade agreements under part 1 of subtitle A expires. Such information shall also be made available to the public.

SEC. 1381. STUDY ON TELECOMMUNICATIONS COMPETITIVENESS IN THE UNITED STATES.

(a) In General.—The Secretary of Commerce, in consultation with the Federal Communications Commission and the United States Trade Representative, shall conduct a study of the competitiveness of the United States telecommunications industry and the effects of foreign telecommunications policies and practices on such industry in order to assist the Congress and the President in determining what actions might be necessary to preserve the competitiveness of the United States telecommunications industry.

(b) Public Comment.—The Secretary of Commerce may, as appropriate, provide notice and reasonable opportunity for public comment as part of the study conducted under subsection (a).

(c) Report.—The Secretary of Commerce shall, by no later than the date that is 1 year after the date of enactment of this Act, submit to the Congress and the President a report on the findings and recommendations reached by the Secretary of Commerce as a result of the study conducted under subsection (a). Such report shall be referred to the appropriate committees of the House of Representatives and of the Senate.

SEC. 1382. INTERNATIONAL OBLIGATIONS.

Nothing in this part may be construed to require actions inconsistent with the international obligations of the United States, including the General Agreement on Tariffs and Trade.

Subtitle D—Adjustment to Import Competition

PART 1—POSITIVE ADJUSTMENT BY INDUSTRIES INJURED BY IMPORTS

SEC. 1401. POSITIVE ADJUSTMENT BY INDUSTRIES INJURED BY IMPORTS.

(a) IN GENERAL.—Chapter 1 of title II of the Trade Act of 1974 (19 U.S.C. 2251-2253) is amended to read as follows:

"CHAPTER 1—POSITIVE ADJUSTMENT BY INDUSTRIES INJURED BY IMPORTS

"SEC. 201. ACTION TO FACILITATE POSITIVE ADJUSTMENT TO IMPORT COMPETITION.

"(a) PRESIDENTIAL ACTION.—If the United States International Trade Commission (hereinafter referred to in this chapter as the 'Commission') determines under section 202(b) that an article is being imported into the United States in such increased quantities as to be a substantial cause of serious injury, or the threat thereof, to the domestic industry producing an article like or directly competitive with the imported article, the President, in accordance with this chapter, shall take all appropriate and feasible action within his power which the President determines will facilitate efforts by the domestic industry to make a positive adjustment to import competition and provide greater economic and social benefits than costs.

"(b) POSITIVE ADJUSTMENT TO IMPORT COMPETITION.—

"(1) For purposes of this chapter, a positive adjustment to import competition occurs when—

"(A) the domestic industry—

"(i) is able to compete successfully with imports after actions taken under section 204 terminate, or

"(ii) the domestic industry experiences an orderly transfer of resources to other productive pursuits; and

"(B) dislocated workers in the industry experience an orderly transition to productive pursuits.

"(2) The domestic industry may be considered to have made a positive adjustment to import competition even though the industry is not of the same size and composition as the industry at the time the investigation was initiated under section 202(b).

"SEC. 202. INVESTIGATIONS, DETERMINATIONS, AND RECOMMENDATIONS BY COMMISSION.

"(a) PETITIONS AND ADJUSTMENT PLANS.—

"(1) A petition requesting action under this chapter for the purpose of facilitating positive adjustment to import competition may be filed with the Commission by an entity, including a trade association, firm, certified or recognized union, or group of workers, which is representative of an industry.

"(2) A petition under paragraph (1)—

"(A) shall include a statement describing the specific purposes for which action is being sought, which may include facilitating the orderly transfer of resources to more productive pursuits, enhancing competitiveness, or other means of adjustment to new conditions of competition; and

"(B) may—

"(i) subject to subsection (d)(1)(C)(i), request provisional relief under subsection (d)(1); or

"(ii) request, or at any time before the 150th day after the date of filing be amended to request, provisional relief under subsection (d)(2).

"(3) Whenever a petition is filed under paragraph (1), the Commission shall promptly transmit copies of the petition to the Office of the United States Trade Representative and other Federal agencies directly concerned.

"(4) A petitioner under paragraph (1) may submit to the Commission and the United States Trade Representative (hereafter in this chapter referred to as the 'Trade Representative'), either with the petition, or at any time within 120 days after the date of filing of the petition, a plan to facilitate positive adjustment to import competition.

"(5)(A) Before submitting an adjustment plan under paragraph (4), the petitioner and other entities referred to in paragraph (1) that wish to participate may consult with the Trade Representative and the officers and employees of any Federal agency that is considered appropriate by the Trade Representative, for purposes of evaluating the adequacy of the proposals being considered for inclusion in the plan in relation to specific actions that may be taken under this chapter.

"(B) A request for any consultation under subparagraph (A) must be made to the Trade Representative. Upon receiving such a request, the Trade Representative shall confer with the petitioner and provide such assistance, including publication of appropriate notice in the Federal Register, as may be practicable in obtaining other participants in the consultation. No consultation may occur under subparagraph (A) unless the Trade Representative, or his delegate, is in attendance.

"(6)(A) In the course of any investigation under subsection (b), the Commission shall seek information (on a confidential basis, to the extent appropriate) on actions being taken, or planned to be taken, or both, by firms and workers in the industry to make a positive adjustment to import competition.

"(B) Regardless whether an adjustment plan is submitted under paragraph (4) by the petitioner, if the Commission makes an affirmative determination under subsection (b), any—

"(i) firm in the domestic industry;

"(ii) certified or recognized union or group of workers in the domestic industry;

"(iii) State or local community;

"(iv) trade association representing the domestic industry; or

"(v) any other person or group of persons,

may, individually, submit to the Commission commitments regarding actions such persons and entities intend to take to facilitate positive adjustment to import competition.

"(7) Nothing in paragraphs (5) and (6) may be construed to provide immunity under the antitrust laws.

"(b) INVESTIGATIONS AND DETERMINATIONS BY COMMISSION.—

"(1)(A) Upon the filing of a petition under subsection (b), the request of the President or the Trade Representative, the resolution of either the Committee on Ways and Means of the House of Representatives or the Committee on Finance of the Senate, or on its own motion, the Commission shall promptly make an investigation to determine whether an article is being imported into the United States in such increased quantities as to be a substantial cause of serious injury, or the threat thereof, to the domestic industry producing an article like or directly competitive with the imported article.

"(B) For purposes of this section, the term 'substantial cause' means a cause which is important and not less than any other cause.

"(2)(A) Except as provided in subparagraph (B), the Commission shall make the determination under paragraph (1) within 120 days after the date on which the petition is filed, the request or resolution is received, or the motion is adopted, as the case may be.

"(B) If before the 100th day after a petition is filed under subsection (a)(1) the Commission determines that the investigation is extraordinarily complicated, the Commission shall make the determination under paragraph (1) within 150 days after the date referred to in subparagraph (A).

"(3)(A) If the Commission makes an affirmative determination under paragraph (1) and the petitioner alleges the existence of critical circumstances, the Commission shall make a determination regarding such allegation—

"(i) on or before the 120th day after the day on which the petition was filed, if such allegation was included in the petition on or before the 90th day after such filing date; or

"(ii) on or before the date the report required under subsection (f) regarding the determination is submitted to the President, if such allegation was included in the petition after the 90th day, and on or before the 150th day, after such filing date.

"(B) For purposes of this paragraph and subsection (d)(2), critical circumstances exist if a substantial increase in imports (either actual or relative to domestic production) over a relatively short period of time has led to circumstances in which a delay in taking action under this chapter would cause harm that would significantly impair the effectiveness of such action.

"(4) In the course of any proceeding under this subsection, the Commission shall, after reasonable notice, hold public hearings and shall afford interested parties and consumers an opportunity to be present, to present evidence, to comment on the adjustment plan, if any, submitted under subsection (a), and to be heard at such hearings.

"(c) FACTORS APPLIED IN MAKING DETERMINATIONS.—

"(1) In making determinations under subsection (b), the Commission shall take into account all economic factors which it considers relevant, including (but not limited to)—

"(A) with respect to serious injury—

"(i) the significant idling of productive facilities in the domestic industry,

"(ii) the inability of a significant number of firms to carry out domestic production operations at a reasonable level of profit, and

"(iii) significant unemployment or underemployment within the domestic industry;

"(B) with respect to threat of serious injury—

"(i) a decline in sales or market share, a higher and growing inventory (whether maintained by domestic producers, importers, wholesalers, or retailers), and a downward trend in production, profits, wages, or employment (or increasing underemployment) in the domestic industry,

"(ii) the extent to which firms in the domestic industry are unable to generate adequate capital to finance the modernization of their domestic plants and equipment, or are unable to maintain existing levels of expenditures for research and development,

"(iii) the extent to which the United States market is the focal point for the diversion of exports of the article concerned by reason of restraints on exports of such article to, or on imports of such article into, third country markets; and

"(C) with respect to substantial cause, an increase in imports (either actual or relative to domestic production) and a decline in the proportion of the domestic market supplied by domestic producers.

"(2) In making determinations under subsection (b), the Commission shall—

"(A) consider the condition of the domestic industry over the course of the relevant business cycle, but may not aggregate the causes of declining demand associated with a recession or economic downturn in the United States economy into a single cause of serious injury or threat of injury; and

"(B) examine factors other than imports which may be a cause of serious injury, or threat of serious injury, to the domestic industry.

The Commission shall include the results of its examination under subparagraph (B) in the report submitted by the Commission to the President under subsection (e).

"(3) The presence or absence of any factor which the Commission is required to evaluate in subparagraphs (A) and (B) of paragraph (1) is not necessarily dispositive of whether an article is being imported into the United States in such increased quantities as to be a substantial cause of serious injury, or the threat thereof, to the domestic industry.

"(4) For purposes of subsection (b), in determining the domestic industry producing an article like or directly competitive with an imported article, the Commission—

"(A) to the extent information is available, shall, in the case of a domestic producer which also imports, treat as part of such domestic industry only its domestic production;

"(B) may, in the case of a domestic producer which produces more than one article, treat as part of such domestic industry only that portion or subdivision of the producer which produces the like or directly competitive article; and

"(C) may, in the case of one or more domestic producers which produce a like or directly competitive article in a major geographic area of the United States and whose production facilities in such area for such article constitute a substantial portion of the domestic industry in the United States and primarily serve the market in such area, and where the imports are concentrated in such area, treat as such domestic industry only that segment of the production located in such area.

"(5) In the course of any proceeding under this subsection, the Commission shall investigate any factor which in its judgment may be contributing to increased imports of the article under investigation. Whenever in the course of its investigation the Commission has reason to believe that the increased imports are attributable in part to circumstances which come within the purview of subtitles A and B of title VII or section 337 of the Tariff Act of 1930, or other remedial provisions of law, the Commission shall promptly notify the appropriate agency so that such action may be taken as is otherwise authorized by such provisions of law.

"(6) For purposes of this subsection:

"(A) The term 'domestic industry' includes producers located in the United States insular possession.

"(B) The term 'significant idling of productive facilities' includes the closing of plants or the underutilization of production capacity.

"(d) Provisional Relief.—

"(1)(A) An entity representing a domestic industry that produces a perishable agricultural product that is like or directly competitive with an imported perishable agricultural product may file a request with the Trade Representative for the monitoring of imports of that product under subparagraph (B). Within 21 days after receiving the request, the Trade Representative shall determine if—

"(i) the imported product is a perishable agricultural product; and

"(ii) there is a reasonable indication that such product is being imported into the United States in such increased quantities as to be, or likely to be, a substantial cause of serious injury, or the threat thereof, to such domestic industry.

"(B) If the determinations under subparagraph (A) (i) and (ii) are affirmative, the Trade Representative shall request, under section 332(g) of the Tariff Act of 1930, the Commission to monitor and investigate the imports concerned for a period not to exceed 2 years. The monitoring and investigation may include the collection and analysis of information that would expedite an investigation under subsection (b).

"(C) If a petition filed under subsection (a)—

"(i) alleges injury from imports of a perishable agricultural product that has been, on the date the allegation is included in the petition, subject to monitoring by the Commission under paragraph (2) for not less than 90 days; and

"(ii) requests that provisional relief be provided under this subsection with respect to such imports;

the Commission shall, not later than the 21st day after the day on which the request was filed, make a determination, on the basis of available information, whether increased imports (either actual or relative to domestic production) of the perishable agricultural product are a substantial cause of serious injury, or the threat thereof, to the domestic industry producing a like or directly competitive perishable product, and whether either—

"(I) the serious injury is likely to be difficult to repair by reason of perishability of the like or directly competitive agricultural product; or

"(II) the serious injury cannot be timely prevented through investigation under subsection (b) and action under section 203.

"(D) At the request of the Commission, the Secretary of Agriculture shall promptly provide to the Commission any relevant information that the Department of Agriculture may have for purposes of making determinations and findings under this subsection.

"(E) Whenever the Commission makes an affirmative preliminary determination under subparagraph (C), the Commission shall find the amount or extent of provisional relief that is necessary to prevent or remedy the serious injury or threat thereof. In carrying out this subparagraph, the Commission shall give preference to increasing or imposing a duty on imports, if such form of relief is feasible and would prevent or remedy the serious injury or threat thereof.

"(F) The Commission shall immediately report to the President its determination under subparagraph (C) and, if the determination is affirmative, the finding under subparagraph (E).

"(G) Within 7 days after receiving a report from the Commission under subparagraph (F) containing an affirmative determination, the President, if he considers provisional relief to be warranted and after taking into account the finding of the Commission under subparagraph (E), shall proclaim such provisional relief that the President considers necessary to prevent or remedy the serious injury or threat thereof.

"(2)(A) The Commission shall, at the same time it makes an affirmative determination under subsection (b)(3)(A) regarding the existence of critical circumstances, find the amount or extent of provisional relief that is appropriate to address such critical circumstances. The Commission shall immediately report to the President each such affirmative determination and finding.

"(B) After receiving a report from the Commission under subparagraph (A), the President shall, within 7 days after the day on which the report is received and after taking into account the finding of the Commission under subparagraph (A), proclaim such provisional relief, if any, that the President considers appropriate to address the critical circumstances.

"(3) If provisional relief is proclaimed under paragraph (1)(G) or (2)(B) in the form of an increase, or the imposition of, a duty, the President shall order the suspension of liquidation of all imported articles subject to the affirmative determination under paragraph (1)(C) or subsection (b)(1), as the case may be, that are entered, or withdrawn from warehouse for consumption, on or after the date of the determination.

"(4)(A) Any provisional relief implemented under this subsection with respect to an imported article shall terminate on the day on which--

"(i) if such relief was proclaimed under paragraph (1)(G), the Commission makes a negative determination under section 203(a) regarding injury or the threat thereof by imports of such article;

"(ii) action described in section 203(a)(3) (A) or (C) takes effect under section 203 with respect to such article;

"(iii) a decision by the President not to take any action under section 203(a) with respect to such article becomes final; or

"(iv) whenever the President determines that, because of changed circumstances, such relief is no longer warranted.

"(B) Any suspension of liquidation ordered under paragraph (3) with respect to an imported article shall terminate on the day on which provisional relief is terminated under subparagraph (A) with respect to the article.

"(C) If an increase in, or the imposition of, a duty that is proclaimed under section 203 on an imported article is different from a duty increase or imposition that was proclaimed for such an article under this section, then the entry of any such article for which liquidation was suspended under paragraph (3) shall be liquidated at whichever of such rates of duty is lower.

"(D) If provisional relief in the form of an increase in, or the imposition of, a duty is proclaimed under this section with respect to an imported article and neither a duty increase nor a duty imposition is proclaimed under section 203 regarding such article, the entry of any such article for which liquidation was suspended under paragraph (3) may be liquidated at the rate of duty that applied before provisional relief was provided.

"(5) For purposes of this subsection:

"(A) A perishable agricultural product is any agricultural article, including livestock, regarding which the Trade Representative considers action under this section to be appropriate after taking into account—

"(i) whether the article has—

"(I) a short shelf life,

"(II) a short growing season, or

"(III) a short marketing period,

"(ii) whether the article is treated as a perishable product under any other Federal law or regulation; and

"(iii) any other factor considered appropriate by the Trade Representative.

The presence or absence of any factor which the Trade Representative is required to take into account under clause (i), (ii), or (iii) is not necessarily dispositive of whether an article is a perishable agricultural product.

"(B) The term 'provisional relief' means—

"(i) any increase in, or imposition of, any duty;

"(ii) any modification or imposition of any quantitative restriction on the importation of an article into the United States; or

"(iii) any combination of actions under clauses (i) and (ii).

"(e) COMMISSION RECOMMENDATIONS.—

"(1) If the Commission makes an affirmative determination under subsection (b)(1), the Commission shall also recommend the action that would address the serious injury, or threat thereof, to the domestic industry and be most effective in facilitating the efforts of the domestic industry to make a positive adjustment to import competition.

"(2) The Commission is authorized to recommend under paragraph (1)—

"(A) an increase in, or the imposition of, any duty on the imported article;

"(B) a tariff-rate quota on the article;

"(C) a modification or imposition of any quantitative restriction on the importation of the article into the United States;

"(D) one or more appropriate adjustment measures, including the provision of trade adjustment assistance under chapter 2; or

"(E) any combination of the actions described in subparagraphs (A) through (D).

"(3) The Commission shall specify the type, amount, and duration of the action recommended by it under paragraph (1). • The limitations set forth in section 203(e) are applicable to the action recommended by the Commission.

"(4) In addition to the recommendation made under paragraph (1), the Commission may also recommend that the President—

"(A) initiate international negotiations to address the underlying cause of the increase in imports of the article or otherwise to alleviate the injury or threat; or

"(B) implement any other action authorized under law that is likely to facilitate positive adjustment to import competition.

"(5) For purposes of making its recommendation under this subsection, the Commission shall—

"(A) after reasonable notice, hold a public hearing at which all interested parties shall be provided an opportunity to present testimony and evidence; and

"(B) take into account—

"(i) the form and amount of action described in paragraph (2) (A), (B), and (C) that would prevent or remedy the injury of threat thereof,

"(ii) the objectives and actions specified in the adjustment plan, if any, submitted under subsection (a)(4),

"(iii) any individual commitment that was submitted to the Commission under subsection (a)(6),

"(iv) any information available to the Commission concerning the conditions of competition in domestic and world markets, and likely developments affecting such conditions during the period for which action is being requested, and

"(v) whether international negotiations may be constructive to address the injury or threat thereof or to facilitate adjustment.

"(6) Only those members of the Commission who agreed to the affirmative determination under subsection (b) are eligible to vote on the recommendation required to be made under paragraph (1) or that may be made under paragraph (3). Members of the Commission who did not agree to the affirmative determination may submit, in the report required under subsection (f), separate views regarding what action, if any, should be taken under section 203.

"(f) REPORT BY COMMISSION.—

"(1) The Commission shall submit to the President a report on each investigation undertaken under subsection (b). The report shall be submitted at the earliest practicable time, but not later than 180 days after the date on which the petition is filed, the request or resolution is received, or the motion is adopted, as the case may be.

"(2) The Commission shall include in the report required under paragraph (1) the following:

"(A) The determination made under subsection (b) and an explanation of the basis for the determination.

"(B) If the determination under subsection (b) is affirmative, the recommendations for action made under subsection (e) and an explanation of the basis for each recommendation.

"(C) Any dissenting or separate views by members of the Commission regarding the determination and any recommendation referred to in subparagraphs (A) and (B).

"(D) The findings required to be included in the report under subsection (c)(2).

"(E) A copy of the adjustment plan, if any, submitted under section 201(b)(4).

"(F) Commitments submitted, and information obtained, by the Commission regarding steps that firms and workers in the domestic industry are taking, or plan to take, to facilitate positive adjustment to import competition.

"(G) A description of—

"(i) the short- and long-term effects that implementation of the action recommended under subection (e) is likely to have on the petitioning domestic industry, on other domestic industries, and on consumers, and

"(ii) the short- and long-term effects of not taking the recommended action on the petitioning domestic industry, its workers and the communities where production facilities of such industry is located, and on other domestic industries.

"(3) The Commission, after submitting a report to the President under paragraph (1), shall promptly make it available to the public (with the exception of the confidential information obtained under section 202(a)(6)(B) and any other information which the Commission determines to be confidential) and cause a summary thereof to be published in the Federal Register.

"(g) EXPEDITED CONSIDERATION OF ADJUSTMENT ASSISTANCE PETITIONS.—If the Commission makes an affirmative determination under subsection (b)(1), the Commission shall promptly notify the Secretary of Labor and the Secretary of Commerce of the determination. After receiving such notification—

"(1) the Secretary of Labor shall give expedited consideration to petitions by workers in the domestic industry for certification for eligibility to apply for adjustment assistance under chapter 2; and

"(2) the Secretary of Commerce shall give expedited consideration to petitions by firms in the domestic industry for certification of eligibility to apply for adjustment assistance under chapter 3.

"(h) LIMITATIONS ON INVESTIGATIONS.—

"(1) Except for good cause determined by the Commission to exist, no investigation for the purposes of this section shall be made with respect to the same subject matter as a previous investigation under this chapter, unless 1 year has elapsed since the Commission made its report to the President of the results of such previous investigation.

"(2) If an article was the subject of an investigation under this section that resulted in any action described in section 203(a)(3) (A), (B), (C), or (E) being taken under section 203, no other investigation under this chapter may be initiated with respect to such article while such action is in effect or during the period beginning on the date on which such action terminates that is equal in duration to the period during which such action was in effect.

"SEC. 203. ACTION BY PRESIDENT AFTER DETERMINATION OF IMPORT INJURY.

"(a) IN GENERAL.—

"(1)(A) After receiving a report under section 202(f) containing an affirmative finding regarding serious injury, or the threat thereof, to a domestic industry, the President shall take all appropriate and feasible action within his power which the President determines will facilitate efforts by the domestic industry to make a positive adjustment to import competition and provide greater economic and social benefits than costs.

"(B) The action taken by the President under subparagraph (A) shall be to such extent, and for such duration, subject to subsection (e)(1), that the President determines to be appropriate and feasible under such subparagraph.

"(C) The interagency trade organization established under section 242(a) of the Trade Expansion Act of 1962 shall, with respect to each affirmative determination reported under section 202(f), make a recommendation to the President as to what action the President should take under subparagraph (A).

"(2) In determining what action to take under paragraph (1), the President shall take into account—

"(A) the recommendation and report of the Commission;

"(B) the extent to which workers and firms in the domestic industry are—

"(i) benefitting from adjustment assistance and other manpower programs, and

"(ii) engaged in worker retraining efforts;

"(C) the efforts being made, or to be implemented, by the domestic industry (including the efforts included in any adjustment plan or commitment submitted to the Commission under section 201(b)) to make a positive adjustment to import competition;

"(D) the probable effectiveness of the actions authorized under paragraph (3) to facilitate positive adjustment to import competition;

"(E) the short- and long-term economic and social costs of the actions authorized under paragraph (3) relative to their short- and long-term economic and social benefits and other considerations relative to the position of the domestic industry in the United States economy;

"(F) other factors related to the national economic interest of the United States, including, but not limited to—

"(i) the economic and social costs which would be incurred by taxpayers, communities, and workers if import relief were not provided under this chapter, "(ii) the effect of the implementation of actions under this section on consumers and on competition in domestic markets for articles, and

"(iii) the impact on United States industries and firms as a result of international obligations regarding compensation;

"(G) the extent to which there is diversion of foreign exports to the United States market by reason of foreign restraints;

"(H) the potential for circumvention of any action taken under this section;

"(I) the national security interests of the United States; and

"(J) the factors required to be considered by the Commission under section 202(e)(5).

"(3) The President may, for purposes of taking action under paragraph (1)—

"(A) proclaim an increase in, or the imposition of, any duty on the imported article;

"(B) proclaim a tariff-rate quota on the article;

"(C) proclaim a modification or imposition of any quantitative restriction on the importation of the article into the United States;

"(D) implement one or more appropriate adjustment measures, including the provision of trade adjustment assistance under chapter 2;

"(E) negotiate, conclude, and carry out orderly marketing agreements with foreign countries limiting the export from foreign countries and the import into the United States of such article;

"(F) proclaim procedures necessary to allocate among importers by the auction of import licenses quantities of the article that are permitted to be imported into the United States;

"(G) initiate international negotiations to address the underlying cause of the increase in imports of the article or otherwise to alleviate the injury or threat thereof;

"(H) submit to Congress legislative proposals to facilitate the efforts of the domestic industry to make a positive adjustment to import competition;

"(I) take any other action which may be taken by the President under the authority of law and which the President considers appropriate and feasible for purposes of paragraph (1); and

"(J) take any combination of actions listed in subparagraphs (A) through (I).

"(4) The President shall take action under paragraph (1) within 60 days after receiving a report from the Commission containing an affirmative determination under section 202(b)(1) (or a determination under such section which he considers to be an affirmative determination by reason of section 330(d) of the Tariff Act of 1930); except that if a supplemental report is requested under paragraph (5), the President shall take action under paragraph (1) within 30 days after the supplemental report is received.

"(5) The President may, within 15 days after the date on which he receives a report from the Commission containing an affirmative determination under section 202(b)(1), request additional information from the Commission. The Commission shall, as soon as practicable but in no event more than 30 days after the date on which it receives the President's request, furnish additional information with respect to the industry in a supplemental report.

"(b) REPORTS TO CONGRESS.—

"(1) On the day the President takes action under subsection (a)(1), the President shall transmit to Congress a document describing the action and the reasons for taking the action. If the action taken by the President differs from the action required to be recommended by the Commission under section 202(e)(1), the President shall state in detail the reasons for the difference.

"(2) On the day on which the President decides that there is no appropriate and feasible action to take under subsection (a)(1) with respect to a domestic industry, the President shall transmit to Congress a document that sets forth in detail the reasons for the decision.

"(3) On the day on which the President takes any action under subsection (a)(1) that is not reported under paragraph (1), the President shall transmit to Congress a document setting forth the action being taken and the reasons therefor.

"(c) IMPLEMENTATION OF ACTION RECOMMENDED BY COMMISSION.—If the President reports under subsection (b)(1) or (2) that—

"(1) the action taken under subsection (a)(1) differs from the action recommended by the Commission under section 202(e)(1); or

"(2) no action will be taken under subsection (a)(1) with respect to the domestic industry;

the action recommended by the Commission shall take effect (as provided in subsection (c)(2)) upon the enactment of a joint resolution described in section 152(a)(1)(A) within the 90-day period beginning on the date on which the document referred to in subsection (b)(1) or (2) is transmitted to the Congress.

"(d) TIME FOR TAKING EFFECT OF CERTAIN RELIEF.—

"(1) Except as provided in paragraph (2), any action described in subsection (a)(3)(A), (B), or (C), that is taken under subsection (a)(1) shall take effect within 15 days after the day on which the President proclaims the action, unless the President announces, on the date he decides to take such action, his intention to negotiate one or more orderly marketing agreements in which case the action under subsection (a)(3)(A), (B), or (C) shall be proclaimed and take effect within 90 days after the date of such decision.

"(2) If the contingency set forth in subsection (c) occurs, the President shall, within 30 days after the date of the enactment of the joint resolution referred to in such subsection, proclaim the action recommended by the Commission under section 202(e)(1).

"(e) LIMITATIONS ON ACTIONS.—

"(1)(A) The duration of the period in which action taken under this section may be in effect shall not exceed 8 years.

"(B) If the initial effective period for action taken under this section is less than 8 years, the President may extend the effective period once, but the aggregate of the initial period and the extension may not exceed 8 years.

"(2) Action may be taken under subsection (a)(1)(A), (B), or (C) or under section 202(d)(2)(B) only to the extent the cumulative impact of such action does not exceed the amount necessary to prevent or remedy the serious injury or threat thereof.

"(3) No action may be taken under this section which would increase a rate of duty to (or impose a rate) which is more than 50 percent ad valorem above the rate (if any) existing at the time the action is taken.

"(4) Any action taken under this section proclaiming a quantitative restriction shall permit the importation of a quantity or value of the article which is not less than the quantity or value of such article imported into the United States during the most recent period that is representative of imports of such article.

"(5) To the extent feasible, an effective period of more than 3 years for an action described in subsection (a)(3)(A), (B), or (C) shall be phased down during the period in which the action is taken, with the first reduction taking effect no later than the close of the day which is 3 years after the day on which such action first takes effect.

"(6)(A) The suspension, pursuant to any action taken under this section, of—

"(i) item 806.30 or 807.00 of the Tariff Schedules of the United States with respect to an article; and

"(ii) the designation of any article as an eligible article for purposes of title V;

shall be treated as an increase in duty.

"(B) No proclamation providing for a suspension referred to in subparagraph (A) with respect to any article may be made by the President, nor may any such suspension be recommended by the Commission under section 203(c), unless the Commission, in addition to making an affirmative determination under section 202(b)(1), determines in the course of its investigation under section 203(a) that the serious injury, or threat thereof, substantially caused by imports to the domestic industry producing a like or directly competitive article results from, as the case may be—

"(A) the application of item 806.30 or item 807.00; or

"(B) the designation of the article as an eligible article for the purposes of title V.

"(f) ORDERLY MARKETING AND OTHER AGREEMENTS.—

"(1) If the President takes action under this section other than the implemention of orderly marketing agreements, the President may, after such action takes effect, negotiate orderly marketing agreements with foreign countries, and may, after such agreements take effect, suspend or terminate, in whole or in part, any action previously taken.

"(2) If an orderly marketing agreement implemented under subsection (a) is not effective, the President may, consistent with the limitations contained in subsection (e), take additional action under subsection (a).

"(g) REGULATIONS.—

"(1) The President shall by regulation provide for the efficient and fair administration of all actions taken for the purpose of providing import relief under this chapter.

"(2) In order to carry out an orderly marketing or other international agreement concluded under this chapter, the President may prescribe regulations governing the entry or withdrawal from warehouse of articles covered by such agreement. In addition, in order to carry out any orderly marketing agreement concluded under this chapter with one or more countries accounting for a major part of United States imports of the article covered by such agreements, including imports into a major geographic area of the United States, the President may issue regulations governing the entry or withdrawal from warehouse of like articles which are the product of countries not parties to such agreement.

"(3) Regulations prescribed under this subsection shall, to the extent practicable and consistent with efficient and fair administration, insure against inequitable sharing of imports by a relatively small number of the larger importers.

"SEC. 204. MONITORING, MODIFICATION, AND TERMINATION OF ACTION.

"(a) MONITORING.—

"(1) So long as any action taken under section 203 remains in effect, the Commission shall monitor developments with respect to the domestic industry, including the progress and specific efforts made by workers and firms in the domestic industry to make a positive adjustment to import competition.

"(2) The Commission shall submit a report on the results of the monitoring under paragraph (1) to the President and to the Congress not later than—

"(A) the 2nd-anniversary of the day on which the action under section 203 first took effect; and

"(B) the last day of each 2-year period occurring after the 2-year period referred to in subparagraph (A).

"(3) In the course of preparing each report under paragraph (2), the Commission shall hold a hearing at which interested persons shall be given a reasonable opportunity to be present, to produce evidence, and to be heard.

"(4) Upon request of the President, the Commission shall advise the President of its judgment as to the probable economic effect on the industry concerned of any extension, reduction, modification, or termination of the action taken under section 203 which is under consideration.

"(b) REDUCTION, MODIFICATION, AND TERMINATION OF ACTION.—

"(1) Action taken under section 203 may be reduced, modified, or terminated by the President (but not before the President receives the report required under subsection (a)(2)(A)) if the President—

"(A) after taking into account any report or advice submitted by the Commission under subsection (a) and after seeking the advice of the Secretary of Commerce and the Secretary of Labor, determines, on the basis that either—

"(i) the domestic industry has not made adequate efforts to make a positive adjustment to import competition, or

"(ii) the effectiveness of the action taken under section 203 has been impaired by changed economic circumstances,

that changed circumstances warrant such reduction, or termination; or

"(B) determines, after a majority of the representatives of the domestic industry submits to the President a petition requesting such reduction, modification, or termination on such basis, that the domestic industry has made a positive adjustment to import competition.

"(2) Notwithstanding paragraph (1), the President is authorized to take such additional action under section 203 as may be necessary to eliminate any circumvention of any action previously taken under such section.

"(d) EVALUATION OF EFFECTIVENESS OF ACTION.—

"(1) After any action taken under section 203 has terminated, the Commission shall evaluate the effectiveness of the actions in facilitating positive adjustment by the domestic industry to import competition, consistent with the reasons set out by the President in the report submitted to the Congress under section 203(b).

"(2) During the course of the evaluation conducted under paragraph (1), the Commission shall, after reasonable public notice, hold a hearing on the effectiveness of the action. All interested persons shall have the opportunity to attend such hearing and to present evidence or testimony at such hearing.

"(3) A report on the evaluation made under paragraph (1) and the hearings held under paragraph (2) shall be submitted by the Commission to the President and to the Congress by no later than the 180th day after the day on which the actions taken under section 203 terminated.

"(e) OTHER PROVISIONS.—

"(1) Action by the President under this chapter may be taken without regard to the provisions of section 126(a) of this Act but only after consideration of the relation of such actions to the international obligations of the United States.

"(2) If the Commission treats as the domestic industry production located in a major geographic area of the United States under section 202(c)(4)(C), then the President shall take into account the geographic concentration of domestic production and of imports in that area in taking any action authorized under paragraph (1).".

(b) CONFORMING AMENDMENTS.—

(1) TRADE ACT OF 1974.—The Trade Act of 1974 is amended as follows:

(A) section 123(b)(4) is amended by striking out "import relief under section 203(h)." and inserting "action under sections 203(e) and 204.".

(B) Sections 224 and 264 (19 U.S.C. 2274 and 2354) are each amended—

(i) by striking out "201" in subsection (a) and inserting "202";

(ii) by striking out "201" in subsection (b) and inserting "202(f)"; and

such section 264 is amended by striking out "201(b)" in subsection (c) and inserting "202(b)".

(2) CARIBBEAN BASIN ECONOMIC RECOVERY ACT.—Section 213 of the Caribbean Basin Economic Recovery Act (19 U.S.C. 2703) is amended—

(A) by striking out "proclaimed pursuant to section 203" in subsection (e)(1) and inserting "provided under chapter 1 of title II";

(B) by striking out "201(d)(1)" in subsection (e)(2) and inserting "202(f)";

(C) by striking out "(a) and (c) of section 203" in subsection (e)(3) and inserting "section 203";

(D) by amending subsection (e)(4)—

(i) by striking out "made under subsections (a) and (c) of section 203" and inserting "taken under section 203";

(ii) by striking out "201(b)" the first place it appears and inserting "202(b)"; and

(iii) by striking out "section 201(b) of such Act" and inserting "such section";

(E) by amending subsection (e)(5)—

(i) by striking out "proclamation issued pursuant to section 203" in subparagraph (A) and inserting "action taken under section 203"; and

(ii) by amending subparagraph (B)—

(I) by striking out "to import relief" and inserting "to any such action",

(II) by striking out "such import relief" and inserting "such action", and

(III) by striking out "subsections (h) and (i) of section 203" and inserting "section 203";

(F) by amending subsection (f)(4)—

(i) by amending subparagraph (A) by striking out "proclamation of import relief pursuant to section 202(a)(1)" and inserting "taking of action under section 203", and

(ii) by amending subparagraph (B) to read as follows:

"(B) on the day a determination by the President not to take action under section 203 of such Act not to take action becomes final,".

(3) **Trade and tariff act of 1984.**—

(A) Title IV of the Tariff and Trade Act of 1984 is amended—

(i) by amending section 403—

(I) by striking out "section 201(d)(1)" in subsection (b) and inserting "section 202(f)",

(II) by striking out "subsections (a) and (c) of" in subsections (c) and (d),

(III) by striking out "201(b)" in subsection (d) and inserting "202(b)", and

(IV) by striking out "subsections (h) and (i) of section 203" in subsection (e)(2) and inserting "sections 203 and 204"; and

(ii) by amending section 404—

(I) by striking out "section 201" in subsection (a) and inserting "section 202(a)",

(II) by striking out "proclamation of import relief under section 202(a)(1)" in subsection (d)(1) and inserting "taking of action under section 203", and

(III) by amending subsection (d)(2) to read as follows:

"(2) on the day a determination of the President under section 203 of such Act not to take action becomes final;".

(4) **Tariff act of 1930.**—Section 330(d) of the Tariff Act of 1930 (19 U.S.C. 1330(d)) is amended—

(A) by amending paragraph (1) by striking out "201" and inserting "202";

(B) by amending paragraph (2)—

(i) by striking out "201" the first place it appears and inserting "202(b)",

(iii) by striking out "201(d)(1)" and inserting "202(e)(1)",

(iv) by striking out "sections 202 and 203" each place it appears and inserting "section 203", and

(v) by striking out "203(b)" in subparagraph (B) and inserting "204(a)"; and

(C) by striking out "203(c)(1)" in paragraph (4) and inserting "203(a)".

(5) TABLE OF CONTENTS.—The entry for such chapter 1 in the table of contents to the Trade Act of 1974 is amended to read as follows:

"CHAPTER 1—POSITIVE ADJUSTMENT BY INDUSTRIES INJURED BY IMPORTS

"Sec. 201. Action to facilitate positive adjustment to import competition.
"Sec. 202. Investigations, determinations, and recommendations by Commission.
"Sec. 203. Action by President after determination of import injury.
"Sec. 204. Monitoring, modification, and termination of action.".

(c) EFFECTIVE DATE.—The amendments made by subsections (a) and (b) shall take effect on the date of the enactment of this Act and shall apply with respect to investigations initiated under chapter 1 of title II of the Trade Act of 1974 on or after that date. Any petition filed under section 201 of such chapter before such date of enactment, and with respect to which the United States International Trade Commission did not make a finding before such date with respect to serious injury or the threat thereof, may be withdrawn and refiled, without prejudice, by the petitioner under section 202(a) of such chapter (as amended by this section).

PART 2—MARKET DISRUPTION

SEC. 1411. MARKET DISRUPTION.

(a) IN GENERAL.—Section 406 of the Trade Act of 1974 (19 U.S.C. 2436) is amended as follows—

(1) Subsection (b) is amended to read as follows:

"(b) With respect to any affirmative determination of the Commission under subsection (a)—

"(1) such determination shall be treated as an affirmative determination made under section 201(b) of this Act (as in effect on the day before the date of the enactment of the Omnibus Trade and Competitiveness Act of 1988); and

"(2) sections 202 and 203 of this Act (as in effect on the day before the date of the enactment of such Act of 1988), rather than the provisions of chapter 1 of title II of this Act as amended by section 1401 of such Act of 1988, shall apply with respect to the taking of subsequent action, if any, by the President in response to such affirmative determination;

except that—

"(A) the President may take action under such sections 202 and 203 only with respect to imports from the country or countries involved of the article with respect to which the affirmative determination was made; and

"(B) if such action consists of, or includes, an orderly marketing agreement, such agreement shall be entered into within 60 days after the import relief determination date.".

(2) Subsection (c) is amended by inserting "referred to in subsection (b)" after "sections 202 and 203".

(3) Subsection (e)(2) is amended—

(A) by inserting "(A)" after "(2)"; and

(B) by inserting at the end thereof the following new subparagraphs:

"(B) For purposes of subparagraph (A):

"(i) Imports of an article shall be considered to be increasing rapidly if there has been a significant increase in such imports (either actual or relative to domestic production) during a recent period of time.

"(ii) The term 'significant cause' refers to a cause which contributes significantly to the material injury of the domestic industry, but need not be equal to or greater than any other cause.

"(C) The Commission, in determining whether market disruption exists, shall consider, among other factors—

"(i) the volume of imports of the merchandise which is the subject of the investigation;

"(ii) the effect of imports of the merchandise on prices in the United States for like or directly competitive articles;

"(iii) the impact of imports of such merchandise on domestic producers of like or directly competitive articles; and

"(iv) evidence of disruptive pricing practices, or other efforts to unfairly manage trade patterns.".

(b) CONFORMING AMENDMENTS REQUIRED BY AMENDMENT OF CHAPTER 1 OF TITLE II OF THE TRADE ACT OF 1974.—Such section 406 is further amended—

(1) by striking out "201(a)(1)" in subsection (a)(1) and subsection (d) and inserting "202(a)"; and

(2) by striking out "subsections (a)(2), (b)(3), and (c) of section 201" in subsection (a)(2) and inserting "subsections (a)(3), (b)(4), and (c)(4) of section 202".

(c) EFFECTIVE DATE.—The amendments made by subsections (a) and (b) apply with respect to investigations initiated under section 406(a) of the Trade Act of 1974 on or after the date of the enactment of this Act.

PART 3—TRADE ADJUSTMENT ASSISTANCE

SEC. 1421. ELIGIBILITY OF WORKERS AND FIRMS FOR TRADE ADJUSTMENT ASSISTANCE.

(a) OIL AND NATURAL GAS INDUSTRY.—

(1)(A) Section 222 of the Trade Act of 1974 (19 U.S.C. 2272) is amended—

(i) by striking out "For purposes of paragraph (3), the term 'contributed importantly' means a cause which is important, but not necessarily more important than any other cause.",

(ii) by striking out "The Secretary" and inserting in lieu thereof "(a) The Secretary", and

(iii) by adding at the end thereof the following new subsection:

"(b) For purposes of subsection (a)(3)—

"(1) The term 'contributed importantly' means a cause which is important but not necessarily more important than any other cause.

"(2)(A) Any firm, or appropriate subdivision of a firm, that engages in exploration or drilling for oil or natural gas shall be considered to be a firm producing oil or natural gas.

"(B) Any firm, or appropriate subdivision of a firm, that engages in exploration or drilling for oil or natural gas, or otherwise produces oil or natural gas, shall be considered to be producing articles directly competitive with imports of oil and with imports of natural gas.".

(B) Notwithstanding section 223(b) of the Trade Act of 1974, or any other provision of law, any certification made under subchapter A of chapter 2 of title II of such Act which—

(i) is made with respect to a petition filed before the date that is 90 days after the date of enactment of this Act, and

(ii) would not have been made if the amendments made by subparagraph (A) had not been enacted into law,

shall apply to any worker whose most recent total or partial separation from the firm, or appropriate subdivision of the firm, described in section 222(a) of such Act occurs after September 30, 1985.

(2) Subsection (c) of section 251 of the Trade Act of 1974 (19 U.S.C. 2341(c)) is amended to read as follows:

"(c)(1) The Secretary shall certify a firm (including any agricultural firm) as eligible to apply for adjustment assistance under this chapter if the Secretary determines—

"(A) that a significant number or proportion of the workers in such firm have become totally or partially separated, or are threatened to become totally or partially separated,

"(B) that—

"(i) sales or production, or both, of such firm have decreased absolutely, or

"(ii) sales or production, or both, of an article that accounted for not less than 25 percent of the total production or sales of the firm during the 12-month period preceding the most recent 12-month period for which data are available have decreased absolutely, and

"(C) increases of imports of articles like or directly competitive with articles which are produced by such firm contributed importantly to such total or partial separation, or threat thereof, and to such decline in sales or production.

"(2) For purposes of paragraph (1)(C)—

"(A) The term 'contributed importantly' means a cause which is important but not necessarily more important than any other cause.

"(B)(i) Any firm which engages in exploration or drilling for oil or natural gas shall be considered to be a firm producing oil or natural gas.

"(ii) Any firm that engages in exploration or drilling for oil or natural gas, or otherwise produces oil or natural gas, shall be considered to be producing articles directly competitive with imports of oil and with imports of natural gas.".

(b) Application to All Industries.—

(1) Paragraph (3) of section 222(a) of the Trade Act of 1974 (19 U.S.C. 2272(a)(3)) is amended to read as follows:

"(3) increases of imports of articles like or directly competitive with articles—

"(A) which are produced by such workers' firm or appropriate subdivision thereof, or

"(B) for which such workers' firm, or appropriate subdivision thereof, provides essential goods or essential services,

contributed importantly to such total or partial separation, or threat thereof, and to such decline in sales or production.".

(2) Subparagraph (C) of section 251(c)(1) of the Trade Act of 1974 (19 U.S.C. 2341(c)(1)(C)) is amended to read as follows:

"(C) increases of imports of articles like or directly competitive with articles—

"(i) which are produced by such firm, or

"(ii) for which such firm provides essential goods or essential services,

contributed importantly to such total or partial separation, or threat thereof, and to such decline in sales or production.".

SEC. 1422. NOTICE TO WORKERS OF BENEFITS UNDER TRADE ADJUSTMENT ASSISTANCE PROGRAM.

Section 225 of the Trade Act of 1974 (19 U.S.C. 2275) is amended—

(1) by striking out "The Secretary" in the first sentence and inserting in lieu thereof "(a) The Secretary", and

(2) by adding at the end thereof the following new subsection:

"(b)(1) The Secretary shall provide written notice through the mail of the benefits available under this chapter to each worker whom the Secretary has reason to believe is covered by a certification made under subchapter A of this chapter—

"(A) at the time such certification is made, if the worker was partially or totally separated from the adversely affected employment before such certification, or

"(B) at the time of the total or partial separation of the worker from the adversely affected employment, if subparagraph (A) does not apply.

"(2) The Secretary shall publish notice of the benefits available under this chapter to workers covered by each certification made under subchapter A in newspapers of general circulation in the areas in which such workers reside.".

SEC. 1423. CASH ASSISTANCE FOR WORKERS.

(a) Participation in Training Program Required.—

(1) Paragraph (5) of section 231(a) of the Trade Act of 1974 (19 U.S.C. 2291(a)(5)) is amended to read as follows:

"(5) Such worker—

"(A) is enrolled in a training program approved by the Secretary under section 236(a),

"(B) has, after the date on which the worker became totally separated, or partially separated, from the adversely affected employment, completed a training program approved by the Secretary under section 236(a), or

"(C) has received a written statement certified under subsection (c)(1) after the date described in subparagraph (B).".

(2) Subsection (b) of section 231 of the Trade Act of 1974 (19 U.S.C. 2291(b)) is amended to read as follows:

"(b)(1) If—

"(A) the Secretary determines that—

"(i) the adversely affected worker—

"(I) has failed to begin participation in the training program the enrollment in which meets the requirement of subsection (a)(5), or

"(II) has ceased to participate in such training program before completing such training program, and

"(ii) there is no justifiable cause for such failure or cessation, or

"(B) the certification made with respect to such worker under subsection (c)(1) is revoked under subsection (c)(2),

no trade readjustment allowance may be paid to the adversely affected worker under this part for the week in which such failure, cessation, or revocation occurred, or any succeeding week, until the adversely affected worker begins or resumes participation in a training program approved under section 236(a).

"(2) The provisions of subsection (a)(5) and paragraph (1) shall not apply with respect to any week of unemployment which begins—

"(A) after the date that is 60 days after the date on which the petition that results in the certification that covers the worker is filed under section 221, and

"(B) before the first week following the week in which such certification is made under subchapter (A).".

(3) Subsection (c) of section 231 of the Trade Act of 1974 (19 U.S.C. 2291(c)) is amended to read as follows:

"(c)(1)(A) If the Secretary finds that it is not feasible or appropriate to approve a training program for a worker under section 236(a), the Secretary shall submit to such worker a written statement certifying such finding.

"(B) If a State or State agency has an agreement with the Secretary under section 239 and the State or State agency finds that it is not feasible or appropriate to approve a training program for a worker pursuant to the requirements of section 236(a), the State or State agency shall—

"(i) submit to such worker a written statement certifying such finding, and

"(ii) submit to the Secretary a written statement certifying such finding and the reasons for such finding.

"(2)(A) If, after submitting to a worker a written statement certified under paragraph (1)(A), the Secretary finds that it is feasible or appropriate to approve a training program for such worker under section 236(a), the Secretary shall submit to such worker a written statement that revokes the certification made under paragraph (1)(A) with respect to such worker.

"(B) If, after submitting to a worker a written statement certified under paragraph (1)(B), a State or State agency finds that it is feasible or appropriate to approve a training program for such worker pursuant to the requirements of section 236(a), the State or State agency shall submit to such worker, and to the Secretary, a written statement that revokes the certification made under paragraph (1)(B) with respect to such worker.

"(3) The Secretary shall submit to the Finance Committee of the Senate and to the Ways and Means Committee of the House of Representatives an annual report on the number of workers who received certifications under paragraph (1) during the preceding year and the number of certifications made under paragraph (1) that were revoked during the preceding year.".

(4) Paragraph (3) of section 239(a) of the Trade Act of 1974 (19 U.S.C. 2311(a)(3)) is amended to read as follows:

"(3) will make any certifications required under section 231(c)(2), and".

(b) WEEKLY AMOUNTS OF READJUSTMENT ALLOWANCES.—Section 232 of the Trade Act of 1974 (19 U.S.C. 2292) is amended—

(1) by striking out ", including on-the-job training," in subsection (b), and

(2) by striking out "under section 231(c) or 236(c)" in subsection (c) and inserting in lieu thereof "under section 231(b)".

(c) LIMITATIONS.—Section 233 of the Trade Act of 1974 (19 U.S.C. 2293) is amended—

(1) by striking out "is approved" in subsection (a)(3)(B) and inserting in lieu thereof "begins",

(2) by striking out "engaged in such training and has not been determined under section 236(c) to be failing to make satisfactory progress in the training" in subsection (a)(3) and inserting in lieu thereof "participating in such training", and

(3) by adding at the end thereof the following new subsection:

"(f) For purposes of this chapter, a worker shall be treated as participating in training during any week which is part of a break in training that does not exceed 14 days if—

"(1) the worker was participating in a training program approved under section 236(a) before the beginning of such break in training, and

"(2) the break is provided under such training program.".

(d) SUPPLEMENTAL WAGE ALLOWANCE DEMONSTRATION PROJECTS.—

(1) Subchapter C of chapter 2 of title II of the Trade Act of 1974 is amended by inserting after section 245 the following new section:

"SEC. 246. SUPPLEMENTAL WAGE ALLOWANCE DEMONSTRATION PROJECTS.

"(a) The Secretary shall establish and carry out one or more demonstration projects during fiscal years 1989 and 1990 for the purpose of—

"(1) determining the attractiveness of a supplemental wage allowance to various categories of workers eligible for assistance under this chapter, based on the amount and duration of the supplement;

"(2) determining the effectiveness of a supplemental wage allowance as an option under this chapter in facilitating the readjustment of adversely affected workers; and

"(3) determining whether a supplemental wage allowance should be made an option under the Trade Adjustment Assistance program for all fiscal years.

"(b)(1) For purposes of this section, the term 'supplemental wage allowance' means a payment that is made to an adversely affected worker who—

"(A) accepts full-time employment at an average weekly wage that is less than the average weekly wage of the worker in the adversely affected employment,

"(B) prior to such acceptance, is eligible for trade readjustment allowances under part I of subchapter B, and

"(C) voluntarily elects to receive such payment in lieu of any trade readjustment allowances that the worker would otherwise be eligible to receive with respect to the period covered by the certification made under subchapter A that applies to such worker.

"(2) A supplemental wage allowance shall be provided under any demonstration project established under subsection (a) to a worker described in paragraph (1) for each week during which the worker performs services in the full-time employment referred to in paragraph (1)(A) in an amount that does not exceed the lesser of—

"(A) the amount of the trade readjustment allowance that the worker would have been eligible to receive for any week under part 1 of subchapter B if the worker had not accepted the full-time employment and had not made the election described in paragraph (1)(C), or

"(B) the excess of—

"(i) an amount equal to 80 percent of the average weekly wage of the worker in the adversely affected employment, over

"(ii) the average weekly wage in the full-time employment.

"(3)(A) Supplemental wage allowances shall not be provided under any demonstration project established under subsection (a) for more than 52 weeks.

"(B) The total amount of supplemental wage allowances that may be paid to any worker under any demonstration project established under subsection (a) with respect to the period covered by the certification applicable to such worker shall not exceed an amount that is equal to the excess of—

"(i) the amount of the limitation imposed under section 233(a)(1) with respect to such worker for such period, over

"(ii) the amount of the trade readjustment allowances paid under part I of subchapter B to such worker for such period.

"(c) The Secretary shall provide for an evaluation of demonstration projects conducted under this section to determine at least the following:

"(1) the extent to which different age groups of eligible recipients utilize the supplemental wage allowance;

"(2) the effect of the amount and duration of the supplemental wage allowance on the utilization of the allowance;

"(3) the extent to which the supplemental wage allowance affects the demand for training and the appropriateness thereof;

"(4) the extent to which the supplemental wage allowance facilitates the readjustment of workers who would not otherwise utilize benefits provided under this chapter;

"(5) the extent to which the allowance affects the cost of carrying out the provisions of this chapter; and

"(6) the effectiveness of the supplemental wage allowance as an option under this chapter in facilitating the readjustment of adversely affected workers.

"(d) By no later than the date that is 3 years after the date of enactment of the Omnibus Trade and Competitiveness Act of 1988, the Secretary shall transmit to the Congress a report that includes—

"(1) an evaluation of the projects authorized under this section that is conducted in accordance with subsection (c), and

"(2) a recommendation as to whether the supplemental wage allowance should be available on a permanent basis as an option for some or all workers eligible for assistance under this chapter.".

(2) For purposes of funding the demonstration projects established under section 246(a) of the Trade Act of 1974, as added by paragraph (1) of this subsection—

(A) the supplemental wage allowances payable under such projects shall be considered to be trade readjustment allowances payable under part I of subchapter B of chapter 2 of title II of the Trade Act of 1974, and

(B) the costs of administering such projects by the States shall be considered to be costs of administering such part I.

(3) The table of contents of the Trade Act of 1974 is amended by inserting after the item relating to section 245 the following new item:

"Sec. 246. Supplemental wage allowance demonstration projects.".

SEC. 1424. JOB TRAINING FOR WORKERS.

(a) IN GENERAL.—Subsection (a) of section 236 of the Trade Act of 1974 (19 U.S.C. 2296(a)) is amended—

(1) by striking out "is available" in paragraph (1)(D) and inserting in lieu thereof "is reasonably available",

(2) by striking out ", and" at the end of subparagraph (D) of paragraph (1),

(3) by adding "and" at the end of subparagraph (E) of paragraph (1),

(4) by inserting after subparagraph (E) of paragraph (1) the following new subparagraph:

"(F) such training is suitable for the worker and available at a reasonable cost,",

(5) by striking out "(to the extent appropriated funds are available)" in the first sentence of paragraph (1),

(6) by inserting "(subject to the limitations imposed by this section)" after "costs of such training" in the second sentence of paragraph (1),

(7) by inserting "directly or through a voucher system" after "by the Secretary" in the second sentence of paragraph (1),

(8) by striking out "and" at the end of subparagraph (C) of paragraph (4),

(9) by redesignating subparagraph (D) of paragraph (4) as subparagraph (F) of paragraph (4),

(10) by inserting after subparagraph (C) of paragraph (4) the following new subparagraphs:

"(D) any program of remedial education,

"(E) any training program (other than a training program described in paragraph (7)) for which all, or any portion, of the costs of training the worker are paid—

"(i) under any Federal or State program other than this chapter, or

"(ii) from any source other than this section, and",

(11) by redesignating paragraphs (2), (3), and (4) as paragraphs (3), (4), and (5), respectively,

(12) by inserting after paragraph (1) the following new paragraph:

"(2)(A) The total amount of payments that may be made under paragraph (1) for any fiscal year shall not exceed $80,000,000.

"(B) If, during any fiscal year, the Secretary estimates that the amount of funds necessary to pay the costs of training approved under this section will exceed the amount of the limitation imposed under subparagraph (A), the Secretary shall decide how the portion of such limitation that has not been expended at the time of such estimate is to be apportioned among the States for the remainder of such fiscal year.", and

(13) by adding at the end of subsection (a) the following new paragraphs:

"(6)(A) The Secretary is not required under paragraph (1) to pay the costs of any training approved under paragraph (1) to the extent that such costs are paid—

"(i) under any Federal or State program other than this chapter, or

"(ii) from any source other than this section.

"(B) Before approving any training to which subparagraph (A) may apply, the Secretary may require that the adversely affected worker enter into an agreement with the Secretary under which the Secretary will not be required to pay under this section the portion of the costs of such training that the worker has reason to believe will be paid under the program, or by the source, described in subparagraph (A) or (B) of paragraph (1).

"(7) The Secretary shall not approve a training program if—

"(A) all or a portion of the costs of such training program are paid under any nongovernmental plan or program,

"(B) the adversely affected worker has a right to obtain training or funds for training under such plan or program, and

"(C) such plan or program requires the worker to reimburse the plan or program from funds provided under this chapter, or from wages paid under such training program, for any portion of the costs of such training program paid under the plan or program.

"(8) The Secretary may approve training for any adversely affected worker who is a member of a group certified under subchapter A at any time after the date on which the group is certified under subchapter A, without regard to whether such worker has exhausted all rights to any unemployment insurance to which the worker is entitled.

"(9) The Secretary shall prescribe regulations which set forth the criteria under each of the subparagraphs of paragraph (1) that will be used as the basis for making determinations under paragraph (1).".

(b) DELAYED INCREASE IN LIMITATION.—Paragraph (2) of section 236(a) of the Trade Act of 1974, as added by subsection (a)(12) of this section, is amended by striking out "$80,000,000" in subparagraph (A) and inserting in lieu thereof "$120,000,000".

(c) ON-THE-JOB TRAINING.—Section 236 of the Trade Act of 1974 (19 U.S.C. 2296) is amended—

(1) by striking out that portion of subsection (d) that precedes paragraph (1) and inserting in lieu thereof the following:

"(d) The Secretary shall pay the costs of any on-the-job training of an adversely affected worker that is approved under subsection (a)(1) in equal monthly installments, but the Secretary may pay such costs, notwithstanding any other provision of this section, only if—",

(2) by striking out subsection (c), and

(3) by redesignating subsections (d), (e), and (f) as subsections (c), (d), and (e), respectively.

(d) AGREEMENTS WITH THE STATES.—

(1)(A) Section 235 of the Trade Act of 1974 (19 U.S.C. 2295) is amended by striking out "cooperating State agencies" and inserting in lieu thereof "the States".

(B) Subsection (e) of section 239 of the Trade Act of 1974 (19 U.S.C. 2311(e)) is amended to read as follows:

"(e) Any agreement entered into under this section shall provide for the coordination of the administration of the provisions for employment services, training, and supplemental assistance under sections 235 and 236 of this Act and under title III of the Job Training Partnership Act upon such terms and conditions as are established by the Secretary in consultation with the States and set forth in such agreement. Any agency of the State jointly administering such provisions under such agreement shall be considered to be a cooperating State agency for purposes of this chapter.".

(2) Subsection (f) of section 239 of the Trade Act of 1974 (19 U.S.C. 2311(f)) is amended to read as follows:

"(f) Each cooperating State agency shall, in carrying out subsection (a)(2)—

"(1) advise each worker who applies for unemployment insurance of the benefits under this chapter and the procedures and deadlines for applying for such benefits,

"(2) facilitate the early filing of petitions under section 221 for any workers that the agency considers are likely to be eligible for benefits under this chapter,

"(3) advise each adversely affected worker to apply for training under section 236(a) before, or at the same time, the worker applies for trade readjustment allowances under part I of subchapter B, and

"(4) as soon as practicable, interview the adversely affected worker regarding suitable training opportunities available to the worker under section 236 and review such opportunities with the worker.".

SEC. 1425. LIMITATION ON PERIOD IN WHICH TRADE READJUSTMENT ALLOWANCES MAY BE PAID.

(a) IN GENERAL.—Paragraph (2) of section 233(a) of the Trade Act of 1974 (19 U.S.C. 2293(a)(2)) is amended to read as follows:

"(2) A trade readjustment allowance shall not be paid for any week occurring after the close of the 104-week period that begins with the first week following the week in which the adversely affected worker was most recently totally separated from adversely affected employment—

"(A) within the period which is described in section 231(a)(1), and

"(B) with respect to which the worker meets the requirements of section 231(a)(2).".

(b) WAIVER OF CERTAIN TIME LIMITATIONS.—

(1) The provisions of subsections (a)(2) and (b) of section 233 of the Trade Act of 1974 shall not apply with respect to any worker who became totally separated from adversely affected employment (within the meaning of section 247 of such Act) during the period that began on August 13, 1981, and ended on April 7, 1986.

(2)(A) Any worker who is otherwise eligible for payment of a trade readjustment allowance under part I of subchapter B of chapter 2 of title II of the Trade Act of 1974 by reason of paragraph (1) of this subsection may receive payments of such allowance only if such worker—

(i) is enrolled in a training program approved by the Secretary under section 236(a) of such Act, and

(ii) has been unemployed continuously since the date on which the worker became totally separated from the adversely affected employment, not taking into account seasonal employment, odd jobs, or part-time, temporary employment.

(B) If the Secretary of Labor determines that—

(i) a worker—

(I) has failed to begin participation in the training program the enrollment in which meets the requirement of subparagraph (A), or

(II) has ceased to participate in such training program before completing such training program, and

(ii) there is no justifiable cause for such failure or cessation,

no trade readjustment allowance may be paid to the worker under part I of subchapter B of chapter 2 of title II of the Trade Act of 1974 for the week in which such failure or cessation occurred, or any succeeding week, until the worker begins or resumes participation in a training program approved under section 236(a) of such Act.

SEC. 1426. AUTHORIZATION OF TRADE ADJUSTMENT ASSISTANCE PROGRAM.

(a) Extension of Sunset.—Subsection (b) of section 285 of the Trade Act of 1974 (19 U.S.C. 2271, preceding note) is amended to read as follows:

"(b) No assistance, vouchers, allowances, or other payments may be provided under chapter 2, no technical assistance may be provided under chapter 3, and no duty shall be imposed under section 287, after September 30, 1993.".

(b) Authorization of Appropriations.—

(1) Section 245 of the Trade Act of 1974 (19 U.S.C. 2317) is amended by striking out "1986, 1987, 1988, 1989, 1990, and 1991" and inserting in lieu thereof "1988, 1989, 1990, 1991, 1992, and 1993".

(2) Subsection (b) of section 256 of the Trade Act of 1974 (19 U.S.C. 2346(b)) is amended by striking out "1986, 1987, 1988, 1989, 1990, and 1991" and inserting in lieu thereof "1988, 1989, 1990, 1991, 1992, and 1993".

(c) Special Rule.—In addition to amounts appropriated for payments under sections 236, 237, and 238 of the Trade Act of 1974 (19 U.S.C. 2296) for fiscal year 1988, such amounts as may be necessary for payments under such sections—

(1) after the date of enactment of this Act, and

(2) before October 1, 1988,

are hereby appropriated and shall be charged to the appropriation for payments under such sections for fiscal year 1989.

SEC. 1427. TRADE ADJUSTMENT ASSISTANCE TRUST FUND.

(a) In General.—Chapter 5 of title II of the Trade Act of 1974 (19 U.S.C. 2391, et seq.) is amended by inserting after section 285 the following new section:

"SEC. 286. TRADE ADJUSTMENT ASSISTANCE TRUST FUND.

"(a) There is hereby established within the Treasury of the United States a trust fund to be known as the Trade Adjustment Assistance Trust Fund (hereinafter in this section referred to as the 'Trust Fund'), consisting of such amounts as may be transferred or credited to the Trust Fund as provided in this section or appropriated to the Trust Fund under subsection (e).

"(b)(1) The Secretary of the Treasury shall transfer to the Trust Fund out of the general fund of the Treasury of the United States amounts determined by the Secretary of the Treasury to be equivalent to the amounts received into such general fund that are attributable to the duty imposed by section 287.

"(2) The amounts which are required to be transferred under paragraph (1) shall be transferred at least quarterly from the general fund of the Treasury of the United States to the Trust Fund on the basis of estimates made by the Secretary of the Treasury of the amounts referred to in paragraph (1) that are received into the Treasury. Proper adjustments shall be made in the amounts subsequently transferred to the extent prior estimates were in excess of, or less than, the amounts required to be transferred.

"(c)(1) The Secretary of the Treasury shall be the trustee of the Trust Fund, and shall submit an annual report to the Committee on Finance of the Senate and the Committee on Ways and Means of the House of Representatives on the financial condition and the results of the operations of the Trust Fund during the fiscal year preceding the fiscal year in which such report is submitted and on the expected condition and operations of the Trust Fund during the fiscal year in which such report is submitted and the 5 fiscal years succeeding such fiscal year. Such report shall be printed as a House document of the session of the Congress to which the report is made.

"(2)(A) The Secretary of the Treasury shall invest such portion of the Trust Fund as is not, in his judgment, required to meet current withdrawals. Such investments may be made only in interest-bearing obligations of the United States. For such purpose, such obligations may be acquired—

"(i) on original issue at the issue price, or

"(ii) by purchase of outstanding obligations at the market price.

"(B) Any obligation acquired by the Trust Fund may be sold by the Secretary of the Treasury at the market price.

"(C) The interest on, and the proceeds from the sale or redemption of, any obligations held in the Trust Fund shall be credited to and form a part of the Trust Fund.

"(d)(1) Amounts in the Trust Fund shall be available—

"(A) for the payment of drawbacks and refunds of the duty imposed by section 287 that are allowable under any other provision of Federal law,

"(B) as provided in appropriation Acts—

"(i) for expenditures that are required to carry out the provisions of chapters 2 and 3, including administrative costs, and

"(ii) for payments required under subsection (e)(2).

"(2) None of the amounts in the Trust Fund shall be available for the payment of loans guaranteed under chapter 3 or for any other expenses relating to financial assistance provided under chapter 3.

"(3)(A) If the total amount of funds expended in any fiscal year to carry out chapters 2 and 3 (including administrative costs) exceeds an amount equal to 0.15 percent of the total value of all articles upon which a duty was imposed by section 287 during the preceding 1-year period, the Secretary of Labor and the Secretary of Commerce (in consultation with the Secretary of the Treasury) shall, notwithstanding any provision of chapter 2 or 3, make a pro rata reduction in—

"(i) the amounts of the trade readjustment allowances that are paid under part I of subchapter B of chapter 2, and

"(ii) the assistance provided under chapter 3,

to ensure (based on estimates of the amount of funds that will be necessary to carry out chapters 2 and 3, and of the amount of revenue that will be raised by section 287, during the remainder of such fiscal year and for the fiscal year succeeding such fiscal year) that all workers and firms eligible for assistance under chapter 2 or 3 receive some assistance under chapter 2 or 3 and that the expenditures made in providing such assistance during the remainder of such fiscal year and the fiscal year succeeding such fiscal year do not exceed the amount of funds available in the Trust Fund to pay for such expenditures.

"(B) No reduction may be made under this paragraph in the amount of any trade readjustment allowance payable under part I of subchapter B of chapter 2 to any worker who received such trade readjustment allowance under such part for the week preceding the first week for which such reduction is otherwise being made under this paragraph.

"(C) If a pro rata reduction made under subparagraph (A) is in effect at the close of a fiscal year, the Secretary of Labor and the Secretary of Commerce, in consultation with the Secretary of the Treasury, may adjust or modify such reduction at the beginning of the fiscal year succeeding such fiscal year, based on estimates of the amount of funds that will be necessary to carry out chapters 2 and 3, and of the amount of revenue that will be raised by section 287, during that succeeding fiscal year.

"(D) Any pro rata reduction made under subparagraph (A), and any pro rata reduction adjusted or modified under subparagraph (C), shall cease to apply after the week in which—

"(i) a 1-year period ends during which the total amount of funds that would have been expended to carry out chapters 2 and 3, including administrative costs, if such reduction were not in effect did not exceed an amount equal to 0.15 percent of the total value of all articles upon which a duty was imposed during such 1-year period, or

"(ii) the Secretary of Labor and the Secretary of Commerce, in consultation with the Secretary of the Treasury, determine that the amount of funds available in the Trust Fund are sufficient to carry out chapters 2 and 3 without such reduction.

"(e)(1)(A) There are authorized to be appropriated to the Trust Fund, as repayable advances, such sums as may from time to time be necessary to make the expenditures described in subsection (d)(1)(B).

"(B) Any advance appropriated to the Trust Fund under the authority of subparagraph (A) may be paid to the Trust Fund only to the extent that the total amount of advances paid during the fiscal year to the Trust Fund from any appropriation authorized under subparagraph (A) that are outstanding after such advance is paid to the Trust Fund does not exceed the lesser of—

"(i) the excess of—

"(I) the total amount of funds that the Secretary of the Treasury (in consultation with the Secretary of Labor and the Secretary of Commerce) estimates will be necessary for the payments and expenditures described in subparagraphs (A) and (B) of subsection (d)(1) for such fiscal year, over

"(II) the total amount of funds that the Secretary of the Treasury estimates will be available in the Trust Fund during the fiscal year (determined without regard to any advances made under this subsection during such fiscal year), or

"(ii) the excess of—

"(I) an amount equal to 0.15 percent of the total value of all articles upon which the Secretary of the Treasury estimates a duty will be imposed by section 287 during such fiscal year, over

"(II) the amount described in clause (i)(II).

"(2) Advances made to the Trust Fund from appropriations authorized under paragraph (1)(A) shall be repaid, and interest on such advances shall be paid, to the general fund of the Treasury of the United States when the Secretary of the Treasury determines that sufficient funds are available in the Trust Fund for such purposes.

"(3) Interest on advances made from appropriations authorized under paragraph (1)(A) shall be at a rate determined by the Secretary of the Treasury (as of the close of the calendar month preceding the month in which the advance is made) to be equal to the current average market yield on outstanding marketable obligations of the United States with remaining periods to maturity comparable to the anticipated period during which the advance will be outstanding.".

(b) CONFORMING AMENDMENT.—The table of contents for the Trade Act of 1974 is amended by inserting, after the item relating to section 285, the following new items:

"Sec. 286. Trade Adjustment Trust Fund.
"Sec. 287. Imposition of additional fee.".

SEC. 1428. IMPOSITION OF SMALL UNIFORM FEE ON ALL IMPORTS.

(a) NEGOTIATIONS.—

(1) The President shall—

(A) undertake negotiations necessary to achieve changes in the General Agreement on Tariffs and Trade that would allow any country to impose a small uniform fee of not more than 0.15 percent on all imports to such country for the purpose of using the revenue from such fee to fund programs which directly assist adjustment to import competition, and

(B) undertake negotiations with any foreign country that has entered into a free trade agreement with the United States under subtitle A or under section 102 of the Trade Act of 1974 to obtain the consent of such country to the imposition of such a fee by the United States.

(2) In the report that is submitted under section 163 of the Trade Act of 1974 for 1989 and 1990, the President shall include a statement on the progress of negotiations conducted under paragraph (1).

(3)(A) On the first day after the date of enactment of this Act on which the General Agreement on Tariffs and Trade allows any country to impose a fee described in paragraph (1), the President shall submit to the Congress, and publish in the Federal Register, a written statement certifying such allowance.

(B) On the first day after the date of enactment of this Act on which any foreign country described in paragraph (1)(B) consents to the imposition of such a fee by the United States, the President shall submit to the Congress, and publish in the Federal Register, a written statement certifying such consent.

(4) If—

(A) the President does not submit to the Congress the written statement described in paragraph (3)(A) before the date that is 2 years after the date of enactment of this Act, and

(B) the President determines on such date that the fee imposed by the amendment made by subsection (b) is not in the national economic interest,

the President shall submit to the Congress, and publish in the Federal Register, written notice of such determination on such date.

(5)(A) Any disapproval resolution that is introduced in the Senate or House of Representatives within the 90-day period beginning on the date that is 2 years after the date of enactment of this Act shall, for purposes of section 152 of the Trade Act of 1974 (19 U.S.C. 2192), be treated as a joint resolution described in section 152(a)(1)(A) of such Act.

(B) For purposes of this part, the term "disapproval resolution" means a joint resolution of the two Houses of the Congress, the matter after the resolving clause of which is as follows: "That the Congress disapproves of the determination made by the President under section 1428(a)(4)(A) of the Omnibus Trade and Competitiveness Act of 1988.".

(b) Imposition of Fee.—Chapter 5 of title II of the Trade Act of 1974 (19 U.S.C. 2391, et seq.), as amended by the preceding section of this Act, is further amended by adding at the end thereof the following new section:

"SEC. 287. IMPOSITION OF ADDITIONAL FEE.

"(a) In addition to any other fee imposed by law, there is hereby imposed a fee on all articles entered, or withdrawn from warehouse, for consumption in the customs territory of the United States during any fiscal year.

"(b)(1) The rate of the fee imposed by subsection (a) shall be a uniform ad valorem rate proclaimed by the President that is equal to the lesser of—

"(A) 0.15 percent, or

"(B) the percentage that is sufficient to provide the funding necessary to—

"(i) carry out the provisions of chapters 2 and 3, and

"(ii) repay any advances made under section 286(e).

"(2) The President shall issue a proclamation setting forth the rate of the fee imposed by subsection (a) by no later than the date that is 15 days before the first date on which a fee is imposed under subsection (a).

"(3)(A) For each fiscal year succeeding the first fiscal year in which a fee is imposed under subsection (a), the President shall issue a proclamation adjusting the rate of the fee imposed by subsection (a) during such fiscal year to the ad valorem rate that meets the requirements of paragraph (1) for such fiscal year.

"(B) Any proclamation issued under subparagraph (A) for a fiscal year shall be issued at least 30 days before the beginning of such fiscal year.

"(c)(1) Except as otherwise provided in this subsection, duty-free treatment provided with respect to any article under any other provision of law shall not prevent the imposition of a fee with respect to such article by subsection (a).

"(2) No fee shall be imposed by subsection (a) with respect to—

"(A) any article (other than an article provided for in item 870.40, 870.45, 870.50, 870.55, or 870.60 of the Tariff Schedules of the United States) that is treated as duty-free under schedule 8 of the Tariff Schedules of the United States, or

"(B) any article which has a value of less than $1,000.".

SEC. 1429. STUDY OF CERTIFICATION METHODS.

(a) IN GENERAL.—The Secretary of Labor, in consultation with the Secretary of Commerce, shall conduct a study of the methods (including, but not limited to, industry-wide certification) that could be used to expedite the certification of workers under subchapter A of chapter 2 of title II of the Trade Act of 1974.

(b) REPORT.—By no later than the date that is 6 months after the date of enactment of this Act, the Secretary of Labor shall submit to the Congress a report on the study conducted under subsection (a). The report shall include the recommendations of the Secretary of Labor regarding the methods that are the subject of the study conducted under subsection (a).

SEC. 1430. EFFECTIVE DATES.

(a) IN GENERAL.—Except as otherwise provided by this section, the amendments made by this part shall take effect on the date of enactment of this Act.

(b) ADDITIONAL FEE.—

(1) Except as otherwise provided in this subsection, the amendment made by section 1428(b) shall apply (if at all) to any article entered, or withdrawn from warehouse for consumption, after the date that is 30 days after the earlier of—

(A) the date on which the President submits to the Congress the written statement described in section 1428(a)(3)(A),

(B) the date that is 2 years after the date of enactment of this Act, or

(C) the date of the enactment of a disapproval resolution that passes both Houses of the Congress within the 90-day period beginning on the date that is 2 years after the date of enactment of this Act.

(2) If the President determines on the date that is 2 years after the date of enactment of this Act that the fee imposed by the amendment made by section 1428(b) is not in the national economic interest, subparagraph (B) of paragraph (1) shall not be taken into account in applying the provisions of paragraph (1).

(3) The amendment made by section 1428(b) shall apply (if at all) to the products of any foreign country described in section

1428(a)(1)(B) that are entered, or withdrawn from warehouse for consumption, after the later of—

(A) the first date on which the fee imposed by such amendment applies with respect to products of foreign countries that are not described in section 1428(a)(1)(B), or

(B) the date on which the President submits to the Congress the written statement described in section 1428(a)(3)(B) certifying the consent of such foreign country to the imposition of the fee.

(c) TRUST FUND.—The amendments made by section 1427 shall take effect on the first date on which the amendment made by section 1428(b) applies with respect to any articles.

(d) ELIGIBILITY OF WORKERS AND FIRMS.—The amendments made by sections 1421(b) and 1424(b) shall take effect on the date that is 1 year after the first date on which the amendment made by section 1428(b) applies with respect to any articles.

(e) NOTIFICATION REQUIREMENTS.—The amendments made by section 1422 shall take effect on the date that is 30 days after the date of enactment of this Act.

(f) TRAINING REQUIREMENT.—The amendments made by subsections (a), (b)(2), and (c)(2) of section 1423 and by paragraphs (2) and (3) of section 1424(c) shall take effect on the date that is 90 days after the date of enactment of this Act.

(g) LIMITATION ON PERIOD FOR WHICH TRADE READJUSTMENT ALLOWANCES MAY BE MADE.—The amendment made by section 1425(a) shall not apply to with respect to any total separation of a worker from adversely affected employment (within the meaning of section 247 of such Act) that occurs before the date of enactment of this Act if the application of such amendment with respect to such total separation would reduce the period for which such worker would (but for such amendment) be allowed to receive trade readjustment allowances under part I of subchapter B of chapter 2 of title II of the Trade Act of 1974.

Subtitle E—National Security

SEC. 1501. IMPORTS THAT THREATEN NATIONAL SECURITY.

(a) IN GENERAL.—Section 232 of the Trade Expansion Act of 1962 (19 U.S.C. 1862) is amended—

(1) by striking out "subsection (b)" each place it appears in subsection (e) and inserting in lieu thereof "subsection (c)",

(2) by redesignating subsections (c), (d), and (e) as subsections (d), (e), and (f), respectively, and

(3) by striking out subsection (b) and inserting in lieu thereof the following new subsections:

"(b)(1)(A) Upon request of the head of any department or agency, upon application of an interested party, or upon his own motion, the Secretary of Commerce (hereafter in this section referred to as the 'Secretary') shall immediately initiate an appropriate investigation to determine the effects on the national security of imports of the article which is the subject of such request, application, or motion.

"(B) The Secretary shall immediately provide notice to the Secretary of Defense of any investigation initiated under this section.

"(2)(A) In the course of any investigation conducted under this subsection, the Secretary shall—

"(i) consult with the Secretary of Defense regarding the methodological and policy questions raised in any investigation initiated under paragraph (1),

"(ii) seek information and advice from, and consult with, appropriate officers of the United States, and

"(iii) if it is appropriate and after reasonable notice, hold public hearings or otherwise afford interested parties an opportunity to present information and advice relevant to such investigation.

"(B) Upon the request of the Secretary, the Secretary of Defense shall provide the Secretary an assessment of the defense requirements of any article that is the subject of an investigation conducted under this section.

"(3)(A) By no later than the date that is 270 days after the date on which an investigation is initiated under paragraph (1) with respect to any article, the Secretary shall submit to the President a report on the findings of such investigation with respect to the effect of the importation of such article in such quantities or under such circumstances upon the national security and, based on such findings, the recommendations of the Secretary for action or inaction under this section. If the Secretary finds that such article is being imported into the United States in such quantities or under such circumstances as to threaten to impair the national security, the Secretary shall so advise the President in such report.

"(B) Any portion of the report submitted by the Secretary under subparagraph (A) which does not contain classified information or proprietary information shall be published in the Federal Register.

"(4) The Secretary shall prescribe such procedural regulations as may be necessary to carry out the provisions of this subsection.

"(c)(1)(A) Within 90 days after receiving a report submitted under subsection (b)(3)(A) in which the Secretary finds that an article is being imported into the United States in such quantities or under such circumstances as to threaten to impair the national security, the President shall—

"(i) determine whether the President concurs with the finding of the Secretary, and

"(ii) if the President concurs, determine the nature and duration of the action that, in the judgment of the President, must be taken to adjust the imports of the article and its derivatives so that such imports will not threaten to impair the national security.

"(B) If the President determines under subparagraph (A) to take action to adjust imports of an article and its derivatives, the President shall implement that action by no later than the date that is 15 days after the day on which the President determines to take action under subparagraph (A).

"(2) By no later than the date that is 30 days after the date on which the President makes any determinations under paragraph (1), the President shall submit to the Congress a written statement of the reasons why the President has decided to take action, or refused to take action, under paragraph (1). Such statement shall be included in the report published under subsection (e).

"(3)(A) If—

"(i) the action taken by the President under paragraph (1) is the negotiation of an agreement which limits or restricts the importation into, or the exportation to, the United States of the article that threatens to impair national security, and "(ii) either—

"(I) no such agreement is entered into before the date that is 180 days after the date on which the President makes the determination under paragraph (1)(A) to take such action, or

"(II) such an agreement that has been entered into is not being carried out or is ineffective in eliminating the threat to the national security posed by imports of such article,

the President shall take such other actions as the President deems necessary to adjust the imports of such article so that such imports will not threaten to impair the national security. The President shall publish in the Federal Register notice of any additional actions being taken under this section by reason of this subparagraph.

"(B) If—

"(i) clauses (i) and (ii) of subparagraph (A) apply, and

"(ii) the President determines not to take any additional actions under this subsection,

the President shall publish in the Federal Register such determination and the reasons on which such determination is based.".

(b) Reports.—

(1) Subsection (e) of section 232 of the Trade Expansion Act of 1962 (19 U.S.C. 1862), as redesignated by subsection (a)(2), is amended to read as follows:

"(d)(1) Upon the disposition of each request, application, or motion under subsection (b), the Secretary shall submit to the Congress, and publish in the Federal Register, a report on such disposition.

"(2) The President shall submit to the Congress an annual report on the operation of the provisions of this section.".

(2) Section 127 (c) of the Trade Act of 1974 (19 U.S.C. 1863) is repealed.

(c) Enforcement of Machine Tool Import Arrangements.—

(1) The Secretary of Commerce is authorized to request the Secretary of the Treasury to carry out such actions as may be necessary or appropriate to ensure the attainment of the objectives of the machine tool decision of the President on May 20, 1986, and to enforce any quantitative limitation, restriction, or other terms contained in related bilateral arrangements. Such actions may include, but are not limited to, requirements that valid export licenses or other documentation issued by a foreign government be presented as a condition for the entry into the United States of assembled and unassembled machine tool products.

(2) For purposes of this subsection, the term "related bilateral arrangement" means any arrangement, agreement, or understanding entered into or undertaken, or previously entered into or undertaken, by the United States and any foreign country or customs union containing such quantitative limitations, restrictions, or other terms relating to the importation into, or exportation to, the United States of categories of assembled and unassembled machine tool products as may be necessary to implement such machine tool decision of May 20, 1986.

(d) Application of Amendments.—

(1) Except as otherwise provided under this subsection, the amendments made by this section shall apply with respect to investigations initiated under section 232(b) of the Trade Expansion Act of 1962 on or after the date of enactment of this Act.

(2) The provisions of subsection (c) of section 232 of the Trade Expansion Act of 1962, as amended by this section, shall apply with respect to any report submitted by the Secretary of Commerce to the President under section 232(b) of such Act after the date of enactment of this Act.

(3) By no later than the date that is 90 days after the date of enactment of this Act, the President shall make the determinations described in section 232(c)(1)(A) of the Trade Expansion Act of 1962, as amended by this section, with respect to any report—

(A) which was submitted by the Secretary of Commerce to the President under section 232(b) of such Act before the date of enactment of this Act, and

(B) with respect to which no action has been taken by the President before the date of enactment of this Act.

Subtitle F—Trade Agencies; Advice, Consultation, and Reporting Regarding Trade Matters

PART 1—FUNCTIONS AND ORGANIZATION OF TRADE AGENCIES

Subpart A—Office of the United States Trade Representative

SEC. 1601. FUNCTIONS.

(a) In General.—Section 141(c) of the Trade Act of 1974 (19 U.S.C. 2171(c)) is amended—

(1) by amending paragraph (1) to read as follows:

"(c)(1) The United States Trade Representative shall—

"(A) have primary responsibility for developing, and for coordinating the implementation of, United States international trade policy, including commodity matters, and, to the extent they are related to international trade policy, direct investment matters;

"(B) serve as the principal advisor to the President on international trade policy and shall advise the President on the impact of other policies of the United States Government on international trade;

"(C) have lead responsibility for the conduct of, and shall be the chief representative of the United States for, international trade negotiations, including commodity and direct investment negotiations, in which the United States participates;

"(D) issue and coordinate policy guidance to departments and agencies on basic issues of policy and interpretation arising in the exercise of international trade functions, to the extent necessary to assure the coordination of international trade policy and consistent with any other law;

"(E) act as the principal spokesman of the President on international trade;

"(F) report directly to the President and the Congress regarding, and be responsible to the President and the Congress for the administration of, trade agreements programs;

"(G) advise the President and Congress with respect to nontariff barriers to international trade, international commodity agreements, and other matters which are related to the trade agreements programs;

"(H) be responsible for making reports to Congress with respect to matters referred to in subparagraphs (C) and (F);

"(I) be chairman of the interagency trade organization established under section 242(a) of the Trade Expansion Act of 1962, and shall consult with and be advised by such organization in the performance of his functions; and

"(J) in addition to those functions that are delegated to the United States Trade Representative as of the date of the enactment of the Omnibus Trade and Competitiveness Act of 1988, be responsible for such other functions as the President may direct.";

(2) by redesignating paragraphs (2) and (3) as paragraphs (3) and (4), respectively; and

(3) by inserting after paragraph (1) the following:

"(2) It is the sense of Congress that the United States Trade Representative should—

"(A) be the senior representative on any body that the President may establish for the purpose of providing to the President advice on overall economic policies in which international trade matters predominate; and

"(B) be included as a participant in all economic summit and other international meetings at which international trade is a major topic.".

(b) Unfair Trade Practices.—Such section 141 is further amended—

(1) by redesignating subsections (d), (e), and (f) as subsections (e), (f), and (g), respectively; and

(2) by inserting after subsection (c) the following new subsection:

"(d)(1) In carrying out subsection (c) with respect to unfair trade practices, the United States Trade Representative shall—

"(A) coordinate the application of interagency resources to specific unfair trade practice cases;

"(B) identify, and refer to the appropriate Federal department or agency for consideration with respect to action, each act, policy, or practice referred to in the report required under section 181(b), or otherwise known to the United States Trade Representative on the basis of other available information, that may be an unfair trade practice that either—

"(i) is considered to be inconsistent with the provisions of any trade agreement and has a significant adverse impact on United States commerce, or

"(ii) has a significant adverse impact on domestic firms or industries that are either too small or financially weak to initiate proceedings under the trade laws;

"(C) identify practices having a significant adverse impact on United States commerce that the attainment of United States negotiating objectives would eliminate; and

"(D) identify, on a biennial basis, those United States Government policies and practices that, if engaged in by a foreign government, might constitute unfair trade practices under United States law.

"(2) For purposes of carrying out paragraph (1), the United States Trade Representative shall be assisted by an interagency unfair trade practices advisory committee composed of the Trade Representative, who shall chair the committee, and senior representatives of the following agencies, appointed by the respective heads of those agencies:

"(A) The Bureau of Economics and Business Affairs of the Department of State.

"(B) The United States and Foreign Commercial Services of the Department of Commerce.

"(C) The International Trade Administration (other than the United States and Foreign Commercial Service) of the Department of Commerce.

"(D) The Foreign Agricultural Service of the Department of Agriculture.

The United States Trade Representative may also request the advice of the United States International Trade Commission regarding the carrying out of paragraph (1).

"(3) For purposes of this subsection, the term 'unfair trade practice' means any act, policy, or practice that—

"(A) may be a subsidy with respect to which countervailing duties may be imposed under subtitle A of title VII;

"(B) may result in the sale or likely sale of foreign merchandise with respect to which antidumping duties may be imposed under subtitle B of title VII;

"(C) may be either an unfair method of competition, or an unfair act in the importation of articles into the United States, that is unlawful under section 337; or

"(D) may be an act, policy, or practice of a kind with respect to which action may be taken under title III of the Trade Act of 1974.".

Subpart B—United States International Trade Commission

SEC. 1611. SERVICE ON COMMISSION FOR PURPOSES OF DETERMINING ELIGIBILITY FOR DESIGNATION AS CHAIRMAN.

Section 330(c)(A)(i) of the Tariff Act of 1930 (19 U.S.C. 1330(c)(A)(i)) is amended by striking out "most recently appointed to" and inserting "with the shortest period of service on".

SEC. 1612. TREATMENT OF COMMISSION UNDER PAPERWORK REDUCTION ACT.

Section 330 of the Tariff Act of 1930 (19 U.S.C. 1330) is amended by adding at the end thereof the following new subsection:

"(f) The Commission shall be considered to be an independent regulatory agency for purposes of chapter 35 of title 44, United States Code.".

SEC. 1613. TREATMENT OF CONFIDENTIAL INFORMATION BY COMMISSION.

The first sentence of section 332(g) of the Tariff Act of 1930 (19 U.S.C. 1332(g)) is amended by striking out ", and shall report to Congress" and inserting ". However, the Commission may not release information which the Commission considers to be confidential business information unless the party submitting the confidential business information had notice, at the time of submission, that such information would be released by the Commission, or such party subsequently consents to the release of the information. The Commission shall report to Congress.".

SEC. 1614. TRADE REMEDY ASSISTANCE OFFICE.

Section 339 of the Tariff Act of 1930 (19 U.S.C. 1339) is amended—

(1) by amending subsection (a)—

(A) by striking out "a Trade" and inserting "a separate office to be known as the Trade", and

(B) by striking out ", upon request, concerning—" and inserting "upon request and shall, to the extent feasible, provide assistance and advice to interested parties concerning—"; and

(2) by amending subsection (b) to read as follows:

"(b) The Trade Remedy Assistance Office, in coordination with each agency responsible for administering a trade law, shall provide technical and legal assistance and advice to eligible small businesses to enable them—

"(1) to prepare and file petitions and applications (other than those which, in the opinion of the Office, are frivolous); and

"(2) to seek to obtain the remedies and benefits available under the trade laws, including any administrative review or administrative appeal thereunder.".

Subpart C—Interagency Trade Organization

SEC. 1621. FUNCTIONS AND ORGANIZATION.

(a) IN GENERAL.—Section 242 of the Trade Expansion Act of 1962 (19 U.S.C. 1872) is amended as follows:

(1) Subsection (a) is amended to read as follows:

"(a)(1) The President shall establish an interagency organization.

"(2) The functions of the organization are—

"(A) to assist, and make recommendations to, the President in carrying out the functions vested in him by the trade laws and to advise the United States Trade Representative (hereinafter in this section referred to as the 'Trade Representative') in carrying out the functions set forth in section 141 of the Trade Act of 1974;

"(B) to assist the President, and advise the Trade Representative, with respect to the development and implementation of the international trade policy objectives of the United States; and

"(C) to advise the President and the Trade Representative with respect to the relationship between the international trade policy objectives of the United States and other major policy areas which may significantly affect the overall international trade policy and trade competitiveness of the United States.

"(3) The interagency organization shall be composed of the following:

"(A) The Trade Representative, who shall be chairperson.

"(B) The Secretary of Commerce.

"(C) The Secretary of State.

"(D) The Secretary of the Treasury.

"(E) The Secretary of Agriculture.

"(F) The Secretary of Labor.

The Trade Representative may invite representatives from other agencies, as appropriate, to attend particular meetings if subject matters of specific functional interest to such agencies are under consideration. It shall meet at such times and with respect to such matters as the President or the Chairman shall direct.".

(2) Subsection (b) is amended by adding at the end thereof the following:

"In carrying out its functions under this subsection, the organization shall take into account the advice of the congressional advisers and private sector advisory committees, as well as that of any committee or other body established to advise the department, agency, or office which a member of the organization heads.".

(b) SENSE OF CONGRESS.—It is the sense of Congress that the interagency organization established under subsection (a) should be the principal interagency forum within the executive branch on international trade policy matters.

PART 2—ADVICE AND CONSULTATION REGARDING TRADE POLICY, NEGOTIATIONS, AND AGREEMENTS

SEC. 1631. INFORMATION AND ADVICE FROM PRIVATE AND PUBLIC SECTORS RELATING TO TRADE POLICY AND AGREEMENTS.

Section 135 of the Trade Act of 1974 (19 U.S.C. 2155) is amended to read as follows:

"SEC. 135. INFORMATION AND ADVICE FROM PRIVATE AND PUBLIC SECTORS.

"(a) IN GENERAL.—

"(1) ᐧ President shall seek information and advice from representative elements of the private sector and the non-Federal governmental sector with respect to—

"(A) negotiating objectives and bargaining positions before entering into a trade agreement under this title or section 1102 of the Omnibus Trade and Competitiveness Act of 1988;

"(B) the operation of any trade agreement once entered into; and

"(C) other matters arising in connection with the development, implementation, and administration of the trade policy of the United States, including those matters referred to in Reorganization Plan Number 3 of 1979 and Executive Order Numbered 12188, and the priorities for actions thereunder.

To the maximum extent feasible, such information and advice on negotiating objectives shall be sought and considered before the commencement of negotiations.

"(2) The President shall consult with representative elements of the private sector and the non-Federal governmental sector on the overall current trade policy of the United States. The consultations shall include, but are not limited to, the following elements of such policy:

"(A) The principal multilateral and bilateral trade negotiating objectives and the progress being made toward their achievement.

"(B) The implementation, operation, and effectiveness of recently concluded multilateral and bilateral trade agreements and resolution of trade disputes.

"(C) The actions taken under the trade laws of the United States and the effectiveness of such actions in achieving trade policy objectives.

"(D) Important developments in other areas of trade for which there must be developed a proper policy response.

"(3) The President shall take the advice received through consultation under paragraph (2) into account in determining the importance which should be placed on each major objective and negotiating position that should be adopted in order to achieve the overall trade policy of the United States.

"(b) ADVISORY COMMITTEE FOR TRADE POLICY AND NEGOTIATIONS.—

"(1) The President shall establish an Advisory Committee for Trade Policy and Negotiations to provide overall policy advice on matters referred to in subsection (a). The committee shall be composed of not more than 45 individuals and shall include representatives of non-Federal governments, labor, industry, agriculture, small business, service industries, retailers, and consumer interests. The committee shall be broadly representative of the key sectors and groups of the economy, particularly with respect to those sectors and groups which are affected by trade. Members of the committee shall be recommended by the United States Trade Representative and appointed by the President for a term of 2 years. An individual may be reappointed to committee for any number of terms. Appointments to the Committee shall be made without regard to political affiliation.

"(2) The committee shall meet as needed at the call of the United States Trade Representative or at the call of two-thirds of the members of the committee. The chairman of the committee shall be elected by the committee from among its members.

"(3) The United States Trade Representative shall make available to the committee such staff, information, personnel, and administrative services and assistance as it may reasonably require to carry out its activities.

"(c) GENERAL POLICY, SECTORAL, OR FUNCTIONAL ADVISORY COMMITTEES.—

"(1) The President may establish individual general policy advisory committees for industry, labor, agriculture, services, investment, defense, and other interests, as appropriate, to provide general policy advice on matters referred to in subsection (a). Such committees shall, insofar as is practicable, be representative of all industry, labor, agricultural, service, investment, defense, and other interests, respectively, including small business interests, and shall be organized by the United States Trade Representative and the Secretaries of Commerce, Defense, Labor, Agriculture, the Treasury, or other executive departments, as appropriate. The members of such committees shall be appointed by the United States Trade Representative in consultation with such Secretaries.

"(2) The President shall establish such sectoral or functional advisory committees as may be appropriate. Such committees shall, insofar as is practicable, be representative of all industry, labor, agricultural, or service interests (including small business interests) in the sector or functional areas concerned. In organizing such committees, the United States Trade Representative and the Secretaries of Commerce, Labor, Agriculture, the Treasury, or other executive departments, as appropriate, shall—

"(A) consult with interested private organizations; and
"(B) take into account such factors as—
"(i) patterns of actual and potential competition between United States industry and agriculture and foreign enterprise in international trade,
"(ii) the character of the nontariff barriers and other distortions affecting such competition,
"(iii) the necessity for reasonable limits on the number of such advisory committees,
"(iv) the necessity that each committee be reasonably limited in size, and
"(v) in the case of each sectoral committee, that the product lines covered by each committee be reasonably related.

"(3) The President—
"(A) may, if necessary, establish policy advisory committees representing non-Federal governmental interests to provide policy advice—
"(i) on matters referred to in subsection (a), and
"(ii) with respect to implementation of trade agreements, and
"(B) shall include as members of committees established under subparagraph (A) representatives of non-Federal governmental interests if he finds such inclusion appropriate after consultation by the United States Trade Representative with such representatives.

"(4) Appointments to each committee established under paragraph (1), (2), or (3) shall be made without regard to political affiliation.

"(d) POLICY, TECHNICAL, AND OTHER ADVICE AND INFORMATION.—Committees established under subsection (c) shall meet at the call of the United States Trade Representative and the Secretaries of Agriculture, Commerce, Labor, Defense, or other executive departments, as appropriate, to provide policy advice, technical advice and information, and advice on other factors relevant to the matters referred to in subsection (a).

"(e) MEETING OF ADVISORY COMMITTEES AT CONCLUSION OF NEGOTIATIONS.—
"(1) The Advisory Committee for Trade Policy and Negotiations, each appropriate policy advisory committee, and each sectoral or functional advisory committee, if the sector or area which such committee represents is affected, shall meet at the conclusion of negotiations for each trade agreement entered into under section 1102 of the Omnibus Trade and Competitiveness Act of 1988, to provide to the President, to Congress, and to the United States Trade Representative a report on such agreement. Each report that applies to a trade agreement entered into under section 1102 of the Omnibus Trade and Competitiveness Act of 1988 shall be provided under the preceding sentence not later than the date on which the President notifies the Congress under section 1103(a)(1)(A) of such Act of 1988 of his intention to enter into that agreement.

"(2) The report of the Advisory Committee for Trade Policy and Negotiations and each appropriate policy advisory committee shall include an advisory opinion as to whether and to what extent the agreement promotes the economic interests of the United States and achieves the applicable overall and principal negotiating objectives set forth in section 1101 of the Omnibus Trade and Competitiveness Act of 1988, as appropriate.

"(3) The report of the appropriate sectoral or functional committee under paragraph (1) shall include an advisory opinion as to whether the agreement provides for equity and reciprocity within the sector or within the functional area.

"(f) APPLICATION OF FEDERAL ADVISORY COMMITTEE ACT.—The provisions of the Federal Advisory Committee Act apply—

"(1) to the Advisory Committee for Trade Policy and Negotiations established under subsection (b); and

"(2) to all other advisory committees which may be established under subsection (c); except that the meetings of advisory committees established under subsections (b) and (c) shall be exempt from the requirements of subsections (a) and (b) of sections 10 and 11 of the Federal Advisory Committee Act (relating to open meetings, public notice, public participation, and public availability of documents), whenever and to the extent it is determined by the President or his designee that such meetings will be concerned with matters the disclosure of which would seriously compromise the development by the United States Government of trade policy, priorities, negotiating objectives or bargaining positions with respect to matters referred to in subsection (a), and that meetings may be called of such special task forces, plenary meetings of chairmen, or other such groups made up of members of the committees established under subsections (b) and (c).

"(g) TRADE SECRETS AND CONFIDENTIAL INFORMATION.—

"(1) Trade secrets and commercial or financial information which is privileged or confidential, and which is submitted in confidence by the private sector or non-Federal government to officers or employees of the United States in connection with trade negotiations, may be disclosed upon request to—

"(A) officers and employees of the United States designated by the United States Trade Representative;

"(B) members of the Committee on Ways and Means of the House of Representatives and the Committee on Finance of the Senate who are designated as official advisers under section 161(a)(1) or are designated by the chairmen of either such committee under section 161(b)(3)(A) and staff members of either such committee designated by the chairmen under section 161(b)(3)(A); and

"(C) members of any committee of the House or Senate or any joint committee of Congress who are designated as advisers under section 161(a)(2) or designated by the chairman of such committee under section 161(b)(3)(B) and staff members of such committee designated under section 161(b)(3)(B), but disclosure may be made under this subparagraph only with respect to trade secrets or commercial or financial information that is relevant to trade policy matters or negotiations that are within the legislative jurisdiction of such committee;

for use in connection with matters referred to in subsection (a).

"(2) Information other than that described in paragraph (1), and advice submitted in confidence by the private sector or non-Federal government to officers or employees of the United States, to the Advisory Committee for Trade Policy and Negotiations, or to any advisory committee established under subsection (c), in connection with matters referred to in subsection (a), may be disclosed upon request to—

"(A) the individuals described in paragraph (1); and

"(B) the appropriate advisory committee established under this section.

"(3) Information submitted in confidence by officers or employees of the United States to the Advisory Committee for Trade Policy and Negotiations, or to any advisory committee established under subsection (c), may be disclosed in accordance with rules issued by the United States Trade Representative and the Secretaries of Commerce, Labor, Defense, Agriculture, or other executive departments, as appropriate, after consultation with the relevant advisory committees established under subsection (c). Such rules shall define the categories of information which require restricted or confidential handling by such committee considering the extent to which public disclosure of such information can reasonably be expected to prejudice the development of trade policy, priorities, or United States negotiating objectives. Such rules shall, to the maximum extent feasible, permit meaningful consultations by advisory committee members with persons affected by matters referred to in subsection (a).

"(h) Advisory Committee Support.—The United States Trade Representative, and the Secretaries of Commerce, Labor, Defense, Agriculture, the Treasury, or other executive departments, as appropriate, shall provide such staff, information, personnel, and administrative services and assistance to advisory committees established under subsection (c) as such committees may reasonably require to carry out their activities.

"(i) Consultation With Advisory Committees; Procedures; Nonacceptance of Committee Advice or Recommendations.—It shall be the responsibility of the United States Trade Representative, in conjunction with the Secretaries of Commerce, Labor, Agriculture, the Treasury, or other executive departments, as appropriate, to adopt procedures for consultation with and obtaining information and advice from the advisory committees established under subsection (c) on a continuing and timely basis. Such consultation shall include the provision of information to each advisory committee as to—

"(1) significant issues and developments; and

"(2) overall negotiating objectives and positions of the United States and other parties;

with respect to matters referred to in subsection (a). The United States Trade Representative shall not be bound by the advice or recommendations of such advisory committees, but shall inform the advisory committees of significant departures from such advice or recommendations made. In addition, in the course of consultations with the Congress under this title, information on the advice and information provided by advisory committees shall be made available to congressional advisers.

"(j) Private Organizations or Groups.—In addition to any advisory committee established under this section, the President shall provide adequate, timely and continuing opportunity for the submission on an informal basis (and, if such information is submitted under the provisions of subsection (g), on a confidential basis) by private organizations or groups, representing government, labor, industry, agriculture, small business, service industries, consumer interests, and others, of statistics, data and other trade information, as well as policy recommendations, pertinent to any matter referred to in subsection (a).

"(k) SCOPE OF PARTICIPATION BY MEMBERS OF ADVISORY COMMITTEES.—Nothing contained in this section shall be construed to authorize or permit any individual to participate directly in any negotiation of any matters referred to in subsection (a). To the maximum extent practicable, the members of the committees established under subsections (b) and (c), and other appropriate parties, shall be informed and consulted before and during any such negotiations. They may be designated as advisors to a negotiating delegation, and may be permitted to participate in international meetings to the extent the head of the United States delegation deems appropriate. However, they may not speak or negotiate for the United States.

"(l) ADVISORY COMMITTEES ESTABLISHED BY DEPARTMENT OF AGRICULTURE.—The provisions of title XVIII of the Food and Agriculture Act of 1977 (7 U.S.C. 2281 et seq.) shall not apply to any advisory committee established under subsection (c).

"(m) NON-FEDERAL GOVERNMENT DEFINED.—As used in this section, the term 'non-Federal government' means—

"(1) any State, territory, or possession of the United States, or the District of Columbia, or any political subdivision thereof; or

"(2) any agency or instrumentality of any entity described in paragraph (1).".

SEC. 1632. CONGRESSIONAL LIAISON REGARDING TRADE POLICY AND AGREEMENTS.

Section 161 of the Trade Act of 1974 (19 U.S.C. 2211) is amended to read as follows:

"SEC. 161. CONGRESSIONAL ADVISERS FOR TRADE POLICY AND NEGOTIATIONS.

"(a) SELECTION.—

"(1) At the beginning of each regular session of Congress, the Speaker of the House of Representatives, upon the recommendation of the chairman of the Committee on Ways and Means, shall select 5 members (not more than 3 of whom are members of the same political party) of such committee, and the President pro tempore of the Senate, upon the recommendation of the chairman of the Committee on Finance, shall select 5 members (not more than 3 of whom are members of the same political party) of such committee, who shall be designated congressional advisers on trade policy and negotiations. They shall provide advice on the development of trade policy and priorities for the implementation thereof. They shall also be accredited by the United States Trade Representative on behalf of the President as official advisers to the United States delegations to international conferences, meetings, and negotiating sessions relating to trade agreements.

"(2)(A) In addition to the advisers designated under paragraph (1) from the Committee on Ways and Means and the Committee on Finance—

"(i) the Speaker of the House may select additional members of the House, for designation as congressional advisers regarding specific trade policy matters or negotiations, from any other committee of the House or joint committee of Congress that has jurisdiction over legislation likely to be affected by such matters or negotiations; and

"(ii) the President pro tempore of the Senate may select additional members of the Senate, for designation as congressional advisers regarding specific trade policy matters or negotiations, from any other committee of the Senate or joint committee of Congress that has jurisdiction over legislation likely to be affected by such matters or negotiations.

Members of the House and Senate selected as congressional advisers under this subparagraph shall be accredited by the United States Trade Representative.

"(B) Before designating any member under subparagraph (A), the Speaker or the President pro tempore shall consult with—

"(i) the chairman and ranking member of the Committee on Ways and Means or the Committee on Finance, as appropriate; and

"(ii) the chairman and ranking minority member of the committee from which the member will be selected.

"(C) Not more than 3 members (not more than 2 of whom are members of the same political party) may be selected under this paragraph as advisers from any committee of Congress.

"(b) BRIEFING.—

"(1) The United States Trade Representative shall keep each official adviser designated under subsection (a)(1) currently informed on matters affecting the trade policy of the United States and, with respect to possible agreements, negotiating objectives, the status of negotiations in progress, and the nature of any changes in domestic law or the administration thereof which may be recommended to Congress to carry out any trade agreement or any requirement of, amendment to, or recommendation under, such agreement.

"(2) The United States Trade Representative shall keep each official adviser designated under subsection (a)(2) currently informed regarding the trade policy matters and negotiations with respect to which the adviser is designated.

"(3)(A) The chairmen of the Committee on Ways and Means and the Committee on Finance may designate members (in addition to the official advisers under subsection (a)(1)) and staff members of their respective committees who shall have access to the information provided to official advisers under paragraph (1).

"(B) The Chairman of any committee of the House or Senate or any joint committee of Congress from which official advisers are selected under subsection (a)(2) may designate other members of such committee, and staff members of such committee, who shall have access to the information provided to official advisers under paragraph (2).

"(c) COMMITTEE CONSULTATION.—The United States Trade Representative shall consult on a continuing basis with the Committee on Ways and Means of the House of Representatives, the Committee on Finance of the Senate, and the other appropriate committees of the House and Senate on the development, implementation, and administration of overall trade policy of the United States. Such consultations shall include, but are not limited to, the following elements of such policy:

"(1) The principal multilateral and bilateral negotiating objectives and the progress being made toward their achievement.

"(2) The implementation, administration, and effectiveness of recently concluded multilateral and bilateral trade agreements and resolution of trade disputes.

"(3) The actions taken, and proposed to be taken, under the trade laws of the United States and the effectiveness, or anticipated effectiveness, of such actions in achieving trade policy objectives.

"(4) The important developments and issues in other areas of trade for which there must be developed proper policy response.

When necessary, meetings shall be held with each Committee in executive session to review matters under negotiation.".

PART 3—ANNUAL REPORTS AND NATIONAL TRADE POLICY AGENDA

SEC. 1641. REPORTS AND AGENDA.

Section 163 of the Trade Act of 1974 (19 U.S.C. 2213) is amended to read as follows:

"SEC. 163. REPORTS.

"(a) ANNUAL REPORT ON TRADE AGREEMENTS PROGRAM AND NATIONAL TRADE POLICY AGENDA.—

"(1) The President shall submit to the Congress during each calendar year (but not later than March 1 of that year) a report on—

"(A) the operation of the trade agreements program, and the provision of import relief and adjustment assistance to workers and firms, under this Act during the preceding calendar year; and

"(B) the national trade policy agenda for the year in which the report is submitted.

"(2) The report shall include, with respect to the matters referred to in paragraph (1)(A), information regarding—

"(A) new trade negotiations;

"(B) changes made in duties and nontariff barriers and other distortions of trade of the United States;

"(C) reciprocal concessions obtained;

"(D) changes in trade agreements (including the incorporation therein of actions taken for import relief and compensation provided therefor);

"(E) the extension or withdrawal of nondiscriminatory treatment by the United States with respect to the products of foreign countries;

"(F) the extension, modification, withdrawal, suspension, or limitation of preferential treatment to exports of developing countries;

"(G) the results of actions to obtain the removal of foreign trade restrictions (including discriminatory restrictions) against United States exports and the removal of foreign practices which discriminate against United States service industries (including transportation and tourism) and investment;

"(H) the measures being taken to seek the removal of other significant foreign import restrictions;

"(I) each of the referrals made under section 141(d)(1)(B) and any action taken with respect to such referral;

"(J) other information relating to the trade agreements program and to the agreements entered into thereunder; and

"(K) the number of applications filed for adjustment assistance for workers and firms, the number of such applications which were approved, and the extent to which adjustment assistance has been provided under such approved applications.

"(3)(A) The national trade policy agenda required under paragraph (1)(B) for the year in which a report is submitted shall be in the form of a statement of—

"(i) the trade policy objectives and priorities of the United States for the year, and the reasons therefor;

"(ii) the actions proposed, or anticipated, to be undertaken during the year to achieve such objectives and priorities, including, but not limited to, actions authorized under the trade laws and negotiations with foreign countries;

"(iii) any proposed legislation necessary or appropriate to achieve any of such objectives or priorities; and

"(iv) the progress that was made during the preceding year in achieving the trade policy objectives and priorities included in the statement provided for that year under this paragraph.

"(B) The President may separately submit any information referred to in subparagraph (A) to the Congress in confidence if the President considers confidentiality appropriate.

"(C) Before submitting the national trade policy agenda for any year, the President shall seek advice from the appropriate advisory committees established under section 135 and shall consult with the appropriate committees of the Congress.

"(D) The United States Trade Representative (hereafter referred to in this section as the 'Trade Representative') and other appropriate officials of the United States Government shall consult periodically with the appropriate committees of the Congress regarding the annual objectives and priorities set forth in each national trade policy agenda with respect to—

"(i) the status and results of the actions that have been undertaken to achieve the objectives and priorities; and

"(ii) any development which may require, or result in, changes to any of such objectives or priorities.

"(b) Annual Trade Projection Report.—

"(1) In order for the Congress to be informed of the impact of foreign trade barriers and macroeconomic factors on the balance of trade of the United States, the Trade Representative and the Secretary of the Treasury shall jointly prepare and submit to the Committee on Finance of the Senate and the Committee on Ways and Means of the House of Representatives (hereafter referred to in this subsection as the 'Committees') on or before March 1 of each year a report which consists of—

"(A) a review and analysis of—

"(i) the merchandise balance of trade,

"(ii) the goods and services balance of trade,

"(iii) the balance on the current account,

"(iv) the external debt position,

"(v) the exchange rates,

"(vi) the economic growth rates,

"(vii) the deficit or surplus in the fiscal budget, and

"(viii) the impact on United States trade of market barriers and other unfair practices,

of countries that are major trading partners of the United States, including, as appropriate, groupings of such countries;

"(B) projections for each of the economic factors described in subparagraph (A) (except those described in clauses (v) and (viii)) for each of the countries and groups of countries referred to in subparagraph (A) for the year in which the report is submitted and for the succeeding year; and

"(C) conclusions and recommendations, based upon the projections referred to in subparagraph (B), for policy changes, including trade policy, exchange rate policy, fiscal policy, and other policies that should be implemented to improve the outlook.

"(2) To the extent that subjects referred to in paragraph (1) (A), (B), or (C) are covered in the national trade policy agenda required under subsection (a)(1)(B) or in other reports required by this Act or other law, the Trade Representative and the Secretary of the Treasury may, as appropriate, draw on the information, analysis, and conclusions, if any, in those reports for the purposes of preparing the report required by this subsection.

"(3) The Trade Representative and the Secretary of the Treasury shall consult with the Chairman of the Board of Governors of the Federal Reserve System in the preparation of each report required under this subsection.

"(4) The Trade Representative and the Secretary of the Treasury may separately submit any information, analysis, or conclusion referred to in paragraph (1) to the Committees in confidence if the Trade Representative and the Secretary consider confidentiality appropriate.

"(5) After submission of each report required under paragraph (1), the Trade Representative and the Secretary of the Treasury shall consult with each of the Committees with respect to the report.

"(c) ITC REPORTS.—The United States International Trade Commission shall submit to the Congress, at least once a year, a factual report on the operation of the trade agreements program.".

Subtitle H—Miscellaneous Customs, Trade, and Other Provisions

PART 1—CUSTOMS PROVISIONS

SEC. 1901. ENFORCEMENT OF THE RESTRICTIONS AGAINST IMPORTED PORNOGRAPHY.

(a) IN GENERAL.—Section 305 of the Tariff Act of 1930 (19 U.S.C. 1305) is amended as follows:

(1) The second paragraph of subsection (a) is designated as subsection (b) and the following side heading, appropriately indented, is inserted before "Upon" at the beginning of the paragraph: "(b) ENFORCEMENT PROCEDURES.—".

(2) The second sentence of subsection (b) (as redesignated by paragraph (1)) is amended to read as follows: "Upon the seizure of such book or matter, such customs officer shall transmit information thereof to the United States attorney of the district in which is situated either—

"(1) the office at which such seizure took place; or

"(2) the place to which such book or matter is addressed;

and the United States attorney shall institute proceedings in the district court for the forfeiture, confiscation, and destruction of the book or matter seized.".

(3) The following new subsections are added at the end thereof:

"(c) Notwithstanding the provisions of subsections (a) and (b), whenever a customs officer discovers any obscene material after such material has been imported or brought into the United States, or attempted to be imported or brought into the United States, he may refer the matter to the United States attorney for the institution of forfeiture proceedings under this section. Such proceedings shall begin no more than 30 days after the time the material is seized; except that no seizure or forfeiture shall be invalidated for delay if the claimant is responsible for extending the action beyond the allowable time limits or if proceedings are postponed pending the consideration of constitutional issues.

"(d) Upon motion of the United States, a court shall stay such civil forfeiture proceedings commenced under this section pending the completion of any related criminal matter.".

(b) EFFECTIVE DATE.—The amendments made by subsection (a) apply with respect to articles entered, or withdrawn from warehouse for consumption, on or after the 15th day after the date of the enactment of this Act.

SEC. 1902. TARE ON CRUDE OIL AND PETROLEUM PRODUCTS.

(a) IN GENERAL.—Section 507 of the Tariff Act of 1930 (19 U.S.C. 1507) is amended—

(1) by striking out "The Secretary" and inserting in lieu thereof "(a) IN GENERAL.—The Secretary",

(2) by striking out "in no case shall there be" and inserting in lieu thereof "(except as otherwise provided in this section) there shall not be", and

(3) by adding at the end thereof the following new subsection:

"(b) CRUDE OIL AND PETROLEUM PRODUCTS.—In ascertaining tare on imports of crude oil, and on imports of petroleum products, allowance shall be made for all detectable moisture and impurities present in, or upon, the imported crude oil or petroleum products.".

(b) EFFECTIVE DATE.—The amendment made by this section shall apply with respect to articles entered, or withdrawn from warehouse for consumption, after October 1, 1987.

SEC. 1903. ELIGIBLE ARTICLES UNDER THE GENERALIZED SYSTEM OF PREFERENCES.

Section 503(c)(1)(B) of the Trade Act of 1974 (19 U.S.C. 2463(c)(1)(B)) is amended to read as follows:

"(B) watches, except those watches entered after June 30, 1989, that the President specifically determines, after public notice and comment, will not cause material injury to watch or watch band, strap, or bracelet manufacturing and assembly operations in the United States or the United States insular possessions,".

SEC. 1904. CUSTOMS BOND CANCELLATION STANDARDS.

Section 623(c) of the Tariff Act of 1930 (19 U.S.C. 1623(c)) is amended by adding at the end thereof the following new sentence: "In order to assure uniform, reasonable, and equitable decisions, the Secretary of the Treasury shall publish guidelines establishing standards for setting the terms and conditions for cancellation of bonds or charges thereunder.".

SEC. 1905. CUSTOMS SERVICES AT PONTIAC/OAKLAND, MICHIGAN, AIRPORT.

Section 236 of the Trade and Tariff Act of 1984 (19 U.S.C. 586) is amended—

(1) by striking out "and" at the end of subsection (a)(1);

(2) by redesignating paragraph (2) of subsection (a) as paragraph (3);

(3) by inserting after paragraph (1) of subsection (a) the following new paragraph:

"(2) the airport located at Pontiac/Oakland, Michigan, and"; and

(4) by striking out "20" in subsection (c).

SEC. 1906. SENSE OF CONGRESS REQUESTING THE PRESIDENT TO INSTRUCT THE SECRETARY OF THE TREASURY TO ENFORCE SECTION 307 OF THE TARIFF ACT OF 1930 WITHOUT DELAY.

(a) CONGRESSIONAL FINDINGS.—The Congress finds that—

(1) its February 1983 report to the Congress on forced labor in the Union of Soviet Socialist Republics, the Department of State confirmed that Soviet forced labor is used "to produce large amounts of primary and manufactured goods for both domestic and Western export markets", and that such labor is used as an integral part of Soviet national economy;

(2) the Central Intelligence Agency has compiled a list of over three dozen products made by Soviet forced labor and imported by the United States, and that items on the September 27, 1983 list include chemicals, gold, uranium, aluminum, wood products and glassware;

(3) the International Commission on Human Rights has concluded that the Soviet Union "continues the deplorable practice of forced labor in manufacturing and construction projects" and that prisoners "are forced to work under conditions of extreme

hardship including malnutrition, inadequate shelter and clothing, and severe discipline";

(4) the Congress is on record as opposing forced labor, having enacted a prohibition (in section 307 of the Tariff Act of 1930 (19 U.S.C. 1307)) on the importation of goods made with such labor and having passed in the Ninety-eighth Congress by unanimous vote a resolution calling such practices morally reprehensible and calling upon the President to express to the Soviet Union the opposition of the United States to such policies;

(5) the prohibition enacted by the Congress declares that "goods, wares, articles, and merchandise mined, produced or manufactured wholly or in part in any foreign country by convict labor or/and forced labor or/and indentured labor under penal sanctions shall not be entitled to entry at any of the ports of the United States, and the importation thereof is hereby prohibited";

(6) there is ample knowledge of the Soviet forced labor system to require enforcement of the prohibition contained in section 307 of the Tariff Act of 1930 (19 U.S.C. 1307); and

(7) the delay in enforcing the law brings into question the commitment of the United States to protest the inhumane treatment of prisoners in the Soviet Gulag, an estimated ten thousand of whom are political and religious prisoners according to the Department of State.

(b) SENSE OF CONGRESS.—It is the sense of the Congress that the President should express to the Soviet Union in the firmest possible terms the strong moral opposition of the United States to the slave labor policies of the Soviet Union by every means possible, including refusing to permit the importation into the United States of any products made in whole or in part by such labor.

(c) PRESIDENTIAL ACTION.—The President is hereby requested to instruct the Secretary of the Treasury to enforce section 307 of the Tariff Act of 1930 (19 U.S.C. 1307) without delay.

SEC. 1907. IMPORT MARKING PROVISIONS.

(a) INCREASE IN PENALTY FOR VIOLATIONS OF COUNTRY-OF-ORIGIN MARKING REQUIREMENTS.—

(1) Section 304(h) of the Tariff Act of 1930 (19 U.S.C. 1304(h)) is amended to read as follows:

"(h) PENALTIES.—Any person who, with intent to conceal the information given thereby or contained therein, defaces, destroys, removes, alters, covers, obscures, or obliterates any mark required under the provisions of this Act shall—

"(1) upon conviction for the first violation of this subsection, be fined not more than $100,000, or imprisoned for not more than 1 year, or both; and

"(2) upon conviction for the second or any subsequent violation of this subsection, be fined not more than $250,000, or imprisoned for not more than 1 year, or both.".

(2)(A) The amendment made by paragraph (1) applies with respect to acts committed on or after the date of the enactment of this Act.

(B) The conviction of a person under section 304(h) of the Tariff Act of 1930 for an act committed before the date of the enactment of this Act shall be disregarded for purposes of applying paragraph (2) of such subsection (as added by the amendment made by paragraph (1) of this subsection.

(b) MARKING OF CONTAINERS OF IMPORTED MUSHROOMS.—Imported preserved mushrooms shall not be considered to be in compliance with section 304 of the Tariff Act of 1930 (19 U.S.C. 1304) or any other law relating to the marking of imported articles unless the containers thereof indicate in English the country in which the mushrooms were grown.

(c) NATIVE-AMERICAN STYLE JEWELRY AND NATIVE-AMERICAN STYLE ARTS AND CRAFTS.—By no later than the date that is 1 year after the date of enactment of this Act, the Secretary of the Treasury shall prescribe and implement regulations under section 304 of the Tariff Act of 1930 (19 U.S.C. 1304) which require, to the greatest extent possible, that all Native-American style jewelry and Native-American style arts and crafts that are imported into the United States have the English name of the country of origin of such jewelry or arts and crafts indelibly marked in a conspicuous place on such jewelry or arts and crafts by a permanent method of marking.

SEC. 1908. DUTY-FREE SALES ENTERPRISES.

(a) FINDINGS.—The Congress finds that—

(1) duty-free sales enterprises play a significant role in attracting international passengers to the United States and thereby their operations favorably affect our balance of payments;

(2) concession fees derived from the operations of authorized duty-free sales enterprises constitute an important source of revenue for the State, local and other governmental authorities that collect such fees;

(3) there is inadequate statutory and regulatory recognition of, and guidelines for the operation of, duty-free sales enterprises; and

(4) there is a need to encourage uniformity and consistency of regulation of duty-free sales enterprises.

(b) IN GENERAL.—Section 555(b) of the Tariff Act of 1930 (19 U.S.C. 1555(b)) is amended to read as follows:

"(b) DUTY-FREE SALES ENTERPRISES.—

"(1) Duty-free sales enterprises may sell and deliver for export from the customs territory duty-free merchandise in accordance with this subsection and such regulations as the Secretary may prescribe to carry out this subsection.

"(2) A duty-free sales enterprise may be located anywhere within—

"(A) the same port of entry, as established under section 1 of the Act of August 24, 1912 (37 Stat. 434), from which a purchaser of duty-free merchandise departs the customs territory; or

"(B) 25 statute miles from the exit point through which the purchaser of duty-free merchandise will depart the customs territory.

"(3) Each duty-free sales enterprise—

"(A) shall establish procedures to provide reasonable assurance that duty-free merchandise sold by the enterprise will be exported from the customs territory;

"(B) if the duty-free sales enterprise is an airport store, shall establish and enforce, in accordance with such regulations as the Secretary may prescribe, restrictions on the sale of duty-free merchandise to any one individual to personal use quantities;

"(C) shall display in prominent places within its place of business notices which state clearly that any duty-free merchandise purchased from the enterprise—

"(i) has not been subject to any Federal duty or tax,

"(ii) if brought back into the customs territory, must be declared and is subject to Federal duty and tax, and

"(iii) is subject to the customs laws and regulation of any foreign country to which it is taken;

"(D) shall not be required to mark or otherwise place a distinguishing identifier on individual items of merchandise to indicate that the items were sold by a duty-free sales enterprise, unless the Secretary finds a pattern in which such items are being brought back into the customs territory without declaration;

"(E) may unpack merchandise into saleable units after it has been entered for warehouse and placed in a duty-free sales enterprise, without requirement of further permits; and

"(F) shall deliver duty-free merchandise—

"(i) in the case of a duty-free sales enterprise that is an airport store—

"(I) to the purchaser (or a family member or companion traveling with the purchaser) in an area that is within the airport and to which access to passengers is restricted to those departing from the customs territory;

"(II) to the purchaser (or a family member or companion traveling with the purchaser) at the exit point of a specific departing flight;

"(III) by placing the merchandise within the aircraft on which the purchaser will depart for carriage as passenger baggage; or

"(IV) if the duty-free sales enterprise has made a good faith effort to effect delivery for exportation through one of the methods described in subclause (I), (II), or (III) but is unable to do so, by any other reasonable method to effect delivery; or

"(ii) in the case of a duty-free sales enterprise that is a border store—

"(I) at a merchandise storage location at or beyond the exit point; or

"(II) at any location approved by the Secretary before the date of enactment of the Omnibus Trade Act of 1987.

"(4) If a State or local or other governmental authority, incident to its jurisdiction over any airport, seaport, or other exit point facility, requires that a concession or other form of approval be obtained from that authority with respect to the operation of a duty-free sales enterprise under which merchandise is delivered to or through such facility for exportation, merchandise incident to such operation may not be withdrawn from a bonded warehouse and transferred to or through such facility unless the operator of the duty-free sales enterprise demonstrates to the Secretary that the concession or approval required for the enterprise has been obtained.

"(5) This subsection does not prohibit a duty-free sales enterprise from offering for sale and delivering to, or on behalf of, individuals departing from the customs territory merchandise other than duty-free merchandise, except that such other merchandise may not be stored in a bonded warehouse facility other than a bonded facility used for retail sales.

"(6) Merchandise that is purchased in a duty-free sales enterprise is not eligible for exemption from duty under subpart A of part 2 of schedule 8 of the Tariff Schedules of the United States if such merchandise is brought back to the customs territory.

"(7) The Secretary shall by regulation establish a separate class of bonded warehouses for duty-free sales enterprises. Regulations issued to carry out this paragraph shall take into account the unique characteristics of the different types of duty-free sales enterprises.

"(8) For purposes of this subsection—

"(A) The term 'airport store' means a duty-free sales enterprise which delivers merchandise to, or on behalf of, individuals departing from the customs territory from an international airport located within the customs territory.

"(B) The term 'border store' means a duty-free sales enterprise which delivers merchandise to, or on behalf of, individuals departing from the customs territory through a land or water border by a means of conveyance other than an aircraft.

"(C) The term 'customs territory' means the customs territory of the United States and foreign trade zones.

"(D) The term 'duty-free sales enterprise' means a person that sells, for use outside the customs territory, duty-free merchandise that is delivered from a bonded warehouse to an airport or other exit point for exportation by, or on behalf of, individuals departing from the customs territory.

"(E) The term 'duty-free merchandise' means merchandise sold by a duty-free sales enterprise on which neither Federal duty nor Federal tax has been assessed pending exportation from the customs territory.

"(F) The term 'exit point' means the area in close proximity to an actual exit for departing from the customs territory, including the gate holding area in the case of an airport, but only if there is reasonable assurance that duty-free merchandise delivered in the gate holding area will be exported from the customs territory.

"(G) The term 'personal use quantities' means quantities that are only suitable for uses other than resale, and includes reasonable quantities for household or family consumption as well as for gifts to others.".

(c) Effective Date.—The amendment made by this section shall take effect on the date that is 15 days after the date of enactment of this Act.

SEC. 1909. CARIBBEAN BASIN INITIATIVE.

(a) Findings.—The Congress finds that—

(1) Caribbean and Central American countries historically have had close economic, political, and cultural ties to the United States;

(2) promoting economic and political stability in the Caribbean and Central America is in the national security interests of the United States;

(3) the economic and political stability of the nations of the Caribbean and Central America can be stengthened significantly by the attraction of foreign and domestic investment specifically devoted to employment generation; and

(4) the diversification of the economies and expansion of exports, particularly those of a non-traditional nature, of the nations of the Caribbean and Central America is linked directly to fair access to the markets of the United States.

(b) INTENT OF THE CONGRESS.—The Congress hereby expresses its intention to ensure that—

(1) the trade elements of the Caribbean Basin Initiative be strengthened in a manner consistent with the promotion of economic and political stability in the Caribbean and Central America;

(2) to the extent that Congress imposes changes that are intended to improve the competitive environment for United States industry and workers, such changes do not unduly affect the unilateral duty-free trade system available to the beneficiary countries designated under the Caribbean Basin Economic Recovery Act; and

(3) generic changes in the trade laws of the United States do not discriminate against imports from designated beneficiary countries in relation to imports from other United States trading partners.

(c) WITHDRAWAL OR SUSPENSION OF DUTY-FREE TREATMENT TO SPECIFIC ARTICLES.—Subsection (e) of section 212 of the Caribbean Basin Economic Recovery Act (19 U.S.C. 2702(e)) is amended to read as follows:

"(e)(1) The President may, after the requirements of subsection (a)(2) and paragraph (2) have been met—

"(A) withdraw or suspend the designation of any country as a beneficiary country, or

"(B) withdraw, suspend, or limit the application of duty-free treatment under this subtitle to any article of any country,

if, after such designation, the President determines that as a result of changed circumstances such country would be barred from designation as a beneficiary country under subsection (b).

"(2)(A) The President shall publish in the Federal Register notice of the action the President proposes to take under paragraph (1) at least 30 days prior to taking such action.

"(B) The United States Trade Representative shall, within the 30-day period beginning on the date on which the President publishes under subparagraph (A) notice of proposed action—

"(i) accept written comments from the public regarding such proposed action,

"(ii) hold a public hearing on such proposed action, and

"(iii) publish in the Federal Register—

"(I) notice of the time and place of such hearing prior to the hearing, and

"(II) the time and place at which such written comments will be accepted.".

SEC. 1910. ETHYL ALCOHOL AND MIXTURES FOR FUEL USE.

(a) IN GENERAL.—Subsection (b) of section 423 of the Tax Reform Act of 1986 (19 U.S.C. 2703, note) is amended—

(1) by striking out "and 1988" in paragraphs (1) and (2) and inserting in lieu thereof ", 1988, and 1989",

(2) by striking out "an insular possession of the United States or" in paragraph (1)(A),

(3) by striking out "January 1, 1986, or" in paragraph (1)(A) and inserting in lieu thereof "July 1, 1987,",

(4) by inserting "or an insular possession of the United States" after "beneficiary country" in paragraph (1)(B)(ii)(II),

(5) by striking out the period at the end of paragraph (1)(B) and inserting in lieu thereof ", or",

(6) by inserting the following new subparagraph after subparagraph (B) of paragraph (1):

"(C) a distillation facility operated by a corporation which, before the date of enactment of the Omnibus Trade Act of 1987—

"(i) has completed engineering and design of a full-scale fermentation facility in the United States Virgin Islands, and

"(ii) has obtained authorization from authorities of the United States Virgin Islands to operate a full-scale fermentation facility.", and

(7) by striking out "or (B)" in paragraph (2) and inserting in lieu thereof ", (B), or (C)".

(b) STUDIES.—

(1) The United States International Trade Commission and the Comptroller General of the United States shall each immediately undertake a study regarding whether the definition of indigenous ethyl alcohol or mixtures thereof used in applying section 423 of the Tax Reform Act of 1986 is consistent with, and will contribute to the achievement of, the stated policy of Congress to encourage the economic development of the beneficiary countries under the Caribbean Basin Economic Recovery Act and the insular possessions of the United States through the maximum utilization of the natural resources of those countries and possessions. Each study shall specifically include—

(A) an assessment regarding whether the indigenous product percentage requirements set forth in subsection (c)(2)(B) of such section 423 are economically feasible for ethyl alcohol producers; and

(B) if the assessment under subparagraph (A) is negative, recommended modifications to the indigenous product percentage requirements that—

(i) will ensure meaningful production and employment in the region,

(ii) will discourage pass-through operations, and

(iii) will not result in harm to producers of ethyl alcohol, or mixtures thereof, in the United States; and

(C) an assessment of the effects of imports of ethyl alcohol, and mixtures thereof, from such beneficiary countries and possessions on producers of ethyl alcohol, and mixtures thereof, in the United States.

(2) The United States International Trade Commission and the Comptroller General of the United States shall each submit a report containing the findings and conclusions of the study carried out under this subsection to the Committee on Ways and Means of the House of Representatives and the Committee on Finance of the Senate before the 180th day after the date of the enactment of this Act.

SEC. 1911. ENFORCEMENT OF RESTRICTIONS ON IMPORTS FROM CUBA.

The United States Trade Representative shall request that all relevant agencies prepare appropriate recommendations for improving the enforcement of restrictions on the importation of articles from Cuba. Such recommendations should include, but not be limited to, appropriate measures to prevent indirect shipments or other means of circumvention. The United States Trade Representative shall, after considering such recommendations, report to the Congress, within 90 days after the date of enactment of this Act, on any administrative measures or proposed legislation which the United States Trade Representative considers necessary and appropriate to enforce restrictions on imports from Cuba.

SEC. 1912. CUSTOMS FORFEITURE FUND.

Section 613A of the Tariff Act of 1930 (19 U.S.C. 1613b) is amended—

(1) by striking out "beginning on the date of the enactment of this section, and ending on September 30, 1987," in subsection (c) and inserting in lieu thereof "described in subsection (a) for which the fund is available to the United States Customs Service,", and

(2) by striking out "private citizens" in subsection (a)(iii) and inserting in lieu thereof "private persons".

PART 2—MISCELLANEOUS TRADE PROVISIONS

SEC. 1931. TRADE STATISTICS.

(a) Reporting of Import Statistics.—Subsection (e) of section 301 of title 13, United States Code, is amended by striking out the last sentence thereof.

(b) Volumetric Index.—

(1) The Director of the Census, in consultation with the Director of the Bureau of Economic Analysis and the Commissioner of Labor Statistics, shall conduct a study to determine the feasibility of developing, and of publishing, an index that measures the real volume of merchandise trade on a monthly basis, which would be reported simultaneously with the balance of merchandise trade for the United States.

(2) The Director of the Census shall submit to the Committee on Finance of the Senate and the Committee on Ways and Means of the House of Representatives a report on the study conducted under paragraph (1) by no later than the date that is one year after the date of enactment of this Act.

SEC. 1932. ADJUSTMENT OF TRADE STATISTICS FOR INFLATION AND DEFLATION.

Subsection (e) of section 301 of title 13, United States Code, is amended by adding at the end thereof the following new sentence: "The information required to be reported under this subsection shall be reported in a form that is adjusted for economic inflation or deflation (on a constant dollar basis consistent with the reporting of the National Income and Product Accounts), and in a form that is not so adjusted.".

SEC. 1933. COAL EXPORTS TO JAPAN.

It is the sense of the Congress that—

(1) the objectives of the November 1983 Joint Policy Statement on Energy Cooperation, as it relates to United States exports of coal to Japan, have not been achieved;

(2) the President should seek to establish reciprocity with Japan with respect to metallurgical coal exports and steel product imports and should encourage increased purchases by Japan of United States steam coal;

(3) the President should direct the United States Trade Representative, in negotiating a Steel Trade Arrangement with Japan, to take into consideration, consistent with the President's steel program, the amount of coal that Japan purchases from the United States in determining the level of steel, semifinished steel and fabricated structured steel products that can be imported into the United States; and

(4) the President should report to the Congress by November 1, 1988 regarding the results of the outcome of any negotiation undertaken in response to this section.

SEC. 1934. PURCHASES OF UNITED STATES-MADE AUTOMOTIVE PARTS BY JAPAN.

(a) FINDINGS.—The Congress finds that—

(1) the United States merchandise trade deficit reached the unprecedented level of $170,000,000,000 in 1986;

(2) the United States trade deficit with Japan, which reached $59,000,000,000 in 1986, accounted for approximately one-third of the total deficit;

(3) approximately one-half of the United States trade deficit with Japan was in motor vehicles and equipment;

(4) while Japanese automobile firms based in Japan produced 7,800,000 passenger cars in 1986 and exported 2,300,000 cars to the United States, United States exports of auto parts to Japan were only about $300,000,000 in 1986;

(5) United States automotive parts producers meet increasingly rigorous requirements for quality, just-in-time supply, and competitive pricing in the United States market; and

(6) the market-oriented sector specific (MOSS) talks on auto parts are aimed at overcoming substantial market access barriers and increasing the access of United States auto parts producers to the original and replacement parts market represented by Japanese automobiles produced in Japan, the United States, and third countries.

(b) SENSE OF CONGRESS.—The Congress—

(1) strongly supports efforts being made by United States negotiators to expand significantly the opportunities for United States automotive parts producers to supply original and replacement parts for Japanese automobiles, wherever those automobiles may be produced; and

(2) determines that success of the MOSS talks will be measured by a significant increase in sales by United States auto parts companies to Japanese vehicle companies and the

initiation of long-term sourcing relationships between such companies.

(c) REPORT ON OUTCOME.—The United States Trade Representative and the Secretary of Commerce shall report to Congress at the conclusion of the MOSS talks on the outcome of the talks and on any agreements reached with Japan with respect to purchases by Japanese firms of United States automotive parts.

SEC. 1935. EFFECT OF IMPORTS ON CRUDE OIL PRODUCTION AND REFINING CAPACITY IN THE UNITED STATES.

The Secretary of Energy shall send to the Secretary of Commerce the results of the study conducted under section 3102 of the Omnibus Budget Reconciliation Act of 1986. Within 180 days of the receipt of the results of such study, the Secretary of Commerce shall report to the President and the Congress recommendations for actions which may be appropriate to address any impact of imports of crude oil and petroleum products on domestic crude oil exploration and production and the domestic petroleum refining capacity.

SEC. 1936. STUDY OF TRADE BARRIERS ESTABLISHED BY AUTO PRODUCING COUNTRIES TO AUTO IMPORTS AND THE IMPACT ON THE UNITED STATES MARKET.

(a) STUDY.—The United States Trade Representative shall conduct a study of formal and informal barriers which auto producing countries have established toward automobile imports and the impact of such barriers on diverting automobile imports into the United States. The study shall consider the impact of such barriers on automobile imports into the United States in the presence of, and in the absence of, voluntary restraint agreements between the United States and Japan.

(b) REPORT.—The United States Trade Representative shall include the findings of the study conducted under subsection (a) in the first report that is submitted under section 181(b) of the Trade Act of 1974 (19 U.S.C. 2241) after the date of enactment of this Act.

SEC. 1937. LAMB MEAT IMPORTS.

Within 15 days after the date of the enactment of this Act, the United States International Trade Commission, pursuant to section 332(g) of the Tariff Act of 1930 (19 U.S.C. 1332(g)), shall monitor and investigate for a period of 2 years the importation into the United States of articles provided for in item 106.30 of the Tariff Schedules of the United States (19 U.S.C. 1202) (relating to fresh, chilled, and frozen lamb meat). For purposes of any request made under subsection (d) of section 202 of the Trade Act of 1974 (as amended by section 1401 of this Act) within such 2-year period for provisional relief with respect to imports of such articles, the monitoring and investigation required under this section shall be treated as having been requested by the United States Trade Representative under paragraph (1)(B) of such subsection.

TITLE II—EXPORT ENHANCEMENT

SEC. 2001. SHORT TITLE.

This title may be referred to as the "Export Enhancement Act of 1988".

Subtitle A—Trade and Foreign Policy

PART I—RELATIONS WITH CERTAIN COUNTRIES

SEC. 2101. UNITED STATES-MEXICO FRAMEWORK AGREEMENT ON TRADE AND INVESTMENT.

(a) FINDINGS.—The Congress finds that the Bilateral Framework Agreement on Trade and Investment, entered into by the United States and Mexico on November 6, 1987—

(1) provides a useful vehicle for the management of bilateral trade and investment relations, based on shared principles and objectives;

(2) establishes procedures for consultation by the two countries on matters of bilateral trade and investment, and should facilitate resolution of disputes on these matters; and

(3) has led to negotiations between the two countries on important issues, and should continue to facilitate such negotiations.

(b) FURTHER IMPLEMENTATION OF THE AGREEMENT.—Within the context of the Bilateral Framework Agreement on Trade and Investment, the President is urged to continue to pursue consultations with representatives of the Government of Mexico for the purposes of implementing the Agreement and achieving an expansion of mutually beneficial trade and investment.

SEC. 2102. RELATIONS WITH COUNTRIES PROVIDING OFFENSIVE WEAPONRY TO BELLIGERENT COUNTRIES IN THE PERSIAN GULF REGION.

It is the sense of the Congress that the President should use all available appropriate leverage to persuade all countries to desist from any further transfers of offensive weaponry, such as Silkworm missiles, to any belligerent country in the Persian Gulf region.

PART II—FAIR TRADE IN AUTO PARTS

SEC. 2121. SHORT TITLE.

This part may be referred to as the "Fair Trade in Auto Parts Act of 1988".

SEC. 2122. DEFINITION.

For purposes of this part, the term "Japanese markets" refers to markets, including those in the United States and Japan, where automotive parts and accessories, both original equipment and aftermarket, are purchased for use in the manufacture or repair of Japanese automobiles.

SEC. 2123. ESTABLISHMENT OF INITIATIVE ON AUTO PARTS SALES TO JAPAN.

(a) IN GENERAL.—The Secretary of Commerce shall establish an initiative to increase the sale of United States-made auto parts and accessories to Japanese markets.

(b) FUNCTIONS.—In carrying out this section, the Secretary shall—

(1) foster increased access for United States-made auto parts and accessories to Japanese companies, including specific consultations on access to Japanese markets;

(2) facilitate the exchange of information between United States auto parts manufacturers and the Japanese automobile industry;

(3) collect data and market information on the Japanese automotive industry regarding needs, trends, and procurement practices, including the types, volume, and frequency of parts sales to Japanese automobile manufacturers;

(4) establish contacts with Japanese automobile manufacturers in order to facilitate contact between United States auto parts manufacturers and Japanese automobile manufacturers;

(5) report on and attempt to resolve disputes, policies, or practices, whether public or private, that result in barriers to increased commerce between United States auto parts manufacturers and Japanese automobile manufacturers;

(6) take actions to initiate periodic consultations with officials of the Government of Japan regarding sales of United States-made auto parts in Japanese markets; and

(7) submit annual written reports or otherwise report annually to the Congress on the sale of United States-made auto parts in Japanese markets, including the extent to which long-term, commercial relationships exist between United States auto parts manufacturers and Japanese automobile manufacturers.

SEC. 2124. ESTABLISHMENT OF SPECIAL ADVISORY COMMITTEE ON AUTO PARTS SALES IN JAPAN.

(a) IN GENERAL.—The Secretary of Commerce shall seek the advice of the United States automotive parts industry in carrying out this part.

(b) ESTABLISHMENT OF COMMITTEE.—The Secretary of Commerce shall establish a Special Advisory Committee for purposes of carrying out this part.

(c) FUNCTIONS.—The Special Advisory Committee established under subsection (b) shall—

(1) report to the Secretary of Commerce on barriers to sales of United States-made auto parts and accessories in Japanese markets;

(2) review and consider data collected on sales of United States-made auto parts and accessories in Japanese markets;

(3) advise the Secretary of Commerce during consultations with the Government of Japan on issues concerning sales of United States-made auto parts in Japanese markets;

(4) assist in establishing priorities for the initiative established under section 2123, and otherwise provide assistance and direction to the Secretary of Commerce in carrying out the intent of that section; and

(5) assist the Secretary in reporting, or otherwise report to the Congress as requested, on the progress of sales of United States-made auto parts in Japanese markets.

(d) AUTHORITY.—The Secretary of Commerce shall draw on existing budget authority in carrying out this part.

SEC. 2125. EXPIRATION DATE.

The authorities under this part shall expire on December 31, 1993.

Subtitle B—Export Enhancement

PART I—GENERAL PROVISIONS

SEC. 2201. COMMERCIAL PERSONNEL AT THE AMERICAN INSTITUTE OF TAIWAN.

The American Institute of Taiwan shall employ personnel to perform duties similar to those performed by personnel of the United States and Foreign Commercial Service. The number of individuals employed shall be commensurate with the number of United States personnel of the Commercial Service who are permanently assigned to the United States diplomatic mission to South Korea.

SEC. 2202. COUNTRY REPORTS ON ECONOMIC POLICY AND TRADE PRACTICES.

The Secretary of State shall, not later than January 31 of each year, prepare and transmit to the Committee on Foreign Affairs and the Committee on Ways and Means of the House of Representatives, to the Committee on Foreign Relations and the Committee on Finance of the Senate, and to other appropriate committees of the Congress, a detailed report regarding the economic policy and trade practices of each country with which the United States has an economic or trade relationship. The Secretary may direct the appropriate officers of the Department of State who are serving overseas, in consultation with appropriate officers or employees of other departments and agencies of the United States, including the Department of Agriculture and the Department of Commerce, to coordinate the preparation of such information in a country as is necessary to prepare the report under this section. The report shall identify and describe, with respect to each country—

(1) the macroeconomic policies of the country and their impact on the overall growth in demand for United States exports;

(2) the impact of macroeconomic and other policies on the exchange rate of the country and the resulting impact on price competitiveness of United States exports;

(3) any change in structural policies (including tax incentives, regulations governing financial institutions, production standards, and patterns of industrial ownership) that may affect the country's growth rate and its demand for United States exports;

(4) the management of the country's external debt and its implications for trade with the United States;

(5) acts, policies, and practices that constitute significant barriers to United States exports or foreign direct investment in that country by United States persons, as identified under section 181(a)(1) of the Trade Act of 1974 (19 U.S.C. 2241(a)(1));

(6) acts, policies, and practices that provide direct or indirect government support for exports from that country, including exports by small businesses;

(7) the extent to which the country's laws and enforcement of those laws afford adequate protection to United States intellectual property, including patents, trademarks, copyrights, and mask works; and

(8) the country's laws, enforcement of those laws, and practices with respect to internationally recognized worker rights (as defined in section 502(a)(4) of the Trade Act of 1974), the conditions of worker rights in any sector which produces goods in which United States capital is invested, and the extent of such investment.

SEC. 2203. OVERSEAS PRIVATE INVESTMENT CORPORATION.

(a) REAFFIRMATION OF SUPPORT FOR OPIC.—The Congress reaffirms its support for the Overseas Private Investment Corporation as a United States Government agency serving important development assistance goals. In order to enhance the Corporation's ability to meet these goals, the Overseas Private Investment Corporation should increase its loan guaranty and direct investment programs.

(b) INCREASE IN GUARANTIES AND DIRECT INVESTMENTS.—

(1) LOAN GUARANTIES.—Section 235(a) of the Foreign Assistance Act of 1961 (22 U.S.C. 2195(a)) is amended—

(A) in paragraph (2) by striking "$750,000,000" and inserting "$1,000,000,000";

(B) by redesignating paragraph (5) as paragraph (6); and

(C) by inserting after paragraph (4) the following:

"(5) Subject to paragraphs (2), (3), and (4), the Corporation shall issue guaranties under section 234(b) having an aggregate contingent liability with respect to principal of not less than $200,000,000 in each fiscal year, to the extent that there are eligible projects which meet the Corporation's criteria for such guaranties.".

(2) DIRECT INVESTMENT.—Section 235(b) of the Foreign Assistance Act of 1961 is amended—

(A) by striking the comma after "Act of 1981" and inserting a period; and

(B) by striking "and the Corporation shall use" and all that follows through "funding" and inserting the following:

"The Corporation shall make loans under section 234(c) in an aggregate amount of not less than $25,000,000 in each fiscal year, to the extent that there are eligible projects which meet the Corporation's criteria for such loans".

(c) OPERATIONS OF THE OVERSEAS PRIVATE INVESTMENT CORPORATION IN THE PEOPLE'S REPUBLIC OF CHINA.—Section 231A(a) of the Foreign Assistance Act of 1961 is amended by adding at the end the following new paragraph:

"(4) In making a determination under this section for the People's Republic of China, the Corporation shall discuss fully and completely the justification for making such determination with respect to each item set forth in subparagraphs (A) through (E) of section 502(a)(4) of the Trade Act of 1974.".

SEC. 2204. TRADE AND DEVELOPMENT PROGRAM.

(a) REAFFIRMATION OF SUPPORT FOR TRADE AND DEVELOPMENT PROGRAM.—The Congress reaffirms its support for the Trade and Development Program, and believes that the Program's ability to support high priority development projects in developing countries would be enhanced by an increase in the funds authorized for the Program as well as by a clarification of the Program's status as a separate component of the International Development Cooperation Agency.

(b) AUTHORIZATION AND USES OF FUNDS; ESTABLISHMENT AS SEPARATE AGENCY.—

(1) ADDITIONAL USES OF FUNDS.—Section 661(a) of the Foreign Assistance Act of 1961 (22 U.S.C. 2421(a)) is amended by inserting after the first sentence the following: "Funds under this section may be used to provide support for project planning, development, management, and procurement for both bilateral and multilateral projects, including training activities undertaken in connection with a project, for the purpose of promoting the use of United States exports in such projects.".

(2) ESTABLISHMENT AS A SEPARATE AGENCY.—Section 661 of that Act is amended—

(A) by redesignating subsection (b) as subsection (d); and

(B) by inserting after subsection (a) the following:

"(b)(1) The purposes of this section shall be carried out by the Trade and Development Program, which shall be a separate component agency of the International Development Cooperation Agency. The Trade and Development Program shall not be an agency within the Agency for International Development or any other component agency of the International Development Cooperation Agency.

"(2) There shall be at the head of the Trade and Development Program a Director. Any individual appointed as the Director on or after January 1, 1989, shall be appointed by the President, by and with the advice and consent of the Senate.

"(3) The Trade and Development Program should serve as the primary Federal agency to provide information to persons in the private sector concerning trade development and export promotion related to bilateral development projects. The Trade and Development Program shall cooperate with the Office of International Major Projects of the Department of Commerce in providing information to persons in the private sector concerning trade development and export promotion related to multilateral development projects. Other Federal departments and agencies shall cooperate with the Trade and Development Program in order for the Program to more effectively provide informational services in accordance with this paragraph.

"(4) The Director of the Trade and Development Program shall, not later than December 31 of each year, submit to the Committee on Foreign Affairs of the House of Representatives and the Committee on Foreign Relations of the Senate a report on the activities of the Trade and Development Program in the preceding fiscal year.

"(c) The Director of the Trade and Development Program shall, by regulation, establish an advisory board which shall include representatives of the private sector. The purpose of the advisory board shall be to make recommendations to the Director with respect to the Trade and Development Program.".

(3) FUNDING LEVELS.—In addition to funds otherwise available to the President for purposes of section 661 of the Foreign Assistance Act of 1961—

(A) not less than $5,000,000 and not more than $10,000,000 for fiscal year 1988 shall be made available for such purposes, half of which shall be derived from amounts available to carry out section 108 of the Foreign Assistance Act of 1961 for such fiscal year, and half of which shall be derived from amounts available to carry out chapter 4 of part II of the Foreign Assistance Act of 1961 for such fiscal year; and

(B) not less than $5,000,000 and not more than $10,000,000 for fiscal year 1989 shall be made available for such purposes, half of which shall be derived from amounts available to carry out section 108 of the Foreign Assistance Act of 1961 for such fiscal year, and half of which shall be derived from amounts available to carry out chapter 4 of part II of the Foreign Assistance Act of 1961 for such fiscal year.

(4) ADDITIONAL FUNDING.—(A) In addition to the amounts otherwise available to the President for purposes of section 661 of the Foreign Assistance Act of 1961 (including amounts available under paragraph (3) of this subsection) for fiscal years 1988 and 1989, there are authorized to be appropriated $10,000,000 for each such fiscal year for education and training programs undertaken in connection with projects under section 661 of that Act, including the operating expenses incurred in implementing such programs. Particular emphasis shall be placed on including in such programs nationals from the People's Republic of China and the Republic of China (Taiwan). Assistance may be provided for education and training under this paragraph only if there is a reasonable expectation that such education and training will result in increased exports from the United States and will not have a negative impact on employment in the United States.

(B) Of the funds made available to carry out subparagraph (A), 50 percent of such funds shall be available only for education and training programs administered in the United States by small business concerns as defined under section 3 of the Small Business Act (15 U.S.C. 632).

(c) AUTHORITIES UNDER THE TRADE AND DEVELOPMENT ENHANCEMENT ACT OF 1983.—

(1) TRANSFER OF FUNCTIONS FROM AID TO TDP.—(A) Section 644 of the Trade and Development Enhancement Act of 1983 (12 U.S.C. 635q) is amended—

(i) in subsection (a)(2) by striking "Agency for International Development" and inserting "Trade and Development Program";

(ii) in subsection (a)(3)(A)—

(I) by striking "offered by the Agency for International Development" and inserting "made available under section 645(d) of this Act"; and

(II) by striking "Agency for International Development" and inserting "Trade and Development Program"; and

(iii) in subsection (d)—

(I) by striking "offered by the Agency for International Development" and inserting "made available under section 645(d) of this Act"; and

(II) by striking "subsections (c) and (d) of section 645" and inserting "section 645(c)".

(B) Section 645 of that Act (12 U.S.C. 635r) is amended—

(i) in the section heading by striking "IN THE AGENCY FOR INTERNATIONAL DEVELOPMENT" and inserting "ADMINISTERED BY THE TRADE AND DEVELOPMENT PROGRAM";

(ii) in subsection (a)—

(I) by striking "Administrator of the Agency for International Development shall establish within the Agency" and inserting "Director of the Trade and Development Program shall carry out";

(II) in paragraph (1) by striking "offered by the Agency for International Development" and inserting "made available under subsection (d)";

(III) in paragraph (1) by striking "Agency for International Development" and inserting "Trade and Development Program";

(IV) in paragraph (2) by striking "offered by the Agency for International Development" and inserting "made available under subsection (d)"; and

(V) in paragraph (2) by striking "Agency for International Development" and inserting "Trade and Development Program";

(iii) in subsection (c)—

(I) in paragraph (1) by striking "of the Agency for International Development"; and

(II) in paragraph (2) by striking "Administrator of the Agency for International Development" and inserting "Director of the Trade and Development Program"; and

(iv) by amending subsection (d) to read as follows:

"(d) Funds available to carry out chapter 4 of part II of the Foreign Assistance Act of 1961 may be used by the Director of the Trade and Development Program, with the concurrence of the Secretary of State (as provided under section 531 of the Foreign Assistance Act of 1961), for the purposes for which funds made available under this subsection are authorized to be used in section 644 and this section. The Secretary of State shall exercise his authority in cooperation with the Administrator of the Agency for International Development. Funds made available pursuant to this subsection may be used to finance a tied aid credit activity in any country eligible for tied aid credits under this Act.".

(2) FUNCTIONS OF NATIONAL ADVISORY COUNCIL ON INTERNATIONAL MONETARY AND FINANCIAL POLICIES.—Section 646 of the Trade and Development Enhancement Act of 1983 (12 U.S.C. 635s) is amended by adding at the end the following:

"(b) The Trade and Development Program shall be represented at any meetings of the National Advisory Council on International Monetary and Financial Policies for discussion of tied aid credit matters, and the representative of the Trade and Development Program at any such meeting shall have the right to vote on any decisions of the Advisory Council relating to tied aid credit matters.".

(d) ADMINISTRATIVE PROVISIONS.—

(1) PAY OF DIRECTOR OF TDP.—Section 5314 of title 5, United States Code, is amended by adding at the end the following:

"Director, Trade and Development Program.".

(2) TRANSITION PROVISIONS.—(A) The Administrator of the Agency for International Development shall transfer to the Director of the Trade and Development Program all records,

contracts, applications, and any other documents or information in connection with the functions transferred by virtue of the amendments made by subsection (c)(1).

(B) All determinations, regulations, and contracts—

(i) which have been issued, made, granted, or allowed to become effective by the President, the Agency for International Development, or by a court of competent jurisdiction, in the performance of the functions transferred by virtue of the amendments made by subsection (c)(1), and

(ii) which are in effect at the time this section takes effect,

shall continue in effect according to their terms until modified, terminated, superseded, set aside, or revoked in accordance with the law by the President, the Director of the Trade and Development Program, or other authorized official, by a court of competent jurisdiction, or by operation of law.

(C)(i) The amendments made by subsection (c)(1) shall not affect any proceedings, including notices of proposed rulemaking, or any application for any financial assistance, which is pending on the effective date of this section before the Agency for International Development in the exercise of functions transferred by virtue of the amendments made by subsection (c)(1). Such proceedings and applications, to the extent that they relate to functions so transferred, shall be continued.

(ii) Orders shall be issued in such proceedings, appeals shall be taken therefrom, and payments shall be made pursuant to such orders, as if this section had not been enacted. Orders issued in any such proceedings shall continue in effect until modified, terminated, superseded, or revoked by the Director of the Trade and Development Program or other authorized official, by a court of competent jurisdiction, or by operation of law.

(iii) Nothing in this subparagraph shall be deemed to prohibit the discontinuance or modification of any such proceeding under the same terms and conditions and to the same extent that such proceeding could have been discontinued or modified if this section had not been enacted.

(iv) The Director of the Trade and Development Program is authorized to issue regulations providing for the orderly transfer to the Trade and Development Program of proceedings continued under this subparagraph.

(D) With respect to any function transferred by virtue of the amendments made by subsection (c)(1) and exercised on or after the effective date of this section, reference in any other Federal law to the Agency for International Development or any officer shall be deemed to refer to the Trade and Development Program or other official to which such function is so transferred.

SEC. 2205. BARTER AND COUNTERTRADE.

(a) INTERAGENCY GROUP.—

(1) ESTABLISHMENT.—The President shall establish an interagency group on countertrade, to be composed of representatives of such departments and agencies of the United States as the President considers appropriate. The Secretary of Commerce shall be the chairman of the interagency group.

(2) FUNCTIONS.—It shall be the function of the interagency group to—

(A) review and evaluate—

(i) United States policy on countertrade and offsets, in light of current trends in international countertrade and offsets and the impact of those trends on the United States economy;

(ii) the use of countertrade and offsets in United States exports and bilateral United States foreign economic assistance programs; and

(iii) the need for and the feasibility of negotiating with other countries, through the Organization for Economic Cooperation and Development and other appropriate international organizations, to reach agreements on the use of countertrade and offsets; and

(B) make recommendations to the President and the Congress on the basis of the review and evaluation referred to in subparagraph (A).

(3) SHARING OF INFORMATION.—Other departments and agencies of the United States shall provide to the interagency group such information available to such departments and agencies as the interagency group may request, except that the requirements, including penalties for violation thereof, for preserving the confidentiality of such information which are applicable to the officials, employees, experts, or consultants of such departments and agencies shall apply in the same manner to each member of the interagency group and to any other person performing any function under this subsection.

(b) OFFICE OF BARTER.—

(1) ESTABLISHMENT—There is established, within the International Trade Administration of the Department of Commerce, the Office of Barter (hereafter in this section referred to as the "Office").

(2) DIRECTOR.—There shall be at the head of the Office a Director, who shall be appointed by the Secretary of Commerce.

(3) STAFF.—The Secretary of Commerce shall transfer such staff to the Office as the Secretary determines is necessary to enable the Office to carry out its functions under this section.

(4) FUNCTIONS.—It shall be the function of the Office to—

(A) monitor information relating to trends in international barter;

(B) organize and disseminate information relating to international barter in a manner useful to business firms, educational institutions, export-related Federal, State, and local government agencies, and other interested persons, including publishing periodic lists of known commercial opportunities for barter transactions beneficial to United States enterprises;

(C) notify Federal agencies with operations abroad of instances where it would be beneficial to the United States for the Federal Government to barter Government-owned surplus commodities for goods and services purchased abroad by the Federal Government; and

(D) provide assistance to enterprises seeking barter and countertrade opportunities.

SEC. 2206. PROTECTION OF UNITED STATES INTELLECTUAL PROPERTY.

It is the sense of the Congress that—

(1) the Secretary of State should urge international technical organizations, such as the World Intellectual Property

Organization, to provide expertise and cooperate fully in developing effective standards, in the General Agreement on Tariffs and Trade, for the international protection of intellectual property rights; and

(2) development assistance programs administered by the Agency for International Development, especially the reimbursable development program, should, in cooperation with the Copyright Office and the Patent and Trademark Office, include technical training for officials responsible for the protection of patents, copyrights, trademarks, and mask works in those countries that receive such development assistance.

SEC. 2207. REPORT ON WORKER RIGHTS.

The Secretary of State shall conduct an in-depth study with a view to improving the breadth, content, and utility of the annual reports submitted to the Congress pursuant to section 505(c) of the Trade Act of 1974 regarding the status of internationally recognized worker rights in foreign countries. Not later than 6 months after the date of the enactment of this Act, the Secretary shall submit a report to the Congress on the findings of such study and shall include in the report recommendations for upgrading the capacity of the United States Government to monitor and report on other countries' respect for such rights.

SEC. 2208. JAPANESE IMPORTATION OF MANUFACTURED GOODS FROM LESS DEVELOPED COUNTRIES.

(a) FINDINGS.—The Congress finds that—

(1) Japan's merchandise trade surplus rose from $62,000,000,000 in fiscal year 1985 to $101,000,000,000 in fiscal year 1986;

(2) these surpluses pose a grave threat to the free trade system;

(3) Japan's most important contribution to the international trading system would be to commit itself as a nation to import with vigor, just as it has exported with vigor in recent decades;

(4) Japan should particularly increase its imports of manufactured goods; and

(5) Japan's share of the exports of less developed countries has declined from 10.6 percent in 1979 to below 8 percent in 1985.

(b) SENSE OF CONGRESS.—It is the sense of the Congress that—

(1) by taking its proportionate share of the manufactured exports of developing countries, Japan will promote not only its economic development but the economic conditions conducive to democracy;

(2) expanding markets for the manufactured exports of less developed countries will directly benefit the United States, and, if less developed countries are able to increase exports to Japan, these countries will be able to earn more of the hard currency needed to service their foreign debt obligations and make the investments necessary to chart a course of solid economic growth; and

(3) if less developed countries are able to export manufactured goods to Japan, they will be under less pressure to divert exports to the United States market.

SEC. 2209. JAPAN AND THE ARAB BOYCOTT OF ISRAEL.

It is the sense of the Congress that the United States should encourage the Government of Japan in its efforts to expand trade relations with Israel and to end compliance by Japanese commercial enterprises with the Arab economic boycott of Israel.

SEC. 2210. FACILITATION OF JEWELRY TRADE.

It is the sense of the Congress that the United States should become a party to the Convention on the Control and Marking of Articles of Precious Metals in order to facilitate the efforts of the United States jewelry industry in penetrating foreign markets.

SEC. 2211. LOAN GUARANTEES.

Section 108 of the Foreign Assistance Act of 1961 (22 U.S.C. 2151f) is amended by adding at the end the following:

"(i)(1) To carry out the purposes of subsection (a), in addition to the other authorities set forth in this section, the agency primarily responsible for administering this part is authorized to issue guarantees on such terms and conditions as it shall determine assuring against losses incurred in connection with loans made to projects that meet the criteria set forth in subsection (c). The full faith and credit of the United States is hereby pledged for the full payment and performance of such guarantees.

"(2) Loans guaranteed under this subsection shall be on such terms and conditions as the agency may prescribe, except for the following:

"(A) The agency shall issue guarantees only when it is necessary to alleviate a credit market imperfection.

"(B) Loans guaranteed shall provide for complete amortization within a period not to exceed ten years or, if the principal purpose of the guaranteed loan is to finance the construction or purchase of a physical asset with a useful life of less than ten years, within a period not to exceed such useful life.

"(C) No loan guaranteed to any one borrower may exceed 50 percent of the cost of the activity to be financed, or $3,000,000, whichever is less, as determined by the agency.

"(D) No loan may be guaranteed unless the agency determines that the lender is responsible and that adequate provision is made for servicing the loan on reasonable terms and protecting the financial interest of the United States.

"(E) The fees earned from the loan guarantees issued under this subsection shall be deposited in the revolving fund account as part of the guarantee reserve established under paragraph (5) of this subsection. Fees shall be assessed at a level such that the fees received, plus the funds from the revolving fund account placed in the guarantee reserve, satisfy the requirements of paragraph (5). Fees shall be reviewed every twelve months to ensure that the fees assessed on new loan guarantees are at the required level.

"(F) Any guarantee shall be conclusive evidence that such guarantee has been properly obtained, and that the underlying loan as contracted qualifies for such guarantee. Except for fraud or material misrepresentation for which the parties seeking payment under such guarantee are responsible, such guarantee shall be presumed to be valid, legal, and enforceable.

"(G) The agency shall determine that the standards used by the lender for assessing the credit risk of new and existing guaranteed loans are reasonable. The agency shall require that there be a reasonable assurance of repayment before credit assistance is extended.

"(H) Commitments to guarantee loans may be made by the agency only to the extent that the total loan principal, any part of which is guaranteed, will not exceed the amount specified in annual appropriations Acts.

"(3) To the extent that fees are not sufficient as specified under paragraph (2)(E) to cover expected future liabilities, appropriations are authorized to maintain an appropriate reserve.

"(4) The losses guaranteed under this subsection may be in dollars or in other currencies. In the case of loans in currencies other than dollars, the guarantees issued shall be subject to an overall payment limitation expressed in dollars.

"(5) The agency shall segregate in the revolving fund account and hold as a reserve an amount estimated to be sufficient to cover the agency's expected net liabilities on the loan guarantees outstanding under this subsection; except that the amount held in reserve shall not be less than 25 percent of the principal amount of the agency's outstanding contingent liabilities on such guarantees. Any payments made to discharge liabilities arising from the loan guarantees shall be paid first out of the assets in the revolving fund account and next out of other funds made available for this purpose.".

PART II—ASSISTANCE TO POLAND

SEC. 2221. SHORT TITLE.

This part may be cited as the "American Aid to Poland Act of 1988".

SEC. 2222. FUNDING FOR SCIENCE AND TECHNOLOGY AGREEMENT.

(a) FUNDING.—For purposes of implementing the 1987 United States-Polish science and technology agreement, there are authorized to be appropriated to the Secretary of State for fiscal year 1988, $1,000,000.

(b) AVAILABILITY OF FUNDS.—Amounts appropriated under subsection (a) are authorized to remain available until expended.

(c) DEFINITION.—For purposes of this section, the term "1987 United States-Polish science and technology agreement" refers to the draft agreement concluded in 1987 by the United States and Poland, entitled "Agreement Between the Government of the United States of America and the Polish People's Republic on Cooperation in Science and Technology and Its Funding", together with annexes relating thereto.

SEC. 2223. DONATION OF SURPLUS AGRICULTURAL COMMODITIES.

(a) AUTHORITY TO DONATE.—Notwithstanding any other provision of law, the Secretary of Agriculture shall donate, under the applicable provisions of section 416(b) of the Agricultural Act of 1949, for each of the fiscal years 1988 through 1992, 8,000 metric tons of uncommitted stocks of eligible commodities of the Commodity Credit Corporation under an agreement with the Government of Poland that the Government of Poland will sell such commodities and that all the proceeds from such sales will be used by nongovernmental agencies for eligible activities in Poland described in section 416(b)(7)(D)(ii) of that Act (as amended by section 2225 of this Act) that have been approved, upon application, by the joint commission described in section 2226 and by the United States chief of diplomatic mission in Poland.

(b) DEFINITIONS.—For purposes of this section—

(1) the term "eligible commodities" has the same meaning as is given such term in section 416(b)(2) of the Agricultural Act of 1949 and, in addition, includes feed grains; and

(2) the term "nongovernmental agencies" includes nonprofit voluntary agencies, cooperatives, intergovernmental agencies such as the World Food Program, and other multilateral organizations.

SEC. 2224. USE OF POLISH CURRENCIES.

(a) USE OF POLISH CURRENCIES.—Subject to subsection (b), nonconvertible Polish currencies (zlotys) held by the United States on the date of enactment of this Act pursuant to an agreement with the Government of Poland under the Agricultural Trade Development and Assistance Act of 1954 which are not assets of the Commodity Credit Corporation shall be made available, to the extent and in such amounts as are provided in advance in appropriation Acts, for eligible activities in Poland described in section 416(b)(7)(D)(ii) of the Agricultural Act of 1949 (as amended by section 2225 of this Act) and approved, upon application, by the joint commission described in section 2226 and by the United States chief of diplomatic mission in Poland.

(b) AVAILABILITY OF CURRENCIES.—Currencies available under subsection (a) are currencies available after satisfaction of existing commitments to use such currencies for other purposes specified by law.

SEC. 2225. ELIGIBLE ACTIVITIES.

Section 416(b)(7)(D)(ii) of the Agricultural Act of 1949 is amended by adding at the end the following: "In addition, foreign currency proceeds generated in Poland may also be used by such agencies or cooperatives for eligible activities approved by the joint commission established pursuant to section 2226 of the American Aid to Poland Act of 1988 and by the United States chief of diplomatic mission in Poland that would improve the quality of life of the Polish people and would strengthen and support the activities of private, nongovernmental independent institutions in Poland. Activities eligible under the preceding sentence include—

"(I) any project undertaken in Poland under the auspices of the Charitable Commission of the Polish Catholic Episcopate for the benefit of handicapped or orphaned children;

"(II) any project for the reconstruction, renovation, or maintenance of the Research Center on Jewish History and Culture of the Jagiellonian University of Krakow, Poland, established for the study of events related to the Holocaust in Poland; and

"(III) any other project or activity which strengthens and supports private and independent sectors of the Polish economy, especially independent farming and agriculture.".

SEC. 2226. JOINT COMMISSION.

(a) ESTABLISHMENT.—The joint commission referred to in sections 2223 and 2224 and in section 416(b)(7)(D)(ii) of the Agricultural Act of 1949 (as amended by section 2225 of this Act) shall be established under an agreement between the United States Government, the

Government of Poland, and nongovernmental agencies (as defined in section 2223) operating in Poland.

(b) MEMBERSHIP.—The joint commission shall be composed of—

(1) appropriate representatives of the Government of Poland;

(2) appropriate representatives of nongovernmental agencies which are parties to the agreement described in subsection (a); and

(3) representatives from the United States diplomatic mission in Poland, which may include a representative of the Foreign Agricultural Service.

SEC. 2227. PROVISION OF MEDICAL SUPPLIES AND HOSPITAL EQUIPMENT TO POLAND.

In addition to amounts authorized to be appropriated to carry out chapter 4 of part II of the Foreign Assistance Act of 1961 (relating to the economic support fund) for fiscal years 1988 and 1989, there are authorized to be appropriated to carry out that chapter for each such fiscal year $2,000,000, which shall be available only for providing medical supplies and hospital equipment to Poland through private and voluntary organizations, including for the expenses of purchasing, transporting, and distributing such supplies and equipment.

Subtitle C—Export Promotion

SEC. 2301. UNITED STATES AND FOREIGN COMMERCIAL SERVICE.

(a) ESTABLISHMENT.—

(1) IN GENERAL.—The Secretary of Commerce shall establish, within the International Trade Administration, the United States and Foreign Commercial Service. The Secretary shall, to the greatest extent practicable, transfer to the Commercial Service the functions and personnel of the United States and Foreign Commercial Services.

(2) ASSISTANT SECRETARY OF COMMERCE AND DIRECTOR GENERAL; OTHER PERSONNEL.—The head of the Commercial Service shall be the Assistant Secretary of Commerce and Director General of the Commercial Service, who shall be appointed by the President, by and with the advice and consent of the Senate. The Assistant Secretary of Commerce and Director General of the Commercial Service may appoint Commercial Service Officers and such other personnel as may be necessary to carry out the activities of the Commercial Service.

(3) COORDINATION WITH FOREIGN POLICY OBJECTIVES.—The Secretary shall take the necessary steps to ensure that the activities of the Commercial Service are carried out in a manner consistent with United States foreign policy objectives, and the Secretary shall consult regularly with the Secretary of State in order to comply with this paragraph.

(4) AUTHORITY OF CHIEF OF MISSION.—All activities of the Commercial Service shall be subject to section 207 of the Foreign Service Act of 1980 (22 U.S.C. 3927).

(b) STATEMENT OF PURPOSE.—The Commercial Service shall place primary emphasis on the promotion of exports of goods and services from the United States, particularly by small businesses and medium-sized businesses, and on the protection of United States business interests abroad by carrying out activities such as—

(1) identifying United States businesses with the potential to export goods and services and providing such businesses with advice and information on establishing export businesses;

(2) providing United States exporters with information on economic conditions, market opportunities, the status of the intellectual property system in such country, and the legal and regulatory environment within foreign countries;

(3) providing United States exporters with information and advice on the necessary adaptation of product design and marketing strategy to meet the differing cultural and technical requirements of foreign countries;

(4) providing United States exporters with actual leads and an introduction to contacts within foreign countries;

(5) assisting United States exporters in locating reliable sources of business services in foreign countries;

(6) assisting United States exporters in their dealings with foreign governments and enterprises owned by foreign governments; and

(7) assisting the coordination of the efforts of State and local agencies and private organizations which seek to promote United States business interests abroad so as to maximize their effectiveness and minimize the duplication of efforts.

(c) OFFICES.—

(1) IN GENERAL.—The Commercial Service shall conduct its activities at a headquarters office, district offices located in major United States cities, and foreign offices located in major foreign cities.

(2) HEADQUARTERS.—The headquarters of the Commercial Service shall provide such managerial, administrative, research, and other services as the Secretary considers necessary to carry out the purposes of the Commercial Service.

(3) DISTRICT OFFICES.—The Secretary shall establish district offices of the Commercial Service in any United States city in a region in which the Secretary determines that there is a need for Federal Government export assistance.

(4) FOREIGN OFFICES.—(A) The Secretary may, after consultation with the Secretary of State, establish foreign offices of the Commercial Service. These offices shall be located in foreign cities in regions in which the Secretary determines there are significant business opportunities for United States exporters.

(B) The Secretary may, in consultation with the Secretary of State, assign to the foreign offices Commercial Service Officers and such other personnel as the Secretary considers necessary. In employing Commercial Service Officers and such other personnel, the Secretary shall use the Foreign Service personnel system in accordance with the Foreign Service Act of 1980. The Secretary shall designate a Commercial Officer as head of each foreign office.

(C) Upon the request of the Secretary, the Secretary of State shall attach the Commercial Service Officers and other employees of each foreign office to the diplomatic mission of the United States in the country in which that foreign office is located, and shall obtain for them diplomatic privileges and immunities equivalent to those enjoyed by Foreign Service personnel of comparable rank and salary.

(D) For purposes of official representation, the senior Commercial Service Officer in each country shall be considered to be the senior commercial representative of the United States in that country, and the United States chief of mission in that country shall accord that officer all privileges and responsibilities appropriate to the position of senior commercial representative of other countries.

(E) The Secretary of State is authorized, upon the request of the Secretary, to provide office space, equipment, facilities, and such other administrative and clerical services as may be required for the operation of the foreign offices. The Secretary is authorized to reimburse or advance funds to the Secretary of State for such services.

(F) The authority of the Secretary under this paragraph shall be subject to section 103 of the Diplomatic Security Act (22 U.S.C. 4802).

(d) RANK OF COMMERCIAL SERVICE OFFICERS IN FOREIGN MISSIONS.—

(1) MINISTER-COUNSELOR.—Notwithstanding any other provision of law, the Secretary is authorized to designate up to 8 United States missions abroad at which the senior Commercial Service Officer will be able to use the diplomatic title of Minister-Counselor. The Secretary of State shall accord the diplomatic title of Minister-Counselor to the senior Commercial Service Officer assigned to a United States mission so designated.

(2) CONSUL GENERAL.—In any United States consulate in which a vacancy occurs in the position of Consul General, the Secretary of State, in consultation with the Secretary, shall consider filling that vacancy with a Commercial Service Officer if the primary functions of the consulate are of a commercial nature and if there are significant business opportunities for United States exporters in the region in which the consulate is located.

(e) INFORMATION DISSEMINATION.—In order to carry out subsection (b)(7), to lessen the cost of distribution of information produced by the Commercial Service, and to make that information more readily available, the Secretary should establish a system for distributing that information in those areas where no district offices of the Commercial Service are located. Distributors of the information should be State export promotion agencies or private export and trade promotion associations. The distribution system should be consistent with cost recovery objectives of the Department of Commerce.

(f) AUDITS.—The Inspector General of the Department of Commerce shall perform periodic audits of the operations of the Commercial Service, but at least once every 3 years. The Inspector General shall report to the Congress the results of each such audit. In addition to an overview of the activities and effectiveness of Commercial Service operations, the audit shall include—

(1) an evaluation of the current placement of domestic personnel and recommendations for transferring personnel among district offices;

(2) an evaluation of the current placement of foreign-based personnel and recommendations for transferring such personnel in response to newly emerging business opportunities for United States exporters; and

(3) an evaluation of the personnel system and its management, including the recruitment, assignment, promotion, and

performance appraisal of personnel, the use of limited appointees, and the "time-in-class" system.

(g) REPORT BY THE SECRETARY.—Not later than 1 year after the date of the enactment of this Act, the Secretary shall submit a report to the Congress on the feasibility and desirability, the progress to date, the present status, and the 5-year outlook, of the comprehensive integration of the functions and personnel of the foreign and domestic export promotion operations within the International Trade Administration of the Department of Commerce.

(h) PAY OF ASSISTANT SECRETARY AND DIRECTOR GENERAL.—Section 5315 of title 5, United States Code, is amended by adding at the end the following:

"Assistant Secretary of Commerce and Director General of the United States and Foreign Commercial Service.".

(i) DEFINITIONS.—For purposes of this section—

(1) the term "Secretary" means the Secretary of Commerce;

(2) the term "Commercial Service" means the United States and Foreign Commercial Service;

(3) the term "United States exporter" means—

(A) a United States citizen;

(B) a corporation, partnership, or other association created under the laws of the United States or of any State; or

(C) a foreign corporation, partnership, or other association, more than 95 percent of which is owned by persons described in subparagraphs (A) and (B),

that exports, or seeks to export, goods or services produced in the United States;

(4) the term "small business" means any small business concern as defined under section 3 of the Small Business Act (15 U.S.C. 632);

(5) the term "State" means any of the several States, the District of Columbia, or any commonwealth, territory, or possession of the United States; and

(6) the term "United States" means the several States, the District of Columbia, and any commonwealth, territory, or possession of the United States.

SEC. 2302. COMMERCIAL SERVICE OFFICERS AND MULTILATERAL DEVELOPMENT BANK PROCUREMENT.

(a) APPOINTMENT OF COMMERCIAL SERVICE OFFICERS TO SERVE WITH EXECUTIVE DIRECTORS.—The Secretary of Commerce, in consultation with the Secretary of the Treasury, shall appoint a procurement officer, who is a representative of the International Trade Administration or a Commercial Service Officer of the United States and Foreign Commercial Service, to serve, on a full-time or part-time basis, with each of the Executive Directors of the multilateral development banks in which the United States participates.

(b) FUNCTIONS OF OFFICERS.—Each procurement officer appointed under subsection (a) shall assist the United States Executive Director with respect to whom such officer is appointed in promoting opportunities for exports of goods and services from the United States by doing the following:

(1) Acting as the liaison between the business community and the multilateral development bank involved, whether or not the bank has offices in the United States. The Secretary of Commerce shall ensure that the procurement officer has access to, and disseminates to United States businesses, information relat-

ing to projects which are being proposed by the multilateral development bank, and bid specifications and deadlines for projects about to be developed by the bank. The procurement officer shall make special efforts to disseminate such information to small and medium-sized businesses interested in participating in such projects. The procurement officer shall explore opportunities for disseminating such information through private sector, nonprofit organizations.

(2) Taking actions to assure that United States businesses are fully informed of bidding opportunities for projects for which loans have been made by the multilateral development bank involved.

(3) Taking actions to assure that United States businesses can focus on projects in which they have a particular interest or competitive advantage, and to permit them to compete and have an equal opportunity in submitting timely and conforming bidding documents.

(c) DEFINITION.—As used in this section, the term "multilateral development bank" includes the International Bank for Reconstruction and Development, the International Development Association, the International Finance Corporation, the Inter-American Development Bank, the Inter-American Investment Corporation, the Asian Development Bank, the African Development Bank, and the African Development Fund.

SEC. 2303. MARKET DEVELOPMENT COOPERATOR PROGRAM.

(a) AUTHORITY OF SECRETARY OF COMMERCE.—In order to promote further the exportation of goods and services from the United States, the Secretary of Commerce is authorized to establish, in the International Trade Administration of the Department of Commerce, a Market Development Cooperator Program. The purpose of the program is to develop, maintain, and expand foreign markets for nonagricultural goods and services produced in the United States.

(b) IMPLEMENTATION OF THE PROGRAM.—The Secretary of Commerce shall carry out the Market Development Cooperator Program by entering into contracts with—

(1) nonprofit industry organizations,

(2) trade associations,

(3) State departments of trade and their regional associations, including centers for international trade development, and

(4) private industry firms or groups of firms in cases where no entity described in paragraph (1), (2), or (3) represents that industry,

(in this section referred to as "cooperators") to engage in activities in order to carry out the purpose of the Market Development Cooperator Program set forth in subsection (a). The costs of activities under such a contract shall be shared equitably among the Department of Commerce, the cooperator involved, and, whenever appropriate, foreign businesses. The Department of Commerce shall undertake to support direct costs of activities under such a contract, and the cooperator shall undertake to support indirect costs of such activities. Activities under such a contract shall be carried out by the cooperator with the approval and assistance of the Secretary.

(c) COOPERATOR PARTNERSHIP PROGRAM.—

(1) IN GENERAL.—(A) As part of the Market Development Cooperator Program established under subsection (a), the Secretary of Commerce shall establish a partnership program with

cooperators under which a cooperator may detail individuals, subject to the approval of the Secretary, to the United States and Foreign Commercial Service for a period of not less than 1 year or more than 2 years to supplement the Commercial Service.

(B) Any individual detailed to the United States and Foreign Commercial Service under this subsection shall be responsible for such duties as the Secretary may prescribe in order to carry out the purpose of the Market Development Cooperator Program set forth in subsection (a).

(C) Individuals detailed to the United States and Foreign Commercial Service under this subsection shall not be considered to be employees of the United States for the purposes of any law administered by the Office of Personnel Management, except that the Secretary of State may determine the applicability to such individuals of section 2(f) of the State Department Basic Authorities Act of 1956 (22 U.S.C. 2669(f)) and of any other law administered by the Secretary of State concerning the detail of such individuals abroad.

(2) QUALIFICATIONS OF PARTICIPANTS.—In order to qualify for the program established under this subsection, individuals shall have demonstrated expertise in the international business arena in at least 2 of the following areas: marketing, market research, and computer data bases.

(3) EXPENSES OF THE PROGRAM.—(A) The cooperator who details an individual to the United States and Foreign Commercial Service under this subsection shall be responsible for that individual's salary and related expenses, including health care, life insurance, and other noncash benefits, if any, normally paid by such cooperator.

(B) The Secretary of Commerce shall pay transportation and housing costs for each individual participating in the program established under this subsection.

(d) BUDGET ACT.—Contracts may be entered into under this section in a fiscal year only to such extent or in such amounts as are provided in appropriations Acts.

SEC. 2304. TRADE SHOWS.

(a) AUTHORITY OF THE SECRETARY OF COMMERCE.—In order to facilitate exporting by United States businesses, the Secretary of Commerce shall provide assistance for trade shows in the United States which bring together representatives of United States businesses seeking to export goods or services produced in the United States and representatives of foreign companies or governments seeking to buy such goods or services from these United States businesses.

(b) RECIPIENTS OF ASSISTANCE.—Assistance under subsection (a) may be provided to—

(1) nonprofit industry organizations,

(2) trade associations,

(3) foreign trade zones, and

(4) private industry firms or groups of firms in cases where no entity described in paragraph (1), (2), or (3) represents that industry,

to provide the services necessary to operate trade shows described in subsection (a).

(c) ASSISTANCE TO SMALL BUSINESSES.—In providing assistance under this section, the Secretary of Commerce shall, in consultation with the Administrator of the Small Business Administration, make special efforts to facilitate participation by small businesses and companies new to export.

(d) USES OF ASSISTANCE.—Funds appropriated to carry out this section shall be used to—

(1) identify potential participants for trade show organizers,

(2) provide information on trade shows to potential participants,

(3) supply language services for participants, and

(4) provide information on trade shows to small businesses and companies new to export.

(e) DEFINITIONS.—As used in this section—

(1) the term "United States business" means—

(A) a United States citizen;

(B) a corporation, partnership, or other association created under the laws of the United States or of any State (including the District of Columbia or any commonwealth, territory, or possession of the United States); or

(C) a foreign corporation, partnership, or other association, more than 95 percent of which is owned by persons described in subparagraphs (A) and (B); and

(2) the term "small business" means any small business concern as defined under section 3 of the Small Business Act (15 U.S.C. 632).

SEC. 2305. AUTHORIZATION OF APPROPRIATIONS FOR EXPORT PROMOTION PROGRAMS.

(a) DEFINITION OF EXPORT PROMOTION PROGRAM.—Section 201(d) of the Export Administration Amendments Act of 1985 (15 U.S.C. 4051(d)) is amended—

(1) in paragraph (3) by striking "and" after the semicolon;

(2) in paragraph (4) by striking the period and inserting "; and"; and

(3) by adding at the end the following:

"(5) the Market Development Cooperator Program established under section 2303 of the Export Enhancement Act of 1988, and assistance for trade shows provided under section 2304 of that Act.".

(b) AUTHORIZATION OF APPROPRIATIONS.—(1) Section 202 of the Export Administration Amendments Act of 1985 (15 U.S.C. 4052) is amended to read as follows:

"There are authorized to be appropriated to the Department of Commerce to carry out export promotion programs $123,922,000 for the fiscal year 1988, and $146,400,000 for each of the fiscal years 1989 and 1990.".

(2) In addition to funds otherwise available, there are authorized to be appropriated to the Department of Commerce to carry out sections 2303 and 2304 of this Act $6,000,000 for each of the fiscal years 1988, 1989, and 1990.

SEC. 2306. UNITED STATES AND FOREIGN COMMERCIAL SERVICE PACIFIC RIM INITIATIVE.

(a) IN GENERAL.—In order to encourage the export of United States goods and services to Japan, South Korea, and Taiwan, the

United States and Foreign Commercial Service shall make a special effort to—

(1) identify United States goods and services which are not being exported to the markets of Japan, South Korea, and Taiwan but which could be exported to these markets under competitive market conditions;

(2) identify and notify United States persons who sell or provide such goods or services of potential opportunities identified under paragraph (1);

(3) present, periodically, a list of the goods and services identified under paragraph (1), together with a list of any impediments to the export of such goods and services, to appropriate authorities in Japan, South Korea, and Taiwan, with a view toward liberalizing markets to such goods and services;

(4) facilitate the entrance into such markets by United States persons identified and notified under paragraph (2); and

(5) monitor and evaluate the results of efforts to increase the sale of goods and services in such markets.

(b) REPORTS TO THE CONGRESS.—The Secretary of Commerce shall report periodically to the Congress on activities carried out under subsection (a).

(c) DEFINITION.—As used in this section, the term "United States person" means—

(1) a United States citizen; or

(2) a corporation, partnership, or other association created under the laws of the United States or any State (including the District of Columbia or any commonwealth, territory, or possession of the United States).

SEC. 2307. INDIAN TRIBES EXPORT PROMOTION.

(a) ASSISTANCE AUTHORIZED.—The Secretary of Commerce is authorized to provide assistance to eligible entities for the development of foreign markets for authentic American Indian arts and crafts. Eligible entities under this section include Indian tribes, tribal organizations, tribal enterprises, craft guilds, marketing cooperatives, and individual Indian-owned businesses.

(b) ACTIVITIES ELIGIBLE FOR ASSISTANCE.—Activities eligible for assistance under this section include, but are not limited to, conduct of market surveys, development of promotional materials, financing of trade missions, participation in international trade fairs, direct marketing, and other market development activities.

(c) ADMINISTRATION OF ASSISTANCE.—Assistance under this section shall be administered by the Secretary of Commerce under guidelines developed by the Secretary. Priority shall be given to projects which support the establishment of long term, stable international markets for American Indian arts and crafts and which are designed to provide the greatest economic benefit to American Indian artisans.

(d) TECHNICAL AND OTHER ASSISTANCE.—The Secretary of Commerce shall provide technical assistance and support services to applicants eligible for and entities receiving assistance under this section for the purpose of helping them in identifying and entering appropriate foreign markets, complying with foreign and domestic legal and banking requirements regarding the export and import of arts and crafts, and utilizing import and export financial arrangements, and shall provide such other assistance as may be necessary to support the development of export markets for American Indian arts and crafts.

(e) LIMITATION ON ASSISTANCE.—No assistance shall be provided under this section in support of any activity which includes the sale or marketing of any craft items other than authentic arts and crafts hand made or hand crafted by American Indian artisans.

SEC. 2308. PRINTING AT OVERSEAS LOCATIONS.

(a) PRINTING IN CONJUNCTION WITH EXPORT PROMOTION PROGRAMS.—Section 201 of the Export Administration Amendments Act of 1985 (15 U.S.C. 4051) is amended by adding at the end the following:

"(e) PRINTING OUTSIDE THE UNITED STATES.—(1) Notwithstanding the provisions of section 501 of title 44, United States Code, and consistent with other applicable law, the Secretary of Commerce, in carrying out any export promotion program, may authorize—

"(A) the printing, distribution, and sale of documents outside the contiguous United States, if the Secretary finds that the implementation of such export promotion program would be more efficient, and if such documents will be distributed primarily and sold exclusively outside the United States; and

"(B) the acceptance of private notices and advertisements in connection with the printing and distribution of such documents.

"(2) Any fees received by the Secretary pursuant to paragraph (1) shall be deposited in a separate account or accounts which may be used to defray directly the costs incurred in conducting activities authorized by paragraph (1) or to repay or make advances to appropriations or other funds available for such activities.".

SEC. 2309. LOCAL CURRENCIES UNDER PUBLIC LAW 480.

Section 108(i) of the Agricultural Trade Development and Assistance Act of 1954 (7 U.S.C. 1708(i)) is amended—

(1) in paragraph (1) by striking "and";

(2) in paragraph (2) by striking the period and inserting "; and"; and

(3) by adding at the end the following:

"(3) the terms 'private sector development activity' and 'private enterprise investment' include the construction of low- and medium-income housing and shelter.".

SEC. 2310. OFFICE OF EXPORT TRADE.

Section 104 of the Export Trading Company Act of 1982 (15 U.S.C. 4003) is amended by adding at the end the following: "The office shall establish a program to encourage and assist the operation of other export intermediaries, including existing and newly formed export management companies.".

SEC. 2311. REPORT ON EXPORT TRADING COMPANIES.

Not later than 18 months after the date of the enactment of this Act, the Secretary of Commerce shall submit a report to the Committee on Banking, Housing, and Urban Affairs of the Senate, and to the Committee on Banking, Finance and Urban Affairs, the Committee on Foreign Affairs, and the Committee on the Judiciary of the House of Representatives, on the activities of the Department of Commerce to promote and encourage the formation of new and the operation of existing and new export promotion intermediaries, including export management companies, export trade associations, bank export trading companies, and export trading companies. The report shall include a survey of the activities of export management companies, export trade associations, and those bank export trading companies and export trading companies established pursuant to the amendments made by title II of the Export Trading Company Act of 1982, and pursuant to title III of that Act. The report shall not contain any information subject to the protections from disclosure provided in that Act.

Subtitle D—Export Controls

SEC. 2401. REFERENCE TO THE EXPORT ADMINISTRATION ACT OF 1979.

For purposes of this subtitle, the Export Administration Act of 1979 shall be referred to as "the Act".

PART I—EXPORT CONTROLS GENERALLY

SEC. 2411. EXPORT LICENSE FEES.

Section 4 of the Act (50 U.S.C. App. 2403) is amended by adding at the end the following:

"(g) FEES.—No fee may be charged in connection with the submission or processing of an export license application.".

SEC. 2412. MULTIPLE LICENSE AUTHORITY.

Section 4(a)(2) of the Act (50 U.S.C. App. 2403(a)(2)) is amended—

(1) in subparagraph (A) by striking the period at the end of the first sentence and inserting ", except that the Secretary may establish a type of distribution license appropriate for consignees in the People's Republic of China."; and

(2) in subparagraph (B) in the first sentence by inserting "(except the People's Republic of China)" after "controlled countries".

SEC. 2413. DOMESTIC SALES TO COMMERCIAL ENTITIES OF CONTROLLED COUNTRIES.

Section 5(a)(1) of the Act (50 U.S.C. App. 2404(a)(1)) is amended by inserting after the second sentence the following: "For purposes of the preceding sentence, the term 'affiliates' includes both governmental entities and commercial entities that are controlled in fact by controlled countries.".

SEC. 2414. AUTHORITY FOR REEXPORTS.

Section 5(a) of the Act (50 U.S.C. App. 2404(a)) is amended by adding at the end the following:

"(4)(A) No authority or permission may be required under this section to reexport any goods or technology subject to the jurisdiction of the United States to any country which maintains export controls on such goods or technology cooperatively with the United States pursuant to the agreement of the group known as the Coordinating Committee, or pursuant to an agreement described in subsection (k) of this section. The Secretary may require any person reexporting any goods or technology under this subparagraph to notify the Secretary of such reexports.

"(B) Notwithstanding subparagraph (A), the Secretary may require authority or permission to reexport the following:

"(i) supercomputers;

"(ii) goods or technology for sensitive nuclear uses (as defined by the Secretary);

"(iii) devices for surreptitious interception of wire or oral communications; and

"(iv) goods or technology intended for such end users as the Secretary may specify by regulation.

"(5)(A) Except as provided in subparagraph (B), no authority or permission may be required under this section to reexport any goods or technology subject to the jurisdiction of the United States from any country when the goods or technology to be reexported are incorporated in another good and—

"(i) the value of the controlled United States content of that other good is 25 percent or less of the total value of the good; or

"(ii) the export of the goods or technology to a controlled country would require only notification of the participating governments of the Coordinating Committee.

For purposes of this paragraph, the 'controlled United States content' of a good means those goods or technology subject to the jurisdiction of the United States which are incorporated in the good, if the export of those goods or technology from the United States to a country, at the time that the good is exported to that country, would require a validated license.

"(B) The Secretary may by regulation provide that subparagraph (A) does not apply to the reexport of a supercomputer which contains goods or technology subject to the jurisdiction of the United States.

"(6) Not later than 90 days after the date of the enactment of this paragraph, the Secretary shall issue regulations to carry out paragraphs (4) and (5). Such regulations shall define the term 'supercomputer' for purposes of those paragraphs.".

SEC. 2415. EXPORTS TO COUNTRIES OTHER THAN CONTROLLED COUNTRIES.

(a) COCOM COUNTRIES.—Section 5(b)(2) of the Act (50 U.S.C. App. 2404(b)(2)) is amended to read as follows:

"(2)(A) Except as provided in subparagraph (B), no authority or permission may be required under this section to export goods or technology to a country which maintains export controls on such goods or technology cooperatively with the United States pursuant to the agreement of the group known as the Coordinating Committee or pursuant to an agreement described in subsection (k) of this section, if the export of such goods or technology to the People's Republic of China or a controlled country on the date of the enactment of the Export Enhancement Act of 1988 would require only notification of the participating governments of the Coordinating Committee.

"(B)(i) The Secretary may require a license for the export of goods or technology described in subparagraph (A) to such end users as the Secretary may specify by regulation.

"(ii) The Secretary may require any person exporting goods or technology under this paragraph to notify the Secretary of those exports.

"(C) The Secretary shall, within 3 months after the date of the enactment of the Export Enhancement Act of 1988, determine which countries referred to in subparagraph (A) are implementing an effective export control system consistent with principles agreed to in the Coordinating Committee, including the following:

"(i) national laws providing appropriate civil and criminal penalties and statutes of limitations sufficient to deter potential violations;

"(ii) a program to evaluate export license applications that includes sufficient technical expertise to assess the licensing status of exports and ensure the reliability of end-users;

"(iii) an enforcement mechanism that provides authority for trained enforcement officers to investigate and prevent illegal exports;

"(iv) a system of export control documentation to verify the movement of goods and technology; and

"(v) procedures for the coordination and exchange of information concerning violations of the agreement of the Coordinating Committee.

The Secretary shall, at least once each year, review the determinations made under the preceding sentence with respect to all countries referred to in subparagraph (A). The Secretary may, as appropriate, add countries to, or remove countries from, the list of countries that are implementing an effective export control system in accordance with this subparagraph. No authority or permission to export may be required for the export of goods or technology to a country on such list.".

(b) COUNTRIES OTHER THAN COCOM COUNTRIES.—Section 5(b) of the Act (50 U.S.C. App. 2404(b)) is amended by adding at the end the following:

"(3)(A) No authority or permission may be required under this section to export to any country, other than a controlled country, any goods or technology if the export of the goods or technology to controlled countries would require only notification of the participating governments of the Coordinating Committee.

"(B) The Secretary may require any person exporting any goods or technology under subparagraph (A) to notify the Secretary of those exports.".

SEC. 2416. CONTROL LIST.

(a) RESOLUTION OF DISPUTES.—Section 5(c)(2) of the Act (50 U.S.C. App. 2404(c)(2)) is amended by striking the last sentence and inserting the following: "If the Secretary and the Secretary of Defense are unable to concur on such items, as determined by the Secretary, the Secretary of Defense may, within 20 days after receiving notification of the Secretary's determination, refer the matter to the President for resolution. The Secretary of Defense shall notify the Secretary of any such referral. The President shall, not later than 20 days after such referral, notify the Secretary of his determination with respect to the inclusion of such items on the list. Failure of the Secretary of Defense to notify the President or the Secretary, or failure of the President to notify the Secretary, in accordance with this paragraph, shall be deemed by the Secretary to constitute concurrence in the implementation of the actions proposed by the Secretary regarding the inclusion of such items on the list.".

(b) CONDUCT OF LIST REVIEWS.—

(1) CONTROL LIST.—Section 5(c)(3) of the Act is amended to read as follows:

"(3) The Secretary shall conduct partial reviews of the list established pursuant to this subsection at least once each calendar quarter in order to carry out the policy set forth in section 3(2)(A) of this Act and the provisions of this section, and shall promptly make such revisions of the list as may be necessary after each such review. Before beginning each quarterly review, the Secretary shall publish notice of that review in the Federal Register. The Secretary shall provide a 30-day period during each review for comment and the submission of data, with or without oral presentation, by interested Government agencies and other affected or potentially affected parties. After consultation with appropriate Government agencies, the Secretary shall make a determination of any revisions in the list within 30 days after the end of the review period. The concurrence or approval of any other department or agency is not required before any such revision is made. The Secretary shall publish in the Federal Register any revisions in the list, with an explanation of the reasons for the revisions. The Secretary shall use the data developed from each review in formulating United States proposals relating to multilateral export controls in the group known as the Coordinating Committee. The Secretary shall further assess, as part of each review, the availability from sources outside the United States of goods and technology comparable to those subject to export controls imposed under this section. All goods and technology on the list shall be reviewed at least once each year. The provisions of this paragraph apply to revisions of the list which consist of removing items from the list or making changes in categories of, or other specifications in, items on the list.".

(2) LIST OF MILITARILY CRITICAL TECHNOLOGIES.—Section 5(d)(5) of the Act (50 U.S.C. App. 2404(d)(5)) is amended in the first sentence by striking "at least annually" and inserting "on an ongoing basis".

(3) TECHNICAL ADVISORY COMMITTEES.—(A) Section 5(c) of the Act is amended by adding at the end the following:

"(4) The appropriate technical advisory committee appointed under subsection (h) of this section shall be consulted by the Secretary with respect to changes, pursuant to paragraph (2) or (3), in the list established pursuant to this subsection, and such technical advisory committee may submit recommendations to the Secretary with respect to such changes. The Secretary shall consider the recommendations of the technical advisory committee and shall inform the committee of the disposition of its recommendations.".

(c) CONTROL LIST REDUCTION.—

(1) IN GENERAL.—Section 5(c) of the Act (50 U.S.C. App. 2404(c)) (as amended by subsection (b)(3) of this section) is further amended by adding at the end the following:

"(5)(A) Not later than 6 months after the date of the enactment of this paragraph, the following shall no longer be subject to export controls under this section:

"(i) All goods or technology the export of which to controlled countries on the date of the enactment of the Export Enhancement Act of 1988 would require only notification of the participating governments of the Coordinating Committee, except for those goods or technology on which the Coordinating Committee agrees to maintain such notification requirement.

"(ii) All medical instruments and equipment, subject to the provisions of subsection (m) of this section.

"(B) The Secretary shall submit to the Congress annually a report setting forth the goods and technology from which export controls have been removed under this paragraph.".

(2) ELIMINATION OF UNILATERAL CONTROLS.—Section 5(c) of the Act (as amended by subsection (b)(3) and paragraph (1) of this subsection) is further amended by adding at the end the following:

"(6)(A) Notwithstanding subsection (f) or (h)(6) of this section, any export control imposed under this section which is maintained unilaterally by the United States shall expire 6 months after the date of the enactment of this paragraph, or 6 months after the export control is imposed, whichever date is later, except that—

"(i) any such export controls on those goods or technology for which a determination of the Secretary that there is no foreign availability has been made under subsection (f) or (h)(6) of this section before the end of the applicable 6-month period and is in effect may be renewed for periods of not more than 6 months each, and

"(ii) any such export controls on those goods or technology with respect to which the President, by the end of the applicable 6-month period, is actively pursuing negotiations with other countries to achieve multilateral export controls on those goods or technology may be renewed for 2 periods of not more than 6 months each.

"(B) Export controls on goods or technology described in clause (i) or (ii) of subparagraph (A) may be renewed only if, before each renewal, the President submits to the Congress a report setting forth all the controls being renewed and stating the specific reasons for such renewal.".

(3) REVIEW OF CERTAIN LOW TECHNOLOGY ITEMS.—Section 5(c) of the Act (as amended by subsection (b)(3) and paragraphs (1) and (2) of this subsection) is further amended by adding at the end the following:

"(7) Notwithstanding any other provision of this subsection, after 1 year has elapsed since the last review in the Federal Register on any item within a category on the control list the export of which to the People's Republic of China would require only notification of the members of the group known as the Coordinating Committee, an export license applicant may file an allegation with the Secretary that such item has not been so reviewed within such 1-year period. Within 90 days after receipt of such allegation, the Secretary—

"(A) shall determine the truth of the allegation;

"(B) shall, if the allegation is confirmed, commence and complet the review of the item; and

"(C) shall, pursuant to such review, submit a finding for publication in the Federal Register.

In such finding, the Secretary shall identify those goods or technology which shall remain on the control list and those goods or technology which shall be removed from the control list. If such review and submission for publication are not completed within that 90-day period, the goods or technology encompassed by such item shall immediately be removed from the control list.".

SEC. 2417. TRADE SHOWS.

Section 5(e) of the Act (50 U.S.C. App. 2404(e)) is amended by adding at the end the following:

"(6) Any application for a license for the export to the People's Republic of China of any good on which export controls are in effect under this section, without regard to the technical specifications of the good, for the purpose of demonstration or exhibition at a trade show shall carry a presumption of approval if—

"(A) the United States exporter retains title to the good during the entire period in which the good is in the People's Republic of China; and

"(B) the exporter removes the good from the People's Republic of China no later than at the conclusion of the trade show.".

SEC. 2418. FOREIGN AVAILABILITY.—

(a) In General.—Section 5(f) of the Act (50 U.S.C. App. 2404(f)) is amended to read as follows:

"(f) Foreign Availability.—

"(1) Foreign availability to controlled countries.—(A) The Secretary, in consultation with the Secretary of Defense and other appropriate Government agencies and with appropriate technical advisory committees established pursuant to subsection (h) of this section, shall review, on a continuing basis, the availability to controlled countries, from sources outside the United States, including countries which participate with the United States in multilateral export controls, of any goods or technology the export of which requires a validated license under this section. In any case in which the Secretary determines, in accordance with procedures and criteria which the Secretary shall by regulation establish, that any such goods or technology are available in fact to controlled countries from such sources in sufficient quantity and of comparable quality so that the requirement of a validated license for the export of such goods or technology is or would be ineffective in achieving the purpose set forth in subsection (a) of this section, the Secretary may not, after the determination is made, require a validated license for the export of such goods or technology during the period of such foreign availability, unless the President determines that the absence of export controls under this section on the goods or technology would prove detrimental to the national security of the United States. In any case in which the President determines under this paragraph that export controls under this section must be maintained notwithstanding foreign availability, the Secretary shall publish that determination, together with a concise statement of its basis and the estimated economic impact of the decision.

"(B) The Secretary shall approve any application for a validated license which is required under this section for the export of any goods or technology to a controlled country and which meets all other requirements for such an application, if the Secretary determines that such goods or technology will, if the license is denied, be available in fact to such country from sources outside the United States, including countries which participate with the United States in multilateral export controls, in sufficient quantity and of comparable quality so that denial of the license would be ineffective in achieving the purpose set forth in subsection (a) of this section, unless the President determines that approving the license application would prove detrimental to the national security of the United States. In any case in which the Secretary makes a determination of foreign availability under this subparagraph with respect to any goods or technology, the Secretary shall determine whether a determination of foreign availability under subparagraph (A) with respect to such goods or technology is warranted.

"(2) FOREIGN AVAILABILITY TO OTHER THAN CONTROLLED COUNTRIES.—(A) The Secretary shall review, on a continuing basis, the availability to countries other than controlled countries, from sources outside the United States, of any goods or technology the export of which requires a validated license under this section. If the Secretary determines, in accordance with procedures which the Secretary shall establish, that any goods or technology in sufficient quantity and of comparable quality are available in fact from sources outside the United States (other than availability under license from a country which maintains export controls on such goods or technology cooperatively with the United States pursuant to the agreement of the group known as the Coordinating Committee or pursuant to an agreement described in subsection (k) of this section), the Secretary may not, after the determination is made and during the period of such foreign availability, require a validated license for the export of such goods or technology to any country (other than a controlled country) to which the country from which the goods or technology is available does not place controls on the export of such goods or technology. The requirement with respect to a validated license in the preceding sentence shall not apply if the President determines that the absence of export controls under this section on the goods or technology would prove detrimental to the national security of the United States. In any case in which the President determines under this paragraph that export controls under this section must be maintained notwithstanding foreign availability, the Secretary shall publish that determination, together with a concise statement of its basis and the estimated economic impact of the decision.

"(B) The Secretary shall approve any application for a validated license which is required under this section for the export of any goods or technology to a country (other than a controlled country) and which meets all other requirements for such an application, if the Secretary determines that such goods or technology are available from foreign sources to that country under the criteria established in subparagraph (A), unless the President determines that approving the license application would prove detrimental to the national security of the United States. In any case in which the Secretary makes a determination of foreign availability under this subparagraph with respect to any goods or technology, the Secretary shall determine whether a determination of foreign availability under subparagraph (A) with respect to such goods or technology is warranted.

"(3) PROCEDURES FOR MAKING DETERMINATIONS.—(A) The Secretary shall make a foreign availability determination under paragraph (1) or (2) on the Secretary's own initiative or upon receipt of an allegation from an export license applicant that such availability exists. In making any such determination, the Secretary shall accept the representations of applicants made in writing and supported by reasonable evidence, unless such representations are contradicted by reliable evidence, including scientific or physical examination, expert opinion based upon adequate factual information, or intelligence information. In making determinations of foreign availability, the Secretary may consider such factors as cost, reliability, the availability and reliability of spare parts and the cost and quality thereof, maintenance programs, durability, quality of end products produced by the item proposed for export, and scale of production. For purposes of this subparagraph, 'evidence' may include such items as foreign manufacturers' catalogues, brochures, or operations or maintenance manuals, articles from reputable trade publications, photographs, and depositions based upon eyewitness accounts.

"(B) In a case in which an allegation is received from an export license applicant, the Secretary shall, upon receipt of the allegation, submit for publication in the Federal Register notice of such receipt. Within 4 months after receipt of the allegation, the Secretary shall determine whether the foreign availability exists, and shall so notify the applicant. If the Secretary has determined that the foreign availability exists, the Secretary shall, upon making such determination, submit the determination for review to other departments and agencies as the Secretary considers appropriate. The Secretary's determination of foreign availability does not require the concurrence or approval of any official, department, or agency to which such a determination is submitted. Not later than 1 month after the Secretary makes the determination, the Secretary shall respond in writing to the applicant and submit for publication in the Federal Register, that—

"(i) the foreign availability does exist and—

"(I) the requirement of a validated license has been removed,

"(II) the President has determined that export controls under this section must be maintained notwithstanding the foreign availability and the applicable steps are being taken under paragraph (4), or

"(III) in the case of a foreign availability determination under paragraph (1), the foreign availability determination will be submitted to a multilateral review process in accordance with the agreement of the Coordinating Committee for a period of not more than 4 months beginning on the date of the publication; or

"(ii) the foreign availability does not exist.

In any case in which the submission for publication is not made within the time period specified in the preceding sentence, the Secretary may not thereafter require a license for the export of the goods or technology with respect to which the foreign availability allegation was made. In the case of a foreign availability determination under paragraph (1) to which clause (i)(III) applies, no license for such export may be required after the end of the 9-month period beginning on the date on which the allegation is received.

"(4) NEGOTIATIONS TO ELIMINATE FOREIGN AVAILABILITY.—(A) In any case in which export controls are maintained under this section notwithstanding foreign availability, on account of a determination by the President that the absence of the controls would prove detrimental to the national security of the United States, the President shall actively pursue negotiations with the governments of the appropriate foreign countries for the purpose of eliminating such availability. No later than the commencement of such negotiations, the President shall notify in writing the Committee on Banking, Housing, and Urban Affairs of the Senate and the Committee on Foreign Affairs of the House of Representatives that he has begun such negotiations and why he believes it is important to national security that export controls on the goods or technology involved be maintained.

"(B) If, within 6 months after the President's determination that export controls be maintained, the foreign availability has not been eliminated, the Secretary may not, after the end of that 6-month period, require a validated license for the export of the goods or technology involved. The President may extend the 6-month period described in the preceding sentence for an additional period of 12 months if the President certifies to the Congress that the negotiations involved are progressing and that the absence of the export controls involved would prove detrimental to the national security of the United States. Whenever the President has reason to believe that goods or technology subject to export controls for national security purposes by the United States may become available from other countries to controlled countries and that such availability can be prevented or eliminated by means of negotiations with such other countries, the President shall promptly initiate negotiations with the governments of such other countries to prevent such foreign availability.

"(C) After an agreement is reached with a country pursuant to negotiations under this paragraph to eliminate or prevent foreign availability of goods or technology, the Secretary may not require a validated license for the export of such goods or technology to that country.

"(5) EXPEDITED LICENSES FOR ITEMS AVAILABLE TO COUNTRIES OTHER THAN CONTROLLED COUNTRIES.—(A) In any case in which the Secretary finds that any goods or technology from foreign sources is of similar quality to goods or technology the export of which requires a validated license under this section and is available to a country other than a controlled country without effective restrictions, the Secretary shall designate such goods or technology as eligible for export to such country under this paragraph.

"(B) In the case of goods or technology designated under subparagraph (A), then 20 working days after the date of formal filing with the Secretary of an individual validated license application for the export of those goods or technology to an eligible country, a license for the transaction specified in the application shall become valid and effective and the goods or technology are authorized for export pursuant to such license unless the license has been denied by the Secretary on account of an inappropriate end user. The Secretary may extend the 20-day period provided in the preceding sentence for an additional period of 15 days if the Secretary requires additional time to consider the application and so notifies the applicant.

"(C) The Secretary may make a foreign availability determination under subparagraph (A) on the Secretary's own initiative, upon receipt of an allegation from an export license applicant that such availability exists, or upon the submission of a certification by a technical advisory committee of appropriate jurisdiction that such availability exists. Upon receipt of such an allegation or certification, the Secretary shall publish notice of such allegation or certification in the Federal Register and shall make the foreign availability determination within 30 days after such receipt and publish the determination in the Federal Register. In the case of the failure of the Secretary to make and publish such determination within that 30-day period, the goods or technology involved shall be deemed to be designated as eligible for export to the country or countries involved, for purposes of subparagraph (B).

"(D) The provisions of paragraphs (1), (2), (3), and (4) do not apply with respect to determinations of foreign availability under this paragraph.

"(6) OFFICE OF FOREIGN AVAILABILITY.—The Secretary shall establish in the Department of Commerce an Office of Foreign Availability, which shall be under the direction of the Under Secretary of Commerce for Export Administration. The Office shall be responsible for gathering and analyzing all the necessary information in order for the Secretary to make determinations of foreign availability under this Act. The Secretary shall make available to the Committee on Foreign Affairs of the House of Representatives and the Committee on Banking, Housing, and Urban Affairs of the Senate at the end of each 6-month period during a fiscal year information on the operations of the Office, and on improvements in the Government's ability to assess foreign availability, during that 6-month period, including information on the training of personnel, the use of computers, and the use of Commercial Service Officers of the United States and Foreign Commercial Service. Such information shall also include a description of representative determinations made under this Act during that 6-month period that foreign availability did or did not exist (as the case may be), together with an explanation of such determinations.

"(7) SHARING OF INFORMATION.—Each department or agency of the United States, including any intelligence agency, and all contractors with any such department or agency, shall, upon the request of the Secretary and consistent with the protection of intelligence sources and methods, furnish information to the Office of Foreign Availability concerning foreign availability of goods and technology subject to export controls under this Act. Each such department or agency shall allow the Office of Foreign Availability access to any information from a laboratory or other facility within such department or agency.

"(8) REMOVAL OF CONTROLS ON LESS SOPHISTICATED GOODS OR TECHNOLOGY.—In any case in which Secretary may not, pursuant to paragraph (1), (2), (3), or (4) of this subsection or paragraph (6) of subsection (h) of this section, require a validated license for the export of goods or technology, then the Secretary may not require a validated license for the export of any similar goods or technology whose function, technological approach, performance thresholds, and other attributes that form the basis for export controls under this section do not exceed the technical parameters of the goods or technology from which the validated license requirement is removed under the applicable paragraph.

"(9) NOTICE OF ALL FOREIGN AVAILABILITY ASSESSMENTS.—Whenever the Secretary undertakes a foreign availability assessment under this subsection or subsection (h)(6), the Secretary shall publish notice of such assessment in the Federal Register.

"(10) AVAILABILITY DEFINED.—For purposes of this subsection and subsections (f) and (h), the term 'available in fact to controlled countries' includes production or availability of any goods or technology in any country—

"(A) from which the goods or technology is not restricted for export to any controlled country; or

"(B) in which such export restrictions are determined by the Secretary to be ineffective.

For purposes of subparagraph (B), the mere inclusion of goods or technology on a list of goods or technology subject to bilateral or multilateral national security export controls shall not alone constitute credible evidence that a country provides an effective means of controlling the export of such goods or technology to controlled countries.".

(b) TECHNICAL ADVISORY COMMITTEE DETERMINATIONS.—Section 5(h)(6) of the Act (50 U.S.C. App. 2404(h)(6)) is amended by adding at the end the following: "After an agreement is reached with a country pursuant to negotiations under this paragraph to eliminate foreign availability of goods or technology, the Secretary may not require a validated license for the export of such goods or technology to that country.".

(c) TECHNICAL AMENDMENT.—Section 14(a)(8) of the Act (50 U.S.C. 2413(a)(8)) is amended by striking "5(f)(5)" and inserting "5(f)(6)".

SEC. 2419. REVIEW OF TECHNOLOGY LEVELS.

Section 5(g) of the Act (50 U.S.C. 2404(g)) is amended—

(1) by inserting "(1)" immediately before the first sentence; and

(2) by adding at the end the following:

"(2)(A) In carrying out this subsection, the Secretary shall conduct annual reviews of the performance levels of goods or technology—

"(i) which are eligible for export under a distribution license,

"(ii) below which exports to the People's Republic of China require only notification of the governments participating in the group known as the Coordinating Committee, and

"(iii) below which no authority or permission to export may be required under subsection (b)(2) or (b)(3) of this section.

The Secretary shall make appropriate adjustments to such performance levels based on these reviews.

"(B) In any case in which the Secretary receives a request which—

"(i) is to revise the qualification requirements or minimum thresholds of any goods eligible for export under a distribution license, and

"(ii) is made by an exporter of such goods, representatives of an industry which produces such goods, or a technical advisory committee established under subsection (h) of this section,

the Secretary, after consulting with other appropriate Government agencies and technical advisory committees established under subsection (h) of this section, shall determine whether to make such revision, or some other appropriate revision, in such qualification requirements or minimum thresholds. In making this determination, the Secretary shall take into account the availability of the goods from sources outside the United States. The Secretary shall make a determination on a request made under this subparagraph within 90 days after the date on which the request is filed. If the

Secretary's determination pursuant to such a request is to make a revision, such revision shall be implemented within 120 days after the date on which the request is filed and shall be published in the Federal Register.".

SEC. 2420. FUNCTIONS OF TECHNICAL ADVISORY COMMITTEES.

(a) CONSULTATION ON REVISIONS OF CONTROL LIST AND ON REGULATIONS.—Section 5(h)(2) of the Act (50 U.S.C. 2404(h)(2)) is amended—

(1) by redesignating clause (E) as clause (F); and

(2) by striking clause (D) and inserting the following: "(D) revisions of the control list (as provided in subsection (c)(4)), including proposed revisions of multilateral controls in which the United States participates, (E) the issuance of regulations, and".

(b) REVIEW OF REGULATIONS.—Section 15(b) of the Act (50 U.S.C. App. 2414(b)) is amended in the third sentence—

(1) by striking "and such other" and inserting "such other"; and

(2) by inserting after "appropriate" the following: ", and the appropriate technical advisory committee".

SEC. 2421. NEGOTIATIONS WITH COCOM.

(a) NEGOTIATING OBJECTIVES.—Section 5(i) of the Act (50 U.S.C. App. 2404(i)) is amended by striking "The President" and inserting "Recognizing the ineffectiveness of unilateral controls and the importance of uniform enforcement measures to the effectiveness of multilateral controls, the President".

(b) INDUSTRY REPRESENTATIVE TO COCOM.—Section 5(i) of the Act is amended by adding at the end the following:

"For purposes of reviews of the International Control List, the President may include as advisors to the United States delegation to the Committee representatives of industry who are knowledgeable with respect to the items being reviewed.".

SEC. 2422. GOODS CONTAINING MICROPROCESSORS OR CERTAIN OTHER PARTS OR COMPONENTS.

Section 5(m) of the Act (50 U.S.C. 2404(m)) is amended to read as follows:

"(m) GOODS CONTAINING CONTROLLED PARTS AND COMPONENTS.—Export controls may not be imposed under this section, or under any other provision of law, on a good solely on the basis that the good contains parts or components subject to export controls under this section if such parts or components—

"(1) are essential to the functioning of the good,

"(2) are customarily included in sales of the good in countries other than controlled countries, and

"(3) comprise 25 percent or less of the total value of the good, unless the good itself, if exported, would by virtue of the functional characteristics of the good as a whole make a significant contribution to the military potential of a controlled country which would prove detrimental to the national security of the United States.".

SEC. 2423. FOREIGN POLICY CONTROLS.

(a) DIPLOMATIC ALTERNATIVES.—Section 6(a) of the Act (50 U.S.C. 2405(a)) is amended by adding at the end the following:

"(6) Before imposing, expanding, or extending export controls under this section on exports to a country which can use goods, technology, or information available from foreign sources and so incur little or no economic costs as a result of the controls, the President should, through diplomatic means, employ alternatives to export controls which offer opportunities of distinguishing the United States from, and expressing the displeasure of the United States with, the specific actions of that country in response to which the controls are proposed. Such alternatives include private discussions with foreign leaders, public statements in situations where private diplomacy is unavailable or not effective, withdrawal of ambassadors, and reduction of the size of the diplomatic staff that the country involved is permitted to have in the United States.".

(b) SPARE PARTS.—Section 6 of the Act (50 U.S.C. App. 2405) is amended by adding at the end the following:

"(p) SPARE PARTS.—(1) At the same time as the President imposes or expands export controls under this section, the President shall determine whether such export controls will apply to replacement parts for parts in goods subject to such export controls.

"(2) With respect to export controls imposed under this section before the date of the enactment of this subsection, an individual validated export license shall not be required for replacement parts which are exported to replace on a one-for-one basis parts that were in a good that was lawfully exported from the United States, unless the President determines that such a license should be required for such parts.".

SEC. 2424. EXPORTS OF DOMESTICALLY PRODUCED CRUDE OIL.

(a) TECHNICAL AMENDMENT.—Section 7(d) of the Act (50 U.S.C. App. 2406(d)) is amended by striking paragraph (4).

(b) CRUDE OIL STUDY.—

(1) REVIEW OF EXPORT RESTRICTIONS ON CRUDE OIL.—The Secretary of Commerce, in consultation with the Secretary of Energy, shall undertake a comprehensive review to assess whether existing statutory restrictions on the export of crude oil produced in the contiguous United States are adequate to protect the energy and national security interests of the United States and American consumers. Taking into account exports licensed since 1983 and potential exports of heavy crude oil produced in California, the review shall assess the effect of increased exports of crude oil produced in the contiguous United States on—

(A) the adequacy of domestic supplies of crude oil and refined petroleum products in meeting United States energy and national security needs;

(B) the quantity, quality, and retail price of petroleum products available to consumers in the United States generally and on the West Coast in particular;

(C) the overall trade deficit of the United States;

(D) acquisition costs of crude oil by domestic petroleum refiners;

(E) the financial viability of sectors of the domestic petroleum industry (including independent refiners, distributors, marketers, and pipeline carriers); and

(F) the United States tanker fleet (and the industries that support it), with particular emphasis on the availability of militarily useful tankers to meet anticipated national defense requirements.

(2) PUBLIC HEARING AND COMMENT.—The Secretary of Commerce shall provide notice and a reasonable opportunity for public hearing and comment on the review conducted pursuant to this subsection.

(3) CONSULTATIONS WITH OTHER AGENCIES.—The Secretary of Commerce shall consult with the Secretary of Defense, the Secretary of the Interior, and the Secretary of Transportation, in addition to the Secretary of Energy, in undertaking the review pursuant to this subsection.

(4) FINDINGS, OPTIONS, AND RECOMMENDATIONS.—After taking public comment and consulting with appropriate State and Federal officials, the Secretary of Commerce, in consultation with the Secretary of Energy, shall develop findings, options, and recommendations regarding the adequacy of existing statutory restrictions on the export of crude oil produced in the contiguous United States in protecting the energy and national security interests of the United States and American consumers.

(5) CONSULTATIONS AND REPORT.—In carrying out this subsection, the Secretary of Commerce shall consult with the Committee on Foreign Affairs and the Committee on Energy and Commerce of the House of Representatives and the Committee on Banking, Housing, and Urban Affairs, the Committee on Commerce, Science, and Transportation, and the Committee on Energy and Natural Resources of the Senate. Not later than 12 months after the date of the enactment of this Act, the Secretary shall transmit to each of those committees a report which contains the results of the review undertaken pursuant to this subsection and the findings, options, and recommendations developed under paragraph (4).

SEC. 2425. PROCEDURES FOR LICENSE APPLICATIONS.

(a) REVIEW OF LICENSE APPLICATIONS BY THE SECRETARY OF DEFENSE.—Section 10(g) of the Act (50 U.S.C. App. 2409(g)) is amended—

(1) in paragraph (2)(A) by inserting "and the Secretary" after "to the President";

(2) by inserting before the last sentence of paragraph (2) the following:

"Whenever the Secretary of Defense makes a recommendation to the President pursuant to paragraph (2)(A), the Secretary shall also submit his recommendation to the President on the request to export if the Secretary differs with the Secretary of Defense.";

(3) by adding at the end of paragraph (2) the following: "If the Secretary of Defense fails to make a recommendation or notification under this paragraph within the 20-day period specified in the third sentence, or if the President, within 20 days after receiving a recommendation from the Secretary of Defense with respect to an export, fails to notify the Secretary that he approves or disapproves the export, the Secretary shall approve or deny the request for a license or other authority to export without such recommendation or notification."; and

(4) by striking paragraph (4).

(b) REPORT BY SECRETARIES OF COMMERCE AND DEFENSE.—The Secretary of Commerce and the Secretary of Defense shall each evaluate and, not later than 4 months after the date of the enactment of this Act, shall jointly prepare and submit a report to the

Committee on Foreign Affairs of the House of Representatives and the Committee on Banking, Housing, and Urban Affairs of the Senate on the review by the Department of Defense for national security purposes as provided in the Export Administration Act of 1979, of export license applications for exports to countries other than controlled countries under section 5(b)(1) of that Act

(c) REPORT ON SMALL BUSINESSES.—Section 10(m) of the Act (50 U.S.C. App. 2409(m)) is amended by adding at the end the following: "The Secretary shall, not later than 120 days after the date of the enactment of the Export Enhancement Act of 1988, report to the Congress on steps taken to implement the plan developed under this subsection to assist small businesses in the export licensing application process.".

SEC. 2426. VIOLATIONS.

Section 11(h) of the Act (50 U.S.C. App. 2410(h)) is amended—

(1) in the first sentence—

(A) by inserting "(1)" before "No"; and

(B) by inserting after "violation of" the following: "this Act (or any regulation, license, or order issued under this Act), any regulation, license, or order issued under the International Emergency Economic Powers Act,"; and

(2) by adding at the end the following:

"(2) The Secretary may exercise the authority under paragraph (1) with respect to any person related, through affiliation, ownership, control, or position of responsibility, to any person convicted of any violation of law set forth in paragraph (1), upon a showing of such relationship with the convicted party, and subject to the procedures set forth in section 13(c) of this Act.".

SEC. 2427. ENFORCEMENT.

Section 12(a)(2)(B) of the Act (50 U.S.C. App. 2411(a)(2)(B)) is amended by adding at the end the following: "The Customs Service may not detain for more than 20 days any shipment of goods or technology eligible for export under a general license under section 4(a)(3). In a case in which such detention is on account of a disagreement between the Secretary and the head of any other department or agency with export license authority under other provisions of law concerning the export license requirements for such goods or technology, such disagreement shall be resolved within that 20-day period. At the end of that 20-day period, the Customs Service shall either release the goods or technology, or seize the goods or technology as authorized by other provisions of law.".

SEC. 2428. ADMINISTRATIVE PROCEDURE AND JUDICIAL REVIEW.

(a) JUDICIAL REVIEW.—(1) Section 13(c) of the Act (50 U.S.C. App. 2412(c)) is amended—

(A) in the last sentence of paragraph (1) by inserting before the period ", except as provided in paragraph (3)";

(B) by redesignating paragraph (3) as paragraph (4); and

(C) by inserting after paragraph (2) the following:

"(3) The order of the Secretary under paragraph (1) shall be final except that the charged party may, within 15 days after the order is issued, appeal the order in the United States Court of Appeals for the District of Columbia Circuit, which shall have jurisdiction of the appeal. The court may, while the appeal is pending, stay the order of the Secretary. The court may review only those issues necessary to determine liability for the civil penalty or other sanction involved. In an appeal filed under this paragraph, the court shall set aside any finding of fact for which the court finds there is not substantial evidence on the record and any conclusion of law which the court finds to be arbitrary, capricious, an abuse of discretion, or otherwise not in accordance with law.".

(2) Section 13(d) of the Act (50 U.S.C. App. 2412(d)) is amended—

(A) in the fifth sentence of paragraph (2) by inserting before the period ", except as provided in paragraph (3)"; and

(B) by adding at the end of paragraph (2) the following: "All materials submitted to the administrative law judge and the Secretary shall constitute the administrative record for purposes of review by the courts.

"(3) An order of the Secretary affirming, in whole or in part, the issuance of a temporary denial order may, within 15 days after the order is issued, be appealed by a person subject to the order to the United States Court of Appeals for the District of Columbia Circuit, which shall have jurisdiction of the appeal. The court may review only those issues necessary to determine whether the standard for issuing the temporary denial order has been met. The court shall vacate the Secretary's order if the court finds that the Secretary's order is arbitrary, capricious, an abuse of discretion, or otherwise not in accordance with law.".

(b) ISSUANCE OF TEMPORARY DENIAL ORDERS.—Section 13(d)(1) of the Act (50 U.S.C. App. 2412(d)(1)) is amended in the second sentence by striking "60" each place it appears and inserting "180".

SEC. 2429. RESPONSIBILITIES OF THE UNDER SECRETARY OF COMMERCE FOR EXPORT ADMINISTRATION.

Section 15(a) of the Act (50 U.S.C. App. 2414(a)) is amended by inserting "and such other statutes that relate to national security" after "functions of the Secretary under this Act".

SEC. 2430. AUTHORIZATION OF APPROPRIATIONS.

Section 18(b) of the Act (50 U.S.C. App. 2417(b)) is amended—

(1) in paragraph (1)—

(A) by striking "each of the fiscal years 1987 and 1988" and inserting "the fiscal year 1988";

(B) by striking "for each such year" each place it appears, and

(C) by striking "and" after the semicolon; and

(2) by striking paragraph (2) and inserting the following:

"(2) $46,913,000 for the fiscal year 1989, of which $15,000,000 shall be available only for enforcement, $5,000,000 shall be available only for foreign availability assessments under subsections (f) and (h)(6) of section 5, $4,000,000 shall be available only for regional export control assistance centers, and $22,913,000 shall be available for all other activities under this Act; and

"(3) such additional amounts for each of the fiscal years 1988 and 1989 as may be necessary for increases in salary, pay, retirement, other employee benefits authorized by law, and other nondiscretionary costs.".

SEC. 2431. TERMINATION DATE.

Section 20 of the Act (50 U.S.C. 2419) is amended by striking "1989" and inserting "1990".

SEC. 2432. MONITORING OF WOOD EXPORTS.

The Secretary of Commerce shall, for a period of 2 years beginning on the date of the enactment of this Act, monitor exports of processed and unprocessed wood to all countries of the Pacific Rim. The Secretary shall include the results of such monitoring in monthly reports setting forth, with respect to each item monitored, actual exports, the destination by country, and the domestic and worldwide price, supply, and demand. The Secretary shall transmit such reports to the Committee on Foreign Affairs of the House of Representatives and the Committee on Banking, Housing, and Urban Affairs of the Senate.

SEC. 2433. STUDY ON NATIONAL SECURITY EXPORT CONTROLS.

(a) ARRANGEMENTS FOR AND CONTENTS OF STUDY.—

(1) ARRANGEMENTS FOR CONDUCTING STUDY.—The Secretary of Commerce and the Secretary of Defense, not later than 60 days after the date of the enactment of this Act, shall enter into appropriate arrangements with the National Academy of Sciences and the National Academy of Engineering (hereafter in this section referred to as the "Academies") to conduct a comprehensive study of the adequacy of the current export administration system in safeguarding United States national security while maintaining United States international competitiveness and Western technological preeminence.

(2) REQUIREMENTS OF STUDY.—Recognizing the need to minimize the disruption of United States trading interests while preventing Western technology from enhancing the development of the military capabilities of controlled countries, the study shall—

(A) identify those goods and technologies which are likely to make crucial differences in the military capabilities of controlled countries, and identify which of those goods and technologies controlled countries already possess or are available to controlled countries from other sources;

(B) develop implementable criteria by which to define those goods and technologies;

(C) demonstrate how such criteria would be applied to the control list by the relevant agencies to revise the list, eliminate ineffective controls, and strengthen controls;

(D) develop proposals to improve United States and multilateral assessments of foreign availability of goods and technology subject to export controls; and

(E) develop proposals to improve the administration of the export control program, including procedures to ensure timely, predictable, and effective decision-making.

(b) ADVISORY PANEL.—In conducting the study under subsection (a), the Academies shall appoint an Advisory Panel of not more than 24 members who shall be selected from among individuals in private life who, by virtue of their experience and expertise, are knowledgeable in relevant scientific, business, legal, or administrative matters. No individual may be selected as a member who, at the time of his or her appointment, is an elected or appointed official or employee in the executive, legislative, or judicial branch of the Government In selecting members of the Advisory Panel, the Academies shall seek suggestions from the President, the Congress, and representatives of industry and the academic community.

(c) EXECUTIVE BRANCH COOPERATION.—The Secretary of Commerce, the Secretary of Defense, the Secretary of State, the Director of the Central Intelligence Agency, and the head of any department or agency that exercises authority in export administration—

(1) shall furnish to the Academies, upon request and under appropriate safeguards, classified or unclassified information which the Academies determine to be necessary for the purposes of conducting the study required by this section; and

(2) shall work with the Academies on such problems related to the study as the Academies consider necessary.

(d) REPORT.—Under the direction of the Advisory Panel, the Academies shall prepare and submit to the President and the Congress, not later than 18 months after entering into the arrangements referred to in subsection (a), a report which contains a detailed statement of the findings and conclusions of the Academies pursuant to the study conducted under subsection (a), together with their recommendations for such legislative or regulatory reforms as they consider appropriate.

(e) AUTHORIZATION OF APPROPRIATIONS.—There are authorized to be appropriated $900,000 to carry out this section.

PART II—MULTILATERAL EXPORT CONTROL ENHANCEMENT

SEC. 2441. SHORT TITLE.

This part may be cited as the "Multilateral Export Control Enhancement Amendments Act".

SEC. 2442. FINDINGS.

The Congress makes the following findings:

(1) The diversion of advanced milling machinery to the Soviet Union by the Toshiba Machine Company and Kongsberg Trading Company has had a serious impact on United States and Western security interests.

(2) United States and Western security is undermined without the cooperation of the governments and nationals of all countries participating in the group known as the Coordinating Committee (hereafter in this part referred to as "COCOM") in enforcing the COCOM agreement.

(3) It is the responsibility of all governments participating in COCOM to place in effect strong national security export control laws, to license strategic exports carefully, and to enforce those export control laws strictly, since the COCOM system is only as strong as the national laws and enforcement on which it is based.

(4) It is also important for corporations to implement effective internal control systems to ensure compliance with export control laws.

(5) In order to protect United States national security, the United States must take steps to ensure the compliance of foreign companies with COCOM controls, including, where necessary conditions have been met, the imposition of sanctions against violators of controls commensurate with the severity of the violation.

SEC. 2443. MANDATORY SANCTIONS AGAINST TOSHIBA AND KONGSBERG.

(a) SANCTIONS AGAINST TOSHIBA MACHINE COMPANY, KONGSBERG TRADING COMPANY, AND CERTAIN OTHER FOREIGN PERSONS.—(1) The President shall impose, for a period of 3 years—

(1) a prohibition on contracting with, and procurement of products and services from—

(A) Toshiba Machine Company and Kongsberg Trading Company, and

(B) any other foreign person whom the President finds to have knowingly facilitated the diversion of advanced milling machinery by Toshiba Machine Company and Kongsberg Trading Company to the Soviet Union,

by any department, agency, or instrumentality of the United States Government; and

(2) a prohibition on the importation into the United States of all products produced by Toshiba Machine Company, Kongsberg Trading Company, and any foreign person described in paragraph (1)(B).

(b) SANCTIONS AGAINST TOSHIBA CORPORATION AND KONGSBERG VAAPENFABRIKK.—The President shall impose, for a period of 3 years, a prohibition on contracting with, and procurement of products and services from, the Toshiba Corporation and Kongsberg Vaapenfabrikk, by any department, agency, or instrumentality of the United States Government.

(c) EXCEPTIONS.—The President shall not apply sanctions under this section—

(1) in the case of procurement of defense articles or defense services—

(A) under existing contracts or subcontracts, including exercise of options for production quantities to satisfy United States operational military requirements;

(B) if the President determines that the company or foreign person to whom the sanctions would otherwise be applied is a sole source supplier of essential defense articles or services and no alternative supplier can be identified; or

(C) if the President determines that such articles or services are essential to the national security under defense coproduction agreements; or

(2) to—

(A) products or services provided under contracts or other binding agreements (as such terms are defined by the President in regulations) entered into before June 30, 1987;

(B) spare parts;

(C) component parts, but not finished products, essential to United States products or production;

(D) routine servicing and maintenance of products; or

(E) information and technology.

(d) DEFINITIONS.—For purposes of this section—

(1) the term "component part" means any article which is not usable for its intended functions without being imbedded or integrated into any other product and which, if used in production of a finished product, would be substantially transformed in that process;

(2) the term "finished product" means any article which is usable for its intended functions without being imbedded in or integrated into any other product, but in no case shall such

term be deemed to include an article produced by a person other than a sanctioned person that contains parts or components of the sanctioned person if the parts or components have been substantially transformed during production of the finished product; and

(3) the term "sanctioned person" means a company or other foreign person upon whom prohibitions have been imposed under subsection (a) or (b).

SEC. 2444. MANDATORY SANCTIONS FOR FUTURE VIOLATIONS.

The Act is amended by inserting after section 11 the following new section:

"MULTILATERAL EXPORT CONTROL VIOLATIONS

"SEC. 11A. (a) DETERMINATION BY THE PRESIDENT.—The President, subject to subsection (c), shall apply sanctions under subsection (b) for a period of not less than 2 years and not more than 5 years, if the President determines that—

"(1) a foreign person has violated any regulation issued by a country to control exports for national security purposes pursuant to the agreement of the group known as the Coordinating Committee, and

"(2) such violation has resulted in substantial enhancement of Soviet and East bloc capabilities in submarine or antisubmarine warfare, ballistic or antiballistic missile technology, strategic aircraft, command, control, communications and intelligence, or other critical technologies as determined by the President, on the advice of the National Security Council, to represent a serious adverse impact on the strategic balance of forces.

The President shall notify the Congress of each action taken under this section. This section, except subsections (h) and (j), applies only to violations that occur after the date of the enactment of the Export Enhancement Act of 1988.

"(b) SANCTIONS.—The sanctions referred to in subsection (a) shall apply to the foreign person committing the violation, as well as to any parent, affiliate, subsidiary, and successor entity of the foreign person, and, except as provided in subsection (c), are as follows:

"(1) a prohibition on contracting with, and procurement of products and services from, a sanctioned person, by any department, agency, or instrumentality of the United States Government, and

"(2) a prohibition on importation into the United States of all products produced by a sanctioned person.

"(c) EXCEPTIONS.—The President shall not apply sanctions under this section—

"(1) in the case of procurement of defense articles or defense services—

"(A) under existing contracts or subcontracts, including the exercise of options for production quantities to satisfy United States operational military requirements;

"(B) if the President determines that the foreign person or other entity to which the sanctions would otherwise be applied is a sole source supplier of essential defense articles or services and no alternative supplier can be identified; or

"(C) if the President determines that such articles or services are essential to the national security under defense coproduction agreements; or

"(2) to—

"(A) products or services provided under contracts or other binding agreements (as such terms are defined by the President in regulations) entered into before the date on which the President notifies the Congress of the intention to impose the sanctions;

"(B) spare parts;

"(C) component parts, but not finished products, essential to United States products or production;

"(D) routine servicing and maintenance of products; or

"(E) information and technology.

"(d) Exclusion.—The President shall not apply sanctions under this section to a parent, affiliate, subsidiary, and successor entity of a foreign person if the President determines that—

"(1) the parent, affiliate, subsidiary, or successor entity (as the case may be) has not knowingly violated the export control regulation violated by the foreign person, and

"(2) the government of the country with jurisdiction over the parent, affiliate, subsidiary, or successor entity had in effect, at the time of the violation by the foreign person, an effective export control system consistent with principles agreed to in the Coordinating Committee, including the following:

"(A) national laws providing appropriate civil and criminal penalties and statutes of limitations sufficient to deter potential violations;

"(B) a program to evaluate export license applications that includes sufficient technical expertise to assess the licensing status of exports and ensure the reliability of end-users;

"(C) an enforcement mechanism that provides authority for trained enforcement officers to investigate and prevent illegal exports;

"(D) a system of export control documentation to verify the movement of goods and technology; and

"(E) procedures for the coordination and exchange of information concerning violations of the agreement of the Coordinating Committee.

"(e) Definitions.—For purposes of this section—

"(1) the term 'component part' means any article which is not usable for its intended functions without being imbedded in or integrated into any other product and which, if used in production of a finished product, would be substantially transformed in that process;

"(2) the term 'finished product' means any article which is usable for its intended functions without being imbedded or integrated into any other product, but in no case shall such term be deemed to include an article produced by a person other than a sanctioned person that contains parts or components of the sanctioned person if the parts or components have been substantially transformed during production of the finished product; and

"(3) the term 'sanctioned person' means a foreign person, and any parent, affiliate, subsidiary, or successor entity of the foreign person, upon whom sanctions have been imposed under this section.

"(f) SUBSEQUENT MODIFICATIONS OF SANCTIONS.—The President may, after consultation with the Congress, limit the scope of sanctions applied to a parent, affiliate, subsidiary, or successor entity of the foreign person determined to have committed the violation on account of which the sanctions were imposed if the President determines that—

"(1) the parent, affiliate, subsidiary, or successor entity (as the case may be) has not, on the basis of available evidence, itself violated the export control regulation involved, either directly or through a course of conduct;

"(2) the government with jurisdiction over the parent, affiliate, subsidiary, or successor entity has improved its export control system as measured by the criteria set forth in subsection (d)(2);

"(3) the parent, affiliate, subsidiary, or successor entity, has instituted improvements in internal controls sufficient to detect and prevent violations of the export control regime implemented under paragraph (2); and

"(4) the impact of the sanctions imposed on the parent, affiliate, subsidiary, or successor entity is proportionate to the increased defense expenditures imposed on the United States.

Notwithstanding the preceding sentence, the President may not limit the scope of the sanction referred to in subsection (b)(1) with respect to the parent of the foreign person determined to have committed the violation, until that sanction has been in effect for at least 2 years.

"(g) REPORTS TO CONGRESS.—The President shall include in the annual report submitted under section 14, a report on the status of any sanctions imposed under this section, including any exceptions, exclusions, or modifications of sanctions that have been applied under subsection (c), (d), or (f).

"(h) DISCRETIONARY IMPOSITION OF SANCTIONS.—If the President determines that a foreign person has violated a regulation issued by a country to control exports for national security purposes pursuant to the agreement of the group known as the Coordinating Committee, but in a case in which subsection (a)(2) may not apply, the President may apply the sanctions referred to in subsection (b) against that foreign person for a period of not more than 5 years.

"(i) COMPENSATION FOR DIVERSION OF MILITARILY CRITICAL TECHNOLOGIES TO CONTROLLED COUNTRIES.—(1) In cases in which sanctions have been applied against a foreign person under subsection (a), the President shall initiate discussions with the foreign person and the government with jurisdiction over that foreign person regarding compensation on the part of the foreign person in an amount proportionate to the costs of research and development and procurement of new defensive systems by the United States and the allies of the United States to counteract the effect of the technological advance achieved by the Soviet Union as a result of the violation by that foreign person.

"(2) The President shall, at the time that discussions are initiated under paragraph (1), report to the Congress that such discussions are being undertaken, and shall report to the Congress the outcome of those discussions.

"(j) OTHER ACTIONS BY THE PRESIDENT.—Upon making a determination under subsection (a) or (h), the President shall—

"(1) initiate consultations with the foreign government with jurisdiction over the foreign person who committed the violation involved, in order to seek prompt remedial action by that government;

"(2) initiate discussions with the governments participating in the Coordinating Committee regarding the violation and means to ensure that similar violations do not occur; and

"(3) consult with and report to the Congress on the nature of the violation and the actions the President proposes to take, or has taken, to rectify the situation.

"(k) DAMAGES FOR CERTAIN VIOLATIONS.—(1) In any case in which the President makes a determination under subsection (a), the Secretary of Defense shall determine the costs of restoring the military preparedness of the United States on account of the violation involved. The Secretary of Defense shall notify the Attorney General of his determination, and the Attorney General may bring an action for damages, in any appropriate district court of the United States, to recover such costs against the person who committed the violation, any person that is owned or controlled by the person who committed the violation, and any person who owns and controls the person who committed the violation.

"(3) The total amount awarded in any case brought under paragraph (2) shall be determined by the court in light of the facts and circumstances, but shall not exceed the amount of the net loss to the national security of the United States. An action under this subsection shall be commenced not later than 3 years after the violation occurs, or one year after the violation is discovered, whichever is later.

"(l) DEFINITION.—For purposes of this section, the term 'foreign person' means any person other than a United States person.".

SEC. 2445. ANNUAL REPORT OF DEFENSE IMPACT.

Section 14 of the Act (50 U.S.C. App. 2413) is amended by adding at the end the following new subsection:

"(f) ANNUAL REPORT OF THE PRESIDENT.—The President shall submit an annual report to the Congress estimating the additional defense expenditures of the United States arising from illegal technology transfers, focusing on estimated defense costs arising from illegal technology transfers that resulted in a serious adverse impact on the strategic balance of forces. These estimates shall be based on assessment by the intelligence community of any technology transfers that resulted in such serious adverse impact. This report may have a classified annex covering any information of a sensitive nature.".

SEC. 2446. IMPROVED MULTILATERAL COOPERATION.

Section 5(i) of the Act (50 U.S.C. App. 2404) (relating to multilateral export controls), as amended by section 2421 of this Act, is further amended by striking paragraphs (1) through (9) and inserting the following:

"(1) Enhanced public understanding of the Committee's purpose and procedures, including publication of the list of items controlled for export by agreement of the Committee, together with all notes, understandings, and other aspects of such agreement of the Committee, and all changes thereto.

"(2) Periodic meetings of high-level representatives of participating governments for the purpose of coordinating export control policies and issuing policy guidance to the Committee.

"(3) Strengthened legal basis for each government's export control system, including, as appropriate, increased penalties and statutes of limitations.

"(4) Harmonization of export control documentation by the participating governments to verify the movement of goods and technology subject to controls by the Committee.

"(5) Improved procedures for coordination and exchange of information concerning violations of the agreement of the Committee.

"(6) Procedures for effective implementation of the agreement through uniform and consistent interpretations of export controls agreed to by the governments participating in the Committee.

"(7) Coordination of national licensing and enforcement efforts by governments participating in the Committee, including sufficient technical expertise to assess the licensing status of exports and to ensure end-use verification.

"(8) More effective procedures for enforcing export controls, including adequate training, resources, and authority for enforcement officers to investigate and prevent illegal exports.

"(9) Agreement to provide adequate resources to enhance the functioning of individual national export control systems and of the Committee.

"(10) Improved enforcement and compliance with the agreement through elimination of unnecessary export controls and maintenance of an effective control list.

"(11) Agreement to enhance cooperation among members of the Committee in obtaining the agreement of governments outside the Committee to restrict the export of goods and technology on the International Control List, to establish an ongoing mechanism in the Committee to coordinate planning and implementation of export control measures related to such agreements, and to remove items from the International Control List if such items continue to be available to controlled countries or if the control of the items no longer serves the common strategic objectives of the members of the Committee.".

SEC. 2447. TECHNICAL AND CONFORMING AMENDMENTS.

(a) Trade Expansion Act of 1962.—Section 233 of the Trade Expansion Act of 1962 (19 U.S.C 1864) is amended—

(1) by striking out "(a)"; and

(2) by striking out subsection (b).

(b) Department of Defense Appropriations Act, 1988.—Sections 8124 and 8129 of the Department of Defense Appropriations Act, 1988 (as contained in section 101(d) of Public Law 100-202) are repealed.

Subtitle E—Miscellaneous Provisions

SEC. 2501. TRADING WITH THE ENEMY ACT.

(a) Termination of Office of Alien Property.—(1) The Trading with the Enemy Act is amended by striking subsections (b) through

(e) of section 39 (50 U.S.C. App. 39) and inserting the following new subsection:

"(b) The Attorney General shall cover into the Treasury, to the credit of miscellaneous receipts, all sums from property vested in or transferred to the Attorney General under this Act—

"(1) which the Attorney General receives after the date of the enactment of the Export Enhancement Act of 1988, or

"(2) which the Attorney General received before that date and which, as of that date, the Attorney General had not covered into the Treasury for deposit in the War Claims Fund, other than any such sums which the Attorney General determines in his or her discretion are the subject matter of any judicial action or proceeding.".

(2) Subsection (f) of such section is amended—

(A) by striking "(f)" and inserting "(c)"; and

(B) by striking "through (d)" and inserting "and (b)".

(b) REMOVAL OF REPORTING REQUIREMENT.—Section 6 of such Act (50 U.S.C. App. 6) is amended in the next to the last sentence by striking ": *Provided further,*" and all that follows through the end of the section and inserting a period.

SEC. 2502. LIMITATION ON EXERCISE OF EMERGENCY AUTHORITIES.

(a) TRADING WITH THE ENEMY ACT.—(1) Section 5(b) of the Trading With the Enemy Act (50 U.S.C. App. 5(b)) is amended by adding at the end the following new paragraph:

"(4) The authority granted to the President in this subsection does not include the authority to regulate or prohibit, directly or indirectly, the importation from any country, or the exportation to any country, whether commercial or otherwise, of publications, films, posters, phonograph records, photographs, microfilms, microfiche, tapes, or other informational materials, which are not otherwise controlled for export under section 5 of the Export Administration Act of 1979 or with respect to which no acts are prohibited by chapter 37 of title 18, United States Code.".

(2) The authorities conferred upon the President by section 5(b) of the Trading With the Enemy Act, which were being exercised with respect to a country on July 1, 1977, as a result of a national emergency declared by the President before such date, and are being exercised on the date of the enactment of this Act, do not include the authority to regulate or prohibit, directly or indirectly, any activity which, under section 5(b)(4) of the Trading With the Enemy Act, as added by paragraph (1) of this subsection, may not be regulated or prohibited.

(b) INTERNATIONAL EMERGENCY ECONOMIC POWERS ACT.—(1) Section 203(b) of the International Emergency Economic Powers Act (50 U.S.C. 1702(b)) is amended—

(A) in paragraph (1) by striking "or" after the semicolon;

(B) in paragraph (2) by striking the period and inserting "; or"; and

(C) by adding at the end the following:

"(3) the importation from any country, or the exportation to any country, whether commercial or otherwise, of publications, films, posters, phonograph records, photographs, microfilms, microfiche, tapes, or other informational materials, which are not otherwise controlled for export under section 5 of the Export Administration Act of 1979 or with respect to which no acts are prohibited by chapter 37 of title 18, United States Code.".

(2) The amendments made by paragraph (1) apply to actions taken by the President under section 203 of the International Emergency Economic Powers Act before the date of the enactment of this Act which are in effect on such date of enactment, and to actions taken under such section on or after such date of enactment.

SEC. 2503. BUDGET ACT.

Any new spending authority (within the meaning of section 401 of the Congressional Budget Act of 1974) which is provided under this title shall be effective for any fiscal year only to the extent or in such amounts as are provided in appropriation Acts.

TITLE III—INTERNATIONAL FINANCIAL POLICY

Subtitle A—Exchange Rates and International Economic Policy Coordination

SEC. 3001. SHORT TITLE.

This subtitle may be cited as the "Exchange Rates and International Economic Policy Coordination Act of 1988".

SEC. 3002. FINDINGS.

The Congress finds that—

(1) the macroeconomic policies, including the exchange rate policies, of the leading industrialized nations require improved coordination and are not consistent with long-term economic growth and financial stability;

(2) currency values have a major role in determining the patterns of production and trade in the world economy;

(3) the rise in the value of the dollar in the early 1980's contributed substantially to our current trade deficit;

(4) exchange rates among major trading nations have become increasingly volatile and a pattern of exchange rates has at times developed which contribute to substantial and persistent imbalances in the flow of goods and services between nations, imposing serious strains on the world trading system and frustrating both business and government planning;

(5) capital flows between nations have become very large compared to trade flows, respond at times quickly and dramatically to policy and economic changes, and, for these reasons, contribute significantly to uncertainty in financial markets, the volatility of exchange rates, and the development of exchange rates which produce imbalances in the flow of goods and services between nations;

(6) policy initiatives by some major trading nations that manipulate the value of their currencies in relation to the United States dollar to gain competitive advantage continue to create serious competitive problems for United States industries;

(7) a more stable exchange rate for the dollar at a level consistent with a more appropriate and sustainable balance in the United States current account should be a major focus of national economic policy;

(8) procedures for improving the coordination of macroeconomic policy need to be strengthened considerably; and

(9) under appropriate circumstances, intervention by the United States in foreign exchange markets as part of a coordinated international strategic intervention effort could produce more orderly adjustment of foreign exchange markets and, in combination with necessary macroeconomic policy changes, assist adjustment toward a more appropriate and sustainable balance in current accounts.

SEC. 3003. STATEMENT OF POLICY.

It is the policy of the United States that—

(1) the United States and the other major industrialized countries should take steps to continue the process of coordinating monetary, fiscal, and structural policies initiated in the Plaza Agreement of September 1985;

(2) the goal of the United States in international economic negotiations should be to achieve macroeconomic policies and exchange rates consistent with more appropriate and sustainable balances in trade and capital flows and to foster price stability in conjunction with economic growth;

(3) the United States, in close coordination with the other major industrialized countries should, where appropriate, participate in international currency markets with the objective of producing more orderly adjustment of foreign exchange markets and, in combination with necessary macroeconomic policy changes, assisting adjustment toward a more appropriate and sustainable balance in current accounts; and

(4) the accountability of the President for the impact of economic policies and exchange rates on trade competitiveness should be increased.

SEC. 3004. INTERNATIONAL NEGOTIATIONS ON EXCHANGE RATE AND ECONOMIC POLICIES.

(a) MULTILATERAL NEGOTIATIONS.—The President shall seek to confer and negotiate with other countries—

(1) to achieve—

(A) better coordination of macroeconomic policies of the major industrialized nations; and

(B) more appropriate and sustainable levels of trade and current account balances, and exchange rates of the dollar and other currencies consistent with such balances; and

(2) to develop a program for improving existing mechanisms for coordination and improving the functioning of the exchange rate system to provide for long-term exchange rate stability consistent with more appropriate and sustainable current account balances.

(b) BILATERAL NEGOTIATIONS.—The Secretary of the Treasury shall analyze on an annual basis the exchange rate policies of foreign countries, in consultation with the International Monetary Fund, and consider whether countries manipulate the rate of exchange between their currency and the United States dollar for purposes of preventing effective balance of payments adjustments or gaining unfair competitive advantage in international trade. If the Secretary considers that such manipulation is occurring with respect to countries that (1) have material global current account surpluses; and (2) have significant bilateral trade surpluses with the United

States, the Secretary of the Treasury shall take action to initiate negotiations with such foreign countries on an expedited basis, in the International Monetary Fund or bilaterally, for the purpose of ensuring that such countries regularly and promptly adjust the rate of exchange between their currencies and the United States dollar to permit effective balance of payments adjustments and to eliminate the unfair advantage. The Secretary shall not be required to initiate negotiations in cases where such negotiations would have a serious detrimental impact on vital national economic and security interests; in such cases, the Secretary shall inform the chairman and the ranking minority member of the Committee on Banking, Housing, and Urban Affairs of the Senate and of the Committee on Banking, Finance and Urban Affairs of the House of Representatives of his determination.

SEC. 3005. REPORTING REQUIREMENTS.

(a) Reports Required.—In furtherance of the purpose of this title, the Secretary, after consultation with the Chairman of the Board, shall submit to the Committee on Banking, Finance and Urban Affairs of the House of Representatives and the Committee on Banking, Housing, and Urban Affairs of the Senate, on or before October 15 of each year, a written report on international economic policy, including exchange rate policy. The Secretary shall provide a written update of developments six months after the initial report. In addition, the Secretary shall appear, if requested, before both committees to provide testimony on these reports.

(b) Contents of Report.—Each report submitted under subsection (a) shall contain—

(1) an analysis of currency market developments and the relationship between the United States dollar and the currencies of our major trade competitors;

(2) an evaluation of the factors in the United States and other economies that underlie conditions in the currency markets, including developments in bilateral trade and capital flows;

(3) a description of currency intervention or other actions undertaken to adjust the actual exchange rate of the dollar;

(4) an assessment of the impact of the exchange rate of the United States dollar on—

(A) the ability of the United States to maintain a more appropriate and sustainable balance in its current account and merchandise trade account;

(B) production, employment, and noninflationary growth in the United States;

(C) the international competitive performance of United States industries and the external indebtedness of the United States;

(5) recommendations for any changes necessary in United States economic policy to attain a more appropriate and sustainable balance in the current account;

(6) the results of negotiations conducted pursuant to section 3004;

(7) key issues in United States policies arising from the most recent consultation requested by the International Monetary Fund under article IV of the Fund's Articles of Agreement; and

(8) a report on the size and composition of international capital flows, and the factors contributing to such flows, includ-

ing, where possible, an assessment of the impact of such flows on exchange rates and trade flows.

(c) REPORT BY BOARD OF GOVERNORS.—Section 2A(1) of the Federal Reserve Act (12 U.S.C. 225a(1)) is amended by inserting after "the Nation" the following: ", including an analysis of the impact of the exchange rate of the dollar on those trends".

SEC. 3006. DEFINITIONS.

As used in this subtitle:

(1) SECRETARY.—The term "Secretary" means the Secretary of the Treasury.

(2) BOARD.—The term "Board" means the Board of Governors of the Federal Reserve System.

Subtitle B—International Debt

PART I—FINDINGS, PURPOSES, AND STATEMENT OF POLICY

SEC. 3101. SHORT TITLE.

This subtitle may be cited as the "International Debt Management Act of 1988".

SEC. 3102. FINDINGS.

The Congress finds that—

(1) the international debt problem threatens the safety and soundness of the international financial system, the stability of the international trading system, and the economic development of the debtor countries;

(2) orderly reduction of international trade imbalances requires very substantial growth in all parts of the world economy, particularly in the developing countries;

(3) growth in developing countries with substantial external debts has been significantly constrained over the last several years by a combination of high debt service obligations and insufficient new flows of financial resources to these countries;

(4) substantial interest payment outflows from debtor countries, combined with inadequate net new capital inflows, have produced a significant net transfer of financial resources from debtor to creditor countries;

(5) negative resource transfers at present levels severely depress both investment and growth in the debtor countries, and force debtor countries to reduce imports and expand exports in order to meet their debt service obligations;

(6) current adjustment policies in debtor countries, which depress domestic demand and increase production for export, help to depress world commodity prices and limit the growth of export markets for United States industries;

(7) the United States has borne a disproportionate share of the burden of absorbing increased exports from debtor countries, while other industrialized countries have increased their imports from developing countries only slightly;

(8) current approaches to the debt problem should not rely solely on new lending as a solution to the debt problem, and should focus on other financing alternatives including a reduction in current debt service obligations;

(9) new international mechanisms to improve the management of the debt problem and to expand the range of financing options available to developing countries should be explored; and

(10) industrial countries with strong current account surpluses have a disproportionate share of the world's capital resources, and bear an additional responsibility for contributing to a viable long-term solution to the debt problem.

SEC. 3103. PURPOSES.

The purposes of this subtitle are—

(1) to expand the world trading system and raise the level of exports from the United States to the developing countries in order to reduce the United States trade deficit and foster economic expansion and an increase in the standard of living throughout the world;

(2) to alleviate the current international debt problem in order to make the debt situation of developing countries more manageable and permit the resumption of sustained growth in those countries; and

(3) to increase the stability of the world financial system and ensure the safety and soundness of United States depository institutions.

SEC. 3104. STATEMENT OF POLICY.

It is the policy of the United States that—

(1) increasing growth in the developing world is a major goal of international economic policy;

(2) it is necessary to broaden the range of options in dealing with the debt problem to include improved mechanisms to restructure existing debt;

(3) active consideration of a new multilateral authority to improve the management of the debt problem and to share the burdens of adjustment more equitably must be undertaken; and

(4) countries with strong current account surpluses bear a major responsibility for providing the financial resources needed for growth in the developing world.

PART II—THE INTERNATIONAL DEBT MANAGEMENT AUTHORITY

SEC. 3111. INTERNATIONAL INITIATIVE.

(a) Directive.—

(1) Study.—The Secretary of the Treasury shall study the feasibility and advisability of establishing the International Debt Management Authority described in this section.

(2) Explanation of determinations.—If the Secretary of the Treasury determines that initiation of international discussions with regard to such authority would (A) result in material increase in the discount at which sovereign debt is sold, (B) materially increase the probability of default on such debt, or (C) materially enhance the likelihood of debt service failure or disruption, the Secretary shall include in his interim reports to the Congress an explanation in detail of the reasons for such determination.

(3) INITIATION OF DISCUSSIONS.—Unless such a determination is made, the Secretary of the Treasury shall initiate discussions with such industrialized and developing countries as the Secretary may determine to be appropriate with the intent to negotiate the establishment of the International Debt Management Authority, which would undertake to—

(A) purchase sovereign debt of less developed countries from private creditors at an appropriate discount;

(B) enter into negotiations with the debtor countries for the purpose of restructuring the debt in order to—

(i) ease the current debt service burden on the debtor countries; and

(ii) provide additional opportunities for economic growth in both debtor and industrialized countries; and

(C) assist the creditor banks in the voluntary disposition of their Third World loan portfolio.

(b) OBJECTIVES.—In any discussions initiated under subsection (a), the Secretary should include the following specific proposals:

(1) That any loan restructuring assistance provided by such an authority to any debtor nation should involve substantial commitments by the debtor to (A) economic policies designed to improve resource utilization and minimize capital flight, and (B) preparation of an economic management plan calculated to provide sustained economic growth and to allow the debtor to meet its restructured debt obligations.

(2) That support for such an authority should come from industrialized countries, and that greater support should be expected from countries with strong current account surpluses.

(3) That such an authority should have a clearly defined close working relationship with the International Monetary Fund and the International Bank for Reconstruction and Development and the various regional development banks.

(4) That such an authority should be designed to operate as a self-supporting entity, requiring no routine appropriation of resources from any member government, and to function subject to the prohibitions contained in the first sentence of section 3112(a).

(5) That such an authority should have a defined termination date and a clear proposal for the restoration of creditworthiness to debtor countries within this timeframe.

(c) INTERIM REPORTS.—At the end of the 6-month period beginning on the date of enactment of this Act and at the end of the 12-month period beginning on such date of enactment, the Secretary of the Treasury shall submit a report on the progress being made on the study or in discussions described in subsection (a) to the Committee on Banking, Finance and Urban Affairs of the House of Representatives and the Committee on Banking, Housing, and Urban Affairs and the Committee on Foreign Relations of the Senate, and shall consult with such committees after submitting each such report.

(d) FINAL REPORT.—On the conclusion of the study or of discussions described in subsection (a), the Secretary shall transmit a report containing a detailed description thereof to the Committee on Banking, Finance and Urban Affairs of the House of Representatives and the Committee on Banking, Housing, and Urban Affairs and the Committee on Foreign Relations of the Senate, together with such recommendations for legislation which the Secretary may determine to be necessary or appropriate for the establishment of the International Debt Management Authority.

SEC. 3112. ACTIONS TO FACILITATE CREATION OF THE AUTHORITY.

(a) In General.—No funds, appropriations, contributions, callable capital, financial guarantee, or any other financial support or obligation or contingent support or obligation on the part of the United States Government may be used for the creation, operation, or support of the International Debt Management Authority specified in section 3111, without the express approval of the Congress through subsequent law, nor shall any expenses associated with such authority, either directly or indirectly, accrue to any United States person without the consent of such person. Except as restricted in the preceding sentence, the Secretary of the Treasury shall review all potential resources available to the multilateral financial institutions which could be used to support the creation of the International Debt Management Authority. In the course of this review, the Secretary shall direct—

(1) the United States Executive Director of the International Monetary Fund to determine the amount of, and alternative methods by which, gold stock of the Fund which, subject to action by its Board of Governors, could be pledged as collateral to obtain financing for the activities of the authority specified in section 3111; and

(2) the United States Executive Director to the International Bank for Reconstruction and Development to determine the amount of, and alternative methods by which, liquid assets controlled by such Bank and not currently committed to any loan program which, subject to action by its Board of Governors, could be pledged as collateral for obtaining financing for the activities of the authority specified in section 3111.

The Secretary of the Treasury shall include a report on the results of the review in the first report submitted under section 3111(c).

(b) Construction of Section.—Subsection (a) shall not be construed to affect any provision of the Articles of Agreement of the International Monetary Fund or of the International Bank for Reconstruction and Development or any agreement entered into under either of such Agreements.

SEC. 3113. IMF-WORLD BANK REVIEW.

(a) IMF Review.—The United States Executive Director of the International Monetary Fund shall request the management of the International Monetary Fund to prepare a review and analysis of the debt burden of the developing countries, with particular attention to alternatives for dealing with the debt problem including new lending instruments, rescheduling and refinancing of existing debt, securitization and debt conversion techniques, discounted debt repurchases, and the International Debt Management Authority described in section 3111 no later than 1 year after the date of the enactment of this Act.

(b) World Bank Review.—The United States Executive Director to the International Bank for Reconstruction and Development shall request the management of the International Bank for Reconstruction and Development to prepare a review and analysis of the debt burden of the developing countries, with particular attention to alternatives for dealing with the debt problem including new lending instruments, rescheduling and refinancing of existing debt, securitization and debt conversion techniques, discounted debt repurchases, and the International Debt Management Authority described in section 3111 no later than 1 year after the date of the enactment of this Act.

PART III—REGULATORY PROVISIONS AFFECTING INTERNATIONAL DEBT

SEC. 3121. PROVISIONS RELATING TO THE REGULATION OF DEPOSITORY INSTITUTIONS.

(a) REGULATORY OBJECTIVES.—It is the sense of the Congress that regulations prescribed by Federal banking regulatory agencies which affect the international assets of United States commercial banks should grant the widest possible latitude to the banks for negotiating principal and interest reductions with respect to obligations of heavily indebted sovereign borrowers.

(b) FLEXIBILITY IN DEBT RESTRUCTURING.—It is the intent of the Congress that, in applying generally accepted accounting standards, Federal agencies which regulate and oversee the operations of depository institutions (within the meaning given to such term by clauses (i) through (vi) of section 19(b)(1)(A) of the Federal Reserve Act) apply to such institutions maximum flexibility in determining the asset value of restructured loans to heavily indebted sovereign borrowers and in accounting for the effects of such restructuring prospectively.

(c) RECAPITALIZATION.—It is the intent of the Congress that Federal agencies which regulate and oversee the operations of depository institutions (within the meaning given to such term by clauses (i) through (vi) of section 19(b)(1)(A) of the Federal Reserve Act) should require depository institutions with substantial amounts of loans to heavily indebted sovereign borrowers to seek, as appropriate, expanded recapitalization through equity financing to ensure that prudent institutional capital-to-total asset ratios are established and maintained.

(d) RESERVES FOR LOAN LOSSES.—It is the intent of the Congress that Federal agencies which regulate and oversee the operations of depository institutions (within the meaning given to such term by clauses (i) through (vi) of section 19(b)(1)(A) of the Federal Reserve Act) should seek to ensure that appropriate levels of reserves be established by depository institutions engaged in substantial lending to heavily indebted sovereign borrowers in accordance with both the credit and country risks associated with such lending.

(e) DATA ON BANKS FOREIGN LOAN RISKS.—Section 913 of the International Lending Supervision Act of 1983 is amended by adding at the end thereof the following new subsection:

"(d) To ensure that Congress is fully informed of the risks to our banking system posed by troubled foreign loans, the Federal banking agencies, before March 31, 1989, and on April 30 of each succeeding year, shall jointly submit to the Committee on Banking, Housing, and Urban Affairs of the Senate and Committee on Banking, Finance and Urban Affairs of the House of Representatives a report that shall include the following:

"(1) The level of loan exposure of those banking institutions under the jurisdiction of each agency which is rated 'value-impaired', 'substandard', 'other transfer risk problems', or in any other troubled debt category as may be established by the banking agencies. This tabulation shall clearly identify aggregate loan exposures of the 9 largest United States banks under the agencies' jurisdiction, the aggregate loan exposures of the next 13 largest banks, and the aggregate exposure of all other such banks which have significant country risk exposures. This tabulation shall include a separate section identifying, to the extent feasible, new bank loans to countries with debt service problems which were made within the past year preceding the date on which the report required under this subsection is due, and shall include the amount of sovereign loans written off or sold by such banks during the preceding year.

"(2) Progress that has been achieved by the appropriate Federal banking agencies and by banking institutions in reducing the risk to the economy of the United States posed by the exposure of banking institutions to troubled international loans through appropriate voluntary or regulatory policies, including increases in capital and reserves of banking institutions.

"(3) The relationship between lending activity by the United States banks and foreign banks in countries experiencing debt service difficulties and exports from the United States and other lending countries to these markets, and the extent to which United States banking institutions can be encouraged to continue to make credit available to finance necessary growth in international trade, and particularly to finance United States exports.

"(4) The response of regulatory agencies in other countries to the international debt problems, including measures which encourage the building of capital and reserves by foreign banking institutions, tax treatment of reserves, encouragement of new lending to promote international trade, and measures which may place United States banking institutions at a competitive disadvantage when compared with foreign banking institutions.

"(5) Steps that have been taken during the previous year by countries experiencing debt service difficulties to enhance conditions for private direct investment (including investment by United States persons) and to eliminate production subsidies, attain price stability, and undertake such other steps as will remove the causes of their debt service difficulties.

Each appropriate Federal banking agency may provide data in the aggregate to the extent necessary to preserve the integrity and confidentiality of the regulatory and examination process.".

SEC. 3122. STUDIES RELATING TO THE REGULATION OF DEPOSITORY INSTITUTIONS.

(a) Regulatory Study Required.—The Comptroller of the Currency, the Board of Governors of the Federal Reserve System, and the Federal Deposit Insurance Corporation shall conduct a study to determine the extent of any regulatory obstacle to negotiated reductions in the debt service obligations associated with foreign debt.

(b) Specific Factors To Be Studied.—The study required by subsection (a) shall include an analysis of regulatory and accounting obstacles to various forms of debt restructuring, including negotiated interest reduction, the amortization of loan losses, securitization and debt conversion techniques, and discounted debt repurchases, as well as an analysis of the profitability of commercial bank lending to developing countries during the 10-year period ending on December 31, 1986. The analysis should include an assessment of the impact of the various forms of debt restructuring on the development of a secondary market in developing country debt and on the safety and soundness of the United States banking system.

(c) REPORT REQUIRED.—Within 6 months after the date of the enactment of this Act, the Comptroller of the Currency, the Board of Governors of the Federal Reserve System, and the Federal Deposit Insurance Corporation shall transmit to the Congress a report containing the findings and conclusions of such agencies with respect to the study required under subsection (a), together with any recommendations concerning legislation which such agencies determine to be necessary or appropriate to remove regulatory obstacles to negotiated reductions in the debt service obligations associated with sovereign debt.

SEC. 3123. LIMITED PURPOSE SPECIAL DRAWING RIGHTS FOR THE POOREST HEAVILY INDEBTED COUNTRIES.

(a) STUDY REQUIRED.—

(1) IN GENERAL.—The Secretary of the Treasury, in consultation with the directors and staff of the International Monetary Fund and such other interested parties as the Secretary may determine to be appropriate, shall conduct a study of the feasibility and the efficacy of reducing the international debt of the poorest of the heavily indebted countries through a one-time allocation by the International Monetary Fund of limited purpose Special Drawing Rights to such countries in accordance with a plan which provides that—

(A) the allocation be made without regard to the quota established for any such country under the Articles of Agreement of the Fund;

(B) limited purpose Special Drawing Rights be used only to repay official debt of any such country;

(C) the allocation of limited purpose Special Drawing Rights to any such country not be treated as an allocation on which such country must pay interest to the Fund; and

(D) the use of limited purpose Special Drawing Rights by any such country to repay official debt shall be treated as an allocation of regular Special Drawing Rights to the creditor.

(2) ADDITIONAL FACTORS TO BE STUDIED.—The study required under paragraph (1) shall include the following:

(A) To the extent the creation and allocation of the limited purpose Special Drawing Rights described in paragraph (1) would require an amendment of the Articles of Agreement of the International Monetary Fund, an assessment of the period of time within which such amendment could be ratified by the member nations, based on discussions with the major members of the Fund.

(B) An assessment of other means for achieving the objectives of principal and interest reduction on official debt of the poorest heavily indebted countries through the use of Special Drawing Rights.

(C) A comparative evaluation of proposals of other members of the International Monetary Fund, the directors and staff of the Fund, and other interested parties.

(D) An analysis of the effect the implementation of the provisions in paragraph (1) would have on bilateral and multilateral lenders, the international monetary system, and such other provisions of this Act as may be appropriate.

(E) A comparative analysis of the available alternatives identified under subparagraph (B) or (C).

(b) REPORT REQUIRED.—Within 3 months after the date of the enactment of this Act, the Secretary of the Treasury shall submit a report to the Committee on Banking, Finance and Urban Affairs of the House of Representatives and the Committee on Banking, Housing, and Urban Affairs and the Committee on Foreign Relations of the Senate containing the findings and conclusions of the Secretary pursuant to the study required under subsection (a), together with—

(1) the recommendation of the Secretary as to which, of all the alternatives for providing relief for the poorest of the heavily indebted countries which were assessed in connection with such study, represents the best available option; and

(2) recommendations for such legislation and administrative action as the Secretary determines to be necessary and appropriate to implement such option.

Subtitle C—Multilateral Development Banks

SEC. 3201. SHORT TITLE.

This subtitle may be cited as the "Multilateral Development Banks Procurement Act of 1988".

SEC. 3202. MULTILATERAL DEVELOPMENT BANK PROCUREMENT.

(a) EXECUTIVE DIRECTORS.—The Secretary of the Treasury shall instruct the United States Executive Director of each multilateral development bank to attach a high priority to promoting opportunities for exports for goods and services from the United States and, in carrying out this function, to investigate thoroughly any complaints from United States bidders about the awarding of procurement contracts by the multilateral development banks to ensure that all contract procedures and rules of the banks are observed and that United States firms are treated fairly.

(b) OFFICER OF PROCUREMENT.—

(1) ESTABLISHMENT.—The Secretary of the Treasury shall designate, within the Office of International Affairs in the Department of the Treasury, an officer of multilateral development bank procurement.

(2) FUNCTION.—The officer shall act as the liaison between the Department of the Treasury, the Department of Commerce, and the United States Executive Directors' offices in the multilateral development banks, in carrying out this section. The officer shall cooperate with the Department of Commerce in efforts to improve opportunities for multilateral development bank procurement by United States companies.

(b) MULTILATERAL DEVELOPMENT BANK DEFINED.—As used in this section, the term "multilateral development bank" includes the International Bank for Reconstruction and Development, the International Development Association, the International Finance Corporation, the Inter-American Development Bank, the Inter-American Investment Corporation, the Asian Development Bank, the African Development Bank, and the African Development Fund.

Subtitle D—Export-Import Bank and Tied Aid Credit Amendments

SEC. 3301. SHORT TITLE.

This subtitle may be cited as the "Export-Import Bank and Tied Aid Credit Amendments of 1988".

SEC. 3302. PROVISIONS RELATING TO TIED AID CREDIT.

(a) FINDINGS.—The Congress finds that—

(1) negotiations have led to an international agreement to increase the grant element required in tied aid credit offers;

(2) concern continues to exist that countries party to the agreement may continue to offer tied aid credits that deviate from the agreement;

(3) in such cases, the United States could continue to lose export sales in connection with the aggressive, and in some cases, unfair, tied aid practices of such countries; and

(4) in such cases, the Export-Import Bank of the United States should continue to use the Tied Aid Credit Fund established by section 15(c) of the Export-Import Bank Act of 1945 to discourage the use of such predatory financing practices.

(b) EXTENSION OF TIED AID CREDIT FUND.—Subsections (c)(2) and (e)(1) of section 15 of the Export-Import Bank Act of 1945 (12 U.S.C. 635i-3 (c)(2) and (e)(1)) are each amended by striking out "and 1988" and inserting in lieu thereof "1988, and 1989".

(c) REPORT.—

(1) IN GENERAL.—On or before December 31, 1988, the President and Chairman of the Export-Import Bank of the United States, in cooperation with other appropriate government agencies, shall submit to the Speaker of the House of Representatives and the President pro tempore of the Senate a written report identifying and analyzing the tied aid credit practices of other countries and shall make recommendations for dealing with such practices.

(2) CONSULTATION.—In preparing the report described in paragraph (1), the Export-Import Bank shall consult with appropriate international organizations such as the International Bank for Reconstruction and Development, the International Monetary Fund, and the Development Assistance Committee of the Organization for Economic Cooperation and Development, and with the countries which are party to the Arrangement on Guidelines for Officially Supported Export Credits adopted by the Organization for Economic Cooperation and Development in November 1987.

SEC. 3303. REPORT ON UNITED STATES EXPORTS TO DEVELOPING COUNTRIES.

Within 90 days after the date of the enactment of this Act, the President and Chairman of the Export-Import Bank of the United States shall submit to the Committee on Banking, Finance and Urban Affairs of the House of Representatives and the Committee on Banking, Housing, and Urban Affairs of the Senate a written report which contains—

(1) an assessment of the effectiveness of recent program changes in increasing United States exports to developing countries; and

(2) an identification of additional specific policy and program changes which—

(A) would enable the Bank to increase the financing of United States exports to developing countries; and

(B) would encourage greater private sector participation in such financing efforts.

SEC. 3304. AMENDMENTS TO SECTION 2(e) OF THE EXPORT-IMPORT BANK ACT OF 1945.

(a) TIME FOR DETERMINING SUPPLIES.—Section 2(e)(1)(A)(i) of the Export-Import Bank Act of 1945 (12 U.S.C. 635(e)(1)(A)(i)) is amended by striking out "productive capacity is expected to become operative" and inserting in lieu thereof "commodity will first be sold".

(b) MAKING COMPARATIVE INJURY DETERMINATIONS.—Section 2(e)(2) of such Act (12 U.S.C. 635(e)(2)) is amended—

(1) by inserting "short- and long-term" before "injury to United States producers"; and

(2) by inserting "and employment" before "of the same, similar, or competing commodity".

(c) SUBSTANTIAL INJURY DEFINED FOR EXPORT-IMPORT BANK DETERMINATIONS.—Section 2(e) of such Act (12 U.S.C. 635(e)) is amended by adding at the end the following:

"(3) DEFINITION.—For purposes of paragraph (1)(B), the extension of any credit or guarantee by the Bank will cause substantial injury if the amount of the capacity for production established, or the amount of the increase in such capacity expanded, by such credit or guarantee equals or exceeds 1 percent of United States production.".

Subtitle E—Export Trading Company Act Amendments

SEC. 3401. SHORT TITLE.

This subtitle may be cited as the "Export Trading Company Act Amendments of 1988".

SEC. 3402. EXPORT TRADING COMPANY AC. AMENDMENTS.

(a) STANDARDS FOR DETERMINATION OF EXPORT TRADING COMPANY STATUS.—Section 4(c)(14) of the Bank Holding Company Act of 1956 (12 U.S.C. 1843(c)(14)) is amended by inserting after subparagraph (F) the following new subparagraph:

"(G) DETERMINATION OF STATUS AS EXPORT TRADING COMPANY.—

"(i) TIME PERIOD REQUIREMENTS.—For purposes of determining whether an export trading company is operated principally for the purposes described in subparagraph (F)(i)—

"(I) the operations of such company during the 2-year period beginning on the date such company commences operations shall not be taken into account in making any such determination; and

"(II) not less than 4 consecutive years of operations of such company (not including any portion of the period referred to in subclause (I)) shall be taken into account in making any such determination.

"(ii) EXPORT REVENUE REQUIREMENTS.—A company shall not be treated as operated principally for the purposes described in subparagraph (F)(i) unless—

"(I) the revenues of such company from the export, or facilitating the export, of goods or services produced in the United States exceed the revenues of such company from the import, or facilitating the import, into the United States of goods or services produced outside the United States; and

"(II) at least ⅓ of such company's total revenues are revenues from the export, or facilitating the export, of goods or services produced in the United States by persons not affiliated with such company.".

(b) LEVERAGE.—Section 4(c)(14)(A) of the Bank Holding Company Act of 1956 (12 U.S.C. 1843(c)(14)(A)) is amended by redesignating clauses (v) and (vi) as clauses (vi) and (vii), respectively, and by inserting after clause (iv) the following new clause:

"(v) LEVERAGE.—The Board may not disapprove any proposed investment solely on the basis of the anticipated or proposed asset-to-equity ratio of the export trading company with respect to which such investment is proposed, unless the anticipated or proposed annual average asset-to-equity ratio is greater than 20-to-1.".

(c) INVENTORY.—Section 4(c)(14)(A)) of the Bank Holding Company Act of 1956 (12 U.S.C. 1843(c)(14)) is amended by inserting after subparagraph (G) (as added by subsection (a) of this section) the following new subparagraph:

"(H) INVENTORY.—

"(i) NO GENERAL LIMITATION.—The Board may not prescribe by regulation any maximum dollar amount limitation on the value of goods which an export trading company may maintain in inventory at any time.

"(ii) SPECIFIC LIMITATION BY ORDER.—Notwithstanding clause (i), the Board may issue an order establishing a maximum dollar amount limitation on the value of goods which a particular export trading company may maintain in inventory at any time (after such company has been operating for a reasonable period of time) if the Board finds that, under the facts and circumstances, such limitation is necessary to prevent risks that would affect the financial or managerial resources of an investor bank holding company to an extent which would be likely to have a materially adverse effect on the safety and soundness of any subsidiary bank of such bank holding company.".

Subtitle F—Primary Dealers

SEC. 3501. SHORT TITLE.

This subtitle may be cited as the "Primary Dealers Act of 1988".

SEC. 3502. REQUIREMENT OF NATIONAL TREATMENT IN UNDERWRITING GOVERNMENT DEBT INSTRUMENTS.

(a) FINDINGS.—The Congress finds that—

(1) United States companies can successfully compete in foreign markets if they are given fair access to such markets;

(2) a trade surplus in services could offset the deficit in manufactured goods and help lower the overall trade deficit significantly;

(3) in contrast to the barriers faced by United States firms in Japan, Japanese firms generally have enjoyed access to United States financial markets on the same terms as United States firms; and

(4) United States firms seeking to compete in Japan face or have faced a variety of discriminatory barriers effectively precluding such firms from fairly competing for Japanese business, including—

(A) limitations on membership on the Tokyo Stock Exchange;

(B) high fixed commission rates (ranging as high as 80 percent) which must be paid to members of the exchange by nonmembers for executing trades;

(C) unequal opportunities to participate in and act as lead manager for equity and bond underwritings;

(D) restrictions on access to automated teller machines;

(E) arbitrarily applied employment requirements for opening branch offices;

(F) long delays in processing applications and granting approvals for licenses to operate; and

(G) restrictions on foreign institutions' participation in Ministry of Finance policy advisory councils.

(b) DESIGNATION OF CERTAIN PERSONS AS PRIMARY DEALERS PROHIBITED.—

(1) GENERAL RULE.—Neither the Board of Governors of the Federal Reserve System nor the Federal Reserve Bank of New York may designate, or permit the continuation of any prior designation of, any person of a foreign country as a primary dealer in government debt instruments if such foreign country does not accord to United States companies the same competitive opportunities in the underwriting and distribution of government debt instruments issued by such country as such country accords to domestic companies of such country.

(2) CERTAIN PRIOR ACQUISITIONS EXCEPTED.—Paragraph (1) shall not apply to the continuation of the prior designation of a company as a primary dealer in government debt instruments if—

(A) such designation occurred before July 31, 1987; and

(B) before July 31, 1987—

(i) control of such company was acquired from a person (other than a person of a foreign country) by a person of a foreign country; or

(ii) in conjunction with a person of a foreign country, such company informed the Federal Reserve Bank of New York of the intention of such person to acquire control of such company.

(c) EXCEPTION FOR COUNTRIES HAVING OR NEGOTIATING BILATERAL AGREEMENTS WITH THE UNITED STATES.—Subsection (b) shall not apply to any person of a foreign country if—

(1) that country, as of January 1, 1987, was negotiating a bilateral agreement with the United States under the authority of section 102(b)(4)(A) of the Trade Act of 1974 (19 U.S.C. 2112(b)(4)(A)); or

(2) that country has a bilateral free trade area agreement with the United States which entered into force before January 1, 1987.

(d) PERSON OF A FOREIGN COUNTRY DEFINED.—For purposes of this section, a person is a "person of a foreign country" if that person, or any other person which directly or indirectly owns or controls that person, is a resident of that country, is organized under the laws of that country, or has its principal place of business in that country.

(e) EFFECTIVE DATE.—This section shall take effect 12 months after the date of the enactment of this Act.

Subtitle G—Financial Reports

SEC. 3601. SHORT TITLE.

This subtitle may be cited as the "Financial Reports Act of 1988".

SEC. 3602. QUADRENNIAL REPORTS ON FOREIGN TREATMENT OF UNITED STATES FINANCIAL INSTITUTIONS.

Not less frequently than every 4 years, beginning December 1, 1990, the Secretary of the Treasury, in conjunction with the Secretary of State, the Board of Governors of the Federal Reserve System, the Comptroller of the Currency, the Federal Deposit Insurance Corporation, the Securities and Exchange Commission, and the Department of Commerce, shall report to the Congress on (1) the foreign countries from which foreign financial services institutions have entered into the business of providing financial services in the United States, (2) the kinds of financial services which are being offered, (3) the extent to which foreign countries deny national treatment to United States banking organizations and securities companies, and (4) the efforts undertaken by the United States to eliminate such discrimination. The report shall focus on those countries in which there are significant denials of national treatment which impact United States financial firms. The report shall also describe the progress of discussions pursuant to section 3603.

SEC. 3603. FAIR TRADE IN FINANCIAL SERVICES.

(a) DISCUSSIONS.—When advantageous the President or his designee shall conduct discussions with the governments of countries that are major financial centers, aimed at:

(1) ensuring that United States banking organizations and securities companies have access to foreign markets and receive national treatment in those markets;

(2) reducing or eliminating barriers to, and other distortions of, international trade in financial services;

(3) achieving reasonable comparability in the types of financial services permissible for financial service companies; and

(4) developing uniform supervisory standards for banking organizations and securities companies, including uniform capital standards.

(b) CONSULTATION BEFORE DISCUSSIONS.—Before entering into those discussions, the President or his designee shall consult with the committees of jurisdiction in the Senate and the House of Representatives.

(c) RECOMMENDATIONS.—After completing those discussions and after consultation with the committees of jurisdiction, the President shall transmit to the Congress any recommendations that have emerged from those discussions. Any recommendations for changes in United States financial laws or practices shall be accompanied by a description of the changes in foreign financial laws or practices that would accompany action by the Congress, and by an explanation of the benefits that would accrue to the United States from adoption of the recommendations.

(d) CONSTRUCTION OF SECTION.—Nothing in this section may be construed as prior approval of any legislation which may be necessary to implement any recommendations resulting from discussions under this section.

SEC. 3604. BANKS LOAN LOSS RESERVES.

The Federal Reserve Board shall submit to the Committee on Banking, Housing, and Urban Affairs of the Senate and the Committee on Banking, Finance and Urban Affairs of the House of Representatives a report on the issues raised by including loan loss reserves as part of banks' primary capital for regulatory purposes by March 31, 1989. Such report shall include a review of the treatment of loan loss reserves and the composition of primary capital of banks in other major industrialized countries, and shall include an analysis as to whether loan loss reserves should continue to be counted as primary capital for regulatory purposes.

TITLE IV—AGRICULTURAL TRADE

SEC. 4001. SHORT TITLE.

This title may be cited as the "Agricultural Competitiveness and Trade Act of 1988".

Subtitle A—Findings, Policy, and Purpose

SEC. 4101. FINDINGS.

Congress finds that—

(1) United States agricultural exports have declined by more than 36 percent since 1981, from $43,800,000,000 in 1981 to $27,900,000,000 in 1987;

(2) the United States share of the world market for agricultural commodities and products has dropped by 20 percent during the last 6 years;

(3) for the first time in 15 years, the United States incurred monthly agricultural trade deficits in 1986;

(4) the loss of $1,000,000,000 in United States agricultural exports causes the loss of 35,000 agricultural jobs and the loss of 60,000 nonagricultural jobs;

(5) the loss of agricultural exports threatens family farms and the economic well-being of rural communities in the United States;

(6) factors contributing to the loss of United States agricultural exports include changes in world agricultural markets such as—

(A) the addition of new exporting nations;

(B) innovations in agricultural technology;

(C) increased use of export subsidies designed to lower the price of commodities on the world market;

(D) the existence of barriers to agricultural trade;

(E) the slowdown in the growth of world food demand in the 1980's due to cyclical economic factors, including currency fluctuations and a debt-related slowdown in the economic growth of agricultural markets in certain developing countries; and

(F) the rapid buildup of surplus stocks as a consequence of favorable weather for agricultural production during the 1980's;

(7) increasing the volume and value of exports is important to the financial well-being of the farm sector in the United States and to increasing farm income in the United States;

(8) in order to increase agricultural exports and improve prices for farmers and ranchers in the United States, it is necessary that all agricultural export programs of the United States be used in an expeditious manner, including programs established under the Agricultural Trade Development and Assistance Act of 1954 (7 U.S.C. 1691 et seq.), the Commodity Credit Corporation Charter Act (15 U.S.C. 714 et seq.), and section 416 of the Agricultural Act of 1949 (7 U.S.C. 1431);

(9) greater use should be made by the Secretary of Agriculture of the authorities established under section 4 of the Food for Peace Act of 1966 (7 U.S.C. 1707a), the Agricultural Trade Development and Assistance Act of 1954 (7 U.S.C. 1691 et seq.), section 416 of the Agricultural Act of 1949 (7 U.S.C. 1431), and the Commodity Credit Corporation Charter Act (15 U.S.C. 714 et seq.) to provide intermediate credit financing and other assistance for the establishment of facilities in importing countries to—

(A) improve the handling, marketing, processing, storage, and distribution of imported agricultural commodities and products; and

(B) increase livestock production to enhance the demand for United States feed grains;

(10) food aid and export assistance programs in developing countries stimulate economic activity which causes incomes to rise, and, as incomes rise, diets improve and the demand for and ability to purchase food increases;

(11) private voluntary organizations and cooperatives are important and successful partners in our food aid and development programs; and

(12) in addition to meeting humanitarian needs, food aid used in sales and barter programs by private voluntary organizations and cooperatives—

(A) provides communities with health care, credit systems, and tools for development; and

(B) establishes the infrastructure that is essential to the expansion of markets for United States agricultural commodities and products.

SEC. 4102. POLICY.

It is the policy of the United States—

(1) to provide, through all possible means, agricultural commodities and products for export at competitive prices, with full assurance of quality and reliability of supply;

(2) to support the principle of free trade and the promotion of fair trade in agricultural commodities and products;

(3) to support fully the negotiating objectives set forth in section 1101(b) of this Act to eliminate or reduce substantially constraints on fair and open trade in agricultural commodities and products;

(4) to use statutory authority to counter unfair foreign trade practices and to use all available means, including export promotion programs, and, if necessary, restrictions on United States imports of agricultural commodities and products, in order to encourage fair and open trade; and

(5) to provide for increased representation of United States agricultural trade interests in the formulation of national fiscal and monetary policy affecting trade.

SEC. 4103. PURPOSE.

It is the purpose of this title—

(1) to increase the effectiveness of the Department of Agriculture in agricultural trade policy formulation and implementation and in assisting United States agricultural producers to participate in international agricultural trade, by strengthening the operations of the Department of Agriculture; and

(2) to improve the competitiveness of United States agricultural commodities and products in the world market.

Subtitle B—Agricultural Trade Initiatives

PART 1—GENERAL PROVISIONS

SEC. 4201. LONG-TERM AGRICULTURAL TRADE STRATEGY REPORTS.

(a) CONTENTS.—The Secretary of Agriculture shall prepare annually, and the President shall submit together with the budget for each fiscal year, a Long-Term Agricultural Trade Strategy Report establishing recommended policy goals for United States agricultural trade and exports, and recommended levels of spending on international activities of the Department of Agriculture, for 1-, 5-, and 10-fiscal year periods. In preparing each such report, the Secretary shall consult with the United States Trade Representative to ensure that the report is coordinated with the annual national trade policy agenda included in the annual report for the relevant fiscal year prepared under section 163 of the Trade Act of 1974 (19 U.S.C. 2213). Each such report shall include—

(1) findings with respect to trends in the comparative position of the United States and other countries in the export of

agricultural commodities and products, organized by major commodity group and including a comparative analysis of the cost of production of such commodities and products;

(2) findings with respect to new developments in research conducted by other countries that may affect the competitiveness of United States agricultural commodities and products;

(3) findings and recommendations with respect to the movement of United States agricultural commodities and products in nonmarket economies;

(4) as appropriate, the agricultural trade goals for each agricultural commodity and value-added product produced in the United States for the period involved, expressed in both physical volume and monetary value;

(5) recommended Federal policy and programs to meet such agricultural trade goals;

(6) recommended levels of Federal spending on international programs and activities of the Department of Agriculture to meet such agricultural trade goals;

(7) recommended levels of Federal spending on programs and activities of agencies other than the Department of Agriculture to meet such agricultural trade goals; and

(8) recommended long-term strategies for growth in agricultural trade and exports—

(A) taking into account United States competitiveness, trade negotiations, and international monetary and exchange rate policies; and

(B) including specific recommendations with respect to export enhancement programs (including credit programs and export payment-in-kind programs), market development activities, and foreign agricultural and economic development assistance activities needed to implement such strategies.

(b) Treatment as Annual Budget Submission.—Provisions of each Long-Term Agricultural Trade Strategy Report that relate to recommended levels of spending on international activities of the Department of Agriculture for the upcoming fiscal year shall be treated as the President's annual budget submission to Congress for such activities for such fiscal year, and shall be submitted along with the budget request for other programs of the Department of Agriculture for such fiscal year

(c) Succeeding Reports.—The Secretary of Agriculture, in each annual Long-Term Agricultural Trade Strategy Report, shall identify any recommendations in such report that might modify the long-term policy contained in any previous report.

(d) Recommendations for Changes In Law.—The President shall include in each annual budget submission recommendations for such changes in law as are required to meet the long-term goals established in the Report.

SEC. 4202. TECHNICAL ASSISTANCE IN TRADE NEGOTIATIONS.

The Secretary of Agriculture shall provide technical services to the United States Trade Representative on matters pertaining to agricultural trade and with respect to international negotiations on issues related to agricultural trade.

SEC. 4203. JOINT DEVELOPMENT ASSISTANCE AGREEMENTS WITH CERTAIN TRADING PARTNERS.

(a) DEVELOPMENT OF PLAN.—With respect to any country that has a substantial positive trade balance with the United States, the Secretary of Agriculture, in consultation with the Secretary of State and (through the Secretary of State) representatives of such country, may develop an appropriate plan under which that country would purchase United States agricultural commodities or products for use in development activities in developing countries. In developing such plan, the Secretary of Agriculture shall take into consideration the agricultural economy of such country, the nature and extent of such country's programs to assist developing countries, and other relevant factors. The Secretary of Agriculture shall submit each such plan to the President as soon as practicable.

(b) AGREEMENT.—The President may enter into an agreement with any country that has a positive trade balance with the United States under which that country would purchase United States agricultural commodities or products for use in agreed-on development activities in developing countries.

SEC. 4204. REORGANIZATION EVALUATION.

The Secretary of Agriculture shall evaluate the reorganization proposal recommended by the National Commission on Agricultural Trade and Export Policy and other proposals to improve management of international trade activities of the Department of Agriculture. To assist the Secretary in the evaluation, the Secretary shall appoint a private sector advisory committee of not less than 4 members, who shall be appointed from among individuals representing farm and commodity organizations, market development cooperators, and agribusiness. Not later than April 30, 1989, the Secretary shall report the findings of the evaluation to Congress, together with the views and recommendations of the private sector advisory committee.

SEC. 4205. CONTRACTING AUTHORITY TO EXPAND AGRICULTURAL EXPORT MARKETS.

(a) IN GENERAL.—The Secretary of Agriculture may contract with individuals for services to be performed outside the United States as the Secretary determines necessary or appropriate for carrying out programs and activities to maintain, develop, or enhance export markets for United States agricultural commodities and products.

(b) NOT EMPLOYEES OF THE UNITED STATES.—Such individuals shall not be regarded as officers or employees of the United States.

SEC. 4206. ESTABLISHMENT OF TRADE ASSISTANCE OFFICE.

(a) ESTABLISHMENT WITHIN THE FOREIGN AGRICULTURAL SERVICE.—The Secretary of Agriculture shall establish an office within the Foreign Agricultural Service to carry out the duties described in subsections (b) and (c) under the direction of the Administrator of the Foreign Agricultural Service.

(b) PRIMARY RESPONSIBILITY.—The office established under subsection (a) shall provide trade assistance and information to persons who are interested in exporting United States agricultural commodities and products or who believe they have been injured by unfair trade practices with respect to trade in agricultural commodities and products.

(c) DUTIES.—The office established under subsection (a) shall—

(1) compile and make readily available international trade information, including information concerning trade practices carried out by other countries to promote the export of agricultural commodities and products, trade barriers imposed by other countries, unfair trade practices of other countries, and remedies under United States law that might be available to persons injured by unfair trade practices; and

(2) provide information and assistance to persons interested in participating in programs carried out by the Foreign Agricultural Service, the Commodity Credit Corporation, and other agencies with respect to the international marketing and export of domestically produced agricultural commodities and products or who believe they have been injured by unfair trade practices of other countries with respect to trade in agricultural commodities and products.

(d) REPORT.—

(1) DEADLINE FOR SUBMISSION.—Not later than 60 days after the end of each fiscal year, the Administrator of the Foreign Agricultural Service shall submit a report described in paragraphs (2) and (3) to the Committee on Agriculture of the House of Representatives and the Committee on Agriculture, Nutrition, and Forestry of the Senate.

(2) CONTENTS OF EACH REPORT.—Each such report shall describe—

(A) the type of information that is currently available through the office established by this section; and

(B) the type of assistance provided to persons during the previous fiscal year.

(3) ADDITIONAL CONTENTS FOR FIRST REPORT.—In the first report submitted under this section, the Administrator shall also—

(A) provide an analysis of the information currently available concerning foreign agricultural trade practices and domestic agricultural trade promotion programs and the methods used to disseminate such information;

(B) provide recommendations with respect to additional information and assistance that should be made available to interested persons; and

(C) provide an analysis of the degree that overlapping information and reports concerning agricultural trade are prepared.

PART 2—FOREIGN AGRICULTURAL SERVICE

SEC. 4211. PERSONNEL OF THE SERVICE.

(a) INCREASED LEVEL.—To ensure that the agricultural export programs of the United States are carried out in an effective manner, the authorized number of personnel for the Foreign Agricultural Service of the Department of Agriculture (hereinafter in this part referred to as the "Service") shall not be less than 900 full-time employees during each of the fiscal years 1989 and 1990.

(b) RANK OF FOREIGN AGRICULTURAL SERVICE OFFICERS IN FOREIGN MISSIONS.—Notwithstanding any other provision of law, the Secretary of State shall, upon the request of the Secretary of Agriculture, accord the diplomatic title of Minister-Counselor to the senior Service officer assigned to any United States mission abroad.

The number of Service officers holding such diplomatic title at any time may not exceed eight.

SEC. 4212. AGRICULTURAL ATTACHE EDUCATIONAL PROGRAM.

The Administrator of the Service (hereinafter in this part referred to as the "Administrator") shall establish a program within the Service that directs attaches of the Service who are reassigned from abroad to the United States, and other personnel of the Service, to visit and consult with producers and exporters of agricultural commodities and products and State officials throughout the United States concerning various methods to increase exports of United States agricultural commodities and products.

SEC. 4213. PERSONNEL RESOURCE TIME.

(a) IN GENERAL.—In planning the overall allocation of personnel resource time of agricultural attaches of the Service, the Administrator shall ensure that the maximum quantity practicable of the overall personnel resource time of agricultural attaches of the Service be devoted to activities designed to increase markets for United States agricultural commodities and products.

(b) REPORTS.—The Administrator shall submit reports to the Committee on Agriculture of the House of Representatives and the Committee on Agriculture, Nutrition, and Forestry of the Senate that describe the allocation of personnel resource time of agricultural attaches during the 1988 and 1989 fiscal years. The report for fiscal year 1988 shall be submitted not later than September 30, 1988, or 30 days after the date of the enactment of this Act, whichever is later. The report for fiscal year 1989 shall be submitted not later than September 30, 1989.

SEC. 4214. COOPERATOR ORGANIZATIONS.

(a) SENSE OF CONGRESS.—It is the sense of Congress that the foreign market development cooperator program of the Service, and the activities of individual foreign market cooperator organizations, have been among the most successful and cost-effective means to expand United States agricultural exports. Congress affirms its support for the program and the activities of the cooperator organizations. The Administrator and the private sector should work together to ensure that the program, and the activities of cooperator organizations, are expanded in the future.

(b) COMMODITIES FOR COOPERATOR ORGANIZATIONS.—The Secretary of Agriculture may make available to cooperator organizations agricultural commodities owned by the Commodity Credit Corporation, for use by such cooperators in projects designed to expand markets for United States agricultural commodities and products.

(c) RELATION TO FUNDS.—Commodities made available to cooperator organizations under this section shall be in addition to, and not in lieu of, funds appropriated for market development activities of such cooperator organizations.

(d) CONFLICTS OF INTEREST.—The Secretary shall take appropriate action to prevent conflicts of interest among cooperator organizations participating in the cooperator program.

(e) EVALUATION.—It is the sense of Congress that the Secretary should establish a consistent, objective means for the evaluation of cooperator programs.

SEC. 4215. AUTHORIZATION OF ADDITIONAL APPROPRIATIONS.

There are authorized to be appropriated for the Service, in addition to any sums otherwise authorized to be appropriated by any provision of law other than this section, $20,000,000 for each of the fiscal years 1988, 1989, and 1990 for market development activities, including—

(1) expansion of the agricultural attache service;

(2) expansion of international trade policy activities of the Service;

(3) enhancement of the Service worldwide market information system;

(4) increasing the number of trade shows and exhibitions conducted by the Service and upgrading the quality of United States representation at trade shows and exhibitions; and

(5) developing markets for value-added beef, pork, and poultry products.

Subtitle C—Existing Agricultural Trade Programs

SEC. 4301. TRIGGERED MARKETING LOANS AND EXPORT ENHANCEMENT.

(a) CERTIFICATION TO CONGRESS.—Notwithstanding any other provision of law, if, before January 1, 1990, a law has not been enacted in accordance with section 151 of the Trade Act of 1974 (19 U.S.C. 2191) that implements an agreement negotiated under the Uruguay round of multilateral trade negotiations conducted under the General Agreement on Tariffs and Trade (hereinafter in this section referred to as "GATT negotiations") concerning agricultural trade, the President, not later than 45 days after such date—

(1) shall submit a report to the Committee on Agriculture, the Committee on Foreign Affairs, and the Committee on Ways and Means of the House of Representatives and the Committee on Agriculture, Nutrition, and Forestry and the Committee on Finance of the Senate describing the status of the GATT negotiations concerning agricultural trade, the progress that has been made to date in the negotiations, the general areas of disagreement, the anticipated date of completion of the negotiations, and the changes in domestic farm programs that are likely to be necessary on conclusion of the negotiations; and

(2) shall certify to Congress whether or not significant progress has been made in the negotiations.

(b) MARKETING LOAN.—

(1) IMPLEMENTATION.—Except as provided in paragraph (2), if the President does not certify that significant progress has been made towards reaching a GATT agreement concerning agricultural trade, the President shall, not later than 60 days before the beginning of the marketing year for the 1990 crop of wheat, instruct the Secretary of Agriculture to permit producers to repay loans made under sections 107D(a), 105C(a), and 201(i) of the Agricultural Act of 1949 (7 U.S.C. 1445b-3(a), 1444e(a), and 1446(i)) for each of the 1990 crops of wheat, feed grains, and soybeans at a level that is the lesser of—

(A) the loan level determined for each such crop; or

(B) the prevailing world market price for each such crop, as determined by the Secretary.

(2) WAIVER.—The President may waive the application of paragraph (1) by certifying to Congress that implementation of the marketing loan would harm further negotiations.

(3) DISCONTINUANCE.—If, after the implementation of a marketing loan in accordance with paragraph (1), the President certifies to Congress that substantial progress is being made in the GATT negotiations and that continuation of the marketing loan program implemented in accordance with paragraph (1) would harm such progress, the President may instruct the Secretary of Agriculture to discontinue the marketing loan program.

(c) EXPORT ENHANCEMENT.—

(1) IN GENERAL.—Except as provided in paragraph (4), if the President exercises the authority to waive or discontinue the marketing loan program provided for in paragraph (2) or (3) of subsection (b), the President shall instruct the Secretary of Agriculture to make agricultural commodities and products acquired by the Commodity Credit Corporation equaling at least $2,000,000,000 in value available during the 1990 through 1992 fiscal years to United States exporters of domestically produced agricultural commodities and products for the purpose of making exports of such commodities and products available on the world market at competitive prices.

(2) NONDISPLACEMENT.—Commodities and products made available in accordance with this subsection shall be in addition to, and not in lieu of, other commodities and products made available for the purpose of enhancing the export of United States commodities and products.

(3) USE OF COMMODITY CREDIT CORPORATION.—The Secretary of Agriculture may use the funds, facilities, and authorities of the Commodity Credit Corporation to carry out this subsection.

(4) EXCEPTION.—The President may waive the application of paragraph (1) by certifying to Congress that implementation of the export enhancement program provided for by this subsection would be a substantial impediment to achieving a successful agreement under the GATT.

(5) DISCONTINUANCE.—If, after the implementation of paragraph (1), the President certifies to Congress that substantial progress is being made in the GATT negotiations and that continuation of the export enhancement program implemented in accordance with paragraph (1) would harm such progress, the President may, not before 60 days after the consultation required under subsection (d) with respect to such certification, instruct the Secretary of Agriculture to suspend the implementation of such program.

(d) CONSULTATION.—The President may not make a certification to Congress under this section unless the United States Trade Representative—

(1) consults about the certification with—

(A) the Committee on Agriculture, the Committee on Foreign Affairs, and the Committee on Ways and Means of the House of Representatives; and

(B) the Committee on Agriculture, Nutrition, and Forestry and the Committee on Finance of the Senate; and

(2) reports to the President the results of such consultation.

SEC. 4302. PRICE SUPPORT PROGRAMS FOR SUNFLOWER SEEDS AND COTTONSEED.

(a) SUNFLOWER SEEDS.—If producers are permitted to repay loans for the 1990 crop of soybeans under section 201(i) of the Agricultural Act of 1949 (7 U.S.C. 1446(i)) at a level that is less than the full amount of the loan pursuant to section 4301 of this Act, the Secretary shall support the price of sunflower seeds through loans and purchases for the 1990 crop of sunflowers in accordance with section 201(l) of the Agricultural Act of 1949.

(b) COTTONSEED.—If a producer is permitted to repay a loan for the 1990 crop of soybeans under section 201(i) of the Agricultural Act of 1949 (7 U.S.C. 1446(i)) at a level that is less than the full amount of the loan pursuant to section 4301 of this Act, the Secretary shall support the price of the 1990 crop of cottonseed at such level as the Secretary determines will cause cottonseed to compete on equal terms with soybeans on the market. The Secretary shall carry out this subsection using the funds, facilities, and authorities of the Commodity Credit Corporation.

(c) DISCONTINUANCE.—If the marketing loan program for the 1990 crop of soybeans is discontinued under section 4301(b)(3) of this Act, the Secretary shall discontinue the price support programs for sunflower seeds and cottonseed required by this section.

SEC. 4303. MULTIYEAR AGREEMENTS UNDER THE FOOD FOR PROGRESS PROGRAM.

Section 1110 of the Food Security Act of 1985 (7 U.S.C. 1736o) is amended—

(1) by redesignating subsection (k) as subsection (l); and

(2) by inserting after subsection (j) the following:

"(k) In carrying out this section, the President shall, on request and subject to the availability of commodities, approve agreements that provide for commodities to be made available for distribution or sale by recipient countries on a multiyear basis if the agreements otherwise meet the requirements of this section.".

SEC. 4304. TARGETED EXPORT ASSISTANCE.

(a) LEVEL OF PROGRAM.—Section 1124(a) of the Food Security Act of 1985 (7 U.S.C. 1736s(a)) is amended—

(1) in paragraph (1)—

(A) by striking out "1988" and inserting in lieu thereof "1987"; and

(B) by striking out "and" at the end; and

(2) by striking out paragraph (2) and inserting in lieu thereof the following:

"(2) for the fiscal year 1988, the Secretary shall use under this section not less than $215,000,000 of the funds of, or commodities owned by, the Corporation, except that the Secretary shall use funds or commodities of the Corporation in excess of $110,000,000 only to the extent appropriations to reimburse the Corporation for such additional expenditures of funds or distribution of commodities are made available in advance to carry out this section; and

"(3) for each of the fiscal years 1989 and 1990, the Secretary shall use under this section not less than $325,000,000 of the funds of, or commodities owned by, the Corporation.".

(b) COUNTERVAILING DUTY ACTION.—Section 1124(b) of such Act is amended—

(1) in paragraph (1), by striking out "Funds" and inserting in lieu thereof "Except as provided in paragraph (3), funds"; and

(2) by adding at the end thereof the following new paragraph:

"(3)(A) Funds or commodities made available for use under this section may be used by the Secretary to assist organizations consisting of producers or processors of United States agricultural commodities in amounts necessary to compensate the organizations for reasonable expenses incurred in defending countervailing duty actions instituted after January 1, 1986, in foreign countries to offset the benefits of the agricultural programs provided for under the Agricultural Act of 1949 (7 U.S.C. 1421 et seq.). In no event may such assistance exceed $500,000 for the defense of any one countervailing duty action.

"(B) If the Secretary declines to make funds or commodities available under this paragraph, the Secretary shall notify the Committee on Agriculture of the House of Representatives and the Committee on Agriculture, Nutrition, and Forestry of the Senate of the reasons for declining to make the funds or commodities available.".

SEC. 4305. EXPORT CREDIT GUARANTEE PROGRAM.

It is the sense of Congress that, to the extent that the Commodity Credit Corporation makes a specified allocation of credit guarantees available under the export credit guarantee program referred to in section 1125 of the Food Security Act of 1985 (7 U.S.C. 1736t) for short-term credit extended to finance the export sales of United States agricultural commodities and products, such allocation should be made on a country-only basis and not on a commodity basis or a commodity and country basis.

SEC. 4306. AGRICULTURAL EXPORT ENHANCEMENT PROGRAM.

(a) PRIORITIES.—Section 1127(b) of the Food Security Act of 1985 (7 U.S.C. 1736v(b)) is amended by striking out paragraph (2) and inserting in lieu thereof the following new paragraph:

"(2) may consider for participation all interested United States exporters, processors, and users and interested foreign purchasers, and may give priority to sales to countries that have traditionally purchased United States agricultural commodities and products;".

(b) LEVEL OF FUNDING.—Section 1127(i) of such Act is amended—

(1) by striking out "1988" and inserting in lieu thereof "1990"; and

(2) by striking out "$1,500,000,000" and inserting in lieu thereof "$2,500,000,000".

SEC. 4307. AGRICULTURAL ATTACHE REPORTS.

Subsection (b) of section 1132 of the Food Security Act of 1985 (7 U.S.C. 1736x(b)) is amended to read as follows:

"(b) The Secretary shall—

"(1) annually compile the information contained in such reports;

"(2) in consultation with the agricultural technical advisory committees established under section 135(c) of the Trade Act of 1974 (19 U.S.C. 2155(c)), include in the compilation a priority ranking of those trade barriers identified in subsection (a) by commodity group;

"(3) include in the compilation a list of actions undertaken to reduce or eliminate such trade barriers; and

"(4) make the compilation available to Congress, the trade assistance office created under section 4602 of the Agricultural Competitiveness and Trade Act of 1988, the agricultural policy advisory committee, and other interested parties.".

SEC. 4308. DAIRY EXPORT INCENTIVE PROGRAM.

Paragraphs (2) through (3) of section 153(d) of the Food Security Act of 1985 (15 U.S.C. 713a-14(d)) are amended to read as follows:

"(2) If payments in commodities are authorized, such payments shall be made through the issuance of generic certificates redeemable in commodities.

"(3) If generic certificates issued in accordance with the program provided for by this section are exchanged for dairy products owned by the Commodity Credit Corporation, the regulations issued by the Secretary shall ensure that—

"(A) such dairy products, or an equal quantity of other dairy products, will be sold for export by the entity; and

"(B) any such export sales by the entity—

"(i) will be in addition to, and not in place of, export sales of dairy products that the entity would otherwise make under the program or in the absence of the program; and

"(ii) to the extent practicable, will not displace commercial export sales of United States dairy products by other exporters.".

SEC. 4309. BARTER OF AGRICULTURAL COMMODITIES.

In recognition of the importance of barter programs in expanding agricultural trade, it is the sense of Congress that the Secretary of Agriculture should expedite the implementation of section 416(d) of the Agricultural Act of 1949 (7 U.S.C. 1431(d)) and section 1167 of the Food Security Act of 1985 (7 U.S.C. 1727g note and 1736aa), relating to the barter of agricultural commodities.

SEC. 4310. MINIMUM LEVEL OF FOOD ASSISTANCE.

(a) ANNUAL MINIMUM.—It is the sense of Congress that—

(1) the United States should maintain its historic proportion of food assistance constituting one-third of all United States foreign economic assistance; and

(2) accordingly, the total amount of food assistance made available to foreign countries under the Agricultural Trade Development and Assistance Act of 1954 (7 U.S.C. 1691 et seq.) and section 416(b) of the Agricultural Act of 1949 (7 U.S.C. 1431(b)) should not be less than one-third of the total amount of foreign economic assistance provided for each fiscal year.

(b) DEFINITION.—For purposes of this section, the term "foreign economic assistance" includes—

(1) assistance under chapter 1 of part I of the Foreign Assistance Act of 1961 (22 U.S.C. 2151 et seq.), the Agricultural Trade Development and Assistance Act of 1954 (7 U.S.C. 1691 et seq.), section 416(b) of the Agricultural Act of 1949 (7 U.S.C. 1431(b)), or any other law authorizing economic assistance for foreign countries; and

(2) United States contributions to the International Bank for Reconstruction and Development, the International Development Association, the Inter-American Development Bank, the

Asian Development Bank, the African Development Bank, or any other multilateral development bank.

SEC. 4311. FOOD AID AND MARKET DEVELOPMENT.

(a) POLICY STATEMENT.—It is the policy of the United States to use food aid and agriculturally-related foreign economic assistance programs more effectively to develop markets for United States agricultural commodities and products.

(b) REQUIREMENT.—The President (or, as appropriate, the Secretary of Agriculture) shall encourage recipient countries under food assistance agreements entered into under any program administered by the Secretary to agree to give preference to United States food and food products in future food purchases.

Subtitle D—Wood and Wood Products

SEC. 4401. DEVELOPING MARKETS FOR WOOD AND WOOD PRODUCTS UNDER PUBLIC LAW 480.

Section 104(b)(1) of the Agricultural Trade Development and Assistance Act of 1954 (7 U.S.C. 1704(b)(1)) is amended by inserting "(including wood and processed wood products of the United States)" after "agricultural commodities" the first place it appears.

SEC. 4402. DEVELOPING MARKETS FOR WOOD AND WOOD PRODUCTS UNDER THE SHORT-TERM AND INTERMEDIATE-TERM EXPORT CREDIT GUARANTEE PROGRAMS.

(a) SHORT-TERM EXPORT CREDIT GUARANTEES.—Section 1125 of the Food Security Act of 1985 (7 U.S.C. 1736t) is amended—

(1) in subsection (b), by inserting ", including wood and processed wood products" after "agricultural commodities and the products thereof"; and

(2) by adding at the end thereof the following:

"(d) For the purpose of this section, the term 'wood and processed wood products' includes but is not limited to logs, lumber (boards, timber, millwork, molding, flooring, and siding), veneer, panel products (plywood, particle board, and fiberboard), utility and telephone poles, other poles and posts, railroad ties, wood pulp, and wood chips.".

(b) INTERMEDIATE-TERM EXPORT CREDIT.—Section 4(b)(1) of the Food for Peace Act of 1966 (7 U.S.C. 1707a(b)(1)) is amended by adding at the end thereof the following: "For the purpose of this paragraph, the term 'agricultural commodities' includes wood and processed wood products, as defined in section 1125(d) of the Food Security Act of 1985 (7 U.S.C. 1736t(d)).".

SEC. 4403. COOPERATIVE NATIONAL FOREST PRODUCTS MARKETING PROGRAM.

The Cooperative Forestry Assistance Act of 1978 (16 U.S.C. 2101 et seq.) is amended by adding at the end thereof the following:

"SEC. 15. COOPERATIVE NATIONAL FOREST PRODUCTS MARKETING PROGRAM.

"(a) FINDINGS AND PURPOSES.—

"(1) FINDINGS.—Congress finds that—

"(A) the health and vitality of the domestic forest products industry is important to the well-being of the economy of the United States;

"(B) the domestic forest products industry has a significant potential for expansion in both domestic and foreign markets;

"(C) many small-sized to medium-sized forest products firms lack the tools that would enable them to meet the increasing challenge of foreign competition in domestic and foreign markets; and

"(D) a new cooperative forest products marketing program will improve the competitiveness of the United States forest products industry.

"(2) PURPOSES.—The purposes of this section are to—

"(A) provide direct technical assistance to the United States forest products industry to improve marketing activities;

"(B) provide cost-share grants to States to support State and regional forest products marketing programs; and

"(C) target assistance to small-sized and medium-sized producers of solid wood and processed wood products, including pulp.

"(b) PROGRAM AUTHORITY.—

"(1) IN GENERAL.—The Secretary shall establish a cooperative national forest products marketing program under this Act that provides—

"(A) technical assistance to States, landowners, and small-sized to medium-sized forest products firms on ways to improve domestic and foreign markets for forest products; and

"(B) grants of financial assistance with matching requirements to the States to assist in State and regional forest products marketing efforts targeted to aid small-sized to medium-sized forest products firms and private, nonindustrial forest landowners.

"(2) INTERSTATE COOPERATIVE AGREEMENTS.—Grant agreements shall encourage the establishment of interstate cooperative agreements by the States for the purpose of promoting the development of domestic and foreign markets for forest products.

"(c) LIMITATIONS.—

"(1) COOPERATION WITH OTHER FEDERAL AGENCIES.—In carrying out this section, the Secretary shall cooperate with Federal departments and agencies to avoid the duplication of efforts and to increase program efficiency.

"(2) DOMESTIC PROGRAM.—The program authorized under this section shall be carried out within the United States and not be extended to Department of Agriculture activities in foreign countries.

"(d) AUTHORIZATION FOR APPROPRIATIONS.—There are authorized to be appropriated $5,000,000 for each of the fiscal years 1988 through 1991, to carry out this section.

"(e) PROGRAM REPORT.—The Secretary shall report to Congress annually on the activities taken under the marketing program established under this section. A final report including recommendations for program changes and the need and desirability of the reauthorization of this authority, and required levels of funding, shall be submitted to Congress not later than September 30, 1990.".

SEC. 4404. USE OF DEPARTMENT OF AGRICULTURE PROGRAMS.

The Secretary of Agriculture shall actively use Department of Agriculture concessional programs and export credit guarantee programs to promote the export of wood and processed wood products.

Subtitle E—Studies and Reports

SEC. 4501. STUDY OF CANADIAN WHEAT IMPORT LICENSING REQUIREMENTS.

(a) FINDINGS.—Congress finds that—

(1) Canadian importers of wheat or products containing a minimum of 25 percent wheat (except packaged wheat products for retail sale) from the United States must obtain import licenses from the Canadian Wheat Board;

(2) the Canadian Wheat Board requires such importers of United States wheat and wheat products to prove that the wheat or wheat products to be imported are not readily available in Canada before issuance of an import license, and therefore, for all practical purposes, such licenses are not granted by the Canadian Wheat Board;

(3) the licensing requirements of the Canadian Wheat Board's import licensing program result in a trade barrier on the importation of United States wheat and wheat products; and

(4) Canada is a member of the General Agreement on Tariffs and Trade and, under such agreement, member countries should, in general, eliminate import licensing programs that operate as nontariff trade barriers.

(b) STUDY.—The Secretary of Agriculture shall conduct a study of the Canadian Wheat Board's import licensing program to—

(1) assess the effect of the Canadian Wheat Board's import licensing program referred to in subsection (a) on wheat producers, processors, and exporters in the United States; and

(2) determine—

(A) the nature and extent of the licensing requirements of the Canadian Wheat Board's import licensing program; and

(B) the estimated effect of the Canadian Wheat Board's import licensing program in reducing exports of United States wheat and wheat products to Canada.

(c) SUBMISSION OF RESULTS.—Not later than 90 days after the date of enactment of this Act, the Secretary shall submit the results of the study conducted under subsection (b) to the United States Trade Representative.

(d) CONSULTATION WITH CONGRESS.—Not later than 90 days after the results of the study are submitted, the Secretary and the United States Trade Representative shall consult with the Committee on Agriculture and the Committee on Ways and Means of the House of Representatives and the Committee on Agriculture, Nutrition, and Forestry and the Committee on Finance of the Senate on the status of efforts to negotiate the elimination of such Canadian licensing requirements.

SEC. 4502. IMPORT INVENTORY.

(a) COMPILATION AND REPORT ON IMPORTS.—The Secretary of Agriculture, in consultation with the Secretary of Commerce, the International Trade Commission, the United States Trade Representative, and the heads of all other appropriate Federal agencies, shall compile and report to the public statistics on the total value and quantity of imported raw and processed agricultural products. The report shall be limited to those statistics that such agencies already obtain for other purposes.

(b) COMPILATION AND REPORT ON CONSUMPTION.—The Secretary shall compile and report to the public data on the total quantity of production and consumption of domestically produced raw and processed agricultural products.

(c) ISSUING OF DATA.—The reports required by this section shall be made in a format that correlates statistics for the quantity and value of imported agricultural products to the production and consumption of domestic agricultural products. The Secretary shall issue such reports on an annual basis, with the first report required not later than 1 year after the date of enactment of this Act.

SEC. 4503. STUDY RELATING TO HONEY.

(a) STUDY.—The Secretary of Agriculture shall conduct a study to determine the effect of imported honey on United States honey producers, the availability of honey bee pollination within the United States, and whether there is reason to believe imports of honey tend to interfere with or render ineffective the honey price support program of the Department of Agriculture.

(b) REPORT.—Not later than 90 days after the date of the enactment of this Act, the Secretary shall report the results of such study to the Committee on Agriculture and the Committee on Ways and Means of the House of Representatives and to the Committee on Agriculture, Nutrition, and Forestry and the Committee on Finance of the Senate.

SEC. 4504. STUDY OF DAIRY IMPORT QUOTAS.

(a) STUDY.—Not later than 180 days after the date of enactment of this Act, the Secretary of Agriculture shall conduct a study to determine whether, and to what extent, the price support program for milk established under section 201(d) of the Agricultural Act of 1949 (7 U.S.C. 1446(d)) would be affected by a reduction in, or elimination of, limitations imposed on the importation of certain dairy products under section 22 of the Agricultural Adjustment Act (7 U.S.C. 624), reenacted with amendments by the Agricultural Marketing Agreement Act of 1937, as a result of multilateral trade negotiations, including negotiations under the General Agreement on Tariffs and Trade. In conducting this study, the Secretary shall assess the likelihood of other nations' agreeing to reduce or eliminate their domestic dairy price stabilization, export subsidization, or import control programs in such multilateral negotiations.

(b) REPORT.—The Secretary shall submit a report describing the results of the study, together with any recommendations, to the Committee on Agriculture and the Committee on Ways and Means of the House of Representatives, and the Committee on Agriculture, Nutrition, and Forestry and the Committee on Finance of the Senate.

SEC. 4505. REPORT ON INTERMEDIATE EXPORT CREDIT.

Not later than 180 days after the date of the enactment of this Act, the Secretary of Agriculture shall submit a report to the Committee on Agriculture and the Committee on Foreign Affairs of the House of Representatives and the Committee on Agriculture, Nutrition, and Forestry of the Senate, on the use of authorities established under section 4 of the Food for Peace Act of 1966 (7 U.S.C. 1707a), the Agricultural Trade Development and Assistance Act of 1954 (7 U.S.C. 1691 et seq.), section 416 of the Agricultural Act of 1949 (7 U.S.C. 1431), and the Commodity Credit Corporation Charter Act (15 U.S.C. 714 et seq.), to provide intermediate credit financing and other trade assistance for the establishment of facilities in importing countries—

(1) to improve the handling, marketing, processing, storage, and distribution of imported agricultural commodities and products;

(2) to increase livestock production in order to enhance the demand for United States feed grains; and

(3) to increase markets for United States livestock and livestock products.

SEC. 4506. IMPORTED MEAT, POULTRY PRODUCTS, EGGS, AND EGG PRODUCTS.

(a) REPORT.—Not later than 90 days after the date of the enactment of this Act, the Secretary of Agriculture shall submit a report to Congress—

(1) specifying the planned distribution, in fiscal years 1988 and 1989, of the resources of the Department of Agriculture available for sampling imported covered products to ensure compliance with the requirements of the Federal Meat Inspection Act (21 U.S.C. 601 et seq.), the Poultry Products Inspection Act (21 U.S.C. 451 et seq.), and the Egg Products Inspection Act (21 U.S.C. 1031 et seq.) that govern the level of residues of pesticides, drugs, and other products permitted in or on such products;

(2) describing current methods used by the Secretary to enforce the requirements of such Acts with respect to the level of residues of pesticides, drugs, and other products permitted in or on such products;

(3) responding to the audit report of the Inspector General of the Department of Agriculture, Number 38002—2—hy, dated January 14, 1987;

(4) providing a summary with respect to the importation of covered products during fiscal years 1987 and 1988 that specifies—

(A) the number of samples of each such product taken during each such fiscal year in carrying out the requirements described in paragraph (1); and

(B) for each violation of such requirements during each such fiscal year—

(i) the covered products with respect to which such violation occurred;

(ii) the residue in or on such product in violation of such requirements;

(iii) the country exporting such product;

(iv) the actions taken in response to such violation and the reasons for such actions; and

(v) the level of testing conducted by the countries exporting such products;

(5) describing any research conducted by the Secretary to develop improved methods to detect residues subject to such requirements in or on covered products; and

(6) providing any recommendations the Secretary considers appropriate for legislation to add or modify penalties for violations of laws, regulations, and other enforcement requirements governing the level of residues that are permitted in or on imported covered products.

(b) REVISION.—Not later than November 15, 1989, the Secretary of Agriculture shall revise, as necessary, the report prepared under subsection (a) and submit the revision to Congress.

(c) DEFINITION.—As used in this section, the term "covered products" means meat, poultry products, eggs, and egg products.

SEC. 4507. STUDY OF CIRCUMVENTION OF AGRICULTURAL QUOTAS.

(a) IN GENERAL.—Not later than 180 days after the date of enactment of this Act, the Comptroller General of the United States shall conduct a study with respect to—

(1) whether articles containing dairy products (including chocolate in blocks of at least 10 pounds and other such products) are being imported into the United States in such a manner or in such quantities as to circumvent or avoid the limitations imposed on imports of dairy products under section 22 of the Agricultural Adjustment Act (7 U.S.C. 624), reenacted with amendments by the Agricultural Marketing Agreement Act of 1937; and

(2) whether products containing refined sugar are being imported into the United States in such a manner or in such quantities as to circumvent or avoid the limitations imposed on imports of refined sugar and sugar containing products imposed under Federal law.

(b) REQUIREMENTS.—In conducting the study required under subsection (a), the Comptroller General shall investigate—

(1) the efforts undertaken by the United States Customs Service in the enforcement of the existing quantitative limitations described in subsection (a);

(2) the change in the composition, volume, and pattern of imports containing sugar and imports containing dairy products subsequent to the initial imposition of the quantitative limitations;

(3) the effectiveness of section 22 of the Agricultural Adjustment Act (7 U.S.C. 624), reenacted with amendments by the Agricultural Marketing Agreement Act of 1937, in preventing the circumvention or avoidance of the quantitative limitations; and

(4) the use of United States foreign trade zones to circumvent the quantitative limitations.

(c) REPORT.—On completion of the study required by this section, the Comptroller General shall report the results of the study to the Committee on Agriculture and the Committee on Ways and Means of the House of Representatives, and the Committee on Agriculture, Nutrition, and Forestry and the Committee on Finance of the Senate.

SEC. 4508. STUDY OF LAMB MEAT IMPORTS.

(a) Study.—The Secretary of Agriculture shall conduct a study of the market for lamb meat products in the United States, focusing on production, demand, rate of return on investment, marketing and trends with respect to the level of imports of live lamb and lamb meat products, and the effects of such imports on the production of lamb meat in the United States.

(b) Report.—Not later than 180 days after the date of enactment of this Act, the Secretary shall submit to the Committee on Ways and Means and the Committee on Agriculture of the House of Representatives and the Committee on Finance and the Committee on Agriculture, Nutrition, and Forestry of the Senate a report setting forth the results of such study. If appropriate, the report should include proposals on ways to bring about a long-term increase in per capita consumption of lamb meat products and ways to encourage a more profitable and productive domestic industry to ensure a plentiful and affordable supply of lamb meat.

SEC. 4509. ROSE STUDY.

(a) Study.—Not later than 240 days after the date of enactment of this Act, the United States International Trade Commission shall, pursuant to section 332 of the Tariff Act of 1930 (19 U.S.C. 1332), complete a study with respect to—

(1) competitive factors affecting the domestic rose-growing industry, including competition from imports;

(2) the effect that the European Community's tariff rate for imported roses has on world trade of roses; and

(3) the extent to which unfair trade practices and foreign barriers to trade are impeding the marketing abroad of domestically produced roses.

(b) Report.—The Commission shall report the results of the study conducted in accordance with subsection (a) as soon as the study is completed to—

(1) the Committee on Agriculture and the Committee on Ways and Means of the House of Representatives;

(2) the Committee on Agriculture, Nutrition, and Forestry and the Committee on Finance of the Senate;

(3) the United States Trade Representative;

(4) the Secretary of Commerce; and

(5) the Secretary of Agriculture.

(c) Review.—It is the sense of Congress that the United States Trade Representative, the Secretary of Commerce, and the Secretary of Agriculture, should use all available remedies, programs, and policies within their respective jurisdictions to assist the domestic rose industry to maintain and enhance its ability to compete in the domestic and world market for roses if, after their review of the study and report required by this section, such officials determine that such action is appropriate to counter any adverse effects on the domestic rose industry caused by unfair trade practices of foreign competitors

Subtitle F—Miscellaneous Agricultural Provisions

SEC. 4601. ALLOCATION OF CERTAIN MILK.

Section 8c(5) of the Agricultural Adjustment Act (7 U.S.C. 608c(5)), reenacted with amendments by the Agricultural Marketing Agreement Act of 1937, is amended by adding at the end the following:

"(K)(i) Notwithstanding any other provision of law, milk produced by dairies—

"(I) owned or controlled by foreign persons; and

"(II) financed by or with the use of bonds the interest on which is exempt from Federal income tax under section 103 of the Internal Revenue Code of 1986;

shall be treated as other-source milk, and shall be allocated as milk received from producer-handlers for the purposes of classifying producer milk, under the milk marketing program established under this Act. For the purposes of this subparagraph, the term 'foreign person' has the meaning given such term under section 9(3) of the Agricultural Foreign Investment Disclosure Act of 1978 (7 U.S.C. 3508(3)).

"(ii) The Secretary of Agriculture shall prescribe regulations to carry out this subparagraph.

"(iii) This subparagraph shall not apply with respect to any dairy that began operation before May 6, 1986.".

SEC. 4602. PAID ADVERTISING FOR FLORIDA-GROWN STRAWBERRIES UNDER MARKETNG ORDERS.

The first proviso of section 8c(6)(I) of the Agricultural Adjustment Act (7 U.S.C. 608c(6)(I)), reenacted with amendments by the Agricultural Marketing Agreement Act of 1937, is amended by striking out "or tomatoes" and inserting in lieu thereof "tomatoes, or Florida-grown strawberries,".

SEC. 4603. APPLICATION OF MARKETNG ORDERS TO IMPORTS.

Section 8e of the Agricultural Adjustment Act (7 U.S.C. 608e-1), reenacted with amendments by the Agricultural Marketing Agreement Act of 1937, is amended—

(1) by inserting "(a)" at the beginning of the first sentence; and

(2) by adding at the end thereof the following new subsection:

"(b)(1) The Secretary may provide for a period of time (not to exceed 35 days) in addition to the period of time covered by a marketing order during which the marketing order requirements would be in effect for a particular commodity during any year if the Secretary determines that such additional period of time is necessary—

"(A) to effectuate the purposes of this Act; and

"(B) to prevent the circumvention of the grade, size, quality, or maturity standards of a seasonal marketing order applicable to a commodity produced in the United States by imports of such commodity.

"(2) In making the determination required by paragraph (1), the Secretary, through notice and comment procedures, shall consider—

"(A) to what extent, during the previous year, imports of a commodity that did not meet the requirements of a marketing order applicable to such commodity were marketed in the United States during the period that such marketing order requirements were in effect for available domestic commodities (or would have been marketed during such time if not for any additional period established by the Secretary):

"(B) if the importation into the United States of such commodity did, or was likely to, circumvent the grade, size, quality or maturity standards of a seasonal marketing order applicable to such commodity produced in the United States; and

"(C) the availability and price of commodities of the variety covered by the marketing order during any additional period the marketing order requirements are to be in effect.

"(3) An additional period established by the Secretary in accordance with this subsection shall be—

"(A) announced not later than 30 days before the date such additional period is to be in effect; and

"(B) reviewed by the Secretary on request, through notice and comment procedures, at least every 3 years in order to determine if the additional period is still needed to prevent circumvention of the seasonal marketing order by imported commodities.

"(4) For the purposes of carrying out this subsection, the Secretary is authorized to make such reasonable inspections as may be necessary.".

SEC. 4604. RECIPROCAL MEAT INSPECTION REQUIREMENT.

(a) IN GENERAL.—Section 20 of the Federal Meat Inspection Act (21 U.S.C. 620) is amended by adding at the end thereof the following new subsection:

"(h)(1) As used in this subsection:

"(A) The term 'meat articles' means carcasses, meat and meat food products of cattle, sheep, swine, goats, horses, mules, or other equines, that are capable of use as human food.

"(B) The term 'standards' means inspection, building construction, sanitary, quality, species verification, residue, and other standards that are applicable to meat articles.

"(2) On request of the Committee on Agriculture or the Committee on Ways and Means of the House of Representatives or the Committee on Agriculture, Nutrition, and Forestry or the Committee on Finance of the Senate, or at the initiative of the Secretary, the Secretary shall, as soon as practicable, determine whether a particular foreign country applies standards for the importation of meat articles from the United States that are not related to public health concerns about end-product quality that can be substantiated by reliable analytical methods.

"(3) If the Secretary determines that a foreign country applies standards described in paragraph (2)—

"(A) the Secretary shall consult with the United States Trade Representative; and

"(B) within 30 days after the determination of the Secretary under paragraph (2), the Secretary and the United States Trade Representative shall recommend to the President whether action should be taken under paragraph (4).

"(4) Within 30 days after receiving a recommendation for action under paragraph (3), the President shall, if and for such time as the President considers appropriate, prohibit imports into the United

States of any meat articles produced in such foreign country unless it is determined that the meat articles produced in that country meet the standards applicable to meat articles in commerce within the United States.

"(5) The action authorized under paragraph (4) may be used instead of, or in addition to, any other action taken under any other law.".

(b) REPORTS.—Section 20(e) of such Act is amended—

(1) by striking out "and" at the end of paragraph (4);

(2) by striking out the period at the end of paragraph (5) and inserting in lieu thereof "; and"; and

(3) by adding at the end thereof the following new paragraph:

"(6) the name of each foreign country that applies standards for the importation of meat articles from the United States that are described in subsection (h)(2).".

SEC. 4605. STUDY OF INTERNATIONAL MARKETING IN LAND GRANT COLLEGES AND UNIVERSITIES.

It is the sense of Congress that—

(1) land grant colleges and universities (as defined in section 1404(10) of the National Agricultural Research, Extension, and Teaching Policy Act of 1977 (7 U.S.C. 3103(10)) should encourage the study and career objective of international marketing of agricultural commodities and products;

(2) because marketing complements production, international agricultural marketing specialists are needed in a globally competitive world; and

(3) enhanced foreign marketing of United States agricultural commodities and products will help relieve stress in the rural economy.

SEC. 4606. INTERNATIONAL TRADE IN EGGS AND EGG PRODUCTS.

(a) FINDINGS.—Congress finds that—

(1) the system of basic and variable levies of the European Community has severely restricted the export of United States eggs and egg products to European Community member countries;

(2) export subsidies of the European Community have caused displacement of United States egg exports in international markets; and

(3) the Secretary of Agriculture is in the process of certifying the Netherland's inspection procedures for egg products for the purpose of importation into the United States of egg products of the Netherlands.

(b) SENSE OF CONGRESS.—It is the sense of Congress that the United States Trade Representative should enter into negotiations with the European Community concerning—

(1) duties, tariffs, and other means used by the European Community to limit the access of United States eggs and egg products to European Community markets; and

(2) European Community export subsidies that have had the effect of excluding United States eggs and egg products from other world markets.

SEC. 4607. UNITED STATES ACCESS TO THE KOREAN BEEF MARKET

(a) FINDINGS.—Congress finds that—

(1) the 1986 United States trade deficit with the Republic of Korea was $7,600,000,000;

(2) the Republic of Korea has banned beef imports since May 1985;

(3) this beef import ban is in contravention of Korea's obligations under the General Agreement on Tariffs and Trade and impairs United States rights under such agreement;

(4) Korea imposes an unreasonably high 20 percent ad valorem tariff on meat products; and

(5) if the Korean beef market were liberalized, the United States, due to comparative advantage, could supply a significant portion of the Korean market for beef, thereby increasing profit opportunities for the United States beef industry while benefiting Korean consumers.

(b) SENSE OF CONGRESS.—It is the sense of Congress that—

(1) the Republic of Korea should take immediate action to fulfill its obligations under the General Agreement on Tariffs and Trade and permit access to its market for United States beef;

(2) the United States should aggressively pursue negotiations to gain access to the Korean market for United States beef;

(3) such negotiations, in addition to elimination of the beef import ban, should address the high tariffs set by the Republic of Korea and the means by which imported beef is distributed in Korea; and

(4) if the Republic of Korea does not show clear evidence that it is engaging in meaningful liberalization of its market for United States beef, the United States should use all available and appropriate means to encourage the Republic of Korea to open its market to United States beef imports.

SEC. 4608. UNITED STATES ACCESS TO JAPANESE AGRICULTURAL MARKETS.

(a) FINDINGS.—Congress finds that—

(1) the United States requested establishment of a panel pursuant to Article XXIII of the General Agreement on Tariffs and Trade (hereinafter in this section referred to as "GATT") to examine Japanese import restrictions on 12 categories of agricultural products;

(2) the GATT panel found that Japanese quantitative restrictions on 10 of the 12 product categories are inconsistent with Article XI of the GATT and recommended that Japan eliminate them or otherwise take action to bring them into conformity with the GATT; and

(3) the rationale behind the GATT panel finding can also be applied to other restrictions that Japan maintains on imports from the United States, including—

(A) a virtual ban on imports of United States rice;

(B) a very restrictive quota on imports of United States beef; and

(C) high tariffs and restrictive quotas on imports of United States citrus.

(b) SENSE OF CONGRESS.—It is the sense of Congress that—

(1) the Government of Japan should immediately take actions to comply with the findings of the GATT panel report;

(2) the Government of Japan should immediately liberalize its trade policies by lowering high tariffs and removing quotas on

agricultural imports from the United States, including those imposed on rice, beef, and citrus, in order to avoid any damage to the close relations between Japan and the United States; and

(3) the United States should continue efforts to persuade the Government of Japan to remove its trade barriers.

SEC. 4609. SENSE OF CONGRESS RELATING TO SECTION 22.

It is the sense of Congress that—

(1) the amounts of assessments collected under the no-net-cost tobacco program can be an indicator of import injury and material interference with the tobacco price support program administered by the Secretary of Agriculture; and

(2) for purposes of any investigation conducted under section 22(a) of the Agricultural Adjustment Act (7 U.S.C. 624(a)), re-enacted with amendments by the Agricultural Marketing Agreement Act of 1937, with respect to tobacco, or articles containing tobacco, imported into the United States, the International Trade Commission should take into account, as if they are costs to the Federal government, contributions and assessments imposed under sections 106A and 106B of the Agricultural Act of 1949 (7 U.S.C. 1445-1 and 1445-2) in determining whether such imported tobacco or articles containing tobacco materially interfere with the tobacco price support program carried out by the Secretary of Agriculture.

TITLE V—FOREIGN CORRUPT PRACTICES AMENDMENTS; INVESTMENT; AND TECHNOLOGY

Subtitle A—Foreign Corrupt Practices Act Amendments; Review of Certain Acquisitions

PART I—FOREIGN CORRUPT PRACTICES ACT AMENDMENTS

SEC. 5001. SHORT TITLE.

This part may be cited as the "Foreign Corrupt Practices Act Amendments of 1988".

SEC. 5002. PENALTIES FOR VIOLATIONS OF ACCOUNTING STANDARDS.

Section 13(b) of the Securities Exchange Act of 1934 (15 U.S.C. 78m(b)) is amended by adding at the end thereof the following:

"(4) No criminal liability shall be imposed for failing to comply with the requirements of paragraph (2) of this subsection except as provided in paragraph (5) of this subsection.

"(5) No person shall knowingly circumvent or knowingly fail to implement a system of internal accounting controls or knowingly falsify any book, record, or account described in paragraph (2).

"(6) Where an issuer which has a class of securities registered pursuant to section 12 of this title or an issuer which is required to file reports pursuant to section 15(d) of this title holds 50 per centum or less of the voting power with respect to a domestic or foreign firm, the provisions of paragraph (2) require only that the issuer proceed in good faith to use its influence, to the extent reasonable under the issuer's circumstances, to cause such domestic or foreign firm to devise and maintain a system of internal accounting controls consistent with paragraph (2). Such circumstances include the relative degree of the issuer's ownership of the domestic or foreign firm and the laws and practices governing the business operations of the country in which such firm is located. An issuer which demonstrates good faith efforts to use such influence shall be conclusively presumed to have complied with the requirements of paragraph (2).

"(7) For the purpose of paragraph (2) of this subsection, the terms 'reasonable assurances' and 'reasonable detail' mean such level of detail and degree of assurance as would satisfy prudent officials in the conduct of their own affairs.".

SEC. 5003. FOREIGN CORRUPT PRACTICES ACT AMENDMENTS.

(a) PROHIBITED TRADE PRACTICES BY ISSUERS.—Section 30A of the Securities Exchange Act of 1934 (15 U.S.C. 78dd-1) is amended to read as follows:

"PROHIBITED FOREIGN TRADE PRACTICES BY ISSUERS

"SEC. 30A. (a) PROHIBITION.—It shall be unlawful for any issuer which has a class of securities registered pursuant to section 12 of this title or which is required to file reports under section 15(d) of this title, or for any officer, director, employee, or agent of such issuer or any stockholder thereof acting on behalf of such issuer, to make use of the mails or any means or instrumentality of interstate commerce corruptly in furtherance of an offer, payment, promise to pay, or authorization of the payment of any money, or offer, gift, promise to give, or authorization of the giving of anything of value to—

"(1) any foreign official for purposes of—

"(A)(i) influencing any act or decision of such foreign official in his official capacity, or (ii) inducing such foreign official to do or omit to do any act in violation of the lawful duty of such official, or

"(B) inducing such foreign official to use his influence with a foreign government or instrumentality thereof to affect or influence any act or decision of such government or instrumentality,

in order to assist such issuer in obtaining or retaining business for or with, or directing business to, any person;

"(2) any foreign political party or official thereof or any candidate for foreign political office for purposes of—

"(A)(i) influencing any act or decision of such party, official, or candidate in its or his official capacity, or (ii) inducing such party, official, or candidate to do or omit to do an act in violation of the lawful duty of such party, official, or candidate,

"(B) inducing such party, official, or candidate to use its or his influence with a foreign government or instrumentality thereof to affect or influence any act or decision of such government or instrumentality,

in order to assist such issuer in obtaining or retaining business for or with, or directing business to, any person; or

"(3) any person, while knowing that all or a portion of such money or thing of value will be offered, given, or promised, directly or indirectly, to any foreign official, to any foreign political party or official thereof, or to any candidate for foreign political office, for purposes of—

"(A)(i) influencing any act or decision of such foreign official, political party, party official, or candidate in his or its official capacity, or (ii) inducing such foreign official, political party, party official, or candidate to do or omit to do any act in violation of the lawful duty of such foreign official, political party, party official, or candidate, or

"(B) inducing such foreign official, political party, party official, or candidate to use his or its influence with a foreign government or instrumentality thereof to affect or influence any act or decision of such government or instrumentality,

in order to assist such issuer in obtaining or retaining business for or with, or directing business to, any person.

"(b) EXCEPTION FOR ROUTINE GOVERNMENTAL ACTION.—Subsection (a) shall not apply to any facilitating or expediting payment to a foreign official, political party, or party official the purpose of which is to expedite or to secure the performance of a routine governmental action by a foreign official, political party, or party official.

"(c) AFFIRMATIVE DEFENSES.—It shall be an affirmative defense to actions under subsection (a) that—

"(1) the payment, gift, offer, or promise of anything of value that was made, was lawful under the written laws and regulations of the foreign official's, political party's, party official's, or candidate's country; or

"(2) the payment, gift, offer, or promise of anything of value that was made, was a reasonable and bona fide expenditure, such as travel and lodging expenses, incurred by or on behalf of a foreign official, party, party official, or candidate and was directly related to—

"(A) the promotion, demonstration, or explanation of products or services; or

"(B) the execution or performance of a contract with a foreign government or agency thereof.

"(d) GUIDELINES BY THE ATTORNEY GENERAL.—Not later than one year after the date of the enactment of the Foreign Corrupt Practices Act Amendments of 1988, the Attorney General, after consultation with the Commission, the Secretary of Commerce, the United States Trade Representative, the Secretary of State, and the Secretary of the Treasury, and after obtaining the views of all interested persons through public notice and comment procedures, shall determine to what extent compliance with this section would be enhanced and the business community would be assisted by further clarification of the preceding provisions of this section and may, based on such determination and to the extent necessary and appropriate, issue—

"(1) guidelines describing specific types of conduct, associated with common types of export sales arrangements and business contracts, which for purposes of the Department of Justice's present enforcement policy, the Attorney General determines would be in conformance with the preceding provisions of this section; and

"(2) general precautionary procedures which issuers may use on a voluntary basis to conform their conduct to the Department of Justice's present enforcement policy regarding the preceding provisions of this section.

The Attorney General shall issue the guidelines and procedures referred to in the preceding sentence in accordance with the provisions of subchapter II of chapter 5 of title 5, United States Code, and those guidelines and procedures shall be subject to the provisions of chapter 7 of that title.

"(e) OPINIONS OF THE ATTORNEY GENERAL.—(1) The Attorney General, after consultation with appropriate departments and agencies of the United States and after obtaining the views of all interested persons through public notice and comment procedures, shall establish a procedure to provide responses to specific inquiries by issuers concerning conformance of their conduct with the Department of Justice's present enforcement policy regarding the preceding provisions of this section. The Attorney General shall, within 30 days after receiving such a request, issue an opinion in response to that request. The opinion shall state whether or not certain specified prospective conduct would, for purposes of the Department of Justice's present enforcement policy, violate the preceding provisions of this section. Additional requests for opinions may be filed with the Attorney General regarding other specified prospective conduct that is beyond the scope of conduct specified in previous requests. In any action brought under the applicable provisions of this section, there shall be a rebuttable presumption that conduct, which is specified in a request by an issuer and for which the Attorney General has issued an opinion that such conduct is in conformity with the Department of Justice's present enforcement policy, is in compliance with the preceding provisions of this section. Such a presumption may be rebutted by a preponderance of the evidence. In considering the presumption for purposes of this paragraph, a court shall weigh all relevant factors, including but not limited to whether the information submitted to the Attorney General was accurate and complete and whether it was within the scope of the conduct specified in any request received by the Attorney General. The Attorney General shall establish the procedure required by this paragraph in accordance with the provisions of subchapter II of chapter 5 of title 5, United States Code, and that procedure shall be subject to the provisions of chapter 7 of that title.

"(2) Any document or other material which is provided to, received by, or prepared in the Department of Justice or any other department or agency of the United States in connection with a request by an issuer under the procedure established under paragraph (1), shall be exempt from disclosure under section 552 of title 5, United States Code, and shall not, except with the consent of the issuer, be made publicly available, regardless of whether the Attorney General responds to such a request or the issuer withdraws such request before receiving a response.

"(3) Any issuer who has made a request to the Attorney General under paragraph (1) may withdraw such request prior to the time the Attorney General issues an opinion in response to such request. Any request so withdrawn shall have no force or effect.

"(4) The Attorney General shall, to the maximum extent practicable, provide timely guidance concerning the Department of Justice's present enforcement policy with respect to the preceding provisions of this section to potential exporters and small businesses that are unable to obtain specialized counsel on issues pertaining to such provisions. Such guidance shall be limited to responses to requests under paragraph (1) concerning conformity of specified prospective conduct with the Department of Justice's present enforcement policy regarding the preceding provisions of this section and general explanations of compliance responsibilities and of potential liabilities under the preceding provisions of this section.

"(f) Definitions.—For purposes of this section:

"(1) The term 'foreign official' means any officer or employee of a foreign government or any department, agency, or instrumentality thereof, or any person acting in an official capacity for or on behalf of any such government or department, agency, or instrumentality.

"(2)(A) A person's state of mind is 'knowing' with respect to conduct, a circumstance, or a result if—

"(i) such person is aware that such person is engaging in

such conduct, that such circumstance exists, or that such result is substantially certain to occur; or

"(ii) such person has a firm belief that such circumstance exists or that such result is substantially certain to occur.

"(B) When knowledge of the existence of a particular circumstance is required for an offense, such knowledge is established if a person is aware of a high probability of the existence of such circumstance, unless the person actually believes that such circumstance does not exist.

"(3)(A) The term 'routine governmental action' means only an action which is ordinarily and commonly performed by a foreign official in—

"(i) obtaining permits, licenses, or other official documents to qualify a person to do business in a foreign country;

"(ii) processing governmental papers, such as visas and work orders;

"(iii) providing police protection, mail pick-up and delivery, or scheduling inspections associated with contract performance or inspections related to transit of goods across country;

"(iv) providing phone service, power and water supply, loading and unloading cargo, or protecting perishable products or commodities from deterioration; or

"(v) actions of a similar nature.

"(B) The term 'routine governmental action' does not include any decision by a foreign official whether, or on what terms, to award new business to or to continue business with a particular party, or any action taken by a foreign official involved in the decisionmaking process to encourage a decision to award new business to or continue business with a particular party.".

(b) Violations.—Section 32(c) of the Securities Exchange Act of 1934 (15 U.S.C. 78ff) is amended to read as follows:

"(c)(1)(A) Any issuer that violates section 30A(a) shall be fined not more than $2,000,000.

"(B) Any issuer that violates section 30A(a) shall be subject to a civil penalty of not more than $10,000 imposed in an action brought by the Commission.

"(2)(A) Any officer or director of an issuer, or stockholder acting on behalf of such issuer, who willfully violates section 30A(a) shall be fined not more than $100,000, or imprisoned not more than 5 years, or both.

"(B) Any employee or agent of an issuer who is a United States citizen, national, or resident or is otherwise subject to the jurisdiction of the United States (other than an officer, director, or stockholder acting on behalf of such issuer), and who willfully violates section 30A(a), shall be fined not more than $100,000, or imprisoned not more than 5 years, or both.

"(C) Any officer, director, employee, or agent of an issuer, or stockholder acting on behalf of such issuer, who violates section 30A(a) shall be subject to a civil penalty of not more than $10,000 imposed in an action brought by the Commission.

"(3) Whenever a fine is imposed under paragraph (2) upon any officer, director, employee, agent, or stockholder of an issuer, such fine may not be paid, directly or indirectly, by such issuer.".

(c) Prohibited Trade Practices by Domestic Concerns.—Section 104 of the Foreign Corrupt Practices Act of 1977 (15 U.S.C. 78dd-2) is amended to read as follows:

"PROHIBITED FOREIGN TRADE PRACTICES BY DOMESTIC CONCERNS

"SEC. 104. (a) PROHIBITION.—It shall be unlawful for any domestic concern, other than an issuer which is subject to section 30A of the Securities Exchange Act of 1934, or for any officer, director, employee, or agent of such domestic concern or any stockholder thereof acting on behalf of such domestic concern, to make use of the mails or any means or instrumentality of interstate commerce curruptly in furtherance of an offer, payment, promise to pay, or authorization of the payment of any money, or offer, gift, promise to give, or authorization of the giving of anything of value to—

"(1) any foreign official for purposes of—

"(A)(i) influencing any act or decision of such foreign official in his official capacity, or (ii) inducing such foreign official to do or omit to do any act in violation of the lawful duty of such official, or

"(B) inducing such foreign official to use his influence with a foreign government or instrumentality thereof to affect or influence any act or decision of such government or instrumentality,

in order to assist such domestic concern in obtaining or retaining business for or with, or directing business to, any person;

"(2) any foreign political party or official thereof or any candidate for foreign political office for purposes of—

"(A)(i) influencing any act or decision of such party, official, or candidate in its or his official capacity, or (ii) inducing such party, official, or candidate to do or omit to do an act in violation of the lawful duty of such party, official, or candidate,

"(B) inducing such party, official, or candidate to use its or his influence with a foreign government or instrumentality thereof to affect or influence any act or decision of such government or instrumentality,

in order to assist such domestic concern in obtaining or retaining business for or with, or directing business to, any person; or

"(3) any person, while knowing that all or a portion of such money or thing of value will be offered, given, or promised, directly or indirectly, to any foreign official, to any foreign political party or official thereof, or to any candidate for foreign political office, for purposes of—

"(A)(i) influencing any act or decision of such foreign official, political party, party official, or candidate in his or its official capacity, or (ii) inducing such foreign official, political party, party official, or candidate to do or omit to do any act in violation of the lawful duty of such foreign official, political party, party official, or candidate, or

"(B) inducing such foreign official, political party, party official, or candidate to use his or its influence with a foreign government or instrumentality thereof to affect or influence any act or decision of such government or instrumentality,

in order to assist such issuer in obtaining or retaining business for or with, or directing business to, any person.

"(b) EXCEPTION FOR ROUTINE GOVERNMENTAL ACTION.—Subsection (a) shall not apply to any facilitating or expediting payment to a foreign official, political party, or party official the purpose of which is to expedite or to secure the performance of a routine governmental action by a foreign official, political party, or party official.

"(c) AFFIRMATIVE DEFENSES.—It shall be an affirmative defense to actions under subsection (a) that—

"(1) the payment, gift, offer, or promise of anything of value

that was made, was lawful under the written laws and regulations of the foreign official's, political party's, party official's, or candidate's country; or

"(2) the payment, gift, offer, or promise of anything of value that was made, was a reasonable and bona fide expenditure, such as travel and lodging expenses, incurred by or on behalf of a foreign official, party, party official, or candidate and was directly related to—

"(A) the promotion, demonstration, or explanation of products or services; or

"(B) the execution or performance of a contract with a foreign government or agency thereof.

"(d) INJUNCTIVE RELIEF.—(1) When it appears to the Attorney General that any domestic concern to which this section applies, or officer, director, employee, agent, or stockholder thereof, is engaged, or about to engage, in any act or practice constituting a violation of subsection (a) of this section, the Attorney General may, in his discretion, bring a civil action in an appropriate district court of the United States to enjoin such act or practice, and upon a proper showing, a permanent injunction or a temporary restraining order shall be granted without bond.

"(2) For the purpose of any civil investigation which, in the opinion of the Attorney General, is necessary and proper to enforce this section, the Attorney General or his designee are empowered to administer oaths and affirmations, subpoena witnesses, take evidence, and require the production of any books, papers, or other documents which the Attorney General deems relevant or material to such investigation. The attendance of witnesses and the production of documentary evidence may be required from any place in the United States, or any territory, possession, or commonwealth of the United States, at any designated place of hearing.

"(3) In case of contumacy by, or refusal to obey a subpoena issued to, any person, the Attorney General may invoke the aid of any court of the United States within the jurisdiction of which such investigation or proceeding is carried on, or where such person resides or carries on business, in requiring the attendance and testimony of witnesses and the production of books, papers, or other documents. Any such court may issue an order requiring such person to appear before the Attorney General or his designee, there to produce records, if so ordered, or to give testimony touching the matter under investigation. Any failure to obey such order of the court may be punished by such court as a contempt thereof. All process in any such case may be served in the judicial district in which such person resides or may be found. The Attorney General may make such rules relating to civil investigations as may be necessary or appropriate to implement the provisions of this subsection.

"(e) GUIDELINES BY THE ATTORNEY GENERAL.—Not later than 6 months after the date of the enactment of the Foreign Corrupt Practices Act Amendments of 1988, the Attorney General, after consultation with the Securities and Exchange Commission, the Secretary of Commerce, the United States Trade Representative, the Secretary of State, and the Secretary of the Treasury, and after obtaining the views of all interested persons through public notice and comment procedures, shall determine to what extent compliance with this section would be enhanced and the business community would be assisted by further clarification of the preceding provisions of this section and may, based on such determination and to the extent necessary and appropriate, issue—

"(1) guidelines describing specific types of conduct, associated with common types of export sales arrangements and business contracts, which for purposes of the Department of Justice's present enforcement policy, the Attorney General determines would be in conformance with the preceding provisions of this section; and

"(2) general precautionary procedures which domestic concerns may use on a voluntary basis to conform their conduct to the Department of Justice's present enforcement policy regarding the preceding provisions of this section.

The Attorney General shall issue the guidelines and procedures referred to in the preceding sentence in accordance with the provisions of subchapter II of chapter 5 of title 5, United States Code, and those guidelines and procedures shall be subject to the provisions of chapter 7 of that title.

"(f) OPINIONS OF THE ATTORNEY GENERAL.—(1) The Attorney General, after consultation with appropriate departments and agencies of the United States and after obtaining the views of all interested persons through public notice and comment procedures, shall establish a procedure to provide responses to specific inquiries by domestic concerns concerning conformance of their conduct with the Department of Justice's present enforcement policy regarding the preceding provisions of this section. The Attorney General shall, within 30 days after receiving such a request, issue an opinion in response to that request. The opinion shall state whether or not certain specified prospective conduct would, for purposes of the Department of Justice's present enforcement policy, violate the preceding provisions of this section. Additional requests for opinions may be filed with the Attorney General regarding other specified prospective conduct that is beyond the scope of conduct specified in previous requests. In any action brought under the applicable provisions of this section, there shall be a rebuttable presumption that conduct, which is specified in a request by a domestic concern and for which the Attorney General has issued an opinion that such conduct is in conformity with the Department of Justice's present enforcement policy, is in compliance with the preceding provisions of this section. Such a presumption may be rebutted by a preponderance of the evidence. In considering the presumption for purposes of this paragraph, a court shall weigh all relevant factors, including but not limited to whether the information submitted to the Attorney General was accurate and complete and whether it was within the scope of the conduct specified in any request received by the Attorney General. The Attorney General shall establish the procedure required by this paragraph in accordance with the provisions of subchapter II of chapter 5 of title 5, United States Code, and that procedure shall be subject to the provisions of chapter 7 of that title.

"(2) Any document or other material which is provided to, received by, or prepared in the Department of Justice or any other department or agency of the United States in connection with a request by a domestic concern under the procedure established under paragraph (1), shall be exempt from disclosure under section 552 of title 5, United States Code, and shall not, except with the consent of the domestic concern, be made publicly available, regardless of whether the Attorney General responds to such a request or the domestic concern withdraws such request before receiving a response.

"(3) Any domestic concern who has made a request to the Attorney General under paragraph (1) may withdraw such request prior to the time the Attorney General issues an opinion in response to such request. Any request so withdrawn shall have no force or effect.

"(4) The Attorney General shall, to the maximum extent practicable, provide timely guidance concerning the Department of Justice's present enforcement policy with respect to the preceding provisions of this section to potential exporters and small businesses that are unable to obtain specialized counsel on issues pertaining to such provisions. Such guidance shall be limited to responses to requests under paragraph (1) concerning conformity of specified prospective conduct with the Department of Justice's present enforcement policy regarding the preceding provisions of this section and general explanations of compliance responsibilities and of potential liabilities under the preceding provisions of this section.

"(g) PENALTIES.—(1)(A) Any domestic concern that violates subsection (a) shall be fined not more than $2,000,000.

"(B) Any domestic concern that violates subsection (a) shall be subject to a civil penalty of not more than $10,000 imposed in an action brought by the Attorney General.

"(2)(A) Any officer or director of a domestic concern, or stockholder acting on behalf of such domestic concern, who willfully violates subsection (a) shall be fined not more than $100,000, or imprisoned not more than 5 years, or both.

"(B) Any employee or agent of a domestic concern who is a United States citizen, national, or resident or is otherwise subject to the jurisdiction of the United States (other than an officer, director, or stockholder acting on behalf of such domestic concern), and who willfully violates subsection (a), shall be fined not more than $100,000, or imprisoned not more than 5 years, or both.

"(C) Any officer, director, employee, or agent of a domestic concern, or stockholder acting on behalf of such domestic concern, who violates subsection (a) shall be subject to a civil penalty of not more than $10,000 imposed in an action brought by the Attorney General.

"(3) Whenever a fine is imposed under paragraph (2) upon any officer, director, employee, agent, or stockholder of a domestic concern, such fine may not be paid, directly or indirectly, by such domestic concern.

"(h) DEFINITIONS.—For purposes of this section:

"(1) The term 'domestic concern' means—

"(A) any individual who is a citizen, national, or resident of the United States; and

"(B) any corporation, partnership, association, joint-stock company, business trust, unincorporated organization, or sole proprietorship which has its principal place of business in the United States, or which is organized under the laws of a State of the United States or a territory, possession, or commonwealth of the United States.

"(2) The term 'foreign official' means any officer or employee of a foreign government or any department, agency, or instrumentality thereof, or any person acting in an official capacity for or on behalf of any such government or department, agency, or instrumentality.

"(3)(A) A person's state of mind is 'knowing' with respect to conduct, a circumstance, or a result if—

"(i) such person is aware that such person is engaging in such conduct, that such circumstance exists, or that such result is substantially certain to occur; or

"(ii) such person has a firm belief that such circumstance exists or that such result is substantially certain to occur.

"(B) When knowledge of the existence of a particular circumstance is required for an offense, such knowledge is established if a person is aware of a high probability of the existence of such circumstance, unless the person actually believes that such circumstance does not exist.

"(4)(A) For purposes of paragraph (1), the term 'routine governmental action' means only an action which is ordinarily and commonly performed by a foreign official in—

"(i) obtaining permits, licenses, or other official documents to qualify a person to do business in a foreign country;

"(ii) processing governmental papers, such as visas and work orders;

"(iii) providing police protection, mail pick-up and delivery, or scheduling inspections associated with contract performance or inspections related to transit of goods across country;

"(iv) providing phone service, power and water supply, loading and unloading cargo, or protecting perishable products or commodities from deterioration; or

"(v) actions of a similar nature.

"(B) The term 'routine governmental action' does not include any decision by a foreign official whether, or on what terms, to award new business to or to continue business with a particular party, or any action taken by a foreign official involved in the decision-making process to encourage a decision to award new business to or continue business with a particular party.

"(5) The term 'interstate commerce' means trade, commerce, transportation, or communication among the several States, or between any foreign country and any State or between any State and any place or ship outside thereof, and such term includes the intrastate use of—

"(A) a telephone or other interstate means of communication, or

"(B) any other interstate instrumentality.".

(d) INTERNATIONAL AGREEMENT.—

(1) NEGOTIATIONS.—It is the sense of the Congress that the President should pursue the negotiation of an international agreement, among the members of the Organization of Economic Cooperation and Development, to govern persons from those countries concerning acts prohibited with respect to issuers and domestic concerns by the amendments made by this section. Such international agreement should include a process by which problems and conflicts associated with such acts could be resolved.

(2) REPORT TO CONGRESS.—(A) Within 1 year after the date of the enactment of this Act, the President shall submit to the Congress a report on—

(i) the progress of the negotiations referred to in paragraph (1),

(ii) those steps which the executive branch and the Congress should consider taking in the event that these negotiations do not successfully eliminate any competitive disadvantage of United States businesses that results when persons from other countries commit the acts described in paragraph (1); and

(iii) possible actions that could be taken to promote cooperation by other countries in international efforts to prevent bribery of foreign officials, candidates, or parties in third countries.

(B) The President shall include in the report submitted under subparagraph (A)—

(i) any legislative recommendations necessary to give the President the authority to take appropriate action to carry out clauses (ii) and (iii) of subparagraph (A);

(ii) an analysis of the potential effect on the interests of the United States, including United States national security, when persons from other countries commit the acts described in paragraph (1); and

(iii) an assessment of the current and future role of private initiatives in curtailing such acts.

PART II—REVIEW OF CERTAIN MERGERS, ACQUISITIONS, AND TAKEOVERS

SEC. 5021. AUTHORITY TO REVIEW CERTAIN MERGERS, ACQUISITIONS, AND TAKEOVERS.

Title VII of the Defense Production Act of 1950 (50 U.S.C. App. 2158 et seq.) is amended by adding at the end thereof the following:

"AUTHORITY TO REVIEW CERTAIN MERGERS, ACQUISITIONS, AND TAKEOVERS

"SEC. 721. (a) INVESTIGATIONS.—The President or the President's designee may make an investigation to determine the effects on national security of mergers, acquisitions, and takeovers proposed or pending on or after the date of enactment of this section by or with foreign persons which could result in foreign control of persons engaged in interstate commerce in the United States. If it is determined that an investigation should be undertaken, it shall commence no later than 30 days after receipt by the President or the President's designee of written notification of the proposed or pending merger, acquisition, or takeover as prescribed by regulations promulgated pursuant to this section. Such investigation shall be completed no later than 45 days after such determination.

"(b) CONFIDENTIALITY OF INFORMATION.—Any information or documentary material filed with the President or the President's designee pursuant to this section shall be exempt from disclosure under section 552 of title 5, United States Code, and no such information or documentary material may be made public, except as may be relevant to any administrative or judicial action or proceeding. Nothing in this subsection shall be construed to prevent disclosure to either House of Congress or to any duly authorized committee or subcommittee of the Congress.

"(c) ACTION BY THE PRESIDENT.—Subject to subsection (d), the President may take such action for such time as the President considers appropriate to suspend or prohibit any acquisition, merger, or takeover, of a person engaged in interstate commerce in the United States proposed or pending on or after the date of enactment of this section by or with foreign persons so that such control will not threaten to impair the national security. The President shall announce the decision to take action pursuant to this subsection not later than 15 days after the investigation described in subsection (a) is completed. The President may direct the Attorney General to seek appropriate relief, including divestment relief, in the district courts of the United States in order to implement and enforce this section.

"(d) FINDINGS OF THE PRESIDENT.—The President may exercise the authority conferred by subsection (c) only if the President finds that—

"(1) there is credible evidence that leads the President to believe that the foreign interest exercising control might take action that threatens to impair the national security, and

"(2) provisions of law, other than this section and the International Emergency Economic Powers Act (50 U.S.C. 1701-1706), do not in the President's judgment provide adequate and appropriate authority for the President to protect the national security in the matter before the President.

The provisions of subsection (d) of this section shall not be subject to judicial review.

"(e) FACTORS TO BE CONSIDERED.—For purposes of this section, the President or the President's designee may, taking into account the requirements of national security, consider among other factors—

"(1) domestic production needed for projected national defense requirements,

"(2) the capability and capacity of domestic industries to meet national defense requirements, including the availability of human resources, products, technology, materials, and other supplies and services, and

"(3) the control of domestic industries and commercial activity by foreign citizens as it affects the capability and capacity of the United States to meet the requirements of national security.

"(f) REPORT TO THE CONGRESS.—If the President determines to take action under subsection (c), the President shall immediately transmit to the Secretary of the Senate and the Clerk of the House of Representatives a written report of the action which the President intends to take, including a detailed explanation of the findings made under subsection (d).

"(g) REGULATIONS.—The President shall direct the issuance of regulations to carry out this section. Such regulations shall, to the extent possible, minimize paperwork burdens and shall to the extent possible coordinate reporting requirements under this section with reporting requirements under any other provision of Federal law.

"(h) EFFECT ON OTHER LAW.—Nothing in this section shall be construed to alter or affect any existing power, process, regulation, investigation, enforcement measure, or review provided by any other provision of law.".

TITLE VIII—SMALL BUSINESS

SEC. 8001. SHORT TITLE.

This title may be cited as the "Small Business International Trade and Competitiveness Act".

SEC. 8002. DECLARATION OF POLICY.

Section 2 of the Small Business Act (15 U.S.C. 631) is amended by redesignating subsections (b) through (e) as subsections (c) through (f), respectively, and by inserting after subsection (a) the following:

"(b)(1) It is the declared policy of the Congress that the Federal Government, through the Small Business Administration, acting in cooperation with the Department of Commerce and other relevant State and Federal agencies, should aid and assist small businesses, as defined under this Act, to increase their ability to compete in international markets by—

"(A) enhancing their ability to export;

"(B) facilitating technology transfers;

"(C) enhancing their ability to compete effectively and efficiently against imports;

"(D) increasing the access of small businesses to long-term capital for the purchase of new plant and equipment used in the production of goods and services involved in international trade;

"(E) disseminating information concerning State, Federal, and private programs and initiatives to enhance the ability of small businesses to compete in international markets; and

"(F) ensuring that the interests of small businesses are adequately represented in bilateral and multilateral trade negotiations.

"(2) The Congress recognizes that the Department of Commerce is the principal Federal agency for trade development and export promotion and that the Department of Commerce and the Small Business Administration work together to advance joint interests. It is the purpose of this Act to enhance, not alter, their respective roles.".

SEC. 8003. CHANGES IN EXISTING SMALL BUSINESS ADMINISTRATION INTERNATIONAL TRADE OFFICE.

Section 22 of the Small Business Act (15 U.S.C. 649) is amended—

(1) by redesignating subsection (b) as subsection (c) and by inserting after subsection (a) the following:

"(b) The Office, working in close cooperation with the Department of Commerce and other relevant Federal agencies, Small Business Development Centers engaged in export promotion efforts, regional and local Administration offices, the small business community, and relevant State and local export promotion programs, shall—

"(1) assist in developing a distribution network for existing trade promotion, trade finance, trade adjustment, trade remedy assistance and trade data collection programs through use of the Administration's regional and local offices and the Small Business Development Center network;

"(2) assist in the aggressive marketing of these programs and the dissemination of marketing information, including computerized marketing data, to the small business community; and

"(3) give preference in hiring or approving the transfer of any employee into the Office or to a position described in paragraph (8) below to otherwise qualified applicants who are fluent in a language in addition to English. Such employees shall accompany foreign trade missions if designated by the director of the Office and shall be available as needed to translate documents, interpret conversations and facilitate multilingual transactions including providing referral lists for translation services if required.";

(2) in subsection (c), as redesignated, by redesignating paragraphs (1) through (3) as (6) through (8), respectively, and by inserting the following before paragraph (6), as redesignated:

"(1) in cooperation with the Department of Commerce, other relevant agencies, regional and local Administration offices, the Small Business Development Center network, and State programs, develop a mechanism for (A) identifying sub-sectors of the small business community with strong export potential; (B) identifying areas of demand in foreign markets; (C) prescreening foreign buyers for commercial and credit purposes; and (D) assisting in increasing international marketing by disseminating relevant information regarding market leads, linking potential sellers and buyers, and catalyzing the formation of joint ventures, where appropriate;

"(2) in cooperation with the Department of Commerce, actively assist small businesses in the formation and utilization of export trading companies, export management companies and research and development pools authorized under section 9 of this Act;

"(3) work in conjunction with other Federal agencies, regional and local offices of the Administration, the Small Business Development Center network, and the private sector to identify and publicize existing translation services, including those available through colleges and universities participating in the Small Business Development Center Program;

"(4) work closely with the Department of Commerce and other relevant Federal agencies to—

"(A) collect, analyze and periodically update relevant data regarding the small business share of United States exports and the nature of State exports (including the production of Gross State Produce figures) and disseminate that data to the public and to Congress;

"(B) make recommendations to the Secretary of Commerce and to Congress regarding revision of the SIC codes to encompass industries currently overlooked and to create SIC codes for export trading companies and export management companies;

"(C) improve the utility and accessibility of existing export promotion programs for small businesses; and

"(D) increase the accessibility of the Export Trading Company contact facilitation service;

"(5) make available to the small business community information regarding conferences on exporting and international trade sponsored by the public and private sector."; and

(3) by adding after subsection (c), as redesignated, the following new subsections:

"(d) The Office shall work in cooperation with the Export-Import Bank of the United States, the Department of Commerce, other relevant Federal agencies, and the States to develop a program through which export specialists in the regional offices of the Administration, regional and local loan officers, and Small Business Development Center personnel can facilitate the access of small businesses to relevant export financing programs of the Export-Import Bank of the United States and to export and pre-export financing programs available from the Administration and the private sector. To accomplish this goal, the Office shall work in cooperation with the Export-Import Bank and the small business community, including small business trade associations, to—

"(1) aggressively market existing Administration export financing and pre-export financing programs;

"(2) identify financing available under various Export-Import Bank programs, and aggressively market those programs to small businesses;

"(3) assist in the development of financial intermediaries and facilitate the access of those intermediaries to existing financing programs;

"(4) promote greater participation by private financial institutions, particularly those institutions already participating in loan programs under this Act, in export finance; and

"(5) provide for the participation of appropriate Administration personnel in training programs conducted by the Export-Import Bank.

"(e) The Office shall—

"(1) work in cooperation with other Federal agencies and the private sector to counsel small businesses with respect to initiating and participating in any proceedings relating to the administration of the United States trade laws; and

"(2) work with the Department of Commerce, the Office of the United States Trade Representative, and the International Trade Commission to increase access to trade remedy proceedings for small businesses.

"(f) The Office shall report to the Committees on Small Business of the House of Representatives and the Senate on an annual basis as to its progress in implementing the requirements under this section.

"(g) The Office, in cooperation, where appropriate, with the Division of Economic Research of the Office of Advocacy, and with other Federal agencies, shall undertake studies regarding the following issues and shall report to the Committees on Small Business of the House of Representatives and the Senate, and to other relevant Committees of the House and Senate within 6 months after the date of enactment of the Small Business International Trade and Competitiveness Act with specific recommendations on—

"(1) the viability and cost of establishing an annual, competitive small business export incentive program similar to the Small Business Innovation Research program and alternative methods of structuring such a program;

"(2) methods of streamlining trade remedy proceedings to increase access for, and reduce expenses incurred by, smaller firms;

"(3) methods of improving the current small business foreign sales corporation tax incentives and providing small businesses with greater benefits from this initiative;

"(4) methods of identifying potential export markets for United States small businesses; maintaining and disseminating current foreign market data; and devising a comprehensive export marketing strategy for United States small business goods and services, and shall include data on the volume and dollar amount of goods and services, identified by type, imported by United States trading partners over the past 10 years; and

"(5) the results of a survey of major United States trading partners to identify the domestic policies, programs and incentives, and the private sector initiatives, which exist to encourage the formation and growth of small business.".

SEC. 8004. AUTHORIZATION OF APPROPRIATIONS.

Section 20 of the Small Business Act (15 U.S.C. 631) is amended by adding the following at the end of subsection (z): "There are hereby authorized to be appropriated to the Administration for each of fiscal years 1988 and 1989, $3,500,000 to carry out the provisions of section 22 of this Act and section 8011 of the Small Business International Trade and Competitiveness Act, of which $350,000 is authorized to reimburse volunteers in the Service Corps of Retired

Executives for their expenses in performing on-site counseling to actual or potential small business exporters, in participating in training sessions for such small businesses, and in preparing materials for use at such training sessions or during counseling.".

SEC. 8005. EXPORT FINANCING PROVIDED BY THE ADMINISTRATION.

Section 7(a)(14) of the Small Business Act (15 U.S.C. 636(a)(14)) is amended to read as follows:

"(14)(A) The Administration under this subsection may provide extensions and revolving lines of credit for export purposes and for pre-export financing to enable small business concerns, including small business export trading companies and small business export management companies, to develop foreign markets. No such extension or revolving line of credit may be made for a period or periods exceeding 18 months. A bank or participating lending institution may establish the rate of interest on extensions and revolving lines of credit as may be legal and reasonable.

"(B) When considering loan or guarantee applications, the Administration shall give weight to export-related benefits, including opening new markets for United States goods and services abroad and encouraging the involvement of small businesses, including agricultural concerns, in the export market.

"(C) The Administration shall aggressively market its export financing program to small businesses.".

SEC. 8006. SMALL BUSINESS DEVELOPMENT CENTERS.

(a) AUTHORIZATION OF APPROPRIATION.—Section 20 of the Small Business Act (15 U.S.C. 631 note) is amended by adding the following at the end of subsection (z): "There are hereby authorized to be appropriated to the Administration for each of the fiscal years 1988 and 1989, $5,000,000 to carry out the provisions of section 21(a)(6).".

(b) SBDC INFORMATION DISSEMINATION AND SERVICE DELIVERY.—Section 21 of the Small Business Act (15 U.S.C. 648) is amended—

(1) in subsection (a)(1), by inserting after "enterprises;" the following: "management and technical assistance regarding small business participation in international markets, export promotion and technology transfer;";

(2) in subsection (a), by redesignating paragraphs (2) through (4) as paragraphs (3) through (5), respectively, and by inserting the following after paragraph (1):

"(2) The Small Business Development Centers shall work in close cooperation with the Administration's regional and local offices, the Department of Commerce, appropriate Federal, State and local agencies and the small business community to serve as an active information dissemination and service delivery mechanism for existing trade promotion, trade finance, trade adjustment, trade remedy and trade data collection programs of particular utility for small businesses.";

(3) by adding at the end of subsection (a) the following new paragraph:

"(6) Any applicant which is funded by the Administration as a Small Business Development Center may apply for an additional grant to be used solely to assist—

"(A) with the development and enhancement of exports by small business concerns; and

"(B) in technology transfer,

as provided under subparagraphs (B) through (G) of subsection (c)(3). Applicants for such additional grants shall comply with all of the provisions of this section, including providing matching funds, except that funding under this paragraph shall be effective for any fiscal year to the extent provided in advance in appropriations Acts and shall be in addition to the dollar program limitations specified in paragraphs (4) and (5). No recipient of funds under this paragraph shall receive a grant which would exceed its pro rata share of a $15,000,000 program based upon the populations to be served by the Small Business Development Center as compared to the total population of the United States. The minimum amount of eligibility for any State shall be $100,000.";

(4) in subsection (c)(3), by striking subparagraph (B) and by inserting the following new subparagraph (B):

"(B) assisting in technology transfer, research and development, including applied research, and coupling from existing sources to small businesses, including—

"(i) working to increase the access of small businesses to the capabilities of automated flexible manufacturing systems;

"(ii) working through existing networks and developing new networks for technology transfer that encourage partnership between the small business and academic communities to help commercialize university-based research and development and introduce university-based engineers and scientists to their counterparts in small technology-based firms; and

"(iii) exploring the viability of developing shared production facilities, under appropriate circumstances;";

(5) in subsection (c)(3), by redesignating subparagraphs (C) through (H) as subparagraphs (H) through (M), respectively, and by inserting the following new subparagraphs after subparagraph (B):

"(C) in cooperation with the Department of Commerce and other relevant Federal agencies, actively assisting small businesses in exporting by identifying and developing potential export markets, facilitating export transactions, developing linkages between United States small business firms and prescreened foreign buyers, assisting small businesses to participate in international trade shows, assisting small businesses in obtaining export financing, and facilitating the development or reorientation of marketing and production strategies; where appropriate, the Small Business Development Center may work in cooperation with the State to establish a State international trade center for these purposes;

"(D) assisting small businesses in developing and implementing marketing and production strategies that will enable them to better compete within the domestic market;

"(E) developing a program in conjunction with the Export-Import Bank and local and regional Administration offices that will enable Small Business Development Centers to serve as an information network and to assist small business applicants for Export-Import Bank financing programs, and otherwise identify and help to make available export financing programs to small businesses;

"(F) working closely with the small business community, small business consultants, State agencies, universities and other appropriate groups to make translation services more readily available to small business firms doing business, or attempting to develop business, in foreign markets;

"(G) in providing assistance under this subsection, applicants shall cooperate with the Department of Commerce and other relevant Federal agencies to increase access to available export market information systems, including the CIMS system;";

(6) in subsection (c), by adding the following new paragraphs:

"(5) In any State (A) in which the Administration has not made a grant pursuant to paragraph (1) of subsection (a), or (B) in which no application for a grant has been made by a Small Business Development Center pursuant to paragraph (6) of such subsection within 60 days after the effective date of any grant under paragraph (a)(1) to such center, the Administration may make grants to a non-profit entity in that State to carry out the activities specified in paragraph (6) of subsection (a). Any such applicants shall comply with the matching funds requirement of paragraph (4) of subsection (a). Such grants shall be effective for any fiscal year only to the extent provided in advance in appropriations Acts, and each State shall be limited to the pro rata share provisions of paragraph (6) of subsection (a).

"(6) In performing the services identified in paragraph (3), the Small Business Development Centers shall work in close cooperation with the Administration's regional and local offices, the local small business community, and appropriate State and local agencies.

"(7) The Deputy Associate Administrator of the Small Business Development Center program, in consultation with the Small Business Development Centers, shall develop and implement an information sharing system which will—

"(A) allow Small Business Development Centers participating in the program to exchange information about their programs; and

"(B) provide information central to technology transfer."; and

(7) by redesignating subsections (d) through (k) as subsections (e) through (l), respectively, and inserting the following new subsection after subsection (c):

"(d) Where appropriate, the Small Business Development Centers shall work in conjunction with the relevant State agency and the Department of Commerce to develop a comprehensive plan for enhancing the export potential of small businesses located within the State. This plan may involve the cofunding and staffing of a State Office of International Trade within the State Small Business Development Center, using joint State and Federal funding, and any other appropriate measures directed at improving the export performance of small businesses within the State.".

SEC. 8007. CAPITAL FORMATION.

(a) LOAN LIMITATIONS.—Section 7(a) of the Small Business Act (15 U.S.C. 636(a)) is amended—

(1) by striking "and" at the end of clause (i) of paragraph (2)(B) and by adding after clause (ii) the following new clauses:

"(iii) not less than 85 per centum of the financing outstanding at the time of disbursement if such financing is a loan under paragraph (16) and is less than $1,176,470; and "(iv) less than 85 per centum of the financing outstanding at the time of disbursement if such financing is a loan under paragraph (16) and exceeds $1,176,470;";

(2) by amending paragraph (3) to read as follows:

"(3) No loan shall be made under this subsection—

"(A) if the total amount outstanding and committed (by participation or otherwise) to the borrower from the business loan and investment fund established by this Act would exceed $750,000, except as provided in subparagraph (B);

"(B) if the total amount outstanding and committed (on a deferred basis) solely for the purposes provided in paragraph (16) to the borrower from the business loan and investment fund established by this Act would exceed $1,000,000, such amount to be in addition to any financing solely for working capital, supplies, or revolving lines of credit for export purposes up to a maximum of $250,000; and

"(C) if effected either directly or in cooperation with banks or other lending institutions through agreements to participate on an immediate basis if the amount would exceed $350,000.";

(3) by adding the following new paragraphs after paragraph (15):

"(16)(A) The Administration may guarantee loans under this paragraph to assist any eligible small business concern in an industry engaged in or adversely affected by international trade in the financing of the acquisition, construction, renovation, modernization, improvement or expansion of productive facilities or equipment to be used in the United States in the production of goods and services involved in international trade, if the Administration determines that the appropriate upgrading of plant and equipment will allow the concern to improve its competitive position. Each such loan shall be secured by a first lien position or first mortgage on the property or equipment financed by the loan. The lender shall agree to sell the loan in the secondary market as authorized in sections 5(f) and 5(g) of this Act within 180 days of the date of disbursement.

"(B) A small business concern shall be considered to be engaged in or adversely affected by international trade for purposes of this provision if such concern is, as determined by the Administration in accordance with regulations that it shall develop—

"(i) in a position to significantly expand existing export markets or develop new export markets; or

"(ii) adversely affected by import competition in that it is—

"(I) confronting increased direct competition with foreign firms in the relevant market; and

"(II) can demonstrate injury attributable to such competition.

"(17) The Administration shall authorize lending institutions and other entities in addition to banks to make loans authorized under this subsection."; and

(4) by redesignating the existing paragraph (16) as paragraph (18).

(b) DEVELOPMENT COMPANY LIMITS.—Section 502(2) of the Small Business Investment Act of 1985 (15 U.S.C. 636(a)(3)) is amended by striking "$500,000" and by inserting in lieu thereof "$750,000"

(c) REPORT.—The Administrator of the Small Business Administration shall report to the Committees on Small Business of the House of Representatives and the Senate within 6 months after the date of enactment of this title as to the viability of creating cooperative Federal-State guarantee programs, particularly for purposes of export financing, to encourage States to coinsure Federal loans, thus permitting the Federal Government to reduce its exposure.

SEC. 8008. SMALL BUSINESS INNOVATION RESEARCH.

Section 6 of Public Law 97-219, as amended by Public Law 99-443, is further amended by adding the following at the end of subsection (a): "The report also shall include the Comptroller General's recommendations as to the advisability of amending the Small Business Innovation Research program to—

"(1) increase each agency's share of research and development expenditures devoted to it by 0.25 per centum per year, until it is 3 per centum of the total extramural research and development funds, and targeting a portion of the increment at products with commercialization or export potential;

"(2) make the Small Business Innovation Research program permanent with a formal congressional review every 10 years, beginning in 1993;

"(3) allocate a modest but appropriate share of each agency's Small Business Innovation Research fund for administrative purposes for effective management, quality maintenance, and the elimination of program delays; and

"(4) include within the Small Business Innovation and Research program all agencies expending between $20,000,000 and $100,000,000 in extramural research and development funds annually.".

SEC. 8009. GLOBALIZATION OF PRODUCTION.

Within one year after the date of enactment of this Act, the Administrator of the Small Business Administration shall submit a written report to the Committees on Small Business of the House of Representatives and the Senate, prepared by the Administration in conjunction with the Bureau of Census and in cooperation with other relevant agencies, that would—

(1) analyze to the extent possible the effect of increased outsourcing and other shifts in production arrangements on small firms, particularly manufacturing firms, within the United States subcontractor tier and to the extent that such data is not available determine methods by which such data may be collected;

(2) assess the impact of specific economic policies, including, but not limited to, procurement, tax and trade policies, in facilitating outsourcing and other international production arrangements; and

(3) make recommendations as to changes in Government policy that would improve the competitive position of smaller United States subcontractors, including recommendations as to incentives which could be provided to larger corporations to maximize their use of United States subcontractors and assist these subcontractors in changing production and marketing

strategies and in obtaining new business in domestic and foreign markets.

SEC. 8010. SMALL BUSINESS TRADE REMEDY ASSISTANCE.

Not later than December 1, 1988, the Comptroller General of the United States shall conduct a study and submit a report to the Committee on Governmental Affairs and the Committee on Small Business of the Senate, as well as to other appropriate committees of the Senate, and to the Committee on Small Business and the Committee on Ways and Means of the House of Representatives on the costs incurred by small businesses in pursuing rights and remedies under the trade laws. Such report shall include an analysis of—

(1) the costs incurred by small businesses (and trade associations whose membership is primarily small business) in pursuing investigations under the trade remedy laws, including—

(A) antidumping investigations and proceedings under title VII of the Tariff Act of 1930;

(B) countervailing duty investigations and proceedings under section 303 or title VII of the Tariff Act of 1930;

(C) unfair trade practice investigations under section 337 of the Tariff Act of 1930;

(D) investigations under chapter 1 of title III of the Tariff Act of 1974;

(E) import relief investigations under chapter 1 of title II of the Trade Act of 1974;

(F) market disruption investigations under section 406 of the Trade Act of 1974; and

(G) national security relief investigations under section 232 of the Trade Expansion Act of 1962;

(2) the extent of assistance and information provided by the Trade Remedy Assistance Office of the United States International Trade Commission;

(3) the ability of small businesses to generate the information and resources needed for such investigations; and

(4) the costs and benefits to the Federal Government of either—

(A) providing reimbursement to small businesses for legal expenses incurred in pursuing trade remedies; or

(B) providing direct legal assistance to small businesses.

SEC. 8011. NATIONAL SEMINAR ON SMALL BUSINESS EXPORTS.

(a) Seminar.—The Administration shall conduct a National Seminar on Small Business Exports within one year following enactment of this Act in order to develop recommendations designed to stimulate exports from small companies. The Seminar shall build upon the information collected by the Administration through previously conducted regional small business trade conferences.

(b) Assistance by Experts.—For the purpose of ascertaining facts and developing policy recommendations concerning the expansion of United States exports from small companies the Seminar shall bring together individuals who are experts in the fields of international trade and small business development and representatives of small businesses, associations, the labor community, academic institutions, and Federal, State and local governments.

(c) Recommendations Concerning Utility of International Conference.—The Seminar shall specifically consider the utility of, and make recommendations regarding, a subsequent International Conference on Small Business and Trade that would—

(1) help establish linkages between United States small business owners and small business owners in foreign countries;

(2) enable United States small business owners to learn how others organize themselves for exporting; and

(3) foster greater consideration of small business concerns in the GATT.

SEC. 8012. TRADE NEGOTIATIONS.

It is the sense of the Congress that the interests of the small business community have not been adequately represented in trade policy formulation and in trade negotiations. Therefore, it is the sense of the Congress that the Administrator of the Small Business Administration should be appointed as a member of the Trade Policy Committee and that the United States Trade Representative should consult with the Small Business Administration and its Office of Advocacy in trade policy formulation and in trade negotiations.

Further, it is the sense of the Congress that the United States Trade Representative would better serve the needs of the small business community with full-time staff assistance with responsibilities for small business trade issues.

Further, it is the sense of the Congress that the United States Trade Representative should appoint a special trade assistant for small business.

SEC. 8013. PROMULGATION OF REGULATIONS.

Notwithstanding any law, rule, or regulation, the Small Business Administration shall promulgate final regulations to carry out the provisions of this title within six months after the date of enactment of this title.

SEC. 8014. EFFECTIVE DATE.

This title shall become effective on the date of its enactment.

TITLE IX—PATENTS

Subtitle A—Process Patents

SEC. 9001. SHORT TITLE.

This subtitle may be cited as the "Process Patent Amendments Act of 1988".

SEC. 9002. RIGHTS OF OWNERS OF PATENTED PROCESSES.

Section 154 of title 35, United States Code, is amended by inserting after "United States" the following: "and, if the invention is a process, of the right to exclude others from using or selling throughout the United States, or importing into the United States, products made by that process,".

SEC. 9003. INFRINGEMENT FOR IMPORTATION, USE, OR SALE.

Section 271 of title 35, United States Code, is amended by adding at the end the following new subsection:

to subsections (b) and (c), shall apply only with respect to products made or imported after the effective date of the amendments made by this subtitle.

(b) EXCEPTIONS.—The amendments made by this subtitle shall not abridge or affect the right of any person or any successor in business of such person to continue to use, sell, or import any specific product already in substantial and continuous sale or use by such person in the United States on January 1, 1988, or for which substantial preparation by such person for such sale or use was made before such date, to the extent equitable for the protection of commercial investments made or business commenced in the United States before such date. This subsection shall not apply to any person or any successor in business of such person using, selling, or importing a product produced by a patented process that is the subject of a process patent enforcement action commenced before January 1, 1987, before the International Trade Commission, that is pending or in which an order has been entered.

(c) RETENTION OF OTHER REMEDIES.—The amendments made by this subtitle shall not deprive a patent owner of any remedies available under subsections (a) through (f) of section 271 of title 35, United States Code, under section 337 of the Tariff Act of 1930, or under any other provision of law.

SEC. 9007. REPORTS TO CONGRESS.

(a) CONTENTS.—The Secretary of Commerce shall, not later than the end of each 1-year period described in subsection (b), report to the Congress on the effect of the amendments made by this subtitle on those domestic industries that submit complaints to the Department of Commerce, during that 1-year period, alleging that their legitimate sources of supply have been adversely affected by the amendments made by this subtitle.

(b) WHEN SUBMITTED.—A report described in subsection (a) shall be submitted with respect to each of the five 1-year periods which occur successively beginning on the effective date of the amendments made by this subtitle and ending five years after that effective date.

Subtitle B—Foreign Filing

SEC. 9101. INCREASED EFFECTIVENESS OF PATENT LAW.

(a) SHORT TITLE.—This section may be cited as the "Patent Law Foreign Filing Amendments Act of 1988".

(b) FILING OF APPLICATIONS IN FOREIGN COUNTRIES.—(1) Section 184 of title 35, United States Code, is amended—

(A) in the third sentence by—

(i) striking out "inadvertently"; and

(ii) inserting "through error and without deceptive intent" after "filed abroad"; and

(B) by adding at the end thereof the following new paragraph:

"The scope of a license shall permit subsequent modifications, amendments, and supplements containing additional subject matter if the application upon which the request for the license is based is not, or was not, required to be made available for inspection under section 181 of this title and if such modifications, amendments, and supplements do not change the general nature of the invention in a manner which would require such application to be made available for inspection under such section 181. In any case in which a license is not, or was not, required in order to file an application in any foreign country, such subsequent modifications, amendments, and supplements may be made, without a license, to the application filed in the foreign country if the United States application was not required to be made available for inspection under section 181 and if such modifications, amendments, and supplements do not, or did not, change the general nature of the invention in a manner which would require the United States application to have been made available for inspection under such section 181.".

(2) Section 185 of title 35, United States Code, is amended by inserting immediately before the period in the last sentence the following: ", unless the failure to procure such license was through error and without deceptive intent, and the patent does not disclose subject matter within the scope of section 181 of this title.".

(3) Section 186 of title 35, United States Code, is amended by inserting "willfully" after "whoever", the second place it appears.

(c) REGULATIONS.—The Commissioner of Patents and Trademarks shall prescribe such regulations as may be necessary to implement the amendments made by this section.

(d) EFFECTIVE DATE.—(1) Subject to paragraphs (2), (3), and (4) of this subsection, the amendments made by this section shall apply to all United States patents granted before, on, or after the date of enactment of this section, to all applications for United States patents pending on or filed after such date of enactment, and to all licenses under section 184 granted before, on, or after the date of enactment of this section.

(2) The amendments made by this section shall not affect any final decision made by a court or the Patent and Trademark Office before the date of enactment of this section with respect to a patent or application for patent, if no appeal from such decision is pending and the time for filing an appeal has expired.

(3) No United States patent granted before the date of enactment of this section shall abridge or affect the right of any person or his successors in business who made, purchased, or used, prior to such date of enactment, anything protected by the patent, to continue the use of, or to sell to others to be used or sold, the specific thing so made, purchased, or used, if the patent claims were invalid or otherwise unenforceable on a ground obviated by this section and the person made, purchased, or used the specific thing in reasonable reliance on such invalidity or unenforceability. If a person reasonably relied on such invalidity or unenforceability, the court before which such matter is in question may provide for the continued manufacture, use, or sale of the thing made, purchased, or used as specified, or for the manufacture, use, or sale of which substantial preparation was made before the date of enactment of this section, and it may also provide for the continued practice of any process practiced, or for the practice of which substantial preparation was made, prior to the date of enactment of this section, to the extent and under such terms as the court deems equitable for the protection of investments made or business commenced before such date of enactment.

(4) The amendments made by this section shall not affect the right of any party in any case pending in court on the date of enactment of this section to have its rights or liabilities—

(A) under any patent before the court, or

(B) under any patent granted after such date of enactment which is related to the patent before the court by deriving priority rights under section 120 or 121 of title 35, United States Code, from a patent or an application for patent common to both patents,

determined on the basis of the substantive law in effect before the date of enactment of this section.

Subtitle A—Foreign Shipping Practices

SEC. 10001. SHORT TITLE.

This subtitle may be cited as the "Foreign Shipping Practices Act of 1988".

SEC. 10002. FOREIGN LAWS AND PRACTICES.

(a) DEFINITIONS.—For purposes of this section—

(1) "common carrier", "marine terminal operator", "non-vessel-operating common carrier", "ocean common carrier", "person", "shipper", "shippers' association", and "United States" have the meanings given each such term, respectively, in section 3 of the Shipping Act of 1984 (46 App. U.S.C. 1702);

(2) "foreign carrier" means an ocean common carrier a majority of whose vessels are documented under the laws of a country other than the United States;

(3) "maritime services" means port-to-port carriage of cargo by the vessels operated by ocean common carriers;

(4) "maritime-related services" means intermodal operations, terminal operations, cargo solicitation, forwarding and agency services, non-vessel-operating common carrier operations, and all other activities and services integral to total transportation systems of ocean common carriers and their foreign domiciled affiliates on their own and others' behalf;

(5) "United States carrier" means an ocean common carrier which operates vessels documented under the laws of the United States; and

(6) "United States oceanborne trade" means the carriage of cargo between the United States and a foreign country, whether direct or indirect, by an ocean common carrier.

(b) AUTHORITY TO CONDUCT INVESTIGATIONS.—The Federal Maritime Commission shall investigate whether any laws, rules, regulations, policies, or practices of foreign governments, or any practices of foreign carriers or other persons providing maritime or maritime-related services in a foreign country result in the existence of conditions that—

(1) adversely affect the operations of United States carriers in United States oceanborne trade; and

(2) do not exist for foreign carriers of that country in the United States under the laws of the United States or as a result of acts of United States carriers or other persons providing maritime or maritime-related services in the United States.

(c) INVESTIGATIONS.—(1) Investigations under subsection (b) of this section may be initiated by the Commission on its own motion or on the petition of any person, including any common carrier, shipper, shippers' association, ocean freight forwarder, or marine terminal operator, or any branch, department, agency, or other component of the Government of the United States.

(2) The Commission shall complete any such investigation and render a decision within 120 days after it is initiated, except that the Commission may extend such 120-day period for an additional 90

days if the Commission is unable to obtain sufficient information to determine whether a condition specified in subsection (b) of this section exists. Any notice providing such an extension shall clearly state the reasons for such extension.

(d) INFORMATION REQUESTS.—(1) In order to further the purposes of subsection (b) of this section, the Commission may, by order, require any person (including any common carrier, shipper, shippers' association, ocean freight forwarder, or marine terminal operator, or any officer, receiver, trustee, lessee, agent or employee thereof) to file with the Commission any periodic or special report, answers to questions, documentary material, or other information which the Commission considers necessary or appropriate. The Commission may require that the response to any such order shall be made under oath. Such response shall be furnished in the form and within the time prescribed by the Commission.

(2) In an investigation under subsection (b) of this section, the Commission may issue subpoenas to compel the attendance and testimony of witnesses and the production of records or other evidence.

(3) Notwithstanding any other provision of law, the Commission may, in its discretion, determine that any information submitted to it in response to a request under this subsection, or otherwise, shall not be disclosed to the public.

(e) ACTION AGAINST FOREIGN CARRIERS.—(1) Whenever, after notice and opportunity for comment or hearing, the Commission determines that the conditions specified in subsection (b) of this section exist, the Commission shall take such action as it considers necessary and appropriate against any foreign carrier that is a contributing cause to, or whose government is a contributing cause to, such conditions, in order to offset such conditions. Such action may include—

(A) limitations on sailings to and from United States ports or on the amount or type of cargo carried;

(B) suspension, in whole or in part, of any or all tariffs filed with the Commission, including the right of an ocean common carrier to use any or all tariffs of conferences in United States trades of which it is a member for such period as the Commission specifies;

(C) suspension, in whole or in part, of the right of an ocean common carrier to operate under any agreement filed with the Commission, including agreements authorizing preferential treatment at terminals, preferential terminal leases, space chartering, or pooling of cargo or revenues with other ocean common carriers; and

(D) a fee, not to exceed $1,000,000 per voyage.

(2) The Commission may consult with, seek the cooperation of, or make recommendations to other appropriate Government agencies prior to taking any action under this subsection.

(3) Before a determination under this subsection becomes effective or a request is made under subsection (f) of this section, the determination shall be submitted immediately to the President who may, within 10 days after receiving such determination, disapprove the determination in writing, setting forth the reasons for the disapproval, if the President finds that disapproval is required for reasons of the national defense or the foreign policy of the United States.

(f) ACTIONS UPON REQUEST OF THE COMMISSION.—Whenever the conditions specified in subsection (b) of this section are found by the Commission to exist, upon the request of the Commission—

(1) the collector of customs at any port or place of destination in the United States shall refuse the clearance required by section 4197 of the Revised Statutes (46 App. U.S.C. 91) to any vessel of a foreign carrier that is identified by the Commission under subsection (e) of this section; and

(2) the Secretary of the department in which the Coast Guard is operating shall deny entry, for purposes of oceanborne trade, of any vessel of a foreign carrier that is identified by the Commission under subsection (e) of this section to any port or place in the United States or the navigable waters of the United States, or shall detain any such vessel at the port or place in the United States from which it is about to depart for any other port or place in the United States.

(g) REPORT.—The Commission shall include in its annual report to Congress—

(1) a list of the twenty foreign countries which generated the largest volume of oceanborne liner cargo for the most recent calendar year in bilateral trade with the United States;

(2) an analysis of conditions described in subsection (b) of this section being investigated or found to exist in foreign countries;

(3) any actions being taken by the Commission to offset such conditions;

(4) any recommendations for additional legislation to offset such conditions; and

(5) a list of petitions filed under subsection (c) of this section that the Commission rejected, and the reasons for each such rejection.

(h) The actions against foreign carriers authorized in subsections (e) and (f) of this section may be used in the administration and enforcement of section 13(b)(5) of the Shipping Act of 1984 (46 App. U.S.C. 1712(b)(5)) or section 19(1)(b) of the Merchant Marine Act, 1920 (46 App. U.S.C. 876).

(i) Any rule, regulation or final order of the Commission issued under this section shall be reviewable exclusively in the same forum and in the same manner as provided in section 2342(3)(B) of title 28, United States Code.

Subtitle B—International Air Transportation

SEC. 10011. MAXIMUM PERIOD FOR TAKING ACTION WITH RESPECT TO COMPLAINTS.

Section 2(b)(2) of the International Air Transportation Fair Competitive Practices Act of 1974 (49 U.S.C. App. 1159b(b)(2)) is amended—

(1) in the third sentence by striking out "but in no event may" and all that follows through "180 days" and inserting in lieu thereof "but the aggregate period for taking action under this subsection may not exceed 90 days"; and

(2) by inserting after the third sentence the following new sentence: "However, if on the last day of such 90-day period, the Secretary finds that—

"(A) negotiations with the foreign government have progressed to a point that a satisfactory resolution of the complaint appears imminent;

"(B) no United States air carrier has been subject to economic injury by the foreign government or an instrumentality of the foreign government (including a foreign air carrier) as a result of the filing of the complaint; and

"(C) public interest requires additional time before the taking of action with respect to the complaint;

the Secretary may extend such 90-day period for not to exceed an additional 90 days.".

SEC. 10012. VIEWS OF THE DEPARTMENT OF COMMERCE AND OFFICE OF THE UNITED STATES TRADE REPRESENTATIVE.

Section 2(b) of the International Air Transportation Fair Competitive Practices Act of 1974 (49 U.S.C. App. 1159b(b)) is amended—

(1) by redesignating paragraph (3), and any references thereto, as paragraph (4);

(2) by striking out the last sentence of paragraph (2); and

(3) by inserting after paragraph (2) the following new paragraph:

"(3) In considering any complaint, or in any proceedings under its own initiative, under this subsection, the Secretary shall—

"(A) solicit the views of the Department of State, the Department of Commerce, and the Office of the United States Trade Representative; and

"(B) provide any affected air carrier or foreign air carrier with reasonable notice and such opportunity to file written evidence and argument as is consistent with acting on the complaint within the time limits set forth in this subsection.".

SEC. 10013. REPORTING ON ACTIONS TAKEN WITH RESPECT TO COMPLAINTS.

Section 2 of the International Air Transportation Fair Competitive Practices Act of 1974 (49 U.S.C. App. 1159b) is amended by adding at the end thereof the following new subsection:

"(e) Not later than the 30th day after taking action with respect to a complaint under this section, the Secretary of Transportation shall report to the Committee on Public Works and Transportation of the House Representatives and the Committee on Commerce, Science, and Transportation of the Senate on actions that have been taken under this section with respect to the complaint.".

Approved August 23, 1988.

LEGISLATIVE HISTORY—H.R. 4848:

CONGRESSIONAL RECORD, Vol. 134 (1988):
July 13, considered and passed House.
Aug. 2, 3, considered and passed Senate.
WEEKLY COMPILATION OF PRESIDENTIAL DOCUMENTS, Vol. 24 (1988):
Aug. 23, Presidential remarks.

UNITED STATES-CANADA FREE-TRADE AGREEMENT IMPLEMENTATION ACT OF 1988

An Act to implement the United States-Canada Free-Trade Agreement.

Date: September 28, 1988

Bill No.: H.R. 5090

Public Law No.: 100-449

Cite: 102 STAT. 1851

Sections reprinted:

Section 410 - Termination of agreement.

TITLE V - EFFECTIVE DATES AND SEVERABILITY

Section 501 - Effective dates.

Section 502 - Severability.

Note: The United States-Canada Free Trade Agreement of 1987 is numbered KAV 270 in the *United States Treaty Index.*

Public Law 100-449
100th Congress

An Act

To implement the United States-Canada Free-Trade Agreement.

Be it enacted by the Senate and House of Representatives of the United States of America in Congress assembled,

SECTION 1. SHORT TITLE AND TABLE OF CONTENTS.

(a) SHORT TITLE.—This Act may be cited as the "United States-Canada Free-Trade Agreement Implementation Act of 1988".

(b) TABLE OF CONTENTS.—

SEC. 2. PURPOSES.

The purposes of this Act are—

(1) to approve and implement the Free-Trade Agreement between the United States and Canada negotiated under the authority of section 102 of the Trade Act of 1974;

(2) to strengthen and develop economic relations between the United States and Canada for their mutual benefit;

(3) to establish a free-trade area between the two nations through the reduction and elimination of barriers to trade in goods and services and to investment; and

(4) to lay the foundation for further cooperation to expand and enhance the benefits of such Agreement.

TITLE I—APPROVAL OF UNITED STATES-CANADA FREE-TRADE AGREEMENT AND RELATIONSHIP OF AGREEMENT TO UNITED STATES LAW

SEC. 101. APPROVAL OF UNITED STATES-CANADA FREE-TRADE AGREEMENT.

(a) Approval of Agreement and Statement of Administrative Action.—Pursuant to sections 102 and 151 of the Trade Act of 1974 (19 U.S.C. 2112 and 2191), the Congress approves—

(1) the United States-Canada Free-Trade Agreement (hereinafter in this Act referred to as the "Agreement") entered into on January 2, 1988, and submitted to the Congress on July 25, 1988;

(2) the letters exchanged between the Governments of the United States and Canada—

(A) dated January 2, 1988, relating to negotiations regarding articles 301 (Rules of Origin) and 401 (Tariff Elimination) of the Agreement, and

(B) dated January 2, 1988, relating to negotiations regarding article 2008 (Plywood Standards) of the Agreement; and

(3) the statement of administrative action proposed to implement the Agreement that was submitted to the Congress on July 25, 1988.

(b) Conditions for Entry Into Force of the Agreement.—At such time as the President determines that Canada has taken measures necessary to comply with the obligations of the Agreement, the President is authorized to exchange notes with the Government of Canada providing for the entry into force, on or after January 1, 1989, of the Agreement with respect to the United States.

(c) Report on Canadian Practices.—Within 60 days after the date of the enactment of this Act (but not later than December 15, 1988), the United States Trade Representative shall submit to the

Congress a report identifying, to the maximum extent practicable, major current Canadian practices (and the legal authority for such practices) that, in the opinion of the United States Trade Representative—

(1) are not in conformity with the Agreement; and

(2) require a change of Canadian law, regulation, policy, or practice to enable Canada to conform with its international obligations under the Agreement.

SEC. 102. RELATIONSHIP OF THE AGREEMENT TO UNITED STATES LAW.

(a) UNITED STATES LAWS TO PREVAIL IN CONFLICT.—No provision of the Agreement, nor the application of any such provision to any person or circumstance, which is in conflict with any law of the United States shall have effect.

(b) RELATIONSHIP OF AGREEMENT TO STATE AND LOCAL LAW.—

(1) The provisions of the Agreement prevail over—

(A) any conflicting State law; and

(B) any conflicting application of any State law to any person or circumstance;

to the extent of the conflict.

(2) Upon the enactment of this Act, the President shall, in accordance with section 306(c)(2)(A) of the Trade and Tariff Act of 1984 (19 U.S.C. 2114c), initiate consultations with the State governments on the implementation of the obligations of the United States under the Agreement. Such consultations shall be held—

(A) through the intergovernmental policy advisory committees on trade established under such section for the purpose of achieving conformity of State laws and practices with the Agreement; and

(B) with the individual States as necessary to deal with particular questions that may arise.

(3) The United States may bring an action challenging any provision of State law, or the application thereof to any person or circumstance, on the ground that the provision or application is inconsistent with the Agreement.

(4) For purposes of this subsection, the term "State law" includes—

(A) any law of a political subdivision of a State; and

(B) any State law regulating or taxing the business of insurance.

(c) EFFECT OF AGREEMENT WITH RESPECT TO PRIVATE REMEDIES.—No person other than the United States shall—

(1) have any cause of action or defense under the Agreement or by virtue of congressional approval thereof, or

(2) challenge, in any action brought under any provision of law, any action or inaction by any department, agency, or other instrumentality of the United States, any State, or any political subdivision of a State on the ground that such action or inaction is inconsistent with the Agreement.

(d) INITIAL IMPLEMENTING REGULATIONS.—Initial regulations necessary or appropriate to carry out the actions proposed in the statement of administrative action submitted under section 101(a)(3) to implement the Agreement shall, to the maximum extent feasible, be issued within 1 year after the date of entry into force of the Agreement. In the case of any implementing action that takes effect after the date of entry into force of the Agreement, initial regulations to carry out that action shall, to the maximum extent feasible, be issued within 1 year after such effective date.

(e) CHANGES IN STATUTES TO IMPLEMENT A REQUIREMENT, AMENDMENT, OR RECOMMENDATION.—The provisions of section 3(c) of the Trade Agreements Act of 1979 (19 U.S.C. 2504(c)) shall apply as if the Agreement were an agreement approved under section 2(a) of that Act whenever the President determines that it is necessary or appropriate to amend, repeal, or enact a statute of the United States in order to implement any requirement of, amendment to, or recommendation, finding or opinion under, the Agreement; but such provisions shall not apply to any bill to implement any such requirement, amendment, recommendation, finding, or opinion that is submitted to the Congress after the close of the 30th month after the month in which the Agreement enters into force.

SEC. 103. CONSULTATION AND LAY-OVER REQUIREMENTS FOR, AND EFFECTIVE DATE OF, PROCLAIMED ACTIONS.

(a) CONSULTATION AND LAY-OVER REQUIREMENTS.—If a provision of this Act provides that the implementation of an action by the President by proclamation is subject to the consultation and lay-over requirements of this section, such action may be proclaimed only if—

(1) the President has obtained advice regarding the proposed action from—

(A) the appropriate advisory committees established under section 135 of the Trade Act of 1974, and

(B) the United States International Trade Commission;

(2) the President has submitted a report to the Committee on Ways and Means of the House of Representatives and the Committee on Finance of the Senate that sets forth—

(A) the action proposed to be proclaimed and the reasons therefor, and

(B) the advice obtained under paragraph (1);

(3) a period of at least 60 calendar days that begins on the first day on which the President has met the requirements of paragraphs (1) and (2) with respect to such action has expired; and

(4) the President has consulted with such Committees regarding the proposed action during the period referred to in paragraph (3).

(b) EFFECTIVE DATE OF CERTAIN PROCLAIMED ACTIONS.—No action proclaimed by the President under the authority of this Act, if such action is not subject to the consultation and lay-over requirements under subsection (a), may take effect before the 15th day after the date on which the text of the proclamation is published in the Federal Register.

SEC. 104. HARMONIZED SYSTEM.

(a) DEFINITION.—As used in this Act, the term "Harmonized System" means the nomenclature system established under the International Convention on the Harmonized Commodity Description and Coding System (done at Brussels on June 14, 1983, and the protocol thereto, done at Brussels on June 24, 1986) as implemented under United States law.

(b) INTERIM APPLICATION OF TSUS.—The following apply if the International Convention, and the protocol thereto, referred to in subsection (a) are not implemented under United States law before the Agreement enters into force:

(1) The President, subject to subsection (c), shall proclaim such modifications to the Tariff Schedules of the United States (19 U.S.C. 1202) as may be necessary to give effect, until such time as such Convention and protocol are so implemented, to the rules of origin, schedule of rate reductions, and other provisions that would, but for the absence of such implementation, be proclaimed under the authority of this Act to, or in terms of, the Harmonized System to implement the obligations of the United States under the Agreement.

(2) Until such time as such Convention and protocol are so implemented, any reference in this Act to the nomenclature of such Convention and protocol shall be treated as a reference to the corresponding nomenclature of the Tariff Schedules of the United States as modified under paragraph (1).

(c) RESTRICTIONS.—

(1) No modification described in subsection (b)(1) that is to take effect concurrently with the entry into force of the Agreement may be proclaimed unless the text of the modification is published in the Federal Register at least 30 days before the date of entry into force.

(2) All modifications proclaimed under the authority of subsection (b)(1) after the Agreement enters into force with respect to the United States are subject to the consultation and lay-over requirements of section 103(a).

SEC. 105. IMPLEMENTING ACTIONS IN ANTICIPATION OF ENTRY INTO FORCE.

Subject to section 103 or 104(c), as appropriate, and any other applicable restriction or limitation in this Act on the proclaiming of actions or the issuing of regulations to carry out this Act or any amendment made by this Act, after the date of the enactment of this Act—

(1) the President may proclaim such actions; and

(2) other appropriate officers of the United States Government may issue such regulations;

as may be necessary to ensure that any provision of this Act, or amendment made by this Act, that takes effect on the date the Agreement enters into force is appropriately implemented on such date, but no such proclamation or regulation may have an effective date earlier than the date of entry into force.

TITLE II—TARIFF MODIFICATIONS, RULES OF ORIGIN, USER FEES, DRAWBACK, ENFORCEMENT, AND OTHER CUSTOMS PROVISIONS

SEC. 201. TARIFF MODIFICATIONS.

(a) TARIFF MODIFICATIONS SPECIFIED IN THE AGREEMENT.—The President may proclaim—

(1) such modifications or continuance of any existing duty;

(2) such continuance of existing duty-free or excise treatment; or

(3) such additional duties;

as the President determines to be necessary or appropriate to carry out article 401 of the Agreement and the schedule of duty reductions with respect to Canada set forth in Annexes 401.2 and 401.7 to the Agreement, as approved under section 101(a)(1). For purposes of proclaiming necessary modifications under such Annex 401.2, any article covered under subheading 9813.00.05 (contained in the United States Schedule in such Annex) shall, unless such article is a drawback eligible good under section 204(a), be treated as being subject to any otherwise applicable customs duty if the article, or merchandise incorporating such article, is exported to Canada.

(b) OTHER TARIFF MODIFICATIONS.—Subject to the consultation and lay-over requirements of section 103(a), the President may proclaim—

(1) such modifications as the United States and Canada may agree to regarding the staging of any duty treatment set forth in Annexes 401.2 and 401.7 of the Agreement;

(2) such modifications or continuance of any existing duty;

(3) such continuance of existing duty-free or excise treatment; or

(4) such additional duties;

as the President determines to be necessary or appropriate to maintain the general level of reciprocal and mutually advantageous concessions with respect to Canada provided for by the Agreement.

(c) MODIFICATIONS AFFECTING PLYWOOD.—

(1) The Congress encourages the President to facilitate the preparation, and the implementation with Canada, of common performance standards for the use of softwood plywood and other structural panels in construction applications in the United States and Canada.

(2) The President shall report to the Congress on the incorporation of common plywood performance standards into building codes in the United States and Canada and may implement the provisions of article 2008 of the Agreement when he determines that the necessary conditions have been met.

(3) Any tariff reduction undertaken pursuant to paragraph (2) shall be in equal annual increments ending January 1, 1998, unless those reductions commence after January 1, 1991.

SEC. 202. RULES OF ORIGIN.

(a) IN GENERAL.—

(1) For purposes of implementing the tariff treatment contemplated under the Agreement, goods originate in the territory of a Party if—

(A) they are wholly obtained or produced in the territory of either Party or both Parties; or

(B) they—

(i) have been transformed in the territory of either Party or both Parties so as to be subject to a change in tariff classification as described in the Annex rules or to such other requirements as the Annex rules may provide when no change in tariff classifications occurs, and

(ii) meet the other conditions set out in the Annex.

(2) A good shall not be considered to originate in the territory of a party under paragraph (1)(B) merely by virtue of having undergone—

(A) simple packaging or, except as expressly provided by the Annex rules, combining operations;

(B) mere dilution with water or another substance that does not materially alter the characteristics of the good; or

(C) any process or work in respect of which it is established, or in respect of which the facts as ascertained clearly justify the presumption, that the sole object was to circumvent the provisions of chapter 3 of the Agreement.

(3) Accessories, spare parts, or tools delivered with any piece of equipment, machinery, apparatus, or vehicle that form part of its standard equipment shall be treated as having the same origin as that equipment, machinery, apparatus, or vehicle if the quantities and values of such accessories, spare parts, or tools are customary for the equipment, machinery, apparatus, or vehicle.

(b) TRANSSHIPMENT.—Goods exported from the territory of one Party originate in the territory of that Party only if—

(1) the goods meet the applicable requirements of subsection (a) and are shipped to the territory of the other Party without having entered the commerce of any third country;

(2) the goods, if shipped through the territory of a third country, do not undergo any operation other than unloading, reloading, or any operation necessary to transport them to the territory of the other Party or to preserve them in good condition; and

(3) the documents related to the exportation and shipment of the goods from the territory of a Party show the territory of the other Party as their final destination.

(c) INTERPRETATION.—In interpreting this section, the following apply:

(1) Whenever the processing or assembly of goods in the territory of either Party or both Parties results in one of the changes in tariff classification described in the Annex rules, such goods shall be considered to have been transformed in the territory of that Party and shall be treated as goods originating in the territory of that Party if—

(A) such processing or assembly occurs entirely within the territory of either Party or both Parties; and

(B) such goods have not subsequently undergone any processing or assembly outside the territories of the Parties that improves the goods in condition or advances them in value.

(2) Whenever the assembly of goods in the territory of a Party fails to result in a change of tariff classification because either—

(A) the goods were imported into the territory of the Party in an unassembled or a disassembled form and were classified as unassembled or disassembled goods pursuant to General Rule of Interpretation 2(a) of the Harmonized System; or

(B) the tariff subheading for the goods provides for both the goods themselves and their parts;

such goods shall not be treated as goods originating in the territory of a Party.

(3) Notwithstanding paragraph (2), goods described in that paragraph shall be considered to have been transformed in the

territory of a Party and be treated as goods originating in the territory of the Party if—

(A) the value of materials originating in the territory of either Party or both Parties used or consumed in the production of the goods plus the direct cost of assembling the goods in the territory of either Party or both Parties constitute not less than 50 percent of the value of the goods when exported to the territory of the other Party; and

(B) the goods have not subsequent to assembly undergone processing or further assembly in a third country and they meet the requirements of subsection (b).

(4) The provisions of paragraph (3) shall not apply to goods of chapters 61-63 of the Harmonized System.

(5) In making the determination required by paragraph (3)(A) and in making the same or a similar determination when required by the Annex rules, where materials originating in the territory of either Party or both Parties and materials obtained or produced in a third country are used or consumed together in the production of goods in the territory of a Party, the value of materials originating in the territory of either Party or both Parties may be treated as such only to the extent that it is directly attributable to the goods under consideration.

(6) In applying the Annex rules, a specific rule shall take precedence over a more general rule.

(d) Annex Rules.—

(1) The President is authorized to proclaim, as a part of the Harmonized System, the rules set forth under the heading "Rules" in Annex 301.2 of the Agreement. For purposes of carrying out this paragraph—

(A) the phrase "headings 2207-2209" in paragraph 7 of section IV of such Annex 301.2 shall be treated as a reference to headings 2203-2209; and

(B) the phrase "any other heading" in paragraph 11 of section XV in such Annex 301.2 shall be treated as a reference to any other heading of chapter 74 of the Harmonized System.

(2) Subject to the consultation and lay-over requirements of section 103, the President is authorized to proclaim such modifications to the rules as may from time-to-time be agreed to by the United States and Canada.

(e) Automotive Products.—

(1) The President is authorized to proclaim such modifications to the definition of Canadian articles (relating to the administration of the Automotive Products Trade Act of 1965) in the general notes of the Harmonized System as may be necessary to conform that definition with chapter 3 of the Agreement.

(2) For purposes of administering the value requirement (as defined in section 304(c)(3)) with respect to vehicles, the Secretary of the Treasury shall prescribe regulations governing the averaging of the value content of vehicles of the same class, or of sister vehicles, assembled in the same plant as an alternative to the calculation of the value content of each vehicle.

(f) Definitions.—For purposes of this section:

(1) The term "Annex" means—

(A) the interpretative guidelines set forth in subsection (c); and

(B) the Annex rules.

(2) The term "Annex rules" means the rules proclaimed under subsection (d).

(3) The term "direct cost of processing or direct cost of assembling" means the costs directly incurred in, or that can reasonably be allocated to, the production of goods, including—

(A) the cost of all labor, including benefits and on-the-job training, labor provided in connection with supervision, quality control, shipping, receiving, storage, packaging, management at the location of the process or assembly, and other like labor, whether provided by employees or independent contractors;

(B) the cost of inspecting and testing the goods;

(C) the cost of energy, fuel, dies, molds, tooling, and the depreciation and maintenance of machinery and equipment, without regard to whether they originate within the territory of a Party;

(D) development, design, and engineering costs;

(E) rent, mortgage interest, depreciation on buildings, property insurance premiums, maintenance, taxes and the cost of utilities for real property used in the production of goods; and

(F) royalty, licensing, or other like payments for the right to the goods;

but not including—

(i) costs relating to the general expense of doing business, such as the cost of providing executive, financial, sales, advertising, marketing, accounting and legal services, and insurance;

(ii) brokerage charges relating to the importation and exportation of goods;

(iii) the costs for telephone, mail, and other means of communication;

(iv) packing costs for exporting the goods;

(v) royalty payments related to a licensing agreement to distribute or sell the goods;

(vi) rent, mortgage interest, depreciation on buildings, property insurance premiums, maintenance, taxes, and the cost of utilities for real property used by personnel charged with administrative functions; or

(vii) profit on the goods.

(4) The term "goods wholly obtained or produced in the territory of either Party or both Parties" means—

(A) mineral goods extracted in the territory of either Party or both Parties;

(B) goods harvested in the territory of either Party or both Parties;

(C) live animals born and raised in the territory of either Party or both Parties;

(D) goods (fish, shellfish, and other marine life taken from the sea by vessels registered or recorded with a Party and flying its flag;

(E) goods produced on board factory ships from the goods referred to in subparagraph (D) provided such factory ships are registered or recorded with that Party and fly its flag;

(F) goods taken by a Party or a person of a Party from the seabed or beneath the seabed outside territorial waters, provided that Party has rights to exploit such seabed;

(G) goods taken from space, provided they are obtained by a Party or a person of a Party and not processed in a third country;

(H) waste and scrap derived from manufacturing operations and used goods, provided they were collected in the territory of either Party or both Parties and are fit only for the recovery of raw materials; and

(I) goods produced in the territory of either Party or both Parties exclusively from goods referred to in subparagraphs (A) to (H) inclusive or from their derivatives, at any stage of production.

(5) The term "materials" means goods, other than those included as part of the direct cost of processing or assembling, used or consumed in the production of other goods.

(6) The term "Party" means Canada or the United States.

(7) The term "territory" means—

(A) with respect to Canada, the territory to which its customs laws apply, including any areas beyond the territorial seas of Canada within which, in accordance with international law and its domestic laws, Canada may exercise rights with respect to the seabed and subsoil and their natural resources; and

(B) with respect to the United States—

(i) the customs territory of the United States, which includes the fifty States, the District of Columbia and the Commonwealth of Puerto Rico,

(ii) the foreign trade zones located in the United States, and the Commonwealth of Puerto Rico, and

(iii) any area beyond the territorial seas of the United States within which, in accordance with international law and its domestic laws, the United States may exercise rights with respect to the seabed and subsoil and their natural resources.

(8) The term "third country" means any country other than Canada or the United States or any territory not a part of the territory of either.

(9) The term "value of materials originating in the territory of either Party or both Parties" means the aggregate of—

(A) the price paid by the producer of an exported good for materials originating in the territory of either Party or both Parties or for materials imported from a third country used or consumed in the production of such originating materials; and

(B) when not included in that price, the following costs related thereto—

(i) freight, insurance, packing, and all other costs incurred in transporting any of the materials referred to in subparagraph (A) to the location of the producer;

(ii) duties, taxes, and brokerage fees on such materials paid in the territory of either Party or both Parties;

(iii) the cost of waste or spoilage resulting from the use or consumption of such materials, less the value of renewable scrap or byproduct; and

(iv) the value of goods and services relating to such materials determined in accordance with subparagraph 1(b) of article 8 of the Agreement on Implementation of article VII of the General Agreement on Tariffs and Trade.

(10) The term "value of the goods when exported to the territory of the other Party" means the aggregate of—

(A) the price paid by the producer for all materials, whether or not the materials originate in either Party or both Parties, and, when not included in the price paid for the materials, the costs related to—

(i) freight, insurance, packing, and all other costs incurred in transporting all materials to the location of the producer;

(ii) duties, taxes, and brokerage fees on all materials paid in the territory of either Party or both Parties;

(iii) the cost of waste or spoilage resulting from the use or consumption of such materials, less the value of renewable scrap or byproduct; and

(iv) the value of goods and services relating to all materials determined in accordance with subparagraph 1(b) of article 8 of the Agreement on Implementation of article VII of the General Agreement on Tariffs and Trade; and

(B) the direct cost of processing or the direct cost of assembling the goods.

(g) SPECIAL PROVISION REGARDING APPLICATION OF RULES OF ORIGIN TO CERTAIN APPAREL.—The Secretary of Commerce is authorized to issue regulations governing the exportation to Canada of apparel products that are cut, or knit to shape, and sewn, or otherwise assembled, in either Party from fabric produced or obtained in a third country for the purpose of establishing which exports of such products shall be permitted to claim preferential tariff treatment under the rules of origin of the Agreement, to the extent that the Agreement provides for quantitative limits on the availability of preferential tariff treatment for such products.

SEC. 203. CUSTOMS USER FEES.

Section 13031(b) of the Consolidated Omnibus Reconciliation Act of 1985 (19 U.S.C. 58c(b)) is amended by adding at the end thereof the following new paragraph:

"(10) The fee charged under subsection (a)(10) of this section with respect to goods of Canadian origin (as determined under section 202 of the United States-Canada Free-Trade Agreement Implementation Act of 1988) shall be in accordance with article 403 of the United States-Canada Free-Trade Agreement. Any service for which an exemption from such fee is provided by reason of this paragraph may not be funded with money contained in the Customs User Fee Account.".

SEC. 204. DRAWBACK.

(a) DEFINITION.—For purposes of this section, the term "drawback eligible goods" means—

(1) goods provided for under paragraph 8 of article 404 of the Agreement;

(2) goods provided for under paragraphs 4 and 5 of such article; and

(3) goods other than those referred to in paragraphs (1) and (2) that the United States and Canada agree are not subject to paragraphs 1, 2, and 3 of such article.

No drawback may be paid with respect to countervailing duties or antidumping duties imposed on drawback eligible goods.

(b) IMPLEMENTATION OF ARTICLE 404.—The President is authorized—

(1) to proclaim the identity, in accordance with the nomenclature of the Harmonized System, of goods referred to in subsection (a)(1); and

(2) subject to the consultation and lay-over requirements of section 103(a), to proclaim—

(A) the identity, in accordance with the nomenclature of the Harmonized System, of goods referred to in subsection (a)(3); and

(B) a delay in the taking effect of article 404 of the Agreement to a date later than January 1, 1994, with respect to any merchandise if the United States and Canada agree to the delay under paragraph 7 of such article.

(c) CONSEQUENTIAL AMENDMENTS.—

(1) BONDED MANUFACTURING WAREHOUSES.—Section 311 of the Tariff Act of 1930 (19 U.S.C. 1311) is amended by adding at the end thereof the following new paragraph:

"No article manufactured in a bonded warehouse, except to the extent that such article is made from an article that is a drawback eligible good under section 204(a) of the United States-Canada Free-Trade Agreement Implementation Act of 1988, may be withdrawn from such warehouse for exportation to Canada on or after January 1, 1994, or such later date as may be proclaimed by the President under section 204(b)(2)(B) of such Act of 1988, without payment of a duty on such imported merchandise in its condition, and at the rate of duty in effect, at the time of importation.".

(2) BONDED SMELTING AND REFINING WAREHOUSES.—Section 312 of the Tariff Act of 1930 (19 U.S.C. 1312) is further amended—

(A) by inserting after "exportation" in each of paragraphs (1) and (4) of subsection (b) the following: "(other than exportation to Canada on or after January 1, 1994, or such later date as may be proclaimed by the President under section 204(b)(2)(B) of the United States-Canada Free-Trade Agreement Implementation Act of 1988, except to the extent that the metal-bearing materials were of Canadian origin as determined in accordance with section 202 of such Act of 1988)"; and

(B) by inserting after "exportation" in subsection (d) the following: "(other than exportation to Canada on or after January 1, 1994, or such later date as may be proclaimed by the President under section 204(b)(2)(B) of the United States-Canada Free-Trade Agreement Implementation Act of 1988, except to the extent that the product is a drawback eligible good under section 204(a) of such Act of 1988)".

(3) DRAWBACK.—Section 313 of the Tariff Act of 1930 (19 U.S.C. 1313) is amended by adding at the end thereof the following new subsections:

"(n) For purposes of subsections (a), (b), (f), (h), and (j)(2), the shipment on or after January 1, 1994, or such later date as may be proclaimed by the President under section 204(b)(2)(B) of the United States-Canada Free-Trade Agreement Implementation Act of 1988, to Canada of an article made from or substituted for, as appropriate, a drawback eligible good under section 204(a) of such Act of 1988 does not constitute an exportation.

"(o) For purposes of subsection (g), vessels built for Canadian account and ownership, or for the Government of Canada, may not be considered to be built for any foreign account and ownership, or for the government of any foreign country, except to the extent that the materials in such vessels are drawback eligible goods under section 204(a) of the United States-Canada Free-Trade Agreement Implementation Act of 1988.".

(4) MANIPULATION IN WAREHOUSE.—The second sentence of section 562 of the Tariff Act of 1930 (19 U.S.C. 1562) is amended by striking out the proviso thereto and the colon preceding such proviso and inserting the following: "; except that upon permission therefor being granted by the Secretary of the Treasury, and under customs supervision, at the expense of the proprietor, merchandise may be cleaned, sorted, repacked, or otherwise changed in condition, but not manufactured, in bonded warehouses established for that purpose and be withdrawn therefrom without payment of duties—

"(1) for exportation to Canada, but on or after January 1, 1994, or such later date as may be proclaimed by the President under section 204(b)(2)(B) of the United States-Canada Free-Trade Agreement Implementation Act of 1988, such exemption from the payment of duties applies only in the case of the exportation to Canada of merchandise that—

"(A) is only cleaned, sorted, or repacked in a bonded warehouse, or

"(B) is a drawback eligible good under section 204(a) of such Act of 1988;

"(2) for exportation to any foreign country except Canada; and

"(3) for shipment to the Virgin Islands, American Samoa, Wake Island, Midway Island, Kingman Reef, Johnston Island or the island of Guam.

Merchandise may be withdrawn from bonded warehouse for consumption, or for exportation to Canada if the duty exemption under paragraph (1) of the preceding sentence does not apply, upon the payment of duties accruing thereon, in its condition and quantity, and at its weight, at the time of withdrawal from warehouse, with such additions to or deductions from the final appraised value as may be necessary by reason of change in condition.".

(5) FOREIGN TRADE ZONES.—Section 3(a) of the Act of June 18, 1934 (commonly known as the "Foreign Trade Zones Act"; 19 U.S.C. 81c) is further amended by adding before the period at the end thereof the following: "*Provided, further*, That with the exception of drawback eligible goods under section 204(a) of the United States-Canada Free-Trade Agreement Implementation Act of 1988, no article manufactured or otherwise changed in condition (except a change by cleaning, testing or repacking) shall be exported to Canada on or after January 1, 1994, or such later date as may be proclaimed by the President under section 204(b)(2)(B) of such Act of 1988, without the payment of a duty that shall be payable on the article in its condition and quantity, and at its weight, at the time of its exportation to Canada unless the privilege in the first proviso to this subsection was requested.".

SEC. 205. ENFORCEMENT.

(a) CERTIFICATIONS OF ORIGIN.—

(1) Any person that certifies in writing that goods exported to Canada meet the rules of origin under section 202 of the United States-Canada Free-Trade Agreement Implementation Act of 1988 shall provide, upon request by any customs official, a copy of that certification.

(2) Any person that fails to provide a copy of a certification requested under paragraph (1) shall be liable to the United States for a civil penalty not to exceed $10,000.

(3) Any person that certifies falsely that goods exported to Canada meet the rules of origin under such section 202 shall be liable to the United States for the same civil penalties provided under section 592 of the Tariff Act of 1930 (19 U.S.C. 1592) for a violation of section 592(a) of such Act by fraud, gross negligence, or negligence, as the case may be. The procedures and provisions of section 592 of such Act that are applicable to a violation under section 592(a) of such Act shall apply with respect to such false certification.

(b) RECORDKEEPING REQUIREMENTS.—Section 508 of the Tariff Act of 1930 (19 U.S.C. 1508) is amended—

(1) by redesignating subsections (b) and (c) as subsections (c) and (d), respectively;

(2) by inserting "and (b)" after "(a)" in subsection (c), as so redesignated;

(3) by adding after subsection (a) the following new subsection:

"(b) Any person who exports, or who knowingly causes to be exported, any merchandise to Canada shall make, keep, and render for examination and inspection such records (including certifications of origin or copies thereof) which pertain to such exportations."; and

(4) by adding at the end thereof the following new subsection:

"(e) Any person who fails to retain records required by subsection (b) or the regulations issued to implement that subsection shall be liable to a civil penalty not to exceed $10,000.".

SEC. 206. EXEMPTION FROM LOTTERY TICKET EMBARGO.

Section 305(a) of the Tariff Act of 1930 (19 U.S.C. 1305(a)) is amended by striking out the period at the end of the first paragraph and inserting the following: ": *Provided further*, That effective January 1, 1993, this section shall not apply to any lottery ticket, printed paper that may be used as a lottery ticket, or advertisement of any lottery, that is printed in Canada for use in connection with a lottery conducted in the United States.".

SEC. 207. PRODUCTION-BASED DUTY REMISSION PROGRAMS WITH RESPECT TO AUTOMOTIVE PRODUCTS.

(a) USTR STUDY.—The United States Trade Representative shall—

(1) undertake a study to determine whether any of the production-based duty remission programs of Canada with respect to automotive products is either—

(A) inconsistent with the provisions of, or otherwise denies the benefits to the United States under, the General Agreement on Tariffs and Trade, or

(B) being implemented inconsistently with the obligations under article 1002 of the Agreement not—

(i) to expand the extent or the application, or

(ii) to extend the duration,

of such programs; and

(2) determine whether to initiate an investigation under section 302 of the Trade Act of 1974 with respect to any of such production-based duty remission programs.

(b) REPORT AND MONITORING.—

(1) The United States Trade Representative shall submit a report to Congress no later than June 30, 1989 (or no later than September 30, 1989, if the Trade Representative considers an extension to be necessary) containing—

(A) the results of the study under subsection (a)(1), as well as a description of the basis used for measuring and verifying compliance with the obligations referred to in subsection (a)(1)(B); and

(B) any determination made under subsection (a)(2) and the reasons therefor.

(2) Notwithstanding the submission of the report under paragraph (1), the Trade Representative shall continue to monitor the degree of compliance with the obligations referred to in subsection (a)(1)(B).

TITLE III—APPLICATION OF AGREEMENT TO SECTORS AND SERVICES

SEC. 301. AGRICULTURE.

(a) SPECIAL TARIFF PROVISIONS FOR FRESH FRUITS AND VEGETABLES.—

(1) The Secretary of Agriculture (hereafter in this section referred to as the "Secretary") may recommend to the President the imposition of a temporary duty on any Canadian fresh fruit or vegetable entered into the United States if the Secretary determines that both of the following conditions exist at the time that imposition of the duty is recommended:

(A) For each of 5 consecutive working days the import price of the Canadian fresh fruit or vegetable is below 90 percent of the corresponding 5-year average monthly import price for such fruit or vegetable.

(B) The planted acreage in the United States for the like fresh fruit or vegetable is no higher than the average planted acreage over the preceding 5 years, excluding the years with the highest and lowest acreage. For the purposes of applying this subparagraph, any acreage increase attributed directly to a reduction in the acreage that was planted to wine grapes as of October 4, 1987, shall be excluded.

Whenever the Secretary makes a determination that the conditions referred to in subparagraphs (A) and (B) regarding any Canadian fresh fruit or vegetable exist, the Secretary shall promptly submit for publication in the Federal Register notice of the determination.

(2) In determining whether to recommend the imposition of a temporary duty to the President under paragraph (1), the Secretary shall consider whether the conditions in subparagraphs (A) and (B) of such paragraph have led to a distortion in trade between the United States and Canada of the fresh fruit or vegetable and, if so, whether the imposition of the duty is

appropriate, including consideration of whether it would significantly correct this distortion.

(3) Not later than 7 days after receipt of a recommendation of the Secretary under paragraph (1), the President, after taking into account the national economic interests of the United States, shall determine whether to impose a temporary duty on the Canadian fresh fruit or vegetable concerned. If the determination is affirmative, the President shall proclaim the imposition and the rate of the temporary duty, but such duty shall not apply to the entry of articles that were in transit to the United States on the first day on which the temporary duty is in effect.

(4) A temporary duty imposed under paragraph (3) shall cease to apply with respect to articles that are entered on or after the earlier of—

(A) the day following the last of 5 consecutive working days with respect to which the Secretary determines that the point of shipment price in Canada for the Canadian fruit or vegetable concerned exceeds 90 percent of the corresponding 5-year average monthly import price; or

(B) the 180th day after the date on which the temporary duty first took effect.

(5) No temporary duty may be imposed under this subsection on a Canadian fresh fruit or vegetable during such time as import relief is provided with respect to such fresh fruit or vegetable under chapter 1 of title II of the Trade Act of 1974.

(6) For purposes of this subsection:

(A) The term "Canadian fresh fruit or vegetable" means any article originating in Canada (as determined in accordance with section 202) and classified within any of the following headings of the Harmonized System:

(i) 07.01 (relating to potatoes, fresh or chilled);

(ii) 07.02 (relating to tomatoes, fresh or chilled);

(iii) 07.03 (relating to onions, shallots, garlic, leeks and other alliaceous vegetables, fresh or chilled);

(iv) 07.04 (relating to cabbages, cauliflowers, kohlrabi, kale and similar edible brassicas, fresh or chilled);

(v) 07.05 (relating to lettuce (lactuca sativa) and chicory (cichorium spp.), fresh or chilled);

(vi) 07.06 (relating to carrots, salad beets or beetroot, salsify, celeriac, radishes and similar edible roots (excluding turnips), fresh or chilled);

(vii) 07.07 (relating to cucumbers and gherkins, fresh or chilled);

(viii) 07.08 (relating to leguminous vegetables, shelled or unshelled, fresh or chilled);

(ix) 07.09 (relating to other vegetables (excluding truffles), fresh or chilled);

(x) 08.06.10 (relating to grapes, fresh);

(xi) 08.08.20 (relating to pears and quinces, fresh);

(xii) 08.09 (relating to apricots, cherries, peaches (including nectarines), plums and sloes, fresh); and

(xiii) 08.10 (relating to other fruit (excluding cranberries and blueberries), fresh).

(B) The term "corresponding 5-year average monthly import price" for a particular day means the average import price of a Canadian fresh fruit or vegetable, for the calendar month in which that day occurs, for that month in each of the preceding 5 years, excluding the years with the highest and lowest monthly averages.

(C) The term "import price" has the meaning given such term in article 711 of the Agreement.

(D) The rate of a temporary duty imposed under this subsection with respect to a Canadian fresh fruit or vegetable means a rate that, including the rate of any other duty in effect for such fruit or vegetable, does not exceed the lesser of—

(i) the duty that was in effect for the fresh fruit or vegetable before January 1, 1989, under column one of the Tariff Schedules of the United States for the applicable season in which the temporary duty is applied; or

(ii) the duty in effect for the fresh fruit or vegetable under column one of such Schedules, or column 1 (General) of the Harmonized System, at the time the temporary duty is applied.

(7)(A) The Secretary shall, to the extent practicable, administer the provisions of this subsection to the 8-digit level of classification under the Harmonized System.

(B) The Secretary may issue such regulations as may be necessary to implement the provisions of this subsection.

(8) For purposes of assisting the Secretary in carrying out this subsection, the Commissioner of Customs and the Director of the Bureau of Census shall cooperate in providing the Secretary with timely information and data relating to the importation of Canadian fresh fruits and vegetables.

(9) The authority to impose temporary duties under this subsection expires on the 20th anniversary of the date on which the Agreement enters into force.

(b) MEAT IMPORT ACT OF 1979.—The Meat Import Act of 1979 (19 U.S.C. 2253 note) is amended—

(1) by inserting at the end of subsection (b)(2) the following flush sentence:

"Such term does not include any article described in subparagraph (A), (B), or (C) originating in Canada (as determined in accordance with section 202 of the United States-Canada Free-Trade Agreement Implementation Act of 1988).";

(2) by striking out "1,204,600,000" in subsection (c) and inserting "1,147,600,000";

(3) by striking out "1,250,000,000 pounds" in subsection (f)(1) and inserting "(A) 1,193,000,000 pounds if no import limitation on Canadian products is in effect under subsection (l), or (B) 1,250,000,000 pounds if an import limitation on Canadian products is in effect under subsection (l)";

(4) by inserting "other than Canada" after "countries" each place it appears in subsection (i); and

(5) by amending subsection (l) to read as follows:

"(l) if the President—

"(1) has—

"(A) proclaimed limitations on meat articles under the preceding provisions of this section, or

"(B) entered into one or more agreements other than with Canada regarding meat articles pursuant to section 204 of the Agricultural Act of 1956; and

"(2) determines that the Government of Canada has not taken equivalent action;

the President may by proclamation limit the total quantities of articles described in subsection (b)(2) (A), (B), and (C) and originating in Canada (as determined in accordance with section 202 of the United States-Canada Free-Trade Agreement Implementation Act of 1988) that may enter the United States. A limitation imposed under the preceding sentence shall be only to the extent that, and only for such period of time as, the President determines sufficient to prevent frustration of the limitations placed on meat articles imported from other countries under this section or actions taken with respect to meat articles under agreements negotiated pursuant to section 204 of the Agricultural Act of 1956.".

(c) AGRICULTURAL ADJUSTMENT ACT.—Section 22(f) of the Agricultural Adjustment Act, as reenacted with amendments by the Agricultural Marketing Agreement Act of 1937 (7 U.S.C. 624(f)), is amended by inserting immediately after "section" the following: "; except that the President may, pursuant to articles 705.5 and 707 of the United States-Canada Free-Trade Agreement, exempt products of Canada from any import restriction imposed under this section".

(d) IMPORTATION OF ANIMAL VACCINES.—The second sentence of the eighth paragraph of the matter under the heading "BUREAU OF ANIMAL INDUSTRY" of the Act of March 4, 1913 (37 Stat. 832, chapter 145; 21 U.S.C. 152) is amended to read as follows: "The importation into the United States of any virus, serum, toxin, or analogous product for use in the treatment of domestic animals, and the importation of any worthless, contaminated, dangerous, or harmful virus, serum, toxin, or analogous product for use in the treatment of domestic animals, is prohibited without (1) a permit from the Secretary of Agriculture, or (2) in the case of an article originating in Canada, such permit or, in lieu of such permit, such certification by Canada as may be prescribed by the Secretary of Agriculture.".

(e) IMPORTATION OF SEEDS.—Subsection (e) of section 302 of the Federal Seed Act (7 U.S.C. 1582(e)) is amended to read as follows:

"(e) The provisions of this title requiring certain seeds to be stained shall not apply—

"(1) to alfalfa or clover seed originating in Canada, or

"(2) when seeds otherwise required to be stained will not be sold within the United States and will be used for seed production only by or for the importer or consignee and the importer of record or consignee files a statement in accordance with the rules and regulations prescribed under section 402 certifying that such seeds will be used only for seed production by or for the importer or consignee.".

(f) PLANT AND ANIMAL HEALTH REGULATIONS.—

(1) Section 103 of the Federal Plant Pest Act (7 U.S.C. 150bb) is amended—

(A) in subsection (a), by striking out "No" and inserting in lieu thereof "Except as provided in subsection (c), no"; and

(B) by adding at the end thereof the following new subsection:

"(c) No person shall move any plant pest from Canada into or through the United States or accept delivery of any plant pest moving from Canada into or through the United States, unless such movement is made in accordance with such regulations as the Secretary may promulgate under this section to prevent the dissemination into the United States of plant pests.".

(2) Section 104 of the Federal Plant Pest Act (7 U.S.C. 150cc) is amended—

(A) in subsection (a), by striking out "Any letter" and inserting in lieu thereof "Except as provided in subsection (b), any letter";

(B) by redesignating subsections (b) and (c) as subsections (c) and (d), respectively, and

(C) by inserting after subsection (a) the following new subsection:

"(b) Any letter, parcel, box, or other package from Canada containing any plant pest, whether sealed as letter-rate postal matter or not, is declared to be nonmailable, and shall not knowingly be conveyed in the mail or delivered from any post office or by any mail carrier, except in accordance with such regulations as the Secretary may promulgate under this section to prevent the dissemination into the United States of plant pests.".

(3) The Act of August 20, 1912 (37 Stat. 315, chapter 308; 7 U.S.C. 154 et seq.) is amended—

(A) in the first section (7 U.S.C. 154), by striking out "*Provided*" the first place it appears and inserting in lieu thereof "*Provided*, That the Secretary of Agriculture may waive the permit requirement for nursery stock imported or offered for entry from Canada: *Provided further*"; and

(B) by adding at the end of section 2 (7 U.S.C. 156) the following new sentence: "This section shall not apply to nursery stock that arrives from, or is imported from, Canada.".

(4) Subsection (a) of section 4 of the Federal Noxious Weed Act of 1974 (7 U.S.C. 2803(a)) is amended to read as follows:

"(a) No person shall knowingly move any noxious weed identified in a regulation promulgated by the Secretary into or through the United States or interstate, unless such movement is—

"(1) from Canada, or authorized under general or specific permit from the Secretary; and

"(2) made in accordance with such conditions as the Secretary may prescribe in the permit and in such regulations as the Secretary may prescribe under this Act to prevent the dissemination into the United States, or interstate, of such noxious weeds.".

(5) Section 306 of the Tariff Act of 1930 (19 U.S.C. 1306) is amended by inserting after subsection (a) the following new subsection:

"(b) Notwithstanding subsection (a), the Secretary of Agriculture may permit, subject to such terms and conditions as the Secretary of Agriculture determines appropriate, the importation of cattle, sheep, or other ruminants, or swine (including embryos of such animals) or the fresh, chilled, or frozen meat of such animals from a region of Canada notwithstanding the existence of rinderpest or foot-and-mouth disease in Canada, if—

"(1) the United States and Canada have entered into an agreement delineating the criteria for recognizing that a geographical region of either country is free from rinderpest or foot-and-mouth disease; and

"(2) the appropriate official of the government of Canada certifies that the region of Canada from which the animal or meat originated is free from rinderpest and foot-and-mouth disease.".

SEC. 302. RELIEF FROM IMPORTS.

(a) Relief From Imports of Canadian Articles.—

(1) A petition requesting action under this section for the purpose of adjusting to the obligations of the United States under the Agreement may be filed with the United States International Trade Commission (hereafter in this section referred to as the "Commission") by an entity, including a trade association, firm, certified or recognized union, or group of workers, which is representative of an industry. The Commission shall transmit a copy of any petition filed under this paragraph to the United States Trade Representative.

(2)(A) Upon the filing of a petition under paragraph (1), the Commission shall promptly initiate an investigation to determine whether, as a result of a reduction or elimination of a duty provided for under the United States-Canada Free-Trade Agreement, an article originating in Canada is being imported into the United States in such increased quantities, in absolute terms, and under such conditions, so that imports of such Canadian article, alone, constitute a substantial cause of serious injury to the domestic industry producing an article like, or directly competitive with, the imported article.

(B) The provisions of—

(i) paragraphs (2), (3), (4), (6), and (7) of subsection (b), other than paragraph (2)(B), and

(ii) subsection (c),

of section 201 of the Trade Act of 1974 (19 U.S.C. 2251), as in effect on June 1, 1988, shall apply with respect to any investigation initiated under subparagraph (A).

(C) By no later than the date that is 120 days after the date on which an investigation is initiated under subparagraph (A), the Commission shall make a determination under subparagraph (A) with respect to such investigation.

(D) If the determination made by the Commission under subparagraph (A) with respect to imports of an article is affirmative, the Commission shall find and recommend to the President the amount of import relief that is necessary to remedy the injury found by the Commission in such affirmative determination, which shall be limited to that set forth in paragraph (3)(C).

(E)(i) By no later than the date that is 30 days after the date on which a determination is made under subparagraph (A) with respect to an investigation, the Commission shall submit to the President a report on the determination and the basis for the determination. The report shall include any dissenting or separate views and a transcript of the hearings and any briefs which were submitted to the Commission in the course of the investigation initiated under subparagraph (A).

(ii) Any finding made under subparagraph (D) shall be included in the report submitted to the President under clause (i).

(F) Upon submitting a report to the President under subparagraph (E), the Commission shall promptly make public such report (with the exception of information which the Commission determines to be confidential) and shall cause a summary thereof to be published in the Federal Register.

(G) For purposes of this subsection—

(i) The provisions of paragraphs (1), (2), and (3) of section 330(d) of the Tariff Act of 1930 (19 U.S.C. 1330(d)) shall be applied with respect to determinations and findings made under this paragraph as if such determinations and findings were made under section 201 of the Trade Act of 1974 (19 U.S.C. 2251).

(ii) The determination of whether an article originates in Canada shall be made in accordance with section 202 (including any proclamations issued under section 202).

(3)(A) By no later than the date that is 30 days after the date on which the President receives the report of the Commission containing an affirmative determination made by the Commission under paragraph (2)(A), the President shall provide relief from imports of the article originating in Canada that is the subject of such determination to the extent that, and for such time (not to exceed 3 years) as the President determines to be necessary to remedy the injury found by the Commission.

(B) The President is not required to provide import relief by reason of this paragraph if the President determines that the provision of such import relief is not in the national economic interest.

(C) The import relief that the President is authorized to provide by reason of this paragraph with respect to an article originating in Canada is limited to—

(i) the suspension of any further reductions provided for under the Agreement in the duty imposed on such article originating in Canada,

(ii) an increase in the rate of duty imposed on such article originating in Canada to a level that does not exceed the lesser of—

(I) the most-favored-nation rate of duty that is imposed by the United States on such article from any other foreign country at the time such import relief is provided, or

(II) the most-favored-nation rate of duty that is imposed by the United States on such article from any other foreign country on the day before the date on which the Agreement enters into force, or

(iii) in the case of a duty applied on a seasonal basis to such article originating in Canada, an increase in the rate of duty imposed on such article originating in Canada to a level that does not exceed the most-favored-nation rate of duty imposed by the United States on such article originating in Canada for the corresponding season immediately prior to the date on which the Agreement enters into force.

(4)(A) No investigation may be initiated under paragraph (2)(A) with respect to any article for which import relief has been provided under this subsection.

(B) No import relief may be provided under this subsection after the date that is 10 years after the date on which the Agreement enters into force.

(5) For purposes of section 123 of the Trade Act of 1974 (19 U.S.C. 2133), any import relief provided by the President under

(1) The objectives of the United States in negotiations conducted under subsection (a)(1)(A) to liberalize trade in services include—

(A) with respect to developing services sectors not covered in the Agreement, the elimination of those tariff, nontariff, and subsidy trade distortions that have potential to affect significant bilateral trade;

(B) the elimination or reduction of measures grandfathered by the Agreement that deny or restrict national treatment in the provision of services;

(C) the elimination of local presence requirements; and

(D) the liberalization of government procurement of services.

In conducting such negotiations, the President shall consult with the services advisory committees established under section 135 of the Trade Act of 1974 (19 U.S.C. 2155).

(2) The objectives of the United States in any negotiations conducted under subsection (a)(1)(B) to liberalize investment rules include—

(A) the elimination of direct investment screening;

(B) the extension of the principles of the Agreement to energy and cultural industries, to the extent such industries are not currently covered by the Agreement;

(C) the elimination of technology transfer requirements and other performance requirements not currently barred by the Agreement; and

(D) the subjection of all investment disputes to dispute resolution under chapter 18 of the Agreement.

In conducting such negotiations, the President shall consult with persons representing diverse interests in the United States in investment.

(3) The objectives of the United States in any negotiations conducted under subsection (a)(1)(C) to improve the protection of intellectual property rights include—

(A) the recognition and adequate protection of intellectual property, including copyrights, patents, process patents, trademarks, mask works, and trade secrets; and

(B) the establishment of dispute resolution procedures and binational enforcement of intellectual property standards.

In conducting such negotiations, the President shall consult with persons representing diverse interests in the United States in intellectual property.

(c) Negotiating Objectives Regarding Automotive Products.—

(1) In conducting negotiations under subsection (a)(1)(D) regarding the value requirement for automotive products, the President shall seek to conclude an agreement by no later than January 1, 1990, to increase the value requirement from 50 percent to at least 60 percent.

(2) The President is authorized, through January 1, 1999, to proclaim any agreed increase in the value requirement.

(3) As used in this section, the term "value requirement" means the minimum percentage of the value of an automotive product that must be accounted for by the value of the materials in the product that originated in the United States or Canada, or both, plus the direct cost of processing or assembly

paragraph (3) shall be treated as action taken under chapter I of title II of such Act.

(b) RELIEF FROM IMPORTS FROM ALL COUNTRIES.—

(1)(A) If, in any investigation initiated under chapter 1 of title II of the Trade Act of 1974, the Commission makes an affirmative determination (or a determination which is treated as an affirmative determination under such chapter by reason of section 330(d) of the Tariff Act of 1930) that an article is being imported into the United States in such increased quantities as to be a substantial cause of serious injury, or the threat thereof, to the domestic industry, the Commission shall also find (and report to the President at the time such injury determination is submitted to the President), whether imports from Canada of the article that is the subject of such investigation are substantial and are contributing importantly to such injury or threat thereof.

(B)(i) In determining under subparagraph (A) whether imports of an article from Canada are substantial, the Commission shall not normally consider imports from Canada in the range of 5 to 10 percent or less of total imports of such article to be substantial.

(ii) For purposes of this paragraph, the term "contributing importantly" means an important cause, but not necessarily the most important cause, of the serious injury or threat thereof caused by imports.

(2)(A) In determining whether to take action under chapter 1 of title II of the Trade Act of 1974 with respect to imports from Canada, the President shall determine whether imports from Canada of such article are substantial and contributing importantly to the serious injury or threat of serious injury found by the Commission.

(B) In determining the nature and extent of action to be taken under chapter 1 of title II of the Trade Act of 1974, the President shall exclude from such action imports from Canada if the President has made a negative determination under subparagraph (A) regarding imports from Canada.

(3)(A) If, under paragraph (2)(B), the President excludes imports from Canada from action taken under chapter 1 of title II of the Trade Act of 1974, the President may, if the President thereafter determines that a surge in imports from Canada of the article that is the subject of the action is undermining the effectiveness of the action, take appropriate action under such chapter with respect to such imports from Canada to include such imports in such action.

(B)(i) If, under paragraph (2)(B), the President excludes imports from Canada from action taken under chapter 1 of title II of the Trade Act of 1974, any entity, including a trade association, firm, certified or recognized union, or group of workers, that is representative of an industry for which such action is being taken under such chapter may request the Commission to conduct an investigation of imports from Canada of the article that is the subject of such action.

(ii) Upon receiving a request under clause (i), the Commission shall conduct an investigation to determine whether a surge in imports from Canada of the article that is the subject of action being taken under chapter 1 of title II of the Trade Act of 1974 undermines the effectiveness of such action. The Commission shall submit the findings of such investigation to the President by no later than the date that is 30 days after the date on which such request is received by the Commission.

(C) For purposes of this paragraph, the term "surge" means a significant increase in imports over the trend for a reasonable, recent base period for which data are available.

(c) Any entity that is representative of an industry may submit a petition for relief under subsection (a), under chapter 1 of title II of the Trade Act of 1974, or under both subsection (a) and such chapter at the same time. If petitions are submitted by such an entity under subsection (a) and such chapter at the same time, the Commission shall consider such petitions jointly.

SEC. 303. ACTS IDENTIFIED IN NATIONAL TRADE ESTIMATES.

With respect to any act, policy, or practice of Canada that is identified in the annual report submitted under section 181 of the Trade Act of 1974 (19 U.S.C. 2241), the United States Trade Representative shall include—

(1) information with respect to the action taken regarding such act, policy, or practice, including but not limited to—

(A) any action under section 301 of the Trade Act of 1974 (including resolution through appropriate dispute settlement procedures),

(B) any action under section 307 of the Trade and Tariff Act of 1984, and

(C) negotiations or consultations, whether on a bilateral or multilateral basis; or

(2) the reasons that no action was taken regarding such act, policy, or practice.

SEC. 304. NEGOTIATIONS REGARDING CERTAIN SECTORS; BIENNIAL REPORTS.

(a) In General.—

(1) The President is authorized to enter into negotiations with the Government of Canada for the purpose of concluding an agreement (including an agreement amending the Agreement) or agreements to—

(A) liberalize trade in services in accordance with article 1405 of the Agreement;

(B) liberalize investment rules;

(C) improve the protection of intellectual property rights;

(D) increase the value requirement applied for purposes of determining whether an automotive product is treated as originating in Canada or the United States; and

(E) liberalize government procurement practices, particularly with regard to telecommunications.

(2) As an exercise of the foreign relations powers of the President under the Constitution, the President will enter into immediate consultations with the Government of Canada to obtain the exclusion from the transport rates established under Canada's Western Grain Transportation Act of agricultural goods that originate in Canada and are shipped via east coast ports for consumption in the United States.

(b) Negotiating Objectives Regarding Services, Investment, and Intellectual Property Rights.—

performed in the United States or Canada, or both, with respect to the product.

(d) NEGOTIATION OF LIMITATION ON POTATO TRADE.—

(1) During the 5-year period beginning on the date of enactment of this Act, the President is authorized to enter into negotiations with Canada for the purpose of obtaining an agreement to limit the exportation and importation of all potatoes between the United States and Canada, including seed potatoes, fresh, chilled or frozen potatoes, dried, desiccated or dehydrated potatoes, and potatoes otherwise prepared or preserved. Any agreement negotiated under this subsection shall provide for an annual limitation divided equally into each half of the year.

(2) For the purpose of conducting negotiations under paragraph (1), the Secretary of Agriculture and the United States Trade Representative shall consult with representatives of the potato producing industry, including the Ad Hoc Potato Advisory Group and the United States/Canada Horticultural Industry Advisory Committee, to solicit their views on negotiations with Canada for reciprocal quantitative limits on the potato trade.

(3) The President is authorized to direct the Secretary of the Treasury to—

(A) carry out such actions as may be necessary or appropriate to ensure the attainment of the objectives of any agreement that is entered into under this section; and

(B) enforce any quantitative limitation, restriction, and other terms contained in the agreement.

Such actions may include, but are not limited to, requirements that valid export licenses or other documentation issued by a foreign government be presented as a condition for the entry into the United States of any article that is subject to the agreement.

(4) The provisions of section 1204 of the Agriculture and Food Act of 1981 (7 U.S.C. 1736j) and the last sentence of section 812 of the Agricultural Act of 1970 (7 U.S.C. 612c-3) shall not apply in the case of actions taken pursuant to this subsection.

(e) CANADIAN CONTROLS ON FISH.—

(1) Within 30 days of the application by Canada of export controls on unprocessed fish under statutes exempted from the Agreement under article 1203, or the application of landing requirements for fish caught in Canadian waters, the President shall take appropriate action to enforce United States rights under the General Agreement on Tariffs and Trade that are retained in article 1205 of the Agreement.

(2) In enforcing the United States rights referred to in paragraph (1), the President has discretion to—

(A) bring a challenge to the offending Canadian practices before the GATT;

(B) retaliate against such offending practices;

(C) seek resolution directly with Canada;

(D) refer the matter for dispute resolution to the Canada-United States Trade Commission; or

(E) take other action that the President considers appropriate to enforce such United States rights.

(f) BIENNIAL REPORT.—The President shall submit to the Congress, at the close of each biennial period occurring after the date on which the Agreement enters into force, a report regarding—

(1) the status of the negotiations regarding agreements that the President is authorized to enter into with Canada under this section;

(2) the effectiveness and operation of any agreement entered into under section 304 that is in force with respect to the United States;

(3) the effectiveness of operation of the Agreement generally; and

(4) the actions taken by the United States and Canada to implement further the objectives of the Agreement.

SEC. 305. ENERGY.

(a) ALASKAN OIL.—Section 7(d)(1) of the Export Administration Act of 1979 (50 U.S.C. App. 2406(d)(1)) is amended—

(1) by striking "or" before "(B)"; and

(2) by inserting after "reenters the United States" the following: ", or (C) is transported to Canada, to be consumed therein, in amounts not to exceed an annual average of 50,000 barrels per day, in addition to exports under subparagraphs (A) and (B), except that any ocean transportation of such oil shall be by vessels documented under section 12106 of title 46, United States Code".

(b) URANIUM.—Section 161(v) of the Atomic Energy Act of 1954 (42 U.S.C. 2201(v)) is amended by inserting "For purposes of this subsection and of section 305 of Public Law 99-591 (100 Stat. 3341-209, 210), 'foreign origin' excludes source or special nuclear material originating in Canada." before "The Commission shall establish".

SEC. 306. LOWERED THRESHOLD FOR GOVERNMENT PROCUREMENT UNDER TRADE AGREEMENTS ACT OF 1979 IN THE CASE OF CERTAIN CANADIAN PRODUCTS.

Section 308(4) of the Trade Agreements Act of 1979 (19 U.S.C. 2518(4)) is amended by inserting after subparagraph (C) the following new subparagraph:

"(D) LOWERED THRESHOLD FOR CERTAIN PRODUCTS AS A CONSEQUENCE OF UNITED STATES-CANADA FREE-TRADE AGREEMENT.—Except as otherwise agreed by the United States and Canada under paragraph 3 of article 1304 of the United States-Canada Free-Trade Agreement, the term 'eligible product' includes a product or service of Canada having a contract value of $25,000 or more that would be covered for procurement by the United States under the GATT Agreement on Government Procurement, but for the SDR threshold provided for in article I(1)(b) of the GATT Agreement on Government Procurement.".

SEC. 307. TEMPORARY ENTRY FOR BUSINESS PERSONS.

(a) NONIMMIGRANT TRADERS AND INVESTORS.—Upon a basis of reciprocity secured by the United States-Canada Free-Trade Agreement, a citizen of Canada, and the spouse and children of any such citizen if accompanying or following to join such citizen, may, if otherwise eligible for a visa and if otherwise admissible into the United States under the Immigration and Nationality Act (8 U.S.C. 1101 et seq.), be considered to be classifiable as a nonimmigrant under section 101(a)(15)(E) of such Act (8 U.S.C. 1101(a)(15)(E)) if entering solely for a purpose specified in Annex 1502.1 (United States of America), Part B—Traders and Investors, of such Agreement, but only if any such purpose shall have been specified in such Annex as of the date of entry into force of such Agreement.

(b) NONIMMIGRANT PROFESSIONALS.—Section 214 of the Immigration and Nationality Act (8 U.S.C. 1184) is amended by adding at the end thereof the following new subsection:

"(e) Notwithstanding any other provision of this Act, an alien who is a citizen of Canada and seeks to enter the United States under and pursuant to the provisions of Annex 1502.1 (United States of America), Part C—Professionals, of the United States-Canada Free-Trade Agreement to engage in business activities at a professional level as provided for therein may be admitted for such purpose under regulations of the Attorney General promulgated after consultation with the Secretaries of State and Labor.".

SEC. 308. AMENDMENT TO SECTION 5136 OF THE REVISED STATUTES.

Paragraph "Seventh" of section 5136 of the Revised Statutes (12 U.S.C. 24 (Seventh)) is amended by adding at the end thereof the following:

"A national banking association may deal in, underwrite, and purchase for such association's own account qualified Canadian government obligations to the same extent that such association may deal in, underwrite, and purchase for such association's own account obligations of the United States or general obligations of any State or of any political subdivision thereof. For purposes of this paragraph—

"(1) the term 'qualified Canadian government obligations' means any debt obligation which is backed by Canada, any Province of Canada, or any political subdivision of any such Province to a degree which is comparable to the liability of the United States, any State, or any political subdivision thereof for any obligation which is backed by the full faith and credit of the United States, such State, or such political subdivision, and such term includes any debt obligation of any agent of Canada or any such Province or any political subdivision of such Province if—

"(A) the obligation of the agent is assumed in such agent's capacity as agent for Canada or such Province or such political subdivision; and

"(B) Canada, such Province, or such political subdivision on whose behalf such agent is acting with respect to such obligation is ultimately and unconditionally liable for such obligation; and

"(2) the term 'Province of Canada' means a Province of Canada and includes the Yukon Territory and the Northwest Territories and their successors.".

SEC. 309. STEEL PRODUCTS.

Nothing in this Act shall preclude any discussion or negotiation between the United States and Canada in order to conclude voluntary restraint agreements or mutually agreed quantitative restrictions on the volume of steel products entering the United States from Canada.

TITLE IV—BINATIONAL PANEL DISPUTE SETTLEMENT IN ANTIDUMPING AND COUNTERVAILING DUTY CASES.

SEC. 401. AMENDMENTS TO SECTION 516A OF THE TARIFF ACT OF 1930.

(a) TIME LIMITS.—Section 516A(a) of the Tariff Act of 1930 (19 U.S.C. 1516a(a)) is amended by adding at the end thereof the following new paragraph.

"(5) TIME LIMITS IN CASES INVOLVING CANADIAN MERCHANDISE.—Notwithstanding any other provision of this subsection, in the case of a determination to which the provisions of subsection (g) apply, an action under this subsection may not be commenced, and the time limits for commencing an action under this subsection shall not begin to run, until the 31st day after—

"(A) the date of publication in the Federal Register of—

"(i) notice of any determination described in paragraph (1)(B) or a determination described in clause (ii) or (iii) of paragraph (2)(B), or

"(ii) an antidumping or countervailing duty order based upon any determination described in clause (i) of paragraph (2)(B), or

"(B) the date on which the Government of Canada receives notice of a determination described in clause (vi) of paragraph (2)(B).".

(b) DEFINITIONS.—Section 516A(f) of the Tariff Act of 1930 (19 U.S.C. 1516a(f)) is amended by adding at the end thereof the following new paragraphs:

"(5) AGREEMENT.—The term 'Agreement' means the United States-Canada Free-Trade Agreement.

"(6) UNITED STATES SECRETARY.—The term 'United States Secretary' means the secretary provided for in paragraph 4 of article 1909 of the Agreement.

"(7) CANADIAN SECRETARY.—The term 'Canadian Secretary' means the secretary provided for in paragraph 5 of article 1909 of the Agreement.".

(c) REVIEW REGARDING CANADIAN MERCHANDISE.—Section 516A of the Tariff Act of 1930 (19 U.S.C. 1516a) is amended by adding at the end thereof the following new subsection:

"(g) REVIEW OF COUNTERVAILING DUTY AND ANTIDUMPING DUTY DETERMINATIONS INVOLVING CANADIAN MERCHANDISE.—

"(1) DEFINITION OF DETERMINATION.—For purposes of this subsection, the term 'determination' means a determination described in—

"(A) paragraph (1)(B) of subsection (a), or

"(B) clause (i), (ii), (iii), or (vi) of paragraph (2)(B) of subsection (a),

if made in connection with a proceeding regarding a class or kind of Canadian merchandise, as determined by the administering authority.

"(2) EXCLUSIVE REVIEW OF DETERMINATION BY BINATIONAL PANELS.—If binational panel review of a determination is requested pursuant to article 1904 of the Agreement, then, except as provided in paragraphs (3) and (4)—

"(A) the determination is not reviewable under subsection (a), and

"(B) no court of the United States has power or jurisdiction to review the determination on any question of law or fact by an action in the nature of mandamus or otherwise.

"(3) EXCEPTION TO EXCLUSIVE BINATIONAL PANEL REVIEW.—

"(A) IN GENERAL.—A determination is reviewable under subsection (a) if the determination sought to be reviewed is—

"(i) a determination as to which neither the United States nor Canada requested review by a binational panel pursuant to article 1904 of the Agreement,

"(ii) a revised determination issued as a direct result of judicial review, commenced pursuant to subsection (a), if neither the United States nor Canada requested review of the original determination, or

"(iii) a determination issued as a direct result of judicial review that was commenced pursuant to subsection (a) prior to the entry into force of the Agreement.

"(B) SPECIAL RULE.—A determination described in subparagraph (A)(i) is reviewable under subsection (a) only if the party seeking to commence review has provided timely notice of its intent to commence such review to the United States Secretary, the Canadian Secretary, all interested parties who were parties to the proceeding in connection with which the matter arises, and the administering authority or the Commission, as appropriate. Such notice is provided timely if the notice is delivered by no later than the date that is 20 days after the date described in subparagraph (A) or (B) of subsection (a)(5) that is applicable to such determination. Such notice shall contain such information, and be in such form, manner, and style, as the administering authority, in consultation with the Commission, shall prescribe by regulations.

"(4) EXCEPTION TO EXCLUSIVE BINATIONAL PANEL REVIEW FOR CONSTITUTIONAL ISSUES.—

"(A) CONSTITUTIONALITY OF BINATIONAL PANEL REVIEW SYSTEM.—An action for declaratory judgment or injunctive relief, or both, regarding a determination on the grounds that any provision of, or amendment made by, the United States-Canada Free-Trade Implementation Agreement Act of 1988 implementing the binational panel dispute settlement system under chapter 19 of the Agreement violates the Constitution may be brought in the United States Court of Appeals for the District of Columbia Circuit. Any action brought under this subparagraph shall be heard and determined by a 3-judge court in accordance with section 2284 of title 28, United States Code.

"(B) OTHER CONSTITUTIONAL REVIEW.—Review is available under subsection (a) with respect to a determination solely concerning a constitutional issue (other than an issue to which subparagraph (A) applies) arising under any law of the United States as enacted or applied. An action for review under this subparagraph shall be assigned to a 3-judge panel of the United States Court of International Trade.

"(C) COMMENCEMENT OF REVIEW.—Notwithstanding the time limits in subsection (a), within 30 days after the date of publication in the Federal Register of notice that binational panel review has been completed, an interested party who is a party to the proceeding in connection with which the matter arises may commence an action under subparagraph (A) or (B) by filing an action in accordance with the rules of the court.

"(D) TRANSFER OF ACTIONS TO APPROPRIATE COURT.—Whenever an action is filed in a court under subparagraph (A) or (B) and that court finds that the action should have been filed in the other court, the court in which the action was filed shall transfer the action to the other court and the action shall proceed as if it had been filed in the court to which it is transferred on the date upon which it was actually filed in the court from which it is transferred.

"(E) FRIVOLOUS CLAIMS.—Frivolous claims brought under subparagraph (A) or (B) are subject to dismissal and sanctions as provided under section 1927 of title 28, United States Code, and the Federal Rules of Civil Procedure.

"(F) SECURITY.—

"(i) SUBPARAGRAPH (A) ACTIONS.—The security requirements of rule 65(c) of the Federal Rules of Civil Procedure apply with respect to actions commenced under subparagraph (A).

"(ii) SUBPARAGRAPH (B) ACTIONS.—No claim shall be heard, and no temporary restraining order or temporary or permanent injunction shall be issued, under an action commenced under subparagraph (B), unless the party seeking review first files an undertaking with adequate security in an amount to be fixed by the court sufficient to recompense parties affected for any loss, expense, or damage caused by the improvident or erroneous issuance of such order or injunction. If a court upholds the constitutionality of the determination in question in such action, the court shall award to a prevailing party fees and expenses, in addition to any costs incurred by that party, unless the court finds that the position of the other party was substantially justified or that special circumstances make an award unjust.

"(G) PANEL RECORD.—The record of proceedings before the binational panel shall not be considered part of the record for review pursuant to subparagraph (A) or (B).

"(H) APPEAL TO SUPREME COURT OF COURT ORDERS ISSUED IN SUBPARAGRAPH (A) ACTIONS.—Notwithstanding any other provision of law, any final judgment of the United States Court of Appeals for the District of Columbia Circuit which is issued pursuant to an action brought under subparagraph (A) shall be reviewable by appeal directly to the Supreme Court of the United States. Any such appeal shall be taken by a notice of appeal filed within 10 days after such order is entered; and the jurisdictional statement shall be filed within 30 days after such order is entered. No stay of an order issued pursuant to an action brought under subparagraph (A) may be issued by a single Justice of the Supreme Court.

"(5) LIQUIDATION OF ENTRIES.—

"(A) APPLICATION.—In the case of a determination for which binational panel review is requested pursuant to article 1904 of the Agreement, the rules provided in this paragraph shall apply, notwithstanding the provisions of subsection (c).

"(B) GENERAL RULE.—In the case of a determination for which binational panel review is requested pursuant to article 1904 of the Agreement, entries of merchandise covered by such determination shall be liquidated in accordance with the determination of the administering authority or the Commission, if they are entered, or withdrawn from warehouse, for consumption on or before the date of publication in the Federal Register by the administering authority of notice of a final decision of a binational panel, or of an extraordinary challenge committee, not in harmony with that determination. Such notice of a decision shall be published within 10 days of the date of the issuance of the panel or committee decision.

"(C) SUSPENSION OF LIQUIDATION.—

"(i) IN GENERAL.—Notwithstanding the provisions of subparagraph (B), in the case of a determination described in clause (iii) or (vi) of subsection (a)(2)(B) for which binational panel review is requested pursuant to article 1904 of the Agreement, the administering authority, upon request of an interested party who was a party to the proceeding in connection with which the matter arises and who is a participant in the binational panel review, shall order the continued suspension of liquidation of those entries of merchandise covered by the determination that are involved in the review pending the final disposition of the review.

"(ii) NOTICE.—At the same time as the interested party makes its request to the administering authority under clause (i), that party shall serve a copy of its request on the United States Secretary, the Canadian Secretary, and all interested parties who were parties to the proceeding in connection with which the matter arises.

"(iii) APPLICATION OF SUSPENSION.—If the interested party requesting continued suspension of liquidation under clause (i) is a foreign manufacturer, producer, or exporter, or a United States importer, the continued suspension of liquidation shall apply only to entries of merchandise manufactured, produced, exported, or imported by that particular manufacturer, producer, exporter, or importer. If the interested party requesting the continued suspension of liquidation under clause (i) is an interested party described in subparagraph (C), (D), (E), or (F) of section 771(9), the continued suspension of liquidation shall apply only to entries which could be affected by a decision of the binational panel convened under chapter 19 of the Agreement.

"(iv) JUDICIAL REVIEW.—Any action taken by the administering authority or the United States Customs Service under this subparagraph shall not be subject to judicial review, and no court of the United States shall have power or jurisdiction to review such action on any question of law or fact by an action in the nature of mandamus or otherwise.

"(6) INJUNCTIVE RELIEF.—Except for cases under paragraph (4)(B), in the case of a determination for which binational panel review is requested pursuant to article 1904 of the Agreement, the provisions of subsection (c)(2) shall not apply.

"(7) IMPLEMENTATION OF INTERNATIONAL OBLIGATIONS UNDER ARTICLE 1904.—

"(A) IN GENERAL.—If a determination is referred to a binational panel or extraordinary challenge committee under the Agreement and the panel or committee makes a decision remanding the determination to the administering authority or the Commission, the administering authority or the Commission shall, within the period specified by the panel or committee, take action not inconsistent with the decision of the panel or committee. Any action taken by the administering authority or the Commission under this paragraph shall not be subject to judicial review, and no court of the United States shall have power or jurisdiction to review such action on any question of law or fact by an action in the nature of mandamus or otherwise.

"(B) APPLICATION IF SUBPARAGRAPH (A) HELD UNCONSTITUTIONAL.—In the event that the provisions of subparagraph (A) are held unconstitutional under the provisions of subparagraphs (A) and (H) of paragraph (4), the provisions of this subparagraph shall take effect. In such event, the President is authorized on behalf of the United States to accept, as a whole, the decision of a binational panel or extraordinary challenge committee remanding the determination to the administering authority or the Commission within the period specified by the panel or committee. Upon acceptance by the President of such a decision, the administering authority or the Commission shall, within the period specified by the panel or committee, take action not inconsistent with such decision. Any action taken by the President, the administering authority, or the Commission under this subparagraph shall not be subject to judicial review, and no court of the United States shall have power or jurisdiction to review such action on any question of law or fact by an action in the nature of mandamus or otherwise.

"(8) REQUESTS FOR BINATIONAL PANEL REVIEW.—

"(A) INTFRESTED PARTY REQUESTS FOR BINATIONAL PANEL REVIEW.—An interested party who was a party to the proceeding in which a determination is made may request binational panel review of such determination by filing a request with the United States Secretary by no later than the date that is 30 days after the date described in subparagraph (A) or (B) of subsection (a)(5) that is applicable to such determination. Receipt of such request by the United States Secretary shall be deemed to be a request for binational panel review within the meaning of article 1904(4) of the Agreement. Such request shall contain such information and be in such form, manner, and style as the administering authority, in consultation with the Commission, shall prescribe by regulations.

"(B) SERVICE OF REQUEST FOR BINATIONAL PANEL REVIEW.—

"(i) SERVICE BY INTERESTED PARTY.—If a request for binational panel review of a determination is filed under subparagraph (A), the party making the request shall serve a copy, by mail or personal service, on any other interested party who was a party to the proceeding in connection with which the matter arises, and on the administering authority or the Commission, as appropriate.

"(ii) SERVICE BY UNITED STATES SECRETARY.—If an interested party to the proceeding requests binational panel review of a determination by filing a request with the Canadian Secretary, the United States Secretary shall serve a copy of the request by mail on any other interested party who was a party to the proceeding in connection with which the matter arises, and on the administering authority or the Commission, as appropriate.

"(C) LIMITATION ON REQUEST FOR BINATIONAL PANEL REVIEW.—Absent a request by an interested party under subparagraph (A), the United States may not request binational panel review under article 1904 of the Agreement of a determination.

"(9) REPRESENTATION IN PANEL PROCEEDINGS.—In the case of binational panel proceedings convened under chapter 19 of the Agreement, the administering authority and the Commission shall be represented by attorneys who are employees of the administering authority or the Commission, respectively. Interested parties who were parties to the proceeding in connection with which the matter arises shall have the right to appear and be represented by counsel before the binational panel.

"(10) NOTIFICATION OF CLASS OR KIND RULINGS.—In the case of a determination which is described in paragraph (2)(B)(vi) of subsection (a) and which is subject to the provisions of paragraph (2), the administering authority, upon request, shall inform any interested person of the date on which the Government of Canada received notice of the determination under article 1904(4) of the Agreement.".

(d) STANDARDS OF REVIEW.—Section 516A(b) of the Tariff Act of 1930 (19 U.S.C. 1516a(b)) is amended by adding a new paragraph (3) as follows:

"(3) EFFECT OF DECISIONS BY UNITED STATES-CANADA BINATIONAL PANELS.—In making a decision in any action brought under subsection (a), a court of the United States is not bound by, but may take into consideration, a final decision of a binational panel or extraordinary challenge committee convened pursuant to article 1904 of the Agreement.".

SEC. 402. AMENDMENTS TO TITLE 28, UNITED STATES CODE.

(a) JURISDICTION OF COURT OF INTERNATIONAL TRADE.—Section 1581(i) of title 28, United States Code, is amended by adding at the end thereof the following flush sentence: "This subsection shall not confer jurisdiction over an antidumping or countervailing duty determination which is reviewable either by the Court of International Trade under section 516A(a) of the Tariff Act of 1930 or by a binational panel under article 1904 of the United States-Canada

Free-Trade Agreement and section 516A(g) of the Tariff Act of 1930.".

(b) RELIEF IN COURT OF INTERNATIONAL TRADE.—Section 2643(c) of title 28, United States Code, is amended—

(1) by striking out "and (4)" in paragraph (1) and inserting in lieu thereof "(4), and (5)"; and

(2) by adding at the end thereof the following new paragraph:

"(5) In any civil action involving an antidumping or countervailing duty proceeding regarding a class or kind of Canadian merchandise, as determined by the administering authority, the Court of International Trade may not order declaratory relief.".

(c) DECLARATORY JUDGMENTS.—Subsection (a) of section 2201 of title 28, United States Code, is amended—

(1) by striking out "1954 or" and inserting in lieu thereof "1986,"; and

(2) by inserting "or in any civil action involving an antidumping or countervailing duty proceeding regarding a class or kind of Canadian merchandise, as determined by the administering authority," after "of title 11,".

(d) ACTIONS UNDER THE AGREEMENT.—

(1) Chapter 95 of title 28, United States Code, is amended by inserting after section 1583 the following new section:

"§ 1584. Civil actions under the United States-Canada Free-Trade Agreement

"The United States Court of International Trade shall have exclusive jurisdiction of any civil action which arises under section 777(d) of the Tariff Act of 1930 and is commenced by the United States to enforce administrative sanctions levied for violation of a protective order or an undertaking.".

(2) The table of contents for chapter 95 of title 28, United States Code, is amended by inserting after the item relating to section 1583 the following new item:

"1584. Civil actions under the United States-Canada Free-Trade Agreement.".

SEC. 403. CONFORMING AMENDMENTS TO THE TARIFF ACT OF 1930.

(a) Section 502(b) of the Tariff Act of 1930 (19 U.S.C. 1502(b)) is amended by striking out all after "recommending the same," and inserting in lieu thereof "a final decision of the United States Court of International Trade, or a final decision of a binational panel pursuant to article 1904 of the United States-Canada Free-Trade Agreement.".

(b) Section 514(b) of the Tariff Act of 1930 (19 U.S.C. 1514(b)) is amended by inserting ", or review by a binational panel of a determination to which section 516A(g)(2) applies is commenced pursuant to section 516A(g) and article 1904 of the United States-Canada Free-Trade Agreement" after "International Trade".

(c) Section 777 of the Tariff Act of 1930 (19 U.S.C. 1677f) is amended by adding at the end thereof the following new subsection:

"(d) DISCLOSURE OF PROPRIETARY INFORMATION UNDER PROTECTIVE ORDERS ISSUED PURSUANT TO THE UNITED STATES-CANADA AGREEMENT.—

"(1) ISSUANCE OF PROTECTIVE ORDERS.—

"(A) IN GENERAL.—If binational panel review of a determination under this title is requested pursuant to article 1904 of the United States-Canada Agreement, or an extraordinary challenge committee is convened under Annex 1904.13 of the United States-Canada Agreement, the administering authority or the Commission, as appropriate, may make available to authorized persons, under a protective order described in paragraph (2), a copy of all proprietary material (but not privileged material as defined by the rules of procedure referred to in article 1904(14) of the United States-Canada Agreement) in the administrative record made during the proceeding in question.

"(B) AUTHORIZED PERSONS.—For purposes of this subsection, the term "authorized persons" means—

"(i) the members of, and the appropriate staff of, the binational panel or the extraordinary challenge committee, as the case may be, and the Secretariat,

"(ii) counsel for parties to such panel or committee proceeding, and employees of such counsel, and

"(iii) any officer or employee of the United States Government designated by the administering authority or the Commission, as appropriate, to whom disclosure is necessary in order to implement the United States-Canada Agreement with respect to such proceeding.

"(C) REVIEW.—A decision concerning the disclosure or nondisclosure of material under protective order by the administering authority or the Commission shall not be subject to judicial review, and no court of the United States shall have power or jurisdiction to review such decision on any question of law or fact by an action in the nature of mandamus or otherwise.

"(2) CONTENTS OF PROTECTIVE ORDER.—Each protective order issued under this subsection shall be in such form and contain such requirements as the administering authority or the Commission may determine by regulation to be appropriate. The administering authority and the Commission shall ensure that regulations issued pursuant to this paragraph shall be designed to provide an opportunity for participation in the binational panel proceeding equivalent to that available for judicial review of determinations by the administering authority or the Commission that are not subject to review by a binational panel.

"(3) PROHIBITED ACTS.—It is unlawful for any person to violate, or to induce the violation of, any provision of a protective order issued under this subsection or to violate, or to induce the violation of, any provision of an undertaking entered into with an authorized agency of Canada to protect proprietary material during binational panel review pursuant to article 1904 of the United States-Canada Agreement.

"(4) SANCTIONS FOR VIOLATION OF PROTECTIVE ORDERS.—Any person who is found by the administering authority or the Commission, as appropriate, after notice and an opportunity for a hearing in accordance with section 554 of title 5, United States Code, to have committed an act prohibited by paragraph (3) shall be liable to the United States for a civil penalty and shall be subject to such other administrative sanctions, including, but not limited to, debarment from practice before the administering authority or the Commission, as the administering authority or the Commission determines to be appropriate. The amount of the civil penalty shall not exceed $100,000 for each violation. Each day of a continuing violation shall constitute a separate violation. The amount of such civil penalty and other sanctions shall be assessed by the administering authority or the Commission by written notice, except that assessment shall be made by the administering authority for violation, or inducement of a violation, of an undertaking entered into by any person with an authorized agency of Canada.

"(5) REVIEW OF SANCTIONS.—Any person against whom sanctions are imposed under paragraph (4) may obtain review of such sanctions by filing a notice of appeal in the United States Court of International Trade within 30 days from the date of the order imposing the sanction and by simultaneously sending a copy of such notice by certified mail to the administering authority or the Commission, as appropriate. The administering authority or the Commission shall promptly file in such court a certified copy of the record upon which such violation was found or such sanction imposed, as provided in section 2112 of title 28, United States Code. The findings and order of the administering authority or the Commission shall be set aside by the court only if the court finds that such findings and order are not supported by substantial evidence, as provided in section 706(2) of title 5, United States Code.

"(6) ENFORCEMENT OF SANCTIONS.—If any person fails to pay an assessment of a civil penalty or to comply with other administrative sanctions after the order imposing such sanctions becomes a final and unappealable order, or after the United States Court of International Trade has entered final judgment in favor of the administering authority or the Commission, an action may be filed in such court to enforce the sanctions. In such action, the validity and appropriateness of the final order imposing the sanctions shall not be subject to review.

"(7) TESTIMONY AND PRODUCTION OF PAPERS.—

"(A) AUTHORITY TO OBTAIN INFORMATION.—For the purpose of conducting any hearing and carrying out other functions and duties under this subsection, the administering authority and the Commission, or their duly authorized agents—

"(i) shall have access to and the right to copy any pertinent document, paper, or record in the possession of any individual, partnership, corporation, association, organization, or other entity,

"(ii) may summon witnesses, take testimony, and administer oaths,

"(iii) and may require any individual or entity to produce pertinent documents, books, or records.

Any member of the Commission, and any person so designated by the administering authority, may sign subpoenas, and members and agents of the administering authority and the Commission, when authorized by the administering authority or the Commission, as appropriate, may administer oaths and affirmations, examine witnesses, take testimony, and receive evidence.

"(B) WITNESSES AND EVIDENCE.—The attendance of witnesses who are authorized to be summoned, and the production of documentary evidence authorized to be ordered, under subparagraph (A) may be required from any place in the United States at any designated place of hearing. In the case of disobedience to a subpoena issued under subparagraph (A), an action may be filed in any district or territorial court of the United States to require the attendance and testimony of witnesses and the production of documentary evidence. Such court, within the jurisdiction of which such inquiry is carried on, may, in case of contumacy or refusal to obey a subpoena issued to any individual, partnership, corporation, association, organization or other entity, issue any order requiring such individual or entity to appear before the administering authority or the Commission, or to produce documentary evidence if so ordered or to give evidence concerning the matter in question. Any failure to obey such order of the court may be punished by the court as a contempt thereof.

"(C) MANDAMUS.—Any court referred to in subparagraph (B) shall have jurisdiction to issue writs of mandamus commanding compliance with the provisions of this subsection or any order of the administering authority or the Commission made in pursuance thereof.

"(D) DEPOSITIONS.—For purposes of carrying out any functions or duties under this subsection, the administering authority or the Commission may order testimony to be taken by deposition. Such deposition may be taken before any person designated by the administering authority or Commission and having power to administer oaths. Such testimony shall be reduced to writing by the person taking the deposition, or under the direction of such person, and shall then be subscribed by the deponent. Any individual, partnership, corporation, association, organization or other entity may be compelled to appear and depose and to produce documentary evidence in the same manner as witnesses may be compelled to appear and testify and produce documentary evidence before the administering authority or Commission, as provided in this paragraph.

"(E) FEES AND MILEAGE OF WITNESSES.—Witnesses summoned before the administering authority or the Commission shall be paid the same fees and mileage that are paid witnesses in the courts of the United States.".

(d) Section 771 of the Tariff Act of 1930 (19 U.S.C. 1677) is amended by adding at the end thereof the following new paragraph (18):

"(18) UNITED STATES-CANADA AGREEMENT.—The term 'United States-Canada Agreement' means the United States-Canada Free-Trade Agreement.".

SEC. 404. AMENDMENTS TO ANTIDUMPING AND COUNTERVAILING DUTY LAW.

Any amendment enacted after the Agreement enters into force with respect to the United States that is made to—

(1) section 303 or title VII of the Tariff Act of 1930, or any successor statute, or

(2) any other statute which—

(A) provides for judicial review of final determinations under such section, title, or statute, or

(B) indicates the standard of review to be applied,

shall apply to Canada only to the extent specified in such amendment.

SEC. 405. ORGANIZATIONAL AND ADMINISTRATIVE PROVISIONS REGARDING THE IMPLEMENTATION OF CHAPTERS 18 AND 19 OF THE AGREEMENT.

(a) APPOINTMENT OF INDIVIDUALS TO PANELS AND COMMITTEES.—

(1)(A) There is established within the interagency organization established under section 242 of the Trade Expansion Act of 1962 (19 U.S.C. 1872) an interagency group which shall—

(i) be chaired by the United States Trade Representative (hereafter in this section referred to as the "Trade Representative"), and

(ii) consist of such officers (or the designees thereof) of the Government of the United States as the Trade Representative considers appropriate.

(B) The interagency group established under subparagraph (A) shall, in a manner consistent with chapter 19 of the Agreement—

(i) prepare by January 3 of each calendar year—

(I) a list of individuals who are qualified to serve as members of binational panels convened under chapter 19 of the Agreement, and

(II) a list of individuals who are qualified to serve on extraordinary challenge committees convened under such chapter,

(ii) if the Trade Representative makes a request under paragraph (5)(A)(i) with respect to a final candidate list during any calendar year, prepare by July 1 of such calendar year a list of those individuals who are qualified to be added to that final candidate list,

(iii) exercise oversight of the administration of the United States Secretariat that is authorized to be established under subsection (e), and

(iv) make recommendations to the Trade Representative regarding the convening of extraordinary challenge committees under chapter 19 of the Agreement.

(2)(A) The Trade Representative shall select individuals from the respective lists prepared by the interagency group under paragraph (1)(B)(i) for placement on a preliminary candidate list of individuals eligible to serve as members of binational panels under Annex 1901.2 of the Agreement and a preliminary candidate list of individuals eligible for selection as members of extraordinary challenge committees under Annex 1904.13 of the Agreement.

(B) The selection of individuals for—

(i) placement on lists prepared by the interagency group under clause (i) or (ii) of paragraph (1)(B),

(ii) placement on preliminary candidate lists under subparagraph (A),

(iii) placement on final candidate lists under paragraph (3),

(iv) placement by the Trade Representative on the rosters described in Annex 1901.2(1) and Annex 1904.13(1) of the Agreement, and

(v) appointment by the Trade Representative for service on binational panels and extraordinary challenge committees convened under chapter 19 of the Agreement,

shall be made on the basis of the criteria provided in Annex 1901.2(1) and Annex 1904.13(1) of the Agreement and shall be made without regard to political affiliation.

(C) For purposes of applying section 1001 of title 18, United States Code, the written or oral responses of individuals to inquiries of the interagency group established under paragraph (1) or the Trade Representative regarding their personal and professional qualifications, and financial and other relevant interests, that bear on their suitability for the placements and appointments described in subparagraph (B), shall be treated as matters within the jurisdiction of an agency of the United States.

(3)(A) By no later than January 3 of each calendar year, the Trade Representative shall submit to the Committee on Finance of the Senate and the Committee on Ways and Means of the House of Representatives (hereafter in this section referred to as the "appropriate Congressional Committees") the preliminary candidate lists of those individuals selected by the Trade Representative under paragraph (2)(A) to be candidates eligible to serve on binational panels or extraordinary challenge committees convened pursuant to chapter 19 of the Agreement during the 1-year period beginning on April 1 of such calendar year.

(B) Upon submission of the preliminary candidate lists under subparagraph (A) to the appropriate Congressional Committees, the Trade Representative shall consult with the appropriate Congressional Committees with regard to the individuals listed on the preliminary candidate lists.

(C) The Trade Representative may add or delete individuals from the preliminary candidate lists submitted under subparagraph (A) after consulting the appropriate Congressional Committees with regard to such addition or deletion. The Trade Representative shall provide to the appropriate Congressional Committees written notice of any addition or deletion of an individual from the preliminary candidate lists.

(4)(A) By no later than March 31 of each calendar year, the Trade Representative shall submit to the appropriate Congressional Committees the final candidate lists of those individuals selected by the Trade Representative to be candidates eligible to serve on binational panels and extraordinary challenge committees convened pursuant to chapter 19 of the Agreement during the 1-year period beginning on April 1 of such calendar year. An individual may be included on a final candidate list only if written notice of the addition of such individual to the preliminary candidate list was submitted to the appropriate Congressional Committees at least 15 days before the date on which that final candidate list is submitted to the appropriate Congressional Committees under this subparagraph.

(B) Except as provided in paragraph (5), no additions may be made to the final candidate lists after the final candidate lists are submitted to the appropriate Congressional Committees under subparagraph (A).

(5)(A) If, after the Trade Representative has submitted the final candidate lists to the appropriate Congressional Committees under paragraph (4)(A) for a calendar year and before July 1 of such calendar year, the Trade Representative determines that additional individuals need to be added to a final candidate list, the Trade Representative shall—

(i) request the interagency group established under paragraph (1)(A) to prepare a list of individuals who are qualified to be added to such candidate list,

(ii) select individuals from the list prepared by the interagency group under paragraph (1)(B)(ii) to be included in a proposed amendment to such final candidate list, and

(iii) by no later than July 1 of such calendar year, submit to the appropriate Congressional Committees the proposed amendments to such final candidate list developed by the Trade Representative under clause (ii).

(B) Upon submission of a proposed amendment under subparagraph (A)(iii) to the appropriate Congressional Committees, the Trade Representative shall consult with the appropriate Congressional Committees with regard to the individuals included in the proposed amendment.

(C) The Trade Representative may add or delete individuals from any proposed amendment submitted under subparagraph (A)(iii) after consulting the appropriate Congressional Committees with regard to such addition or deletion. The Trade Representative shall provide to the appropriate Congressional Committees written notice of any addition or deletion of an individual from the proposed amendment.

(D)(i) If the Trade Representative submits under subparagraph (A)(iii) in any calendar year a proposed amendment to a final candidate list, the Trade Representative shall, by no later than September 30 of such calendar year, submit to the appropriate Congressional Committees the final form of such amendment. On October 1 of such calendar year, such amendment shall take effect and the individuals included in the final form of such amendment shall be added to the final candidate list.

(ii) An individual may be included in the final form of an amendment submitted under clause (i) only if written notice of the addition of such individual to the proposed form of such amendment was submitted to the appropriate Congressional Committees at least 15 days before the date on which the final form of such amendment is submitted under clause (i).

(iii) Individuals added to a final candidate list under clause (i) shall be eligible to serve on binational panels or extraordinary challenge committees convened pursuant to chapter 19 of the Agreement, as the case may be, during the 6-month period beginning on October 1 of the calendar year in which such addition occurs.

(iv) No additions may be made to the final form of an amendment described in clause (i) after the final form of such amendment is submitted to the appropriate Congressional Committees under clause (i).

(6)(A) The Trade Representative is the only officer of the Government of the United States authorized to act on behalf of the Government of the United States in making any selection or appointment of an individual to—

(i) the rosters described in Annex 1901.2(1) and Annex 1904.13(1) of the Agreement, or

(ii) the binational panels or extraordinary challenge committees convened pursuant to chapter 19 of the Agreement,

that is to be made solely or jointly by the Government of the United States under the terms of the Agreement.

(B) Except as otherwise provided in paragraph (7)(B), the Trade Representative may—

(i) select an individual for placement on the rosters described in Annex 1901.2(1) and Annex 1904.13(1) of the Agreement during the 1-year period beginning on April 1 of any calendar year,

(ii) appoint an individual to serve as one of those members of any binational panel or extraordinary challenge committee convened pursuant to chapter 19 of the Agreement during such 1-year period who, under the terms of the Agreement, are to be appointed solely by the Government of the United States, or

(iii) act to make a joint appointment with the Government of Canada, under the terms of the Agreement, of any individual who is a citizen or national of the United States to serve as any other member of such a panel or committee,

only if such individual is on the appropriate final candidate list that was submitted to the appropriate Congressional Committees under paragraph (4)(A) during such calendar year or on such list as it may be amended under paragraph (5)(D)(i).

(7)(A) Except as otherwise provided in this paragraph, no individual may—

(i) be selected by the Government of the United States for placement on the rosters described in Annex 1901.2(1) and Annex 1904.13(1) of the Agreement, or

(ii) be appointed solely or jointly by the Government of the United States to serve as a member of a binational panel or extraordinary challenge committee convened pursuant to chapter 19 of the Agreement,

during the 1-year period beginning on April 1 of any calendar year for which the Trade Representative has not met the requirements of this subsection.

(B)(i) Notwithstanding paragraphs (3), (4), or (6)(B) (other than paragraph (3)(A)), individuals listed on the preliminary candidate lists submitted to the appropriate Congressional Committees under paragraph (3)(A) may—

(I) be selected by the Trade Representative for placement on the rosters described in Annex 1901.2(1) and Annex 1904.13(1) of the Agreement during the 3-month period beginning on the date on which the Agreement enters into force, and

(II) be appointed solely or jointly by the Trade Representative under the terms of the Agreement to serve as members of binational panels or extraordinary challenge committees that are convened pursuant to chapter 19 of the Agreement during such 3-month period.

(ii) If the Agreement enters into force after January 3, 1989, the provisions of this subsection shall be applied with respect to the calendar year in which the Agreement enters into force—

(I) by substituting "the date that is 30 days after the date on which the Agreement enters into force" for "January 3 of each calendar year" in paragraphs (1)(B)(i) and (3)(A), and

(II) by substituting "the date that is 3 months after the date on which the Agreement enters into force" for "March 31 of each calendar year" in paragraph (4)(A).

(b) STATUS OF PANELISTS.—Notwithstanding any other provision of law, individuals appointed by the United States to serve on panels or committees convened pursuant to chapter 19 of the Agreement, and individuals designated to assist such appointed individuals, shall not be considered to be employees or special employees of, or to be otherwise affiliated with, the Government of the United States.

(c) IMMUNITY OF PANELISTS.—With the exception of acts described in section 777f(d)(3) of the Tariff Act of 1930, as added by this Act, individuals serving on panels or committees convened pursuant to chapter 19 of the Agreement, and individuals designated to assist the individuals serving on such panels or committees, shall be immune from suit and legal process relating to acts performed by such individuals in their official capacity and within the scope of their functions as such panelists or committee members or assistants to such panelists or committee members.

(d) REGULATIONS.—The administering authority under title VII of the Tariff Act of 1930, the United States International Trade Commission, and the United States Trade Representative may promulgate such regulations as are necessary or appropriate to carry out actions in order to implement their respective responsibilities under chapters 18 and 19 of the Agreement. Initial regulations to carry out such functions shall be issued prior to the date of entry into force of the Agreement.

(e) ESTABLISHMENT OF UNITED STATES SECRETARIAT.—

(1) The President is authorized to establish within any department or agency of the Federal Government a United States Secretariat which, subject to the oversight of the interagency group established under subsection (a)(1)(A), shall facilitate—

(A) the operation of chapters 18 and 19 of the Agreement, and

(B) the work of the binational panels and extraordinary challenge committees convened under chapters 18 and 19 of the Agreement.

(2) The United States Secretariat established by the President under paragraph (1) shall not be considered to be an agency for purposes of section 552 of title 5, United States Code.

SEC. 406. AUTHORIZATION OF APPROPRIATIONS FOR THE SECRETARIAT, THE PANELS, AND THE COMMITTEES.

(a) THE SECRETARIAT.—There are authorized to be appropriated to the department or agency within which the United States Secretariat described in chapter 19 of the Agreement is established the lesser of—

(1) such sums as may be necessary, or

(2) $5,000,000,

for each fiscal year succeeding fiscal year 1988 for the establishment and operations of such United States Secretariat and for the payment of the United States share of the expenses of the dispute settlement proceedings under chapter 18 of the Agreement.

(b) PANELS AND COMMITTEES.—

(1) There are authorized to be appropriated to the Office of the United States Trade Representative for fiscal year 1989 such sums as may be necessary to pay during such fiscal year the United States share of the expenses of binational panels and

extraordinary challenge committees convened pursuant to chapter 19 of the Agreement.

(2) The United States Trade Representative is authorized to transfer funds appropriated pursuant to the authorization provided under paragraph (1) to any department or agency of the United States in order to facilitate payment of the expenses described in paragraph (1).

(3) Funds appropriated for the payment of expenses described in paragraph (1) during any fiscal year may be expended only to the extent such funds do not exceed the amount authorized to be appropriated under paragraph (1) for such fiscal year. This paragraph shall apply, notwithstanding any law enacted after the date of enactment of this Act, unless such subsequent law specifically provides that this paragraph shall not apply and specifically cites this paragraph.

SEC. 407. TESTIMONY AND PRODUCTION OF PAPERS IN EXTRAORDINARY CHALLENGES.

(a) AUTHORITY OF EXTRAORDINARY CHALLENGE COMMITTEE TO OBTAIN INFORMATION.—If an extraordinary challenge committee (hereinafter referred to in this section as the "committee") is convened pursuant to article 1904(13) of the Agreement, and the allegations before the committee include a matter referred to in article 1904(13)(a)(i) of the Agreement, for the purposes of carrying out its functions and duties under Annex 1904.13 of the Agreement, the committee—

(1) shall have access to, and the right to copy, any document, paper, or record pertinent to the subject matter under consideration, in the possession of any individual, partnership, corporation, association, organization, or other entity,

(2) may summon witnesses, take testimony, and administer oaths,

(3) may require any individual, partnership, corporation, association, organization, or other entity to produce documents, books, or records relating to the matter in question, and

(4) may require any individual, partnership, corporation, association, organization, or other entity to furnish in writing, in such detail and in such form as the committee may prescribe, information in its possession pertaining to the matter.

Any member of the committee may sign subpoenas, and members of the committee, when authorized by the committee, may administer oaths and affirmations, examine witnesses, take testimony, and receive evidence.

(b) WITNESSES AND EVIDENCE.—The attendance of witnesses who are authorized to be summoned, and the production of documentary evidence authorized to be ordered, under subsection (a) may be required from any place in the United States at any designated place of hearing. In the case of disobedience to a subpoena authorized under subsection (a), the committee may request the Attorney General of the United States to invoke the aid of any district or territorial court of the United States in requiring the attendance and testimony of witnesses and the production of documentary evidence. Such court, within the jurisdiction of which such inquiry is carried on, may, in case of contumacy or refusal to obey a subpoena issued to any individual, partnership, corporation, association, organization, or other entity, issue an order requiring such individual or entity to appear before the committee, or to produce documentary evidence if so ordered or to give evidence concerning the matter in question. Any failure to obey such order of the court may be punished by such court as a contempt thereof.

(c) MANDAMUS.—Any court referred to in subsection (b) shall have jurisdiction to issue writs of mandamus commanding compliance with the provisions of this section or any order of the committee made in pursuance thereof.

(d) DEPOSITIONS.—The committee may order testimony to be taken by deposition at any stage of the committee review. Such deposition may be taken before any person designated by the committee and having power to administer oaths. Such testimony shall be reduced to writing by the person taking the deposition, or under the direction of such person, and shall then be subscribed by the deponent. Any individual, partnership, corporation, association, organization or other entity may be compelled to appear and depose and to produce documentary evidence in the same manner as witnesses may be compelled to appear and testify and produce documentary evidence before the committee, as provided in this section.

SEC. 408. REQUESTS FOR REVIEW OF CANADIAN ANTIDUMPING AND COUNTERVAILING DUTY DETERMINATIONS.

(a) REQUESTS FOR REVIEW BY THE UNITED STATES.—In the case of a final antidumping or countervailing duty determination of a competent investigating authority of Canada, as defined in article 1911 of the Agreement, requests by the United States for binational panel review under article 1904 of the Agreement shall be made by the United States Secretary, described in article 1909(4) of the Agreement.

(b) REQUESTS FOR REVIEW BY A PERSON.—In the case of a final antidumping or countervailing duty determination of a competent investigating authority of Canada, as defined in article 1911 of the Agreement, a person, within the meaning of article 1904(5) of the Agreement, may request a binational panel review of such determination by filing with the United States Secretary, described in article 1909(4) of the Agreement, such a request within the time limit provided for in article 1904(4) of the Agreement. The receipt of such request by the United States Secretary shall be deemed to be a request for binational panel review within the meaning of article 1904(4) of the Agreement. Such request shall contain such information and be in such form, manner, and style as the administering authority shall prescribe by regulations. The request for such panel review shall not preclude the United States, Canada, or any other person from challenging before a binational panel the basis for a particular request for review.

(c) SERVICE OF REQUEST FOR REVIEW.—Whenever binational panel review is requested under this section, the United States Secretary shall serve a copy of the request on all persons who would be regarded as interested parties to the proceeding if the determination in question had been made under title VII of the Tariff Act of 1930.

SEC. 409. SUBSIDIES.

(a) NEGOTIATING AUTHORITY.—

(1) The President is authorized to enter into an agreement with Canada, including an agreement to amend the Agreement, on rules applicable to trade between the United States and Canada that

(A) deal with unfair pricing and government subsidization, and

(B) provide for increased discipline on subsidies.

(2)(A) The objectives of the United States in negotiating an agreement under paragraph (1) include (but are not limited to)—

(i) achievement, on an expedited basis, of increased discipline on government production and export subsidies that have a significant impact, directly or indirectly, on bilateral trade between the United States and Canada; and

(ii) attainment of increased and more effective discipline on those Canadian Government (including provincial) subsidies having the most significant adverse impact on United States producers that compete with subsidized products of Canada in the markets of the United States and Canada.

(B) Special emphasis should be given in negotiating an agreement under paragraph (1) to obtain discipline on Canadian subsidy programs that adversely affect United States industries which directly compete with subsidized imports.

(3) The United States members of the working group established under article 1907 of the Agreement shall—

(A) consult regularly with the Committee on Finance of the Senate, the Committee on Ways and Means of the House of Representatives, and advisory committees established under section 135 of the Trade Act of 1974 (19 U.S.C. 2155) regarding—

(i) the issues being considered by the working group, and

(ii) as appropriate, the objectives and strategy of the United States in the negotiations, and

(B) beginning in January 1990, submit an annual report to such Congressional Committees on the progress being made in the negotiations to obtain an agreement that meets the objectives described in paragraph (2).

(4) Notwithstanding any other provision of this Act or of any other law, the provisions of section 151 of the Trade Act of 1974 (19 U.S.C. 2191) shall not apply to any bill or joint resolution that implements an agreement entered into under paragraph (1), unless the President determines and notifies the Congress that such agreement—

(A) will provide greater discipline over government subsidies and no less discipline over unfair pricing practices by producers than that provided by the agreements described in paragraphs (5) and (6) of section 2 of the Trade Agreements Act of 1979 (the Subsidies Code and Antidumping Code), respectively, taking into account the effects of the Agreement, and

(B) will neither undermine such multilateral discipline nor detract from United States efforts to increase such discipline on a multilateral basis in, or subsequent to, the Uruguay Round of multilateral trade negotiations.

(b) IDENTIFICATION OF INDUSTRIES FACING SUBSIDIZED IMPORTS.—

(1) Any entity, including a trade association, firm, certified or recognized union, or group of workers, that is representative of a United States industry and has reason to believe that—

(A)(i) as a result of implementation of provisions of the Agreement, the industry is likely to face increased competition from subsidized Canadian imports with which it directly competes; or

(ii) the industry is likely to face increased competition from subsidized imports with which it directly competes from any other country designated by the President, following consultations with the Congress, as benefitting from a reduction of tariffs or other trade barriers under a trade agreement that enters into force after January 1, 1989; and

(B) the industry is likely to experience a deterioration of its competitive position before rules and disciplines relating to the use of government subsidies have been developed with respect to such country;

may file a petition with the United States Trade Representative (hereafter referred to in this section as the "Trade Representative") to be identified under this section.

(2) Within 90 days of receipt of a petition under paragraph (1), the Trade Representative, in consultation with the Secretary of Commerce, shall decide whether to identify the industry on the basis that there is a reasonable likelihood that the industry may face both the subsidization described in paragraph (1)(A) and the deterioration described in paragraph (1)(B).

(3) At the request of an entity that is representative of an industry identified under paragraph (2), the Trade Representative shall—

(A) compile and make available to the industry information under section 305 of the Trade Act of 1974,

(B) recommend to the President that an investigation by the United States International Trade Commission be requested under section 332 of the Tariff Act of 1930, or

(C) take actions described in both subparagraphs (A) and (B).

The industry may request the Trade Representative to take appropriate action to update (as often as annually) any information obtained under subparagraph (A) or (B), or both, as the case may be, until an agreement on adequate rules and disciplines relating to government subsidies is reached.

(4)(A) The Trade Representative and the Secretary of Commerce shall review information obtained under paragraph (3) and consult with the industry identified under paragraph (2) with a view to deciding whether any action is appropriate under section 301 of the Trade Act of 1974, including the initiation of an investigation under section 302(c) of that Act (in the case of the Trade Representative), or under subtitle A of title VII of the Tariff Act of 1930, including the initiation of an investigation under section 702(a) of that Act (in the case of the Secretary of Commerce).

(B) In determining whether to initiate any investigation under section 301 of the Trade Act of 1974 or any other trade law, other than title VII of the Tariff Act of 1930, the Trade Representative, after consultation with the Secretary of Commerce—

(i) shall seek the advice of the advisory committees established under section 135 of the Trade Act of 1974;

(ii) shall consult with the Committee on Finance of the Senate and the Committee on Ways and Means of the House of Representatives;

(iii) shall coordinate with the interagency committee established under section 242 of the Trade Expansion Act of 1962; and

(iv) may ask the President to request advice from the United States International Trade Commission.

(C) In the event an investigation is initiated under section 302(c) of the Trade Act of 1974 as a result of a review under this paragraph and the President, following such investigation (including any applicable dispute settlement proceedings under the Agreement or any other trade agreement), determines to take action under section 301(a) of such Act, the President shall give preference to actions that most directly affect the products that benefit from governmental subsidies and were the subject of the investigation, unless there are no significant imports of such products or the President otherwise determines that application of the action to other products would be more effective.

(5) Any decision, whether positive or negative, or any action by the Trade Representative or the Secretary of Commerce under this section shall not in any way—

(A) prejudice the right of any industry to file a petition under any trade law,

(B) prejudice, affect, or substitute for, any proceeding, investigation, determination, or action by the Secretary of Commerce, the United States International Trade Commission, or the Trade Representative pursuant to such a petition,

(C) prejudice, affect, substitute for, or obviate any proceeding, investigation, or determination under section 301 of the Trade Act of 1974, title VII of the Tariff Act of 1930, or any other trade law.

(6) Nothing in this subsection may be construed to alter in any manner the requirements in effect before the enactment of this Act for standing under any law of the United States or to add any additional requirements for standing under any law of the United States.

SEC. 410. TERMINATION OF AGREEMENT.

(a) IN GENERAL.—If—

(1) no agreement is entered into between the United States and Canada on a substitute system of rules for antidumping and countervailing duties before the date that is 7 years after the date on which the Agreement enters into force, and

(2) the President decides not to exercise the rights of the United States under article 1906 of the Agreement to terminate the Agreement,

the President shall submit to the Congress a report on such decision which explains why continued adherence to the Agreement is in the national economic interest of the United States.

(b) TRANSITION PROVISIONS.—

(1) If on the date on which the Agreement should cease to be in force an investigation or enforcement proceeding concerning the violation of a protective order issued under section 777(d) of the Tariff Act of 1930 (as amended by this Act) or a Canadian undertaking is pending, such investigation or proceeding shall continue and sanctions may continue to be imposed in accordance with the provisions of such section.

(2) If on the date on which the Agreement should cease to be in force a binational panel review under article 1904 of the Agreement is pending, or has been requested, with respect to a determination to which section 516A(g)(2) of the Tariff Act of 1930 (as added by this Act) applies, such determination shall be reviewable under section 516A(a) of the Tariff Act of 1930. In the case of a determination to which the provisions of this paragraph apply, the time limits for commencing an action under section 516A(a)(2)(A) of the Tariff Act of 1930 shall not begin to run until the date on which the Agreement ceases to be in force.

TITLE V—EFFECTIVE DATES AND SEVERABILITY

SEC. 501. EFFECTIVE DATES.

(a) In General.—Except as provided in subsection (b), the provisions of this Act, and the amendments made by this Act, shall take effect on the date the Agreement enters into force.

(b) Exceptions.—Sections 1 and 2, title I, section 304 (except subsection (f)), section 309, this section and section 502 shall take effect on the date of enactment of this Act.

(c) Termination of Provisions and Amendments if Agreement Terminates.—On the date on which the Agreement ceases to be in force, the provisions of this Act (other than this subsection and section 410(b)), and the amendments made by this Act, shall cease to have effect.

SEC. 502. SEVERABILITY.

If any provision of this Act, any amendment made by this Act, or the application of such a provision or amendment to any person or circumstances is held to be invalid, the remainder of this Act, the remaining amendments made by this Act, and the application of such provision or amendment to persons or circumstances other than those to which it is held invalid, shall not be affected thereby.

Approved September 28, 1988.

LEGISLATIVE HISTORY—H.R. 5090:

HOUSE REPORTS: No. 100-816, Pt. 1 (Comm. on Ways and Means), Pt. 2 (Comm. on Interior and Insular Affairs), Pt. 3 (Comm. on Foreign Affairs), Pt. 4 (Comm. on the Judiciary), Pt. 5 (Comm. on Banking, Finance and Urban Affairs), Pt. 6 (Comm. on Government Operations), Pt. 7 (Comm. on Energy and Commerce), and Pt. 8 (Comm. on Agriculture).

SENATE REPORTS: No. 100-509 (Comm. on Finance; Comm. on Agriculture, Nutrition, and Forestry; Comm. on Energy and Natural Resources; and Comm. on Governmental Affairs).

CONGRESSIONAL RECORD, Vol. 134 (1988):

Aug. 9, considered and passed House.

Sept. 19, considered and passed Senate.

NATIONAL DEFENSE AUTHORIZATION ACT, FISCAL YEAR 1989

An Act to authorize appropriations for fiscal year 1989 for military activities of the Department of Defense, for military construction, and for defense activities of the Department of Energy, to prescribe personnel strengths for such fiscal year for the Armed Forces, and for other purposes.

Date: September 29, 1988

Bill No.: H.R. 4481

Public Law No.: 100-456

Cite: 102 STAT. 1918

Sections reprinted:

TITLE X - MATTERS RELATING NATO COUNTRIES AND OTHER ALLIES

Section 1004 - Sense of Congress on need for modernization of theater nuclear capabilities of NATO.

Section 1009 - Contributions by Japan to global stability.

TITLE XIII - FOREIGN RELATIONS MATTERS

Section 1301 - Sense of Congress concerning the Panama Canal and the United States Southern Command.

Section 1302 - Limitation on assistance to Panamanian Defense Force.

Section 1303 - Sense of Congress concerning indictment of General Noriega of Panama on drug-related charges.

Section 1304 - Sense of Congress on introduction of Armed Forces into Nicaragua for combat.

Section 1305 - Human rights violations by the government of Poland.

Section 1306 - Conditions for sale or other transfer of F-15 aircraft to Saudi Arabia.

Section 1307 - Restriction on sale of defense articles to certain nations.

Section 1308 - United States bases in the Republic of the Philippines.

Section 1309 - Annual assessment of security at United States bases in the Philippines.

Section 1310 - Economic sanctions against Ethiopia.

Public Law 100-456
100th Congress

An Act

To authorize appropriations for fiscal year 1989 for military activities of the Department of Defense, for military construction, and for defense activities of the Department of Energy, to prescribe personnel strengths for such fiscal year for the Armed Forces, and for other purposes.

Be it enacted by the Senate and House of Representatives of the United States of America in Congress assembled,

SECTION 1. SHORT TITLE

This Act may be cited as the "National Defense Authorization Act, Fiscal Year 1989".

TITLE IX—MATTERS RELATING TO ARMS CONTROL

SEC. 901. SENSE OF CONGRESS ON EXPANDING CONFIDENCE-BUILDING MEASURES

(a) FINDINGS.—Congress makes the following findings:

(1) Approximately two years have passed since the Conference on Confidence- and Security-Building Measures and Disarmament in Europe (CDE) adjourned in Stockholm following the adoption of measures designed to increase openness and predictability of military activities in Europe.

(2) To date, there have been seven formal observations and challenge inspections which have been conducted in accordance with the Stockholm agreements.

(3) The military leaders of the North Atlantic Treaty Organization have concluded that the Stockholm observations and inspections have positively contributed to an improved understanding of Warsaw Pact forces and capabilities.

(4) The Conventional Stability Talks (CST), which may begin before the end of 1988, will likely require careful and potentially prolonged negotiation.

(5) New negotiations will also begin under the auspices of the Conference on Security and Cooperation in Europe (CSCE) as a follow-on to the Stockholm conference.

(6) The confidence-building measures established at Stockholm could, if expanded, contribute significantly to the success of the CDE follow-on conference and also to the establishment of a procedural framework for verifying a future CST agreement.

(b) SENSE OF CONGRESS.—It is the sense of Congress that the President should give high priority to developing, in coordination with the North Atlantic Treaty Organization allies of the United States, stabilizing and verifiable proposals for expanding the regime of confidence-building measures in conjunction with the follow-on to the Conference on Confidence- and Security-Building Measures and Disarmament in Europe (CDE) and the new Conventional Stability Talks (CST).

SEC. 902. SENSE OF CONGRESS ON START TALKS

It is the sense of Congress that any agreement negotiated by the President to achieve a reduction and limitation on strategic arms (through the strategic arms reduction talks in Geneva or otherwise)—

(1) should not prevent the United States from deploying a force structure under the agreement which emphasizes survivable strategic systems and, in particular, should not in any way compromise the security of the United States ballistic-missile carrying submarine force, and

(2) should not prohibit or limit the deployment of non-nuclear cruise missiles.

SEC. 903. SENSE OF CONGRESS CONCERNING ROLE OF CONGRESS IN ARMS CONTROL AND DEFENSE POLICIES

It is the sense of Congress—

(1) that Congress, in exercising its authority under the Constitution "to raise and support Armies" and "provide and maintain Navies" and, in the case of the Senate, to advise and consent to the ratification of treaties, has a role to play in formulating arms control and defense policies of the United States, but

(2) that Congress, in exercising that authority, should not usurp, undermine, or interfere with the authority of the President under the Constitution to negotiate and implement treaties, especially in the case of treaties which affect arms control and defense policies of the United States.

SEC. 904. SENSE OF CONGRESS ON THE FIVE-YEAR ABM TREATY REVIEW

(a) FINDINGS.—Congress makes the following findings:

(1) The Treaty Between the United States of America and the Union of Soviet Socialist Republics on the Limitation of Anti-Ballistic Missile Systems, With Associated Protocol (hereinafter in this section referred to as the "ABM Treaty" or the "Treaty") in Article XIV, Paragraph 2, reads as follows: "Five years after entry into force of this Treaty, and at five-year intervals thereafter, the Parties shall together conduct a review of this Treaty.".

(2) Such Treaty entered into force on October 3, 1972, and the third five-year anniversary date specified for the conduct of the review contemplated in the Treaty, therefore, was October 3, 1987.

(3) As a fundamental principle of the canons of legal construction, a specified number of years after a specific and determinable date means the specified anniversary of such date and therefore the third five-year review of the ABM Treaty should have begun on or about October 3, 1987.

(4) The Parties to the Treaty have not met as required by the Treaty because the United States refused to meet on the date specified in the Treaty for such meeting (October 3, 1987) and has refused since such date to propose a date for the meeting.

(b) SENSE OF CONGRESS.—In light of the findings in subsection (a), it is the sense of Congress that the President should, without any further delay, propose an early date to conduct the overdue five-year review of the ABM Treaty. The President shall inform Congress of the results of that review immediately after it takes place.

SEC. 905. REVISION OF ANNUAL REPORT ON SOVIET COMPLIANCE WITH ARMS CONTROL COMMITMENTS

(a) AMENDMENT TO PUBLIC LAW 99-145.—The text of section 1002 of the Department of Defense Authorization Act, 1986 (22 U.S.C. 2592a), is amended to read as follows:

"(a) ANNUAL REPORT.—Not later than December 1 of each year, the President shall submit to Congress a report containing the findings of the President with respect to the compliance of the Soviet Union with its arms control commitments and any additional information necessary to keep Congress currently informed.

"(b) MATTERS TO BE INCLUDED.—The President shall specifically include in each such report the following:

"(1) A summary of the current status of all arms control agreements in effect between the United States and the Soviet Union.

"(2) An assessment of all violations by the Soviet Union of such agreements and the risks such violations pose to the national security of the United States and its allies.

"(3) A net assessment of the aggregate military significance of all such violations.

"(4) A statement of the compliance policy of the United States with respect to violations by the Soviet Union of those agreements.

"(5) What actions, if any, the President has taken or proposes to take to bring the Soviet Union into compliance with its

ing under such program by recipient, including distinguishing between grant aid, loans, and credits.

(c) POLICY ON DISCUSSIONS WITH JAPAN.—It is the sense of Congress that in the discussions with Japan referred to in section 1008 for the purpose of reaching a more equitable distribution of the burden of financial support for the security of the leading industrialized democracies, the objective of such discussions should include the establishment of a schedule for increases in spending under Japan's Official Development Assistance program and its defense programs so that, by 1992, the level of spending on those programs (stated as a percentage of gross national product) will approximate the average of the levels of spending by the member nations of the North Atlantic Treaty Organization on official development assistance and defense programs (stated as a percentage of their respective gross national products).

(d) REPORT.—Not later than 180 days after the date of the enactment of this Act, the President shall submit to Congress a report on the progress of the discussions described in subsection (c) with respect to Japan.

(e) FURTHER CONGRESSIONAL ACTION.—It is the sense of Congress that if, in the judgment of Congress, the report of the President under subsection (d) does not reflect substantial progress toward a more equitable distribution of the burden of maintaining the security of the leading industrialized democracies, Congress should review the extent of the distribution of the mutual security burden between the United States and Japan and should consider whether additional legislation is appropriate.

TITLE XIII—FOREIGN RELATIONS MATTERS

SEC. 1301. SENSE OF CONGRESS CONCERNING THE PANAMA CANAL AND THE UNITED STATES SOUTHERN COMMAND

(a) FINDINGS.—The Congress finds that—

(1) the security of, and the free flow of shipping through, the Panama Canal are vital interests of the United States; and

(2) the continued ability of the United States Southern Command (which currently has its headquarters in the Republic of Panama) to carry out assigned missions, especially the mission of defense of the Panama Canal, is essential to protecting and promoting the interests of the United States.

(b) SENSE OF CONGRESS.—In light of the findings in subsection (a), it is the sense of Congress that the President should take all steps necessary to ensure the continued ability of the United States Southern Command (or any successor command) to carry out assigned missions, especially the mission of defense of the Panama Canal.

SEC. 1302. LIMITATION ON ASSISTANCE TO PANAMANIAN DEFENSE FORCE

(a) LIMITATION.—The President may not use any funds appropriated to or for the use of any department, agency, or other entity of the United States for the purpose of providing assistance to the Panamanian Defense Force. The limitation in the preceding sentence shall cease to apply upon the submission by the President to Congress of a certification by the President—

(1) that no armed forces of the Soviet Union, the Republic of Cuba, or the Republic of Nicaragua are present in the Republic of Panama (other than military attachés accredited to the Republic of Panama); and

(2) that General Manuel Noriega has relinquished command of the Panamanian Defense Force and no longer holds any official position of leadership (either military or civilian) in the Republic of Panama.

(b) CLARIFICATION.—Subsection (a) does not prohibit the President from obligating or expending any funds necessary for—

(1) the defense of the Panama Canal,

(2) the collection of intelligence,

(3) the maintenance of United States Armed Forces in the Republic of Panama, or

(4) the protection of United States interests in the Republic of Panama.

(c) REPORT.—Not later than 30 days after the date of the enactment of this Act, the President shall submit to Congress a detailed report, in both classified and unclassified form, indicating—

(1) whether (and to what extent) military, paramilitary, or intelligence personnel of the Soviet Union, Cuba, or Nicaragua are present in the Republic of Panama; and

(2) whether (and to what extent) the Panamanian Defense Force has coordinated with, cooperated with, supported, or received support from, any such personnel.

SEC. 1303. SENSE OF CONGRESS CONCERNING INDICTMENT OF GENERAL NORIEGA OF PANAMA ON DRUG-RELATED CHARGES

(a) FINDINGS.—The Congress finds that—

(1) General Manuel Noriega, the commander of the Panamanian Defense Force, was indicted on February 5, 1988, in the United States District Courts for the Southern District and for the Middle District of Florida on a number of serious drug-related charges against the laws of the United States, including charges involving trafficking in illegal drugs, protecting and supporting drug traffickers, and laundering of drug-related money; and

(2) there have been reports in the news media and from other sources that discussions between officials of the United States and General Noriega may have occurred concerning arrangements under which General Noriega would give up political power and leave the Republic of Panama in exchange for which the United States would file a motion to dismiss the indictments referred to in paragraph (1).

(b) SENSE OF CONGRESS.—It is the sense of Congress—

(1) that the United States should not conduct or authorize any negotiations or discussions, and should not make any arrangements, with General Manuel Noriega which would involve any effort by the United States to dismiss the indictments referred to in subsection (a)(1); and

(2) that any such negotiation, discussion, or arrangement—

(A) would be incompatible with the high priority that the United States places on the war on drugs;

(B) would not further the prospects for restoring noncorrupt, democratic government to the Republic of Panama; and

(C) would not serve the interests of the United States.

SEC. 1304. SENSE OF CONGRESS ON INTRODUCTION OF ARMED FORCES INTO NICARAGUA FOR COMBAT

Congress hereby reaffirms the sense of Congress expressed in the first session of the 99th Congress (in section 1451 of the Department of Defense Authorization Act, 1986 (Public Law 99-145; 99 Stat. 760)), that United States Armed Forces should not be introduced into or over Nicaragua for combat. However, nothing in this section shall be construed as affecting the authority and responsibility of the President or Congress under the Constitution, statutes, or treaties of the United States in force.

SEC. 1305. HUMAN RIGHTS VIOLATIONS BY THE GOVERNMENT OF POLAND

(a) FINDINGS.—Congress makes the following findings:

(1) The government of Poland, headed by General Wojciech Jaruzelski, has violated internationally recognized human rights of the people of Poland, including the right to peaceably assemble, the right to strike, the right to freely associate, and the right to due process.

(2) The Jaruzelski government has retaliated against the justified, peaceful protests of workers at Nowa Huta, Poland, through the use of violence and force.

(3) The Jaruzelski government has prosecuted and imprisoned a number of persons for politically related offenses.

(4) The Jaruzelski government has to date refused to take steps which would guarantee the right of the people of Poland to participate in the management of the economy of Poland and has refused to accept the principle of pluralism in the national life of Poland.

(b) SENSE OF CONGRESS.—It is, therefore, the sense of Congress—

(1) that the use of force against the workers of Nowa Huta and intimidation against other strikers in Poland should be condemned; and

(2) that improvement in relations between the United States and Poland must be predicated on an improvement in internationally recognized human rights in Poland, including the release of political prisoners, steps toward trade union pluralism and the rights of independent trade unions to organize, and steps toward genuine national reconciliation and dialogue.

SEC. 1306. CONDITIONS FOR SALE OR OTHER TRANSFER OF F-15 AIRCRAFT TO SAUDI ARABIA

(a) Notwithstanding any other provision of law, any sale or other transfer to Saudi Arabia by the United States of F-15 aircraft shall be subject to the following conditions:

(1) Any such F-15 aircraft sold or otherwise transferred to Saudi Arabia shall be limited to models A, B, C, and D.

(2) The United States shall not sell or otherwise transfer to Saudi Arabia the F-15-E with a ground attack capability and shall not upgrade existing Saudi aircraft to that capability.

(3) Saudi Arabia shall not possess more than 60 F-15 aircraft at any time, except that additional replacement F-15 aircraft may be held in the United States, at the expense of Saudi Arabia, for shipment to Saudi Arabia only after the President notifies Congress that the existing inventory of F-15 aircraft held by Saudi Arabia is less than 60 and, then, only on a one-for-one replacement basis as each F-15 aircraft is totally removed from the inventory of Saudi Arabia.

(b) The President may waive subsection (a) if the President certifies to Congress that such action is in the national interest.

SEC. 1307. RESTRICTION ON SALE OF DEFENSE ARTICLES TO CERTAIN NATIONS

(a) RESTRICTION.—During fiscal year 1989, the United States may not make any sale of defense articles subject to section 36(b) of the Arms Export Control Act (22 U.S.C. 2776(b)) to any nation which has acquired intermediate-range ballistic missiles made by the People's

Republic of China.

(b) PRESIDENTIAL CERTIFICATION.—(1) The restriction in subsection (a) shall cease to apply with respect to any nation which has acquired such missiles upon certification by the President to Congress that that nation does not have chemical, biological, or nuclear warheads for those missiles.

(2) If the President makes a certification under paragraph (1) in the case of any nation, the President shall notify Congress promptly of any evidence that, after the date of such certification, such nation has acquired chemical, biological, or nuclear warheads for those missiles.

SEC. 1308. UNITED STATES BASES IN THE REPUBLIC OF THE PHILIPPINES

(a) CONGRESSIONAL FINDINGS.—Congress makes the following findings:

(1) The United States has maintained military bases in the Philippines since 1947 pursuant to the United States-Philippine Military Bases Agreement and maintained military bases in the Philippines for many years before that under other arrangements.

(2) Clark Air Force Base, Subic Bay Naval Base, and the other United States military installations in the Philippines significantly promote the mutual interests of the United States and the Philippines and contribute to regional and global security.

(3) These installations are also important to the development of democratic institutions and to economic progress in the Western Pacific and Southeast Asia.

(4) The United States military installations in the Philippines employ a loyal and highly skilled cadre of Filipinos and make a substantial contribution to the Philippine economy.

(5) The Military Bases Agreement as currently in effect has a fixed term lasting until September 16, 1991, after which it continues in effect subject to termination by either party on one year's notice.

(6) Pursuant to a 1979 amendment to that agreement, the President of the United States pledged to the Government of the Republic of the Philippines to undertake "best efforts" to obtain security assistance for the Philippines, and such pledge was reiterated by the President of the United States in 1983 as part of a five-year review of the agreement.

(7) The United States and the Republic of the Philippines are currently engaged in a second five-year review of the Military Bases Agreement.

(8) Officials of the Government of the Republic of the Philippines have indicated to officials of the United States that the United States should significantly increase compensation for the use by the United States of military bases in the Philippines.

(9) The provision of multilateral economic assistance to the Republic of the Philippines should be considered separately from the provision of security assistance by the United States to the Republic of the Philippines in return for United States basing rights in the Philippines.

(b) REPORT ON FACILITIES.—(1) The Secretary of Defense shall submit to Congress a report on the existing United States military facilities in the Republic of the Philippines. The report shall include analysis of the following:

(A) The costs and benefits of maintaining those facilities, including the costs to the United States of the operation and maintenance of those facilities and any other costs associated with those facilities and the economic and social benefits and other benefits of those facilities to the Republic of the Philippines.

(B) Potential alternative locations for those facilities.

(C) The strategic value to the United States of having military facilities located in the Philippines and of having such facilities at the potential alternative locations considered.

(D) The costs and benefits of relocating those facilities to the potential alternative locations, including—

(i) the cost to the United States of operation and maintenance and other costs,

(ii) the economic, social, and other costs to the Philippines, and

(iii) the economic, social, and other benefits to the government and community at each alternative location.

(E) The availability of skilled indigenous personnel at the potential alternative locations and the cost of training such personnel to work at such installations.

(2) The report shall be prepared in consultation with the Secretary of State and shall be submitted to Congress not later than six months after the date of the enactment of this Act.

SEC. 1309. ANNUAL ASSESSMENT OF SECURITY AT UNITED STATES BASES IN THE PHILIPPINES

The Secretary of Defense shall submit to Congress an annual report assessing security at United States military facilities in the Republic of the Philippines. Each such report shall include an assessment of the cooperation provided by the Philippine Government, at both the national and local level, in improving such security. The report required by this subsection shall be submitted to Congress not later than May 1 each year.

SEC. 1310. ECONOMIC SANCTIONS AGAINST ETHIOPIA

(a) STATEMENTS OF POLICY.—The Congress—

(1) condemns the Government of Ethiopia for its blatant disregard for human life as demonstrated by its use of food as a weapon, its forced resettlement program, and its human rights record;

(2) in the strongest terms possible, urges the Government of Ethiopia to allow foreign relief personnel to return to the north and to allow the international relief campaign to resume operations at its own risk, while retaining full control over its assets and having access to adequate aircraft and fuel;

(3) in the strongest terms possible, urges rebel groups to cease attacks upon relief vehicles and relief distribution points and to respect the impartiality of the international relief campaign;

(4) urges the President and the Secretary of State (through direct representations to the Government of Ethiopia and certain rebel groups and through sustained multilateral initiatives involving other Western donors, the United Nations, and the Organization of African Unity) to focus world pressure and opinion upon the combatants in northern Ethiopia, to press for an "open roads/own risk" policy that will facilitate the resumption of international relief efforts in the north, to press the Government of Ethiopia and the rebel groups to reach a pragmatic, enduring political settlement, and to press the Government of Ethiopia to implement genuine and effective reform of its failed agricultural policies; and

(5) urges the President and the Secretary of State to engage in direct discussion with the Soviet Union in order that the peaceful resolution of the crisis in northern Ethiopia becomes a high

priority of the Soviet Union and that the approach of the Soviet Union is consistent with that of the West.

(b) SANCTIONS.—(1) Notwithstanding any other provision of law, the President is authorized to, and is hereby strongly urged to, impose such economic sanctions upon Ethiopia as the President determines to be appropriate (subject to paragraphs (2) and (3)) if, at any time after the date of the enactment of this Act, the Government of Ethiopia engages in any of the following outrages:

(A) Forced resettlement.

(B) Forced confinement in any resettlement camp.

(C) Diversion of international relief to the military.

(D) Denial of international relief to any persons at risk because of famine.

(E) Seizure of international relief assets provided by the United States.

(F) Prohibition of end-use monitoring of food distribution by international relief personnel.

(2) In imposing sanctions pursuant to paragraph (1) on imports from Ethiopia, the President shall give priority consideration to those products which constitute major imports from Ethiopia, unless the President determines that sanctions against such products would have an adverse effect on economic interests of the United States.

(3) If a sanction imposed pursuant to paragraph (1) involves the prohibition or curtailment of exports to Ethiopia, that sanction may only be imposed under the authority and subject to the requirements of section 6 of the Export Administration Act of 1979.

(c) REPORTS TO CONGRESS.—Not more than 15 days after the date of the enactment of this Act and at the end of each 90-day period thereafter, the President shall submit to Congress a report stating whether or not, during the 90-day period preceding the date of the report, the Government of Ethiopia engaged in any conduct described in subsection (b). Each such report shall describe the response of the United States to any such conduct.

(d) REGULATION AUTHORITY.—The President shall issue such regulations, licenses, and orders as are necessary to implement any sanction imposed under this section.

(e) EXPIRATION.—The authority provided by subsection (b) shall expire on June 1, 1990.

DEPARTMENT OF DEFENSE APPROPRIATION ACT, 1989

An Act making appropriations for the Department of Defense for the fiscal year ending September 30, 1989, and for other purposes.

Date: October 1, 1988

Bill No.: H.R. 4781

Public Law No.: 100-463

Cite: 102 STAT. 2270

Sections reprinted:

Section 8144 - Soviet Union killing of foreign correspondents in Afghanistan.

TITLE IX - ASSISTANCE FOR THE NICARAGUAN RESISTANCE.

Section 9001 - Policy

Section 9002 - Special conditions warranting expedited procedures for legislation concerning transportation of previously appropriated assistance held in title by the Nicaraguan resistance.

Section 9003 - Restrictions regarding the emergency transport of previously appropriated assistance held in title by the Nicaraguan resistance.

Section 9004 - Reports.

Section 9009 - United States policy concerning economic assistance for Central America.

Section 9010 - Economic incentives for democracy in Nicaragua similar to those available to Central American democracies.

*Public Law 100-463
100th Congress

An Act

Making appropriations for the Department of Defense for the fiscal year ending September 30, 1989, and for other purposes.

Be it enacted by the Senate and House of Representatives of the United States of America in Congress assembled, That the following sums are appropriated, out of any money in the Treasury not otherwise appropriated, for the fiscal year ending September 30, 1989, for military functions administered by the Department of Defense, and for other purposes, namely:

SEC. 8144. (a) The Congress finds that—

(1) the armed forces of the Soviet Union have waged a brutal war of conquest against the people of Afghanistan for 8 years;

(2) foreign correspondents attempting to cover the war in Afghanistan have always been subject to extreme danger;

(3) the danger to foreign correspondents became even greater in 1984 when the Soviet Ambassador to Pakistan explicitly threatened foreign journalists entering Afghanistan in the company of the Afghan resistance, known as the mujaheddin;

(4) on September 19, 1985, Charles E. Thornton, a medical reporter for the Arizona Republic, was killed by Soviet troops while preparing a story about volunteer doctors in Afghanistan;

(5) on October 9, 1987, Lee Shapiro, of North Bergen, New Jersey, and Jim Lindelof, of California, were ambushed and murdered by Soviet troops while filming a documentary on the war in Afghanistan;

(6) the statements of Abdul Malik, the Afghan interpreter and guide who accompanied Lee Shapiro and Jim Lindelof and who witnessed their deaths, demonstrate that the two Americans were straffed by helicopter gunships of the Soviet Union and shot by Soviet soldiers who then confiscated their equipment and film; and

(7) Charles E. Thornton, Lee Shapiro, and Jim Lindelof displayed great courage by facing the perils of war and the lethal threat directed against correspondents and ultimately gave their lives to inform the world of the struggle for liberty taking place in Afghanistan.

(b) It is the sense of the Congress that the President should posthumously award the Presidential Medal of Freedom to Charles E. Thornton, Lee Shapiro, and Jim Lindelof in honor of their brave efforts to document the Afghan struggle for freedom.

TITLE IX—ASSISTANCE FOR THE NICARAGUAN RESISTANCE

SEC. 9001. POLICY.

It is the policy of the United States to advance peace and democracy in Central America and to protect American security interests in the region. In pursuing that policy it is the objective of the United States to seek a just and lasting peace for the region in a manner compatible with the Esquipulas Accord of August 7, 1987, the declaration of the Central American presidents at San Jose, Costa Rica, on January 16, 1988, the Sapoa Agreement of March 23, 1988, and United States national security interests in the region.

SEC. 9002. SPECIAL CONDITIONS WARRANTING EXPEDITED PROCEDURES FOR LEGISLATION CONCERNING TRANSPORTATION OF PREVIOUSLY APPROPRIATED ASSISTANCE HELD IN TITLE BY THE NICARAGUAN RESISTANCE.

If, at any time after enactment of this Act and before the adjournment sine die of the second session of the One Hundredth Congress—

(1) the President finds that the Government of Nicaragua has caused an emergency situation in Central America which is having a critical impact on peace and stability of that region, and

(2) the President has consulted with the presidents of Costa Rica, El Salvador, Honduras, and Guatemala regarding that emergency situation, and

(3) the President submits to the Congress the report described in section 9004(a), and

(4) the President requests the Congress to consider legislation which would authorize the transportation to the Nicaraguan Resistance of previously appropriated assistance held in title by the Nicaraguan Resistance and, if necessary, provide authority for (a) the interchangeability of such assistance with equipment of comparable value and purpose which is owned by the United States, and (b) the transportation of humanitarian and military assistance in the same transportation system, and

(5) the House of Representatives has passed legislation, with or without amendments, with respect to the request under paragraph (4),

then a joint resolution described in section 9013(a)(1), shall be considered in the Senate in accordance with the procedures specified in section 9013 of this title.

SEC. 9003. RESTRICTIONS REGARDING THE EMERGENCY TRANSPORT OF PREVIOUSLY APPROPRIATED ASSISTANCE HELD IN TITLE BY THE NICARAGUAN RESISTANCE.

(a) IN GENERAL.—This section shall only apply upon the enactment of legislation, considered in the Senate in accordance with section 9013, authorizing the transportation to the Nicaraguan Resistance of previously appropriated assistance not to exceed $16,500,000 held in title by the Nicaraguan Resistance and, if necessary, providing authority for the interchangeability of such assistance with equipment of comparable value and purpose which is owned by the United States.

(b) FUNDS FOR TRANSPORTATION.—(1) There shall be transferred to the Secretary of State from unobligated funds from appropriations accounts specified in section 9011—

(A) such sums as are necessary to carry out the transportation requirements described in subsection (a), but not to exceed $5,000,000; and

(B) such sums as are necessary to provide for the indemnification of aircraft leased with funds transferred under clause (A), but not to exceed $20,000,000.

(2) The Secretary of State shall transfer the balance, if any, remaining of funds transferred under paragraph (1)(B) to the appropriations accounts from which such funds were transferred under such paragraph when the transportation requirements described in subsection (a) have been met.

(c) MONITORING BY CONGRESSIONAL COMMITTEES.—(1) The chairmen and ranking minority members of the Permanent Select Committee on Intelligence of the House of Representatives and the Select Committee on Intelligence of the Senate shall be kept fully and currently informed regarding the transportation or exchange of any assistance described in subsection (a), including the value and purpose of the items transported or exchanged and the costs of such transportation.

(2) For purposes of this subsection, the term "fully and currently informed" includes the provision of all records, data, and other information necessary to carry out the monitoring of activities described in this subsection.

(d) ROLE OF THE SECRETARY OF STATE.—The Secretary of State (or his designee) shall be responsible for support, coordination, and supervision of the transportation of assistance described in subsection (a). Such support shall involve the provision of funds as well as the provision and transportation of materiel and other assistance.

(e) The authority granted by this section expires upon delivering of previously appropriated assistance and interchanged assistance authorized by this section.

SEC. 9004. REPORTS.

(a) PRESIDENTIAL REPORT.—At the time of the submission to the Congress by the President of any request for the authority described in section 9002(4), the President shall submit to the Congress a report containing—

(1) a detailed discussion and substantial evidence of the nature of the emergency situation in or adjacent to Nicaragua caused by actions taken by the Government of Nicaragua having a critical impact on peace and stability of the Central American region,

(2) a description of the recommendations made by the presidents of the Central American democracies consulted in accordance with section 9002(2), and

(3) the justification for the transport to the Nicaraguan Resistance of previously appropriated assistance held in title by the Nicaraguan Resistance,

including specific information pertaining to at least two of the following three actions:

(A) Sandinista initiation of an unprovoked military attack and any other hostile action directed against the forces of the Nicaraguan Resistance, as well as participation or support of any hostile actions against such forces by any other foreign country or organized group;

(B) Other blatant violations of the Esquipulas Accord of August 7, 1987, such as suppression of the media and the internal political opposition, including a denial of its rights to assemble and to hold peaceful demonstrations, and other human rights violations against the people of Nicaragua; and

(C) A continued unacceptable level of military assistance by Soviet-bloc countries, including Cuba.

(b) MONTHLY REPORT BY THE SECRETARY OF STATE.—The Secretary of State shall, not less than once every 30 days after the date of enactment of this Act until the funds provided under this title are expended, submit to the intelligence committees and foreign relations committees of the Congress a report—

(1) describing the conditions in Nicaragua and the use of the funds provided under this title;

(2) a detailed statement of any progress toward a negotiated settlement of the armed conflict in Central America, as agreed to under the Esquipulas Accord of August 7, 1987;

(3) a detailed discussion of United States efforts since the signing of the Sapoa agreement to encourage the Soviet Union to restrict the shipment of Soviet arms to the Government of Nicaragua and specifying Soviet reaction to such efforts;

(4) a discussion reviewing the status of United States national security interests in Central America, with particular attention to the advisability of entering into bilateral negotiations with the Government of Nicaragua concerning—

(A) the termination of the presence of Soviet and Soviet-bloc (including Cuban) military and security advisors in Nicaragua;

(B) the termination of Soviet and Soviet-bloc (including Cuban) assistance to the Government of Nicaragua; and

(C) a prohibition on the establishment or use of bases in Nicaragua by the Soviet Union or any Soviet-bloc country, including Cuba;

(5) a description of United States diplomatic efforts in support of the Esquipulas Accord of August 7, 1987, and the Sapoa

Agreement of March 23, 1988, and an analysis of the actions taken by the Nicaraguan Resistance and the Government of Nicaragua to negotiate a settlement under the provisions of these agreements;

(6) an evaluation of the effect that additional military assistance for the Nicaraguan Resistance would have on political and economic stability in Honduras, Costa Rica, and El Salvador, as well as how such assistance would advance the process of negotiation and political settlement in Nicaragua;

(7) a description of the progress made by economic development programs that have been implemented in Honduras, El Salvador, and Costa Rica since the Esquipulas Accord of August 7, 1987, was signed and what effect renewed fighting in Nicaragua would have on these programs; and

(8) a discussion of the policies of the European allies of the United States and the Latin American democracies (outside Central America) toward Central America, and the extent of their support for and cooperation with United States policies regarding the Nicaraguan Resistance.

(c) DEFINITIONS.—For purposes of this section—

(1) the term "intelligence committees" refers to the Permanent Select Committee on Intelligence of the House of Representatives and the Select Committee on Intelligence of the Senate; and

(2) the term "foreign relations committees" refers to the Committee on Foreign Relations of the Senate and the Committee on Foreign Affairs of the House of Representatives.

SEC. 9009. UNITED STATES POLICY CONCERNING ECONOMIC ASSISTANCE FOR CENTRAL AMERICA.

As part of an effort to promote democracy and address on a long-term basis the economic causes of regional and political instability in Central America—

(1) in recognition of the recommendations of groups such as the National Bipartisan Commission on Central America, the Inter-American Dialogue, and the Sanford Commission,

(2) to assist in the implementation of these economic plans and to encourage other countries in other parts of the world to join in extending assistance to Central America,

(3) and in the context of an agreement to end military conflict in the region,

the Congress encourages the President to submit proposals for bilateral and multilateral action—

(A) to provide additional economic assistance to the democratic countries of Central America to promote economic stability, expand educational opportunity, foster progress in human rights, bolster democratic institutions, and strengthen institutions of justice;

(B) to facilitate the ability of Central American economies to grow through the development of their infrastructure, expansion of exports, and the strengthening of increased investment opportunities;

(C) to provide a more realistic plan to assist Central American countries in managing their foreign debt; and

(D) to develop these initiatives in concert with Western Europe, Japan, and other democratic allies.

SEC. 9010. ECONOMIC INCENTIVES FOR DEMOCRACY IN NICARAGUA SIMILAR TO THOSE AVAILABLE TO CENTRAL AMERICAN DEMOCRACIES.

(a) CONDITION ON TERMINATION OF TRADE EMBARGO AND PROVISION OF RELOCATION ASSISTANCE.—(1) If the Government of Nicaragua and the Nicaraguan Resistance sign a comprehensive final agreement to provide for peace and democracy in Nicaragua, then—

(A) the President shall terminate the trade embargo imposed against Nicaragua by Executive order 12513 of May 1, 1985; and

(B) there shall be transferred to the President from unobligated funds from the appropriations accounts specified in section 9011, $10,000,000, to remain available for a period of twelve months after the signing of the agreement, to provide assistance for the relocation in Nicaragua and the reintegration into Nicaraguan civil society of members of the Nicaraguan Resistance, and the Nicaraguans outside Nicaragua displaced by the conflict.

(2) Nothing in this section shall be construed to limit the authority of the President under the International Emergency Economic Powers Act.

(b) TRADE BENEFITS.—On or after the date which is 180 days after the date of signing of the agreement described in subsection (a), if the President certifies to the Congress that the Government of Nicaragua is continuing to comply with that agreement, then the President may, notwithstanding any other provision of law—

(1) designate Nicaragua a beneficiary country for purposes of proposals referred to in section 9009 and for purposes of the Caribbean Basin Economic Recovery Act (19 U.S.C. 2701 et seq.);

(2) designate Nicaragua a beneficiary developing country for purposes of title V of the Trade Act of 1974 (relating to the generalized system of preferences); and

(3) authorize loan assistance to Nicaragua under the Export-Import Bank Act of 1945.

(c) INTERPRETATION.—Authority granted by subsections (a) and (b) shall be in addition to, and shall not be construed to limit, authority otherwise available to the President by law.

WILDLIFE CONSERVATION APPROPRIATIONS, 1988-1992

An Act to authorize appropriations to carry out the Endangered Species Act of 1973 during fiscal years 1988, 1989, 1990, 1991, and 1992, and for other purposes.

Date: October 7, 1988

Bill No.: H.R. 1467

Public Law No.: 100-478

Cite: 102 STAT. 2306

Sections reprinted:

Public Law 100-478
100th Congress

An Act

To authorize appropriations to carry out the Endangered Species Act of 1973 during fiscal years 1988, 1989, 1990, 1991, and 1992, and for other purposes.

Be it enacted by the Senate and House of Representatives of the United States of America in Congress assembled,

TITLE II—AFRICAN ELEPHANT CONSERVATION

SEC. 2001. SHORT TITLE.

This title may be cited as the "African Elephant Conservation Act".

SEC. 2002. STATEMENT OF PURPOSE.

The purpose of this title is to perpetuate healthy populations of African elephants.

SEC. 2003. FINDINGS.

The Congress finds the following:

(1) Elephant populations in Africa have declined at an alarming rate since the mid-1970's.

(2) The large illegal trade in African elephant ivory is the major cause of this decline and threatens the continued existence of the African elephant.

(3) The African elephant is listed as threatened under the Endangered Species Act of 1973 (16 U.S.C. 1531 et seq.) and its continued existence will be further jeopardized if this decline is not reversed.

(4) Because African elephant ivory is indistinguishable from Asian elephant ivory, there is a need to ensure that the trade in African elephant ivory does not further endanger the Asian elephant, which is listed as endangered under section 4 of the Endangered Species Act of 1973 (16 U.S.C. 1533) and under Appendix I of CITES.

(5) In response to the significant illegal trade in African elephant ivory, the parties to CITES established the CITES Ivory Control System to curtail the illegal trade and to encourage African countries to manage, conserve, and protect their African elephant populations.

(6) The CITES Ivory Control System entered into force recently and should be allowed to continue in force for a reasonable period of time to assess its effectiveness in curtailing the illegal trade in African elephant ivory.

(7) Although some African countries have effective African elephant conservation programs, many do not have sufficient resources to properly manage, conserve, and protect their elephant populations.

(8) The United States, as a party to CITES and a large market for worked ivory, shares responsibility for supporting and implementing measures to stop the illegal trade in African elephant ivory and to provide for the conservation of the African elephant.

(9) There is no evidence that sport hunting is part of the poaching that contributes to the illegal trade in African elephant ivory, and there is evidence that the proper utilization of well-managed elephant populations provides an important source of funding for African elephant conservation programs.

SEC. 2004. STATEMENT OF POLICY.

It is the policy of the United States—

(1) to assist in the conservation and protection of the African elephant by supporting the conservation programs of African countries and the CITES Secretariat; and

(2) to provide financial resources for those programs.

PART I—AFRICAN ELEPHANT CONSERVATION ASSISTANCE

SEC. 2101. PROVISION OF ASSISTANCE.

(a) IN GENERAL.—The Secretary may provide financial assistance under this part from the African Elephant Conservation Fund for approved projects for research, conservation, management, or protection of African elephants.

(b) PROJECT PROPOSAL.—Any African government agency responsible for African elephant conservation and protection, the CITES Secretariat, and any organization or individual with experience in African elephant conservation may submit to the Secretary a project proposal under this section. Each such proposal shall contain—

(1) the name of the person responsible for conducting the project;

(2) a succinct statement of the need for and purposes of the project;

(3) a description of the qualifications of the individuals who will be conducting the project;

(4) an estimate of the funds and time required to complete the project;

(5) evidence of support of the project by governmental entities of countries within which the project will be conducted, if such support may be important for the success of the project; and

(6) any other information the Secretary considers to be necessary or appropriate for evaluating the eligibility of the project for funding under this title.

(c) PROJECT REVIEW AND APPROVAL.—The Secretary shall review each project proposal to determine if it meets the criteria set forth in subsection (d) and otherwise merits assistance under this title. Not later than six months after receiving a project proposal, and subject to the availability of funds, the Secretary shall approve or disapprove the proposal and provide written notification to the person who submitted the proposal and to each country within which the project is proposed to be conducted.

(d) CRITERIA FOR APPROVAL.—The Secretary may approve a project under this section if the project will enhance programs for African elephant research, conservation, management, or protection by—

(1) developing in a usable form sound scientific information on African elephant habitat condition and carrying capacity, total elephant numbers and population trends, or annual reproduction and mortality; or

(2) assisting efforts—

(A) to ensure that any taking of African elephants in the country is effectively controlled and monitored;

(B) to implement conservation programs to provide for healthy, sustainable African elephant populations; or

(C) to enhance compliance with the CITES Ivory Control System.

(e) PROJECT REPORTING.—Each entity that receives assistance under this section shall provide such periodic reports to the Director of the United States Fish and Wildlife Service as the Director considers relevant and appropriate. Each report shall include all information requested by the Director for evaluating the progress and success of the project.

SEC. 2102. AFRICAN ELEPHANT CONSERVATION FUND.

(a) ESTABLISHMENT.—There is established in the general fund of the Treasury a separate account to be known as the "African Elephant Conservation Fund", which shall consist of amounts deposited into the Fund by the Secretary of the Treasury under subsection (b).

(b) DEPOSITS INTO FUND.—The Secretary of the Treasury shall deposit into the Fund—

(1) subject to appropriations, all amounts received by the United States in the form of penalties under section 2204 which are not used to pay rewards under section 2205;

(2) amounts received by the Secretary of the Interior in the form of donations under subsection (d); and

(3) other amounts appropriated to the Fund to carry out this part.

(c) USE.—

(1) IN GENERAL.—Subject to paragraph (2), amounts in the Fund may be used by the Secretary, without further appropriation, to provide assistance under this part.

(2) ADMINISTRATION.—Not more than three percent of amounts appropriated to the Fund for a fiscal year may be used by the Secretary to administer the Fund for that fiscal year.

(d) ACCEPTANCE AND USE OF DONATIONS.—The Secretary may accept and use donations of funds to provide assistance under this part. Amounts received by the Secretary in the form of such donations shall be transferred by the Secretary to the Secretary of the Treasury for deposit into the Fund.

SEC. 2103. ANNUAL REPORTS.

The Secretary shall submit an annual report to the Congress not later than January 31 of each year regarding the Fund and the status of the African elephant. Each such report shall include with respect to the year for which the report is submitted a description of—

(1) the total amounts deposited into and expended from the Fund;

(2) the costs associated with the administration of the Fund;

(3) a summary of the projects for which the Secretary has provided assistance under this part and an evaluation of those projects; and

(4) an evaluation of African elephant populations and whether the CITES Ivory Control System is functioning effectively to control the illegal trade in African elephant ivory.

PART II—MORATORIA AND PROHIBITED ACTS

SEC. 2201. REVIEW OF AFRICAN ELEPHANT CONSERVATION PROGRAMS.

(a) IN GENERAL.—Within one month after the date of the enactment of this title, the Secretary shall issue a call for information on the African elephant conservation program of each ivory producing country by—

(1) publishing a notice in the Federal Register requesting submission of such information to the Secretary by all interested parties; and

(2) submitting a written request for such information through the Secretary of State to each ivory producing country.

(b) REVIEW AND DETERMINATION.—

(1) IN GENERAL.—The Secretary shall review the African elephant conservation program of each ivory producing country and, not later than one year after the date of the enactment of this title, shall issue and publish in the Federal Register a determination of whether or not the country meets the following criteria:

(A) The country is a party to CITES and adheres to the CITES Ivory Control System.

(B) The country's elephant conservation program is based on the best available information, and the country is making expeditious progress in compiling information on the elephant habitat condition and carrying capacity, total population and population trends, and the annual reproduction and mortality of the elephant populations within the country.

(C) The taking of elephants in the country is effectively controlled and monitored.

(D) The country's ivory quota is determined on the basis of information referred to in subparagraph (B) and reflects the amount of ivory which is confiscated or consumed domestically by the country.

(E) The country has not authorized or allowed the export of amounts of raw ivory which exceed its ivory quota under the CITES Ivory Control System.

(2) DELAY IN ISSUING DETERMINATION.—If the Secretary finds within one year after the date of the enactment of this title that there is insufficient information upon which to make the determination under paragraph (1), the Secretary may delay issuing the determination until no later than December 31, 1989. The Secretary shall issue and publish in the Federal Register at the time of the finding a statement explaining the reasons for any such delay.

SEC. 2202. MORATORIA.

(a) IVORY PRODUCING COUNTRIES.—

(1) IN GENERAL.—The Secretary shall establish a moratorium on the importation of raw and worked ivory from an ivory producing country immediately upon making a determination that the country does not meet all the criteria set forth in section 2201(b)(1).

(2) LATER ESTABLISHMENT.—With regard to any ivory producing country for which the Secretary has insufficient information to make a determination pursuant to section 2201(b), the Secretary shall establish a moratorium on the importation of raw and worked ivory from such country not later than January 1, 1990, unless, based on new information, the Secretary concludes before that date that the country meets all of the criteria set forth in section 2201(b)(1).

(b) INTERMEDIARY COUNTRIES.—The Secretary shall establish a moratorium on the importation of raw and worked ivory from an intermediary country immediately upon making a determination that the country—

(1) is not a party to CITES;

(2) does not adhere to the CITES Ivory Control System;

(3) imports raw ivory from a country that is not an ivory producing country;

(4) imports raw or worked ivory from a country that is not a party to CITES;

(5) imports raw or worked ivory that originates in an ivory producing country in violation of the laws of that ivory producing country;

(6) substantially increases its imports of raw or worked ivory from a country that is subject to a moratorium under this title during the first three months of that moratorium; or

(7) imports raw or worked ivory from a country that is subject to a moratorium under this title after the first three months of that moratorium, unless the ivory is imported by vessel during the first six months of that moratorium and is accompanied by shipping documents which show that it was exported before the establishment of the moratorium.

(c) SUSPENSION OF MORATORIUM.—The Secretary shall suspend a moratorium established under this section if, after notice and public comment, the Secretary determines that the reasons for establishing the moratorium no longer exist.

(d) PETITION.—

(1) IN GENERAL.—Any person may at any time submit a petition in writing requesting that the Secretary establish or suspend a moratorium under this section. Such a petition shall include such substantial information as may be necessary to demonstrate the need for the action requested by the petition.

(2) CONSIDERATION AND RULING.—The Secretary shall publish a notice of receipt of a petition under this subsection in the Federal Register and shall provide an opportunity for the public to comment on the petition. The Secretary shall rule on such petition not later than 90 days after the close of the public comment period.

(e) SPORT-HUNTED TROPHIES.—Individuals may import sport-hunted elephant trophies that they have legally taken in an ivory producing country that has submitted an ivory quota. The Secretary shall not establish any moratorium under this section, pursuant to a petition or otherwise, which prohibits the importation into the United States of sport-hunted trophies from elephants that are legally taken by the importer or the importer's principal in an ivory producing country that has submitted an ivory quota.

(f) CONFISCATED IVORY.—Trade in raw or worked ivory that is confiscated by an ivory producing country or an intermediary country and is disposed of pursuant to the CITES Ivory Control System shall not be the sole cause for the establishment of a moratorium under this part if all proceeds from the disposal of the confiscated ivory are used solely to enhance wildlife conservation programs or conservation purposes of CITES. With respect to any country that was not a party to CITES at the time of such confiscation, this subsection shall not apply until such country develops appropriate measures to assure that persons with a history of illegal dealings in ivory shall not benefit from the disposal of confiscated ivory.

SEC. 2203. PROHIBITED ACTS.

Except as provided in section 2202(e), it is unlawful for any person—

(1) to import raw ivory from any country other than an ivory producing country;

(2) to export raw ivory from the United States;

(3) to import raw or worked ivory that was exported from an ivory producing country in violation of that country's laws or of the CITES Ivory Control System;

(4) to import worked ivory, other than personal effects, from any country unless that country has certified that such ivory was derived from legal sources; or

(5) to import raw or worked ivory from a country for which a moratorium is in effect under section 2202.

SEC. 2204. PENALTIES AND ENFORCEMENT.

(a) CRIMINAL VIOLATIONS.—Whoever knowingly violates section 2203 shall, upon conviction, be fined under title 18, United States Code, or imprisoned for not more than one year, or both.

(b) CIVIL VIOLATIONS.—Whoever violates section 2203 may be assessed a civil penalty by the Secretary of not more than $5,000 for each such violation.

(c) PROCEDURES FOR ASSESSMENT OF CIVIL PENALTY.—Proceedings for the assessment of a civil penalty under this section shall be conducted in accordance with the procedures provided for in section 11(a) of the Endangered Species Act of 1973 (16 U.S.C. 1540(a)).

(d) USE OF PENALTIES.—Subject to appropriations, penalties collected under this section may be used by the Secretary of the Treasury to pay rewards under section 2205 and, to the extent not used to pay such rewards, shall be deposited by the Secretary of the Treasury into the Fund.

(e) ENFORCEMENT.—The Secretary, the Secretary of the Treasury, and the Secretary of the department in which the Coast Guard is operating shall enforce this part in the same manner such Secretaries carry out enforcement activities under section 11(e) of the Endangered Species Act of 1973 (16 U.S.C. 1540(e)). Section 11(c) of the Endangered Species Act of 1973 (16 U.S.C. 1540(c)) shall apply to actions arising under this part.

SEC. 2205. REWARDS.

(a) IN GENERAL.—Upon the recommendation of the Secretary, the Secretary of the Treasury may pay a reward to any person who furnishes information which leads to a civil penalty or a criminal conviction under this title.

(b) AMOUNT.—The amount of a reward under this section shall be equal to not more than one-half of any criminal or civil penalty or fine with respect to which the reward is paid, or $25,000, whichever is less.

(c) LIMITATION ON ELIGIBILITY.—An officer or employee of the United States or of any State or local government who furnishes information or renders service in the performance of his or her official duties shall not be eligible for a reward under this section.

PART III—MISCELLANEOUS

SEC. 2301. PERMISSION TO IMPORT OR EXPORT AFRICAN ELEPHANT IVORY.

Section 9(d) of the Endangered Species Act of 1973 (16 U.S.C. 1538(d)) is amended to read as follows:

"(d) IMPORTS AND EXPORTS.—

"(1) IN GENERAL.—It is unlawful for any person, without first having obtained permission from the Secretary, to engage in business—

"(A) as an importer or exporter of fish or wildlife (other than shellfish and fishery products which (i) are not listed pursuant to section 4 of this Act as endangered species or threatened species, and (ii) are imported for purposes of human or animal consumption or taken in waters under the jurisdiction of the United States or on the high seas for recreational purposes); or

"(B) as an importer or exporter of any amount of raw or worked African elephant ivory.

"(2) REQUIREMENTS.—Any person required to obtain permission under paragraph (1) of this subsection shall—

"(A) keep such records as will fully and correctly disclose each importation or exportation of fish, wildlife, plants, or African elephant ivory made by him and the subsequent disposition made by him with respect to such fish, wildlife, plants, or ivory;

"(B) at all reasonable times upon notice by a duly authorized representative of the Secretary, afford such representative access to his place of business, an opportunity to examine his inventory of imported fish, wildlife, plants, or African elephant ivory and the records required to be kept under subparagraph (A) of this paragraph, and to copy such records; and

"(C) file such reports as the Secretary may require.

"(3) REGULATIONS.—The Secretary shall prescribe such regulations as are necessary and appropriate to carry out the purposes of this subsection.

"(4) RESTRICTION ON CONSIDERATION OF VALUE OR AMOUNT OF AFRICAN ELEPHANT IVORY IMPORTED OR EXPORTED.—In granting permission under this subsection for importation or exportation of African elephant ivory, the Secretary shall not vary the requirements for obtaining such permission on the basis of the value or amount of ivory imported or exported under such permission.".

SEC. 2302. RELATIONSHIP TO ENDANGERED SPECIES ACT OF 1973.

The authority of the Secretary under this title is in addition to and shall not affect the authority of the Secretary under the Endangered Species Act of 1973 (16 U.S.C. 1531 et seq.) or diminish the Secretary's authority under the Lacey Act Amendments of 1981 (16 U.S.C. 3371 et seq.).

SEC. 2303. CERTIFICATION UNDER PELLY AMENDMENT.

If the Secretary finds in administering this title that a country does not adhere to the CITES Ivory Control System, that country is deemed, for purposes of section 8(a)(2) of the Act of August 27, 1954 (22 U.S.C. 1978), to be diminishing the effectiveness of an international program for endangered or threatened species.

SEC. 2304. EFFECTIVENESS OF CITES.

Within 3 months after the completion of the 8th Conference of the Parties to CITES, the Secretary shall determine whether this title, together with the CITES Ivory Control System, has substantially stopped the importation of illegally harvested ivory into the United States. If the Secretary determines that the importation of illegally harvested ivory has not been substantially stopped, the Secretary shall recommend to the Congress amendments to this title or other actions that may be necessary to achieve the purposes of this title, including the establishment of a complete moratorium on the importation of elephant ivory into the United States.

SEC. 2305. DEFINITIONS.

In this title—

(1) the term "African elephant" means any animal of the species loxodonta africana;

(2) the term "CITES" means the Convention on the International Trade in Endangered Species of Wild Fauna and Flora;

(3) the term "CITES Ivory Control System" means the ivory quota and marking system established by CITES to curtail illegal trade in African elephant ivory;

(4) the term "Fund" means the African Elephant Conservation Fund established by section 2102;

(5) the terms "import" and "importation" have the meanings such terms have in the Endangered Species Act of 1973 (16 U.S.C. 1531 et seq.);

(6) the term "intermediary country" means a country that exports raw or worked ivory that does not originate in that country;

(7) the term "ivory producing country" means any African country within which is located any part of the range of a population of African elephants;

(8) the term "ivory quota" means a quota submitted by an ivory producing country to the CITES Secretariat in accordance with the CITES Ivory Control System;

(9) the term "personal effects" means articles which are not intended for sale and are part of a shipment of the household effects of a person who is moving his or her residence to or from the United States, or are included in personal accompanying baggage;

(10) the term "raw ivory" means any African elephant tusk, and any piece thereof, the surface of which, polished or unpolished, is unaltered or minimally carved;

(11) the term "Secretary" means the Secretary of the Interior;

(12) the term "United States" means the fifty States, the District of Columbia, Guam, the Commonwealth of the Northern Mariana Islands, the Commonwealth of Puerto Rico, and the territories and possessions of the United States; and

(13) the term "worked ivory" means any African elephant tusk, and any piece thereof, which is not raw ivory.

CAMBODIA JOINT RESOLUTION, 1988

Joint Resolution in support of the restoration of a free and independent Cambodia, the withdrawal of Vietnamese forces, and the protection of the Cambodian people from a return to power by the genocidal Khmer Rouge.

Date: October 18, 1988

Bill No.: H.J. Res. 602

Public Law No.: 100-502

Cite: 102 STAT. 2504

Sections reprinted: All

Public Law 100-502
100th Congress

Joint Resolution

In support of the restoration of a free and independent Cambodia, the withdrawal of Vietnamese forces, and the protection of the Cambodian people from a return to power by the genocidal Khmer Rouge.

Whereas the people of Cambodia suffered terribly under the despotic regime of the Khmer Rouge and subsequently during the occupation by the Socialist Republic of Vietnam;

Whereas the people of Cambodia have been victims of genocide, enslavement, starvation, and other deliberate acts of cruelty perpetrated by the Khmer Rouge, resulting in the deaths of over one million Cambodian people;

Whereas the Socialist Republic of Vietnam has maintained armed forces within Cambodia, thereby perpetuating their domination and forestalling the realization of self-determination by the Cambodian people;

Whereas the Vietnamese-installed Government of the People's Republic of Kampuchea has seriously abused the human and civil rights of the Cambodian people;

Whereas due to fears of persecution in their homeland, hundreds of thousands of Cambodians have become refugees or displaced persons, seeking first asylum in other Southeast Asian nations and subsequent resettlement in third countries;

Whereas the United States has supported the non-Communist resistance led by Prince Norodom Sihanouk and Son Sann in order to end the Vietnamese occupation of Cambodia and recover for the Cambodian people their sovereign rights;

Whereas Prince Norodom Sihanouk has with courage and conviction devoted his energies to restoring his homeland to independence, neutrality, peace, and harmony;

Whereas the Socialist Republic of Vietnam has declared its intention to withdraw forces from Cambodia by the end of 1990 and has pledged to join negotiations for a resolution of the Cambodian question;

Whereas dialogue and diplomatic discussions have increased on a regional and international basis concerning the future of Cambodia;

Whereas the stability of Southeast Asia can only be assured once peace is restored to Cambodia and the rights of the Cambodian people are universally respected; and

Whereas it is a moral imperative of all nations that the people of Cambodia no longer be made to suffer at the hands of the Khmer Rouge or any other force that would do further harm to the Khmer people or further endanger their cultural and religious heritage: Now, therefore, be it

Resolved by the Senate and House of Representatives of the United States of America in Congress assembled, That the United States—

(1) declares that all parties seeking a settlement of the conflict in Cambodia, including the United States, should have among their highest priorities the restoration of a free and independent Cambodia and the protection of the Cambodian people from a return to power by the genocidal Khmer Rouge;

(2) calls on the Socialist Republic of Vietnam to fully withdraw its armed forces from Cambodia, and further calls on all parties to respect the territorial integrity of Cambodia and to deny safe haven to Khmer Rouge forces seeking the overthrow of a newly formed sovereign Cambodian government;

(3) should seek a Cambodian settlement which contains workable measures to prevent a Khmer Rouge return to power, including a cessation of the flow of war materiel and the accumulation of caches of arms that might ultimately be used to terrorize the Cambodian people and to threaten a legitimate government of Cambodia;

(4) declares that the United States must remain vigilant to ensure that genocide is never tolerated or forgotten anywhere in the world and that those responsible for such heinous crimes should be held accountable under international law, as prescribed by the Convention on the Prevention and Punishment of the Crime of Genocide;

(5) declares that the United States in cooperation with the international community should use all appropriate means available to prevent a return to power of Pol Pot, the top echelon of the Khmer Rouge, and their armed forces, so that the Cambodian people might genuinely be free to pursue self-determination without the spectre of the coercion, intimidation, and torture that are known elements of the Khmer Rouge ideology;

(6) should seek the support of the member nations of the Association of Southeast Asian Nations (ASEAN) and other nations for the inclusion, in declarations and resolutions promulgated by the United Nations pertaining to the Cambodian conflict, of the principle that those responsible for acts of genocide and massive violations of internationally recognized human rights shall not return to positions of political power in Cambodia upon withdrawal of the foreign occupation forces;

(7) declares that the United States, in conjunction with the member nations of the Association of Southeast Asia Nations (ASEAN), should continue to provide assistance, support, and encouragement to the non-Communist Cambodian forces, particularly their efforts to achieve a negotiated settlement that would permit self-determination for the Cambodian people and the return of refugees in safety and dignity to their homeland;

(8) declares that the United States, in consultation with the member nations of the Association of Southeast Asia Nations, should consider whether such a settlement could be facilitated by the convening of an international conference on Cambodia and the provision of an international peacekeeping force that, in addition to performing other appropriate peacekeeping duties, could also supervise the withdrawal of Vietnamese forces and the holding of free and fair elections in Cambodia;

(9) should seek to ensure—

(A) that the refugee camps controlled by the Khmer Rouge are opened to inspection by international organizations, and

(B) that those within those camps have the freedom to move to non-Khmer Rouge controlled camps if they desire to do so; and

(10) should attempt to halt the flow of arms and military equipment to the Khmer Rouge by urging those nations providing assistance to the Khmer Rouge to cease doing so.

Approved October 18, 1988.

LEGISLATIVE HISTORY—H.J. Res. 602:

CONGRESSIONAL RECORD, Vol. 134 (1988):
Aug. 8, considered and passed House.
Sept. 16, considered and passed Senate.

WEEKLY COMPILATION OF PRESIDENTIAL DOCUMENTS, Vol. 24 (1988):
Oct. 18, Presidential statement.

BIOLOGICAL DIVERSITY JOINT RESOLUTION, 1988

Joint Resolution to encourage increased international cooperation to protect biological diversity.

Date: October 25, 1988

Bill No.: H.J. Res. 648

Public Law No.: 100-530

Cite: 102 STAT. 2651

Sections reprinted: All

Public Law 100-530
100th Congress

Joint Resolution

To encourage increased international cooperation to protect biological diversity.

Whereas habitat destruction is a main cause of the accelerating extinction of animal and plant species;

Whereas increased international cooperation is essential to protect species threatened with extinction and to halt the loss of unique and irreplaceable ecosystems; and

Whereas the United States has strongly supported efforts to convene an international convention for preservation of the Earth's biological diversity: Now therefore, be it

Resolved by the Senate and House of Representatives of the United States of America in Congress assembled,

SECTION 1. STATEMENT OF POLICIES.

The Congress—

(1) supports the United States efforts, consistent with section 119(g) of the Foreign Assistance Act of 1961, to initiate discussions to develop an international agreement to preserve biological diversity; and

(2) calls upon the President to continue exerting United States leadership in order to achieve the earliest possible negotiation of an international convention to conserve the Earth's biological diversity, including the protection of a representative system of ecosystems adequate to conserve biological diversity.

SEC. 2. REPORT.

Not later than one year after the date of the enactment of this joint resolution, the President shall submit a report to the Congress on progress toward the goal of negotiating the international convention described in paragraph (2) of section 1.

Approved October 25, 1988.

LEGISLATIVE HISTORY—H.J. Res. 648:

CONGRESSIONAL RECORD, Vol. 134 (1988):
Sept. 20, 22, considered and passed House.
Oct. 7, considered and passed Senate.

BERNE CONVENTION IMPLEMENTATION ACT OF 1988

An Act to amend title 17, United States Code, to implement the Berne Convention for the Protection of Literary and Artistic Works, as revised at Paris on July 24, 1971, and for other purposes.

Date: October 31, 1988

Bill No.: H.R. 4262

Public Law No.: 100-568

Cite: 102 STAT. 2853

Sections reprinted: All.

Public Law 100-568
100th Congress

An Act

To amend title 17, United States Code, to implement the Berne Convention for the Protection of Literary and Artistic Works, as revised at Paris on July 24, 1971, and for other purposes.

Be it enacted by the Senate and House of Representatives of the United States of America in Congress assembled.

SECTION 1. SHORT TITLE AND REFERENCES TO TITLE 17, UNITED STATES CODE.

(a) SHORT TITLE.—This Act may be cited as the "Berne Convention Implementation Act of 1988".

(b) REFERENCES TO TITLE 17, UNITED STATES CODE.—Whenever in this Act an amendment or repeal is expressed in terms of an amendment to or a repeal of a section or other provision, the reference shall be considered to be made to a section or other provision of title 17, United States Code.

SEC. 2. DECLARATIONS.

The Congress makes the following declarations:

(1) The Convention for the Protection of Literary and Artistic Works, signed at Berne, Switzerland, on September 9, 1886, and all acts, protocols, and revisions thereto (hereafter in this Act referred to as the "Berne Convention") are not self-executing under the Constitution and laws of the United States.

(2) The obligations of the United States under the Berne Convention may be performed only pursuant to appropriate domestic law.

(3) The amendments made by this Act, together with the law as it exists on the date of the enactment of this Act, satisfy the obligations of the United States in adhering to the Berne Convention and no further rights or interests shall be recognized or created for that purpose.

SEC. 3. CONSTRUCTION OF THE BERNE CONVENTION.

(a) RELATIONSHIP WITH DOMESTIC LAW.—The provisions of the Berne Convention—

(1) shall be given effect under title 17, as amended by this Act, and any other relevant provision of Federal or State law, including the common law; and

(2) shall not be enforceable in any action brought pursuant to the provisions of the Berne Convention itself.

(b) CERTAIN RIGHTS NOT AFFECTED.—The provisions of the Berne Convention, the adherence of the United States thereto, and satisfaction of United States obligations thereunder, do not expand or reduce any right of an author of a work, whether claimed under Federal, State, or the common law—

(1) to claim authorship of the work; or

(2) to object to any distortion, mutilation, or other modification of, or other derogatory action in relation to, the work, that would prejudice the author's honor or reputation.

SEC. 4. SUBJECT MATTER AND SCOPE OF COPYRIGHTS.

(a) SUBJECT AND SCOPE.—Chapter 1 is amended—

(1) in section 101—

(A) in the definition of "Pictorial, graphic, and sculptural works" by striking out in the first sentence "technical drawings, diagrams, and models" and inserting in lieu thereof "diagrams, models, and technical drawings, including architectural plans";

(B) by inserting after the definition of "Audiovisual works", the following:

"The 'Berne Convention' is the Convention for the Protection of Literary and Artistic Works, signed at Berne, Switzerland, on September 9, 1886, and all acts, protocols, and revisions thereto.

"A work is a 'Berne Convention work' if—

"(1) in the case of an unpublished work, one or more of the authors is a national of a nation adhering to the Berne Convention, or in the case of a published work, one or more of the authors is a national of a nation adhering to the Berne Convention on the date of first publication;

"(2) the work was first published in a nation adhering to the Berne Convention, or was simultaneously first published in a nation adhering to the Berne Convention and in a foreign nation that does not adhere to the Berne Convention;

"(3) in the case of an audiovisual work—

"(A) if one or more of the authors is a legal entity, that author has its headquarters in a nation adhering to the Berne Convention; or

"(B) if one or more of the authors is an individual, that author is domiciled, or has his or her habitual residence in, a nation adhering to the Berne Convention; or

"(4) in the case of a pictorial, graphic, or sculptural work that is incorporated in a building or other structure, the building or structure is located in a nation adhering to the Berne Convention.

For purposes of paragraph (1), an author who is domiciled in or has his or her habitual residence in, a nation adhering to the Berne Convention is considered to be a national of that nation. For purposes of paragraph (2), a work is considered to have been simultaneously published in two or more nations if its dates of publication are within 30 days of one another."; and

(C) by inserting after the definition of "Copyright owner", the following:

"The 'country of origin' of a Berne Convention work, for purposes of section 411, is the United States if—

"(1) in the case of a published work, the work is first published—

"(A) in the United States;

"(B) simultaneously in the United States and another nation or nations adhering to the Berne Convention, whose law grants a term of copyright protection that is the same as or longer than the term provided in the United States;

"(C) simultaneously in the United States and a foreign nation that does not adhere to the Berne Convention; or

"(D) in a foreign nation that does not adhere to the Berne Convention, and all of the authors of the work are nationals, domiciliaries, or habitual residents of, or in the case of an audiovisual work legal entities with headquarters in, the United States;

"(2) in the case of an unpublished work, all the authors of the work are nationals, domiciliaries, or habitual residents of the United States, or, in the case of an unpublished audiovisual work, all the authors are legal entities with headquarters in the United States; or

"(3) in the case of a pictorial, graphic, or sculptural work incorporated in a building or structure, the building or structure is located in the United States.

For the purposes of section 411, the 'country of origin' of any other Berne Convention work is not the United States.";

(2) in section 104(b)—

(A) by redesignating paragraph (4) as paragraph (5); and

(B) by inserting after paragraph (3) the following new paragraph:

"(4) the work is a Berne Convention work; or";

(3) in section 104 by adding at the end thereof the following:

"(c) EFFECT OF BERNE CONVENTION.—No right or interest in a work eligible for protection under this title may be claimed by virtue of, or in reliance upon, the provisions of the Berne Convention, or the adherence of the United States thereto. Any rights in a work eligible for protection under this title that derive from this title, other Federal or State statutes, or the common law, shall not be expanded or reduced by virtue of, or in reliance upon, the provisions of the Berne Convention, or the adherence of the United States thereto."; and

(4) by inserting after section 116 the following new section:

"§ 116A. Negotiated licenses for public performances by means of coin-operated phonorecord players

"(a) APPLICABILITY OF SECTION.—This section applies to any nondramatic musical work embodied in a phonorecord.

"(b) LIMITATION ON EXCLUSIVE RIGHT IF LICENSES NOT NEGOTIATED.—

"(1) APPLICABILITY.—In the case of a work to which this section applies, the exclusive right under clause (4) of section 106 to perform the work publicly by means of a coin-operated phonorecord player is limited by section 116 to the extent provided in this section.

"(2) DETERMINATION BY COPYRIGHT ROYALTY TRIBUNAL.—The Copyright Royalty Tribunal, at the end of the 1-year period beginning on the effective date of the Berne Convention Implementation Act of 1988, and periodically thereafter to the extent necessary to carry out subsection (f), shall determine whether or not negotiated licenses authorized by subsection (c) are in effect so as to provide permission to use a quantity of musical works not substantially smaller than the quantity of such works performed on coin-operated phonorecord players during the 1-year period ending on the effective date of that Act. If the Copyright Royalty Tribunal determines that such negotiated licenses are not so in effect, the Tribunal shall, upon making the determination, publish the determination in the Federal Register. Upon such publication, section 116 shall apply with respect to musical works that are not the subject of such negotiated licenses.

"(c) NEGOTIATED LICENSES.—

"(1) AUTHORITY FOR NEGOTIATIONS.—Any owners of copyright in works to which this section applies and any operators of coin-operated phonorecord players may negotiate and agree upon the terms and rates of royalty payments for the performance of such works and the proportionate division of fees paid among copyright owners, and may designate common agents to negotiate, agree to, pay, or receive such royalty payments.

"(2) ARBITRATION.—Parties to such a negotiation, within such time as may be specified by the Copyright Royalty Tribunal by regulation, may determine the result of the negotiation by arbitration. Such arbitration shall be governed by the provisions of title 9, to the extent such title is not inconsistent with this section. The parties shall give notice to the Copyright Royalty Tribunal of any determination reached by arbitration and any such determination shall, as between the parties to the arbitration, be dispositive of the issues to which it relates.

"(d) LICENSE AGREEMENTS SUPERIOR TO COPYRIGHT ROYALTY TRIBUNAL DETERMINATIONS.—License agreements between one or more copyright owners and one or more operators of coin-operated phonorecord players, which are negotiated in accordance with subsection (c), shall be given effect in lieu of any otherwise applicable determination by the Copyright Royalty Tribunal.

"(e) NEGOTIATION SCHEDULE.—Not later than 60 days after the effective date of the Berne Convention Implementation Act of 1988, if the Chairman of the Copyright Royalty Tribunal has not received notice, from copyright owners and operators of coin-operated phonorecord players referred to in subsection (c)(1), of the date and location of the first meeting between such copyright owners and such operators to commence negotiations authorized by subsection (c), the Chairman shall announce the date and location of such meeting. Such meeting may not be held more than 90 days after the effective date of such Act.

"(f) COPYRIGHT ROYALTY TRIBUNAL TO SUSPEND VARIOUS ACTIVITIES.—The Copyright Royalty Tribunal shall not conduct any rate-making activity with respect to coin-operated phonorecord players unless, at any time more than one year after the effective date of the Berne Convention Implementation Act of 1988, the negotiated licenses adopted by the parties under this section do not provide permission to use a quantity of musical works not substantially smaller than the quantity of such works performed on coin-operated phonorecord players during the one-year period ending on the effective date of such Act.

"(g) TRANSITION PROVISIONS; RETENTION OF COPYRIGHT ROYALTY TRIBUNAL JURISDICTION.—Until such time as licensing provisions are determined by the parties under this section, the terms of the compulsory license under section 116, with respect to the public performance of nondramatic musical works by means of coin-operated phonorecord players, which is in effect on the day before the effective date of the Berne Convention Implementation Act of 1988, shall remain in force. If a negotiated license authorized by this section comes into force so as to supersede previous determinations of the Copyright Royalty Tribunal, as provided in subsection (d), but

thereafter is terminated or expires and is not replaced by another licensing agreement, then section 116 shall be effective with respect to musical works that were the subject of such terminated or expired licenses.".

(b) TECHNICAL AMENDMENTS.—(1) Section 116 is amended—

(A) by amending the section heading to read as follows:

"§ 116. Scope of exclusive rights in nondramatic musical works: Compulsory licenses for public performances by means of coin-operated phonorecord players";

(B) in subsection (a) in the matter preceding paragraph (1), by inserting after "in a phonorecord," the following: "the performance of which is subject to this section as provided in section 116A,"; and

(C) in subsection (e), by inserting "and section 116A" after "As used in this section".

(2) The table of sections at the beginning of chapter 1 is amended by striking out the item relating to section 116, and inserting in lieu thereof the following:

"116. Scope of exclusive rights in nondramatic musical works: Compulsory licenses for public performances by means of coin-operated phonorecord players.

"116A. Negotiated licenses for public performances by means of coin-operated phonorecord players.".

SEC. 5. RECORDATION.

Section 205 is amended—

(1) by striking out subsection (d); and

(2) by redesignating subsections (e) and (f) as subsections (d) and (e), respectively.

SEC. 6. PREEMPTION WITH RESPECT TO OTHER LAWS NOT AFFECTED.

Section 301 is amended by adding at the end thereof the following:

"(e) The scope of Federal preemption under this section is not affected by the adherence of the United States to the Berne Convention or the satisfaction of obligations of the United States thereunder.".

SEC. 7. NOTICE OF COPYRIGHT.

(a) VISUALLY PERCEPTIBLE COPIES.—Section 401 is amended—

(1) in subsection (a), by amending the subsection heading to read as follows:

"(a) GENERAL PROVISIONS.—";

(2) in subsection (a), by striking out "shall be placed on all" and inserting in lieu thereof "may be placed on";

(3) in subsection (b), by striking out "The notice appearing on the copies" and inserting in lieu thereof "If a notice appears on the copies, it"; and

(4) by adding at the end the following:

"(d) EVIDENTIARY WEIGHT OF NOTICE.—If a notice of copyright in the form and position specified by this section appears on the published copy or copies to which a defendant in a copyright infringement suit had access, then no weight shall be given to such a defendant's interposition of a defense based on innocent infringement in mitigation of actual or statutory damages, except as provided in the last sentence of section 504(c)(2).".

(b) PHONORECORDS OF SOUND RECORDINGS.—Section 402 is amended—

(1) in subsection (a), by amending the subsection heading to read as follows:

"(a) GENERAL PROVISIONS.—";

(2) in subsection (a), by striking out "shall be placed on all" and inserting in lieu thereof "may be placed on";

(3) in subsection (b), by striking out "The notice appearing on the phonorecords" and inserting in lieu thereof "If a notice appears on the phonorecords, it"; and

(4) by adding at the end thereof the following new subsection:

"(d) EVIDENTIARY WEIGHT OF NOTICE.—If a notice of copyright in the form and position specified by this section appears on the published phonorecord or phonorecords to which a defendant in a copyright infringement suit had access, then no weight shall be given to such a defendant's interposition of a defense based on innocent infringement in mitigation of actual or statutory damages, except as provided in the last sentence of section 504(c)(2).".

(c) PUBLICATIONS INCORPORATING UNITED STATES GOVERNMENT WORKS.—Section 403 is amended to read as follows:

"Sections 401(d) and 402(d) shall not apply to a work published in copies or phonorecords consisting predominantly of one or more works of the United States Government unless the notice of copyright appearing on the published copies or phonorecords to which a defendant in the copyright infringement suit had access includes a statement identifying, either affirmatively or negatively, those portions of the copies or phonorecords embodying any work or works protected under this title.".

(d) NOTICE OF COPYRIGHT; CONTRIBUTIONS TO COLLECTIVE WORKS.—Section 404 is amended—

(1) in subsection (a), by striking out "to satisfy the requirements of sections 401 through 403", and inserting in lieu thereof "to invoke the provisions of section 401(d) or 402(d), as applicable"; and

(2) in subsection (b), by striking out "Where" and inserting in lieu thereof "With respect to copies and phonorecords publicly distributed by authority of the copyright owner before the effective date of the Berne Convention Implementation Act of 1988, where".

(e) OMISSION OF NOTICE.—Section 405 is amended—

(1) in subsection (a), by striking out "The omission of the copyright notice prescribed by" and inserting in lieu thereof "With respect to copies and phonorecords publicly distributed by authority of the copyright owner before the effective date of the Berne Convention Implementation Act of 1988, the omission of the copyright notice described in";

(2) in subsection (b), by striking out "omitted," in the first sentence and inserting in lieu thereof "omitted and which was publicly distributed by authority of the copyright owner before the effective date of the Berne Convention Implementation Act of 1988,"; and

(3) by amending the section heading to read as follows:

"§ 405. Notice of copyright: Omission of notice on certain copies and phonorecords"

(f) ERROR IN NAME OR DATE.—Section 406 is amended—

(1) in subsection (a) by striking out "Where" and inserting in lieu thereof "With respect to copies and phonorecords publicly distributed by authority of the copyright owner before the

effective date of the Berne Convention Implementation Act of 1988, where";

(2) in subsection (b) by inserting "before the effective date of the Berne Convention Implementation Act of 1988" after "distributed";

(3) in subsection (c)—

(A) by inserting "before the effective date of the Berne Convention Implementation Act of 1988" after "publicly distributed"; and

(B) by inserting after "405" the following: "as in effect on the day before the effective date of the Berne Convention Implementation Act of 1988"; and

(4) by amending the section heading to read as follows:

"§ 406. Notice of copyright: Error in name or date on certain copies and phonorecords".

(g) CLERICAL AMENDMENT.—The table of sections at the beginning of chapter 4 is amended by striking out the items relating to sections 405 and 406 and inserting in lieu thereof the following:

"405. Notice of copyright: Omission of notice on certain copies and phonorecords.
"406. Notice of copyright: Error in name or date on certain copies and phonorecords.".

SEC. 8. DEPOSIT OF COPIES OR PHONORECORDS FOR LIBRARY OF CONGRESS.

Section 407(a) is amended by striking out "with notice of copyright".

SEC. 9. COPYRIGHT REGISTRATION.

(a) REGISTRATION IN GENERAL.—Section 408 is amended—

(1) in subsection (a), by striking out "Subject to the provisions of section 405(a), such" in the second sentence and inserting in lieu thereof "Such";

(2) in subsection (c)(2)—

(A) by striking out "all of the following conditions—" and inserting in lieu thereof "the following conditions:";

(B) by striking out subparagraph (A); and

(C) by redesignating subparagraphs (B) and (C) as subparagraphs (A) and (B), respectively.

(b) INFRINGEMENT ACTIONS.—

(1) REGISTRATION AS A PREREQUISITE.—Section 411 is amended—

(A) by amending the section heading to read as follows:

"§ 411. Registration and infringement actions";

(B) in subsection (a) by striking out "Subject" and inserting in lieu thereof "Except for actions for infringement of copyright in Berne Convention works whose country of origin is not the United States, and subject"; and

(C) in subsection (b)(2) by inserting ", if required by subsection (a)," after "work".

(2) TABLE OF SECTIONS.—The table of sections at the beginning of chapter 4 is amended by striking out the item relating to section 411 and inserting in lieu thereof the following:

"411. Registration and infringement actions.".

SEC. 10. COPYRIGHT INFRINGEMENT AND REMEDIES.

(a) INFRINGEMENT.—Section 501(b) is amended by striking out "sections 205(d) and 411," and inserting in lieu thereof "section 411,".

(b) DAMAGES AND PROFITS.—Section 504(c) is amended—

(1) in paragraph (1)—

(A) by striking out "$250", and inserting in lieu thereof "$500"; and

(B) by striking out "$10,000", and inserting in lieu thereof "$20,000"; and

(2) in paragraph (2)—

(A) by striking out "$50,000.", and inserting in lieu thereof "$100,000."; and

(B) by striking out "$100.", and inserting in lieu thereof "$200.".

SEC. 11. COPYRIGHT ROYALTY TRIBUNAL.

Chapter 8 is amended—

(1) in section 801, by adding at the end of subsection (b) the following: "In determining whether a return to a copyright owner under section 116 is fair, appropriate weight shall be given to—

"(i) the rates previously determined by the Tribunal to provide a fair return to the copyright owner, and

"(ii) the rates contained in any license negotiated pursuant to section 116A of this title."; and

(2) by amending section 804(a)(2)(C) to read as follows:

"(C)(i) In proceedings under section 801(b)(1) concerning the adjustment of royalty rates as provided in section 115, such petition may be filed in 1990 and in each subsequent tenth calendar year, and at any time within 1 year after negotiated licenses authorized by section 116A are terminated or expire and are not replaced by subsequent agreements.

"(ii) If negotiated licenses authorized by section 116A come into force so as to supersede previous determinations of the Tribunal, as provided in section 116A(d), but thereafter are terminated or expire and are not replaced by subsequent agreements, the Tribunal shall, upon petition of any party to such terminated or expired negotiated license agreement, promptly establish an interim royalty rate or rates for the public performance by means of a coin-operated phonorecord player of nondramatic musical works embodied in phonorecords which had been subject to the terminated or expired negotiated license agreement. Such interim royalty rate or rates shall be the same as the last such rate or rates and shall remain in force until the conclusion of proceedings to adjust the royalty rates applicable to such works, or until superseded by a new negotiated license agreement, as provided in section 116A(d).".

SEC. 12. WORKS IN THE PUBLIC DOMAIN.

Title 17, United States Code, as amended by this Act, does not provide copyright protection for any work that is in the public domain in the United States.

SEC. 13. EFFECTIVE DATE; EFFECT ON PENDING CASES.

(a) EFFECTIVE DATE.—This Act and the amendments made by this Act take effect on the date on which the Berne Convention (as defined in section 101 of title 17, United States Code) enters into force with respect to the United States.

(b) EFFECT ON PENDING CASES.—Any cause of action arising under title 17, United States Code, before the effective date of this Act shall be governed by the provisions of such title as in effect when the cause of action arose.

Approved October 31, 1988.

LEGISLATIVE HISTORY—H.R. 4262 (S. 1301):

HOUSE REPORTS: No. 100-609 (Comm. on the Judiciary).
SENATE REPORTS: No. 100-352 accompanying S. 1301 (Comm. on the Judiciary).
CONGRESSIONAL RECORD, Vol. 134 (1988):
May 10, considered and passed House.
Oct. 5, S. 1301 considered and passed Senate; proceedings vacated and H.R. 4262, amended, passed in lieu.
Oct. 12, House concurred in Senate amendment.
WEEKLY COMPILATION OF PRESIDENTIAL DOCUMENTS, Vol. 24 (1988):
Oct. 31, Presidential remarks.

BANGLADESH DISASTER ASSISTANCE ACT OF 1988

An Act concerning disaster assistance for Bangladesh.

Date: October 31, 1988

Bill No.: H.R. 5389

Public Law No.: 100-576

Cite: 102 STAT. 2897

Sections reprinted: All.

Public Law 100-576
100th Congress

An Act

Concerning disaster assistance for Bangladesh.

Be it enacted by the Senate and House of Representatives of the United States of America in Congress assembled,

SECTION 1. SHORT TITLE.

This Act may be cited as the "Bangladesh Disaster Assistance Act of 1988".

SEC. 2. FINDINGS.

The Congress finds that—

(1) as a result of the 1988 floods, two-thirds of Bangladesh has been inundated with flood waters;

(2) over 30 million people in Bangladesh are homeless, over 2,000 dead, tens of thousands ill, and potentially millions at risk of waterborne disease and epidemic because of lack of safe water and overcrowding;

(3) transportation, communications, and normal commerce in Bangladesh have been seriously interrupted, with a potential cost for replacing destroyed or damaged infrastructure of $500,000,000;

(4) agricultural lands have been flooded, with a potential crop loss of nearly $1,000,000,000;

(5) the people of the United States have respected and generously supported the efforts of the people of Bangladesh to maintain their independence, promote equitable economic growth, and strive for political pluralism and greater democracy; and

(6) the Government of Bangladesh has taken quick action to cope with this disaster, one of the most serious in the history of Bangladesh, but must rely on a generous response from the international community for emergency assistance and, even more importantly, for the expertise and resources needed to prevent the continual recurrence of such disastrous floods.

SEC. 3. COMMENDATION OF AND SUPPORT FOR THE PEOPLE OF BANGLADESH.

The Congress—

(1) commends the courage and resourcefulness demonstrated by the people of Bangladesh in response to the 1988 floods;

(2) commends the President for the generous provision by the United States of emergency assistance for Bangladesh;

(3) commends United States private and voluntary organizations, international organizations, foreign governments, and others for their compassionate response to this natural disaster;

(4) expresses its support for the people of Bangladesh at this most critical time;

(5) declares its willingness to work with the President to provide generous levels of emergency humanitarian assistance to the people of Bangladesh;

(6) declares its willingness to work with the Government of Bangladesh and with private and voluntary organizations to ensure that emergency assistance quickly reaches those most in need; and

(7) declares its willingness to work with the international community to seek the means to prevent a recurrence of such natural disasters, and urges the President to promote a regional solution designed to prevent a recurrence of such natural disasters.

SEC. 4. EMERGENCY ASSISTANCE FOR BANGLADESH.

(a) USE OF FOOD FOR DEVELOPMENT LOCAL CURRENCIES FOR DISASTER ASSISTANCE.—(1) Section 301 of the Agricultural Trade Development and Assistance Act of 1954 is amended by adding at the end the following:

"(c) In the event of a serious natural disaster in a country participating in a Food for Development Program, funds accruing from the sale of commodities made available under this title may be used, with the approval of the United States Government, for disaster relief, rehabilitation, and reconstruction assistance in any rural or urban area of that country adversely affected by the disaster. Such assistance may include (but is not limited to) food, medicine and medical supplies, shelter, and in-country transportation.".

(2) Food for Development agreements entered into under title III of that Act before the date of enactment of this Act may be amended in order to implement the amendment made by paragraph (1).

(3) Pending amendment pursuant to paragraph (2) of Food for Development agreements with the Government of Bangladesh, the use of funds accruing under those agreements, with the approval of the United States Government, for flood-related disaster assistance authorized by the amendment made by paragraph (1) shall be deemed to be consistent with the applicable agreement.

(b) ADDITIONAL FUNDS FOR DISASTER ASSISTANCE FOR BANGLADESH.—It is the sense of the Congress that, in order to provide additional resources for disaster assistance for the victims of the 1988 floods in Bangladesh, not less than $100,000,000 of the local currencies generated under Food for Development agreements with the Government of Bangladesh should be used for the disaster relief, rehabilitation, and reconstruction assistance purposes authorized by the amendment made by subsection (a)(1).

(c) REGULAR ASSISTANCE PROGRAMS TO BE MAINTAINED.—Disaster assistance provided for Bangladesh by the United States because of the 1988 floods should be in addition to the regularly programmed assistance for that country for fiscal year 1989 under chapter 1 of part I of the Foreign Assistance Act of 1961 (relating to development assistance) and titles I, II, and III of the Agriculture Trade Development and Assistance Act of 1954 (relating to food assistance); and the level of such regularly programmed assistance should not be reduced because of such disaster assistance.

(d) EXTENSION OF PERIOD FOR USE OF FOOD FOR DEVELOPMENT LOCAL CURRENCIES.—It is the sense of the Congress that the period, during which funds accruing under Food for Development agreements with the Government of Bangladesh must be used, should be extended from September 30, 1989, to at least September 30, 1990.

SEC. 5. REPORT TO CONGRESS.

(a) IN GENERAL.—Not later than 6 months after the date of enactment of this Act, the President shall submit to the Congress a report on efforts by the international community and the governments of the region to develop regional programs for the Ganges basin and the Brahmaputra basin that are designed—

(1) to ensure an equitable and predictable supply of water in the dry season; and

(2) to promote better flood control mechanisms to mitigate in the mid-term, and prevent in the long-term, floods as severe as the 1988 floods in Bangladesh.

(b) SPECIFIC REQUIREMENTS.—The report required by subsection (a)—

(1) shall describe what efforts have been made by international organizations and other international institutions, by bilateral and multilateral assistance donors, and by countries in the region, to achieve the objectives set forth in subsection (a);

(2) shall describe the feasibility studies, planning studies, or actual projects that are in preparation or have been completed to achieve those objectives;

(3) shall analyze the potential costs, the technology obstacles (such as those presented by the earthquakes to which the region is prone), and the political problems that stand in the way of effective flood control in the Ganges basin and the Brahmaputra basin;

(4) shall describe the environmental causes of the flood, particularly deforestation and soil erosion; and

(5) shall describe the efforts made, and the efforts proposed to be made, by the President to promote a regional approach to achieving the objectives set forth in subsection (a).

SEC. 6. OFFICE OF TECHNOLOGY ASSESSMENT.

It is the sense of the Congress that the Office of Technology Assessment—

(1) should cooperate in the effort described in section 5; and

(2) in particular, should provide to the Department of State and the Congress—

(A) a synopsis of all current studies and reports—

(i) on flood control in the Ganges basin and the Brahmaputra basin, or

(ii) on state-of-the-art technology available for the construction and maintenance of flood control projects, and

(B) any cost benefit analysis of efforts to improve water availability in the dry season and to mitigate or prevent severe flooding.

Approved October 31, 1988.

LEGISLATIVE HISTORY—H.R. 5389:

CONGRESSIONAL RECORD, Vol. 134 (1988):
Oct. 4, 6, considered and passed House.
Oct. 14, considered and passed Senate.

GENOCIDE CONVENTION IMPLEMENTATION ACT OF 1987 (PROXMIRE ACT)

An Act to implement the International Convention on the Prevention and Punishment of Genocide.

Date: November 4, 1988.

Bill No.: S.1851

Public Law No.: 100-606

Cite: 102 STAT. 3045

Sections reprinted: All.

Public Law 100-606
100th Congress

An Act

To implement the International Convention on the Prevention and Punishment of Genocide.

Be it enacted by the Senate and House of Representatives of the United States of America in Congress assembled,

SECTION 1. SHORT TITLE.

This Act may be cited as the "Genocide Convention Implementation Act of 1987 (the Proxmire Act)".

SEC. 2. TITLE 18 AMENDMENTS.

(a) IN GENERAL.—Part I of title 18, United States Code, is amended by inserting after chapter 50 the following:

"CHAPTER 50A—GENOCIDE

"Sec.
1091. Genocide.
1092. Exclusive remedies.
1093. Definitions.

"§ 1091. Genocide

"(a) BASIC OFFENSE.—Whoever, whether in time of peace or in time of war, in a circumstance described in subsection (d) and with the specific intent to destroy, in whole or in substantial part, a national, ethnic, racial, or religious group as such—

"(1) kills members of that group;

"(2) causes serious bodily injury to members of that group;

"(3) causes the permanent impairment of the mental faculties of members of the group through drugs, torture, or similar techniques;

"(4) subjects the group to conditions of life that are intended to cause the physical destruction of the group in whole or in part;

"(5) imposes measures intended to prevent births within the group; or

"(6) transfers by force children of the group to another group;

or attempts to do so, shall be punished as provided in subsection (b).

"(b) PUNISHMENT FOR BASIC OFFENSE.—The punishment for an offense under subsection (a) is—

"(1) in the case of an offense under subsection (a)(1), a fine of not more than $1,000,000 and imprisonment for life; and

"(2) a fine of not more than $1,000,000 or imprisonment for not more than twenty years, or both, in any other case.

"(c) INCITEMENT OFFENSE.—Whoever in a circumstance described in subsection (d) directly and publicly incites another to violate subsection (a) shall be fined not more than $500,000 or imprisoned not more than five years, or both.

"(d) REQUIRED CIRCUMSTANCE FOR OFFENSES.—The circumstance referred to in subsections (a) and (c) is that—

"(1) the offense is committed within the United States; or

"(2) the alleged offender is a national of the United States (as defined in section 101 of the Immigration and Nationality Act (8 U.S.C. 1101)).

"(e) NONAPPLICABILITY OF CERTAIN LIMITATIONS.—Notwithstanding section 3282 of this title, in the case of an offense under subsection (a)(1), an indictment may be found, or information instituted, at any time without limitation.

"§ 1092. Exclusive remedies

"Nothing in this chapter shall be construed as precluding the application of State or local laws to the conduct proscribed by this chapter, nor shall anything in this chapter be construed as creating any substantive or procedural right enforceable by law by any party in any proceeding.

"§ 1093. Definitions

"As used in this chapter—

"(1) the term 'children' means the plural and means individuals who have not attained the age of eighteen years;

"(2) the term 'ethnic group' means a set of individuals whose identity as such is distinctive in terms of common cultural traditions or heritage;

"(3) the term 'incites' means urges another to engage imminently in conduct in circumstances under which there is a substantial likelihood of imminently causing such conduct;

"(4) the term 'members' means the plural;

"(5) the term 'national group' means a set of individuals whose identity as such is distinctive in terms of nationality or national origins;

"(6) the term 'racial group' means a set of individuals whose identity as such is distinctive in terms of physical characteristics or biological descent;

"(7) the term 'religious group' means a set of individuals whose identity as such is distinctive in terms of common religious creed, beliefs, doctrines, practices, or rituals; and

"(8) the term 'substantial part' means a part of a group of such numerical significance that the destruction or loss of that part would cause the destruction of the group as a viable entity within the nation of which such group is a part.".

(b) CLERICAL AMENDMENT.—The table of chapters at the beginning of part I of title 18, United States Code, is amended by inserting after the item relating to chapter 50 the following new item:

"50A. Genocide .... 1091".

Approved November 4, 1988.

LEGISLATIVE HISTORY—S. 1851 (H.R. 4243):

HOUSE REPORTS: No. 100-566 accompanying H.R. 4243 (Comm. on the Judiciary).
SENATE REPORTS: No. 100-333 (Comm. on the Judiciary).
CONGRESSIONAL RECORD, Vol. 134 (1988):
  Apr. 25, H.R. 4243 considered and passed House.
  Oct. 14, S. 1851 considered and passed Senate.
  Oct. 19, considered and passed House.
WEEKLY COMPILATION OF PRESIDENTIAL DOCUMENTS, Vol. 24 (1988):
  Nov. 4, Presidential remarks.

FISHERY AGREEMENT WITH THE SOVIET UNION ACT, 1988

An Act to approve the governing international fishery agreement between the United States and the Union of Soviet Socialist Republics, and for other purposes.

Date: November 7, 1988.

Bill No.: H.R. 4919

Public Law No.: 100-629

Cite: 102 STAT. 3286

Sections reprinted:

Section 1 - Soviet Union Fishing Agreement.
Section 5 - North Pacific and Bering Sea Fisheries Advisory Body.

Public Law 100-629
100th Congress

An Act

To approve the governing international fishery agreement between the United States and the Union of Soviet Socialist Republics, and for other purposes.

Be it enacted by the Senate and House of Representatives of the United States of America in Congress assembled,

SECTION 1. SOVIET UNION FISHING AGREEMENT.

That notwithstanding any provision of the Magnuson Fishery Conservation and Management Act (16 U.S.C. 1801 et seq.), the governing international fishery agreement entered into between the Government of the United States and the Government of the Union of Soviet Socialist Republics, as contained in the message to Congress from the President of the United States dated June 22, 1988, is approved by the Congress and shall enter into force and effect with respect to the United States on the date of the enactment of this Act.

SEC. 5. NORTH PACIFIC AND BERING SEA FISHERIES ADVISORY BODY.

(a) IN GENERAL.—The Secretary of State shall establish an advisory body on the fisheries of the North Pacific and the Bering Sea, which shall advise the United States representative to the International Consultative Committee created in accordance with Article XIV of the governing international fishery agreement entered into between the United States and the Union of Soviet Socialist Republics, as contained in the message to Congress from the President of the United States dated June 22, 1988.

(b) MEMBERSHIP.—

(1) IN GENERAL.—The advisory body established pursuant to this section shall consist of 12 members, as follows:

(A) The Director of the Department of Fisheries of the State of Washington.

(B) The Commission of the Department of Fish and Game of the State of Alaska.

(C) Five members appointed by the Secretary of State from among persons nominated by the Governor of Alaska on the basis of their knowledge and experience in commercial harvesting, processing, or marketing of fishery resources.

(D) Five members appointed by the Secretary of State from among persons nominated by the Governor of Washington on the basis of their knowledge and experience in commercial harvesting, processing, or marketing of fishery resources.

(2) NOMINATIONS.—The Governor of Alaska and the Governor of Washington shall each nominate 10 persons for purposes of paragraph (1).

(c) PAY.—Members of the advisory body established pursuant to this section shall receive no pay by reason of their service as members of the advisory body.

(d) EXEMPTION FROM FEDERAL ADVISORY COMMITTEE ACT.—The Federal Advisory Committee Act (5 U.S.C. App. 1 et seq.) shall not apply to an advisory body established pursuant to this section.

LEGISLATIVE HISTORY—H.R. 4919:

HOUSE REPORTS: No. 100-968 (Comm. on Merchant Marine and Fisheries).
CONGRESSIONAL RECORD, Vol. 134 (1988):
Sept. 26, considered and passed House.
Sept. 30, considered and passed Senate, amended.
Oct. 3, 4, House disagreed to Senate amendment.
Oct. 21, Senate receded from its amendment.

INTER-AMERICAN COMMERCIAL ARBITRATION CONVENTION IMPLEMENTATION ACT, 1988.

An Act to implement the Inter-American Convention on International Commercial Arbitration.

Date: November 16, 1988.

Bill No.: S.2204

Public Law No.: 100-669

Cite: 102 STAT. 3969

Sections reprinted: All

Public Law 100-669
100th Congress

An Act

To implement the Inter-American Convention on International Commercial Arbitration.

Be it enacted by the Senate and House of Representatives of the United States of America in Congress assembled,

SECTION 1. Chapter 1 of title 9, United States Code, is amended by adding at the end thereof the following new section:

"§ 15. Inapplicability of the Act of State doctrine

"Enforcement of arbitral agreements, confirmation of arbitral awards, and execution upon judgments based on orders confirming such awards shall not be refused on the basis of the Act of State doctrine.".

SEC. 2. Section 1605(a) of title 28, United States Code, is amended by—

(1) striking out "or" at the end of paragraph (4);

(2) striking out the period at the end of paragraph (5) and inserting in lieu thereof "; or"; and

(3) adding at the end thereof the following:

"(6) in which the action is brought, either to enforce an agreement made by the foreign State with or for the benefit of a private party to submit to arbitration all or any differences which have arisen or which may arise between the parties with respect to a defined legal relationship, whether contractual or not, concerning a subject matter capable of settlement by arbitration under the laws of the United States, or to confirm an award made pursuant to such an agreement to arbitrate, if (A) the arbitration takes place or is intended to take place in the United States, (B) the agreement or award is or may be governed by a treaty or other international agreement in force for the United States calling for the recognition and enforcement of arbitral awards, (C) the underlying claim, save for the agreement to arbitrate, could have been brought in a United States court under this section or section 1607, or (D) paragraph (1) of this subsection is otherwise applicable.".

SEC. 3. Section 1610(a) of title 28, United States Code, is amended by—

(1) striking out the period at the end of paragraph (5) and inserting in lieu thereof ", or"; and

(2) adding at the end thereof the following:

"(6) the judgment is based on an order confirming an arbitral award rendered against the foreign State, provided that attachment in aid of execution, or execution, would not be inconsistent with any provision in the arbitral agreement.".

Approved November 16, 1988.

LEGISLATIVE HISTORY—S. 2204:

CONGRESSIONAL RECORD, Vol. 134 (1988):
Sept. 30, considered and passed Senate.
Oct. 20, considered in House.
Oct. 21, considered and passed House, amended. Senate concurred in House amendment.

ANTI-DRUG ABUSE ACT OF 1988

An Act to prevent the manufacturing, distribution, and use of illegal drugs, and for other purposes.

Date: November 18, 1988.

Bill No.: H.R. 5210

Public Law No.: 100-690

Cite: 102 STAT. 4181

Sections reprinted:

TITLE IV - INTERNATIONAL NARCOTICS CONTROL
- Subtitle A - General provisions
  - Section 4001 - Short title.
  - Section 4002 - Table of contents.
  - Section 4003 - Definitions.
- Subtitle B - Multilateral narcotics control efforts
  - Section 4101 - Regional anti-narcotic forces.
  - Section 4102 - United Nations efforts to stop illegal drug trafficking.
  - Section 4103 - International drug force.
  - Section 4104 - International drug conference.
  - Section 4105 - Integrated regional plan to fight the international narcotics trade.
  - Section 4106 - Regional anti-narcotics training center in the Caribbean.
  - Section 4107 - Authorization of appropriations for multilateral and regional drug abuse programs.
  - Section 4108 - International criminal court.
- Subtitle C - Authorizations and earmarkings of foreign assistance
  - Section 4201 - Authorization for international narcotics control assistance.
  - Section 4202 - Herbicides for aerial coca eradication.
  - Section 4203 - Procurement of weapons to defend aircraft involved in narcotics control efforts.
  - Section 4204 - Training for narcotics control activities.

Public Law 100-690
100th Congress

An Act

To prevent the manufacturing, distribution, and use of illegal drugs, and for other purposes.

Be it enacted by the Senate and House of Representatives of the United States of America in Congress assembled,

TITLE IV—INTERNATIONAL NARCOTICS CONTROL

Subtitle A—General Provisions

SEC. 4001. SHORT TITLE.

This title may be cited as the "International Narcotics Control Act of 1988".

SEC. 4002. TABLE OF CONTENTS.

The table of contents for this title is as follows:

SEC. 4003. DEFINITIONS.

As used in this title, the terms "drug" and "narcotic" mean narcotic and psychotropic drugs and other controlled substances as defined in section 481(i)(3) of the Foreign Assistance Act of 1961.

Subtitle B—Multilateral Narcotics Control Efforts

SEC. 4101. REGIONAL ANTI-NARCOTICS FORCES.

(a) NEED FOR ANTI-NARCOTICS FORCE IN THE WESTERN HEMISPHERE.—It is the sense of Congress that—

(1) the operations of international illegal drug smuggling organizations pose a direct threat to the national security of the member nations of the Organization of American States;

(2) illegal international drug smuggling organizations have grown so large and powerful that they threaten to overwhelm small nations standing alone against them;

(3) to preserve the national sovereignty, protect the public health, and maintain domestic law and order within their borders, member nations of the Organization of American States should coordinate their efforts to fight the illegal drug trade;

(4) recent events in drug source and transit countries in the Western Hemisphere make clear the requirement for international agreement on the formation of a multinational force to conduct operations against these illegal drug smuggling organizations;

(5) the United States should make every effort to initiate diplomatic discussions through the Organization of American States aimed at achieving agreement to establish and operate a Western Hemisphere anti-narcotics force; and

(6) sensitive to the legitimate concerns of other member nations of the Organization of American States, the United States stands ready to provide equipment, training, and financial resources to support the establishment and operation of such an anti-narcotics force, but believes that the personnel for such a force should be provided by those nations facing the most serious threat from drug trafficking organizations

(b) DIPLOMATIC DISCUSSIONS REGARDING WESTERN HEMISPHERE REGIONAL FORCE.—The President shall direct the United States Ambassador to the Organization of American States, under the direction of the Secretary of State, to initiate diplomatic discussions with member nations of the Organization of American States aimed at securing agreement to the formation of a multinational force to conduct operations against international illegal drug smuggling organizations wherever they may be found in the Western Hemisphere.

(c) REPORT TO CONGRESS.—Not later than 6 months after the date of enactment of this Act, the Secretary of State shall report to the Committee on Foreign Relations of the Senate and the Committee on Foreign Affairs of the House of Representatives on the progress United States diplomatic efforts have made toward achieving agreement on the establishment of such a multinational anti-narcotics force for the Western Hemisphere.

(d) BUDGET REQUEST.—If diplomatic efforts toward achieving a multinational anti-narcotics force for the Western Hemisphere demonstrate progress or agreement has been reached on formation of such a force, the President shall submit to the Congress, within 30 days after submission of the report required by subsection (c), supplemental budget requests for fiscal years 1989 and 1990 covering the United States share of the cost of operation and maintenance of such a force.

(e) OTHER REGIONAL ANTI-NARCOTIC FORCES.—The Congress urges the President to seek the establishment, in each of the relevant regions of the world, of a multilateral anti-narcotics force similar to the Western Hemisphere anti-narcotics force contemplated by this section.

SEC. 4102. UNITED NATIONS EFFORTS TO STOP ILLEGAL DRUG TRAFFICKING.

(a) FINDINGS.—The Congress finds that—

(1) the Department of State estimates that in 1987 the worldwide production of opium was between 1,902 and 3,107 metric tons, production of cocaine hydrochloride was between 324 and 422 metric tons, and production of marijuana was between 10,930 and 17,625 metric tons;

(2) it is estimated that the value of the illegal drug trade worldwide is as high as $500,000,000,000 a year;

(3) drug traffickers appear to be intensifying their efforts to distribute drugs to Western industrialized nations, as a source of stable currencies;

(4) drug traffickers also appear to be intensifying their efforts to distribute drugs to developing nations, as a means to increase their market;

(5) it is estimated that there are between 25,000,000 and 30,000,000 drug addicts worldwide;

(6) the American illegal drug market alone, comprised primarily of marijuana, cocaine, and heroin, annually produces between $50,000,000,000 and $100,000,000,000 at the retail level;

(7) approximately 35 percent of the inmates of State prisons were under the influence of illegal drugs at the time they committed the crime for which they were incarcerated;

(8) it is estimated that there are 26,000,000 regular users of illegal drugs in the Nation, slightly more than 10 percent of the Nation's population; and

(9) over 50 percent of the high school seniors in the Nation have used marijuana or hashish.

(b) ENCOURAGEMENT FOR ESTABLISHMENT OF INTERNATIONAL FORCE.—The Congress encourages the United Nations to explore ways and means to establish an international force or mechanism aimed at stopping the trafficking of illegal drugs.

SEC. 4103. INTERNATIONAL DRUG FORCE.

It is the sense of the Congress that the President should call for international negotiations for the purpose of agreeing on the establishment of an international drug force to pursue and apprehend major international drug traffickers.

SEC. 4104. INTERNATIONAL DRUG CONFERENCE.

It is the sense of the Congress that—

(1) the President should convene as soon as possible an international conference to be known as the International Conference on Combatting Illegal Drug Production, Trafficking, and Use in the Western Hemisphere;

(2) this conference should involve the heads of state, the highest-ranking law enforcement officers, and other appropriate officials from every government in the Western Hemisphere that is willing to combat the drug trade, and whose cooperation the President determines is essential to that goal; and

(3) this conference should focus exclusively on combatting the drug trade and, in particular, should emphasize enhancing cooperative efforts among the governments of the Western Hemisphere to—

(A) substantially reduce the production, cultivation, and processing of illicit drugs;

(B) eliminate the transshipment of such drugs through countries in the Western Hemisphere;

(C) curb the demand for and use of such drugs in every country in the Western Hemisphere;

(D) combat the problems of drug-related corruption and drug money laundering; and

(E) share intelligence information, extradite drug traffickers, and take other steps necessary to improve law enforcement efforts against the drug trade.

SEC. 4105. INTEGRATED REGIONAL PLAN TO FIGHT THE INTERNATIONAL COCAINE TRADE.

(a) CONSULTATIONS CONCERNING CREATION OF AN INTEGRATED PLAN.—The Secretary of State shall consult with—

(1) the heads of appropriate agencies and departments of the United States Government,

(2) the governments of those countries in the Western Hemisphere that cultivate, process, or traffic in cocaine, and

(3) the governments of other cocaine consuming countries

about the feasibility of creating a comprehensive, integrated, multi national plan whose objective would be the substantial reduction or elimination of the international cocaine trade.

(b) REPORT ON THE INTEGRATED PLAN.—Not later than 6 months after the date of enactment of this Act, the Secretary of State shall report to the Congress on—

(1) the feasibility of creating a comprehensive, integrated, multinational plan whose objective would be the substantial reduction or elimination of the international cocaine trade;

(2) the measures in such areas as eradication, interdiction, crop substitution, economic development, extradition, money-laundering, precursor chemical control, and related fields, that would be required to achieve such an objective;

(3) the material resources, funding, and technological assistance each producer and transit country would require in order to achieve such an objective; and

(4) the resources, funding, and other assistance each producer, transit, and consuming country would be prepared to make available for such an effort.

SEC. 4106. REGIONAL ANTI-NARCOTICS TRAINING CENTER IN THE CARIBBEAN.

It is the sense of the Congress that the Assistant Secretary of State for International Narcotics Matters—

(1) should seek the establishment of a regional anti-narcotics training center in the Caribbean;

(2) should contribute funds or other resources to such a center; and

(3) should seek such contributions from other countries for such a center.

SEC. 4107. AUTHORIZATION OF APPROPRIATIONS FOR MULTILATERAL AND REGIONAL DRUG ABUSE CONTROL PROGRAMS.

Section 302 of the Foreign Assistance Act of 1961 is amended by adding at the end the following:

"(j) In addition to amounts otherwise available under this section for such purposes, there are authorized to be appropriated to the President $3,000,000 for fiscal year 1989 to be available only for United States contributions to multilateral and regional drug abuse control programs. Of the amount authorized to be appropriated by this subsection—

"(1) $2,000,000 shall be for a United States contribution to the United Nations Fund for Drug Abuse Control;

"(2) $600,000 shall be for the Organization of American States (OAS) Inter-American Drug Abuse Control Commission (CICAD) Legal Development Project, except that the proportion which such amount bears to the total amount of contributions to this specific project may not exceed the proportion which the United States contribution to the budget of the Organization of American States for that fiscal year bears to the total contributions to the budget of the Organization of American States for that fiscal year; and

"(3) $400,000 shall be for the Organization of American States (OAS) Inter-American Drug Abuse Control Commission (CICAD) Law Enforcement Training Project, except that the proportion which such amount bears to the total amount of contributions to this specific project may not exceed the proportion which the United States contribution to the budget of the Organization of American States for that fiscal year bears to the total contributions to the budget of the Organization of American States for that fiscal year.".

SEC. 4108. INTERNATIONAL CRIMINAL COURT.

(a) In General.—It is the sense of the Senate that the President should begin discussions with foreign governments to investigate the feasibility and advisability of establishing an international criminal court to expedite cases regarding the prosecution of persons accused of having engaged in international drug trafficking or having committed international crimes.

(b) United States Citizens.—Such discussions shall not include any commitment that such court shall have jurisdiction over the extradition of United States citizens and shall assure that any international agreement shall recognize the rights and privileges guaranteed to United States citizens under the United States Constitution.

Subtitle C—Authorizations and Earmarkings of Foreign Assistance

SEC. 4201. AUTHORIZATION FOR INTERNATIONAL NARCOTICS CONTROL ASSISTANCE.

Section 482(a) of the Foreign Assistance Act of 1961 is amended by striking out paragraphs (1) and (3) and by inserting the following new paragraph (1) after "(a)":

"(1) To carry out the purposes of section 481, there are authorized to be appropriated to the President $101,000,000 for fiscal year 1989.".

SEC. 4202. HERBICIDES FOR AERIAL COCA ERADICATION.

(a) Earmarking of Funds.—The Secretary of State shall use not less than $500,000 of the funds made available for fiscal year 1989 to carry out chapter 8 of part I of the Foreign Assistance Act of 1961 (relating to international narcotics control) to finance the testing and use of safe and effective herbicides for use in the aerial eradication of coca.

(b) Impact on the Environment and Health.—Section 481(d) of that Act is amended by adding at the end the following:

"(5)(A) The President, with the assistance of appropriate Federal agencies, shall monitor any use under this chapter of a herbicide in the aerial eradication of coca in order to determine the impact of such use on the environment and on the health of individuals.

"(B) The President shall report on such impact in the annual report required by subsection (e).

"(C) If the President determines that any such use is harmful to the environment or the health of individuals, the President shall immediately report that determination to the Committee on Foreign Affairs of the House of Representatives and the Committee on Foreign Relations of the Senate, together with such recommendations as the President deems appropriate.".

SEC. 4203. PROCUREMENT OF WEAPONS TO DEFEND AIRCRAFT INVOLVED IN NARCOTICS CONTROL EFFORTS.

(a) EARMARKING OF MAP FUNDS.—Of the funds available to carry out chapter 2 of part II of the Foreign Assistance Act of 1961 (relating to the grant military assistance program), $1,000,000 for fiscal year 1989 shall be made available to arm, for defensive purposes, aircraft used in narcotics control eradication or interdiction efforts. These funds may only be used to arm aircraft already in the inventory of the recipient country, and may not be used for the purchase of new aircraft.

(b) NOTIFICATION TO CONGRESS.—The Committee on Foreign Affairs of the House of Representatives and the Committee on Foreign Relations of the Senate shall be notified of the use of any such funds for that purpose at least 15 days in advance in accordance with the reprogramming procedures applicable under section 634A of the Foreign Assistance Act of 1961.

SEC. 4204. TRAINING FOR NARCOTICS CONTROL ACTIVITIES.

(a) EARMARKING OF FUNDS.—Not less than $2,000,000 of the funds made available for fiscal year 1989 to carry out chapter 5 of part II of the Foreign Assistance Act of 1961 (relating to international military education and training) shall be available only for—

(1) education and training in the operation and maintenance of equipment used in narcotics control interdiction and eradication efforts of countries in Latin America and the Caribbean which are described in subsection (c); and

(2) the expenses of deploying, upon the request of the government of a foreign country described in subsection (c), Department of Defense mobile training teams in that foreign country to conduct training in military-related individual and collective skills that will enhance that country's ability to conduct tactical operations in narcotics interdiction.

(b) UNITS ELIGIBLE FOR TRAINING.—Education and training may be provided under subsection (a)(1) and training may be provided under subsection (a)(2) only for foreign law enforcement agencies, or other units, that are organized for the specific purpose of narcotics enforcement.

(c) ELIGIBLE COUNTRIES.—Assistance may be provided under this section only for countries—

(1) which are major illicit drug producing or major drug-transit countries (as defined in section 481(i) of the Foreign Assistance Act of 1961);

(2) which have democratic governments; and

(3) whose law enforcement agencies do not engage in a consistent pattern of gross violations of internationally recognized human rights (as defined in section 502B(d)(1) of the Foreign Assistance Act of 1961).

(d) COORDINATION WITH INTERNATIONAL NARCOTICS CONTROL ASSISTANCE PROGRAM.—Assistance under this section shall be coordinated with assistance provided under chapter 8 of part I of the Foreign Assistance Act of 1961 (relating to international narcotics control).

(e) WAIVER OF SECTION 660.—Assistance may be provided pursuant to this section notwithstanding the prohibition contained in section 660 of the Foreign Assistance Act of 1961 (relating to police training).

SEC. 4205. MILITARY ASSISTANCE FOR ANTI-NARCOTICS EFFORTS.

(a) PURPOSES OF ASSISTANCE.—Assistance provided under this section shall be designed to—

(1) enhance the ability of friendly governments to control illicit narcotics production and trafficking;

(2) strengthen the bilateral ties of the United States with friendly governments by offering concrete assistance in this area of great mutual concern; and

(3) strengthen respect for internationally recognized human rights and the rule of law in efforts to control illicit narcotics production and trafficking.

(b) WAIVER OF CERTAIN PROVISIONS.—During fiscal years 1989 and 1990, section 660(a) of the Foreign Assistance Act of 1961 shall not apply with respect to assistance provided under chapter 2 of part II of that Act (relating to the grant military assistance program) to countries described in subsection (c) for the procurement, for use in narcotics control, eradication, and interdiction efforts, of weapons or ammunition for foreign law enforcement agencies, or other units, that are organized for the specific purpose of narcotics enforcement.

(c) ELIGIBLE COUNTRIES.—Assistance may be provided under this section only for countries—

(1) which are major illicit drug producing or major drug-transit countries (as defined in section 481(i) of the Foreign Assistance Act of 1961);

(2) which have democratic governments; and

(3) whose law enforcement agencies do not engage in a consistent pattern of gross violations of internationally recognized human rights (as defined in section 502B(d)(1) of the Foreign Assistance Act of 1961).

(d) REPORTS TO CONGRESS.—Not less than 15 days before funds are obligated to provide assistance authorized by this section, the President shall transmit to the Committee on Foreign Affairs of the House of Representatives and the Committee on Foreign Relations of the Senate, in accordance with the procedures applicable under section 634A of the Foreign Assistance Act of 1961, a written notification which specifies—

(1) the country to which the assistance is to be provided;

(2) the type and value of the assistance to be provided;

(3) the law enforcement agencies or other units that will receive the assistance; and

(4) an explanation of how the proposed assistance will achieve the purposes specified in subsection (a) of this section.

(e) REPORTS ON HUMAN RIGHTS SITUATION.—Section 502B(c) of the Foreign Assistance Act of 1961 (relating to country-specific human rights reports upon the request of the foreign affairs committees) applies with respect to countries for which assistance authorized by this section is proposed or is being provided.

(f) COORDINATION WITH INTERNATIONAL NARCOTICS CONTROL ASSISTANCE PROGRAM.—Assistance under this section shall be coordinated with assistance provided under chapter 8 of part I of the Foreign Assistance Act of 1961 (relating to international narcotics control).

(g) EARMARKING FOR LATIN AMERICA AND THE CARIBBEAN.—Of the amounts made available for fiscal year 1989 to carry out chapter 2 of part II of the Foreign Assistance Act of 1961, $3,500,000 shall be available only to provide assistance authorized by this section for countries in Latin America or the Caribbean.

(h) CONFORMING AMENDMENTS.—(1) Section 578(a) of the Foreign Operations, Export Financing, and Related Programs Appropriations Act, 1989 (Public Law 100–461), is amended—

(A) by striking out paragraph (3);

(B) in paragraph (4), by striking out "except as provided in paragraph (3) of this subsection"; and

(C) by redesignating paragraph (4) as paragraph (3).

(2) The amendments made by paragraph (1) shall be effective as of October 1, 1988.

SEC. 4206. REALLOCATION OF FUNDS WITHHELD FROM COUNTRIES WHICH FAIL TO TAKE ADEQUATE STEPS TO HALT ILLICIT DRUG PRODUCTION OR TRAFFICKING.

(a) REQUIREMENT TO REALLOCATE.—Chapter 8 of part I of the Foreign Assistance Act of 1961 is amended by adding at the end the following:

"SEC. 486. REALLOCATION OF FUNDS WITHHELD FROM COUNTRIES WHICH FAIL TO TAKE ADEQUATE STEPS TO HALT ILLICIT DRUG PRODUCTION OR TRAFFICKING.

"(a) ADDITIONAL ASSISTANCE FOR COUNTRIES TAKING SIGNIFICANT STEPS.—If any funds authorized to be appropriated for any fiscal year for security assistance are not used for assistance for the country for which those funds were allocated because of the requirements of section 481(h) or any other provision of law requiring the withholding of assistance for countries that have not taken adequate steps to halt illicit drug production or trafficking, the President shall use those funds for additional assistance for those countries which have met their illicit drug eradication targets or have otherwise taken significant steps to halt illicit drug production or trafficking, as follows:

"(1) INTERNATIONAL NARCOTICS CONTROL ASSISTANCE.—Those funds may be transferred to and consolidated with the funds appropriated to carry out this chapter in order to provide additional narcotics control assistance for those countries. Funds transferred under this paragraph may only be used to provide increased funding for activities previously justified to the Congress. Transfers may be made under this paragraph without regard to the 20-percent increase limitation contained in section 610(a). This paragraph does not apply with respect to funds made available for assistance under the Arms Export Control Act.

"(2) SECURITY ASSISTANCE.—Any such funds not used under paragraph (1) shall be reprogrammed within the account for which they were appropriated (subject to the regular reprogramming procedures under section 634A) in order to provide additional security assistance for those countries.

"(b) DEFINITION OF SECURITY ASSISTANCE.—As used in this section, the term 'security assistance' means assistance under chapter 2 of part II of this Act (relating to the grant military assistance program), chapter 4 of part II of this Act (relating to the Economic Support Fund), chapter 5 of part II of this Act (relating to international military education and training), or the Arms Export Control Act (relating to foreign military sales financing).".

(b) CONFORMING AMENDMENTS.—(1) The amendment made by subsection (a) of this section supersedes section 578(d) of the Foreign Operations, Export Financing, and Related Programs Appropriations Act, 1989 (Public Law 100–461).

(2) Funds may be transferred pursuant to paragraph (1) of section 486(a) of the Foreign Assistance Act of 1961 (as enacted by this section) notwithstanding section 514 of the Foreign Operations,

Export Financing, and Related Programs Appropriations Act, 1989 (as amended by section 589 of that Act), relating to transfers between accounts.

Subtitle D—Provisions Relating to Specific Countries

SEC. 4301. COOPERATIVE NONMAJOR DRUG-TRANSIT COUNTRIES.

(a) Greater Attention.—The Congress urges the Assistant Secretary of State for International Narcotics Matters to give greater attention, and provide more narcotics control assistance, to those countries which are drug-transit countries but are not major drug-transit countries (as defined in section 481(i)(5) of the Foreign Assistance Act of 1961) and which are cooperating with the United States in its international narcotics control efforts.

(b) Earmarking of Assistance.—Of the amounts made available for fiscal year 1989 to carry out chapter 8 of part I of the Foreign Assistance Act of 1961 (relating to international narcotics control), not less than $1,000,000 shall be available only for assistance to countries described in subsection (a).

SEC. 4302. ASSISTANCE FOR BOLIVIA.

(a) Security Assistance.—For fiscal year 1989, assistance may be provided for Bolivia under chapter 2 (relating to the grant military assistance program), chapter 4 (relating to the Economic Support Fund), and chapter 5 (relating to international military education and training) of part II of the Foreign Assistance Act of 1961 and under chapter 2 of the Arms Export Control Act (relating to foreign military sales financing) only if the President certifies to the Congress that the Government of Bolivia is implementing legislation that—

(1) establishes its legal coca requirements,

(2) provides for the licensing of the number of hectares necessary to produce the legal requirement,

(3) makes unlicensed coca production illegal, and

(4) makes possession and distribution of coca leaf illegal (other than possession and distribution for licit purposes).

(b) Section 481 Certification.—

(1) Conditions on certification.—For fiscal year 1989, the President may make a certification with respect to Bolivia under clause (i) or (ii) of section 481(h)(2)(A) of the Foreign Assistance Act of 1961 only if the Government of Bolivia—

(A) has entered into the narcotics cooperation agreement with the United States specified in section 611(2)(B) of the International Security and Development Cooperation Act of 1985;

(B) has fully achieved the eradication targets contained in that agreement; and

(C) has begun a program of forced eradication of illicit coca cultivation if the targets for voluntary eradication are not being met or are not continued.

(2) Nonwaivability.—The authorities contained in section 614 of the Foreign Assistance Act of 1961 may not be used to waive the requirements of this subsection, and may not be used

to waive the requirements of section 481(h) of that Act for fiscal year 1989 with respect to Bolivia.

(c) DEVELOPMENT ASSISTANCE.—For fiscal year 1989, the project agreement document for a project carried out pursuant to chapter 1 of part I of the Foreign Assistance Act of 1961 (relating to development assistance) shall contain—

(1) in the case of the Chapare Regional Development Project, a clause requiring that project activities be suspended if the Government of Bolivia fails to achieve the coca eradication targets contained in the applicable agreement concerning that project; and

(2) in the case of a project to be carried out in an area in Bolivia in which there is no known illicit coca cultivation as of the date of enactment of this Act, a clause requiring that project activities be suspended if the Government of Bolivia fails to keep the project area free of illicit coca cultivation.

(d) FISCAL YEAR 1989 EARMARKING.—Title II of the Foreign Operations, Export Financing, and Related Programs Appropriations Act, 1989 (Public Law 100–461), is amended in the paragraph under the heading "INTERNATIONAL NARCOTICS CONTROL" by striking out "$15,000,000" in the first proviso and all that follows through "not less than" in the second proviso.

SEC. 4303. ASSISTANCE FOR PERU.

(a) DETERMINATIONS REGARDING NARCOTICS CONTROL COOPERATION.—In making determinations with respect to Peru pursuant to section 481(h)(2)(A)(i) of the Foreign Assistance Act of 1961 for fiscal year 1989, the President shall give foremost consideration to whether the Government of Peru made substantial progress in meeting its coca eradication targets during the previous year.

(b) UPPER HUALLAGA VALLEY PROJECT.—Funds authorized to be appropriated for fiscal year 1989 to carry out chapter 1 of part I of that Act (relating to development assistance) may be made available for the project of the Agency for International Development in the Upper Huallaga Valley of Peru only if the Secretary of State determines, and reports to the Congress, that such project continues to be effective in reducing and eradicating coca leaf production, distribution, and marketing in the Upper Huallaga Valley.

SEC. 4304. ASSISTANCE FOR MEXICO.

(a) LIMITATION ON ASSISTANCE.—(1) Except as provided in paragraph (2), not more than $15,000,000 of the amounts made available for fiscal year 1989 to carry out chapter 8 of part I of the Foreign Assistance Act of 1961 (relating to international narcotics control) may be made available for Mexico.

(2) Assistance in excess of the amount specified in paragraph (1) may be made available for Mexico only if the congressional committees specified in section 634A(a) of the Foreign Assistance Act of 1961 are notified at least 15 days in advance in accordance with the regular reprogramming procedures applicable under that section.

(b) COOPERATION ON DRUG LAW ENFORCEMENT MATTERS.—The Congress urges the Government of Mexico to cooperate fully with the United States on matters of concern to the United States regarding drug law enforcement. In particular, the Congress anticipates that the new Government which will take office on December 1 will move expeditiously to bring to trial and effectively prosecute those responsible for the 1985 murders of Drug Enforcement

Administration agent Enrique Camarena Salazar and his pilot Alfredo Zavala Avelar and those responsible for the 1986 detention and torture of Drug Enforcement Administration agent Victor Cortez, Junior.

(c) Joint Air Operations and Joint Crewing.—In making determinations with respect to Mexico pursuant to section 481(h)(2)(A)(i) of the Foreign Assistance Act of 1961 for fiscal year 1989, the President shall consider whether the Government of Mexico has responded favorably to the United States proposals to establish, and is making measurable progress toward implementing—

(1) a joint United States-Mexico airborne apprehension capability (commonly referred to as "joint air operations"); and

(2) joint air surveillance operations (commonly referred to as "joint crewing").

(d) Banking Information Concerning Money Laundering.—The Congress encourages the Government of Mexico, upon ratification of the Mutual Legal Assistance Treaty between the United States and Mexico, to furnish banking information pursuant to that treaty which would permit the successful investigation and prosecution in the United States of major narco-terrorists who use Mexican financial institutions to "launder" their profits.

SEC. 4305. ASSISTANCE FOR COLOMBIA.

(a) Size of Military Assistance Group.—The third sentence of section 515(c)(1) of the Foreign Assistance Act of 1961 (relating to countries authorized to have more than 6 members of the Armed Forces assigned to carry out international security assistance programs) is amended by inserting "Colombia," after "Honduras,".

(b) Increased Military Assistance.—There are authorized to be appropriated to carry out chapter 2 of part II of the Foreign Assistance Act of 1961 (relating to the grant military assistance program) $15,000,000 as supplemental appropriations for fiscal year 1989, which are authorized to remain available until expended. These funds shall be available only to provide defense articles to the armed forces of Colombia to support their efforts to combat illicit narcotics production and trafficking.

(c) Protection From Narco-Terrorist Attacks.—

(1) Earmark of funds.—Of the funds made available for fiscal year 1989 to carry out chapter 4 of part II of the Foreign Assistance Act of 1961 (relating to the Economic Support Fund), not less than $5,000,000 shall be used to provide to the Government of Colombia such assistance as it may request to provide protection against narco-terrorist attacks on judges, other government officials, and members of the press.

(2) Waiver of prohibition on assistance to police forces.—The assistance provided for in paragraph (1) may be provided without regard to section 660 of the Foreign Assistance Act of 1961.

(3) Notification to congress.—Funds made available pursuant to paragraph (1) may not be obligated until at least 15 days after the Committee on Foreign Affairs of the House of Representatives and the Committee on Foreign Relations of the Senate are notified of the proposed obligation in accordance with the reprogramming procedures applicable under section 634A of the Foreign Assistance Act of 1961.

(4) EXTENSION OF PERIOD FOR OBLIGATION OF FUNDS.—Funds allocated to carry out this subsection shall remain available until expended, notwithstanding any other provision of law.

SEC. 4306. ILLICIT DRUG PRODUCTION AND TRAFFICKING IN PAKISTAN.

In making determinations with respect to Pakistan pursuant to section 481(h)(2)(A)(i) of the Foreign Assistance Act of 1961, the President shall take into account the extent to which the Government of Pakistan—

(1) is increasing the number of illicit laboratories destroyed and is vigorously prosecuting and punishing the owners and operators of such laboratories;

(2) is increasing the number of arrests and successful prosecutions of violators, with particular emphasis on putting major traffickers out of business; and

(3) has made changes in Pakistani legal codes in order to enable Pakistani law enforcement officials to move more effectively against narcotics traffickers, such as new conspiracy laws and new asset seizure laws.

SEC. 4307. UNITED STATES RELIANCE ON LICIT OPIUM GUM FROM FOREIGN SOURCES.

(a) REVIEW REQUIRED.—The President shall conduct a review of United States narcotics raw material policy to determine—

(1) the current and reserve international needs for opium-derived pharmaceutical and chemical products, and the relative capabilities for meeting those needs through the opium gum process and the concentrated poppy straw method of production;

(2) whether the United States should continue to rely on a single foreign country for all its licit opium gum;

(3) whether it should be United States policy to encourage all countries which produce licit opium to use the concentrated poppy straw method of production; and

(4) what options are available, consistent with treaties to which the United States is a party, to reduce United States reliance on licit opium gum from foreign sources.

(b) REPORT TO CONGRESS.—The results of this review shall be reported to the Congress not later than 6 months after the date of enactment of this Act.

SEC. 4308. AFGHANISTAN AS A HEROIN SOURCE.

(a) FINDING.—The Congress finds that Afghanistan remains the source of most of the heroin exported from southwest Asia.

(b) STATEMENT OF POLICY.—It is the sense of the Congress that—

(1) the United States Government should pursue efforts to press the Government of Afghanistan, and should work with the Mujahadeen—

(A) to reduce production and trafficking in areas under their respective control, and

(B) to encourage drug eradication, interdiction, and crop substitution in Afghanistan; and

(2) an initiative should be developed which could be put in place as the Mujahadeen and successors to the present Kabul regime begin to exert more civil authority.

SEC. 4309. INVOLVEMENT OF THE GOVERNMENT OF LAOS IN ILLICIT DRUG PRODUCTION AND TRAFFICKING.

(a) PERIODIC REPORTS.—The President shall prepare and transmit to the Congress, in accordance with subsection (b), periodic reports containing the following determinations:

(1) Does the Government of Laos, as a matter of government policy, encourage or facilitate the production or distribution of illegal drugs?

(2) Does any senior official of the Government of Laos engage in, encourage, or facilitate the production or distribution of illegal drugs?

(3) Do other governments in the region assist the distribution of illegal drugs from Laos?

(b) TIME FOR SUBMISSION OF REPORTS.—The report described in subsection (a) shall be submitted as part of each report required by section 481(e) of the Foreign Assistance Act of 1961 and as part of each report required by section 2013 of the Anti-Drug Abuse Act of 1986.

(c) INFORMATION TO BE INCLUDED.—(1) If an affirmative determination is made under paragraph (1) or (2) of subsection (a), the report shall describe the activities and identities of officials whose activities caused that determination to be made.

(2) If an affirmative determination is made under paragraph (3) of subsection (a), the report shall describe the activities of other governments in the region which caused that determination to be made.

Subtitle E—Annual Report and Certification Process

SEC. 4401. EXPRESSION IN NUMERICAL TERMS OF MAXIMUM ACHIEVABLE REDUCTIONS IN ILLICIT DRUG PRODUCTION

Section 481(e)(4) of the Foreign Assistance Act of 1961 is amended by inserting after the first sentence the following: "Each determination of the President under the preceding sentence shall be expressed in numerical terms, such as the number of acres of illicitly cultivated controlled substances which can be eradicated.".

SEC. 4402. REPORTS ON ASSISTANCE DENIED.

Section 481(e) of the Foreign Assistance Act of 1961 is amended by adding at the end the following:

"(8) Each report pursuant to this subsection shall describe the United States assistance for the preceding fiscal year which was denied, pursuant to subsection (h), to each major illicit drug producing country and each major drug-transit country.".

SEC. 4403. EXCLUSION OF CERTAIN NARCOTICS EDUCATION ACTIVITIES FROM DEFINITION OF UNITED STATES ASSISTANCE.

Section 481(i)(4)(vii) of the Foreign Assistance Act of 1961 is amended by striking out "126 of this Act;" and inserting in lieu thereof "126(b)(2) of this Act (but any such assistance shall be subject to the prior notification procedures applicable to reprogrammings pursuant to section 634A of this Act),".

SEC. 4404. REPORTS AND RESTRICTIONS CONCERNING CERTAIN COUNTRIES.

Section 2013(a) of the Anti-Drug Abuse Act of 1986 is amended—

(1) by striking out "Not later than 6 months after the date of enactment of this Act and every 6 months thereafter, the" and inserting in lieu thereof "The"; and

(2) by inserting ", at the same time as each report is submitted pursuant to section 481(b)(2) of the Foreign Assistance Act of 1961," after "transmit to the Congress".

SEC. 4405. DETERMINING MAJOR DRUG-TRANSIT COUNTRIES.

(a) PROCEDURES FOR DETERMINING.—Section 481 of the Foreign Assistance Act of 1961 is amended by adding at the end the following:

"(k)(1) For each calendar year, the Secretary of State, after consultation with the appropriate committees of the Congress, shall establish numerical standards and other guidelines for determining which countries will be considered to be major drug-transit countries under subsection (i)(5)(A) and (B) of this section.

"(2) Not later than September 1 of each year, the Secretary of State shall make a preliminary determination of the numerical standards and other guidelines to be used pursuant to paragraph (1) with respect to that year and shall notify the appropriate committees of the Congress of those standards and guidelines.

"(3) Not later than October 1 of each year, the Secretary of State shall notify the appropriate committees of the Congress of—

"(A) which countries appear likely, as of that date, to be determined to be major drug-transit countries for that year under the numerical standards and other guidelines developed pursuant to this subsection; and

"(B) which countries appear likely, as of that date, to be determined to be major illicit drug producing countries for that year.

"(4) Each report submitted pursuant to subsection (e) shall discuss—

"(A) any changes made, since the notification provided pursuant to paragraph (2), in the numerical standards and other guidelines used in determining which countries were major drug-transit countries under subsection (i)(5)(A) and (B) during the preceding year; and

"(B) any changes made, since the notification provided pursuant to paragraph (3)—

"(i) in the countries determined to be major drug-transit countries under subsection (i)(5)(A) and (B) during the preceding year; or

"(ii) in the countries determined to be major illicit drug producing countries for that year.".

(b) TRANSITION PROVISION.—With respect to fiscal year 1989, the Secretary of State—

(1) shall take the actions specified in subsection (k)(2) of section 481 of the Foreign Assistance Act of 1961 (as added by subsection (a) of this section) not later than 30 days after the date of enactment of this Act; and

(2) shall take the actions specified in subsection (k)(3) of that section (as added by subsection (a) of this section) not later than 60 days after the date of enactment of this Act.

SEC. 4406. WAIVER OF RESTRICTIONS ON UNITED STATES ASSISTANCE FOR CERTAIN MAJOR DRUG-TRANSIT COUNTRIES.

Section 481(h) of the Foreign Assistance Act of 1961 shall not apply with respect to a major drug-transit country for fiscal year 1989 if the President certifies to the Congress, during that fiscal year, that—

(1) section 481(i)(5)(C) of that Act (relating to money laundering) does not apply to that country;

(2) the country previously was a major illicit drug producing country but, during each of the preceding two years, has effectively eliminated illicit drug production; and

(3) the country is cooperating fully with the United States or has taken adequate steps on its own—

(A) in satisfying the goals agreed to in an applicable bilateral narcotics agreement with the United States (as described in section 481(h)(2) of that Act) or a multilateral agreement which achieves the objectives of that section;

(B) in preventing narcotic and psychotropic drugs and other controlled substances transported through such country from being sold illegally within the jurisdiction of such country to United States Government personnel or their dependents or from being transported, directly or indirectly, into the United States; and

(C) in preventing and punishing bribery and other forms of public corruption which facilitate the production, processing, or shipment of narcotic and psychotropic drugs and other controlled substances, or which discourage the investigation and prosecution of such acts.

SEC. 4407. ANNUAL CERTIFICATION PROCEDURES FOR BILATERAL AND MULTILATERAL ASSISTANCE.

(a) REVISION OF PROCEDURES.—Section 481(h) of the Foreign Assistance Act of 1961 is amended by striking out all that precedes subparagraph (B) of paragraph (4) and inserting in lieu thereof the following:

"(h) ANNUAL CERTIFICATION PROCEDURES.—

"(1) WITHHOLDING OF BILATERAL ASSISTANCE AND OPPOSITION TO MULTILATERAL DEVELOPMENT ASSISTANCE.—(A) Fifty percent of the United States assistance allocated each fiscal year in the report required by section 653(a) for each major illicit drug producing country or major drug-transit country shall be withheld from obligation and expenditure, except as provided in paragraph (2).

"(B) The Secretary of the Treasury shall instruct the United States Executive Director of the International Bank for Reconstruction and Development, the United States Executive Director of the International Development Association, the United States Executive Director of the Inter-American Development Bank, and the United States Executive Director of the Asian Development Bank to vote, on and after March 1 of each year, against any loan or other utilization of the funds of their respective institution to or for any major illicit drug producing country or major drug-transit country, except as provided in paragraph (2).

"(2) CERTIFICATION PROCEDURE.—(A) Subject to paragraph (1), the assistance withheld from a country pursuant to paragraph (1)(A) may be obligated and expended, and the requirement of paragraph (1)(B) to vote against multilateral development bank assistance to a country shall not apply, if the President determines and certifies to the Congress, at the time of the submission of the report required by subsection (e), that—

"(i) during the previous year the country has cooperated fully with the United States, or has taken adequate steps on its own—

"(I) in satisfying the goals agreed to in an applicable bilateral narcotics agreement with the United States (as described in subparagraph (B)) or a multilateral agreement which achieves the objectives of subparagraph (B),

"(II) in preventing narcotic and psychotropic drugs and other controlled substances produced or processed, in whole or in part, in such country or transported through such country, from being sold illegally within the jurisdiction of such country to United States Government personnel or their dependents or from being transported, directly or indirectly, into the United States,

"(III) in preventing and punishing the laundering in that country of drug-related profits or drug-related moneys, and

"(IV) in preventing and punishing bribery and other forms of public corruption which facilitate the production, processing, or shipment of narcotic and psychotropic drugs and other controlled substances, or which discourage the investigation and prosecution of such acts; or

"(ii) for a country that would not otherwise qualify for certification under clause (i), the vital national interests of the United States require that the assistance withheld pursuant to paragraph (1)(A) be provided and that the United States not vote against multilateral development bank assistance for that country pursuant to paragraph (1)(B).

"(B) A bilateral narcotics agreement referred to in subparagraph (A)(i)(I) is an agreement between the United States and a foreign country in which the foreign country agrees to take specific activities, including, where applicable, efforts to—

"(i) reduce drug production, drug consumption, and drug trafficking within its territory, including activities to address illicit crop eradication and crop substitution;

"(ii) increase drug interdiction and enforcement;

"(iii) increase drug treatment;

"(iv) increase the identification of and elimination of illicit drug laboratories;

"(v) increase the identification and elimination of the trafficking of precursor chemicals for the use in production of illegal drugs;

"(vi) increase cooperation with United States drug enforcement officials; and

"(vii) where applicable, increase participation in extradition treaties, mutual legal assistance provisions directed at money laundering, sharing of evidence, and other initiatives for cooperative drug enforcement.

"(C) A country which in the previous year was designated as a major illicit drug producing country or a major drug-transit country may not be determined to be cooperating fully under subparagraph (A)(i) unless it has in place a bilateral narcotics agreement with the United States or a multilateral agreement which achieves the objectives of subparagraph (B).

"(D) If the President makes a certification with respect to a country pursuant to subparagraph (A)(ii), he shall include in such certification—

"(i) a full and complete description of the vital national interests placed at risk if United States bilateral assistance to that country is terminated pursuant to this subsection and multilateral development bank assistance is not provided to such country; and

"(ii) a statement weighing the risk described in clause (i) against the risks posed to the vital national interests of the United States by the failure of such country to cooperate fully with the United States in combating narcotics or to take adequate steps to combat narcotics on its own.

"(E) The President may make a certification under subparagraph (A)(i) with respect to a major illicit drug producing country or major drug-transit country which is also a producer of licit opium only if the President determines that such country has taken steps to prevent significant diversion of its licit cultivation and production into the illicit market, maintains production and stockpiles at levels no higher than those consistent with licit market demand, and prevents illicit cultivation and production.

"(3) MATTERS TO BE CONSIDERED.—In determining whether to make the certification required by paragraph (2) with respect to a country, the President shall consider the following:

"(A) Have the actions of the government of that country resulted in the maximum reductions in illicit drug production which were determined to be achievable pursuant to subsection (e)(4)? In the case of a major illicit drug producing country, the President shall give foremost consideration, in determining whether to make the determination required by paragraph (2), to whether the government of that country has taken actions which have resulted in such reductions.

"(B) Has that government taken the legal and law enforcement measures to enforce in its territory, to the maximum extent possible, the elimination of illicit cultivation and the suppression of illicit manufacturing of and trafficking in narcotic and psychotropic drugs and other controlled substances, as evidenced by seizures of such drugs and substances and of illicit laboratories and the arrest and prosecution of violators involved in the traffic in such drugs and substances significantly affecting the United States?

"(C) Has that government taken the legal and law enforcement steps necessary to eliminate, to the maximum extent possible, the laundering in that country of drug-related profits or drug-related moneys, as evidenced by—

"(i) the enactment and enforcement by that government of laws prohibiting such conduct, "(ii) that government entering into, and cooperating under the terms of, mutual legal assistance agreements with the United States governing (but not limited to) money laundering, and

"(iii) the degree to which that government otherwise cooperates with United States law enforcement authorities on anti-money laundering efforts?

"(D) Has that government taken the legal and law enforcement steps necessary to eliminate, to the maximum extent possible, bribery and other forms of public corruption which facilitate the production, processing, or shipment of narcotic and psychotropic drugs and other controlled substances, or which discourage the investigation and prosecution of such acts, as evidenced by the enactment and enforcement of laws prohibiting such conduct?

"(E) Has that government, as a matter of government policy, encouraged or facilitated the production or distribution of illicit narcotic and psychotropic drugs and other controlled substances?

"(F) Does any senior official of that government engage in, encourage, or facilitate the production or distribution of illicit narcotic and psychotropic drugs and other controlled substances?

"(G) Has that government investigated aggressively all cases in which any member of an agency of the United States Government engaged in drug enforcement activities since January 1, 1985, has been the victim of acts or threats of violence, inflicted by or with the complicity of any law enforcement or other officer of such country or any political subdivision thereof, and energetically sought to bring the perpetrators of such offense or offenses to justice?

"(H) Having been requested to do so by the United States Government, does that government fail to provide reasonable cooperation to lawful activities of United States drug enforcement agents, including the refusal of permission to such agents engaged in interdiction of aerial smuggling into the United States to pursue suspected aerial smugglers a reasonable distance into the airspace of the requested country?

"(I) Has that government made necessary changes in legal codes in order to enable law enforcement officials to move more effectively against narcotics traffickers, such as new conspiracy laws and new asset seizure laws?

"(J) Has that government expeditiously processed United States extradition requests relating to narcotics trafficking?

"(K) Has that government refused to protect or give haven to any known drug traffickers, and has it expeditiously processed extradition requests relating to narcotics trafficking made by other countries?

"(4) CONGRESSIONAL REVIEW.—Paragraph (1) shall apply without regard to paragraph (2) if, within 45 days of continuous session (within the meaning of section 601(b)(1) of the International Security Assistance and Arms Export Control Act of 1976) after receipt of a certification under paragraph (2), the Congress enacts a joint resolution disapproving the determination of the President contained in such certification.

"(5) DENIAL OF ASSISTANCE FOR COUNTRIES DECERTIFIED.—If the President does not make a certification under paragraph (2) with respect to a country or the Congress enacts a joint resolution disapproving such certification, then until such time as the conditions specified in paragraph (6)(A) are satisfied—

"(A) funds may not be obligated for United States assistance for that country, and funds previously obligated for United States assistance for that country may not be expended for the purpose of providing assistance for that country; and

"(B) the requirement to vote against multilateral development bank assistance pursuant to paragraph (1)(B) shall apply with respect to that country, without regard to the date specified in that paragraph.

"(6) RECERTIFICATION.—(A) Paragraph (5) shall apply to a country until—

"(i) the President makes a certification under paragraph (2) with respect to that country, and the Congress does not enact a joint resolution under paragraph (4) disapproving the determination of the President contained in that certification; or

"(ii) the President submits at any other time a certification of the matters described in paragraph (2) with respect to such country, and the Congress enacts a joint resolution approving the determination of the President contained in that certification.".

(b) CONFORMING AMENDMENTS.—(1) Such section 481(h) is further amended—

(A) by striking out existing paragraph (5); and

(B) in subparagraph (B) of paragraph (6), as so redesignated by the amendment made by subsection (a) of this section—

(i) by striking out "such" in clause (i), and

(ii) by inserting "under this subsection" before "shall be" in clause (i); and

(iii) by striking out "resolution" in clause (ii) and inserting in lieu thereof "resolutions".

(2) Section 585 of the Foreign Operations, Export Financing, and Related Programs Appropriations Act, 1988 (as contained in section 101(e) of Public Law 100-202), is amended by striking out subsection (c).

SEC. 4408. ANNUAL CERTIFICATION PROCEDURES FOR TRADE AND AVIATION SANCTIONS.

(a) REVISION OF PROCEDURES.—Paragraphs (1) and (2) of section 802(b) the Trade Act of 1974 (19 U.S.C. 2492(b)(1) and (2)) are amended to read as follows:

"(b)(1)(A) Subject to paragraph (3), subsection (a) shall not apply with respect to a country if the President determines and certifies to the Congress, at the time of the submission of the report required by section 481(e) of the Foreign Assistance Act of 1961, that—

"(i) during the previous year the country has cooperated fully with the United States, or has taken adequate steps on its own—

"(I) in satisfying the goals agreed to in an applicable bilateral narcotics agreement with the United States (as described in paragraph (B)) or a multilateral agreement which achieves the objectives of paragraph (B),

"(II) in preventing narcotic and psychotropic drugs and other controlled substances produced or processed, in whole or in part, in such country or transported through such country, from being sold illegally within the jurisdiction of such country to United States Government personnel or their dependents or from being transported, directly or indirectly, into the United States,

"(III) in preventing and punishing the laundering in that country of drug-related profits or drug-related moneys, and

"(IV) in preventing and punishing bribery and other forms of public corruption which facilitate the production, processing, or shipment of narcotic and psychotropic drugs and other controlled substances, or which discourage the investigation and prosecution of such acts; or

"(ii) for a country that would not otherwise qualify for certification under clause (i), the vital national interests of the United States require that subsection (a) not be applied with respect to that country.

"(B) A bilateral narcotics agreement referred to in subparagraph (A)(i)(I) is an agreement between the United States and a foreign country in which the foreign country agrees to take specific activities, including, where applicable, efforts to—

"(i) reduce drug production, drug consumption, and drug trafficking within its territory, including activities to address illicit crop eradication and crop substitution;

"(ii) increase drug interdiction and enforcement;

"(iii) increase drug treatment;

"(iv) increase the identification of and elimination of illicit drug laboratories;

"(v) increase the identification and elimination of the trafficking of precursor chemicals for the use in production of illegal drugs;

"(vi) increase cooperation with United States drug enforcement officials; and

"(vii) where applicable, increase participation in extradition treaties, mutual legal assistance provisions directed at money laundering, sharing of evidence, and other initiatives for cooperative drug enforcement.

"(C) A country which in the previous year was designated as a major drug producing country or a major drug-transit country may not be determined to be cooperating fully under subparagraph (A)(i) unless it has in place a bilateral narcotics agreement with the United States or a multilateral agreement which achieves the objectives of subparagraph (B).

"(D) If the President makes a certification with respect to a country pursuant to subparagraph (A)(ii), he shall include in such certification—

"(i) a full and complete description of the vital national interests placed at risk if action is taken pursuant to subsection (a) with respect to that country; and

"(ii) a statement weighing the risk described in clause (i) against the risks posed to the vital national interests of the United States by the failure of such country to cooperate fully with the United States in combating narcotics or to take adequate steps to combat narcotics on its own.

"(E) The President may make a certification under subparagraph (A)(i) with respect to a major drug producing country or drug-transit country which is also a producer of licit opium only if the President determines that such country has taken steps to prevent significant diversion of its licit cultivation and production into the illicit market, maintains production and stockpiles at levels no higher than those consistent with licit market demand, and prevents illicit cultivation and production.

"(2) In determining whether to make the certification required by paragraph (1) with respect to a country, the President shall consider the following:

"(A) Have the actions of the government of that country resulted in the maximum reductions in illicit drug production which were determined to be achievable pursuant to section 481(e)(4) of the Foreign Assistance Act of 1961? In the case of a major drug producing country, the President shall give foremost consideration, in determining whether to make the certification required by paragraph (1), to whether the government of that country has taken actions which have resulted in such reductions.

"(B) Has that government taken the legal and law enforcement measures to enforce in its territory, to the maximum extent possible, the elimination of illicit cultivation and the suppression of illicit manufacturing of and trafficking in narcotic and psychotropic drugs and other controlled substances, as evidenced by seizures of such drugs and substances and of illicit laboratories and the arrest and prosecution of violators involved in the traffic in such drugs and substances significantly affecting the United States?

"(C) Has that government taken the legal and law enforcement steps necessary to eliminate, to the maximum extent possible, the laundering in that country of drug-related profits or drug-related moneys, as evidenced by—

"(i) the enactment and enforcement by that government of laws prohibiting such conduct,

"(ii) that government entering into, and cooperating under the terms of, mutual legal assistance agreements with the United States governing (but not limited to) money laundering, and

"(iii) the degree to which that government otherwise cooperates with United States law enforcement authorities on anti-money laundering efforts?

"(D) Has that government taken the legal and law enforcement steps necessary to eliminate, to the maximum extent possible, bribery and other forms of public corruption which facilitate the production, processing, or shipment of narcotic and psychotropic drugs and other controlled substances, or which discourage the investigation and prosecution of such acts, as evidenced by the enactment and enforcement of laws prohibiting such conduct?

"(E) Has that government, as a matter of government policy, encouraged or facilitated the production or distribution of illicit narcotic and psychotropic drugs and other controlled substances?

"(F) Does any senior official of that government engage in, encourage, or facilitate the production or distribution of illicit narcotic and psychotropic drugs and other controlled substances?

"(G) Has that government investigated aggressively all cases in which any member of an agency of the United States Government engaged in drug enforcement activities since January 1, 1985, has been the victim of acts or threats of violence, inflicted by or with the complicity of any law enforcement or other officer of such country or any political subdivision thereof, and has energetically sought to bring the perpetrators of such offense or offenses to justice?

"(H) Having been requested to do so by the United States Government, does that government fail to provide reasonable cooperation to lawful activities of United States drug enforcement agents, including the refusal of permission to such agents engaged in interdiction of aerial smuggling into the United States to pursue suspected aerial smugglers a reasonable distance into the airspace of the requested country?

"(I) Has that government made necessary changes in legal codes in order to enable law enforcement officials to move more effectively against narcotics traffickers, such as new conspiracy laws and new asset seizure laws?

"(J) Has that government expeditiously processed United States extradition requests relating to narcotics trafficking?

"(K) Has that government refused to protect or give haven to any known drug traffickers, and has it expeditiously processed extradition requests relating to narcotics trafficking made by other countries?".

(b) CONGRESSIONAL REVIEW PERIOD.—Section 802(b) of that Act is amended—

(1) in paragraph (3) by striking out "30 days" and inserting in lieu thereof "45 days";

(2) in paragraph (4)(A) by striking out "30 days" and inserting in lieu thereof "45 days"; and

(3) in paragraph (4)(B) by striking out "30 days" and inserting in lieu thereof "45 days".

(c) DETERMINING MAJOR DRUG-TRANSIT COUNTRIES.—Section 802 of that Act is amended by adding at the end the following:

"(e) For each calendar year, the Secretary of State, after consultation with the appropriate committees of the Congress, shall establish numerical standards and other guidelines for determining which countries will be considered to be major drug-transit countries under section 805(3)(A) and (B).".

Subtitle F—Miscellaneous Provisions Relating to Assistance Programs

SEC. 4501. REPORTING ON TRANSFER OF UNITED STATES ASSETS.

(a) 15-DAY ADVANCE NOTIFICATION.—Any transfer by the United States Government to a foreign country for narcotics control purposes of any property seized by or otherwise forfeited to the United States Government in connection with narcotics-related activity shall be subject to the regular reprogramming procedures applicable under section 634A of the Foreign Assistance Act of 1961.

(b) ANNUAL REPORTS.—Section 4601 of this title requires that all such transfers be reported annually to the Congress.

SEC. 4502. IMPORTANCE OF SUPPRESSING INTERNATIONAL NARCOTICS TRAFFICKING.

Section 481(a)(1) of the Foreign Assistance Act of 1961 is amended—

(1) by redesignating subparagraphs (B) through (D) as subparagraphs (C) through (E), respectively; and

(2) by inserting after subparagraph (A) the following:

"(B) suppression of international narcotics trafficking is among the most important foreign policy objectives of the United States;".

SEC. 4503. PROHIBITION ON ASSISTANCE TO DRUG TRAFFICKERS.

Chapter 8 of part I of the Foreign Assistance Act of 1961, as amended by section 4206 of this title, is further amended by adding at the end the following:

"SEC. 487. PROHIBITION ON ASSISTANCE TO DRUG TRAFFICKERS.

"(a) PROHIBITION.—The President shall take all reasonable steps to ensure that assistance under this Act and the Arms Export Control Act is not provided to or through any individual or entity that the President knows or has reason to believe—

"(1) has been convicted of a violation of, or a conspiracy to violate, any law or regulation of the United States, a State or the District of Columbia, or a foreign country relating narcotic or psychotropic drugs or other controlled substances (as defined in section 481(i)(3) of this Act); or

"(2) is or has been an illicit trafficker in any such controlled substance or is or has been a knowing assistor, abettor, conspirator, or colluder with others in the illicit trafficking in any such substance.

"(b) REGULATIONS.—The President shall issue regulations specifying the steps to be taken in carrying out this section.

"(c) CONGRESSIONAL REVIEW OF REGULATIONS.—Regulations issued pursuant to subsection (b) shall be submitted to the Congress before they take effect."

SEC. 4504. PROCUREMENT FOR INTERNATIONAL NARCOTICS CONTROL ASSISTANCE.

The Congress urges the Secretary of State to take appropriate corrective action to improve the Department of State's procurement operations in order to assure that the procurement of property or services for use in providing assistance under chapter 8 of part I of the Foreign Assistance Act of 1961 (relating to international narcotics control assistance) is timely, efficient, and in accordance with applicable procurement statutes and regulations.

SEC. 4505. PROHIBITION ON USE OF NARCOTICS CONTROL ASSISTANCE TO ACQUIRE REAL PROPERTY.

Chapter 8 of part I of the Foreign Assistance Act of 1961, as amended by sections 4206 and 4503 of this title, is further amended by adding at the end the following:

"SEC. 488. PROHIBITION ON USE OF NARCOTICS CONTROL ASSISTANCE TO ACQUIRE REAL PROPERTY.

"Funds made available to carry out this chapter may not be used to acquire (by purchase, lease, or other means) any real property for use by foreign military, paramilitary, or law enforcement forces."

SEC. 4506. REIMBURSEMENT FOR DOD SERVICES USED IN PROVIDING INTERNATIONAL NARCOTICS CONTROL ASSISTANCE.

Section 632(c) of the Foreign Assistance Act of 1961 is amended by inserting after "actual cost," the following: "or, in the case of services procured from the Department of Defense to carry out chapter 8 of part I, the amount of the additional costs incurred by the Department of Defense in providing such services,".

SEC. 4507. PERMISSIBLE USES OF AIRCRAFT AND OTHER EQUIPMENT.

Chapter 8 of part I of the Foreign Assistance Act of 1961, as amended by sections 4206, 4503, and 4505 of this title, is further amended by adding at the end the following:

"SEC. 489. PERMISSIBLE USES OF AIRCRAFT AND OTHER EQUIPMENT.

"(a) IN GENERAL.—The President shall take all reasonable steps to ensure that aircraft and other equipment made available to foreign countries under this chapter are used only in ways that are consistent with the purposes for which such equipment was made available.

"(b) REPORTS.—In the reports submitted pursuant to subsection (e), the President shall discuss—

"(1) any evidence indicating misuse by a foreign country of aircraft or other equipment made available under this chapter, and

"(2) the actions taken by the United States Government to prevent future misuse of such equipment by that foreign country.

"(c) REGULATIONS.—The President shall issue regulations specifying the steps to be taken in carrying out this section.

"(d) CONGRESSIONAL REVIEW OF REGULATIONS.—Regulations issued pursuant to subsection (c) shall be submitted to the Congress before they take effect.".

Subtitle G—Department of State Activities

SEC. 4601. COORDINATION OF ALL UNITED STATES ANTI-NARCOTICS ASSISTANCE TO FOREIGN COUNTRIES.

(a) COORDINATION.—Consistent with subtitle A of title I of this Act, the Secretary of State shall be responsible for coordinating all assistance provided by the United States Government to support international efforts to combat illicit narcotics production or trafficking.

(b) ANNUAL REPORTS.—

(1) REQUIREMENT FOR REPORTS.—At the time that the report required by section 481(e) of the Foreign Assistance Act of 1961 is submitted each year, the Secretary of State, in consultation with appropriate United States Government agencies, shall report to the appropriate committees of the Congress on the assistance provided by the United States Government during the preceding fiscal year to support international efforts to combat illicit narcotics production or trafficking.

(2) SPECIFIC ITEMS TO BE INCLUDED.—(A) Each report pursuant to this subsection shall specify the amount and nature of the assistance provided.

(B) Each report pursuant to this subsection shall include, for each country which is a significant direct or indirect source of illicit narcotic and psychotropic drugs and other controlled substances significantly affecting the United States, a section prepared by the Drug Enforcement Administration, a section prepared by the Customs Service, and a section prepared by the Coast Guard, which describes in detail—

(i) the assistance provided or to be provided (as the case may be) to such country by that agency, and

(ii) the assistance provided or to be provided (as the case may be) to that agency by such country,

with respect to narcotic control efforts during the preceding fiscal year, the current fiscal year, and the next fiscal year

(C) Each report required by this subsection shall also list all transfers, which were made by the United States Government during the preceding fiscal year, to a foreign country for narcotics control purposes of any property seized by or otherwise forfeited to the United States Government in connection with narcotics-related activity, including an estimate of the fair market value and physical condition of each item of property transferred.

(3) REPORTS MAY BE CLASSIFIED.—The reports required by this subsection may be provided on a classified basis to the extent necessary.

(c) RULE OF CONSTRUCTION.—Nothing contained in this section shall be construed to limit or impair the authority or responsibility of any other Federal agency with respect to law enforcement, domestic security operations, or intelligence activities as defined in Executive Order 12333.

SEC. 4602. REWARDS FOR INFORMATION CONCERNING NARCOTICS-RELATED OFFENSES COMMITTED OUTSIDE THE UNITED STATES.

Section 36(g) of the State Department Basic Authorities Act of 1956 is amended by amending the second sentence to read as follows: "In addition to the amount authorized to be appropriated by the preceding sentence, there are authorized to be appropriated, without fiscal year limitation, $5,000,000 for 'Administration of Foreign Affairs' for use in paying rewards for information described in subsection (b)(1).".

SEC. 4603. DENIAL OF PASSPORTS TO CERTAIN CONVICTED DRUG TRAFFICKERS.

Title I of the State Department Basic Authorities Act of 1956 is amended—

(1) by redesignating section 42 as section 43; and

(2) by inserting after section 41 the following:

"SEC. 42. DENIAL OF PASSPORTS TO CERTAIN CONVICTED DRUG TRAFFICKERS.

"(a) INELIGIBILITY FOR PASSPORT.—

"(1) IN GENERAL.—A passport may not be issued to an individual who is convicted of an offense described in subsection (b) during the period described in subsection (c) if the individual used a passport or otherwise crossed an international border in committing the offense.

"(2) PASSPORT REVOCATION.—The Secretary of State shall revoke a passport previously issued to an individual who is ineligible to receive a passport under paragraph (1).

"(b) DRUG LAW OFFENSES.—

"(1) FELONIES.—Subsection (a) applies with respect to any individual convicted of a Federal drug offense, or a State drug offense, if the offense is a felony.

"(2) CERTAIN MISDEMEANORS.—Subsection (a) also applies with respect to an individual convicted of a Federal drug offense, or a State drug offense, if the offense is misdemeanor, but only if the Secretary of State determines that subsection (a) should apply with respect to that individual on account of that offense. This paragraph does not apply to an individual's first conviction for a misdemeanor which involves only possession of a controlled substance.

"(c) PERIOD OF INELIGIBILITY.—Subsection (a) applies during the period that the individual—

"(1) is imprisoned, or is legally required to be imprisoned, as the result of the conviction for the offense described in subsection (b); or

"(2) is on parole or other supervised release after having been imprisoned as the result of that conviction.

"(d) EMERGENCY AND HUMANITARIAN EXCEPTIONS.—Notwithstanding subsection (a), the Secretary of State may issue a passport, in emergency circumstances or for humanitarian reasons, to an individual with respect to whom that subsection applies.

"(e) DEFINITIONS.—As used in this section—

"(1) the term 'controlled substance' has the same meaning as is provided in section 102 of the Controlled Substances Act (21 U.S.C. 802);

"(2) the term 'Federal drug offense' means a violation of—

"(A) the Controlled Substances Act (21 U.S.C. 801 et seq.) or the Controlled Substances Import and Export Act (21 U.S.C. 951 et seq.);

"(B) any other Federal law involving controlled substances; or

"(C) subchapter II of chapter 53 of title 31, United States Code (commonly referred to as the 'Bank Secrecy Act'), or section 1956 or section 1957 of title 18, United States Code (commonly referred to as the 'Money Laundering Act'), if the Secretary of State determines that the violation is related to illicit production of or trafficking in a controlled substance;

"(3) the term 'felony' means a criminal offense punishable by death or imprisonment for more than one year;

"(4) the term 'imprisoned' means an individual is confined in or otherwise restricted to a jail-type institution, a half-way house, a treatment facility, or another institution, on a full or part-time basis, pursuant to the sentence imposed as the result of a conviction;

"(5) the term 'misdemeanor' means a criminal offense other than a felony;

"(6) the term 'State drug offense' means a violation of State law involving the manufacture, distribution, or possession of a controlled substance; and

"(7) the term 'State law' means the law of a State of the United States, the District of Columbia, the Commonwealth of Puerto Rico, the Commonwealth of the Northern Mariana Islands, or a territory or possession of the United States.".

SEC. 4604. MACHINE-READABLE DOCUMENT BORDER SECURITY PROGRAM.

(a) REQUIREMENT TO DEVELOP PROGRAM.—(1) The Department of State, the United States Customs Service, and the Immigration and Naturalization Service shall develop a comprehensive machine-readable travel and identity document border security program that will improve border entry and departure control through automated data capture of machine-readable travel and identity documents.

(2) Within 60 days after the date of enactment of this Act, the Department of State, the Customs Service, and the Immigration and Naturalization Service shall jointly submit a detailed implementation plan to the Congress and the President regarding how they intend to carry out the program required by this section.

(3) The border security program required by this section shall include an integrated cooperative data exchange system that will incorporate law enforcement data on narcotics traffickers, terrorists, convicted criminals, fugitives, and others currently documented in the Lookout Systems of all three agencies and departments.

(4) In developing the border security program mandated in this section, the agencies and departments shall ensure that at least the following documents shall be integrated into the program and be machine-readable: border crossing cards; alien registration; pilots licenses; passports; and visas.

(b) AGENCIES THAT WILL CONTRIBUTE LAW ENFORCEMENT DATA FOR THE SYSTEM.—The following agencies and organizations shall contribute appropriate law enforcement data to the integrated cooperative data exchange system mandated in this section and shall update such information into the system on no less than a monthly basis:

(1) The Drug Enforcement Administration.

(2) The Federal Bureau of Investigation.

(3) The Bureau of Alcohol, Tobacco, and Firearms.

(4) The Internal Revenue Service.

(5) The Federal Aviation Administration.

(6) The United States Marshals Service.

(7) The United States Coast Guard.

(c) AUTHORIZATION OF APPROPRIATIONS.—(1) There are authorized to be appropriated $23,000,000 for fiscal year 1989 for the development, procurement, and implementation of a machine-readable travel and identity document border security program. Of this amount $7,000,000 shall be available only for the United State Customs Service, $7,000,000 shall be available only for the Immigration and Naturalization Service, and $9,000,000 shall be available only for the Department of State to carry out the provisions of this section.

(2) The amounts authorized by paragraph (1) are in addition to other amounts authorized to be appropriated for fiscal year 1989.

(d) CONTINUING FULL IMPLEMENTATION REQUIRED.—All agencie participating in the development and implementation of the border security program and systems mandated in this section shall maintain their participation and contributions to the program and systems authorized under this section at full implementation levels in fiscal years 1990, 1991, and 1992, subject to the availability of appropriations.

SEC. 4605. EXTRADITION AND MUTUAL LEGAL ASSISTANCE TREATIES AND MODEL COMPREHENSIVE ANTIDRUG LAWS.

(a) FINDINGS.—The Congress finds that—

(1) section 133 of the Foreign Relations Authorization Act, Fiscal Years 1986 and 1987 (enacted August 16, 1985), directed the Secretary of State to increase United States efforts to negotiate updated extradition treaties relating to narcotics offenses with each major drug-producing country;

(2) section 803 of the Foreign Relations Authorization Act, Fiscal Years 1988 and 1989 (enacted December 22, 1987) directed the Secretary of State to ensure that an objective of the United States diplomatic mission in each major illicit drug producing or major drug-transit country be to ensure that drug traffickers can be extradited to the United States; and

(3) although some progress has been made pursuant to these directives in increasing international law enforcement cooperation with respect to illicit drug production and trafficking, much greater international law enforcement cooperation is required in combating the illicit drug problem.

(b) GREATER EMPHASIS REQUIRED.—Therefore, the Congress directs the Secretary of State to place greater emphasis on updating extradition treaties, and on negotiating mutual legal assistance treaties, with major illicit drug producing countries and major drug-transit countries.

(c) MODEL TREATIES AND ANTIDRUG LAWS.—The Secretary of State and the Attorney General shall jointly develop a model extradition treaty with respect to narcotics-related violations (including extradition of host country nationals), a model mutual legal assistance treaty, and model comprehensive anti-narcotics legislation. The Secretary of State shall distribute such treaties and legislation to each United States mission abroad.

(d) REPORT TO CONGRESS.—The Secretary of State shall report to the Congress, not later than six months after the date of enactment of this Act, on actions taken to carry out this section.

SEC. 4606. OVERSEAS INVESTIGATIVE PROGRAM.

It is the sense of the Congress that Regional Security Officers and other security personnel at United States embassies and other civilian posts abroad should be directed to expand their investigative activities with respect to illicit drug use and trafficking by United States Government personnel and their dependents.

SEC. 4607. ASSIGNMENT OF MORE DRUG ENFORCEMENT ADMINISTRATION AGENTS TO UNITED STATES EMBASSIES.

The Congress urges the Secretary of State to permit the assignment of additional Drug Enforcement Administration agents to United States diplomatic missions in those foreign countries where illicit narcotics production or trafficking is, or is likely to become, a significant problem.

Subtitle H—International Banking Matters

SEC. 4701. INTERNATIONAL CURRENCY TRANSACTION REPORTING.

(a) FINDINGS.—The Congress finds that—

(1) the success of cash transaction and money laundering control statutes in the United States has been significant; and

(2) the United States should play a leadership role in the development of an international system of a similar kind.

(b) PURPOSE.—It is the purpose of this section to urge the United States Government, to the maximum extent practicable, to seek the active cooperation of other countries in the enforcement of these statutes, since only a truly multilateral approach can be effective in eliminating bank haven loopholes through which money launderers can escape.

(c) ESTABLISHMENT OF INTERNATIONAL AGENCY.—The Congress urges the Secretary of the Treasury to negotiate with finance ministers of foreign countries to establish an international currency control agency to—

(1) serve as a central source of information and database for international drug enforcement agencies;

(2) collect and analyze currency transaction reports filed by member countries; and

(3) encourage the adoption, by member countries, of uniform cash transaction and money laundering statutes.

(d) MAINTENANCE OF DOMESTIC EFFORT.—While establishing a multilateral agency will be the most effective method of combating money laundering, the United States must itself continue to do everything it can to curb international money laundering.

SEC. 4702. RESTRICTIONS ON LAUNDERING OF UNITED STATES CURRENCY.

(a) FINDINGS.—The Congress finds that international currency transactions, especially in United States currency, that involve the proceeds of narcotics trafficking fuel trade in narcotics in the United States and worldwide and consequently are a threat to the national security of the United States.

(b) PURPOSE.—The purpose of this section is to provide for international negotiations that would expand access to information on transactions involving large amounts of United States currency wherever those transactions occur worldwide.

(c) NEGOTIATIONS.—(1) The Secretary of the Treasury (hereinafter in this section referred to as the "Secretary") shall enter into negotiations with the appropriate financial supervisory agencies and other officials of any foreign country the financial institutions of which do business in United States currency. Highest priority shall be attached to countries whose financial institutions the Secretary determines, in consultation with the Attorney General and the Director of National Drug Control Policy, may be engaging in currency transactions involving the proceeds of international narcotics trafficking, particularly United States currency derived from drug sales in the United States.

(2) The purposes of negotiations under this subsection are—

(A) to reach one or more international agreements to ensure that foreign banks and other financial institutions maintain adequate records of large United States currency transactions, and

(B) to establish a mechanism whereby such records may be made available to United States law enforcement officials.

In carrying out such negotiations, the Secretary should seek to enter into and further cooperative efforts, voluntary information exchanges, the use of letters rogatory, and mutual legal assistance treaties.

(d) REPORTS.—Not later than 1 year after the date of enactment of this Act, the Secretary shall submit an interim report to the Committee on Banking, Finance and Urban Affairs of the House of Representatives and the Committee on Banking, Housing, and Urban Affairs of the Senate on progress in the negotiations under subsection (c). Not later than 2 years after such enactment, the Secretary shall submit a final report to such Committees and the President on the outcome of those negotiations and shall identify, in consultation with the Attorney General and the Director of National Drug Control Policy, countries—

(1) with respect to which the Secretary determines there is evidence that the financial institutions in such countries are engaging in currency transactions involving the proceeds of international narcotics trafficking; and

(2) which have not reached agreement with United States authorities on a mechanism for exchanging adequate records on international currency transactions in connection with narcotics investigations and proceedings.

(e) AUTHORITY.—If after receiving the advice of the Secretary and in any case at the time of receipt of the Secretary's report, the Secretary determines that a foreign country—

(1) has jurisdiction over financial institutions that are substantially engaging in currency transactions that effect the United States involving the proceeds of international narcotics trafficking;

(2) such country has not reached agreement on a mechanism for exchanging adequate records on international currency transactions in connection with narcotics investigations and proceedings; and

(3) such country is not negotiating in good faith to reach such an agreement,

the President shall impose appropriate penalties and sanctions, including temporarily or permanently—

(1) prohibiting such persons, institutions or other entities in such countries from participating in any United States dollar clearing or wire transfer system; and

(2) prohibiting such persons, institutions or entities in such countries from maintaining an account with any bank or other financial institution chartered under the laws of the United States or any State.

Any penalties or sanctions so imposed may be delayed or waived upon certification of the President to the Congress that it is in the national interest to do so. Financial institutions in such countries that maintain adequate records shall be exempt from such penalties and sanctions.

(f) DEFINITIONS.—For the purposes of this section—

(1) The term "United States currency" means Federal Reserve Notes and United States coins.

(2) The term "adequate records" means records of United States' currency transactions in excess of $10,000 including the identification of the person initiating the transaction, the person's business or occupation, and the account or accounts affected by the transaction, or other records of comparable effect.

(g) SUNSET.—The authority given the President in subsection (e) shall expire on June 30, 1994.

SEC. 4703. EXPORT-IMPORT BANK FINANCING FOR SALES OF DEFENSE ARTICLES AND SERVICES FOR ANTI-NARCOTICS PURPOSES.

Section 2(b)(6) of the Export-Import Bank Act of 1945 (12 U.S.C. 635(b)(6)) is amended—

(1) by inserting "(A)" before "The Bank";

(2) by striking "paragraph" and inserting in lieu thereof "subparagraph"; and

(3) by adding at the end the following new subparagraphs:

"(B) Subparagraph (A), and section 32 of the Arms Export Control Act, shall not apply to any sale of defense articles or services if—

"(i) the Bank is requested to provide a guarantee or insurance for the sale;

"(ii) the President determines that the defense articles or services are being sold primarily for anti-narcotics purposes;

"(iii) section 481(h)(5) of the Foreign Assistance Act of 1961 does not apply with respect to the purchasing country;

"(iv) the President determines, in accordance with subparagraph (C), that the sale is in the national interest of the United States;

"(v) the Bank determines that, notwithstanding the provision of a guarantee or insurance for the sale, not more than 5 percent of the guarantee and insurance authority available to the Bank in any fiscal year will be used by the Bank to support the sale of defense articles and services; and

"(vi) the sale is made on or before September 30, 1990.

"(C) In determining whether a sale of defense articles or services would be in the national interest of the United States, the President shall take into account whether the sale would—

"(i) be consistent with the anti-narcotics policy of the United States;

"(ii) involve the end use of a defense article or service in a major illicit drug producing or major drug-transit country (as defined in section 481(i) of the Foreign Assistance Act of 1961); and

"(iii) be made to a country with a democratic form of government.

"(D)(i) The Board shall not give approval to guarantee or insure a sale of defense articles or services unless—

"(I) the President determines, in accordance with subparagraph (C), that it is in the national interest of the United States for the Bank to provide such guarantee or insurance; and

"(II) such determination has been reported to the Speaker and the Committee on Banking, Finance and Urban Affairs of the House of Representatives, and to the Committee on Banking, Housing, and Urban Affairs and the Committee on Foreign Relations of the Senate, not less than 25 days of continuous session of the Congress before the date of such approval.

"(ii) For purposes of clause (i), continuity of a session of the Congress shall be considered as broken only by an adjournment of the Congress sine die, and the days on which either House is not in session because of an adjournment of more than 3 days to a day certain shall be excluded in the computation of the 25-day period referred to in such sentence.

"(E) The provision of a guarantee or insurance under subparagraph (B) shall be deemed to be the provision of security assistance for purposes of section 502B of the Foreign Assistance Act of 1961 (relating to governments which engage in a consistent pattern of gross violations of international recognized human rights).

"(F) To the extent that defense articles or services for which a guarantee or insurance is provided under subparagraph (B) are used for a purpose other than anti-narcotics purposes, they may be used only for those purposes for which defense articles and defense services sold under the Arms Export Control Act (relating to the foreign military sales program) may be used under section 4 of such Act.

"(G) As used in this paragraph, the term 'defense articles and services' means articles, services, and related technical data that are designated as defense articles and defense services pursuant to sections 38 and 47(7) of the Arms Export Control Act and listed on the United States Munitions List (part 121 of title 22 of the Code of Federal Regulations).".

Subtitle I—Miscellaneous Provisions

SEC. 4801. INTELLIGENCE COMMUNITY ACTIONS DIRECTED AT ILLICIT INTERNATIONAL DRUG TRAFFICKING.

It is the sense of the Congress that, given the magnitude of the illicit drug problem and the threat it poses to the national security of the United States, agencies of the intelligence community should be more actively involved in the effort to combat illicit international drug trafficking.

SEC. 4802. CORRECTION OF TECHNICAL ERRORS IN PRIOR ACTS.

(a) Anti-Drug Abuse Act of 1986.—(1) Section 2015(b)(1) of the Anti-Drug Abuse Act of 1986 is amended by striking out "effects" and inserting in lieu thereof "efforts".

(2) Section 2030(b) of that Act is amended by striking out "subsection (A)(4)" and inserting in lieu thereof "subsection (a)(4)".

(b) 1986 Drug Act Amendments to Foreign Assistance Act.—Section 481(i)(4)(vi) of the Foreign Assistance Act of 1961 (as amended by section 2005 of the Anti-Drug Abuse Act of 1986) is amended by striking out "section 1049(c)(2)" and inserting in lieu thereof "section 104(c)(2)".

SEC. 4803. RESOURCES FOR CERTAIN DRUG CONTROL ACTIVITIES.

(a) Findings.—The Congress finds that—

(1) there has been a severe, cancer-like growth of youth gangs who abuse, transport, and traffic in illegal drugs;

(2) such youth gangs engage in acts of violence, often on a random basis, resulting in death or serious bodily injury to thousands of people, as well as terrorizing tens of thousands of others;

(3) such youth gangs have spread their activities from southern California to more than 50 cities throughout the United States, thereby clearly indicating that the threat posed by these gangs is national in nature, requiring a strong Federal response;

(4) stopping drugs at the source is one of the critical elements of our Government's war on drugs; and

(5) the Airwing Operations of the Bureau of International Narcotics Matters in the Department of State is an important tool of our Government's policy against narcotics trafficking.

(b) REVIEW.—It is, therefore, the sense of the Congress that the Director of National Drug Control Policy should review the entire drug control problem to determine priorities for new resources or shifting of existing resources, giving particular attention to—

(1) planning for and assistance to the Airwing Operations of the Bureau of International Narcotics Matters in the Department of State; and

(2) assistance to control the present and growing threat posed to the Nation by youth gangs which traffic in illegal drugs.

(c) ADDITIONAL RESOURCES.—Based upon his findings, the Director of National Drug Control Policy should consider, as necessary, recommending significant resources in addition to those specifically allocated in this Act.

CENTRAL AMERICA BIPARTISAN ACCORD ACT, 1989

An Act to implement the Bipartisan Accord on Central America of March 24, 1989.

Date: April 18, 1989

Bill No.: H.R. 1750

Public Law No.: 101-14

Cite: 103 STAT. 37

Sections reprinted: All

Public Law 101-14
101st Congress
An Act

To implement the Bipartisan Accord on Central America of March 24, 1989.

Be it enacted by the Senate and House of Representatives of the United States of America in Congress assembled,

SECTION 1. POLICY.

The purpose of this Act is to implement the Bipartisan Accord on Central America between the President and the Congress signed on March 24, 1989.

SEC. 2. ADDITIONAL HUMANITARIAN ASSISTANCE.

(a) TRANSFER OF FUNDS.—The President may transfer to the Agency for International Development, from unobligated funds from the appropriations accounts specified in section 6—

(1) up to $49,750,000, to provide humanitarian assistance to the Nicaraguan Resistance, to remain available through February 28, 1990;

(2) such funds as may be necessary to provide transportation in accordance with section 3 for assistance authorized by paragraph (1); and

(3) not to exceed $5,000,000 to "Operating Expenses of the Agency for International Development" to meet the necessary administrative expenses to carry out this Act, to remain available through March 31, 1990.

(b) DEFINITION.—For purposes of this section and section 3, the term "humanitarian assistance" means—

(1) food, clothing, and shelter;

(2) medical services, medical supplies, and nonmilitary training for health and sanitation;

(3) nonmilitary training of the recipients with respect to their treatment of civilians and other armed forces personnel, in accordance with internationally accepted standards of human rights;

(4) payment for such items, services, and training;

(5) replacement batteries for existing communications equipment; and

(6) support for voluntary reintegration of and voluntary regional relocation by the Nicaraguan Resistance.

SEC. 3. TRANSPORTATION OF HUMANITARIAN ASSISTANCE.

(a) IN GENERAL.—The transportation of humanitarian assistance on or after the date of enactment of this Act which, before such date, was specifically authorized by law to be provided to the Nicaraguan Resistance, or which is authorized to be provided by section 2, shall be arranged solely by the Agency for International Development in a manner consistent with the Bipartisan Accord on Central America between the President and the Congress signed on March 24, 1989.

(b) Prohibition on Mixed Loads.—Transportation of any military assistance, or of any assistance other than that specified in 2(b), is prohibited.

SEC. 4. MEDICAL ASSISTANCE.

The President may transfer, in addition to funds transferred prior to March 31, 1989, to the Administrator of the Agency for International Development from unobligated funds from appropriations accounts specified in section 6, up to $4,166,000, to be used only for the provision of medical assistance for the civilian victims of the Nicaraguan civil strife to be transported and administered by the Catholic Church in Nicaragua.

SEC. 5. UNITED STATES POLICY CONCERNING ECONOMIC ASSISTANCE FOR CENTRAL AMERICA.

As part of an effort to promote democracy and address on a long-term basis the economic causes of regional and political instability in Central America—

(1) in recognition of the recommendations of groups such as the National Bipartisan Commission on Central America, the Inter-American Dialogue, and the Sanford Commission;

(2) to assist in the implementation of these economic plans and to encourage other countries in other parts of the world to join in extending assistance to Central America; and

(3) in the context of an agreement to end military conflict in the region;

the Congress encourages the President to submit proposals for bilateral and multilateral action—

(A) to provide additional economic assistance to the democratic countries of Central America to promote economic stability, expand educational opportunity, foster progress in human rights, bolster democratic institutions, and strengthen institutions of justice;

(B) to facilitate the ability of Central American economies to grow through the development of their infrastructure, expansion of exports, and the strengthening of increased investment opportunities;

(C) to provide a more realistic plan to assist Central American countries in managing their foreign debt; and

(D) to develop these initiatives in concert with Western Europe, Japan, and other democratic allies.

SEC. 6. SOURCE OF FUNDS; AND RESCISSION.

(INCLUDING TRANSFERS AND RESCISSION)

(a) Source of Funds.—The appropriations accounts from which funds may be transferred pursuant to sections 2 and 4 are the following accounts in amounts not to exceed the following:

(1) Missile Procurement, Army, 1988, $3,500,000.

(2) Procurement of Weapons and Tracked Combat Vehicles, Army, 1987, $12,739,000.

(3) Other Procurement, Army, 1988, $761,000.

(4) Research, Development, Test and Evaluation, Air Force, 1988, $1,902,000.

(5) Weapons Procurement, Navy, 1989, $2,000,000.

(6) Research, Development, Test and Evaluation, Navy, 1989, $13,400,000.

VIENNA CONVENTION ON DIPLOMATIC RELATIONS ACT, 1989

An Act to ratify certain agreements relating to the Vienna Convention on Diplomatic Relations.

Date: July 26, 1989

Bill No.: H.R. 2214

Public Law No.: 101-62

Cite: 103 STAT. 162

Sections reprinted: All

Public Law 101-62
101st Congress

An Act

To ratify certain agreements relating to the Vienna Convention on Diplomatic Relations.

Be it enacted by the Senate and House of Representatives of the United States of America in Congress assembled, That, pursuant to section 101(d) of Public Law 99-239, the following agreements are approved and shall enter into force in accordance with their terms:

(1) "Agreement Between the Government of the United States and the Government of the Republic of the Marshall Islands to Amend the Governmental Representation Provisions of the Compact of Free Association Pursuant to section 432 of the Compact", signed on March 18, 1988; and

(2) "Agreement Between the Government of the United States and the Government of the Federated States of Micronesia to Amend the Governmental Representation Provisions of the Compact of Free Association Pursuant to section 432 of the Compact", signed on March 9, 1988.

Approved July 26, 1989.

LEGISLATIVE HISTORY—H.R. 2214:

HOUSE REPORTS: No. 101-111 (Comm. on Foreign Affairs).
CONGRESSIONAL RECORD, Vol. 135 (1989):
June 27, considered and passed House.
July 13, considered and passed Senate.
WEEKLY COMPILATION OF PRESIDENTIAL DOCUMENTS, Vol. 25 (1989):
July 26, Presidential statement.

DEPARTMENTS OF COMMERCE, JUSTICE, AND STATE, THE JUDICIARY, AND RELATED AGENCIES APPROPRIATIONS ACT, 1990

An Act making appropriations for the Departments of Commerce, Justice, and State, the Judiciary, and related agencies for the fiscal year ending September 30, 1990, and for other purposes.

Date: November 21, 1989

Bill No.: H.R. 2991

Public Law No.: 101-162

Cite: 101 STAT. 988

Sections reprinted:

Section 609 - Sea turtles conservation.
Section 610 - Restrictions on exporting satellites to China

Public Law 101–162
101st Congress

An Act

Making appropriations for the Departments of Commerce, Justice, and State, the Judiciary, and related agencies for the fiscal year ending September 30, 1990, and for other purposes.

SEC. 609. (a) The Secretary of State, in consultation with the Secretary of Commerce, shall, with respect to those species of sea turtles the conservation of which is the subject of regulations promulgated by the Secretary of Commerce on June 29, 1987—

(1) initiate negotiations as soon as possible for the development of bilateral or multilateral agreements with other nations for the protection and conservation of such species of sea turtles;

(2) initiate negotiations as soon as possible with all foreign governments which are engaged in, or which have persons or companies engaged in, commercial fishing operations which, as determined by the Secretary of Commerce, may affect adversely such species of sea turtles, for the purpose of entering into bilateral and multilateral treaties with such countries to protect such species of sea turtles;

(3) encourage such other agreements to promote the purposes of this section with other nations for the protection of specific ocean and land regions which are of special significance to the health and stability of such species of sea turtles;

(4) initiate the amendment of any existing international treaty for the protection and conservation of such species of sea turtles to which the United States is a party in order to make such treaty consistent with the purposes and policies of this section; and

(5) provide to the Congress by not later than one year after the date of enactment of this section—

(A) a list of each nation which conducts commercial shrimp fishing operations within the geographic range of distribution of such sea turtles;

(B) a list of each nation which conducts commercial shrimp fishing operations which may affect adversely such species of sea turtles; and

(C) a full report on—

(i) the results of his efforts under this section; and

(ii) the status of measures taken by each nation listed pursuant to paragraph (A) or (B) to protect and conserve such sea turtles.

(b)(1) IN GENERAL.—The importation of shrimp or products from shrimp which have been harvested with commercial fishing technology which may affect adversely such species of sea turtles shall be prohibited not later than May 1, 1991, except as provided in paragraph (2).

(2) CERTIFICATION PROCEDURE.—The ban on importation of shrimp or products from shrimp pursuant to paragraph (1) shall not apply if the President shall determine and certify to the Congress not later than May 1, 1991, and annually thereafter that—

(A) the government of the harvesting nation has provided documentary evidence of the adoption of a regulatory program governing the incidental taking of such sea turtles in the course of such harvesting that is comparable to that of the United States; and

(B) the average rate of that incidental taking by the vessels of the harvesting nation is comparable to the average rate of incidental taking of sea turtles by United States vessels in the course of such harvesting; or

(C) the particular fishing environment of the harvesting nation does not pose a threat of the incidental taking of such sea turtles in the course of such harvesting.

SEC. 610. (a) No monies appropriated by this Act may be used to reinstate, or approve any export license applications for the launch of United States-built satellites on Soviet- or Chinese-built launch vehicles unless the President makes a report under subsection (b) or (c) of this section.

(b) The restriction on the approval of export licenses for United States-built satellites to the People's Republic of China for launch on Chinese-built launch vehicles is terminated if the President makes a report to the Congress that:

(1) the Government of the People's Republic of China has made progress on a program of political reform throughout the entire country which includes—

(A) lifting of martial law;

(B) halting of executions and other reprisals against individuals for the nonviolent expression of their political beliefs;

(C) release of political prisoners;

(D) increased respect for internationally recognized human rights, including freedom of expression, the press, assembly, and association; and

(E) permitting a freer flow of information, including an end to the jamming of Voice of America and greater access for foreign journalists; or

(c) It is in the national interest of the United States.

FOREIGN OPERATIONS, EXPORT FINANCING, AND RELATED PROGRAMS APPROPRIATIONS ACT, 1990

An Act making appropriations for foreign operations, export financing, and related programs for the fiscal year ending September 30, 1990, and for other purposes.

Date: November 21, 1989

Bill No.: H.R. 3743

Public Law No.: 101-167

Cite: 103 STAT. 1195

Sections reprinted:

Section 527 (a-d) - United Nations voting record (subsection (e), which repeals provisions of some earlier laws, is omitted.)
Section 533 - Energy conservation.
Section 534 - Global warming initiative and tropical forestry assistance.
Section 573 - Modernization of military capabilities of certain countries.
- Subsection (a) - Authority to transfer excess defense articles
- Subsection (b) - Limitations on transfers.
- Subsection (c) - Notification to Congress.
- Subsection (e) - Maintenance of military balance in Eastern Mediterranean.
- Subsection (f) - Major illicit drug producing countries in Latin America and the Caribbean.
- Subsection (g) - Definitions.

Section 598 - International Coffee Agreement.
Section 599 - Latvia, Estonia, and Lithuania.
Section 599B - Human rights in Cuba.

Public Law 101–167
101st Congress

An Act

Making appropriations for foreign operations, export financing, and related programs for the fiscal year ending September 30, 1990, and for other purposes.

UNITED NATIONS VOTING RECORD

SEC. 527. (a) IN GENERAL.—Not later than March 31 of each year, the Secretary of State shall transmit to the Speaker of the House of Representatives and the President of the Senate a full and complete annual report which assesses for the prior calendar year, with respect to each foreign country member of the United Nations, the voting practices of the governments of such countries at the United Nations, and evaluates General Assembly and Security Council actions and the responsiveness of those governments to United States policy on issues of special importance to the United States.

(b) INFORMATION ON VOTING PRACTICES IN THE UNITED NATIONS.—Such report shall include, with respect to voting practices and plenary actions in the United Nations during the preceding year, information to be compiled and supplied by the Permanent Representative of the United States to the United Nations, consisting of—

(1) an analysis and discussion, prepared in consultation with the Secretary of State, of the extent to which member countries supported United States policy objectives at the United Nations;

(2) an analysis and discussion, prepared in consultation with the Secretary of State, of actions taken by the United Nations by consensus;

(3) with respect to plenary votes of the United Nations General Assembly—

(A) a listing of all such votes on issues which directly affected important United States interests and on which the United States lobbied extensively and a brief description of the issues involved in each such vote;

(B) a listing of the votes described in subparagraph (A) which provides a comparison of the vote cast by each member country with the vote cast by the United States;

(C) a country-by-country listing of votes described in subparagraph (A); and

(D) a listing of votes described in subparagraph (A) displayed in terms of United Nations regional caucus groups;

(4) a listing of all plenary votes cast by member countries of the United Nations in the General Assembly which provides a comparison of the vote cast by each member country with the vote cast by the United States;

(5) an analysis and discussion, prepared in consultation with the Secretary of State, of the extent to which other members supported United States policy objectives in the Security Council and a separate listing of all Security Council votes of each member country in comparison with the United States; and

(6) a side-by-side comparison of agreement on important and overall votes for each member country and the United States.

(c) FORMAT.—Information required pursuant to subsection (b)(3) shall also be submitted, together with an explanation of the statistical methodology, in a format identical to that contained in chapter II of the March 14, 1988, Report to Congress on Voting Practices in the United Nations.

(d) STATEMENT BY THE SECRETARY OF STATE.—Each report under subsection (a) shall contain a statement by the Secretary of State discussing the measures which have been taken to inform United States diplomatic missions of United Nations General Assembly and Security Council activities.

ENVIRONMENTAL CONCERNS

SEC. 533. (a) It is the policy of the United States that sustainable economic growth must be predicated on the sustainable management of natural resources. The Secretary of the Treasury shall instruct the United States Executive Directors of each multilateral development bank (MDB) to promote vigorously within each MDB the expansion of programs in areas which address the problems of global climate change through requirements to—

(1) augment and expand the professional staff of each MDB with expertise in end-use energy efficiency and conservation and renewable energy;

(2) develop methodologies which allow borrowing countries to include investments in end-use energy efficiency and renewable energy as explicit alternatives in the "least cost" energy sector investments plans they prepare with MDB assistance. Such plans shall give priority to projects and programs which support energy conservation, end-use efficiency and renewable energy sources in major economic sectors, and shall compare the economic and environmental costs of those actions with the economic and environmental costs of investments in conventional energy supplies;

(3) provide analysis for each proposed loan to support additional power generating capacity, comparing the economic and environmental costs of investments in demand reduction, including energy conservation and end-use energy efficiency, with the economic and environmental costs of the proposal;

(4) assure that systematic, detailed environmental impact assessments (EIA) of proposed energy projects, or projects with potential significant environmental impacts, are conducted early in the project cycle. Assessments should include but not be limited to—

(A) consideration of a wide range of alternatives to the proposed project including, where feasible, alternative investments in end-use energy efficiency and non-conventional renewable energy; and

(B) encouragement and adoption of policies which allow for public participation in the EIA process;

(5) include environmental costs in the economic assessment of the proposed projects with significant potential environmental impacts, or power projects, and if possible for all projects which involve expansion of generating capacity of more than 10 MW, develop a standard increase in project cost as a surrogate for the environmental costs;

(6) encourage and promote end-use energy efficiency and renewable energy in negotiations of policy-based energy sector lending, and MDBs should consider not proceeding with policy-based sector loans which do not contain commitments from the borrowing country to devote a significant portion of its sector investments toward energy efficiency and renewable energy;

(7) provide technical assistance as a component of all energy sector lending to help borrowing countries identify and pursue end-use energy efficiency investments. This technical assistance shall include support for detailed audits of energy use and the development of institutional capacity to promote end-use energy efficiency and conservation;

(8) work with borrowing countries, with input from the public in both borrowing and donor countries, to develop loans for end-use energy efficiency and renewable energy, where possible "bundling" small projects into larger, more easily financed projects; and

(9) seek the convening of a special seminar for board members and senior staff of each MDB concerning alternate energy investment opportunities and end-use energy efficiency and conservation.

(b) The Secretary of the Treasury as a part of the annual report to the Congress shall describe in detail, progress made by each of the MDBs in adopting and implementing programs meeting the standards set out in subsection (a), including in particular—

(1) efforts by the Department of Treasury to assure implementation by each of the MDBs of programs substantially equivalent to those set out in this section, and results of such efforts;

(2) progress made by each MDB in drafting and implementing least cost energy plans for each recipient country which meets requirements outlined in subsection (a)(2);

(3) the absolute dollar amounts, and proportion of total lending in the energy sector, of loans and portions of loans, approved by each MDB in the previous year for projects or programs of end-use energy efficiency and conservation and renewable energy.

(c) Not later than April 1, 1990, the Secretary of the Treasury shall request each MDB to prepare an analysis of the impact its current forestry sector loans will have on borrowing country emissions of CO_2 and the status of proposals for specific forestry sector activities to reduce CO_2 emissions.

(d)(1) The Administrator of the Agency for International Development shall issue guidance to all Agency missions and bureaus detailing the elements of a "Global Warming Initiative" which will emphasize the need to reduce emissions of greenhouse gases, especially CO_2, through strategies consistent with their continued economic development. This initiative shall emphasize the need to accelerate sustainable development strategies in areas such as reforestation, biodiversity, end-use energy efficiency, least-cost energy planning, and renewable energy, and shall encourage mission directors to incorporate the elements of this initiative in developing their country programs.

(2) The Agency for International Development shall—

(A) increase the number and expertise of personnel devoted to end-use energy efficiency, renewable energy, and environmental activities in all bureaus and missions;

(B) devote increased resources to technical training of mission directors, in energy planning, energy conservation, end-use energy efficiency, renewable energy, reforestation, and biodiversity;

(C) accelerate the activities of the Multi-Agency Working Group on Power Sector Innovation to enable completion of case studies of at least ten countries in fiscal year 1990; and

(D) devote at least 10 percent of the resources allocated for forestry activities to the preservation and restoration (as opposed to management for extraction) of natural forests.

(3) Funds appropriated by this Act to carry out the provisions of sections 103 to 106 of the Foreign Assistance Act of 1961 may be used to reimburse the full cost of technical personnel detailed or assigned to, or contracted by, the Agency for International Development to provide expertise in the environmental sector.

(4)(A) Section 119(b) of the Foreign Assistance Act of 1961 is amended by inserting ", notwithstanding section 660," after "this part".

(B) Not less than $10,000,000 of the funds appropriated to carry out the provisions of sections 103 through 106 of such Act (including funds for sub-Saharan Africa) shall be made available for biological diversity activities, of which $2,000,000 shall be made available for the Parks in Peril project, pursuant to the authority of section 119(b) and $1,000,000 shall be available for the National Science Foundation's international biological diversity program.

(C) Funds obligated in prior fiscal years pursuant to the authority of section 119(b) may be expended in fiscal year 1990 pursuant to the authority of such section as amended by subparagraph (A).

(e) The Secretary of the Treasury shall—

(1) instruct the United States Executive Directors to the International Bank for Reconstruction and Development, the International Development Association, the Inter-American Development Bank, the African Development Bank, the Asian Development Bank, and the International Monetary Fund, to actively support lending portfolios which allow debtor developing countries to reduce or restructure debt in concert with the sustainable use of their natural resources. As a part of any such debt restructuring program, the United States Executive Director should require a thorough review of opportunities this initiative may offer for providing additional financial resources for the management of natural resources. The Secretary shall submit a report to the Committees on Appropriations on the progress of this program by April 30, 1990;

(2) instruct the United States Executive Directors to the international financial institutions to seek the support of other donor countries in the implementation of this policy; and

(3) instruct the United States Executive Director to the International Bank for Reconstruction and Development to actively seek the implementation by the World Bank of the recommendations set forth in its April 1, 1988, report on "Debt-for-Nature swaps", including the setting up of a pilot debt-for-nature swap program in one or more interested countries. The Secretary shall submit a progress report on the implementation of this program to the Committees on Appropriations by April 1, 1990.

(f) The Secretary of the Treasury shall seek to incorporate natural resource management initiatives throughout the implementation of the Brady Plan. The Secretary shall submit to the Committees on Appropriations a report by April 15, 1990, describing how such initiatives have been incorporated into the Brady Plan and identifying any such initiatives undertaken to date.

(g) The Secretary of the Treasury shall instruct the United States Executive Director to the Inter-American Development Bank to—

(1) seek implementation of the environmental reform measures agreed to as part of the Bank's 7th Replenishment;

(2) seek adoption of Bank policies regarding indigenous people, relations with nongovernmental organizations, and the protection of wildlife and unique natural and cultural features;

(3) require the Bank to demonstrate how it has improved, and will improve, the monitoring of environmental and social components of loans; and

(4) within four months after the date of enactment of this Act report to the Committees on Appropriations on the progress the Bank has made in implementing each of these reforms.

GLOBAL WARMING INITIATIVE

SEC. 534. (a) TROPICAL FORESTRY ASSISTANCE.—(1) In order to achieve the maximum impact from activities relating to tropical forestry, the Agency for International Development shall focus tropical forestry assistance programs on the key middle- and low-income developing countries (hereinafter "key countries") which are projected to contribute large amounts of greenhouse gases related to global warming as a result of industrialization and the burning of fossil fuels, and destruction of tropical forests.

(2) Funds appropriated to carry out the provisions of sections 103 and 106 of the Foreign Assistance Act of 1961, as amended, may be used by the Agency for International Development, notwithstanding any other provision of law, for the purpose of supporting tropical forestry programs aimed at reducing emissions of greenhouse gases with regard to the key countries in which deforestation makes a significant contribution to global warming, except that such assistance shall be subject to sections 116, 502B, and 620A of the Foreign Assistance Act of 1961.

(3) In providing assistance relating to tropical forests, the Administrator of that Agency shall, to the extent feasible and appropriate, assist countries in developing a systematic analysis of the appropriate use of their total tropical forest resources, with the goal of developing a national program for sustainable forestry.

(b) ENERGY ASSISTANCE.—(1) In order to achieve the maximum impact from activities relating to energy, the Agency for International Development shall focus energy assistance activities on the key countries, where assistance would have the greatest impact on reducing emissions from greenhouse gases. Such assistance shall be focused on improved energy efficiency, increased use of renewable energy resources and national energy plans (such as least-cost energy plans) which include investment in end-use efficiency and renewable energy resources.

(2) Funds appropriated to carry out the provisions of sections 103 and 106 of the Foreign Assistance Act of 1961, as amended, may be used by the Agency for International Development, notwithstanding any other provision of law, for the purpose of supporting energy programs aimed at reducing emissions of greenhouse gases related to global warming with regard to the key countries, except that such assistance shall be subject to sections 116, 502B, and 620A of the Foreign Assistance Act of 1961.

(3) It is the sense of the Congress that the Agency for International Development should increase its efforts in the fields of energy efficiency, renewable energy, and energy planning. Such increase should take place with respect to key countries and countries with large Economic Support Fund project assistance. Such efforts should include—

(A) an increase in the number of Agency for International Development staff with energy expertise, including staff with expertise in renewable energy technologies and end-use efficiency;

(B) assistance to develop analyses of energy-sector actions that could minimize emissions of greenhouse gases at least cost, while at the same time meeting basic economic and social development needs. Such assistance should include country-specific analyses which compare the economic and environmental costs of actions to promote energy efficiency and nonconventional renewable energy with the economic and environmental costs of investments to provide additional conventional energy supplies;

(C) assistance to develop energy-sector plans that employ end-use analysis and other techniques to identify the most cost-effective actions to minimize increased reliance on fossil fuels, ensuring to the maximum extent feasible that nongovernmental organizations and academic institutions are involved in this planning;

(D) insuring that AID energy assistance—including support for private-sector initiatives—is consistent with the analyses and plans described in subparagraphs (B) and (C) above, and that environmental impacts (including that on global warming) and alternatives have been fully analyzed;

(E) assistance to improve efficiency in the production, transmission, distribution, and use of energy. Such assistance should focus on the development of institutions to (i) promote energy efficiency in all sectors of energy production and use, (ii) provide training and technical assistance to help energy producers and users identify cost-effective actions to improve energy efficiency, (iii) finance specific investments in energy efficiency in all sectors of energy production and use, and (iv) improve local capabilities in the research, development, and sale of energy efficient technologies;

(F) assistance in exploiting nonconventional renewable energy resources, including wind, solar, small-hydro, geothermal, and advanced biomass systems. This assistance should also promote efficient use of traditional biomass fuels through improved fuelwood management and improved methods of charcoal production;

(G) expanding efforts to meet the energy needs of the rural poor through the methods described in subparagraphs (E) and (F). Specifically these efforts should promote improved efficiency in the use of biomass fuels for household energy, improved systems of fuelwood management, and the development of the nonconventional renewable energy systems described in subparagraph (F);

(H) encouraging host countries to sponsor meetings with officials from the United States utility sector who are leaders in energy efficiency and other United States experts to discuss the application of least-cost planning techniques;

(I) developing a cadre of United States experts from industry, academia, nonprofit organizations, and government agencies capable of providing technical assistance to developing countries concerning energy policy and planning, energy efficiency and renewable energy resources;

(J) in cooperation with the Department of Energy, the Environmental Protection Agency, the World Bank, and the Development Assistance Committee of the OECD, supporting research concerning the ways developing nations can meet their energy needs while minimizing global warming and how to meet those needs; and

(K) strengthening the Agency for International Development's partnership with the Department of Energy in order to ensure that the Agency's energy efforts take full advantage of United States expertise and technology.

(c) Reports and Authorities.—(1) The Agency for International Development, in consultation with the Environmental Protection Agency (EPA), the Department of State, and other appropriate agencies, shall submit to Congress no later than April 15, 1990, a report which (1) examines the potential contributions of developing countries to future global emissions of greenhouse gases under different economic growth scenarios, (2) estimates the relative contributions of those countries to global greenhouse gas emissions, and

(3) identifies specific key countries which stand to contribute significantly to global greenhouse gas emissions, and in which actions to promote energy efficiency, reliance on renewable energy resources, and conservation of forest resources could significantly reduce emissions of greenhouse gases. This report should utilize existing data, including the models and methodologies already developed by the EPA for their report to Congress on policy options for stabilizing global climate.

(2) Of the funds appropriated to carry out the provisions of sections 103 and 106 of the Foreign Assistance Act of 1961, as amended, the Agency for International Development may use such amounts as may be necessary to reimburse United States Government agencies, agencies of State governments, and institutions of higher learning for the full costs of employees detailed or assigned to the Agency for International Development for the purpose of carrying out activities relating to forestry and energy programs aimed at reducing emissions of greenhouse gases related to global warming. Personnel who are detailed or assigned for the purposes of this section shall not be included within any personnel ceiling applicable to any United States Government agency during the period of detail or assignment.

(d) EXPORT-IMPORT BANK.—(1) Of the financing provided by the Export-Import Bank that is utilized for the support of exports for the energy sector, the Bank shall seek to provide not less than 5 per centum of such financing for renewable energy projects.

(2) The Export-Import Bank shall take all appropriate steps to finance information exchanges and training whose purpose it is to help link United States producers in the renewable energy sector with assistance programs and potential foreign customers.

(3) Beginning on April 15, 1990, the Chairman of the Export-Import Bank shall submit an annual report to the Committees on Appropriations on the Bank's implementation of this subsection.

MODERNIZATION OF MILITARY CAPABILITIES OF CERTAIN COUNTRIES

SEC. 573. (a) AUTHORITY TO TRANSFER EXCESS DEFENSE ARTICLES.—

(1) NATO SOUTHERN FLANK COUNTRIES.—The President may transfer—

(A) to any NATO southern flank country which is eligible for United States security assistance and which is integrated into NATO's military structure; and

(B) to any major non-NATO ally on the southern and southeastern flank of NATO which is eligible for United States security assistance, such excess defense articles as may be necessary to help modernize the defense capabilities of such country.

(2) MAJOR ILLICIT DRUG PRODUCING COUNTRIES.—Subject to subsection (f), the President may transfer to any country—

(A) which is a major illicit drug producing country,

(B) which has a democratic government, and

(C) whose armed forces do not engage in a consistent pattern of gross violations of internationally recognized human rights, such excess defense articles as may be necessary to carry out subsection (f)(1).

(3) TERMS OF TRANSFERS.—Excess defense articles may be transferred under this section without cost to the recipient country.

(b) LIMITATIONS ON TRANSFERS.—The President may transfer excess defense articles under this section only if—

(1) they are drawn from existing stocks of the Department of Defense;

(2) funds available to the Department of Defense for the procurement of defense equipment are not expended in connection with the transfer; and

(3) the President determines that the transfer of the excess defense articles will not have an adverse impact on the military readiness of the United States.

(c) NOTIFICATION TO CONGRESS.—

(1) ADVANCE NOTICE.—The President may not transfer excess defense articles under this section until thirty days after the President has provided notice of the proposed transfer to the committees specified in paragraph (2). This notification shall include—

(A) a certification of the need for the transfer;

(B) an assessment of the impact of the transfer on the military readiness of the United States; and

(C) the value of the excess defense articles to be transferred.

(2) COMMITTEES TO BE NOTIFIED.—Notice shall be provided pursuant to paragraph (1) to the Committee on Foreign Affairs, and the Committee on Appropriations of the House of Representatives and the Committee on Armed Services, the Committee on Foreign Relations, and the Committee on Appropriations of the Senate.

(e) MAINTENANCE OF MILITARY BALANCE IN EASTERN MEDITERRANEAN.—

(1) UNITED STATES POLICY.—The Congress intends that excess defense articles be made available under this section consistent with the United States policy, established by section 841 of the International Cooperation Act of 1989, of maintaining the military balance in the Eastern Mediterranean.

(2) MAINTENANCE OF BALANCE.—Accordingly, the President shall ensure that, over the three-year period beginning on October 1, 1989, the ratio of—

(A) the value of excess defense articles made available for Turkey under this section, to

(B) the value of excess defense articles made available for Greece under this section, closely approximates the ratio of—

(i) the amount of foreign military financing provided for Turkey, to

(ii) the amount of foreign military financing provided for Greece.

(3) EXCEPTION TO REQUIREMENT.—This subsection shall not apply if either Greece or Turkey ceases to be eligible to receive excess defense articles under subsection (a).

(f) MAJOR ILLICIT DRUG PRODUCING COUNTRIES IN LATIN AMERICA AND THE CARIBBEAN.—

(1) PURPOSE.—Excess defense articles shall be transferred under subsection (a)(2) for the purpose of encouraging the military forces of an eligible country in Latin America and the Caribbean to participate with local law enforcement agencies in a comprehensive national antinarcotics program, conceived and developed by the government of that country, by conducting activities within that country and on the high seas to prevent the production, processing, trafficking, transportation, and consumption of illicit narcotic or psychotrophic drugs or other controlled substances.

(2) USES OF EXCESS DEFENSE ARTICLES.—Excess defense articles may be furnished to a country under subsection (a)(2) only if that country ensures that those excess defense articles will be used only in support of antinarcotics activities.

(3) ROLE OF THE SECRETARY OF STATE.—The Secretary of State shall determine the eligibility of countries to receive excess defense articles under subsection (a)(2) and insure that any transfer is coordinated with other antinarcotics enforcement programs assisted by the United States Government.

(4) LIMITATION.—The aggregate value of excess defense articles transferred to a country under subsection (a)(2) in any fiscal year may not exceed $10,000,000.

(g) DEFINITIONS.—As used in this section—

(1) the term "excess defense article" has the meaning given that term by section 644(g);

(2) the term "made available" means that a good faith offer is made by the United States to furnish the excess defense articles to a country;

(3) the term "major non-NATO ally" includes Australia, Egypt, Israel, Japan, and New Zealand;

(4) the term "NATO" means the North Atlantic Treaty Organization; and

(5) the term "NATO southern flank countries" means Greece, Italy, Portugal, Spain, and Turkey.

INTERNATIONAL COFFEE AGREEMENT

SEC. 598. It is the Sense of the Congress that the International Coffee Agreement is an important measure in promoting economic and political stability in many developing countries, including Colombia, that the collapse of the Agreement would seriously undermine Colombia's efforts at fighting illegal drugs, and that the Administration should undertake every possible effort to successfully conclude a renewal of the Agreement.

LATVIA, ESTONIA, AND LITHUANIA

SEC. 599. (a) The Congress finds that—

(1) the Baltic states of Latvia, Estonia, and Lithuania gained their independence from the Russian Socialist Federative Soviet Republic in 1918, a fact recognized by the government of the Russian Socialist Federative Soviet Republic in 1920;

(2) the governments of the Latvian Democratic Republic and the Russian Socialist Federative Soviet Republic (RSFSR) signed a Treaty of Peace in Riga, Latvia on August 11, 1920, in which the RSFSR "establishes the right of self-determination for all nations, even to the point of total separation from the States with which they have been incorporated" and declares that "Russia unreservedly recognizes the independence, self-subsistency and sovereignty of the Latvian State and voluntarily and forever renounces all sovereign rights over the Latvian people and territory which formerly belonged to Russia";

(3) similar treaties were signed by both the Republic of Estonia and the Republic of Lithuania with the RSFSR on February 2, 1920 and July 12, 1920, respectively";

(4) the independent republics of Latvia, Estonia, and Lithuania swiftly recovered from the ravages of World War I and became active in the World community, gaining membership in the League of Nations on September 22, 1921 and full recognition by the United States on July 28, 1922;

(5) the sovereign rights of the independent states of Latvia, Estonia, and Lithuania were violated by the Union of Soviet Socialist Republics in a Secret Protocol to the Nazi-Soviet Treaty of Nonaggression of August 23, 1939, which divided

Eastern Europe into Nazi and Soviet "spheres of influence";

(6) the Union of Soviet Socialist Republics coerced the governments of Latvia, Estonia, and Lithuania to sign Pacts of Mutual Assistance in October 1939, which stipulated that the "contracting parties undertake not to enter into any alliances or to participate in any coalitions directed against one of the contracting parties" and that "the carrying into effect of the present pact must in no way affect the sovereign rights of the contracting parties, in particular their political structure, their economic and social system, and their military measures";

(7) the Union of Soviet Socialist Republics violated not only those bilateral agreements with the independent Baltic states but also international conventions on the changing of international borders by force when the Soviet Union issued ultimatums to the three independent nations on June 15–16, 1940, demanding the formation of governments to their liking, followed by armed invasions of Lithuania, Latvia, and Estonia on June 16–17, 1940;

(8) the occupation of the Baltic states was confirmed on July 14–15, 1940, with the irregular and illegal "election" of new parliaments, which then petitioned for admission into the Soviet Union, and these petitions were accepted by the Soviet Union, as follows: Lithuania's on August 3, 1940, Latvia's on August 4, 1940, and Estonia's on August 5, 1940;

(9) the Government of the United States continues its policy of standing by the 1922 recognition of the de jure independent governments in the Baltic states, and of refusing to recognize the forced incorporation of the Baltic states into the Soviet Union;

(10) the peoples of Latvia, Estonia, and Lithuania have never accepted the occupation of their native lands, and have demonstrated their resolve on numerous occasions since 1940, most notably in the last three years. The most striking demonstration of the desires of the Baltic people took place on August 23, 1989, the fiftieth anniversary of the Nazi-Soviet Treaty of Nonaggression, when nearly two million citizens of Latvia, Estonia, and Lithuania joined hands in a four-hundred-mile human chain stretching across the Baltic states from the Estonian capital of Tallinn, through the Latvian capital, Riga, to the Lithuanian capital of Vilninus;

(11) the people of the Baltic states, through their elected representatives in the Popular Front of Latvia, the Popular Front of Estonia, and the Lithuanian Movement in Support of Perestroika "Sajudis", have declared their desire for the restoration of independence in the Baltic states; and

(12) even the Communist officials and regimes in each of the Baltic states have begun to respond to the drive for more autonomy.

(b) The Congress urges the President—

(1) to raise the issue of the political rights of the Baltic peoples in all diplomatic contacts with the Soviet Union including during the meeting between President Bush and President Gorbachev in December, 1989 and during the Presidential summit scheduled in 1990 between the United States and the Soviet Union; and

(2) to call upon the Soviet Union—

(A) to honor the international agreements it has voluntarily entered into, such as the Final Act of the Helsinki Conference on Security and Cooperation in Europe and the United Nations Declaration of Human Rights, as well as the bilateral agreements it has voluntarily entered into with the independent governments of Latvia, Estonia, and Lithuania,

(B) to allow the people of Latvia, Estonia, and Lithuania their right of self-determination, as guaranteed by the RSFSR in 1920 as well as by the current constitution of the Soviet Union,

(C) to recognize the human rights of all peoples both within the Soviet Union and under Soviet influence, and

(D) to replace the policy of aggressive industrialization in the Baltic states, which has poisoned the land, air, and water of Latvia, Estonia, and Lithuania, with one of environmental responsibility.

HUMAN RIGHTS IN CUBA

SEC. 599B. (1) FINDINGS.—The Congress finds that—

(A) the United Nations in 1989 issued its first report on humans rights in Cuba this year, the result of a year-long investigation that concluded on the 30th year of Fidel Castro's rise to power;

(B) the report extensively documented across-the-board human rights abuses that include cases of torture, missing people, religious persecution, violations of civil and political rights and violations of economic and social rights;

(C) the United Nations received 137 complaints of "torture, cruel, inhuman or degrading treatment or punishment";

(D) among the abuses reported to the United Nations were sensory deprivation, immersion in a pit latrine, mock executions, overcrowding in special cells, deafening loudspeakers, keeping prisoners naked in front of relatives, and forcing a prisoner about to be executed to carry his own coffin or dig his own grave;

(E) the United Nations commissioners also charged the Cuban regime with carrying out reprisals against Cuban citizens who offered testimony to the United Nations group, a clear violation of the Castro's government's promise not to harass those who complained about human rights;

(F) at least 22 Cuban human rights activists who were arrested are currently serving prison sentences or being held without trial;

(G) the Human Rights Commission approved a resolution on March 9, 1989, calling on the Cuban government to cooperate with the Secretary General of the United Nations in settling unresolved issues raised by the human rights study group;

(H) since March 9, 1989, the United Nations has failed to take any substantive action to follow up on the March 9 resolution.

The United Nations also has failed to intervene on behalf of those who are now imprisoned because of their attempts to testify before the United Nations human rights investigative group last fall.

(2) STATEMENT OF POLICY.—In the interest of promoting respect for human rights in Cuba, the Congress—

(A) calls on the Secretary General of the United Nations to act upon the resolution approved by the Commission on Human Rights March 9, 1989, calling on the Secretary General to take appropriate follow up action on the Commission's report;

(B) calls on the Secretary General to specifically urge the Cuban government to release the 22 persons still being held in detention because of their human rights activities;

(C) calls on the United States Ambassador to the United Nations to make known in the strongest terms the dissatisfaction of the United States with the failure by the United Nations to continue to act on its own resolution; and

(D) calls on the Secretary of the United Nations to expand the United Nation's investigation of Cuba to include an examination of labor rights in recognition of current Cuban law which prohibits the formation of independent unions and which has led to the imprisonment of those Cuban workers who have tried to organize themselves.

SUPPORT FOR EAST EUROPEAN DEMOCRACY (SEED) ACT OF 1989

An Act to promote political democracy and economic pluralism in Poland and Hungary by assisting those nations during a critical period of transition and abetting the development in those nations of private business sectors, labor market reforms, and democratic institutions; to establish, through these steps, the framework for a composite program of support for East European Democracy (SEED).

Date: November 28, 1989.

Bill No.: H.R. 3402

Public Law No.: 101-179

Cite No.: 103 STAT. 1298

Sections reprinted: All

Public Law 101-179
101st Congress

An Act

To promote political democracy and economic pluralism in Poland and Hungary by assisting those nations during a critical period of transition and abetting the development in those nations of private business sectors, labor market reforms, and democratic institutions; to establish, through these steps, the framework for a composite program of support for East European Democracy (SEED).

Be it enacted by the Senate and House of Representatives of the United States of America in Congress assembled,

SECTION 1. SHORT TITLE AND TABLE OF CONTENTS.

(a) SHORT TITLE.—This Act may be cited as the "Support for East European Democracy (SEED) Act of 1989".

(b) TABLE OF CONTENTS.—The table of contents for this Act is as follows:

TITLE VI—ADDITIONAL SEED PROGRAM ACTIONS

TITLE VII—REPORTS TO CONGRESS

TITLE VIII—MISCELLANEOUS PROVISIONS

SEC. 2. SUPPORT FOR EAST EUROPEAN DEMOCRACY (SEED) PROGRAM.

(a) SEED PROGRAM.—The United States shall implement, beginning in fiscal year 1990, a concerted Program of Support for East European Democracy (which may also be referred to as the "SEED Program"). The SEED Program shall be comprised of diverse undertakings designed to provide cost-effective assistance to those countries of Eastern Europe that have taken substantive steps toward institutionalizing political democracy and economic pluralism.

(b) OBJECTIVES OF SEED ASSISTANCE.—The President should ensure that the assistance provided to East European countries pursuant to this Act is designed—

(1) to contribute to the development of democratic institutions and political pluralism characterized by—

(A) the establishment of fully democratic and representative political systems based on free and fair elections,

(B) effective recognition of fundamental liberties and individual freedoms, including freedom of speech, religion, and association,

(C) termination of all laws and regulations which impede the operation of a free press and the formation of political parties,

(D) creation of an independent judiciary, and

(E) establishment of non-partisan military, security, and police forces;

(2) to promote the development of a free market economic system characterized by—

(A) privatization of economic entities,

(B) establishment of full rights to acquire and hold private property, including land and the benefits of contractual relations,

(C) simplification of regulatory controls regarding the establishment and operation of businesses,

(D) dismantlement of all wage and price controls,

(E) removal of trade restrictions, including on both imports and exports,

(F) liberalization of investment and capital, including the repatriation of profits by foreign investors;

(G) tax policies which provide incentives for economic activity and investment,

(H) establishment of rights to own and operate private banks and other financial service firms, as well as unrestricted access to private sources of credit, and

(I) access to a market for stocks, bonds, and other instruments through which individuals may invest in the private sector; and

(3) not to contribute any substantial benefit—

(A) to Communist or other political parties or organizations which are not committed to respect for the democratic process, or

(B) to the defense or security forces of any member country of the Warsaw Pact.

(c) SEED ACTIONS.—Assistance and other activities under the SEED Program (which may be referred to as "SEED Actions") shall include activities such as the following:

(1) LEADERSHIP IN THE WORLD BANK AND INTERNATIONAL MONETARY FUND.—United States leadership in supporting—

(A) loans by the International Bank for Reconstruction and Development and its affiliated institutions in the World Bank group that are designed to modernize industry, agriculture, and infrastructure, and

(B) International Monetary Fund programs designed to stimulate sound economic growth.

(2) CURRENCY STABILIZATION LOANS.—United States leadership in supporting multilateral agreement to provide government-to-government loans for currency stabilization where such loans can reduce inflation and thereby foster conditions necessary for the effective implementation of economic reforms.

(3) DEBT REDUCTION AND RESCHEDULING.—Participation in multilateral activities aimed at reducing and rescheduling a country's international debt, when reduction and deferral of debt payments can assist the process of political and economic transition.

(4) AGRICULTURAL ASSISTANCE.—Assistance through the grant and concessional sale of food and other agricultural commodities and products when such assistance can ease critical shortages but not inhibit agricultural production and marketing in the recipient country.

(5) ENTERPRISE FUNDS.—Grants to support private, nonprofit "Enterprise Funds", designated by the President pursuant to law and governed by a Board of Directors, which undertake loans, grants, equity investments, feasibility studies, technical assistance, training, and other forms of assistance to private enterprise activities in the Eastern European country for which the Enterprise Fund so is designated.

(6) LABOR MARKET-ORIENTED TECHNICAL ASSISTANCE.—Technical assistance programs directed at promoting labor market reforms and facilitating economic adjustment.

(7) TECHNICAL TRAINING.—Programs to provide technical skills to assist in the development of a market economy.

(8) PEACE CORPS.—Establishment of Peace Corps programs.

(9) SUPPORT FOR INDIGENOUS CREDIT UNIONS.—Support for the establishment of indigenous credit unions.

(10) GENERALIZED SYSTEM OF PREFERENCES.—Eligibility for trade benefits under the Generalized System of Preferences.

(11) Most favored nation trade status.—The granting of temporary or permanent nondiscriminatory treatment (commonly referred to as "most favored nation status") to the products of an East European country through the application of the criteria and procedures established by section 402 of the Trade Act of 1974 (19 U.S.C. 2432; commonly referred to as the "Jackson-Vanik amendment").

(12) Overseas private investment corporation.—Programs of the Overseas Private Investment Corporation.

(13) Export-import bank programs.—Programs of the Export-Import Bank of the United States.

(14) Trade and development program activities.—Trade and Development Program activities under the Foreign Assistance Act of 1961.

(15) Investment treaties.—Negotiation of bilateral investment treaties.

(16) Special tax treatment of below-market loans.—Exempting bonds from Internal Revenue Code rules relating to below-market loans.

(17) Exchange activities.—Expanded exchange activities under the Fulbright, International Visitors, and other programs conducted by the United States Information Agency.

(18) Cultural centers.—Contributions toward the establishment of reciprocal cultural centers that can facilitate educational and cultural exchange and expanded understanding of Western social democracy.

(19) Sister institutions.—Establishment of sister institution programs between American and East European schools and universities, towns and cities, and other organizations in such fields as medicine and health care, business management, environmental protection, and agriculture.

(20) Scholarships.—Scholarships to enable students to study in the United States.

(21) Science and technology exchanges.—Grants for the implementation of bilateral agreements providing for cooperation in science and technology exchange.

(22) Assistance for democratic institutions.—Assistance designed to support the development of legal, legislative, electoral, journalistic, and other institutions of free, pluralist societies.

(23) Environmental assistance.—Environmental assistance directed at overcoming crucial deficiencies in air and water quality and other determinants of a healthful society.

(24) Medical assistance.—Medical assistance specifically targeted to overcome severe deficiencies in pharmaceuticals and other basic health supplies.

(25) Encouragement for private investment and voluntary assistance.—Encouraging private investment and voluntary private assistance, using a variety of means including a SEED Information Center System and the provision by the Department of Defense of transportation for private nonfinancial contributions.

TITLE I—STRUCTURAL ADJUSTMENT

SEC. 101. MULTILATERAL SUPPORT FOR STRUCTURAL ADJUSTMENT IN POLAND AND HUNGARY.

(a) MULTILATERAL ASSISTANCE FOR POLAND AND HUNGARY.—

(1) IN GENERAL.—To the extent that Poland and Hungary continue to evolve toward pluralism and democracy and to develop and implement comprehensive economic reform programs, the United States Government shall take the leadership in mobilizing international financial institutions, in particular the International Monetary Fund and the International Bank for Reconstruction and Development and its affiliated institutions in the World Bank group, to provide timely and appropriate resources to help Poland and Hungary.

(2) WORLD BANK STRUCTURAL ADJUSTMENT LOAN FOR POLAND.—In furtherance of paragraph (1), the Secretary of the Treasury shall direct the United States Executive Director of the International Bank for Reconstruction and Development to urge expeditious approval and disbursement by the Bank of a structural adjustment loan to Poland in an appropriate amount in time to facilitate the implementation of major economic reforms scheduled for early 1990, including the termination of energy, export, and agricultural subsidies and wage indexation.

(b) STABILIZATION ASSISTANCE, DEBT RELIEF, AND AGRICULTURAL ASSISTANCE FOR POLAND.—To the extent that Poland continues to evolve toward pluralism and democracy and to develop and implement comprehensive economic reform programs, the United States Government shall do the following:

(1) STABILIZATION ASSISTANCE.—The United States Government, in conjunction with other member governments of the Organization of Economic Cooperation and Development (OECD) and international financial institutions (including the International Monetary Fund), shall support the implementation of a plan of the Government of Poland to attack hyperinflation and other structural economic problems, address pressing social problems, carry out comprehensive economic reform, and relieve immediate and urgent balance of payments requirements in Poland, through the use of mechanisms such as—

(A) the Exchange Stabilization Fund pursuant to section 5302 of title 31, United States Code, and in accordance with established Department of the Treasury policies and procedures; and

(B) the authority provided in section 102(c) of this Act.

(2) DEBT RELIEF.—The United States Government—

(A) shall urge all members of the "Paris Club" of creditor governments and other creditor governments to adopt, and participate in, a generous and early rescheduling program for debts owed by the Government of Poland; and

(B) in coordination with other creditor governments, shall seek to expedite consultations between the Government of Poland and its major private creditors in order to facilitate a rescheduling and reduction of payments due on debt owed to such creditors in a manner consistent with the international debt policy announced by the Secretary of the Treasury on March 10, 1989.

(3) AGRICULTURAL ASSISTANCE.—The United States Government shall provide agricultural assistance for Poland in accordance with section 103.

SEC. 102. STABILIZATION ASSISTANCE FOR POLAND.

(a) IMMEDIATE EMERGENCY ASSISTANCE.—To the extent that the ongoing International Monetary Fund review of the Polish economy projects a probable balance of payments shortage for the fourth quarter of 1989, the United States Government, in carrying out paragraph (1) of section 101(b)—

(1) should work closely with the European Community and international financial institutions to determine the extent of emergency assistance required by Poland for the fourth quarter of 1989, and

(2) should consider extending a bridge loan to relieve immediate and urgent balance of payments requirements using the Exchange Stabilization Fund in accordance with paragraph (1)(A) of section 101(b).

(b) IMMEDIATE, MULTILATERAL RESPONSE TO POLAND'S ECONOMIC STABILIZATION NEEDS.—In furtherance of section 101(b)(1), the President, acting in coordination with the European Community, should seek to ensure that the industrialized democracies undertake an immediate, multilateral effort to respond to Poland's request for $1,000,000,000 to support its economic stabilization program.

(c) ADDITIONAL AUTHORITY TO PROVIDE STABILIZATION ASSISTANCE.—

(1) AUTHORITY.—In order to carry out paragraph (1) of section 101(b), the President is authorized to furnish assistance for Poland, notwithstanding any other provision of law, to assist in the urgent stabilization of the Polish economy and ultimately to promote longer-term economic growth and stability, based on movement toward free market principles. Such assistance may be provided for balance of payments support (including commodity import programs), support for private sector development, or for other activities to further efforts to develop a free market-oriented economy in Poland.

(2) AUTHORIZATION OF APPROPRIATIONS.—For purposes of providing the assistance authorized by this subsection, there are authorized to be appropriated $200,000,000 for fiscal year 1990 to carry out chapter 4 of part II of the Foreign Assistance Act of 1961 (22 U.S.C. 2346 and following; relating to the economic support fund), in addition to amounts otherwise available for such purposes.

SEC. 103. AGRICULTURAL ASSISTANCE.

(a) AGRICULTURAL ASSISTANCE STRATEGY.—

(1) UNITED STATES ASSISTANCE.—A principal component of the SEED Program shall be the provision by the United States of food and other agricultural commodities and products to alleviate crucial shortages that may be created in an East European country by the transition from state-directed controls to a free market economy.

(2) ASSISTANCE FROM OTHER COUNTRIES.—In order to ensure the necessary quantity and diversity of agricultural assistance for that purpose, the United States shall take all appropriate steps to encourage parallel efforts by the European Community and other agricultural surplus countries.

(3) Avoiding disincentives to private agricultural production and marketing.—In participating in such multilateral agricultural assistance, the United States shall seek to strike a balance wherein agricultural commodities and products are supplied in such quantities as will be effective in overcoming severe shortages and dampening inflation but without impeding the development of incentives for private agricultural production and marketing in the recipient country.

(b) Agricultural Assistance for Poland.—Pursuant to section 101(b)(3), the United States Government—

(1) shall make available to Poland, in coordination with the European Community, United States agricultural assistance—

(A) to alleviate immediate food shortages (such assistance to be specifically targeted toward elements of the Polish population most vulnerable to hunger and malnutrition, in particular the infirm, the elderly, and children), and

(B) to facilitate the transition from state-directed controls to a free market economy, while avoiding disincentives to domestic agricultural production and reform; and

(2) in order to ensure the necessary quantity and diversity of such agricultural assistance, shall take all appropriate steps to encourage parallel efforts by the European Community and other agricultural surplus countries.

(c) FY 1990 Minimum Level of Agricultural Assistance for Poland.—In carrying out subsection (b) of this section, the level of assistance for Poland for fiscal year 1990 under section 416(b) of the Agricultural Act of 1949 (7 U.S.C. 1431(b)), the Agricultural Trade Development and Assistance Act of 1954 (7 U.S.C. 1691 and following), and the Food for Progress Act of 1985 (7 U.S.C. 1736o) should not be less than $125,000,000. Such assistance—

(1) to the maximum extent practicable, shall be provided through nongovernmental organizations; and

(2) shall emphasize feed grains.

(d) Consistency With Budget Requirements.—Subsection (c) should not be construed to authorize or require any budgetary obligations or outlays that are inconsistent with House Concurrent Resolution 106 of the 101st Congress (setting forth the congressional budget for the United States Government for fiscal year 1990).

SEC. 104. DEBT-FOR-EQUITY SWAPS AND OTHER SPECIAL TECHNIQUES.

(a) Reduction of Debt Burden.—The President shall take all appropriate actions to explore and encourage innovative approaches to the reduction of the government-to-government and commercial debt burden of East European countries which have taken substantive steps toward political democracy and economic pluralism.

(b) Authority for Discounted Sales of Debt.—Notwithstanding any other provision of law, the President may undertake the discounted sale, to private purchasers, of United States Government debt obligations of an East European country which has taken substantive steps toward political democracy and economic pluralism, subject to subsection (c).

(c) Condition.—An obligation may be sold under subsection (b) only if the sale will facilitate so-called debt-for-equity or debt-for-development swaps wherein such newly privatized debt is exchanged by the new holder of the obligation for—

(1) local currencies, policy commitments, or other assets needed for development or other economic activities, or

(2) for an equity interest in an enterprise theretofore owned by the particular East European government.

TITLE II—PRIVATE SECTOR DEVELOPMENT

SEC. 201. ENTERPRISE FUNDS FOR POLAND AND HUNGARY.

(a) PURPOSES.—The purposes of this section are to promote—

(1) development of the Polish and Hungarian private sectors, including small businesses, the agricultural sector, and joint ventures with United States and host country participants, and

(2) policies and practices conducive to private sector development in Poland and Hungary,

through loans, grants, equity investments, feasibility studies, technical assistance, training, insurance, guarantees, and other measures.

(b) AUTHORIZATION OF APPROPRIATIONS.—To carry out the purposes specified in subsection (a), there are authorized to be appropriated to the President—

(1) $240,000,000 to support the Polish-American Enterprise Fund; and

(2) $60,000,000 to support the Hungarian-American Enterprise Fund.

Such amounts are authorized to be made available until expended.

(c) NONAPPLICABILITY OF OTHER LAWS.—The funds appropriated under subsection (b) may be made available to the Polish-American Enterprise Fund and the Hungarian-American Enterprise Fund and used for the purposes of this section notwithstanding any other provision of law.

(d) DESIGNATION OF ENTERPRISE FUNDS.—

(1) DESIGNATION.—The President is authorized to designate two private, nonprofit organizations as eligible to receive funds and support pursuant to this section upon determining that such organizations have been established for the purposes specified in subsection (a). For purposes of this Act, the organizations so designated shall be referred to as the Polish-American Enterprise Fund and the Hungarian-American Enterprise Fund (hereinafter in this section referred to as the "Enterprise Funds").

(2) CONSULTATION WITH CONGRESS.—The President shall consult with the leadership of each House of Congress before designating an organization pursuant to paragraph (1).

(3) BOARD OF DIRECTORS.—(A) Each Enterprise Fund shall be governed by a Board of Directors comprised of private citizens of the United States, and citizens of the respective host country, who have demonstrated experience and expertise in those areas of private sector development in which the Enterprise Fund is involved.

(B) A majority of the members of the Board of Directors of each Enterprise Fund shall be United States citizens.

(C) A host country citizen who is not committed to respect for democracy and a free market economy may not serve as a member of the Board of Directors of an Enterprise Fund.

(4) ELIGIBILITY OF ENTERPRISE FUNDS FOR GRANTS.—Grants may be made to an Enterprise Fund under this section only if the Enterprise Fund agrees to comply with the requirements specified in this section.

(5) Private character of enterprise funds.—Nothing in this section shall be construed to make an Enterprise Fund an agency or establishment of the United States Government, or to make the officers, employees, or members of the Board of Directors of an Enterprise Fund officers or employees of the United States for purposes of title 5, United States Code.

(e) Grants to Enterprise Funds.—Funds appropriated to the President pursuant to subsection (b) shall be granted to the Enterprise Funds by the Agency for International Development to enable the Enterprise Funds to carry out the purposes specified in subsection (a) and for the administrative expenses of each Enterprise Fund.

(f) Eligible Programs and Projects.—

(1) In general.—The Enterprise Funds may provide assistance pursuant to this section only for programs and projects which are consistent with the purposes set forth in subsection (a).

(2) Employee stock ownership plans.—Funds available to the Enterprise Funds may be used to encourage the establishment of Employee Stock Ownership Plans (ESOPs) in Poland and Hungary.

(3) Indigenous credit unions.—Funds available to the Enterprise Funds may be used for technical and other assistance to support the development of indigenous credit unions in Poland and Hungary. As used in this paragraph, the term "credit union" means a member-owned, nonprofit, cooperative depository institution—

(A) which is formed to permit individuals in the field of membership specified in such institution's charter to pool their savings, lend the savings to one another, and own the organization where they save, borrow, and obtain related financial services; and

(B) whose members are united by a common bond and democratically operate the institution.

(4) Telecommunications modernization in Poland.—The Polish-American Enterprise Fund may use up to $25,000,000 for grants for projects providing for the early introduction in Poland of modern telephone systems and telecommunications technology, which are crucial in establishing the conditions for successful transition to political democracy and economic pluralism.

(5) Economic foundation of NSZZ Solidarność.—Funds available to the Polish-American Enterprise Fund may be used to support the Economic Foundation of NSZZ Solidarność.

(g) Matters To Be Considered by Enterprise Funds.—In carrying out this section, each Enterprise Fund shall take into account such considerations as internationally recognized worker rights and other internationally recognized human rights, environmental factors, United States economic and employment effects, and the likelihood of commercial viability of the activity receiving assistance from the Enterprise Fund.

(h) Retention of Interest.—An Enterprise Fund may hold funds granted to it pursuant to this section in interest-bearing accounts, prior to the disbursement of such funds for purposes specified in subsection (a), and may retain for such program purposes any interest earned on such deposits without returning such interest to the Treasury of the United States and without further appropriation by the Congress.

(i) USE OF UNITED STATES PRIVATE VENTURE CAPITAL.—In order to maximize the effectiveness of the activities of the Enterprise Funds, each Enterprise Fund may conduct public offerings or private placements for the purpose of soliciting and accepting United States venture capital which may be used, separately or together with funds made available pursuant to this section, for any lawful investment purpose that the Board of Directors of the Enterprise Fund may determine in carrying out this section. Financial returns on Enterprise Fund investments that include a component of private venture capital may be distributed, at such times and in such amounts as the Board of Directors of the Enterprise Fund may determine, to the investors of such capital.

(j) FINANCIAL INSTRUMENTS FOR INDIVIDUAL INVESTMENT IN POLAND.—In order to maximize the effectiveness of the activities of the Polish-American Enterprise Fund, that Enterprise Fund should undertake all possible efforts to establish financial instruments that will enable individuals to invest in the private sectors of Poland and that will thereby have the effect of multiplying the impact of United States grants to that Enterprise Fund.

(k) NONAPPLICABILITY OF OTHER LAWS.—Executive branch agencies may conduct programs and activities and provide services in support of the activities of the Enterprise Funds notwithstanding any other provision of law.

(l) LIMITATION ON PAYMENTS TO ENTERPRISE FUND PERSONNEL.—No part of the funds of either Enterprise Fund shall inure to the benefit of any board member, officer, or employee of such Enterprise Fund, except as salary or reasonable compensation for services.

(m) INDEPENDENT PRIVATE AUDITS.—The accounts of each Enterprise Fund shall be audited annually in accordance with generally accepted auditing standards by independent certified public accountants or independent licensed public accountants certified or licensed by a regulatory authority of a State or other political subdivision of the United States. The report of each such independent audit shall be included in the annual report required by this section.

(n) GAO AUDITS.—The financial transactions undertaken pursuant to this section by each Enterprise Fund may be audited by the General Accounting Office in accordance with such principles and procedures and under such rules and regulations as may be prescribed by the Comptroller General of the United States, so long as the Enterprise Fund is in receipt of United States Government grants.

(o) RECORDKEEPING REQUIREMENTS.—The Enterprise Funds shall ensure—

(1) that each recipient of assistance provided through the Enterprise Funds under this section keeps—

(A) separate accounts with respect to such assistance;

(B) such records as may be reasonably necessary to disclose fully the amount and the disposition by such recipient of the proceeds of such assistance, the total cost of the project or undertaking in connection with which such assistance is given or used, and the amount and nature of that portion of the cost of the project or undertaking supplied by other sources; and

(C) such other records as will facilitate an effective audit; and

(2) that the Enterprise Funds, or any of their duly authorized representatives, have access for the purpose of audit and examination to any books, documents, papers, and records of the recipient that are pertinent to assistance provided through the Enterprise Funds under this section.

(p) ANNUAL REPORTS.—Each Enterprise Fund shall publish an annual report, which shall include a comprehensive and detailed description of the Enterprise Fund's operations, activities, financial condition, and accomplishments under this section for the preceding fiscal year. This report shall be published not later than January 31 each year, beginning in 1991.

SEC. 202. LABOR MARKET TRANSITION IN POLAND AND HUNGARY.

(a) TECHNICAL ASSISTANCE.—The Secretary of Labor (hereinafter in this section referred to as the "Secretary"), in consultation with representatives of labor and business in the United States, shall—

(1) provide technical assistance to Poland and Hungary for the implementation of labor market reforms; and

(2) provide technical assistance to Poland and Hungary to facilitate adjustment during the period of economic transition and reform.

(b) TYPES OF TECHNICAL ASSISTANCE AUTHORIZED.—In carrying out subsection (a), the Secretary is authorized to provide technical assistance regarding policies and programs for training and retraining, job search and employment services, unemployment insurance, occupational safety and health protection, labor-management relations, labor statistics, analysis of productivity constraints, entrepreneurial support for small businesses, market-driven systems of wage and income determinations, job creation, employment security, the observance of internationally recognized worker rights (including freedom of association and the right to organize and bargain collectively), and other matters that the Secretary may deem appropriate regarding free labor markets and labor organizations.

(c) ADMINISTRATIVE AUTHORITIES.—In carrying out subsection (a), the Secretary is authorized to do the following:

(1) Solicit and accept in the name of the Department of Labor, and employ or dispose of in furtherance of the purposes of this section, any money or property, real, personal, or mixed, tangible or intangible, received by gift, devise, bequest, or otherwise. Gifts and donations of property which are no longer required for the discharge of the purposes of this section shall be reported to the Administrator of General Services for transfer, donation, or other disposal in accordance with the Federal Property and Administrative Services Act of 1949 (40 U.S.C. 471 and following).

(2) Solicit and accept voluntary and uncompensated services notwithstanding section 1342 of title 31, United States Code. A volunteer under this paragraph shall not be deemed to be an employee of the United States except for the purposes of—

(A) the tort claims provisions of title 28, United States Code, and

(B) subchapter I of chapter 81 of title 5, United States Code, relating to compensation for work injuries.

(3) Enter into arrangements or agreements with appropriate departments, agencies, and establishments of Poland and Hungary.

(4) Enter into arrangements or agreements with appropriate private and public sector United States parties, and international organizations.

(d) CONSULTATION WITH APPROPRIATE OFFICERS.—In carrying out the responsibilities established by this section, the Secretary shall seek information and advice from, and consult with, appropriate officers of the United States.

(e) CONSULTATION WITH LABOR AND BUSINESS REPRESENTATIVES.—For purposes of this section, consultation between the Secretary and United States labor and business representatives shall not be subject to the Federal Advisory Committee Act (5 U.S.C. App.).

(f) DELEGATION OF RESPONSIBILITIES.—The Secretary shall delegate the authority to carry out the programs authorized by this section to the head of the Bureau of International Labor Affairs of the Department of Labor.

(g) AUTHORIZATION OF APPROPRIATIONS.—There are authorized to be appropriated to the Department of Labor for the 3-year period beginning October 1, 1989, to carry out this section—

(1) $4,000,000 for technical assistance to Poland; and

(2) $1,000,000 for technical assistance to Hungary.

SEC. 203. TECHNICAL TRAINING FOR PRIVATE SECTOR DEVELOPMENT IN POLAND AND HUNGARY.

(a) TECHNICAL TRAINING PROGRAM.—The Agency for International Development shall develop and implement a program for extending basic agribusiness, commercial, entrepreneurial, financial, scientific, and technical skills to the people of Poland and Hungary to enable them to better meet their needs and develop a market economy. This program shall include management training and agricultural extension activities.

(b) PARTICIPATION BY ENTERPRISE FUNDS AND OTHER AGENCIES AND ORGANIZATIONS.—In carrying out subsection (a), the Agency for International Development may utilize the Polish-American Enterprise Fund and the Hungarian-American Enterprise Fund and other appropriate Government and private agencies, programs, and organizations such as—

(1) the Department of Agriculture;

(2) the Farmer-to-Farmer Program under section 406(a) (1) and (2) of the Agricultural Trade Development and Assistance Act of 1954 (7 U.S.C. 1736(a) (1) and (2));

(3) the International Executive Service Corps;

(4) the Foundation for the Development of Polish Agriculture;

(5) the World Council of Credit Unions; and

(6) other United States, Polish, and Hungarian private and voluntary organizations and private sector entities.

(c) NONAPPLICABILITY OF OTHER PROVISIONS OF LAW.—Assistance provided pursuant to subsection (a) under the authorities of part I of the Foreign Assistance Act of 1961 may be provided notwithstanding any other provision of law.

(d) AUTHORIZATION OF APPROPRIATIONS.—For purposes of implementing this section, there are authorized to be appropriated $10,000,000 for the 3-year period beginning October 1, 1989, to carry out chapter 1 of part I of the Foreign Assistance Act of 1961 (22 U.S.C. 2151 and following; relating to development assistance), in addition to amounts otherwise available for such purposes.

(e) LIMITATION WITH RESPECT TO FARMER-TO-FARMER PROGRAM.—Any activities carried out pursuant to this Act through the Farmer-to-Farmer Program under section 406(a) (1) and (2) of the Agricultural Trade Development and Assistance Act of 1954 shall be funded with funds authorized to be appropriated by this Act and local currencies made available under section 205, and shall not be funded with funds made available pursuant to section 1107 of the Food Security Act of 1985 (7 U.S.C. 1736 note) or a similar, subsequent provision of law.

SEC. 204. PEACE CORPS PROGRAMS IN POLAND AND HUNGARY.

There are authorized to be appropriated to carry out programs in Poland and Hungary under the Peace Corps Act, $6,000,000 for the 3-year period beginning October 1, 1989, in addition to amounts otherwise available for such purposes. Such programs shall include the use of Peace Corps volunteers—

(1) to provide English language training, and

(2) to extend the technical skills described in section 203(a) to the people of Poland and Hungary, using the Associate Volunteer Program to the extent practicable.

SEC. 205. USE OF POLISH CURRENCY GENERATED BY AGRICULTURAL ASSISTANCE.

(a) ADDITIONAL ASSISTANCE FOR POLAND.—A portion of the agricultural commodities described in subsection (c) may be made available and sold or bartered in Poland to generate local currencies to be used—

(1) to complement the assistance for Poland authorized by sections 103(b), 201, and 203 of this Act, and

(2) to support the activities of the joint commission established pursuant to section 2226 of the American Aid to Poland Act of 1988 (7 U.S.C. 1431 note),

notwithstanding section 416(b)(7) of the Agricultural Act of 1949 (7 U.S.C. 1431(b)(7)) or any other provision of law.

(b) EMPHASIS ON AGRICULTURAL DEVELOPMENT.—The uses of local currencies generated under this section should emphasize the development of agricultural infrastructure, agriculture-related training, and other aspects of agricultural development in Poland.

(c) COMMODITIES SUBJECT TO REQUIREMENTS.—Subsection (a) applies with respect to agricultural commodities made available for Poland for fiscal years 1990, 1991, and 1992 under section 416(b) of the Agricultural Act of 1949 (7 U.S.C. 1431(b)), the Agricultural Trade Development and Assistance Act of 1954 (7 U.S.C. 1691 and following), and the Food for Progress Act of 1985 (7 U.S.C. 1736o).

(d) OTHER USES NOT PRECLUDED.—The uses of agricultural commodities and local currencies specified in subsection (a) are in addition to other uses authorized by law.

SEC. 206. UNITED STATES POLICY OF PRIVATE FINANCIAL SUPPORT FOR POLISH AND HUNGARIAN CREDIT UNIONS.

(a) IN GENERAL.—In order to facilitate the development of indigenous credit unions in Poland and Hungary, it is the policy of the United States that—

(1) United States citizens, financial institutions (other than federally insured depository institutions), and other persons may make contributions and loans to, make capital deposits in, and provide other forms of financial and technical assistance to credit unions in Poland and Hungary; and

(2) federally insured depository institutions may provide technical assistance to credit unions in Poland and Hungary, to the extent that the provision of such assistance is prudent and not inconsistent with safe and sound banking practice.

(b) AMENDMENT TO FEDERAL CREDIT UNION ACT.—Section 107 of the Federal Credit Union Act (12 U.S.C. 1757) is amended by redesignating paragraph (16) as paragraph (17) and by inserting after paragraph (15) the following new paragraph:

"(16) subject to such regulations as the Board may prescribe, to provide technical assistance to credit unions in Poland and Hungary; and".

(c) DEFINITIONS.—For purposes of subsection (a)—

(1) the term "credit union" means a member-owned, nonprofit, cooperative depository institution—

(A) which is formed to permit individuals in the field of membership specified in such institution's charter to pool their savings, lend the savings to one another, and own the organization where they save, borrow, and obtain related financial services; and

(B) whose members are united by a common bond and democratically operate the institution; and

(2) the term "federally insured depository institution" means—

(A) any insured depository institution (as defined in section 3(c)(2) of the Federal Deposit Insurance Act); and

(B) any insured credit union (as defined in section 101(7) of the Federal Credit Union Act).

TITLE III—TRADE AND INVESTMENT

SEC. 301. ELIGIBILITY OF POLAND FOR GENERALIZED SYSTEM OF PREFERENCES.

Subsection (b) of section 502 of the Trade Act of 1974 (19 U.S.C. 2462(b)) is amended by striking out "Poland" in the table within such subsection.

SEC. 302. OVERSEAS PRIVATE INVESTMENT CORPORATION PROGRAMS FOR POLAND AND HUNGARY.

(a) ELIGIBILITY OF POLAND AND HUNGARY FOR OPIC PROGRAMS.—Section 239(f) of the Foreign Assistance Act of 1961 (22 U.S.C. 2199(f)) is amended by inserting ", Poland, Hungary," after "Yugoslavia".

(b) ENHANCEMENT OF NONGOVERNMENTAL SECTOR.—In accordance with its mandate to foster private initiative and competition and enhance the ability of private enterprise to make its full contribution to the development process, the Overseas Private Investment Corporation shall support projects in Poland and Hungary which will result in enhancement of the nongovernmental sector and reduction of state involvement in the economy.

(c) AVOIDANCE OF DUPLICATIVE AMENDMENTS.—If the Foreign Operations, Export Financing, and Related Programs Appropriations Act, 1990, contains the same amendment that is made by subsection (a) of this section, the amendment made by that Act shall not be effective.

SEC. 303. EXPORT-IMPORT BANK PROGRAMS FOR POLAND AND HUNGARY.

(a) AUTHORITY TO EXTEND CREDIT TO POLAND AND HUNGARY.—Notwithstanding section 2(b)(2) of the Export-Import Bank Act of 1945 (12 U.S.C. 635(b)(2)), the Export-Import Bank of the United States may guarantee, insure, finance, extend credit, and participate in the extension of credit in connection with the purchase or lease of any product by the Republic of Hungary or any agency or national thereof or by the Polish People's Republic or any agency or national thereof.

(b) PRIVATE FINANCIAL INTERMEDIARIES TO FACILITATE EXPORTS TO POLAND.—Consistent with the provisions of the Export-Import Bank Act of 1945 (12 U.S.C. 635 and following), the Export-Import Bank of the United States shall work with private financial intermediaries in Poland to facilitate the export of goods and services to Poland.

SEC. 304. TRADE CREDIT INSURANCE PROGRAM FOR POLAND.

(a) ESTABLISHMENT OF PROGRAM.—Chapter 2 of part I of the Foreign Assistance Act of 1961 is amended by inserting after section 224 (22 U.S.C 2184) the following new section:

"SEC. 225. TRADE CREDIT INSURANCE PROGRAM FOR POLAND.

"(a) GENERAL AUTHORITY.—

"(1) ASSURANCE TO EXPORT-IMPORT BANK OF REPAYMENT.—The President is authorized to provide guarantees to the Bank for liabilities described in paragraph (2) in order to satisfy the requirement of section 2(b)(1)(B) of the Export-Import Bank Act of 1945 (12 U.S.C. 635(b)(1)(B)) that the Bank have reasonable assurance of repayment.

"(2) LIABILITIES WHICH MAY BE GUARANTEED.—The liabilities that may be guaranteed under paragraph (1) are liabilities incurred by the Bank in connection with guarantees or insurance provided under the Export-Import Bank Act of 1945 for financing for transactions involving the export of goods and services for the use of the private sector in Poland.

"(b) GUARANTEES AVAILABLE ONLY FOR SHORT-TERM GUARANTEES AND INSURANCE.—Guarantees provided under subsection (a) shall be for short-term guarantees and insurance extended by the Bank which shall be repayable within a period not to exceed one year from the date of arrival at the port of importation of the goods and services covered by such guarantees or insurance.

"(c) AGREEMENT ON CRITERIA AND PROCEDURES.—Guarantees or insurance extended by the Bank and guaranteed pursuant to subsection (a) shall be provided by the Bank in accordance with criteria and procedures agreed to by the Administrator and the Bank.

"(d) RESERVE FUND.—The agreement referred to in subsection (c) shall also provide for the establishment of a reserve fund by the administering agency, with such funds made available to the reserve as the Administrator deems necessary to discharge liabilities under guarantees provided under subsection (a).

"(e) DISCHARGE OF LIABILITIES.—

"(1) FUNDS WHICH MAY BE USED.—Such amounts of the funds made available to carry out chapter 4 of part II of this Act (relating to the economic support fund) as the President determines are necessary may be made available to discharge liabilities under guarantees entered into under subsection (a).

"(2) CREDITING OF SUBSEQUENT PAYMENTS.—To the extent that any of the funds made available pursuant to paragraph (1) are paid out for a claim arising out of liabilities guaranteed under subsection (a), amounts received after the date of such payment, with respect to such claim, shall be credited to the reserve fund established pursuant to subsection (d), shall be merged with the funds in such reserve, and shall be available for the purpose of payments by the Administrator to the Bank for guarantees under subsection (a).

"(f) APPROPRIATIONS ACTION REQUIRED.—Commitments to guarantee under subsection (a) are authorized only to the extent and in the amounts provided in advance in appropriations Acts.

"(g) LIMITATION ON OUTSTANDING COMMITMENTS.—The aggregate amount of outstanding commitments under subsection (a) may not exceed $200,000,000 of contingent liability for loan principal during any fiscal year.

"(h) BIANNUAL REPORTS TO CONGRESS.—Every 6 months, the Administrator and the President of the Bank shall prepare and transmit to the Speaker of the House of Representatives and the Chairman of the Committee on Foreign Relations of the Senate a report on the amount and extension of guarantees and insurance provided by the Bank and guaranteed under this section during the preceding 6-month period.

"(i) ADMINISTRATIVE AND TECHNICAL ASSISTANCE.—The Bank shall provide, without reimbursement, such administrative and technical assistance to the administering agency as the Bank and the Administrator determine appropriate to assist the administering agency in carrying out this section.

"(j) FEES AND PREMIUMS.—The Bank is authorized to charge fees and premiums, in connection with guarantees or insurance guaranteed by the administering agency under subsection (a), that are commensurate (in the judgment of the Bank) with the Bank's administrative costs and the risks covered by the agency's guarantees. Any amounts received by the Bank in excess of the estimated costs incurred by the Bank in administering such guarantees or insurance—

"(1) shall be credited to the reserve fund established pursuant to subsection (d),

"(2) shall be merged with the funds in such reserve, and

"(3) shall be available for the purpose of payments by the administering agency to the Bank for guarantees under subsection (a).

"(k) RESTRICTIONS NOT APPLICABLE.—Prohibitions on the use of foreign assistance funds for assistance for Poland shall not apply with respect to the funds made available to carry out this section.

"(l) EXPIRATION OF AUTHORITY.—The President may not enter into any commitments to guarantee under subsection (a) after September 30, 1992.

"(m) DEFINITIONS.—For purposes of this section—

"(1) the term 'administering agency' means the Agency for International Development;

"(2) the term 'Administrator' means the Administrator of the Agency for International Development; and

"(3) the term 'Bank' means the Export-Import Bank of the United States.".

(b) CONFORMING AMENDMENT.—Section 224 of that Act is amended by inserting "FOR CENTRAL AMERICA" after "PROGRAM" in the section caption.

(c) Conforming Reference.—With respect to Poland, any reference in the Foreign Operations, Export Financing, and Related Programs Appropriations Act, 1990, to section 224 of the Foreign Assistance Act of 1961 shall be deemed to be a reference to section 225 of that Act (as enacted by this section).

SEC. 305. TRADE AND DEVELOPMENT PROGRAM ACTIVITIES FOR POLAND AND HUNGARY.

In order to permit expansion of the Trade and Development Program into Poland and Hungary, there are authorized to be appropriated $6,000,000 for the 3-year period beginning October 1, 1989, to carry out section 661 of the Foreign Assistance Act of 1961 (22 U.S.C. 2241), in addition to amounts otherwise available for such purpose.

SEC. 306. BILATERAL INVESTMENT TREATIES WITH POLAND AND HUNGARY.

The Congress urges the President to seek bilateral investment treaties with Poland and Hungary in order to establish a more stable legal framework for United States investment in those countries.

SEC. 307. CERTAIN POLISH BONDS NOT SUBJECT TO INTERNAL REVENUE CODE RULES RELATING TO BELOW-MARKET LOANS.

(a) In General.—Paragraph (5) of section 1812(b) of the Tax Reform Act of 1986 is amended—

(1) by inserting "or Poland" after "Israel" in the text thereof, and

(2) by inserting "or polish" after "israel" in the heading thereof.

(b) Effective Date.—The amendments made by this section shall apply to obligations issued after the date of the enactment of this Act.

TITLE IV—EDUCATIONAL, CULTURAL, AND SCIENTIFIC ACTIVITIES

SEC. 401. EDUCATIONAL AND CULTURAL EXCHANGES AND SISTER INSTITUTIONS PROGRAMS WITH POLAND AND HUNGARY.

(a) Educational and Cultural Exchanges.—

(1) Support for expanded u.s. participation.—The United States should expand its participation in educational and cultural exchange activities with Poland and Hungary, using the full array of existing government-funded and privately-funded programs, with particular emphasis on the J. William Fulbright Educational Exchange Program, the International Visitors Program, the Samantha Smith Memorial Exchange Program, the exchange programs of the National Academy of Sciences, youth and student exchanges through such private organizations as The Experiment in International Living, The American Field Service Committee, and Youth for Understanding, and research exchanges sponsored by the International Research and Exchanges Board (IREX).

(2) Emphasis on skills in business and economics.—The United States should place particular emphasis on expanding its participation in educational exchange activities that will assist in developing the skills in business and economics that

are necessary for the development of a free market economy in Poland and Hungary.

(b) BINATIONAL FULBRIGHT COMMISSIONS.—The United States should take all appropriate action to establish binational Fulbright commissions with Poland and Hungary in order to facilitate and enhance academic and scholarly exchanges with those countries.

(c) RECIPROCAL CULTURAL CENTERS.—The President should consider the establishment of reciprocal cultural centers in Poland and the United States and in Hungary and the United States to facilitate government-funded and privately-funded cultural exchanges.

(d) SISTER INSTITUTIONS PROGRAMS.—The President shall act to encourage the establishment of "sister institution" programs between American and Polish organizations and between American and Hungarian organizations, including such organizations as institutions of higher education, cities and towns, and organizations in such fields as medicine and health care, business management, environmental protection, and agricultural research and marketing.

(e) AUTHORIZATION OF APPROPRIATIONS.—To enable the United States Information Agency to support the activities described in this section, there are authorized to be appropriated $12,000,000 for the 3-year period beginning October 1, 1989, in addition to amounts otherwise available for such purposes.

SEC. 402. POLAND-HUNGARY SCHOLARSHIP PARTNERSHIP.

(a) ESTABLISHMENT OF SCHOLARSHIP PROGRAM.—The Administrator of the Agency for International Development is authorized to establish and administer a program of scholarship assistance, in cooperation with State governments, universities, community colleges, and businesses, to provide scholarships to enable students from Poland and Hungary to study in the United States.

(b) EMPHASIS ON BUSINESS AND ECONOMICS.—The scholarship program provided for in this section shall emphasize scholarships to enable students from Poland and Hungary to study business and economics in the United States. Such scholarships may be provided for study in programs that range from the standard management courses to more specialized assistance in commercial banking and the creation of a stock market.

(c) GRANTS TO STATES.—In carrying out this section, the Administrator may make grants to States to provide scholarship assistance for undergraduate or graduate degree programs, and training programs of one year or longer, in study areas related to the critical development needs of Poland and Hungary.

(d) CONSULTATION WITH STATES.—The Administrator shall consult with the participating States with regard to the educational opportunities available within each State and on the assignment of scholarship recipients.

(e) FEDERAL SHARE.—The Federal share for each year for which a State receives payments under this section shall not be more than 50 percent.

(f) NON-FEDERAL SHARE.—The non-Federal share of payments under this section may be in cash, including the waiver of tuition or the offering of in-State tuition or housing waivers or subsidies, or in-kind fairly evaluated, including the provision of books or supplies.

(g) FORGIVENESS OF SCHOLARSHIP ASSISTANCE.—The obligation of any recipient to reimburse any entity for any or all scholarship assistance provided under this section shall be forgiven upon the recipient's prompt return to Poland or Hungary, as the case may be, for a period which is at least one year longer than the period spent studying in the United States with scholarship assistance.

(h) PRIVATE SECTOR PARTICIPATION.—To the maximum extent practicable, each participating State shall enlist the assistance of the private sector to enable the State to meet the non-Federal share of payments under this section. Wherever appropriate, each participating State shall encourage the private sector to offer internships or other opportunities consistent with the purposes of this section to students receiving scholarships under this section.

(i) FUNDING.—Grants to States pursuant to this section shall be made with funds made available to carry out chapter 1 of part I of the Foreign Assistance Act of 1961 (22 U.S.C. 2151 and following; relating to development assistance) or chapter 4 of part II of that Act (22 U.S.C. 2346 and following; relating to the economic support fund). In addition to amounts otherwise available for such purpose under those chapters, there are authorized to be appropriated $10,000,000 for the 3-year period beginning October 1, 1989, for use in carrying out this section.

(j) RESTRICTIONS NOT APPLICABLE.—Prohibitions on the use of foreign assistance funds for assistance for Poland and Hungary shall not apply with respect to the funds made available to carry out this section.

(k) DEFINITION OF STATE.—As used in this section, the term "State" means each of the several States, the District of Columbia, the Commonwealth of Puerto Rico, Guam, American Samoa, the Virgin Islands, the Trust Territory of the Pacific Islands, and the Commonwealth of the Northern Mariana Islands.

SEC. 403. SCIENCE AND TECHNOLOGY EXCHANGE WITH POLAND AND HUNGARY.

(a) AGREEMENT WITH POLAND.—There are authorized to be appropriated to the Secretary of State for purposes of continuing to implement the 1987 United States-Polish science and technology agreement—

(1) $1,500,000 for fiscal year 1990,

(2) $2,000,000 for fiscal year 1991, and

(3) $2,000,000 for fiscal year 1992.

(b) AGREEMENT WITH HUNGARY.—There are authorized to be appropriated to the Secretary of State for purposes of implementing the 1989 United States-Hungarian science and technology agreement—

(1) $500,000 for fiscal year 1990,

(2) $1,000,000 for fiscal year 1991, and

(3) $1,000,000 for fiscal year 1992.

(c) DEFINITION OF AGREEMENTS BEING FUNDED.—For purposes of this section—

(1) the term "1987 United States-Polish science and technology agreement" refers to the agreement concluded in 1987 by the United States and Poland, entitled "Agreement Between the Government of the United States of America and the Polish People's Republic on Cooperation in Science and Technology and Its Funding", together with annexes relating thereto; and

(2) the term "1989 United States-Hungarian science and technology agreement" refers to the agreement concluded in 1989 by the United States and Hungary, entitled "Agreement Between the Government of the United States of America and the Government of the Hungarian People's Republic for Scientific

and Technology Cooperation", together with annexes relating thereto.

TITLE V—OTHER ASSISTANCE PROGRAMS

SEC. 501. ASSISTANCE IN SUPPORT OF DEMOCRATIC INSTITUTIONS IN POLAND AND HUNGARY.

(a) Authorization of Assistance.—In addition to amounts otherwise available for such purposes, there are authorized to be appropriated to carry out chapter 4 of part II of the Foreign Assistance Act of 1961 (22 U.S.C. 2346 and following; relating to the economic support fund) $12,000,000 for the 3-year period beginning October 1, 1989, which shall be available only for the support of democratic institutions and activities in Poland and Hungary.

(b) Nonapplicability of Other Laws.—Assistance may be provided under this section notwithstanding any other provision of law.

SEC. 502. ENVIRONMENTAL INITIATIVES FOR POLAND AND HUNGARY.

(a) Priority for the Control of Pollution.—The Congress recognizes the severe pollution problems affecting Poland and Hungary and the serious health problems which ensue from such pollution. The Congress therefore directs that a high priority be given in the implementation of assistance to Poland and Hungary to the control of pollution and the restoration of the natural resource base on which a sustainable, healthy economy depends.

(b) EPA Activities Generally.—In addition to specific authorities contained in any of the environmental statutes administered by the Environmental Protection Agency, the Administrator of that Agency (hereinafter in this section referred to as the "Administrator") is authorized to undertake such educational, policy training, research, and technical and financial assistance, monitoring, coordinating, and other activities as the Administrator may deem appropriate, either alone or in cooperation with other United States or foreign agencies, governments, or public or private institutions, in protecting the environment in Poland and Hungary.

(c) EPA Activities in Poland.—The Administrator shall cooperate with Polish officials and experts to—

(1) establish an air quality monitoring network in the Krakow metropolitan area as a part of Poland's national air monitoring network; and

(2) improve both water quality and the availability of drinking water in the Krakow metropolitan area.

(d) EPA Activities in Hungary.—The Administrator shall work with other United States and Hungarian officials and private parties to establish and support a regional center in Budapest for facilitating cooperative environmental activities between governmental experts and public and private organizations from the United States and Eastern and Western Europe.

(e) Funding of EPA Activities.—To enable the Environmental Protection Agency to carry out subsections (b), (c), and (d), there are authorized to be appropriated $10,000,000 for the 3-year period beginning October 1, 1989, to carry out chapter 1 of part I of the Foreign Assistance Act of 1961 (22 U.S.C. 2151 and following; relating to development assistance) or chapter 4 of Part II of that Act (22 U.S.C. 2346 and following; relating to the economic support fund). These funds may be used to carry out those subsections notwithstanding any provision of law relating to the use of foreign assistance funds.

(f) DEPARTMENT OF ENERGY ACTIVITIES RELATING TO FOSSIL FUELS.—

(1) CLEAN COAL.—The Secretary of Energy shall cooperate with Polish officials and experts to retrofit a coal-fired commercial powerplant in the Krakow, Poland, region with advanced clean coal technology that has been successfully demonstrated at a comparably scaled powerplant in the United States. Such retrofit shall be carried out by one or more United States companies using United States technology and equipment manufactured in the United States. The Secretary may vest title in any property acquired under this paragraph in an entity other than the United States.

(2) EQUIPMENT ASSESSMENT.—The Secretary of Energy shall cooperate with Polish officials and experts and companies within the United States to assess and develop the capability within Poland to manufacture or modify boilers, furnaces, smelters, or other equipment that will enable industrial facilities within Poland to use fossil fuels cleanly. The Secretary may vest title in any property acquired under this paragraph in an entity other than the United States.

(3) AUTHORIZATION OF APPROPRIATIONS.—To carry out paragraphs (1) and (2) of this subsection, there are authorized to be appropriated $30,000,000 for the 3-year period beginning October 1, 1989. Not more than $10,000,000 of the funds appropriated under this paragraph may be used to carry out the requirements of paragraph (1).

(g) PRIORITY FOR EFFICIENT ENERGY USE.—In view of the high energy usage per unit of output in Hungary and Poland, the Secretary of Energy shall give high priority to assisting officials of Poland and Hungary in improving the efficiency of their energy use, through emphasis on such measures as efficient motors, lights, gears, and appliances and improvements in building insulation and design.

(h) ALTERNATIVE INVESTMENTS IN ENERGY IN HUNGARY.—It is the sense of the Congress that the Executive branch should work with the Government of Hungary to achieve environmentally safe alternative investments in energy efficiency, particularly with regard to projects along the Danube River.

SEC. 503. MEDICAL SUPPLIES, HOSPITAL EQUIPMENT, AND MEDICAL TRAINING FOR POLAND.

(a) AUTHORIZATION OF ASSISTANCE.—In addition to amounts otherwise available for such purposes, there are authorized to be appropriated to carry out chapter 4 of part II of the Foreign Assistance Act of 1961 (22 U.S.C. 2346 and following; relating to the economic support fund) $4,000,000 for the 3-year period beginning October 1, 1989, which shall be available only—

(1) for providing medical supplies and hospital equipment to Poland through private and voluntary organizations, including for the expenses of purchasing, transporting, and distributing such supplies and equipment, and

(2) for training of Polish medical personnel.

(b) NONAPPLICABILITY OF OTHER LAWS.—Assistance may be provided under this section notwithstanding any other provision of law, other than—

(1) section 104(f) of the Foreign Assistance Act of 1961 (22 U.S.C. 2151b(f); relating to the prohibition on the use of funds for abortions and involuntary sterilizations), and

(2) any provision of the annual Foreign Operations, Export Financing, and Related Programs Appropriations Act that relates to abortion.

TITLE VI—ADDITIONAL SEED PROGRAM ACTIONS

SEC. 601. POLICY COORDINATION OF SEED PROGRAM.

The President shall designate, within the Department of State, a SEED Program coordinator who shall be directly responsible for overseeing and coordinating all programs described in this Act and all other activities that the United States Government conducts in furtherance of the purposes of this Act.

SEC. 602. SEED INFORMATION CENTER SYSTEM.

(a) ESTABLISHMENT.—The President shall establish a SEED Information Center System, using existing Executive branch agencies and acting in cooperation with the Government of Poland and the Government of Hungary.

(b) FUNCTIONS.—

(1) IN GENERAL.—The SEED Information Center System shall serve as a central clearinghouse mechanism for information relating to—

(A) business needs and opportunities in Eastern Europe, and

(B) voluntary assistance to countries in Eastern Europe.

(2) PRIVATE ENTERPRISE DEVELOPMENT.—The SEED Information Center System shall be organized, among other purposes, to encourage—

(A) the submission of economically sound proposals to the Polish-American Enterprise Fund and Hungarian-American Enterprise Fund, and

(B) other sources of finance for the development of private enterprise in Eastern Europe.

(c) LOCATION.—The SEED Information Center System shall be based jointly in Washington, District of Columbia; Warsaw, Poland; and Budapest, Hungary; and should it become appropriate, the capitals of other East European countries.

SEC. 603. ENCOURAGING VOLUNTARY ASSISTANCE FOR POLAND AND HUNGARY.

(a) ENCOURAGING PRIVATE CONTRIBUTIONS.—It is the sense of the Congress that the President should take all possible steps to encourage across the Nation a massive outpouring of private contributions of money and nonperishable foods, to be collected by civic, religious, school, and youth organizations, for assistance to Poland and to refugees from Romania who are in Hungary.

(b) TRANSPORTATION TO POLAND OF PRIVATE CONTRIBUTIONS.—In further of subsection (a), the President—

(1) using all available authorities, including section 402 of title 10, United States Code (relating to transportation of humanitarian relief supplies), should use resources of the Department of Defense (including the National Guard) to transport nonfinancial private contributions to Poland,

(2) should request additional authorities as needed for the use of those resources for that purpose; and

(3) should encourage maximum participation by such recognized private and voluntary organizations as the Polish-American Congress in the transportation of nonfinancial private contributions to Poland.

SEC. 604. ECONOMIC AND COMMERCIAL OFFICERS AT UNITED STATES EMBASSIES AND MISSIONS IN POLAND AND HUNGARY.

It is the sense of the Congress that, to the extent practicable—

(1) the United States Embassy in Budapest, Hungary, should be assigned one additional economic and commercial officer;

(2) the United States Embassy in Warsaw, Poland, should be assigned one additional economic officer and one additional commercial officer;

(3) the United States Trade Center in Warsaw, Poland, should be assigned one additional economic and commercial officer; and

(4) the United States mission in Krakow, Poland, should be assigned one additional economic and commercial officer.

TITLE VII—REPORTS TO CONGRESS

SEC. 701. REPORT ON INITIAL STEPS TAKEN BY UNITED STATES AND ON POLAND'S REQUIREMENT FOR AGRICULTURAL ASSISTANCE.

(a) INITIAL REPORT.—Not later than 60 days after the date of enactment of this Act, the President shall submit a report to the Congress—

(1) describing the steps taken by the United States Government pursuant to title I, in particular sections 102 (a) and (b);

(2) assessing Poland's requirements for additional agricultural assistance during fiscal year 1990 and its requirements for agricultural assistance during fiscal years 1991 and 1992; and

(3) specifying how much agricultural assistance the President proposes be provided by the United States to meet those requirements.

(b) UPDATING ASSESSMENTS.—As additional information becomes available, the President shall provide to the Congress revised assessments of Poland's requirements for agricultural assistance during fiscal years 1991 and 1992, specifying how much agricultural assistance the President proposes be provided by the United States to meet those requirements.

SEC. 702. REPORT ON CONFIDENCE BUILDING MEASURES BY POLAND AND HUNGARY.

Not later than 180 days after the date of enactment of this Act, the President shall submit a report to the Congress identifying—

(1) the confidence building measures Poland and Hungary could undertake to facilitate the negotiation of agreements, including bilateral customs and technology transfer agreements, that would encourage greater direct private sector investment in that country; and

(2) the confidence building measures Poland and Hungary could undertake with respect to the treatment accorded those countries under the Export Administration Act of 1979.

SEC. 703. REPORT ON ENVIRONMENTAL PROBLEMS IN POLAND AND HUNGARY.

The first report submitted pursuant to section 704 shall include the following:

(1) Assessment of problems.—An overall assessment of the environmental problems facing Poland and Hungary, including—

(A) a relative ranking of the severity of the problems and their effects on both human health and the general environment;

(B) a listing of the geographical areas of each country that have suffered the heaviest environmental damage, and a description of the source and scope of the damage; and

(C) an assessment of the environmental performance of leading industrial polluters in those countries and the expected effect on pollution levels of industrial modernization.

(2) Priorities and costs for action.—An analysis of the priorities that Poland and Hungary should each assign in addressing its environmental problems, and an estimate of the capital and human resources required to undertake a comprehensive program of environmental protection in that country.

(3) Role of United States and multilateral assistance.—A statement of strategy for United States assistance for the next 5 years to address environmental problems in Poland and Hungary, including—

(A) recommendations for appropriate levels and forms of bilateral financial and technical assistance;

(B) recommendations concerning United States participation in cooperative multilateral undertakings;

(C) an assessment of the feasibility of debt-for-nature swaps as a technique of environmental protection in each country; and

(D) recommendations for minimizing further environmental damage to Krakow, and for the protection and restoration of historic sites in that city.

SEC. 704. ANNUAL SEED PROGRAM REPORT.

(a) Findings.—The Congress finds that—

(1) in order to provide the President with maximum flexibility and opportunity for innovation in implementation of the SEED Program, this Act sets forth general goals and modalities for the support of democracy and economic pluralism in Eastern Europe;

(2) prompt United States action in devising specific measures to achieve the goals outlined in this Act will be crucial in generating the public awareness, and the international commitment, necessary for United States leadership of a successful multilateral program of assistance in Eastern Europe; and

(3) clear-cut delineation of such United States actions at an early date is integral to United States leadership of this effort.

(b) Initial Seed Program Report.—Accordingly, the first report pursuant to subsection (c) shall be a comprehensive report that includes a full description of all SEED Actions taken pursuant to each provision of this Act since the enactment of this Act.

(c) ANNUAL SEED PROGRAM REPORT.—Not later than January 31 of each year (beginning in 1991), the President shall submit to the Congress a "Report on the United States Program of Support for East European Democracy (the SEED Program)". Each such report shall describe the assistance provided to each East European country under this Act during the preceding fiscal year. In addition, each such report shall contain an assessment of the progress made by each such recipient country in—

(1) implementing economic policies designed to promote sustained economic growth, develop economic freedom, and increase opportunities for the people of that country; and

(2) adopting and implementing constitutional, legal, and administrative measures that—

(A) affect the powers of the executive and legislative authorities and the independence of the judiciary,

(B) affect the formation and operation of independent political parties, groups, associations, or organizations, or

(C) affect fundamental human rights and civil liberties.

SEC. 705. REPORTS ON CERTAIN ACTIVITIES.

At the same time each report is submitted pursuant to section 704(c), the President shall submit to the appropriate committees of the Congress a report on the extent of espionage activities against the United States and other member countries of the North Atlantic Treaty Organization by operatives of the government of any East European country that is receiving assistance under this Act. Such reports may be submitted in classified form.

SEC. 706. NOTIFICATIONS TO CONGRESS REGARDING ASSISTANCE.

Section 634A of the Foreign Assistance Act of 1961 (22 U.S.C. 2394-1; relating to reprogramming notifications) applies with respect to obligations of funds made available under that Act to carry out this Act, notwithstanding any other provision of this Act.

TITLE VIII—MISCELLANEOUS PROVISIONS

SEC. 801. SUSPENSION OF SEED ASSISTANCE.

The President should suspend all assistance to an East European country pursuant to this Act if the President determines, and reports to the Congress, that—

(1) that country is engaged in international activities directly and fundamentally contrary to United States national security interests;

(2) the president or any other government official of that country initiates martial law or a state of emergency for reasons other than to respond to a natural disaster or a foreign invasion; or

(3) any member who was elected to that country's parliament has been removed from that office or arrested through extraconstitutional processes.

SEC. 802. DECLARATION OF THE REPUBLIC OF HUNGARY.

(a) FINDINGS.—The Congress finds that—

(1) on October 23, 1989, in a public ceremony in Budapest, the acting President of Hungary declared the Hungarian state to be an independent, democratic Republic of Hungary;

(2) this public ceremony was held on the 33d anniversary of Hungary's 1956 revolution that was bloodily suppressed by Soviet troops;

(3) this public ceremony was held in the same Kossuth Square where the first mass rally of the 1956 revolution was held;

(4) as a further symbol of Hungary's faithfulness to the legacy of the revolution of 1956, the declaration by the acting President was made from the same balcony from which Imre Nagy, the martyred Prime Minister of the revolutionary government of 1956, addressed the citizens of Budapest 33 years before;

(5) the heroic revolt and freedom fight of the Hungarian people in 1956 was an inspirational event, reminding a generation of Americans of the sacrifices people are willing to undertake as the price of liberty; and

(6) the present efforts of the Hungarian people to validate the legacy of the revolution of 1956 by establishing a free, independent, and prosperous Hungary have gained the sympathy and admiration of the American people.

(b) CONGRESSIONAL DECLARATIONS.—The Congress—

(1) congratulates the people of Hungary on the declaration of a Republic of Hungary committed to democratic principles; and

(2) expresses its desire to enhance the friendly relations between the people of Hungary and the people of the United States and between their respective governments.

SEC. 803. ADMINISTRATIVE EXPENSES OF THE AGENCY FOR INTERNATIONAL DEVELOPMENT.

For the purpose of paying administrative expenses incurred in connection with carrying out its functions under this Act, the Agency for International Development may use up to $500,000 each fiscal year of the funds made available to the Agency under this Act.

SEC. 804. RELATION OF PROVISIONS OF THIS ACT TO CERTAIN PROVISIONS OF APPROPRIATIONS ACTS.

Any provision of the annual Foreign Operations, Export Financing, and Related Programs Appropriations Act that provides that assistance for Poland or Hungary under that Act may be provided "notwithstanding any other provision of law" shall not supersede any otherwise applicable provision of this Act. This section shall not, however, be construed to apply with respect to section 599C(b) of the Foreign Operations, Export Financing, and Related Programs Appropriations Act, 1990 (or a corresponding provision of a subsequent such appropriations Act).

SEC. 805. CERTAIN USES OF EXCESS FOREIGN CURRENCIES.

(a) AUTHORITY TO USE.—During fiscal year 1990, the Administrator of the Agency for International Development may use, for the purposes described in subsection (b), such sums of foreign currencies described in subsection (c) as the Administrator may determine, subject to subsection (f).

(b) PURPOSES FOR WHICH CURRENCY MAY BE USED.—Foreign currencies may be used under this section—

(1) for the same purposes for which assistance may be provided under part I of the Foreign Assistance Act of 1961 (22 U.S.C. 2151 and following; relating to economic assistance), and

(2) for the support of any institution providing education for a significant number of United States nationals (who may include

members of the United States Armed Forces or the Foreign Service or dependents of such members).

(c) CURRENCIES WHICH MAY BE USED.—The foreign currencies which may be used under this section are United States-owned excess foreign currencies that are in excess of amounts necessary for satisfaction of preexisting commitments to use such currencies for other purposes specified by law.

(d) WHERE CURRENCIES MAY BE USED.—Foreign currencies may be used under this section in the country where such currencies are held or in other foreign countries.

(e) NONAPPLICABILITY OF OTHER PROVISIONS OF LAW.—Foreign currencies may be used under this section notwithstanding section 1306 of title 31, United States Code, or any other provision of law.

(f) REQUIREMENT FOR APPROPRIATIONS ACTION.—The authority of this section may be exercised only to such extent or in such amount as may be provided in advance in an appropriation Act.

Approved November 28, 1989.

LEGISLATIVE HISTORY—H.R. 3402:

HOUSE REPORTS: No. 101-278, Pt. 1 (Comm. on Ways and Means), Pt. 2 (Comm. on Foreign Affairs), and Pt. 3 (Comm. on Public Works and Transportation); and No. 101-377 (Comm. of Conference).
CONGRESSIONAL RECORD, Vol. 135 (1989):
Oct. 19, considered and passed House.
Nov. 14, considered and passed Senate, amended.
Nov. 16, House concurred in Senate amendments with an amendment.
Nov. 17, House and Senate agreed to conference report.
WEEKLY COMPILATION OF PRESIDENTIAL DOCUMENTS, Vol. 25 (1989):
Nov. 28, Presidential statement.

NATIONAL DEFENSE AUTHORIZATION ACT FOR FISCAL YEARS 1990 AND 1991

An Act to authorize appropriations for fiscal years 1990 and 1991 for military activities of the Department of Defense, for military construction, and for defense activities of the Department of Energy, to prescribe personnel strengths for such fiscal years for the Armed Forces, and for other purposes.

Date: November 29, 1989

Bill No.: H.R. 2461

Public Law No.: 101-189

Cite: 103 STAT. 1352

Sections reprinted:

TITLE IX - MATTERS RELATING TO NATO MEMBER NATIONS AND OTHER ALLIES

Part A - Conventional Force Reductions in Europe

Section 901 - Framework for determining conventional force requirements in a changing threat environment.

Section 902 - Implications of mutual reductions in conventional forces in Europe by NATO and Warsaw Pact member nations.

Section 903 - Report on verification measures for possible conventional arms control agreement.

Part B - Burden Sharing

Section 912 - Active-duty forces in Europe of member nations of NATO.

Section 913 - Contributions by Japan to global security.

Section 915 - United States-Republic of Korea security relationship and other security matters in East Asia.

Part C - Expenditures in Europe

Section 922 - Sense of Congress concerning United States military facilities in NATO member countries.

TITLE X - MATTERS RELATING TO ARMS CONTROL

Section 1001 - Presidential report on possible effects of a strategic arms reduction agreement on Trident program.

Section 1002 - Presidential report on the verification work that has been conducted with regard to mobile ICBMs under a START agreement.

Section 1003 - Sense of Congress on START talks.

Section 1004 - Report on asymmetrics in capabilities of United States and Soviet Union to produce and deploy ballistic missile defense systems.

Section 1005 - Sense of the Congress with respect to accidental launch protection.

Section 1006 - Congressional findings and sense of Congress concerning the Krasnoyarsk radar.

Section 1007 - Sense of Congress concerning exploring the feasibility of treaty limitations on weapons capable of threatening military satellites.

Section 1008 - Report on satellite survivability.

Section 1009 - Report on the desirability of negotiations with the Soviet Union regarding limitations on antisatellite capabilities.

Section 1010 - Report on verification of compliance with agreements to limit nuclear testing.

Section 1011 - Sense of Congress on arms control negotiations and United States modernization policy.

Section 1012 - Report on effect of space nuclear reactors on gamma-ray astronomy missions.

Section 1013 - Sense of Congress on chemical weapons negotiations.

Public Law 101-189
101st Congress

An Act

To authorize appropriations for fiscal years 1990 and 1991 for military activities of the Department of Defense, for military construction, and for defense activities of the Department of Energy, to prescribe personnel strengths for such fiscal years for the Armed Forces, and for other purposes.

Be it enacted by the Senate and House of Representatives of the United States of America in Congress assembled,

SECTION 1. SHORT TITLE

This Act may be cited as the "National Defense Authorization Act for Fiscal Years 1990 and 1991".

TITLE IX—MATTERS RELATING TO NATO MEMBER NATIONS AND OTHER ALLIES

PART A—CONVENTIONAL FORCE REDUCTIONS IN EUROPE

SEC. 901. FRAMEWORK FOR DETERMINING CONVENTIONAL FORCE REQUIREMENTS IN A CHANGING THREAT ENVIRONMENT

(a) EVALUATION OF EFFECT OF WARSAW PACT REDUCTIONS AND OF POSSIBLE CFE AGREEMENT.—The Secretary of Defense shall submit to the congressional defense committees a report providing the Secretary's evaluation of the effect upon requirements of the United States for conventional forces and for military spending that could be anticipated under the following assumptions:

(1) The full implementation of the unilateral force reductions in, and subsequent reorganization of, forces of the Soviet Union described by the President of the Soviet Union on December 7, 1988, and the unilateral force reductions subsequently announced by the other members of the Warsaw Pact.

(2) Entry into force of a conventional arms control agreement establishing rough parity in conventional forces in Europe between forces of the North Atlantic Treaty Organization and the Warsaw Pact at equal levels (at approximately 85 to 90 percent of NATO's current inventory) of tanks, artillery, armored troop carriers, combat helicopters, and land-based combat aircraft.

(b) MATTERS TO BE INCLUDED IN EVALUATION.—In carrying out the evaluation required by subsection (a) of the unilateral force reductions referred to in paragraph (1) of that subsection and the potential effect of an agreement referred to in paragraph (2) of that subsection, the Secretary shall include in the evaluation (at a minimum) the following (stated for both the near-term and mid-term):

(1) An assessment of the threat to NATO under the assumptions specified in each of paragraphs (1) and (2) of subsection (a).

(2) The effect on the defense strategy of the United States for meeting its NATO commitments in the changing threat environment, including the effect on the ability of NATO to defend against an attack by the Warsaw Pact (A) on short warning, or (B) during a crisis in Europe.

(3) The effect on—

(A) the mix of active and reserve forces of the United States;

(B) the ratio of (i) conventional forces of the United States deployed in the European theater, to (ii) conventional forces of the United States deployed in the continental United States; and

(C) air and sea lift requirements.

(3) The effect on operational military concepts of the United States and NATO (such as Follow-on Forces Attack (FOFA), AirLand Battle, Maritime Strategy, and Rapid Reinforcement) that were initially developed to counter the large advantage of the Warsaw Pact in conventional land forces in the European theater.

(4) The effect on equipment requirements of the United States for meeting its commitments to NATO in the 1990s.

(c) TIME FOR SUBMISSION.—The report required by subsection (a) shall be submitted concurrently with the submission to Congress of the President's budget for fiscal year 1991 pursuant to section 1105 of title 31, United States Code. The report shall be submitted in both classified and unclassified form.

SEC. 902. IMPLICATIONS OF MUTUAL REDUCTIONS IN CONVENTIONAL FORCES IN EUROPE BY NATO AND WARSAW PACT MEMBER NATIONS

(a) COMMENDATION OF PRESIDENT'S CONVENTIONAL ARMS REDUCTION INITIATIVE.—Congress commends and supports the President's conventional arms control initiative announced in Brussels on May 29, 1989, in which the President proposed, and the North Atlantic Treaty Organization (NATO) agreed, that NATO expand its negotiating position at the negotiations on reductions in conventional forces in Europe (begun in Vienna on March 9, 1989, and known as the "CFE Talks") to include—

(1) substantial reductions by each side to equal ceilings of helicopters and combat aircraft; and

(2) a reduction to a common ceiling of United States military personnel stationed in Western Europe and Soviet military personnel stationed in Eastern Europe.

(b) PRESIDENTIAL REPORT.—(1) Not later than six months after the date of the enactment of this Act, the President shall submit to Congress an unclassified report, with classified annexes as necessary, on the foreign policy and military implications to NATO and to the Warsaw Pact of significant reductions of conventional forces by NATO and Warsaw Pact countries to a ceiling which is the same for both sides.

(2) The report shall address possible force reduction scenarios for a second round of CFE negotiations and shall be based upon two different assumptions with regard to the level of reductions in personnel and equipment to be made. Under the first assumption, personnel and equipment would be reduced to a level 25 percent below current NATO levels. Under the second assumption, personnel and equipment would be reduced to a level 50 percent below current NATO levels.

(3) The report shall include the following:

(A) A comprehensive net assessment of the current balance between NATO forces and Warsaw Pact forces and of the overall trends in that balance, including an assessment of the trends in active and reserve forces and in total equipment holdings in stationed and indigenous forces.

(B) A description of the likely alternative force postures that could be adopted by member nations of both alliances (particularly by the United States and the Soviet Union) under each of the assumptions analyzed, together with a description of the possible effects of restructuring of both NATO and Warsaw Pact forces in Europe for defensive purposes.

(C) A statement of the costs (or savings) to the United States, over at least a seven-year period, estimated to be associated with each force posture described under subparagraph (B), together with an analysis of how those costs (or savings) were determined.

(D) An analysis of the implications for NATO strategy, security, and military policy under each of the reduction levels referred to in paragraph (2), including a net assessment of the resulting balance between NATO forces and Warsaw Pact forces.

(E) An assessment of the effects under each of the reduction levels referred to in paragraph (2) (including the alternative force postures under each assumption) upon the stability of the conventional balance of forces in Europe.

(F) An assessment of the ability of NATO to defend Europe under each of the assumed reduction levels in the event of an attack by the Warsaw Pact (i) on short warning, or (ii) during a crisis in Europe.

(G) An assessment of the effects under each of the reduction levels referred to in paragraph (2) on—

(i) the short-range nuclear force requirements of NATO;

(ii) the requirements of the United States for POMCUS and war-reserve stocks;

(iii) the requirements of NATO for airlift and sealift based in the United States and for reinforcing units from the United States; and

(iv) the ability of the United States to meet global military requirements.

SEC. 903. REPORT ON VERIFICATION MEASURES FOR POSSIBLE CONVENTIONAL ARMS CONTROL AGREEMENT

(a) REPORT.—The President shall submit to Congress a report on the types of measures that would be required to verify the proposal for reductions in conventional forces in Europe adopted by the member nations of the North Atlantic Treaty Organization (NATO) on May 30, 1989.

(b) MATTERS TO BE INCLUDED IN REPORT.—The President shall include in the report under subsection (a) the following:

(1) A discussion of the types of information that it would be necessary for the parties to such an agreement to exchange for such verification.

(2) A discussion of the range of options under consideration by the executive branch for defining what constitutes a militarily significant violation of a conventional arms control agreement.

(3) A description of the national technical means, on-site inspections, and other cooperative measures that would be necessary to detect violations of such an agreement, including—

(A) an analysis of the measures that would be required to monitor (i) the withdrawal and demobilization of military personnel, and (ii) the withdrawal and (if required by the agreement) the destruction of military equipment provided for in any such agreement; and

(B) the President's judgment on those on-site inspections and confidence building measures under consideration that are the most acceptable, and the least acceptable, to the NATO alliance and the Warsaw Pact, including an assessment of the counterintelligence aspects of such measures for NATO.

(4) A discussion of the procedures the NATO alliance would follow in the event of a violation of such an agreement by a member of the Warsaw Treaty Organization.

(c) DATA BASE ANALYSIS.—(1) The report under subsection (a) shall also include a comprehensive analysis of—

(A) the uncertainties in the data bases to be used by United States intelligence with respect to the military forces of NATO member nations and Warsaw Pact member nations located in the proposed areas of reduction;

(B) the uncertainties in the estimates of the trends in such forces; and

(C) the differences in the data bases and counting rules used by the United States, the allies of the United States, and the Warsaw Pact member nations.

(2) The analysis under paragraph (1) shall address separately the uncertainties in the estimates of each of the following:

(A) Active forces.

(B) Reserve forces.

(C) Equipment subject to reductions and ceilings.

(D) Indigenous forces.

(E) Stationed forces.

(d) Submission of Report.—The report required by subsection (a) shall be submitted not later than March 1, 1990. The report shall include such comments and recommendations as the President determines appropriate. The report shall be submitted in both classified and unclassified versions.

SEC. 912. ACTIVE-DUTY FORCES IN EUROPE OF MEMBER NATIONS OF NATO

(a) Findings.—Congress makes the following findings:

(1) Member nations of the North Atlantic Treaty Organization (NATO), at the initiative of the President, have presented to the nations of the Warsaw Pact a comprehensive proposal concerning reductions in conventional forces in Europe for consideration in the negotiations on Conventional Armed Forces in Europe (CFE).

(2) An agreement based on that proposal would significantly enhance security and stability in Europe and the cause of peace worldwide.

(3) Irrespective of developments in the CFE negotiations, several member nations of NATO are considering making significant unilateral reductions over the next several years in the number of their active-duty forces in Europe.

(4) Such unilateral reductions in active-duty forces before an agreement on CFE enters into force would—

(A) undercut efforts by NATO to improve its conventional defense posture in Europe, increase reliance by NATO on the threat of the early use of nuclear weapons to deter aggression, and undermine the NATO arms control negotiating posture in the CFE negotiations; and

(B) exacerbate longstanding burdensharing tensions among member nations of NATO.

(5) Despite shifts in relative economic power from the United States to some of the major allies of the United States, the costs of mutual defense continue to be borne disproportionately by the United States.

(6) Adjustments in burdensharing are long overdue.

(b) Definitions.—For purposes of this section:

(1) The term "active-duty forces in Europe" means those active-duty military personnel assigned to permanent duty ashore in European member nations of NATO, except that such term does not include INF-related forces.

(2) The term "INF-related forces" means those active-duty military personnel assigned to permanent duty ashore in European member nations of NATO who are to be demobilized or withdrawn from Europe as a result of the elimination of the intermediate-range nuclear weapons of the United States pursuant to the Treaty between the United States of America and the Union of Soviet Socialist Republics on the Elimination of their Intermediate-range and Shorter-range Missiles, signed on December 8, 1987 (commonly referred to as the "INF Treaty").

(3) The term "U.S. end-strength level in Europe" means the actual number of active-duty forces in Europe of the Armed Forces of the United States at the end of a fiscal year.

(4) The term "allied forces end-strength level in Europe" means the actual number of active-duty forces in Europe of the armed forces of member nations of NATO (other than the United States) in Europe at the end of a fiscal year.

(c) BASELINE REPORT ON ACTIVE-DUTY FORCES IN EUROPE.—(1) Not later than 60 days after the date of the enactment of this Act, the Secretary of Defense shall submit to the congressional defense committees, the Committee on Foreign Relations of the Senate, and the Committee on Foreign Affairs of the House of Representatives a report on the number of the active-duty forces in Europe of the member nations of NATO. The report shall identify the following:

(1) The U.S. end-strength level in Europe for fiscal year 1989.

(2) The allied forces end-strength level in Europe for fiscal year 1989.

(3) The actual number of active-duty forces in Europe of the armed forces of each member nation of NATO (other than the United States) at the end of fiscal year 1989.

(4) The ratio (expressed in terms of a percentage) of—

(A) the U.S. end-strength level in Europe; to

(B) the allied forces end-strength level in Europe.

(d) U.S.-ALLIED FORCES RATIO.—(1) The ratio identified for fiscal year 1989 under subsection (c)(4) is hereinafter in this section referred to as the "baseline U.S.-allied forces ratio".

(2) The ratio identified in an annual report under subsection (e) is hereinafter in this section referred to as the "U.S.-allied forces ratio".

(e) ANNUAL REPORT ON MAINTAINING ACTIVE-DUTY FORCES IN EUROPE.—(1) During each of the fiscal years 1991, 1992, and 1993, the Secretary of Defense shall prepare a report identifying for the preceding fiscal year the following:

(A) The U.S. end-strength level in Europe for the fiscal year covered by the report.

(B) The allied forces end-strength level in Europe for such fiscal year.

(C) The ratio (expressed in terms of a percentage) of the U.S. end-strength level in Europe to the allied forces end-strength level in Europe for the fiscal year covered by the report.

(2) The Secretary shall include in each such report the following:

(A) A statement of whether there has been any change in the U.S.-allied forces ratio for such fiscal year compared with—

(i) the baseline U.S.-allied forces ratio; and

(ii) after fiscal year 1991, the U.S-allied forces ratio for the fiscal year immediately preceding the fiscal year covered by such report.

(B) In the case of a change in the U.S.-allied forces ratio for such fiscal year, a description of the amount of such change and any explanation of the cause for such change.

(C) A discussion of any action taken by the United States during such fiscal year to encourage member nations of NATO (other than the United States) to increase the number of their active-duty forces in Europe and the results of that action.

(3)(A) Except as provided in subparagraph (B), the report required by paragraph (1) shall be submitted to the congressional defense committees, the Committee on Foreign Relations of the Senate, and the Committee on Foreign Affairs of the House of Representatives not later than April 1 of each fiscal year referred to in such paragraph.

(B) The Secretary shall be considered to have complied with subparagraph (A) in a fiscal year if the Secretary includes the information required by paragraphs (1) and (2) in the report submitted in such year pursuant to section 1002(d)(2) of the Department of Defense Authorization Act, 1985 (22 U.S.C. 1928 note).

(f) LIMITATION ON OBLIGATION OF FUNDS.—(1) If the Secretary of Defense states in a report prepared under subsection (e) that the U.S.-allied forces ratio for the fiscal year covered by such report is greater than the baseline U.S.-allied forces ratio by more than one-tenth of one percentage point—

(A) the President shall undertake appropriate diplomatic initiatives to persuade the member nations of NATO (other than the United States) to increase the number of their active-duty forces in Europe so that the U.S.-allied forces ratio no longer exceeds the baseline U.S.-allied forces ratio; and

(B) funds appropriated to or for the use of the Department of Defense may not be obligated or expended for the next fiscal year to support active-duty forces in Europe of the Armed Forces of the United States at an end-strength level that would cause the U.S-allied forces ratio in such fiscal year to exceed the baseline U.S.-allied forces ratio by more than one-tenth of one percentage point.

(2) The President may waive the provisions of paragraph (1) if the President determines that such action is critical to the national security of the United States. The President shall immediately notify Congress of such a waiver and the reasons for such waiver.

(3) Paragraph (1) shall not apply in the event of a declaration of war or an armed attack on any member nation of NATO or in the event that a comprehensive arms reduction agreement enters into force as a result of the negotiations on Conventional Armed Forces in Europe (CFE).

(g) END-STRENGTH PERMANENT CEILING.—Nothing in this section shall be construed to permit the obligation or expenditure of funds to support an end-strength level of members of the Armed Forces of the United States assigned to permanent duty ashore in European member nations of NATO at any level in excess of the permanent ceiling specified in section 1002(c)(1) of the Department of Defense Authorization Act, 1985 (22 U.S.C. 1928 note).

SEC. 913. CONTRIBUTIONS BY JAPAN TO GLOBAL SECURITY

(a) FINDINGS.—Congress finds—

(1) that extraordinary political, economic, and social changes have occurred in Japan since World War II; and

(2) that, as a result of such changes, Japan is capable of assuming increased responsibility for its own security.

(b) SENSE OF CONGRESS.—It is the sense of Congress that, in view of the changes referred to in subsection (a), Japan should—

(1) assume increased responsibility for its own security;

(2) offset the direct costs incurred by the United States in deploying military forces for the defense of Japan, including costs (other than pay and allowances) related to the presence of United States military personnel in Japan; and

(3) make a contribution to the common defense that is more commensurate with its economic status by taking the following actions:

(A) Increasing expenditures for its Official Development Assistance program and its defense programs so that, by

1992, the level of spending by Japan on those programs (stated as a percentage of gross national product) will approximate the average of the levels of spending by the member nations of the North Atlantic Treaty Organization (NATO) on official development assistance and defense programs (stated as a percentage of their respective gross national products).

(B) Devoting any increase in its spending for such Official Development Assistance program primarily to the Republic of the Philippines and to countries in regions of importance to global stability outside of East Asia, particularly to countries in Latin America, the Caribbean area, and the Mediterranean area.

(C) Devoting any increase in spending for that program primarily to untied grants and increasing the portion of total expenditures made in that program for those multilateral financial institutions of which Japan is a member.

(D) Designating those nations that are to be recipients of increased development assistance referred to in subparagraphs (A) through (C) after consultation with Japan's security partners.

(E) Completing, after consultation with the United States, the 5-year defense program of Japan for fiscal years 1986 through 1990 and, at the earliest possible date after the completion of that program, fulfilling the pledge made by the Prime Minister of Japan in May 1981 to defend the territory, airspace, and sea lanes of Japan to a distance of 1,000 nautical miles.

(F) Acquiring "off-the-shelf" military equipment from the United States (including completely equipped, long-range early warning aircraft, additional AEGIS weapon systems, refueling aircraft, munitions, and spare parts) in developing the capabilities called for in Japan's current and subsequent 5-year defense programs.

(c) NEGOTIATIONS AND CONSULTATIONS.—At the earliest practicable date after the enactment of this Act, the President shall—

(1) enter into negotiations with Japan for the purpose of achieving an agreement under which Japan agrees to make contributions sufficient in value to meet the direct cost of deploying United States forces for the defense of Japan; and

(2) issue an invitation to the Government of Japan and other governments of Pacific allies of the United States to engage in annual multilateral consultations on security concerns, consistent with the constitutions and national defense requirements of the respective countries.

(d) REPORTS.—(1) In order that Congress may determine whether further action is appropriate, not later than April 1, 1990, the President shall submit to the congressional committees described in paragraph (3) an initial report on the status and results of—

(A) the negotiations with Japan referred to in subsection (c)(1); and

(B) the invitation required under subsection (c)(2), including any consultations resulting from such invitation.

(2) Not later than one year after the date of the enactment of this Act, the President shall submit to such congressional committees a second report on the status and results of the matters referred to in paragraph (1).

(3) The congressional committees referred to in this subsection are the congressional defense committees, the Committee on Foreign Relations of the Senate, and the Committee on Foreign Affairs of the House of Representatives.

SEC. 915. UNITED STATES-REPUBLIC OF KOREA SECURITY RELATIONSHIP AND OTHER SECURITY MATTERS IN EAST ASIA

(a) FINDINGS.—Congress makes the following findings:

(1) Since the end of the Korean conflict, the Republic of Korea has made tremendous progress in rebuilding its economic and military strength.

(2) Despite this progress, an indigenous military balance has not yet been achieved on the Korean peninsula, and the Democratic People's Republic of Korea continues to pose a serious threat to the security of the Republic of Korea.

(3) The alliance between the United States and the Republic of Korea has contributed greatly to the security of both countries.

(4) The Republic of Korea has dedicated a large share of its national resources to its security, as shown by the fact that defense expenditures comprise approximately one-third of the national budget of the Republic of Korea.

(5) The United States has contributed a large amount of national resources, including approximately 44,000 military personnel, to protecting the security interests that it shares with the Republic of Korea.

(6) The presence of United States military personnel in the Republic of Korea contributes to the preservation of peace on the Korean peninsula, serves as a military deterrent, and is a tangible manifestation of the commitment of the United States to the defense of the Republic of Korea.

(7) In accordance with its obligations under the 1954 Mutual Defense Treaty with the Republic of Korea, the United States remains committed to the security and territorial integrity of the Republic of Korea.

(b) SENSE OF CONGRESS ON THE UNITED STATES-REPUBLIC OF KOREA SECURITY RELATIONSHIP.—(1) It is the sense of Congress that—

(A) the United States should review the missions, force structure, and locations of its military forces in the Republic of Korea and East Asia;

(B) the Republic of Korea should assume increased responsibility for its own security;

(C) the Republic of Korea should offset more of the direct costs incurred by the United States in deploying military forces for the defense of the Republic of Korea; and

(D) the United States and the Republic of Korea should consult on the feasibility and desirability of partial, gradual reductions of United States military forces in the Republic of Korea.

(2) In order that Congress may determine whether further action is appropriate, not later than April 1, 1990, the President shall submit to the congressional committees described in subsection (d) an initial report on the status and results of any consultations held by the United States and the Republic of Korea on the matter referred to in paragraph (1)(D).

(3) Not later than one year after the date of the enactment of this Act, the President shall submit to such congressional committees a second report on the status and results of the consultations referred to in paragraph (1)(D).

(c) REPORT ON MILITARY PRESENCE IN EAST ASIA.—(1) Not later than April 1, 1990, the President shall submit to the congressional committees described in subsection (d) a report on the military presence of the United States in East Asia, including the Republic of Korea. The President shall include in such report a strategic plan relating to the continued United States military presence in East Asia.

(2) The report required by this subsection shall specifically include the following:

(A) An assessment of the implications of recent developments in the Soviet Union and the People's Republic of China for United States and allied security planning in East Asia.

(B) Identification of any changes in the missions, force structure, and locations of United States forces in East Asia that could strengthen the capabilities of such forces and lower the costs of maintaining such forces.

(C) A discussion of ways in which increased defense responsibilities and costs presently borne by the United States can be transferred to the allies of the United States in East Asia.

(D) Identification of the additional actions that the Republic of Korea can take to contribute more to its own security.

(E) A discussion of the feasibility of restructuring United States military forces stationed in Okinawa with the objective of improving civil-military relations and increasing United States training opportunities.

(F) A discussion of the status and prospects of negotiations between the United States and the Republic of the Philippines on the continued use of United States military installations in the Republic of the Philippines.

(G) An assessment of whether a requirement still exists for a regional security role for United States forces stationed in the Republic of Korea.

(3) The report required by this subsection shall also include a five-year plan with respect to the United States military presence in the Republic of Korea, including a discussion of the feasibility and desirability of the following:

(A) Partial, gradual reductions in the number of United States military personnel stationed in the Republic of Korea.

(B) Larger offsets by the Republic of Korea for the direct costs incurred by the United States in deploying military forces in defense of the Republic of Korea.

(C) The relocation of United States military personnel and facilities within the Republic of Korea that can be made to reduce friction between such personnel and the people of the Republic of Korea.

(D) Changes in the United Nations and United States-Republic of Korea bilateral command arrangements that would facilitate a transfer of certain military missions and command to the Republic of Korea.

(E) Confidence-building measures that could be promoted in northeast Asia to lessen tensions in the region.

(F) Additional actions the Republic of Korea could take to assume more responsibility for its own security.

(d) CONGRESSIONAL COMMITTEES TO RECEIVE REPORTS.—The congressional committees referred to in this section are the congressional defense committees, the Committee on Foreign Relations of the Senate, and the Committee on Foreign Affairs of the House of Representatives.

PART C—EXPENDITURES IN EUROPE

SEC. 922. SENSE OF CONGRESS CONCERNING UNITED STATES MILITARY FACILITIES IN NATO MEMBER COUNTRIES

(a) NATO POLICY.—It is the sense of Congress that the North Atlantic Treaty Organization (NATO) should adopt as its policy the following views expressed by the North Atlantic Assembly in its 1987 report entitled "NATO in the 1990s":

(1) The member nations of NATO should examine further measures that could be taken to relieve the United States from the burdens of its military presence in Europe.

(2) Such nations should consider the provision of base facilities for allied forces and equipment as a part of their national contributions to Western security.

(3) Such nations should not expect compensation for providing facilities that the NATO alliance decides are essential to implement NATO security strategy.

(4) All wealthier member nations of NATO should assist Portugal, Greece, and Turkey to ensure that NATO remains politically, economically, and militarily strong in its southern region as well as in its central and northern regions.

(b) UNITED STATES PAYMENT FOR USE OF BASE FACILITIES IN NATO COUNTRIES.—It is further the sense of Congress that the United

TITLE X—MATTERS RELATING TO ARMS CONTROL

SEC. 1001. PRESIDENTIAL REPORT ON POSSIBLE EFFECTS OF A STRATEGIC ARMS REDUCTION AGREEMENT ON TRIDENT PROGRAM

(a) REPORT.—Not later than April 1, 1990, the President shall submit to Congress a comprehensive report on the Trident program under a possible Strategic Arms Reduction Talks (START) agreement. The report shall address the following issues:

(1) The objective for the size of the Trident submarine force fleet both with and without a START agreement.

(2) The implications for United States strategic force posture under a START agreement of a fleet of 21 or more Trident submarines, each with 192 warheads on 24 ballistic missiles, under two different assumptions, as follows:

(A) All such warheads are accountable under START limits.

(B) The warheads on one-to-three Trident submarines are not accountable under START limits.

(3) A net assessment of the implications for United States security of a START agreement that allows the Soviet Union as well as the United States to have an equivalent number of warheads on submarines that are not accountable under START limits.

States should not provide economic or security assistance to any NATO member nation as compensation or rent for the use of base facilities in that nation.

(4) The technical feasibility and cost implications of various options for reducing the number of warheads on Trident submarines, including those submarines already built, those under construction, and those yet to be built.

(5) The verification challenges to the United States posed by such options if the Soviet Union were to adopt them in its ballistic missile submarine forces.

(b) FORM OF REPORT.—The President shall submit the report under subsection (a) in both classified and unclassified versions.

(c) WAIVER.—The President may waive the requirements of subsection (a) if he has signed a START agreement or other strategic arms reduction agreement with the Soviet Union before the date by which the report is otherwise required to be submitted.

SEC. 1002. PRESIDENTIAL REPORT ON THE VERIFICATION WORK THAT HAS BEEN CONDUCTED WITH REGARD TO MOBILE ICBMs UNDER A START AGREEMENT

(a) FINDINGS.—Congress makes the following findings:

(1) The United States must have confidence that any agreement achieved through the Strategic Arms Limitation Talks (START) in Geneva will be effectively verifiable.

(2) The position of the United States at the START negotiations, from 1985 until September 1989, was to ban the deployment of mobile intercontinental ballistic missiles (ICBMs) under a START regime unless an effective verification regime could be identified and implemented. In September 1989, the United States announced that it was withdrawing its proposal for the ban of mobile ICBMs, contingent upon Congress providing funds for mobile ICBMs to be deployed by the United States.

(3) The Soviet Union has deployed two mobile ICBM systems, the SS-24 and the SS-25.

(4) The President conducted a strategic review during the period between January 20, 1989, and the resumption of the START negotiations on June 15, 1989.

(b) PRESIDENTIAL REPORT.—Not later than March 31, 1990, the President shall submit to Congress a report (in classified and unclassified form) describing all studies that have been performed between March 1985 and August 1989 by agencies of the United States Government with regard to the capability of the United States to monitor and verify a START agreement which allows mobile ICBMs. The report shall include the following:

(1) A description of each study conducted by United States Government agencies during the strategic review referred to in subsection (a)(4) to determine the ability of the United States to verify limitations on mobile ICBMs of the Soviet Union under a START agreement, including a summary of the conclusions reached under each such study.

(2) A description of any so-called "Red Team" study conducted between March 1985 and August 1989 with regard to the existence of mobile ICBMs under a START regime, including a summary of the conclusions reached under each such study

(3) A description of each study conducted by United States Government agencies between March 1989 and August 1989 to assess the value of various options relating to the verification of mobile ICBMs (such options to include the option known as "tagging" and the establishment of designated deployment

areas), including a summary of the conclusions reached under each such study.

SEC. 1003. SENSE OF CONGRESS ON START TALKS

Congress hereby reaffirms the sense of Congress expressed in the second session of the 100th Congress (in section 902 of the National Defense Authorization Act, Fiscal Year 1989 (Public Law 100–456; 102 Stat. 2031)) that any agreement negotiated by the President to achieve a reduction and limitation on strategic arms (through the Strategic Arms Reduction Talks in Geneva or otherwise)—

(1) should not prevent the United States from deploying a force structure under the agreement which emphasizes survivable strategic systems and, in particular, should not in any way compromise the security of the United States ballistic-missile carrying submarine force; and

(2) should not prohibit or limit the deployment of non-nuclear cruise missiles.

SEC. 1004. REPORT ON ASYMMETRIES IN CAPABILITIES OF UNITED STATES AND SOVIET UNION TO PRODUCE AND DEPLOY BALLISTIC MISSILE DEFENSE SYSTEMS

(a) STUDY REQUIRED.—The Secretary of Defense shall conduct a study on the asymmetry in the near-term capabilities of the United States and the Soviet Union to deploy ballistic missile defenses beyond those permitted under the 1972 ABM Treaty. The study shall be conducted in coordination with the Director of Central Intelligence.

(b) MATTERS TO BE INCLUDED IN STUDY.—Subject to subsection (e), the study shall include the following:

(1) An assessment of the likelihood of a breakout by the Soviet Union from the 1972 ABM Treaty in the next five years and the assumptions used for that assessment.

(2) An assessment of the capability of the Soviet Union to exploit a situation in which the limitations of the 1972 ABM Treaty do not apply, including a detailed assessment of the capabilities of the Soviet Union to produce—

(A) space-based anti-ballistic missile (ABM) launchers and interceptors;

(B) ground-based ABM launchers and interceptors; and

(C) the infrastructure for ABM battle management command, control, and communications.

(3) An assessment of the production base of the United States for production of the elements specified in subparagraphs (A), (B), and (C) of paragraph (2), including an estimate of how quickly the United States could respond to a breakout by the Soviet Union in each of those elements.

(c) STUDY TO ASSESS POSSIBLE UNITED STATES RESPONSE TO SOVIET BREAKOUT.—(1) The study shall also include an assessment of the immediate and long-term actions that could be taken by the United States to respond to redress any asymmetry in the potential of the United States and the Soviet Union to exploit a breakout by the Soviet Union from the 1972 ABM Treaty.

(2) That assessment shall include an evaluation of the actions that would be necessary to support—

(A) a one-site ABM system (as allowed under the Treaty); or

(B) an expanded ABM system unconstrained by the limitations of the 1972 ABM Treaty.

(3) Such assessment shall specifically address the required actions, and the costs associated with those actions, to support both the one-site ABM system and the expanded ABM system to be evaluated under paragraph (2), including (A) the upgrading and expansion of the existing United States radar network, (B) the use of existing inactive ABM components at Grand Forks, North Dakota, and (C) the development and deployment of other required components.

(d) REPORT.—Not later than the date on which the budget for fiscal year 1991 is submitted to Congress pursuant to section 1105 of title 31, United States Code, the Secretary of Defense shall submit to Congress a report on the study under subsection (a). The report shall be submitted in both classified and unclassified form. The report shall specify the results of the study under subsection (a), including each matter required to be included in the study under this section.

(e) WAIVER OF REQUIRED STUDY FEATURE.—The study under subsection (a) need not include the assessment referred to in subsection (b)(1) if, before the date of the submission of the report required by subsection (d) with respect to the study, the President submits to Congress the report required by section 907 of the National Defense Authorization Act, Fiscal Year 1989 (Public Law 100–456; 102 Stat. 2034), regarding antiballistic missile capabilities and activities of the Soviet Union (such report having been required by subsection (c) of such section to be submitted not later than January 1, 1989).

(f) 1972 ABM TREATY DEFINED.—For purposes of this section, the term "1972 ABM Treaty" means the Treaty Between the United States of America and the Union of Soviet Socialist Republics on the Limitations of Anti-Ballistic Missiles, signed at Moscow on May 26, 1972.

SEC. 1005. SENSE OF THE CONGRESS WITH RESPECT TO ACCIDENTAL LAUNCH PROTECTION

(a) FINDINGS.—Congress makes the following findings:

(1) The Strategic Defense Initiative (SDI) has made substantial progress in developing technologies to defend the United States from a possible ballistic missile attack, be it deliberate or accidental.

(2) Ground-based elements and their associated adjuncts and technologies represent the most mature technologies within the SDI program and should therefore receive priority by the Strategic Defense Initiative Organization.

(3) The United States is a signatory to the 1972 Anti-Ballistic Missile Treaty.

(4) There have been several accidents involving ballistic missiles, including the loss of a submarine of the Soviet Union due to inadvertent missile ignition and the inadvertent landing in China of a test missile of the Soviet Union.

(5) The continued proliferation of offensive ballistic missile forces by non-superpower countries hostile to the United States and our allies raises the possibility of future nuclear threats.

(b) REAFFIRMATION OF SENSE OF CONGRESS.—Congress hereby reaffirms the sense of Congress expressed in section 224(b) of the National Defense Authorization Act, Fiscal Year 1989 (Public Law 100–456; 102 Stat. 1942) stating—

(1) that the Secretary of Defense should direct the Strategic Defense Initiative Organization to give priority to development of technologies and systems for a system capable of protecting

the United States from the accidental launch of a strategic ballistic missile against the continental United States; and

(2) that such development of an accidental launch protection system should be carried out with an objective of ensuring that such system is in compliance with the 1972 Anti-Ballistic Missile Treaty.

(c) SUBMISSION OF PREVIOUSLY REQUIRED REPORT.—The Secretary of Defense shall submit to Congress forthwith the report on the status of planning for development of a deployment option for such an accidental launch protection system that was required by section 224(c) of that Act to be submitted not later than March 1, 1989.

SEC. 1006. CONGRESSIONAL FINDINGS AND SENSE OF CONGRESS CONCERNING THE KRASNOYARSK RADAR

(a) REAFFIRMATION OF PRIOR FINDINGS.—Congress hereby reaffirms the findings made with respect to the large phased-array radar of the Soviet Union known as the "Krasnoyarsk radar" in paragraphs (1) through (6) of section 902(a) of the National Defense Authorization Act for Fiscal Years 1988 and 1989 (Public Law 100–180; 101 Stat. 1135), as follows:

(1) The 1972 Anti-Ballistic Missile Treaty prohibits each party from deploying ballistic missile early warning radars except at locations along the periphery of its national territory and oriented outward.

(2) The 1972 Anti-Ballistic Missile Treaty prohibits each party from deploying an ABM system to defend its national territory and from providing a base for any such nationwide defense.

(3) Large phased-array radars were recognized during negotiation of the Anti-Ballistic Missile Treaty as the critical long lead-time element of a nationwide defense against ballistic missiles.

(4) In 1983 the United States discovered the construction, in the interior of the Soviet Union near the town of Krasnoyarsk, of a large phased-array radar that has subsequently been judged to be for ballistic early warning and tracking.

(5) The Krasnoyarsk radar is more than 700 kilometers from the Soviet-Mongolian border and is not directed outward but instead faces the northeast Soviet border more than 4,500 kilometers away.

(6) The Krasnoyarsk radar is identical to other Soviet ballistic missile early warning radars and is ideally situated to fill the gap that would otherwise exist in a nationwide Soviet ballistic missile early warning radar network.

(b) FURTHER FINDINGS.—In addition to the findings referred to in subsection (a), Congress finds with respect to the Krasnoyarsk radar that—

(1) in 1987 the President declared that radar to be a clear violation of the 1972 Anti-Ballistic Missile Treaty;

(2) until the meeting between the Secretary of State and the Foreign Minister of the Soviet Union at Jackson Hole, Wyoming, in September 1989, the Soviet Union had rejected demands by the United States that it dismantle that radar without conditions, but the joint statment issued following that meeting states that the government of the Soviet Union "had decided to completely dismantle the Krasnoyarsk radar station"; and

(3) on October 23, 1989, the Foreign Minister of the Soviet Union conceded that the Krasnoyarsk radar is a violation of the 1972 Anti-Ballistic Missile Treaty.

(c) SENSE OF CONGRESS.—It is the sense of Congress—

(1) that the Soviet Union should dismantle the Krasnoyarsk radar (as announced in the joint statement referred to in subsection (b)(2)) expeditiously and without conditions; and

(2) that until such radar is completely dismantled it will remain a clear violation of the 1972 Anti-Ballistic Missile Treaty.

SEC. 1007. SENSE OF CONGRESS CONCERNING EXPLORING THE FEASIBILITY OF TREATY LIMITATIONS ON WEAPONS CAPABLE OF THREATENING MILITARY SATELLITES

It is the sense of Congress that, as soon as practicable, the President should explore the feasibility of a mutual and verifiable treaty with the Soviet Union which places the strictest possible limitations, consistent with the security interests of the United States and its allies, on the development, testing, production, and deployment of weapons capable of directly threatening United States military satellites.

SEC. 1008. REPORT ON SATELLITE SURVIVABILITY

(a) REQUIREMENT FOR REPORT.—The President shall submit to Congress a comprehensive report on United States antisatellite weapon activities and the survivability of United States satellites against current and potential antisatellite weapons deployed by the Soviet Union. The report shall be submitted by March 15, 1990, and shall be submitted in both classified and unclassified versions.

(b) MATTERS TO BE INCLUDED IN REPORT.—The report required by subsection (a) shall include the following:

(1) Detailed information (including funding profiles, expected capabilities, and schedules for development, testing, and deployment) on all United States antisatellite weapon programs.

(2) An analysis of the antisatellite potential of the anticipated deployed version of each Strategic Defense Initiative technology capable of damaging or destroying objects in space.

(3) An assessment of the threat that would be posed to satellites of the United States if the technologies described in paragraphs (1) and (2) were to be tested by the Soviet Union, at levels of performance equal to those intended by the United States, and developed into weapons for damaging or destroying objects in space.

(4) A review of arms control options and satellite survivability measures (including cost data) that would improve the survivability of current and future United States military satellite systems.

(5) A review of alternative means of providing the support to military forces of the United States that is currently provided by United States satellites if those satellites become vulnerable to attack as the result of the deployment by the Soviet Union of antisatellite weapons with the levels of performance contemplated in paragraph (3).

SEC. 1009. REPORT ON THE DESIRABILITY OF NEGOTIATIONS WITH THE SOVIET UNION REGARDING LIMITATIONS ON ANTISATELLITE CAPABILITIES

(a) REPORT BY THE PRESIDENT.—The President shall submit to Congress a comprehensive report regarding the desirability of an agreement with the Soviet Union to impose limitations on antisatellite capabilities. The President shall include in such report his determination of whether a ban or other limitations on some or all antisatellite weapons would be verifiable and, if so, whether such a ban or other limitation would be in the national interest of the United States.

(b) MATTERS RELATING TO VERIFICATION.—In making the determination referred to in subsection (a), the President shall—

(1) consider the extent to which on-site inspection measures (as well as national technical means for verification) can increase confidence in the ability of the United States to monitor and verify various agreed-upon antisatellite limitations; and

(2) examine various arms control possibilities, including—

(A) a total ban on antisatellite capability by both the United States and the Soviet Union;

(B) a ban or other limitation on antisatellite weapons with the potential to attack satellites at altitudes above the Van Allen belt; and

(C) a ban or other limitation on antisatellite weapons that operate only in low-Earth orbit.

(c) MATTERS RELATING TO DETERRENCE AND WAR FIGHTING REQUIREMENTS.—In the report required by subsection (a), the President shall also address the following:

(1) The contribution an antisatellite capability of the United States can make toward enhancing deterrence.

(2) The contribution an antisatellite capability can make toward meeting the war fighting requirements of the United States and how such a capability enhances force survivability.

(3) The extent to which (based upon a net assessment) the United States would be better able to meet its war fighting requirements and deterrence objectives if—

(A) the Soviet Union possessed an antisatellite capability and the United States did not possess an antisatellite capability;

(B) neither the United States nor the Soviet Union possessed an antisatellite capability;

(C) the United States and the Soviet Union both possessed a limited antisatellite capability;

(D) the United States and the Soviet Union both possessed an unrestricted antisatellite capability.

(d) SUBMISSION OF REPORT.—The report required by subsection (a) shall be submitted to Congress not later than May 1, 1990, and shall be submitted in both classified and unclassified versions.

SEC. 1010. REPORT ON VERIFICATION OF COMPLIANCE WITH AGREEMENTS TO LIMIT NUCLEAR TESTING

(a) REPORT REQUIREMENT.—The Secretary of Energy shall prepare a report, in classified form, assessing the possible effects on the abilities of the United States to verify compliance by the Soviet Union with any agreement (presently in effect or under negotiation) to limit testing of nuclear devices should any information or data now obtained under any cooperative agreement with any controlled country and used to verify the degree of such compliance be curtailed or become unavailable due to a change in, or severing of, diplomatic relations with such a controlled country. The report shall assess, in particular, whether compliance by the Soviet Union with any such agreement to limit testing of nuclear devices can be fully and reliably verified should such a cooperative agreement be curtailed or terminated. The report shall be prepared in consultation with the Secretary of Defense.

(b) SUBMISSION OF REPORT.—The report prepared under subsection (a) shall be submitted to Congress not later than six months after the date of the enactment of this Act.

(c) CONTROLLED COUNTRY DEFINITION.—For purposes of this section, the term "controlled country" means a country listed in section 620(f)(1) of the Foreign Assistance Act of 1961 (22 U.S.C. 2370(f)(1)).

SEC. 1011. SENSE OF CONGRESS ON ARMS CONTROL NEGOTIATIONS AND UNITED STATES MODERNIZATION POLICY

(a) FINDINGS.—Congress makes the following findings:

(1) The United States is currently engaged in a wide range of arms control negotiations in the areas of strategic nuclear forces, strategic defenses, conventional force levels, chemical weapons, and security and confidence building measures.

(2) On May 30, 1989, the North Atlantic Treaty Organization issued a "Comprehensive Concept on Arms Control and Disarmament" which placed a special emphasis on arms control as a means of enhancing security and stability in Europe.

(3) The President has stated that arms control is one of the highest priorities of the United States in the area of security and foreign policy and that the United States will pursue a dynamic, active arms control dialogue with the Soviet Union and the other Warsaw Pact countries.

(4) The United States has already made major proposals at the Conventional Forces in Europe Talks, convened on March 6, 1989, which would result in a dramatic reduction in Soviet and Warsaw Pact conventional forces.

(5) The President, on September 25, 1989, made a major new arms control proposal in the area of chemical weapons.

(b) SENSE OF CONGRESS.—It is the sense of Congress that—

(1) the President is to be commended for pursuing a wide array of arms control initiatives in the context of a multitude of arms control negotiations, all of which have been designed to enhance global security and result in meaningful, militarily significant reductions in military forces;

(2) Congress fully supports the arms control efforts of the President and encourages the government of the Soviet Union to respond favorably to United States arms control proposals which would require the Soviet Union to reduce its massive quantitative superiority in military weaponry;

(3) the President should seek arms control agreements that would not limit the United States to levels of forces inferior to the limits provided for the Soviet Union; and

(4) the President's efforts to negotiate such agreements is dependent upon the maintenance of a vigorous research and development and modernization program as required for a prudent defense posture.

(c) REAFFIRMATION OF PROHIBITION RELATING TO ENTERING INTO CERTAIN ARMS CONTROL AGREEMENTS.—Congress hereby reaffirms the proviso in the first sentence of section 33 of the Arms Control and Disarmament Act (22 U.S.C. 2573) that no action may be taken under that Act or any other Act that will obligate the United States to disarm or to reduce or limit the Armed Forces or armaments of the United States, except pursuant to the treatymaking power of the President under the Constitution or unless authorized by further affirmative legislation by the Congress.

SEC. 1012. REPORT ON EFFECT OF SPACE NUCLEAR REACTORS ON GAMMA-RAY ASTRONOMY MISSIONS

Not later than April 30, 1990, the President shall submit to Congress a report on the potential for interference with gamma-ray astronomy missions that could be caused by the placement in Earth orbit of space nuclear reactors.

SEC. 1013. SENSE OF CONGRESS ON CHEMICAL WEAPONS NEGOTIATIONS

(a) FINDINGS.—Congress makes the following findings:

(1) The proliferation of chemical weapons and the repeated use of chemical weapons represent a grave threat to the security and interests of the United States.

(2) The most comprehensive and effective response to the threat posed by the proliferation of chemical weapons is the completion of an effectively verifiable treaty banning the production and stockpiling of all chemical weapons.

(3) The successful completion of a treaty banning all chemical weapons through the negotiations at the multinational United Nations Conference on Disarmament in Geneva should be one of the highest arms control priorities of the United States.

(b) SENSE OF CONGRESS.—In light of the findings in subsection (a), it is the sense of Congress that—

(1) the President should continue ongoing efforts to establish an agreement with the Soviet Union and other countries establishing a mutual and effectively verifiable agreement to stop the production, proliferation, and stockpiling of all lethal chemical weapons; and

(2) the United States negotiators in Geneva should take concrete steps to initiate proposals regarding the composition of the verification regime for such an agreeement that will meet the legitimate concerns of other parties while addressing the security concerns of the United States.

SEC. 1014. UNITED STATES PROGRAM FOR ON-SITE INSPECTIONS UNDER ARMS CONTROL AGREEMENTS

(a) FINDINGS CONCERNING ON-SITE INSPECTION PERSONNEL.—Congress makes the following findings:

(1) The United States is currently engaged in multilateral and bilateral negotiations seeking to achieve treaties or agreements to reduce or eliminate various types of military weapons and to make certain reductions in military personnel levels. These negotiations include negotiations for (A) reductions in strategic forces, conventional armaments, and military personnel levels, (B) regimes for monitoring nuclear testing, and (C) the complete elimination of chemical weapons.

(2) Requirements for monitoring these possible treaties or agreements will be extensive and will place severe stress on the monitoring capabilities of United States national technical means.

(3) In the case of the INF Treaty, the United States and the Soviet Union negotiated, and are currently using, on-site inspection procedures to complement and support monitoring by national technical means. Similar on-site inspection procedures are being negotiated for inclusion in possible future treaties and agreements referred to in paragraph (1).

(4) During initial implementation of the provisions of the INF Treaty, the United States was not fully prepared for the personnel requirements for the conduct of on-site inspections. The Director of Central Intelligence has stated that on-site inspection requirements for any strategic arms reduction treaty or agreement will be far more extensive than those for the INF Treaty. The number of locations within the Soviet Union that would possibly be subject to on-site inspections under a START agreement have been estimated to be approximately 2,500 (compared to 120 for the INF Treaty).

(5) On-site inspection procedures are likely to be an integral part of any future arms control treaty or agreement.

(6) Personnel requirements will be extensive for such on-site inspection procedures, both in terms of numbers of personnel and technical and linguistic skills. Since verification requirements for the INF Treaty are already placing severe stress on current personnel resources, the requirements for verification under START and other possible future treaties and agreements may quickly exceed the current number of verification personnel having necessary technical and language skills.

(7) There is a clear need for a database of the names of individuals who are members of the Armed Forces or civilian employees of the United States Government, or of other citizens and nationals of the United States, who are qualified (by reason of technical or language skills) to participate in on-site inspections under an arms control treaty or agreement.

(8) The organization best suited to establish such a database is the On-Site Inspection Agency (OSIA) of the Department of Defense, which was created by the President to implement (for the United States) the on-site inspection provisions of the INF Treaty.

(b) STATUS OF THE OSIA.—(1) Congress finds that—

(A) the Director of the OSIA (currently a brigadier general of the Army) is appointed by the Secretary of Defense with the concurrence of the Secretary of State and the approval of the President;

(B) the Secretary of Defense provides to the Director appropriate policy guidance formulated by the interagency arms control mechanism established by the President;

(C) most of the personnel of the OSIA are members of the Armed Forces (who are trained and paid by the military departments within the Department of Defense) and include linguists, weapons specialists, and foreign area specialists;

(D) the Department of Defense provides the OSIA with substantially all of its administrative and logistic support (including military air transportation for inspections in the Soviet Union and Eastern Europe); and

(E) the facilities in Europe and the United States at which OSIA personnel escort personnel of the Soviet Union conducting inspections under the on-site inspection terms of the INF Treaty are under the jurisdiction of the Department of Defense (or under the jurisdiction of entities that are contractors with the Department of Defense).

(2) In light of the findings in paragraph (1) and the report submitted pursuant to section 909 of Public Law 100–456 entitled "Report to the Congress on U.S. Monitoring and Verification Activities Related to the INF Treaty" (submitted on July 27, 1989), Congress hereby determines that by locating the On-Site Inspection Agency within the Department of Defense for the purposes of administrative and logistic support and operational guidance, and integrating on-site inspection responsibilities under the INF Treaty with existing organizational activities of that Department, the President has been able to ensure that sensitive national security assets are protected and that obligations of the United States under that treaty are fulfilled in an efficient and cost-effective manner.

(c) ESTABLISHMENT OF PERSONNEL DATABASE.—(1) In light of the findings in subsection (a), the Director of the On-Site Inspection Agency shall establish a database consisting of the names of individuals who could be assigned or detailed (in the case of Government personnel) or employed (in the case of non-Government personnel) to participate in the conduct of on-site inspections under any future arms control treaty or agreement that includes provisions for such inspections.

(2) The database should be composed of the names of individuals with skills (including linguistic and technical skills) necessary for the conduct of on-site inspections.

(d) INF TREATY DEFINED.—For purposes of this section, the term "INF Treaty" means the Treaty Between the United States and the Union of Soviet Socialist Republics on the Elimination of Their Intermediate-Range and Shorter-Range Missiles, signed in Washington, DC, on December 8, 1987.

TITLE XI—DEPARTMENT OF DEFENSE ORGANIZATION AND MANAGEMENT MATTERS

PART A—FORCE STRUCTURE

SEC. 1101. STUDY OF TOTAL FORCE POLICY, FORCE MIX, AND MILITARY FORCE STRUCTURE

(a) FINDINGS.—Congress makes the following findings:

(1) Since the inception of the Total Force Policy in the Department of Defense in 1973, there has never been a comprehensive, authoritative study done by the Department on the operation and effectiveness of that policy.

(2) Decisions within the Department of Defense with respect to military force mix appear to be made in a fragmented and decentralized manner.

(3) A comprehensive study of the Total Force Policy, force mix, and military force structure is long overdue.

(b) STUDY.—(1) The Secretary of Defense shall convene a study group to review the operation, effectiveness, and soundness of the following policies and practices of the Department of Defense and to make recommendations to the Secretary for improvement of those policies and practices:

(A) The Total Force Policy.

(B) Assignment of missions within and between the active and reserve components of the armed forces.

(C) Force structure of the active and reserve components of the armed forces.

(2) The study group shall include—

(A) senior-level active-duty officers from each branch of the armed forces;

(B) senior-level reserve-component officers from each of the seven reserve components;

(C) civilian officials of the Department of Defense; and

(D) such participants from outside the Department of Defense as the Secretary considers appropriate.

(3) The Chairman of the Joint Chiefs of Staff shall provide such joint staff support to the study group as necessary. He shall participate in the activities of the study group in accordance with the provisions of section 153 of title 10, United States Code, including the responsibility to assess the conformance of manpower programs and policies with strategic plans and to advise the study group about the extent to which program recommendations and budget proposals conform with the priorities established in strategic plans and for the combatant commands.

(4) The Secretary shall ensure that the study group, in carrying out its duties and responsibilities, has access to federally funded research centers (FFRCs) and other necessary support.

(5) The Secretary of Defense shall consult with the Secretary of Transportation with respect to the functions of the study group insofar as they relate to the Selected Reserve of the Coast Guard Reserve.

(6) Meetings of the study group may be closed to the public in connection with the consideration of classified material.

(c) Matters To Be Considered.—(1) In carrying out the study required by subsection (a), the study group shall evaluate and make recommendations to the Secretary concerning each of the following matters (with each such matter to be evaluated separately insofar as it relates to each policy or practice set forth in subparagraphs (A) through (C) of subsection (b)(1)):

(1) With respect to the Total Force Policy of the Department of Defense, the basic tenets of that policy, how well that policy has been implemented, and what changes (if any) are desirable to improve upon that policy and its implementation.

(2) The effectiveness of the existing chain of management and command responsibility in evaluating and integrating force requirements among the armed forces, and between the active components and the reserve components.

(3) The extent to which officials responsible for such evaluation and integration of force requirements currently (and should in the future) participate in the budget and resource allocation processes of the Department of Defense.

(4) The adequacy of the methodology used by the Department of Defense in the assignment of missions between the active and reserve components and, within each active and reserve component, the assignment of missions among various major types of units, including—

(A) the extent to which that methodology includes the use of cost-benefit analyses; and

(B) the methodology for the manner by which force reductions are distributed within individual units and between active and reserve components.

(5) The scope and size of force reductions with respect to major units (such as air wings, carrier groups, and divisions) that would result in an irreversible change of the capability of those units to perform assigned missions, with emphasis on considerations such as mobilization, loss of skilled manpower, equipment, and training.

(d) ADDITIONAL MATTERS TO BE CONSIDERED.—(1) In carrying out its study and making its recommendations, the study group shall also evaluate the process by which decisions within the Department of Defense respecting force mix and force structure are made with regard to the readiness, sustainability, and overall mission capability of the active and reserve forces. The study group shall also consider whether the Department of Defense has a cogent strategy for making such decisions with respect to force mix that anticipates a substantially smaller military force structure in the future and whether the Department has developed a system for regular and systematic top-level evaluation of decisions respecting force mix or reductions in force structure.

(2) In carrying out the evaluation required by paragraph (1), the study group shall consider (among other matters it considers appropriate) the following:

(A) The optimal structure of military forces required to meet the threat as described in net assessments prepared pursuant to section 153 of title 10, United States Code, taking into account currently available and projected budget resources.

(B) The appropriateness of the missions that have been assigned to major units (such as air wings, carrier groups, and divisions) in each of the active and reserve components in view of the status of those units with respect to personnel and equipment resources and training systems.

(C) The response times for the deployment of such units in the event of a mobilization.

(D) An evaluation of the readiness and sustainability of each of the active and reserve components and of the contributions of each such component to the overall military capability of the United States.

(E) The extent to which the active and reserve component units that are identified for use during the first 30 days of a mobilization are prepared to undertake wartime missions (as measured against the standards established by the Chairman of the Joint Chiefs of Staff in accordance with section 153 of title 10, United States Code), the reasons for any lack of preparedness for such missions, and recommendations for measures that would be necessary for those units to become fully mission capable.

(F) The adequacy of equipment distribution and modernization in the active and reserve components, including consideration of the importance of prepositioning of light and heavy equipment in the mobilization process.

(G) The adequacy of the current base of military personnel and equipment available for short notice rotation and deployment in order to meet worldwide defense commitments.

(H) The capability of each component of the active and reserve forces to meet assigned and projected missions at each step in the mobilization process and the adequacy of current airlift and sealift capability.

(I) The resources (including funds) needed for sufficient personnel, equipment, and training to achieve desired force structure and mission capability in both the active and reserve components.

(J) The capability of the active and reserve components, jointly and separately, to respond to mobilization requirements at each stage of the mobilization process.

(d) REPORTS.—(1) The study group shall submit to the Secretary of Defense an interim report on its findings and recommendations at such time as the Secretary may require, but not later than September 1, 1990. The Secretary shall submit the interim report to the Committees on Armed Services of the Senate and the House of Representatives not later than September 15, 1990.

(2) The study group shall submit its final report, including its findings and recommendations, to the Secretary not later than December 1, 1990. The Secretary shall submit the final report of the study group, together with any comment and recommendation of the Secretary, to those committees not later than December 31, 1990.

(e) LIMITATION ON OBLIGATION OF CERTAIN FUNDS IF REPORTS SUBMITTED LATE.—If either of the reports required by subsection (d) is not submitted to those committees by the date specified in that subsection for the report to be submitted, the Secretary of Defense may not, on or after that date, obligate any funds for a new contract for advisory, consultant, or assistance services until the report is submitted.

SEC. 1102. STUDIES OF CLOSE SUPPORT FOR LAND FORCES

(a) SECRETARY OF DEFENSE STUDY.—The Secretary of Defense shall conduct a study of close support, including close air support.

(b) CONTRACTOR STUDY.—In conducting the study required by subsection (a), the Secretary shall provide for a study to be conducted by the Institute for Defense Analysis, a Federal contract research center. The Institute shall submit a report to the Secretary on such study at such time before March 1, 1990, as the Secretary may require.

(c) JCS STUDY.—The Chairman of the Joint Chiefs of Staff shall conduct a study of close support, including close air support. The Chairman shall submit a report to the Secretary of Defense on such study at such time before March 1, 1990, as the Secretary may require.

(d) STUDIES TO BE INDEPENDENT.—Each study under subsections (a), (b), and (c) shall be conducted independently of the others.

(e) MATTERS TO BE INCLUDED.—The studies conducted under subsections (a), (b), and (c) shall include consideration of each of the following:

(1) The nature of the present, and anticipated future, battlefield across a representative set of conflict levels.

(2) The requirements of the land force for close support across this representative set of conflict levels in terms of targets and time, including the lessons of recent combat experience.

(3) With regard to the battlefields and close support requirements identified pursuant to paragraphs (1) and (2), the current and anticipated ground and air systems capable of meeting these requirements.

(4) With regard to these major systems, their significant characteristics in terms of effectiveness, integration with allies, command and control, survivability, and life-cycle cost.

(5) The implications (in terms of roles and missions) of the selection of, or failure to select, each of these major systems as part of an appropriate force structure.

(f) Report to Congress.—The Secretary of Defense shall submit to Congress a report on the studies conducted under this section. The report shall include—

(1) the findings, conclusions, and recommendations of the Secretary in the study conducted by the Secretary under subsection (a) with respect to each of the matters set forth in subsection (e);

(2) copies of the reports to the Secretary under subsections (b) and (c), including the findings, conclusions, and recommendations contained in those reports; and

(3) such comments on those reports as the Secretary considers appropriate.

(g) Time for Submission.—The report required under subsection (f) shall be submitted not later than March 1, 1990.

(h) Close Air Support Defined.—For purposes of this section, the term "close air support", as defined in Joint Chiefs of Staff Publication 1, dated June 1, 1987, means air action against hostile targets which are in close proximity to friendly forces and which require detailed integration of each air mission with the fire and movement of those forces.

SEC. 1103. STRATEGIC AIR DEFENSE ALERT MISSION

(a) Readiness of Air National Guard Units.—The Secretary of Defense shall ensure that those units of the Air National Guard that are assigned to carry out the strategic air defense mission in the northern portion of the United States retain the capability to generate and maintain a readiness posture that meets the needs of all operations plans of the North American Aerospace Defense Command (NORAD).

(b) Fiscal Year 1990 Limitation.—During fiscal year 1990, the Secretary of Defense may not reduce the man years or flying hours of the units described in subsection (a).

(c) Report.—Not later than March 1, 1990, the Secretary of the Air Force shall submit to the Committees on Armed Services of the Senate and House of Representatives a report on the strategic air defense alert mission. The report shall describe the following:

(1) The rationale and goals for the strategic air defense modernization program undertaken jointly by the United States and Canada.

(2) The operational requirements of NORAD in crisis and wartime for generating and forward deploying air defense forces of the Air National Guard based in the northern portion of the United States.

(3) The plans of the Air Force for maintaining the readiness of aircraft, flight crews, maintenance personnel, control tower personnel, and security forces of the air defense units described in subsection (a) to implement NORAD operations plans.

(4) The plans of the Air Force for transitioning from current interceptor aircraft and current peacetime unit alert mission and training practices to new aircraft and new unit alert mis-

sion and training practices, including the effect of such transition on unit manning levels and combat mission readiness.

(5) The current ability of the forward operating bases in Canada to accommodate forward deployment of air defense units on a sustained basis and plans of the Air Force for the improvement of such bases.

(6) The current and planned radars, intercept systems, communications systems, and command elements (together with deployment schedules for those which are planned) that are intended to detect, identify, track, and intercept intruders into northern Canadian airspace during peacetime, during periods of heightened tension, and during hostilities.

(d) REPEAL.—Section 713 of the National Defense Authorization Act, Fiscal Year 1989 (Public Law 100–456; 102 Stat. 1998), is repealed.

ARMS CONTROL AND DISARMAMENT AMENDMENTS ACT OF 1989

An Act to amend the Arms Control and Disarmament Act to authorize appropriations for the Arms Control and Disarmament Agency, and for other purposes.

Date: December 11, 1989

Bill No.: H.R. 1495

Public Law No.: 101-216

Cite: 103 STAT. 1853

Sections reprinted:

TITLE I - ARMS CONTROL AND DISARMAMENT AGENCY
- Section 104 - Arms control implementation and compliance resolution.
- Section 105 - Arms control verification.

TITLE II - ON-SITE INSPECTION ACTIVITIES
- Section 201 - On-site inspection agency.

Public Law 101-216
101st Congress

An Act

To amend the Arms Control and Disarmament Act to authorize appropriations for the Arms Control and Disarmament Agency, and for other purposes.

Be it enacted by the Senate and House of Representatives of the United States of America in Congress assembled,

SECTION 1. SHORT TITLE.

This Act may be cited as the "Arms Control and Disarmament Amendments Act of 1989".

SEC. 104. ARMS CONTROL IMPLEMENTATION AND COMPLIANCE RESOLUTION.

The Director of the United States Arms Control and Disarmament Agency should study, and report to the Congress on, the advisability of establishing in the Agency an arms control implementation and compliance resolution bureau, or other organizational unit, that would be responsible for—

(1) managing the implementation of existing and future arms control agreements;

(2) coordinating the activities of the Special Verification Commission and the Standing Consultative Commission; and

(3) preparing comprehensive analyses and policy positions regarding the effective resolution of arms control compliance questions.

SEC. 105. ARMS CONTROL VERIFICATION.

(a) ESTABLISHMENT OF WORKING GROUP.—The President should establish a working group—

(1) to examine verification approaches to a strategic arms reduction agreement and other arms control agreements; and

(2) to assess the relevance for such agreements of the verification provisions of the Treaty Between the United States and the Union of Soviet Socialist Republics on the Elimination of Their Intermediate-Range and Shorter-Range Missiles (signed at Washington, December 8, 1987).

(b) INFORMATION AND DATA BASE.—(1) The Agency shall allocate sufficient resources to develop and maintain a comprehensive information and data base on verification concepts, research, technologies, and systems. The Agency shall collect, maintain, analyze, and disseminate information pertaining to arms control verification and monitoring, including information regarding—

(A) all current United States bilateral and multilateral arms treaties; and

(B) proposed, prospective, and potential bilateral or multilateral arms treaties in the areas of nuclear, conventional, chemical, and space weapons.

(2) The Agency shall seek to improve United States verification and monitoring activities through the monitoring and support of relevant research and analysis.

(3) The Agency shall provide detailed information on the activities pursuant to this section in its annual report to the Congress.

TITLE II—ON-SITE INSPECTION ACTIVITIES

SEC. 201. ON-SITE INSPECTION AGENCY.

The Arms Control and Disarmament Act is amended by adding at the end the following:

"TITLE V—ON-SITE INSPECTION ACTIVITIES

"SEC. 61. FINDINGS.

"The Congress finds that—

"(1) under this Act, the United States Arms Control and Disarmament Agency is charged with the 'formulation and implementation of United States arms control and disarmament policy in a manner which will promote the national security';

"(2) as defined in this Act, the terms 'arms control' and 'disarmament' mean 'the identification, verification, inspection, limitation, control, reduction, or elimination, of armed forces and armaments of all kinds under international agreement to establish an effective system of international control';

"(3) the On-Site Inspection Agency was established in 1988 pursuant to the INF Treaty to implement, on behalf of the United States, the inspection provisions of the INF Treaty;

"(4) on-site inspection activities under the INF Treaty include—

"(A) inspections in the Soviet Union, Czechoslovakia, and the German Democratic Republic,

"(B) escort duties for Soviet teams visiting the United States and the Basing Countries,

"(C) establishment and operation of the Portal Monitoring Facility in the Soviet Union, and

"(D) support for the Soviet inspectors at the Portal Monitoring Facility in Utah;

"(5) the personnel of the On-Site Inspection Agency include civilian technical experts, civilian support personnel, and members of the Armed Forces; and

"(6) the senior officials of the On-Site Inspection Agency include representatives from the United States Arms Control and Disarmament Agency and the Department of State.

"SEC. 62. POLICY COORDINATION CONCERNING IMPLEMENTATION OF ON-SITE INSPECTION PROVISIONS.

"(a) Interagency Coordination.—OSIA should receive policy guidance which is formulated through an interagency mechanism established by the President.

"(b) Role of the Secretary of Defense.—The Secretary of Defense should provide to OSIA appropriate policy guidance formulated through the interagency mechanism described in subsection (a) and operational direction, consistent with section 113(b) of title 10, United States Code.

"(c) Role of the Director.—The Director should provide to the interagency mechanism described in subsection (a) appropriate recommendations for policy guidance to OSIA consistent with sections 2(d), 22, and 34(c) of this Act.

"SEC. 64. DEFINITIONS.

"As used in this title—

"(1) the term 'INF Treaty' means the Treaty Between the United States and the Union of Soviet Socialist Republics on the Elimination of Their Intermediate-Range and Shorter-Range Missiles (signed at Washington, December 8, 1987); and

"(2) the term 'OSIA' means the On-Site Inspection Agency established by the President, or such other agency as may be designated by the President to carry out the on-site inspection provisions of the INF Treaty.".

Approved December 11, 1989.

LEGISLATIVE HISTORY—H.R. 1495 (S. 1868):

HOUSE REPORTS: No. 101-72, Pt. 1 (Comm. on Foreign Affairs) and Pt. 2 (Comm. on Armed Services).
SENATE REPORTS: No. 101-195, accompanying S. 1868 (Comm. on Foreign Relations).
CONGRESSIONAL RECORD, Vol. 135 (1989):
Sept. 19, considered and rejected in House.
Oct. 12, considered and passed House.
Nov. 17, considered and passed Senate, amended.
Nov. 19, House concurred in Senate amendment.
WEEKLY COMPILATION OF PRESIDENTIAL DOCUMENTS, Vol. 25 (1989):
Dec. 11, Presidential statement.

PALAU JOINT RESOLUTION

Joint resolution to authorize entry into force of the Compact of Free Association between the United States and the Government of Palau, and for other purposes.

Date: December 12, 1989

Bill No.: H.J. Res. 175

Public Law No.: 101-219

Cite: 103 STAT. 1870

Sections reprinted:

TITLE I - IMPLEMENTATION OF COMPACT OF FREE ASSOCIATION WITH PALAU (Sections 101-113)

Public Law 101-219
101st Congress

Joint Resolution

To authorize entry into force of the Compact of Free Association between the United States and the Government of Palau, and for other purposes.

Resolved by the Senate and House of Representatives of the United States of America in Congress assembled,

TITLE I—IMPLEMENTATION OF COMPACT OF FREE ASSOCIATION WITH PALAU

SEC. 101. ENTRY INTO FORCE OF COMPACT.

Notwithstanding the provisions of Section 101(d)(1)(B) of Public Law 99-658, entry into force of the Compact of Free Association between the United States and Palau (set forth in title II of Public Law 99-658 and hereafter in this joint resolution referred to as the "Compact") in accordance with subsections (a) and (d) of section 101 of Public Law 99-658 (100 Stat. 3673) is hereby authorized—

(1) subject to the condition that the Compact, as approved by the Congress in Public Law 99-658, is approved by the requisite percentage of the votes cast in a referendum conducted pursuant to the Constitution of Palau, and such approval is free from any legal challenge, and

(2) upon expiration of 30 days, in which either the House of Representatives or the Senate of the United States is in session, after the President notifies the Committees on Interior and Insular Affairs and Foreign Affairs of the House of Representatives and the Committee on Energy and Natural Resources of the Senate of the effective date of the Compact.

SEC. 102. FISCAL PROCEDURES ASSISTANCE.

Upon request of the Government of Palau, the Secretary of the Interior shall provide assistance to the Government of Palau to develop and promulgate regulations for the effective expenditure of funds received pursuant to this joint resolution, Public Laws 99-658 and 99-239, or any other Act of Congress.

SEC. 103. ANTIDRUG PROGRAM.

(a) PLAN.—The Department of the Interior shall develop, in cooperation with the Government of Palau and the National Drug Control Policy Office, a plan for an antidrug program in Palau. The plan shall be submitted to the Committees on Interior and Insular Affairs, Foreign Affairs, and Appropriations of the House of Representatives and the Committees on Energy and Natural Resources and Appropriations of the Senate by April 1, 1990. The plan shall: (1) identify the specific needs and costs of such an antidrug program; (2) shall identify all existing resources to be allocated for its implementation by the Government of the United States and the Government of Palau; and (3) shall recommend priority use for additional resources, assuming such resources are made available.

(b) AGREEMENT.—Following completion of the plan, the President and the Government of Palau shall negotiate an agreement to facilitate implementation of the plan. Such agreement may include—

(1) that the Government of Palau may request, on a long-term or case-by-case basis, that the officers of United States law enforcement agencies may conduct investigations consistent with implementation of the plan in cooperation with the law enforcement agencies of the Government of Palau;

(2) that the Government of Palau or the Government of the United States may agree to provide specific resources, on a one-time or a multiyear basis, to strengthen the antidrug program; and

(3) a specific description of the technical assistance, training, and equipment to be provided to Palau by the United States necessary to implement the plan.

SEC. 104. PUBLIC AUDITOR AND SPECIAL PROSECUTOR.

(a) Upon request of the Government of Palau the President shall provide, on a nonreimbursable basis, appropriate technical assistance to the public auditor or special prosecutor. The assistance provided pursuant to this subsection for the first five years after the effective date of the Compact shall, upon the request of the Government of Palau, and to the extent personnel are available, include (but not be limited to) the full time services of—

(1) an auditor or accountant, as determined by the public auditor, for the office of public auditor; and

(2) an attorney or investigator, as determined by the special prosecutor, for the office of special prosecutor.

SEC. 105. POWER GENERATION.

Section 104(e) of Public Law 99–658 is amended to read as follows:

"(e) Neither the Secretary of the Treasury nor any other officer or agent of the United States shall pay or transfer any portion of the sum and amounts payable to the Government of Palau pursuant to this joint resolution to any party other than the Government of Palau, except under the procedures established by the Compact and its related agreements. No funds appropriated pursuant to the Compact, this Act, or any other Act for grants or other assistance to Palau may be used to satisfy any obligation or expense incurred by Palau prior to November 14, 1986, with respect to any contract or debt related to any electrical generating plant or related facilities entered into or incurred by Palau which has not been specifically authorized by Congress in advance, except that the Government of Palau may use any portion of the annual grant under section 211(b) not required to be devoted to the energy needs of those parts of Palau not served by its central power generating facilities and any portion of the funds under section 212(b) of the Compact for such purpose.".

SEC. 106. AUDIT CERTIFICATION.

The chief officer of any agency conducting an audit pursuant to paragraph (1) of sections 102(c) and 103(m) of the Compact of Free Association Act of 1985 (Public Law 99–239) and section 101(d)(1)(C) of Public Law 99–658 shall certify that audit.

SEC. 107. ACQUISITION OF DEFENSE SITES.

The provisions of title III of the Compact relating to future use by the United States of defense sites in Palau do not restrict the authority of the President of the United States to—

(1) request additional funding, subject to appropriation, related to the use of privately owned land in Palau pursuant to article II of title III of the Compact as may be appropriate in light of actual land use requirements, independent appraisals of such privately owned land accepted by both governments, and other appropriate documentation of actual land use costs; and

(2) consent to an extension of the time set forth in a subsidiary agreement to such article in which the Government of Palau is required to make such land available to the United States.

SEC. 108. FEDERAL PROGRAMS COORDINATION PERSONNEL.

The Secretary of the Interior shall station at least one professional staff person in each of the Offices of the United States Representatives in the Republic of Palau, the Federated States of Micronesia, and the Republic of the Marshall Islands to provide Federal program coordination and technical assistance to such governments as authorized under Public Laws 99-239 and 99-658. In meeting the purposes of this section the Secretary shall select qualified persons following consultations with the Interagency Group on Freely Associated State Affairs.

SEC. 109. REFERENDUM COSTS.

The Secretary of the Interior shall provide such sums as may be necessary for a further referendum on approval of the Compact, if one is required, or other appropriate costs associated with the approval process in Palau.

SEC. 110. AGREEMENTS.

(a) EFFECTIVE DATE OF CERTAIN AGREEMENTS.—An agreement between the United States and the Government of the Republic of Palau consistent with the agreements approved by Public Law 101-62 (101 Stat. 162) shall take effect without further authorization thirty days after submission to Congress.

(b) EXTENSIONS.—The provisions of article IX, paragraph 5(a) of the Agreement referred to in section 462(e) of the Compact of Free Association as approved by Public Law 99-239, and article IX, paragraph 5(a) of the agreement referred to in section 462(f) of the Compact of Free Association for Palau as approved by Public Law 99-658, are extended, in accordance with the terms thereof, until October 1, 1998, unless earlier terminated or further extended by the laws of the United States.

(c) AUTHORIZATION.—Funding to implement the provisions of this title, and for assistance to the central health care facility and the prison in Palau, and the offices of Public Auditor and Special Prosecutor as proposed in the agreement entitled "Agreement Concerning Special Programs related to the Entry into Force of the Compact of Free Association Between the Government of the United States and the Government of the Republic of Palau" signed on May 26, 1989, shall be available pursuant to the authorization in section 105(c) of Public Law 99-239 as referenced by section 102(b) of Public Law 99-658 or from funds appropriated for technical assistance to the Secretary of the Interior.

SEC. 111. MODIFICATION OF ENERGY ASSISTANCE FUNDING.

(a) The President is authorized to negotiate and conclude an agreement, including the obligation of United States funds, with the Government of Palau which shall provide the following:

(1) The sum of $28,000,000, adjusted by section 215 of the Compact at the time of its availability to Palau, shall be provided to Palau pursuant to section 211(b) of the Compact and upon entry into force of the Compact.

(2) Palau shall pay to the United States, on or before the 15th anniversary of the effective date of the Compact, an amount equal to the net economic cost to the United States of making available the section 211(b) funds in the manner specified in this subsection rather than as provided in section 211(b).

(3) Such economic cost shall reflect the time value of money and be determined using the rate determined for an equivalent loan by the Federal Financing Bank as of the date these funds are advanced, and using an inflation rate consistent with the determinations made under the provisions of section 215 of the Compact.

(4) If the Government of Palau has not paid such net economic costs to the United States by the 15th anniversary of the effective date of the Compact, then the United States shall be automatically paid such sums from the fund established under section 211(f) of the Compact.

(5) The provision of section 211(b) funds, as appropriated by Public Law 99-349 and pursuant to this subsection, shall be in fulfillment of all United States obligations under such section 211(b) of the Compact and shall be subject to section 236 of the Compact.

(b) Subject to the provisions of subsection (a) and upon the request of the Government of Palau, the sum of $28 million appropriated by Public Law 99-349 to fulfill the obligations of the United States under section 211(b) of the Compact (approved in Public Law 99-658), adjusted by section 215 of such Compact, shall be provided to Palau upon entry into force of the Compact.

(c) Funding provided in Public Law 101-121 under the "Trust Territory of the Pacific Islands" appropriation account shall remain available until expended.

SEC. 112. SUBMISSION OF AGREEMENTS.

Any agreement concluded with the Government of Palau pursuant to this joint resolution including the agreement entitled "Agreement Concerning Special Programs related to the Entry into Force of the Compact of Free Association Between the Government of the United States and the Government of the Republic of Palau" signed on May 26, 1989, and any agreement which would amend, change, or terminate any such agreement, or portion thereof, shall be submitted to the Congress and may not take effect until after 30 days after the date on which such agreement is so submitted. An amendment or agreement substituting or in addition to the subsidiary agreement negotiated under section 212(a) of the Compact or its annex shall take effect only when approved by an Act of Congress.

SEC. 113. TRANSITION FUNDING.

For the purposes of applying section 105(c)(2) of the Compact of Free Association Act of 1985 (99 Stat. 1792) to Palau, the terms "fiscal year 1987", "fiscal year 1988", and "fiscal year 1989" in section 104(c) of Public Law 99-658 shall be deemed to be the first, second, and third fiscal years, respectively, beginning after the effective date of the Compact.

ANTI-TERRORISM AND ARMS EXPORT AMENDMENTS ACT OF 1989

An Act to prohibit exports of military equipment to countries supporting international terrorism, and for other purposes.

Date: December 12, 1989

Bill No.: H.R. 91

Public Law No.: 101-222

Cite: 103 STAT. 1892

Sections reprinted: All

Public Law 101-222
101st Congress

An Act

To prohibit exports of military equipment to countries supporting international terrorism, and for other purposes.

Be it enacted by the Senate and House of Representatives of the United States of America in Congress assembled,

SECTION 1. SHORT TITLE AND TABLE OF CONTENTS.

(a) SHORT TITLE.—This Act may be cited as the "Anti-Terrorism and Arms Export Amendments Act of 1989".

(b) TABLE OF CONTENTS.—The table of contents for this Act is as follows:

SEC. 2. PROHIBITION ON ARMS TRANSACTIONS WITH COUNTRIES SUPPORTING TERRORISM.

(a) PROHIBITION.—Section 40 of the Arms Export Control Act (22 U.S.C. 2780) is amended to read as follows:

"SEC. 40. TRANSACTIONS WITH COUNTRIES SUPPORTING ACTS OF INTERNATIONAL TERRORISM.

"(a) PROHIBITED TRANSACTIONS BY THE UNITED STATES GOVERNMENT.—The following transactions by the United States Government are prohibited:

"(1) Exporting or otherwise providing (by sale, lease or loan, grant, or other means), directly or indirectly, any munitions item to a country described in subsection (d) under the authority of this Act, the Foreign Assistance Act of 1961, or any other law (except as provided in subsection (h)). In implementing this paragraph, the United States Government—

"(A) shall suspend delivery to such country of any such item pursuant to any such transaction which has not been completed at the time the Secretary of State makes the determination described in subsection (d), and

"(B) shall terminate any lease or loan to such country of any such item which is in effect at the time the Secretary of State makes that determination.

"(2) Providing credits, guarantees, or other financial assistance under the authority of this Act, the Foreign Assistance Act of 1961, or any other law (except as provided in subsection (h)), with respect to the acquisition of any munitions item by a country described in subsection (d). In implementing this paragraph, the United States Government shall suspend expenditures pursuant to any such assistance obligated before the Secretary of State makes the determination described in subsection (d). The President may authorize expenditures otherwise required to be suspended pursuant to the preceding sentence if the President has determined, and reported to the Congress, that suspension of those expenditures causes undue financial hardship to a supplier, shipper, or similar person and allowing the expenditure will not result in any munitions item being made available for use by such country.

"(3) Consenting under section 3(a) of this Act, under section 505(a) of the Foreign Assistance Act of 1961, under the regulations issued to carry out section 38 of this Act, or under any other law (except as provided in subsection (h)), to any transfer of any munitions item to a country described in subsection (d). In implementing this paragraph, the United States Government shall withdraw any such consent which is in effect at the time the Secretary of State makes the determination described in subsection (d), except that this sentence does not apply with respect to any item that has already been transferred to such country.

"(4) Providing any license or other approval under section 38 of this Act for any export or other transfer (including by means of a technical assistance agreement, manufacturing licensing agreement, or coproduction agreement) of any munitions item to a country described in subsection (d). In implementing this paragraph, the United States Government shall suspend any such license or other approval which is in effect at the time the Secretary of State makes the determination described in subsection (d), except that this sentence does not apply with respect to any item that has already been exported or otherwise transferred to such country.

"(5) Otherwise facilitating the acquisition of any munitions item by a country described in subsection (d). This paragraph applies with respect to activities undertaken—

"(A) by any department, agency, or other instrumentality of the Government,

"(B) by any officer or employee of the Government (including members of the United States Armed Forces), or

"(C) by any other person at the request or on behalf of the Government.

The Secretary of State may waive the requirements of the second sentence of paragraph (1), the second sentence of paragraph (3), and the second sentence of paragraph (4) to the extent that the Secretary determines, after consultation with the Congress, that unusual and compelling circumstances require that the United States Government not take the actions specified in that sentence.

"(b) Prohibited Transactions by United States Persons.—

"(1) In general.—A United States person may not take any of the following actions:

"(A) Exporting any munitions item to any country described in subsection (d).

"(B) Selling, leasing, loaning, granting, or otherwise providing any munitions item to any country described in subsection (d).

"(C) Selling, leasing, loaning, granting, or otherwise providing any munitions item to any recipient which is not the government of or a person in a country described in subsection (d) if the United States person has reason to know that the munitions item will be made available to any country described in subsection (d).

"(D) Taking any other action which would facilitate the acquisition, directly or indirectly, of any munitions item by the government of any country described in subsection (d), or any person acting on behalf of that government, if the United States person has reason to know that that action will facilitate the acquisition of that item by such a government or person.

"(2) LIABILITY FOR ACTIONS OF FOREIGN SUBSIDIARIES, ETC.—A United States person violates this subsection if a corporation or other person that is controlled in fact by that United States person (as determined under regulations, which the President shall issue) takes an action described in paragraph (1) outside the United States.

"(3) APPLICABILITY TO ACTIONS OUTSIDE THE UNITED STATES.—Paragraph (1) applies with respect to actions described in that paragraph which are taken either within or outside the United States by a United States person described in subsection (l)(3)(A) or (B). To the extent provided in regulations issued under subsection (l)(3)(D), paragraph (1) applies with respect to actions described in that paragraph which are taken outside the United States by a person designated as a United States person in those regulations.

"(c) TRANSFERS TO GOVERNMENTS AND PERSONS COVERED.—This section applies with respect to—

"(1) the acquisition of munitions items by the government of a country described in subsection (d); and

"(2) the acquisition of munitions items by any individual, group, or other person within a country described in subsection (d), except to the extent that subparagraph (D) of subsection (b)(1) provides otherwise.

"(d) COUNTRIES COVERED BY PROHIBITION.—The prohibitions contained in this section apply with respect to a country if the Secretary of State determines that the government of that country has repeatedly provided support for acts of international terrorism.

"(e) PUBLICATION OF DETERMINATIONS.—Each determination of the Secretary of State under subsection (d) shall be published in the Federal Register.

"(f) RESCISSION.—A determination made by the Secretary of State under subsection (d) may not be rescinded unless the President submits to the Speaker of the House of Representatives and the chairman of the Committee on Foreign Relations of the Senate—

"(1) before the proposed rescission would take effect, a report certifying that—

"(A) there has been a fundamental change in the leadership and policies of the government of the country concerned;

"(B) that government is not supporting acts of international terrorism; and

"(C) that government has provided assurances that it will not support acts of international terrorism in the future; or

"(2) at least 45 days before the proposed rescission would take effect, a report justifying the rescission and certifying that—

"(A) the government concerned has not provided any support for international terrorism during the preceding 6-month period; and

"(B) the government concerned has provided assurances that it will not support acts of international terrorism in the future.

"(g) WAIVER.—The President may waive the prohibitions contained in this section with respect to a specific transaction if—

"(1) the President determines that the transaction is essential to the national security interests of the United States; and

"(2) not less than 15 days prior to the proposed transaction, the President—

"(A) consults with the Committee on Foreign Affairs of the House of Representatives and the Committee on Foreign Relations of the Senate; and

"(B) submits to the Speaker of the House of Representatives and the chairman of the Committee on Foreign Relations of the Senate a report containing—

"(i) the name of any country involved in the proposed transaction, the identity of any recipient of the items to be provided pursuant to the proposed transaction, and the anticipated use of those items;

"(ii) a description of the munitions items involved in the proposed transaction (including their market value) and the actual sale price at each step in the transaction (or if the items are transferred by other than sale, the manner in which they will be provided);

"(iii) the reasons why the proposed transaction is essential to the national security interests of the United States and the justification for such proposed transaction;

"(iv) the date on which the proposed transaction is expected to occur; and

"(v) the name of every United States Government department, agency, or other entity involved in the proposed transaction, every foreign government involved in the proposed transaction, and every private party with significant participation in the proposed transaction.

To the extent possible, the information specified in subparagraph (B) of paragraph (2) shall be provided in unclassified form, with any classified information provided in an addendum to the report.

"(h) EXEMPTION FOR TRANSACTIONS SUBJECT TO NATIONAL SECURITY ACT REPORTING REQUIREMENTS.—The prohibitions contained in this section do not apply with respect to any transaction subject to reporting requirements under title V of the National Security Act of 1947 (50 U.S.C. 413 et seq.; relating to congressional oversight of intelligence activities).

"(i) RELATION TO OTHER LAWS.—

"(1) IN GENERAL.—With regard to munitions items controlled pursuant to this Act, the provisions of this section shall apply notwithstanding any other provision of law, other than section 614(a) of the Foreign Assistance Act of 1961 (22 U.S.C. 2364(a)).

"(2) SECTION 614(a) WAIVER AUTHORITY.—If the authority of section 614(a) of the Foreign Assistance Act of 1961 is used to permit a transaction under that Act or the Arms Export Control Act which is otherwise prohibited by this section, the written policy justification required by that section shall include the information specified in subsection (g)(2)(B) of this section.

"(j) CRIMINAL PENALTY.—Any person who willfully violates this section shall be fined for each violation not more than $1,000,000, imprisoned not more than 10 years, or both.

"(k) CIVIL PENALTIES; ENFORCEMENT.—In the enforcement of this section, the President is authorized to exercise the same powers concerning violations and enforcement which are conferred upon departments, agencies, and officials by sections 11(c), 11(e), 11(g), and 12(a) of the Export Administration Act of 1979 (subject to the same terms and conditions as are applicable to such powers under that Act), except that, notwithstanding section 11(c) of that Act, the civil penalty for each violation of this section may not exceed $500,000.

"(l) DEFINITIONS.—As used in this section—

"(1) the term 'munitions item' means any item enumerated on the United States Munitions list (without regard to whether the item is imported into or exported from the United States);

"(2) the term 'United States', when used geographically, means the several States, the District of Columbia, the Commonwealth of Puerto Rico, the Commonwealth of the Northern Mariana Islands, and any territory or possession of the United States; and

"(3) the term 'United States person' means—

"(A) any citizen or permanent resident alien of the United States;

"(B) any sole proprietorship, partnership, company, association, or corporation having its principal place of business within the United States or organized under the laws of the United States, any State, the District of Columbia, the Commonwealth of Puerto Rico, the Commonwealth of the Northern Mariana Islands, or any territory or possession of the United States;

"(C) any other person with respect to that person's actions while in the United States; and

"(D) to the extent provided in regulations issued by the Secretary of State, any person that is not described in subparagraph (A), (B), or (C) but—

"(i) is a foreign subsidiary or affiliate of a United States person described in subparagraph (B) and is controlled in fact by that United States person (as determined in accordance with those regulations), or

"(ii) is otherwise subject to the jurisdiction of the United States,

with respect to that person's actions while outside the United States.".

(b) CONFORMING AMENDMENT.—Section 3(f) of the Arms Export Control Act (22 U.S.C. 2753(f)) is repealed.

SEC. 3. CONSIDERATIONS IN ISSUANCE OF ARMS EXPORT LICENSES AND IN ARMS SALES.

(a) EXPORT LICENSES.—Section 38(a)(2) of the Arms Export Control Act (22 U.S.C. 2778) is amended by inserting "support international terrorism," after "arms race,".

(b) ARMS SALES.—Section 36(b)(1)(D) of that Act (22 U.S.C. 2776(b)(1)(D)) is amended—

(1) by redesignating clauses (ii) through (iv) as clauses (iii) through (v), respectively; and

(2) by inserting the following new clause (ii) after clause (i):
"(ii) support international terrorism;".

SEC. 4. EXPORTS TO COUNTRIES SUPPORTING TERRORISM.

Section 6(j) of the Export Administration Act of 1979 (50 U.S.C. App 2405(j)) is amended to read as follows:

"(j) COUNTRIES SUPPORTING INTERNATIONAL TERRORISM.—(1) A validated license shall be required for the export of goods or technology to a country if the Secretary of State has made the following determinations:

"(A) The government of such country has repeatedly provided support for acts of international terrorism.

"(B) The export of such goods or technology could make a significant contribution to the military potential of such country, including its military logistics capability, or could enhance the ability of such country to support acts of international terrorism.

"(2) The Secretary and the Secretary of State shall notify the Committee on Foreign Affairs of the House of Representatives and the Committee on Banking, Housing, and Urban Affairs and the Committee on Foreign Relations of the Senate at least 30 days before issuing any validated license required by paragraph (1).

"(3) Each determination of the Secretary of State under paragraph (1)(A), including each determination in effect on the date of the enactment of the Antiterrorism and Arms Export Amendments Act of 1989, shall be published in the Federal Register.

"(4) A determination made by the Secretary of State under paragraph (1)(A) may not be rescinded unless the President submits to the Speaker of the House of Representatives and the chairman of the Committee on Banking, Housing, and Urban Affairs and the chairman of the Committee on Foreign Relations of the Senate—

"(A) before the proposed rescission would take effect, a report certifying that—

"(i) there has been a fundamental change in the leadership and policies of the government of the country concerned;

"(ii) that government is not supporting acts of international terrorism; and

"(iii) that government has provided assurances that it will not support acts of international terrorism in the future; or

"(B) at least 45 days before the proposed rescission would take effect, a report justifying the rescission and certifying that—

"(i) the government concerned has not provided any support for international terrorism during the preceding 6-month period; and

"(ii) the government concerned has provided assurances that it will not support acts of international terrorism in the future.".

SEC. 5. PROHIBITION ON ASSISTANCE TO COUNTRIES SUPPORTING INTERNATIONAL TERRORISM.

Section 620A of the Foreign Assistance Act of 1961 (22 U.S.C. 2371) is amended to read as follows:

"SEC. 620A. PROHIBITION ON ASSISTANCE TO GOVERNMENTS SUPPORTING INTERNATIONAL TERRORISM.

"(a) PROHIBITION.—The United States shall not provide any assistance under this Act, the Agricultural Trade Development and Assistance Act of 1954, the Peace Corps Act, or the Export-Import Bank Act of 1945 to any country if the Secretary of State determines that the government of that country has repeatedly provided support for acts of international terrorism.

"(b) PUBLICATION OF DETERMINATIONS.—Each determination of the Secretary of State under subsection (a), including each determination in effect on the date of the enactment of the Antiterrorism and Arms Export Amendments Act of 1989, shall be published in the Federal Register.

"(c) RESCISSION.—A determination made by the Secretary of State under subsection (a) may not be rescinded unless the President submits to the Speaker of the House of Representatives and the chairman of the Committee on Foreign Relations of the Senate—

"(1) before the proposed rescission would take effect, a report certifying that—

"(A) there has been a fundamental change in the leadership and policies of the government of the country concerned;

"(B) that government is not supporting acts of international terrorism; and

"(C) that government has provided assurances that it will not support acts of international terrorism in the future; or

"(2) at least 45 days before the proposed rescission would take effect, a report justifying the rescission and certifying that—

"(A) the government concerned has not provided any support for international terrorism during the preceding 6-month period; and

"(B) the government concerned has provided assurances that it will not support acts of international terrorism in the future.

"(d) WAIVER.—Assistance prohibited by subsection (a) may be provided to a country described in that subsection if—

"(1) the President determines that national security interests or humanitarian reasons justify a waiver of subsection (a), except that humanitarian reasons may not be used to justify assistance under part II of this Act (including chapter 4, chapter 6, and chapter 8), or the Export-Import Bank Act of 1945; and

"(2) at least 15 days before the waiver takes effect, the President consults with the Committee on Foreign Affairs of the House of Representatives and the Committee on Foreign Relations of the Senate regarding the proposed waiver and submits a report to the Speaker of the House of Representatives and the chairman of the Committee on Foreign Relations of the Senate containing—

"(A) the name of the recipient country;

"(B) a description of the national security interests or humanitarian reasons which require the waiver;

"(C) the type and amount of and the justification for the assistance to be provided pursuant to the waiver; and

"(D) the period of time during which such waiver will be effective.

The waiver authority granted in this subsection may not be used to provide any assistance under the Foreign Assistance Act of 1961 which is also prohibited by section 40 of the Arms Export Control Act.".

SEC. 6. DESIGNATION OF ITEMS ON THE MUNITIONS LIST.

Section 38 of the Arms Export Control Act (22 U.S.C. 2278) is amended by adding at the end the following:

"(h) The designation by the President (or by an official to whom the President's functions under subsection (a) have been duly delegated), in regulations issued under this section, of items as defense articles or defense services for purposes of this section shall not be subject to judicial review.".

SEC. 7. QUARTERLY REPORTS ON THIRD COUNTRY TRANSFERS AND ON DOD TRANSFERS TO OTHER AGENCIES.

(a) QUARTERLY REPORTS.—Section 36(a) of the Arms Export Control Act (22 U.S.C. 2776(a)) is amended—

(1) by striking out "and" at the end of paragraph (8);

(2) by striking out the period at the end of paragraph (9) and inserting in lieu thereof a semicolon; and

(3) by inserting after paragraph (9) the following:

"(10) a listing of the consents to third-party transfers of defense articles or defense services which were granted, during the quarter for which such report is submitted, for purposes of section 3(a)(2) of this Act, the regulations issued under section 38 of this Act, or section 505(a)(1)(B) of the Foreign Assistance Act of 1961, if the value (in terms of original acquisition cost) of the defense articles or defense services to be transferred is $1,000,000 or more; and

"(11) a listing of all munitions items (as defined in section 40(l)(1)) which were sold, leased, or otherwise transferred by the Department of Defense to any other department, agency, or other entity of the United States Government during the quarter for which such report is submitted (including the name of the recipient Government entity and a discussion of what that entity will do with those munitions items) if—

"(A) the value of the munitions items was $250,000 or more; or

"(B) the value of all munitions items transferred to that Government department, agency, or other entity during that quarter was $250,000 or more;

excluding munitions items transferred (i) for disposition or use solely within the United States, or (ii) for use in connection with intelligence activities subject to reporting requirements under title V of the National Security Act of 1947 (50 U.S.C. 413 et seq.; relating to congressional oversight of intelligence activities).".

(b) CLASSIFICATION OF REPORTS.—That section is amended in the parenthetical clause in the text preceding paragraph (1) by inserting ", and any information provided under paragraph (11) of this subsection may also be provided in a classified addendum" after "(b)(1) of this section".

SEC. 8. SPECIAL AUTHORITIES.

The second sentence of section 614(c) of the Foreign Assistance Act of 1961 (22 U.S.C. 2364(c)) is amended to read as follows: "The

President shall fully inform the chairman and ranking minority member of the Committee on Foreign Affairs of the House of Representatives and the chairman and ranking minority member of the Committee on Foreign Relations of the Senate of each use of funds under this subsection prior to the use of such funds.".

SEC. 9. HOSTAGE ACT.

Section 2001 of the Revised Statutes of the United States (22 U.S.C. 1732) is amended by inserting "and not otherwise prohibited by law" after "acts of war".

SEC. 10. SELF-DEFENSE IN ACCORDANCE WITH INTERNATIONAL LAW.

The use by any government of armed force in the exercise of individual or collective self-defense in accordance with applicable international agreements and customary international law shall not be considered an act of international terrorism for purposes of the amendments made by this Act.

Approved December 12, 1989.

LEGISLATIVE HISTORY—H.R. 91 (S. 347):

HOUSE REPORTS: No. 101-296 (Comm. on Foreign Affairs).
SENATE REPORTS: No. 101-173 accompanying S. 347 (Comm. on Foreign Relations).
CONGRESSIONAL RECORD, Vol. 135 (1989):
Oct. 23, considered and passed House.
Nov. 21, considered and passed Senate, amended. House concurred in Senate amendments.
WEEKLY COMPILATION OF PRESIDENTIAL DOCUMENTS, Vol. 25 (1989):
Dec. 12, Presidential statement.

INTERNATIONAL NARCOTICS CONTROL ACT OF 1989

An Act to combat international narcotics production and trafficking.

Date: Dec. 13, 1989

Bill No.: H.R. 3611

Public Law No.: 101-231

Cite: 103 STAT. 1954

Sections reprinted: All

Public Law 101-231
101st Congress

An Act

To combat international narcotics production and trafficking.

Be it enacted by the Senate and House of Representatives of the United States of America in Congress assembled,

SECTION 1. SHORT TITLE AND TABLE OF CONTENTS.

(a) SHORT TITLE.—This Act may be cited as the "International Narcotics Control Act of 1989".

(b) TABLE OF CONTENTS.—The table of contents for this Act is as follows:

SEC. 2. ANDEAN DRUG INITIATIVE.

(a) FINDINGS RELATING TO ECONOMIC ASSISTANCE NEEDS.—The Congress finds that—

(1) it is crucial to international antidrug efforts that funds be made available for crop substitution programs and alternative employment opportunities to provide alternative sources of income for those individuals in major coca producing countries who are dependent on illicit drug production activities, as well as for eradication, enforcement, rehabilitation and treatment, and education programs in those countries; and

(2) the United States and other major donor countries (including European countries and Japan) should provide increased economic assistance, on an urgent basis, to those major coca producing countries which have taken concrete steps to attack illicit coca production, processing, and trafficking, by eradication, interdiction, or other methods which significantly reduce the flow of cocaine to the world market.

(b) PLAN TO ADDRESS NEED FOR ASSISTANCE.—The Congress, therefore, urges the Director of National Drug Control Policy to submit to the Congress in February 1990, as part of the National Drug Control

Strategy report required by section 1005 of the Anti-Drug Abuse Act of 1988 (21 U.S.C. 1504), a plan which addresses the need outlined in subsection (a).

(c) ANDEAN SUMMIT.—The Congress urges the President in the strongest possible terms to include the following issues on the formal agenda of the meeting between the President and the heads of government of Bolivia, Colombia, and Peru, scheduled for early February 1990:

(1) Bilateral and multilateral antidrug efforts that make funds available for crop substitution programs and alternative employment opportunities in major coca producing countries, as well as for eradication, enforcement, rehabilitation and treatment, and education programs in those countries.

(2) Initiatives to improve and expand antidrug efforts in the Andean region, including through the use of United States international economic, commercial, and other policies.

(3) Prior bilateral discussions aimed at increasing multilateral economic development assistance from Japan, Canada, and Western European countries for antidrug efforts in the Andean region.

(4) Debt-for-drugs exchanges that forgive Andean bilateral debt held by the United States and other creditor countries in return for commitments by Andean governments to use the savings in debt service for antidrug programs, pursuant to agreements negotiated under section 481(h)(2)(B) of the Foreign Assistance Act of 1961 (22 U.S.C. 2291(h)(2)(B)) and other international agreements and initiatives.

(5) Bilateral and multilateral efforts to halt the transfer of arms, precursor chemicals, and sophisticated communications equipment and technology from legitimate sources to drug trafficking organizations.

(d) REPORT ON ANDEAN SUMMIT MEETING.—Not later than 30 days after the conclusion of the Andean summit meeting described in subsection (c), the President shall report to the Congress on the outcome of that meeting.

(e) SUPPLEMENTAL BUDGET REQUESTS.—At the same time as he submits the report required by subsection (d), the President shall submit to the Congress such supplemental budget requests for fiscal years 1990 and 1991 as may be necessary to cover the United States share of the cost of additional economic assistance to implement an Andean antidrug strategy, including the commitments made at the Andean summit meeting described in subsection (c).

SEC. 3. MILITARY AND LAW ENFORCEMENT ASSISTANCE FOR BOLIVIA, COLOMBIA, AND PERU.

(a) PURPOSES OF ASSISTANCE.—Assistance provided under this section shall be designed to—

(1) enhance the ability of the Government of Bolivia, the Government of Colombia, and the Government of Peru to control illicit narcotics production and trafficking;

(2) strengthen the bilateral ties of the United States with those governments by offering concrete assistance in this area of great mutual concern; and

(3) strengthen respect for internationally recognized human rights and the rule of law in efforts to control illicit narcotics production and trafficking.

(b) MILITARY ASSISTANCE AND TRAINING.—Subject to the requirements of this section, the President is authorized to use the funds made available to carry out this section to provide defense articles, defense services, and international military education and training to Bolivia, Colombia, and Peru. Such assistance shall be provided under the authorities of section 23 of the Arms Export Control Act (22 U.S.C. 2763; relating to the foreign military financing program) and chapter 5 of part II of the Foreign Assistance Act of 1961 (22 U.S.C. 2347 and following; relating to international military education and training). Such assistance is in addition to any other such assistance made available to those countries.

(c) LAW ENFORCEMENT TRAINING.—

(1) AUTHORIZED FORMS AND RECIPIENTS OF ASSISTANCE.—Subject to paragraph (2), up to $6,500,000 of the funds made available to carry out this section may be used, notwithstanding section 660 of the Foreign Assistance Act of 1961 (22 U.S.C. 2420; relating to the prohibition on law enforcement assistance)—

(A) to provide to law enforcement agencies, or other units, that are organized for the specific purpose of narcotics enforcement by the Government of Bolivia, the Government of Colombia, or the Government of Peru, education and training in the operation and maintenance of equipment used in narcotics control interdiction and eradication efforts; and

(B) for the expenses of deploying, upon the request of the Government of Bolivia, the Government of Colombia, or the Government of Peru, Department of Defense mobile training teams in that country to conduct training in military-related individual and collective skills that will enhance that country's ability to conduct tactical operations in narcotics interdiction.

(2) OFFSETTING REDUCTION.—The amount that may be used under paragraph (1) shall be reduced by the amount of any assistance provided for Bolivia, Colombia, or Peru under the Foreign Operations, Export Financing, and Related Programs Appropriations Act, 1990, for the purposes specified in subparagraph (A) or (B) of paragraph (1).

(d) EQUIPMENT FOR LAW ENFORCEMENT UNITS.—

(1) AUTHORIZED FORMS AND RECIPIENTS OF ASSISTANCE.—Subject to paragraph (2), up to $12,500,000 of the funds made available to carry out this section may be used, notwithstanding section 660 of the Foreign Assistance Act of 1961 (22 U.S.C. 2420; relating to the prohibition on law enforcement assistance), for the procurement of defense articles for use in narcotics control, eradication, and interdiction efforts by law enforcement agencies, or other units, that are organized for the specific purpose of narcotics enforcement.

(2) OFFSETTING REDUCTION.—The amount that may be used under paragraph (1) shall be reduced by the amount of any assistance provided for Bolivia, Colombia, or Peru under the Foreign Operations, Export Financing, and Related Programs Appropriations Act, 1990, for the procurement of weapons or ammunition in accordance with the general authorities contained in section 481(a) of the Foreign Assistance Act of 1961.

(e) CONDITIONS OF ELIGIBILITY.—Assistance may be provided under this section to Bolivia, Colombia, or Peru only—

(1) so long as that country has a democratic government; and

(2) the law enforcement agencies of that country do not engage in a consistent pattern of gross violations of internationally recognized human rights (as defined in section 502B(d)(1) of the Foreign Assistance Act of 1961 (22 U.S.C. 2304(d)(1)).

(f) NOTIFICATIONS TO CONGRESS.—Not less than 15 days before funds are obligated pursuant to this section, the President shall transmit to the congressional committees specified in section 634A of the Foreign Assistance Act of 1961 (22 U.S.C. 2394-1) a written notification in accordance with the procedures applicable to reprogrammings under that section. Such notification shall specify—

(1) the country to which the assistance is to be provided;

(2) the type and value of the assistance to be provided;

(3) the law enforcement agencies or other units that will receive the assistance; and

(4) an explanation of how the proposed assistance will achieve the purposes specified in subsection (a) of this section.

(g) REPORTS ON HUMAN RIGHTS SITUATION.—Section 502B(c) of the Foreign Assistance Act of 1961 (22 U.S.C. 2304(c); relating to country-specific human rights reports upon the request of the foreign affairs committees) applies with respect to countries for which assistance authorized by this section is proposed or is being provided.

(h) COORDINATION WITH INTERNATIONAL NARCOTICS CONTROL ASSISTANCE PROGRAM.—Assistance under this section shall be coordinated with assistance provided under chapter 8 of part I of the Foreign Assistance Act of 1961 (22 U.S.C. 2291 and following; relating to international narcotics control assistance).

(i) AUTHORIZATION OF APPROPRIATIONS.—There are authorized to be appropriated $125,000,000 for fiscal year 1990 to carry out this section, which amount is authorized to be made available until expended.

SEC. 4. ACQUISITION BY SPECIAL DEFENSE ACQUISITION FUND OF DEFENSE ARTICLES FOR NARCOTICS CONTROL PURPOSES.

Section 51(a) of the Arms Export Control Act (22 U.S.C. 2795(a)) is amended by adding at the end the following:

"(4)(A) The Fund shall also be used to acquire defense articles that are particularly suited for use for narcotics control purposes and are appropriate to the needs of recipient countries, such as small boats, planes (including helicopters), and communications equipment.

"(B) Each report pursuant to section 53(a) shall designate the defense articles that have been acquired or are to be acquired pursuant to this paragraph and the defense articles acquired under this chapter that were transferred for use in narcotics control purposes.".

SEC. 5. EXCESS DEFENSE ARTICLES FOR CERTAIN MAJOR ILLICIT DRUG PRODUCING COUNTRIES.

Chapter 2 of part II of the Foreign Assistance Act of 1961 (22 U.S.C. 2311 and following) is amended by adding at the end the following:

"SEC. 517. MODERNIZATION OF MILITARY CAPABILITIES OF CERTAIN MAJOR ILLICIT DRUG PRODUCING COUNTRIES.

"(a) AUTHORITY TO TRANSFER EXCESS DEFENSE ARTICLES.—Subject to the limitations in this section, the President may transfer to a country—

"(1) which is a major illicit drug producing country (as defined in section 481(i)(2)) in Latin America and the Caribbean,

"(2) which has a democratic government, and

"(3) whose armed forces do not engage in a consistent pattern of gross violations of internationally recognized human rights (as defined in section 502B(d)(1)),

such excess defense articles as may be necessary to carry out subsection (b).

"(b) PURPOSE.—Excess defense articles may be transferred under subsection (a) only for the purpose of encouraging the military forces of an eligible country in Latin America and the Caribbean to participate with local law enforcement agencies in a comprehensive national antinarcotics program, conceived and developed by the government of that country, by conducting activities within that country and on the high seas to prevent the production, processing, trafficking, transportation, and consumption of illicit narcotic or psychotropic drugs or other controlled substances (as defined in section 481(i)(3)).

"(c) USES OF EXCESS DEFENSE ARTICLES.—Excess defense articles may be furnished to a country under subsection (a) only if that country ensures that those excess defense articles will be used only in support of antinarcotics activities.

"(d) ROLE OF THE SECRETARY OF STATE.—The Secretary of State shall determine the eligibility of countries to receive excess defense articles under subsection (a). In accordance with section 4601 of the International Narcotics Control Act of 1988, the Secretary shall ensure that the transfer of excess defense articles under subsection (a) is coordinated with other antinarcotics enforcement programs assisted by the United States Government.

"(e) DOLLAR LIMITATION.—The aggregate value of excess defense articles transferred to a country under subsection (a) in any fiscal year may not exceed $10,000,000.

"(f) CONDITIONS ON TRANSFERS.—The President may transfer excess defense articles under this section only if—

"(1) they are drawn from existing stocks of the Department of Defense;

"(2) funds available to the Department of Defense for the procurement of defense equipment are not expended in connection with the transfer; and

"(3) the President determines that the transfer of the excess defense articles will not have an adverse impact on the military readiness of the United States.

"(g) TERMS OF TRANSFERS.—Excess defense articles may be transferred under this section without cost to the recipient country.

"(h) WAIVER OF REQUIREMENT FOR REIMBURSEMENT OF DOD EXPENSES.—Section 632(d) does not apply with respect to transfers of excess defense articles under this section.

"(i) NOTIFICATION TO CONGRESS.—

"(1) ADVANCE NOTICE.—The President may not transfer excess defense articles under this section until 30 days after the President has provided notice of the proposed transfer to the committees specified in paragraph (2). This notification shall include—

"(A) a certification of the need for the transfer;

"(B) an assessment of the impact of the transfer on the military readiness of the United States; and

"(C) a statement of the value of the excess defense articles to be transferred.

"(2) COMMITTEES TO BE NOTIFIED.—Notice shall be provided pursuant to paragraph (1) to the Committee on Armed Services, the Committee on Foreign Affairs, and the Committee on Appropriations of the House of Representatives and the Committee on Armed Services, the Committee on Foreign Relations, and the Committee on Appropriations of the Senate.".

SEC. 6. WAIVER OF BROOKE-ALEXANDER AMENDMENT FOR MAJOR COCA PRODUCING COUNTRIES.

During fiscal year 1990, section 620(q) of the Foreign Assistance Act of 1961 (22 U.S.C. 2370(q)) and section 518 of the Foreign Operations, Export Financing, and Related Programs Appropriation Act, 1990, do not apply with respect to narcotics-related assistance for a country which is a major illicit drug producing country (as defined in section 481(i)(2) of the Foreign Assistance Act of 1961) because of its coca production.

SEC. 7. MEXICO.

(a) LIMITATION ON NARCOTICS CONTROL ASSISTANCE.—

(1) LIMITATION.—Except as provided in paragraph (2), not more than $15,000,000 of the amounts made available for fiscal year 1990 to carry out chapter 8 of part I of the Foreign Assistance Act of 1961 (22 U.S.C. 2291 and following; relating to international narcotics control assistance) may be made available for Mexico.

(2) PROCEDURE FOR ADDITIONAL ASSISTANCE.—Assistance in excess of the amount specified in paragraph (1) may be made available for Mexico only if the congressional committees specified in section 634A of the Foreign Assistance Act of 1961 (22 U.S.C. 2394-1) are notified at least 15 days in advance in accordance with the procedures applicable to reprogrammings under that section.

(b) SENATE POLICY TOWARD THE CONTROL OF ILLEGAL DRUGS IN MEXICO.—

(1) FINDINGS.—The Senate finds that—

(A) the Foreign Assistance Act of 1961 requires, except in cases of vital national interest, that all countries determined to be a major illicit drug producing country or a major drug-transit country must be "cooperating fully" with United States antinarcotics activities in order to continue receiving various forms of United States foreign assistance;

(B) relations between the United States and Mexico have suffered since the 1985 kidnapping and murder of Drug Enforcement Administration agent Enrique Camarena and the 1986 torture of DEA agent Victor Cortez;

(C) testimony before the Senate dating to 1986 has indicated that high-ranking Mexican government, military, and law enforcement officials have been involved in illegal narcotics operations, including narcotics trafficking operations into the United States;

(D) Mexico has been determined to be the primary producer of marijuana and heroin entering the United States and the transit point for up to 50 percent of the cocaine being smuggled into this country;

(E) there have been three drug-related mass murders involving more than 30 victims along the southwest border in recent months involving Mexican drug trafficking organizations;

(F) the United States continues to seek, with Mexican cooperation, hot pursuit and overflight authority for United States law enforcement agencies, access to bank records, verification of eradication figures, information on those who have been tried, charged, sentenced, and served time for narcotics-related crimes, and extradition of criminal figures;

(G) there was sworn in a new president and Government of Mexico on December 1, 1988, creating a new era of opportunity for increased cooperation and mutual friendship;

(H) the new President of Mexico, Carlos Salinas de Gortari, has indicated a strong willingness to expand and improve Mexico's antinarcotics activities;

(I) the Chief of the Mexico City Police Investigative Service, Miguel Nazar Haro, who is under indictment in the United States, has been fired;

(J) the Government of Mexico has arrested Miguel Angel Felix-Gallardo, one of the most notorious drug trafficking figures in Mexico;

(K) Mexican officials have for the first time conceded that corrupt Mexican officials, including law enforcement, government, and military officials, have previously protected Mr. Gallardo; and

(L) criminal charges of electoral fraud against the mayor of Hermosillo, Carlos Robles, and homicide and arms charges against the head of Mexico's Oil Workers Union, Joaquin Hernandez Galicia, have been filed.

(2) SENATE POLICY.—It is the sense of the Senate that—

(A) President Salinas should be supported in his expressed willingness to end the narcotics-related corruption that has permeated the Government of Mexico in the past;

(B) Mexico should conclude the prosecution of the murders of Drug Enforcement Administration agent Camarena, the perpetrators of torture against DEA agent Cortez, and make progress in the prosecution of Felix-Gallardo;

(C) Mexico should demonstrate its commitment to cooperating fully in antinarcotics activities by entering into negotiations with the United States on—

(i) joint overflight and hot pursuit operations, involving Mexican law enforcement officials traveling on United States interdiction aircraft with Mexican officers having responsibility for actual arrests of suspects;

(ii) participation of United States law enforcement agencies in air surveillance flights for interdiction efforts and joint United States-Mexico border enforcement and interdiction operations;

(iii) United States requests for access to bank records to assist in carrying out narcotics-related investigations; and

(iv) United States requests for verification of eradication statistics, including ground verification; and

(D) the people of Mexico should be supported in their efforts to rid their country of illicit narcotics, bribery and corruption, and electoral fraud.

SEC. 8. NONAPPLICABILITY OF CERTIFICATION PROCEDURES TO CERTAIN MAJOR DRUG-TRANSIT COUNTRIES.

Section 481(h) of the Foreign Assistance Act of 1961 shall not apply with respect to a major drug-transit country for fiscal year 1990 if the President certifies to the Congress, during that fiscal year, that—

(1) subparagraph (C) of section 481(i)(5) of that Act, relating to money laundering, does not apply to that country;

(2) the country previously was a major illicit drug producing country but, during each of the preceding two years, has effectively eliminated illicit drug production; and

(3) the country is cooperating fully with the United States or has taken adequate steps on its own—

(A) in satisfying the goals agreed to in an applicable bilateral narcotics agreement with the United States (as described in section 481(h)(2)(B) of that Act) or a multilateral agreement which achieves the objectives of that section;

(B) in preventing narcotic and psychotropic drugs and other controlled substances transported through such country from being sold illegally within the jurisdiction of such country to United States Government personnel or their dependents or from being transported, directly or indirectly, into the United States; and

(C) in preventing and punishing bribery and other forms of public corruption which facilitate the production, processing, or shipment of narcotic and psychotropic drugs and other controlled substances, or which discourage the investigation and prosecution of such acts.

SEC. 9. COORDINATION OF UNITED STATES TRADE POLICY AND NARCOTICS CONTROL OBJECTIVES.

(a) Need for Coordination.—It is the sense of the Congress that United States trade policy should be coordinated with United States narcotics control objectives, particularly with respect to issues such as the International Coffee Agreement.

(b) Presidential Review.—The Congress commends the President for reviewing whether the International Coffee Agreement negotiations should be resumed and whether the trade benefits provided in the Caribbean Basin Economic Recovery Act (19 U.S.C. 2701 and following) should be extended to the major coca producing countries of Latin America.

SEC. 10. DEBT-FOR-DRUGS EXCHANGES.

(a) Authority.—The President may release Bolivia, Colombia, or Peru from its obligation to make payments to the United States Government of principal and interest on account of a loan made to that country under the Foreign Assistance Act of 1961 (22 U.S.C.

2151 and following; relating to foreign assistance programs) or credits extended for that country under section 23 of the Arms Export Control Act (22 U.S.C. 2763; relating to foreign military sales credits) if the President determines that that country is implementing programs to reduce the flow of cocaine to the United States in accordance with a formal bilateral or multilateral agreement, to which the United States is a party, that contains specific, quantitative and qualitative, performance criteria with respect to those programs.

(b) CONGRESSIONAL REVIEW OF AGREEMENTS.—The President shall submit any such agreement with Bolivia, Colombia, or Peru to the Committee on Foreign Affairs of the House of Representatives and the Committee on Foreign Relations of the Senate at least 15 days before exercising the authority of section (a) with respect to that country.

(b) COORDINATION WITH MULTILATERAL DEBT RELIEF ACTIVITIES.—The authority provided in subsection (a) shall be exercised in coordination with multilateral debt relief activities.

(c) EFFECTIVE DATE.—Subsection (a) takes effect on October 1, 1990.

SEC. 11. MULTILATERAL ANTINARCOTICS STRIKE FORCE.

(a) FINDINGS.—The Congress finds that—

(1) the Congress has, in the past, indicated its support for a multilateral, regional approach to narcotics control efforts;

(2) a proposal to create a multilateral, international antinarcotics force for the Western Hemisphere, is a plan worthy of praise and strong United States support;

(3) the development of a greater capability to assist the governments of Latin America and the Caribbean, including the Caribbean Basin nations, is an essential component of efforts to interdict the flow of narcotics to the United States; and

(4) regional leadership in the promotion of a multilateral, paramilitary force to combat the drug cartels is welcomed and encouraged.

(b) SENSE OF CONGRESS.—It is therefore the sense of the Congress that—

(1) the proposal for the promotion of a regional multilateral antinarcotics force for the Western Hemisphere should be endorsed; and

(2) the United States should work through the United Nations, the Organization of American States, and other multilateral organizations to determine the feasibility of such a force and should assist in the establishment of this force if it is found to be feasible.

SEC. 12. WEAPONS TRANSFERS TO INTERNATIONAL NARCOTICS TRAFFICKERS.

(a) HALTING WEAPONS TRANSFERS TO NARCOTICS TRAFFICKERS.—The Congress urges the President to seek agreement by the relevant foreign countries, especially the member countries of the North Atlantic Treaty Organization and the member countries of the Warsaw Pact, to join with the United States in taking the necessary steps to halt transfers of weapons to narcotics traffickers in Latin America.

(b) COORDINATION OF UNITED STATES EFFORTS TO TRACK ILLEGAL ARMS TRANSFERS.—The Congress urges the President to improve the coordination of United States Government efforts—

(1) to track the flow of weapons illegally from the United States and other countries to international narcotics traffickers, and

(2) to prevent such illegal shipments from the United States.

(c) INTERPOL.—The Congress calls upon the President to direct the United States representative to INTERPOL to urge that organization to study the feasibility of creating an international database on the flow of those types of weapons that are being acquired illegally by international narcotics traffickers.

(d) REPORT TO CONGRESS.—Not later than 6 months after the date of enactment of this Act, the President shall report to the Congress on the steps taken in accordance with this section.

SEC. 13. REWARDS FOR INFORMATION CONCERNING ACTS OF INTERNATIONAL TERRORISM.

(a) AMENDMENT.—Subject to subsection (b), section 36(c) of the State Department Basic Authorities Act of 1956 (22 U.S.C. 2708(c)) is amended by striking out "$500,000" and inserting in lieu thereof "$2,000,000".

(b) AVOIDING DUPLICATIVE AMENDMENTS.—If the Foreign Relations Authorization Act, Fiscal Years 1990 and 1991, is enacted before this Act, and that Act makes the same amendment as is described in subsection (a), then subsection (a) shall not take effect. If, however, this Act is enacted before the Foreign Relations Authorization Act, Fiscal Years 1990 and 1991, and that Act would make the same amendment as is made by subsection (a), then that amendment as proposed to be made by that Act shall not take effect.

SEC. 14. WAIVER OF BUMPERS AMENDMENT.

(a) ASSISTANCE FOR CROP SUBSTITUTION ACTIVITIES.—During fiscal year 1990, the provisions described in subsection (b) do not apply with respect to assistance for crop substitution activities undertaken in furtherance of narcotics control objectives.

(b) BUMPERS AMENDMENT.—The provisions made inapplicable by subsection (a) are any provisions of the annual Foreign Operations, Export Financing, and Related Programs Appropriations Act that prohibit the use of funds made available to carry out part I of the Foreign Assistance Act of 1961 for activities in connection with the growth or production in a foreign country of an agricultural commodity for export which would compete with a similar commodity grown or produced in the United States.

SEC. 15. PARTICIPATION IN FOREIGN POLICE ACTIONS.

Section 481(c) of the Foreign Assistance Act of 1961 (22 U.S.C. 2291(c)) is amended to read as follows:

"(c) PARTICIPATION IN FOREIGN POLICE ACTIONS.—

"(1) PROHIBITION ON EFFECTING AN ARREST.—No officer or employee of the United States may directly effect an arrest in any foreign country as part of any foreign police action with respect to narcotics control efforts, notwithstanding any other provision of law.

"(2) PARTICIPATION IN ARREST ACTIONS.—Paragraph (1) does not prohibit an officer or employee of the United States, with the approval of the United States chief of mission, from being present when foreign officers are effecting an arrest or from assisting foreign officers who are effecting an arrest.

"(3) EXCEPTION FOR EXIGENT, THREATENING CIRCUMSTANCES.—Paragraph (1) does not prohibit an officer or employee from taking direct action to protect life or safety if exigent circumstances arise which are unanticipated and which pose an immediate threat to United States officers or employees, officers or employees of a foreign government, or members of the public.

"(4) EXCEPTION FOR MARITIME LAW ENFORCEMENT.—With the agreement of a foreign country, paragraph (1) does not apply with respect to maritime law enforcement operations in the territorial sea of that country.

"(5) INTERROGATIONS.—No officer or employee of the United States may interrogate or be present during the interrogation of any United States person arrested in any foreign country with respect to narcotics control efforts without the written consent of such person.

"(6) EXCEPTION FOR STATUS OF FORCES ARRANGEMENTS.—This subsection does not apply to the activities of the United States Armed Forces in carrying out their responsibilities under applicable Status of Forces arrangements.".

SEC. 16. AUTHORIZATION OF APPROPRIATIONS FOR INTERNATIONAL NARCOTICS CONTROL ASSISTANCE.

Section 482(a)(1) of the Foreign Assistance Act of 1961 (22 U.S.C. 2292(a)(1)) is amended by striking out "$101,000,000 for fiscal year 1989" and inserting in lieu thereof "$115,000,000 for fiscal year 1990".

SEC. 17. REVISIONS OF CERTAIN NARCOTICS-RELATED PROVISIONS OF THE FOREIGN ASSISTANCE ACT.

(a) PLANS BY SIGNATORIES TO 1961 SINGLE CONVENTION.—Section 481(a)(1) of the Foreign Assistance Act of 1961 (22 U.S.C. 2291(a)(1)) is amended by striking out the last sentence.

(b) QUARTERLY AND MID-YEAR REPORTS.—Section 481(b) of that Act (22 U.S.C. 2291(b)) is amended by striking out "(1)" and all that follows through "August" in paragraph (2) and inserting in lieu thereof "MID-YEAR REPORT.—Not later than September".

(c) USE OF HERBICIDES FOR AERIAL ERADICATION.—Section 481(d) of that Act (22 U.S.C. 2291(d)) is amended to read as follows:

"(d) USE OF HERBICIDES FOR AERIAL ERADICATION.—

"(1) MONITORING.—The President, with the assistance of appropriate Federal agencies, shall monitor any use under this chapter of a herbicide for aerial eradication in order to determine the impact of such use on the environment and on the health of individuals.

"(2) NOTICE TO HHS AND EPA.—The Secretary of State shall inform the Secretary of Health and Human Services and the Administrator of the Environmental Protection Agency of the use or intended use by any country or international organization of any herbicide for aerial eradication in a program receiving assistance under this chapter.

"(3) ANNUAL REPORTS.—In the annual report required by subsection (e), the President shall report on the impact on the environment and the health of individuals of the use under this chapter of a herbicide for aerial eradication.

"(4) REPORT UPON DETERMINATION OF HARM TO ENVIRONMENT OR HEALTH.—If the President determines that any such use is harmful to the environment or the health of individuals, the President shall immediately report that determination to the Committee on Foreign Affairs of the House of Representatives and the Committee on Foreign Relations of the Senate, together with such recommendations as the President deems appropriate.".

(d) DEFINITION OF COOPERATION.—Section 481(h) of that Act (22 U.S.C. 2291(h)) is amended—

(1) in paragraph (2)(A)(i)(IV), by inserting "illicit" before "production";

(2) in paragraph (2)(B)(iii), by striking out "treatment" and inserting in lieu thereof "education and treatment programs";

(3) in paragraph (2)(B)(v), by inserting "essential" before "precursor"; and

(4) in paragraph (3)(D), by inserting "illicit" before "production".

(e) DEFINITION OF MAJOR ILLICIT DRUG PRODUCING COUNTRY.—Section 481(i)(2) of that Act (22 U.S.C. 2291(i)(2)) is amended to read as follows:

"(2) the term 'major illicit drug producing country' means a country that illicitly produces during a fiscal year 5 metric tons or more of opium or opium derivative, 500 metric tons or more of coca, or 500 metric tons or more of marijuana;".

(f) DETERMINING MAJOR ILLICIT DRUG PRODUCING AND DRUG-TRANSIT COUNTRIES.—Section 481(k) of that Act (22 U.S.C. 2291(k)) is amended by striking out paragraph (4).

(g) CONTRIBUTION BY RECIPIENT COUNTRY.—Section 482(d) of that Act (22 U.S.C. 2292(d)) is amended to read as follows:

"(d) CONTRIBUTION BY RECIPIENT COUNTRY.—To ensure local commitment to the activities assisted under this chapter, a country receiving assistance under this chapter should bear an appropriate share of the costs of any narcotics control program, project, or activity for which such assistance is to be provided. A country may bear such costs on an 'in kind' basis.".

(h) CONFORMING AMENDMENTS TO NARCOTICS CONTROL TRADE ACT.—The Narcotics Control Trade Act (19 U.S.C. 2492 and following) is amended—

(1) in section 802(b)(1)(A)(i)(IV), by inserting "illicit" before "production";

(2) in section 802(b)(1)(B)(iii), by striking out "treatment" and inserting in lieu thereof "education and treatment programs";

(3) in section 802(b)(1)(B)(v), by inserting "essential" before "precursor";

(4) in section 802(b)(2)(D), by inserting "illicit" before "production";

and

(5) in section 805, by amending paragraph (2) to read as follows:

"(2) the term 'major drug producing country' means a country that illicitly produces during a fiscal year 5 metric tons or more of opium or opium derivative, 500 metric tons or more of coca, or 500 metric tons or more of marijuana; and".

Approved December 13, 1989.

LEGISLATIVE HISTORY—H.R. 3611 (S. 1735):

HOUSE REPORTS: No. 101-342, Pt. 1 (Comm. on Foreign Affairs) and No. 101-383 (Comm. of Conference).
CONGRESSIONAL RECORD, Vol. 135 (1989):
Oct. 5, S. 1735 considered and passed Senate.
Nov. 13, H.R. 3611 considered and passed House.
Nov. 15, considered and passed Senate, amended, in lieu of S. 1735.
Nov. 21, House and Senate agreed to conference report.
WEEKLY COMPILATION OF PRESIDENTIAL DOCUMENTS, Vol. 25 (1989):
Dec. 13, Presidential statement.

INTERNATIONAL DEVELOPMENT AND FINANCE ACT OF 1989

An Act to reauthorize the Export-Import Bank tied aid credit fund and pilot interest subsidy program, to provide for the participation of the United States in a replenishment of the Inter-American Development Bank and in the Enhanced Structural Adjustment Facility of the International Monetary Fund, to improve the safety and soundness of the United States banking system and encourage the reduction of the debt burdens of the highly indebted countries, to encourage the multilateral development banks to engage in environmentally sustainable lending practices and give greater priority to poverty alleviation, and for other purposes.

Date: December 18, 1989

Bill No.: H.R. 2494

Public Law No.: 101-240

Cite: 103 STAT. 2492

Sections reprinted: All (except section 101 amends some provisions of the Export-Import Bank Act).

Public Law 101-240
101st Congress

An Act

To reauthorize the Export-Import Bank tied aid credit fund and pilot interest subsidy program, to provide for the participation of the United States in a replenishment of the Inter-American Development Bank and in the Enhanced Structural Adjustment Facility of the International Monetary Fund, to improve the safety and soundness of the United States banking system and encourage the reduction of the debt burdens of the highly indebted countries, to encourage the multilateral development banks to engage in environmentally sustainable lending practices and give greater priority to poverty alleviation, and for other purposes.

Be it enacted by the Senate and House of Representatives of the United States of America in Congress assembled,

SECTION 1. SHORT TITLE; TABLE OF CONTENTS.

(a) SHORT TITLE.—This Act may be cited as the "International Development and Finance Act of 1989".

(b) TABLE OF CONTENTS.—

TITLE I—EXPORT-IMPORT BANK ACT AMENDMENTS

SEC. 102. EXTENSION OF CREDIT BY EXPORT-IMPORT BANK WITH RESPECT TO ANGOLA PROHIBITED UNLESS CERTAIN CONDITIONS ARE MET.

Section 2(b) of the Export-Import Bank Act of 1945 (12 U.S.C. 635(b)) is amended by adding at the end the following:

"(12) PROHIBITION RELATING TO ANGOLA.—Notwithstanding any determination by the President under paragraph (2) or (11), the Bank may not guarantee, insure, or extend (or participate in the extension of) credit in connection with any export of any good (other than food or an agricultural commodity) or service to the People's Republic of Angola until the President certifies to the Congress that free and fair elections have been held in Angola in which all participants were afforded free and fair access, and that the government of Angola—

"(A) is willing, and is actively seeking, to achieve an equitable political settlement of the conflict in Angola, including free and fair elections, through a mutual cease-fire and a dialogue with the opposition armed forces;

"(B) has demonstrated progress in protecting internationally recognized human rights, and particularly in—

"(i) ending, through prosecution or other means, involvement of members of the military and security forces in political violence and abuses of internationally recognized human rights;

"(ii) vigorously prosecuting persons engaged in political violence who are connected with the government; and

"(iii) bringing to justice those responsible for the abduction, torture, and murder of citizens of Angola and citizens of the United States; and

"(C) has demonstrated progress in its respect for, and protection of—

"(i) the freedom of the press;

"(ii) the freedom of speech;

"(iii) the freedom of assembly;

"(iv) the freedom of association (including the right to organize for political purposes);

"(v) internationally recognized worker rights; and

"(vi) other attributes of political pluralism and democracy.

The President shall include in each report made pursuant to this paragraph a detailed statement with respect to each of the conditions set forth in this paragraph. This paragraph shall not be construed to impose any requirement with respect to Angola that is more restrictive than any requirement imposed by this section generally on all other countries.".

SEC. 103. EXPORT-IMPORT PROGRAMS TO THE PEOPLE'S REPUBLIC OF CHINA PROHIBITED UNLESS CERTAIN CONDITIONS ARE MET.

(a) Notwithstanding any other provision of law and subject to the provisions of subsections (b) and (c), the Export-Import Bank of the United States shall not finance any trade with, nor extend any loan, credit, credit guarantee, insurance or reinsurance to the People's Republic of China.

(b) The prohibitions described in subsection (a) of this section shall not apply to food or agricultural commodities.

(c) The President may waive the prohibitions in subsection (a) if he makes a report to Congress either—

(1) that the Government of the People's Republic of China has made progress on a program of political reform throughout the country, as well as in Tibet, which includes—

(A) lifting of martial law;

(B) halting of executions and other reprisals against individuals for the nonviolent expression of their political beliefs;

(C) release of political prisoners;

(D) increased respect for internationally recognized human rights, including freedom of expression, the press, assembly, and association; and

(E) permitting a freer flow of information, including an end to the jamming of Voice of America and greater access for foreign journalists; or

(2) it is in the national interest of the United States to terminate a suspension under subsection (a).

TITLE II—INTER-AMERICAN DEVELOPMENT BANK

SEC. 201. PARTICIPATION BY THE UNITED STATES IN A CAPITAL INCREASE OF THE INTER-AMERICAN DEVELOPMENT BANK; INCREASE IN RESOURCES OF FUND FOR SPECIAL OPERATIONS.

The Inter-American Development Bank Act (22 U.S.C. 283 et seq.) is amended by adding at the end the following:

"SEC. 33. CAPITAL INCREASE; INCREASE IN RESOURCES OF FUND FOR SPECIAL OPERATIONS.

"(a) AUTHORITY TO VOTE FOR, AND TO SUBSCRIBE AND CONTRIBUTE TO, INCREASE IN AUTHORIZED CAPITAL STOCK OF BANK AND INCREASE IN RESOURCES OF FUND FOR SPECIAL OPERATIONS.—

"(1) VOTE AUTHORIZED.—The United States Governor of the Bank is authorized to vote for resolutions which—

"(A) were transmitted by the Board of Executive Directors to the Governors of the Bank by resolution of April 19, 1989;

"(B) are pending before the Board of Governors of the Bank; and

"(C) provide for—

"(i) an increase in the authorized capital stock of the Bank and subscriptions to the Bank; and

"(ii) an increase in the resources of the Fund for Special Operations and contributions to the Fund.

"(2) SUBSCRIPTION AND CONTRIBUTION AUTHORITY.—To the extent and in the amounts provided in advance in appropriations Acts, on adoption of the resolutions described in paragraph (1), the United States Governor of the Bank may, on behalf of the United States—

"(A) subscribe to 760,112 shares of the increase in the authorized capital stock of the Bank; and

"(B) contribute $82,304,000 to the Fund for Special Operations.

"(b) LIMITATION ON AUTHORIZATION OF APPROPRIATIONS.—To pay for the subscription and contribution authorized under subsection (a), there are authorized to be appropriated, without fiscal year limitation, for payment by the Secretary of the Treasury—

"(1) $9,169,559,712, for the United States subscription to the capital stock of the Bank; and

"(2) $82,304,000, for the United States contribution to the Fund for Special Operations.

"(c) ORGANIZATIONAL CHANGES REQUIRED TO BE MADE BEFORE PAYMENT FOR SUBSCRIPTION TO CAPITAL STOCK AND CONTRIBUTION TO THE FUND FOR SPECIAL OPERATIONS.—The Secretary of the Treasury may not make any payment for the subscription and contribution authorized under subsection (a) unless the Bank—

"(1) has established an environmental unit with responsibility for the development, evaluation, and integration of Bank policies, projects, and programs designed to promote environmentally sustainable development in borrower countries;

"(2) has increased the number of the staff of the Bank with environmentally oriented responsibilities and training;

"(3) provides for an increase in the number of environmentally beneficial projects and programs financed by the Bank; and

"(4) has designed a process for ensuring the access of indigenous non-governmental organizations to the process for designing projects and programs.

"(d) Certification of Access to Bank Records Required Before Payment for Subscription to Capital Stock and Contribution to Fund for Special Operations.—The Secretary of the Treasury shall not make any payment for the subscription and contribution authorized under subsection (a) until the Secretary, after consultation with the United States Executive Director of the Bank, certifies to the Congress that—

"(1) the Bank has given the Comptroller General of the United States access to the audit memorandum issued by the Auditor General of the Bank with respect to the November 1987 disbursement of funds to the Government of Nicaragua;

"(2) the Bank has implemented and is continuing to implement revised procedures issued in 1988 for collecting loan services payments in arrears;

"(3) the revised procedures referred to in paragraph (2) satisfy the recommendations of the Auditor General of the Bank; and

"(4) the Comptroller General of the United States has access to all documents of the Bank on the same terms and under the same conditions as such documents are made available to the United States Executive Director of the Bank.".

SEC. 202. INVESTMENT IN HUMAN CAPITAL.

(a) Promotion of Lending in Support of Human Capital.—The Inter-American Development Bank Act (22 U.S.C. 283 et seq.) is amended by adding after the section added by section 201 of this Act the following:

"SEC. 34. INVESTMENT IN HUMAN CAPITAL.

"(a) In General.—The Secretary of the Treasury shall instruct the United States Executive Director of the Inter-American Development Bank to propose and use the voice and vote of such director, during the 4-year period beginning on January 1, 1990, to vigorously promote an increase in the proportion of Bank lending in support of projects and programs which support investments in human capital and to seek the rapid implementation by the Bank of systematic mechanisms of consultation with locally affected populations in borrower countries either directly or through appropriate representative non-governmental organizations.

"(b) Investments in Human Capital Defined.—As used in subsection (a), the term 'investments in human capital' means investments in projects, policies, and programs designed to improve urban and rural health care and sanitation, basic nutrition, education, the small-producer private sector, the economic activities of women, and the development of indigenous non-governmental organizations.".

(b) Report to the Congress.—The Chairman of the National Advisory Council on International Monetary and Financial Policies shall include in the report required by section 1701 of the International Financial Institutions Act for fiscal year 1991 a report on the efforts undertaken by the United States Executive Director of the Inter-American Development Bank, and the progress to date, in achieving the objectives of section 34 of the Inter-American Development Bank Act.

burden of such country) during the 4-year period beginning on January 1, 1990, to 25 percent of the aggregate value of all loans made by the Bank during such 4-year period;

"(2) take all necessary steps to encourage the Bank to limit the aggregate value of the policy based loans made by the Bank to the government of a particular country during such 4-year period, to 50 percent of the aggregate value of all loans made by the Bank to such government during such 4-year period;

"(3) instruct the United States Executive Director of the Bank to explore with the other Executive Directors of the Bank ways to use a portion of the resources made available to the Bank by reason of the subscription and contribution described in section 33(a)(2) for debt reduction and debt service reduction for countries described in paragraph (1); and

"(4) before the end of the 12-month period beginning on the date of the enactment of this section, report to the Congress on the matters described in paragraph (3).".

SEC. 204. INCREASE IN INTER-AMERICAN DEVELOPMENT BANK LENDING TO THE CARIBBEAN.

The Inter-American Development Bank Act (22 U.S.C. 283 et seq.) is amended by adding after the section added by section 203 of this Act the following:

"SEC. 36. INCREASE IN LENDING TO THE CARIBBEAN.

"The Secretary of the Treasury shall instruct the United States Executive Director of the Bank to enter into discussions with the management of the Bank and with other member country governments to seek to increase Bank lending to the Caribbean region, directly or through appropriate financial intermediaries, for viable projects which will—

"(1) result in expanded regional economic integration, diversification, and industrial and agricultural production, and improved infrastructure; and

"(2) seek to ensure equitable and environmentally sustainable economic growth.".

SEC. 205. SENSE OF THE CONGRESS THAT INTER-AMERICAN DEVELOPMENT BANK LOANS SHOULD REDUCE DEPENDENCE ON ILLICIT NARCOTICS.

It is the sense of the Congress that, whenever possible and appropriate, loans made by the Inter-American Development Bank during the 4-year period beginning on January 1, 1990, should promote economic development which will reduce the growing economic dependence on the production and transit of illicit narcotics in certain borrower countries.

SEC. 206. DIRECTIVES REGARDING GOVERNMENT-OWNED ENTERPRISES IN COUNTRIES RECEIVING IADB LOANS.

The International Financial Institutions Act (22 U.S.C. 262c et seq.) is amended by redesignating section 1612 as section 1613 and by inserting after section 1611 the following:

"SEC. 1612. DIRECTIVES REGARDING GOVERNMENT-OWNED ENTERPRISES IN COUNTRIES RECEIVING IADB LOANS.

"(a) FINDING.—The Congress finds that a principal focus of United States Government policy in the multilateral development banks has been and should be to foster greater development of the private sector in member borrowing countries of such banks.

"(b) TECHNICAL ASSISTANCE TO TRANSFORM GOVERNMENT-OWNED ENTERPRISES INTO PRIVATELY OWNED ENTERPRISES.—In order to assist and strengthen the advancement of ongoing efforts to have the Inter-American Development Bank play a key role in building a viable private sector in member borrowing countries of such bank, and to further assist such bank in its determination to facilitate the transfer of government-owned enterprises in such countries to private ownership, the Secretary of the Treasury shall instruct the United States Executive Director of such bank to vigorously encourage the provision of technical assistance to such countries to transform enterprises owned, in whole or in part, by the governments of such countries into privately owned, self-sufficient enterprises. Such technical assistance may involve the valuation of the assets of such government-owned enterprises, the assessment of tender offers, and the creation or strengthening of market-based mechanisms to facilitate such a transfer of ownership.".

TITLE III—INTERNATIONAL MONETARY FUND ENHANCED STRUCTURAL ADJUSTMENT FACILITY

SEC. 301. CONTRIBUTION TO THE INTEREST SUBSIDY ACCOUNT OF THE ENHANCED STRUCTURAL ADJUSTMENT FACILITY OF THE INTERNATIONAL MONETARY FUND.

The Bretton Woods Agreements Act (22 U.S.C. 286 et seq.) is amended by adding at the end the following:

"SEC. 54. CONTRIBUTION TO THE INTEREST SUBSIDY ACCOUNT OF THE ENHANCED STRUCTURAL ADJUSTMENT FACILITY OF THE INTERNATIONAL MONETARY FUND.

"(a) CONTRIBUTION AUTHORIZED.—

"(1) IN GENERAL.—Subject to paragraph (2), the United States Governor of the Fund may contribute $150,000,000 to the Interest Subsidy Account of the Enhanced Structural Adjustment Facility of the Fund on behalf of the United States.

"(2) CONDITION.—The United States Governor of the Fund may not make a commitment to contribute any amount authorized to be contributed under paragraph (1) before an amount equal to such amount has been appropriated for such purpose.

"(b) LIMITATION ON AUTHORIZATION OF APPROPRIATIONS.—To pay for the contribution authorized by subsection (a), there are authorized to be appropriated not to exceed $150,000,000, without fiscal year limitation, for payment by the Secretary of the Treasury.".

SEC. 302. DISCUSSIONS TO ENHANCE THE CAPACITY OF THE INTERNATIONAL MONETARY FUND TO ALLEVIATE THE POTENTIALLY ADVERSE IMPACTS OF FUND PROGRAMS ON THE POOR AND THE ENVIRONMENT.

The Bretton Woods Agreements Act (22 U.S.C. 286 et seq.) is amended by adding after the section added by section 301 of this Act the following:

"SEC. 55. DISCUSSIONS TO ENHANCE THE CAPACITY OF THE FUND TO ALLEVIATE THE POTENTIALLY ADVERSE IMPACTS OF FUND PROGRAMS ON THE POOR AND THE ENVIRONMENT.

"The Secretary of the Treasury shall instruct the United States Executive Director of the Fund to seek policy changes by the Fund, through formal initiatives and through bilateral discussions, which will result in—

"(1) the initiation of a systematic review of policy prescriptions implemented by the Fund, for the purpose of determining whether the Fund's objectives were met and the social and environmental impacts of such policy prescriptions; and

"(2) the establishment of procedures which ensure the inclusion, in future economic reform programs approved by the Fund, of policy options which eliminate or reduce the potential adverse impact on the well-being of the poor or the environment resulting from such programs.".

TITLE IV—INTERNATIONAL DEBT PROVISIONS

SEC. 401. SHORT TITLE.

This title may be cited as the "Foreign Debt Reserving Act of 1989".

SEC. 402. ADDITIONAL RESERVE REQUIREMENTS.

(a) FINDINGS.—The Congress finds that—

(1) since the adoption of the International Lending Supervision Act of 1983, the credit quality of loans by United States banking institutions to highly indebted countries has deteriorated and the prospects for full repayment of such loans have diminished;

(2) in general during this period, the level of country exposure and transfer risk associated with loans by United States banking institutions to highly indebted countries has not been adequately reflected in the reserve levels established by many individual United States banking institutions or the reserve requirements imposed by Federal banking agencies pursuant to such Act;

(3) during the last 3 years and particularly in recent months, United States banking institutions have increased their reserves for possible losses from loans to highly indebted countries but such reserves remain, in some cases, significantly lower than reserves established by banking institutions in a number of foreign countries and may not be adequate to deal with potential risks; and

(4) in order to fulfill the purposes of such Act, the Federal banking agencies should take a more active role in reviewing reserve levels established by United States banking institutions for potential losses from loans to highly indebted countries and in requiring appropriate levels of both special and general reserves to reflect the increased risk of such loans.

(b) IN GENERAL.—The International Lending Supervision Act of 1983 (12 U.S.C. 3901 et seq.) is amended by inserting after section 905 the following new section:

"SEC. 905A. ADDITIONAL RESERVE REQUIREMENTS.

"(a) IN GENERAL.—Each appropriate Federal banking agency shall review the exposure to risk of United States banking institutions arising from the medium- and long-term loans made by such institutions that are outstanding to any highly indebted country. Each agency shall provide direction to such institutions regarding additions to general reserves maintained by each banking institution for potential loan losses and special reserves required by such agency arising from such review.

"(b) DETERMINATION OF INSTITUTIONAL EXPOSURE TO RISK.—In determining the exposure of an institution to risk for purposes of subsection (a), the appropriate Federal banking agency—

"(1) shall determine whether any country exposure that is, and has been for at least 2 years, rated in the category 'Other Transfer Risk Problems' or the category 'Substandard' by the Interagency Country Exposure Review Committee should be reevaluated;

"(2) may exempt, in full or in part, from reserve requirements established pursuant to subsection (a), any loan—

"(A) to a country that enters into a debt reduction, debt service reduction, or financing program with its bank creditors that is supported by the International Bank for Reconstruction and Development or the International Monetary Fund; or

"(B) secured, in whole or in part, by appropriate collateral for payment of interest or principal;

"(3) take into account any other factors which bear on such exposure and the particular circumstances of the institution; and

"(4) shall consider as indicators of risk, where appropriate, the average reserve levels maintained by or required of banking institutions in foreign countries and secondary market prices for such loans.

"(c) TIMING AND REPORT.—

"(1) DETERMINED BY AGENCY.—Except as provided in paragraph (3), each appropriate Federal banking agency shall determine the timing of any addition to reserves required by subsection (a).

"(2) REPORT.—Each appropriate Federal banking agency shall include in each report required to be made under section 913(d) after 1989 a report on the actions taken pursuant to this section.

"(3) DEADLINE.—Each Federal agency required to undertake a review described in subsection (a) shall complete the review not later than December 31, 1990.

"(d) HIGHLY INDEBTED COUNTRY DEFINED.—As used in this section, the term 'highly indebted country' means any country designated as a 'Highly Indebted Country' in the annual World Debt Tables most recently published by the International Bank for Reconstruction and Development before the date of the enactment of this section.".

SEC. 403. REPORT ON MARK TO MARKET ACCOUNTING.

(a) REPORT REQUIRED.—Before the end of the 90-day period beginning on the date of the enactment of this section, the Board of Governors of the Federal Reserve System, the Federal Deposit Insurance Corporation, and the Comptroller of the Currency shall jointly report to the Committee on Banking, Finance and Urban Affairs of the House of Representatives and the Committee on

Banking, Housing, and Urban Affairs of the Senate on the merits of mark to market accounting treatment as an appropriate accounting treatment for the sovereign debt of highly indebted countries which is held by United States commercial banks.

(b) CONTENTS OF REPORT.—The report required under subsection (a) shall include—

(1) a discussion of the merits of mark to market accounting treatment as the appropriate accounting treatment for the sovereign debt of highly indebted countries which is held by United States commercial banks; and

(2) a description of the factors which the Board of Governors of the Federal Reserve System, the Federal Deposit Insurance Corporation, and the Comptroller of the Currency will consider in future assessments of the applicability of mark to market accounting to such debt.

SEC. 404. STUDY ON ELIMINATION OF CAPITAL FLIGHT.

(a) IN GENERAL.—The Secretary of the Treasury shall instruct the United States Executive Director of the International Monetary Fund to propose that the Fund conduct a study on multilateral means by which the banking industry might help reverse capital flight from countries which are engaged in debt restructuring, including—

(1) the feasibility of disclosing the names of account holders whose accounts may consist of flight capital, and the balances of such accounts;

(2) the usefulness of such disclosures in deterring the creation and maintenance of such accounts, and how such deterrence would operate or be defeated;

(3) the extent to which any such information is gathered and to whom such information is made available;

(4) the receptiveness of such countries to the disclosure of such information;

(5) the difficulties in, and the cost of, collecting such information and overcoming legal obstacles used to disguise the true ownership of such deposits, including the feasibility of using the threat of confiscatory penalties to prevent the disguising of the ownership of deposits;

(6) the usefulness of using taxes as a means to encourage the repatriation of flight capital; and

(7) the applicability (if any) of efforts to facilitate the identification, tracing, seizure, and forfeiture of drug crime proceeds, and to prevent the use of the banking system and of financial institutions for the purpose of money laundering.

(b) FLIGHT CAPITAL DEFINED.—As used in subsection (a), the term "flight capital" means any asset—

(1)(A) which is deposited in a banking institution for safekeeping or investment purposes; or

(B) for which a financial institution serves as a conduit, an agent, or a fiduciary in a transaction; and

(2) the owner of which may be a legal resident of a country other than the country in which the institution is located.

(c) REPORT TO THE CONGRESS.—Not later than the end of the 180-day period beginning on the date of the enactment of this Act, the Secretary of the Treasury shall submit to the Chairman of the Committee on Banking, Finance and Urban Affairs of the House of Representatives, and the Committee on Banking, Housing, and

Urban Affairs of the Senate a report on the actions taken and studies completed as required by subsection (a).

SEC. 405. FACTORS TO BE TAKEN INTO ACCOUNT IN DEVELOPING UNITED STATES POLICY TOWARD DEBT REDUCTION FOR CERTAIN HIGHLY INDEBTED COUNTRIES; REPORT TO THE CONGRESS.

(a) FACTORS TO BE TAKEN INTO ACCOUNT.—In developing the policy of the United States Government with respect to debt reduction for each highly indebted country which has a substantial share of the export market for 1 or more agricultural commodities the export market for which the United States also has a substantial share, the Secretary of the Treasury shall consider among other factors the effects of such policy on:

(1) United States exports of such commodities.

(2) The world price of such commodities.

(3) Domestic agricultural production and land distribution patterns in such country.

(4) The volume of exports from such country of agricultural commodities the export market for which such country has a substantial share of.

(5) Basic nutrition levels in such country.

(b) REPORT TO THE CONGRESS.—Before the end of the 12-month period beginning on the date of the enactment of this section, the Secretary of the Treasury shall submit a report to the Congress on the potential impact of such policy on such factors in the highly indebted countries.

(c) HIGHLY INDEBTED COUNTRY DEFINED.—As used in this section, the term "highly indebted country" means any country designated as a "Highly Indebted Country" in the annual World Debt Tables most recently published by the International Bank for Reconstruction and Development before the date of the enactment of this section.

SEC. 406. SENSE OF THE CONGRESS THAT AGREEMENTS TO REDUCE DEBT BURDEN SHOULD BE ACCOMPANIED BY TRADE LIBERALIZATION.

(a) FINDINGS.—The Congress finds that—

(1) Third World debtor nations have often been forced to raise trade barriers in order to accumulate foreign exchange surpluses to repay debt obligations;

(2) trade flows between such nations and the United States have lessened due to the debt crisis;

(3) the reduction of trade barriers would benefit the world economy and promote economic growth; and

(4) the Brady plan encourages debt reduction agreements on behalf of domestic financial institutions.

(b) SENSE OF THE CONGRESS.—It is the sense of Congress that the Secretary of the Treasury should continue to encourage trade liberalization as an element of economic reform programs.

SEC. 407. LINKAGE OF DEBT REDUCTION LOANS TO REDUCTION IN DRUG TRAFFICKING; REPORT TO CONGRESS.

(a) FINDINGS.—The Congress finds that—

(1) the Brady Initiative is a positive step, recognizing as it does the need for reducing the debt and debt service burdens of the indebted developing countries;

(2) the multilateral development banks should, as part of this debt reduction process, encourage such countries to further reform their economies by reducing their dependence on production and trafficking of illicit narcotics; and

(3) reduction of debt should relieve some of the financial burden on these countries, and thereby enable them to rely on legal income-generating activities.

(b) INSTRUCTION OF UNITED STATES EXECUTIVE DIRECTORS.—The Secretary of the Treasury shall instruct the United States Executive Director of each multilateral development bank that, in voting with respect to loans from the multilateral development bank to reduce the debt and debt burden of borrowing countries which are major producers, processors, traffickers, or exporters of illegal drugs to the United States, the Executive Director shall give preference to those countries which show marked improvement in reducing the volume of cultivation, processing, trafficking, and export to the United States of illegal drugs. In making a determination under the preceding sentence with respect to a country's improvement, the Secretary of the Treasury shall consult with the heads of the relevant agencies.

(c) REPORT TO CONGRESS.—The Secretary of the Treasury shall include, in the detailed accounting required by section 2018(c) of the International Narcotics Control Act of 1986 (22 U.S.C. 2191 note), relating to multilateral development bank assistance for drug eradication and crop substitution programs, an additional discussion of the steps taken and the progress made in implementing the goals set forth in subsection (b) of this section, and further steps needed to secure the achievement of these goals.

(d) DEFINITIONS.—As used in this section—

(1) the term "multilateral development bank" includes the International Bank for Reconstruction and Development, the International Development Association, the International Finance Corporation, the Inter-American Development Bank, the Inter-American Investment Corporation, the Asian Development Bank, the African Development Bank, and the African Development Fund; and

(2) the term "illegal drugs" means "narcotic and psychotropic drugs and other controlled substances", as defined in section 481(i)(3) of the Foreign Assistance Act of 1961 (22 U.S.C. 2291(i)(3)).

TITLE V—ALLEVIATION OF POVERTY; ENVIRONMENTAL PROVISIONS; DEBT-FOR-DEVELOPMENT SWAPS; CONSOLIDATION OF REPORTING REQUIREMENTS

Subtitle A—Alleviation of Poverty

SEC. 501. INCREASING THE PRODUCTIVE ECONOMIC PARTICIPATION OF THE POOR.

The International Financial Institutions Act (22 U.S.C. 262c et seq.) is amended by redesignating section 1613 (as so redesignated by section 206 of this Act) as section 1614 and by inserting after section 1612 (as added by such section 206) the following:

"SEC. 1613. DISCUSSIONS TO INCREASE THE PRODUCTIVE ECONOMIC PARTICIPATION OF THE POOR; REPORTS.

"(a) IN GENERAL.—The Secretary of the Treasury shall instruct the United States Executive Director for each multilateral development bank to vigorously and continually advocate, in all replenishment negotiations and in discussion with other directors of such bank and with such bank, the following:

"(1) A major objective of such bank's operations and financing in each borrowing country, as a long term priority, should be to increase the productive role of the poor in the economy of such country.

"(2) Such bank should encourage and assist each borrowing country to develop sustainable national plans and strategies to eliminate the causes and alleviate the manifestations of poverty which keep the poor from leading economically and socially productive lives. Such plans and strategies should give attention to—

"(A) the enhancement of human resources, including programs for basic nutrition, primary health services, basic education, and safe water and basic sanitation;

"(B) access to income-generating activities, employment, and productive assets such as land and credit; and

"(C) consultation with public sector social agencies and local non-governmental organizations.

"(3) As an integral element of ongoing policy dialogue with each borrowing country to design structural adjustment plans and project lending programs, such bank should provide assistance consistent with achieving the objectives of the country's national plan for increasing the productive economic participation of the poor. Such dialogue should be conducted with government agencies working in social and economic sectors and with non-governmental groups in the borrowing country, especially those that have grassroots involvement with poor people.

"(4) In an annual review document, such bank should describe the extent to which the goal of increasing the productive economic participation of the poor is being advanced or retarded and the steps that are being taken to overcome obstacles to its fulfillment. Such review should be based on information contained in the bank's country implementation review documents and in the country strategy documents for each borrowing country. Such country strategy documents should describe the national strategy for productive economic participation of the poor and the steps the bank plans to take to assist the borrowing country during the period covered by the country strategy document.

"(5) Such bank should assist countries in assessing and monitoring progress in achieving poverty alleviation goals and targets through measurement by appropriate social indicators.

"(6) Such bank should adopt procedures and budgetary allocations for administrative purposes, and establish appropriate staffing levels, to ensure that adequate resources are available to implement the bank's program for enhancing the productive economic participation of the poor, in consultation with non-governmental groups.

"(7) Such bank should adopt, as a separate and major criterion in the allocation of concessional financing resources, a preferential allocation to each country which undertakes significant efforts to enhance the productive economic participation of the poor.

"(8) Such bank should require each country which receives structural adjustment assistance to have in place, after a reasonable phase-in period, a strategy to enhance the productive economic participation of the poor.

"(b) PROGRESS REPORT.—Before the end of the 1-year period beginning on the date of the enactment of this section, the Secretary of the Treasury shall submit to the Committee on Banking, Finance and Urban Affairs and the Committee on Appropriations of the House of Representatives, and the Committee on Foreign Relations and the Committee on Appropriations of the Senate, a report on the following:

"(1) The status of advocacy and progress being made to implement the objectives of subsection (a), describing the success to date, the obstacles encountered, and future expectations of progress.

"(2) A description of the progress to date in achieving the purposes of section 1611, including the institutional capacity and effort devoted to assisting in the development of statistical measures to assess the well-being of the poor.

"(3) A description and evaluation of the progress to date in developing effective mechanisms for involving non-governmental organizations, directly or indirectly, in the design, implementation, and monitoring of development projects, programs, and policies of the multilateral development banks.".

Subtitle B—International Debt Exchanges and the Environment

SEC. 511. SENSE OF THE CONGRESS RESOLUTION REGARDING ENVIRONMENTAL POLICY AND INTERNATIONAL DEBT EXCHANGES.

It is the sense of the Congress that—

(1) the Secretary of the Treasury should include support for sustainable development and conservation projects when providing a framework for negotiating or facilitating exchanges or reductions of commercial debt of foreign countries; and

(2) that in assisting or facilitating the reduction of debt of heavily indebted foreign countries, through multilateral institutions such as the International Monetary Fund or the International Bank for Reconstruction and Development, the Secretary of State and the Secretary of the Treasury should—

(A) support efforts to provide adequate resources for sustainable development and conservation projects as a component of the restructured commercial bank debt of that country; and

(B) in providing such support, seek to assure that—

(i) the host government, or a local nongovernmental organization acting with the support of the host government, has identified conservation or sustainable development projects it will target for assistance;

(ii) there will be in place an organization, either governmental or nongovernmental, that will have the commitment to assure the long-term viability of the project; and

(iii) the allocation of the resources provided for conservation and sustainable development projects through the debt restructuring agreement is done in a manner that will not overwhelm or distort economic conditions in the host country.

SEC. 512. MULTILATERAL DEVELOPMENT BANKS AND DEBT-FOR-NATURE EXCHANGES.

The International Financial Institutions Act (22 U.S.C. 262c et seq.) is amended by redesignating section 1614 (as so redesignated by section 501 of this Act) as section 1617, and by inserting after section 1613 (as added by such section 501) the following:

"SEC. 1614. MULTILATERAL DEVELOPMENT BANKS AND DEBT-FOR-NATURE EXCHANGES.

"(a) DIRECTIONS TO THE UNITED STATES EXECUTIVE DIRECTORS.—The Secretary of the Treasury shall direct the United States Executive Directors of the multilateral development banks to—

"(1) negotiate for the creation in each respective multilateral development bank, except where the Secretary of the Treasury determines that the provisions of this subsection have previously been met, of a department that will—

"(A) be responsible for environmental protection and resource conservation, including support for restoration, protection, and sustainable use policies;

"(B) develop and monitor strict environmental guidelines and policies to govern lending activities; and

"(C) actively promote, coordinate and facilitate debt-for-nature exchanges and the restoration, protection, and sustainable use of tropical forests, renewable natural resources, endangered ecosystems and species in debtor countries;

"(2) support and encourage the approval of multilateral development bank loans which include provisions that foster and facilitate the implementation of a sound and effective environmental policy in the borrowing country;

"(3) encourage the banks to assist such countries in reducing and restructuring private debt through the use of a portion of a project or policy based environmental loan in ways which will enable such countries to buy back private debt at a rate of discount available for such debt, at auction in the secondary market or through negotiations with creditors holding such debt;

"(4) seek to ensure that staff of each bank facilitate debtor countries' collaboration with local and international nongovernmental or private organizations in implementing debt-for-nature exchanges; and

"(5) seek to ensure that each bank adopts policy guidelines which to the maximum extent possible provide for—

"(A) the inclusion of sustainable use policies in loan agreements negotiated with borrower members;

"(B) the adoption of economic programs to foster sound environmental policies; and

"(C) the provision of debtor countries' policy changes or significant increases in financial resources for use in at least 1 of the following—

"(i) restoration, protection, or sustainable use of the world's oceans and atmosphere;

"(ii) restoration, protection, or sustainable use of diverse animal and plant species;

"(iii) establishment, restoration, protection, and maintenance of parks and reserves;

"(iv) development and implementation of sound systems of natural resource management;

"(v) development and support of local conservation programs;

"(vi) training programs to strengthen conservation institutions and increase scientific, technical, and managerial capabilities of individuals and organizations involved in conservation efforts;

"(vii) efforts to generate knowledge, increase understanding, and enhance public commitment to conservation;

"(viii) design and implementation of sound programs of land and ecosystem management; and

"(ix) promotion of regenerative approaches in farming, forestry, and watershed management.

"(b) NEGOTIATION OF GUIDELINES FOR RESTORATION, PROTECTION, OR SUSTAINABLE USE POLICIES.—The United States Executive Directors of the multilateral development banks shall seek to negotiate with the other executive directors to provide guidelines for restoration, protection, or sustainable use policies. Pending the outcome of such negotiations, the United States Executive Directors shall consider restoration, protection, or sustainable use policies to be those which—

"(1) support development that maintains and restores the renewable natural resource base so that present and future needs of debtor countries' populations can be met, while not impairing critical ecosystems and not exacerbating global environmental problems;

"(2) are environmentally sustainable in that resources are conserved and managed in an effort to remove pressure on the natural resource base and to make judicious use of the land so as to sustain growth and the availability of all natural resources;

"(3) support development that does not exceed the limits imposed by local hydrological cycles, soil, climate, vegetation, and human cultural practices;

"(4) promote the maintenance and restoration of soils, vegetation, hydrological cycles, wildlife, critical ecosystems (tropical forests, wetlands, and coastal marine resources), biological diversity and other natural resources essential to economic growth and human well-being and shall, when using natural resources, be implemented to minimize the depletion of such natural resources; and

"(5) take steps, wherever feasible, to prevent pollution that threatens human health and important biotic systems and to achieve patterns of energy consumption that meet human needs and rely on renewable resources.

"(c) INCLUSION OF CERTAIN ITEMS IN GUIDELINES.—The United States Executive Directors shall endeavor to include the provisions of paragraphs (1) through (5) of subsection (b) in the guidelines developed through the negotiations specified in this section.

"SEC. 1615. PROMOTION OF LENDING FOR THE ENVIRONMENT.

"The Secretary of the Treasury shall instruct the United States Executive Director of the International Bank for Reconstruction and Development to initiate discussions with the other executive directors of such bank and the management of such bank and propose that, in order to reduce the future need for bank lending for reforestation and restoration of environmentally degraded areas, the bank establish a project and policy based environmental lending program (including a loan a portion of which could be used to reduce and restructure private debt), to be made available to interested countries with a demonstrated commitment to natural resource conservation, which would be based on—

"(1) the estimated long-term economic return which could be expected from the sustainable use and protection of tropical forests, including the value of tropical forests for indigenous people and for science;

"(2) the value derived from such services as—

"(A) watershed management;

"(B) soil erosion control;

"(C) the maintenance and improvement of—

"(i) fisheries;

"(ii) water supply regulation for industrial development;

"(iii) food;

"(iv) fuel;

"(v) fodder; and

"(vi) building materials for local communities;

"(D) the extraction of naturally occurring products from locally controlled protected areas; and

"(E) indigenous knowledge of the management and use of natural resources; and

"(3) the long-term benefits expected to be derived from maintaining biological diversity and climate stabilization.

"SEC. 1616. PROMOTION OF INSTITUTION-BUILDING FOR NONGOVERNMENTAL ORGANIZATIONS CONCERNED WITH THE ENVIRONMENT.

"The Secretary of the Treasury shall instruct the United States Executive Directors of the multilateral development banks to vigorously promote the adoption of policies and procedures which seek to—

"(1) increase collaboration with, and, where necessary, strengthen, nongovernmental organizations in such countries which are concerned with environmental protection by providing appropriate assistance and support for programs and activities on environmental protection; and

"(2) encourage international collaboration for information exchange and project enhancement with nongovernmental organizations in developing countries which are concerned with environmental protection and government agencies and private voluntary organizations in developed countries which are concerned with environmental protection.".

Subtitle C—Environmental Impact Assessments

SEC. 521. ASSESSMENT OF ENVIRONMENTAL IMPACT OF PROPOSED MULTILATERAL DEVELOPMENT BANK ACTIONS.

Title XIII of the International Financial Institutions Act (22 U.S.C. 262m et seq.) is amended by adding at the end the following:

"SEC. 1308. ASSESSMENT OF ENVIRONMENTAL IMPACT OF PROPOSED MULTILATERAL DEVELOPMENT BANK ACTIONS.

"(a) ASSESSMENT REQUIRED BEFORE FAVORABLE VOTE ON ACTION.—

"(1) IN GENERAL.—Beginning 2 years after the date of the enactment of this section, the Secretary of the Treasury shall instruct the United States Executive Director of each multilateral development bank not to vote in favor of any action proposed to be taken by the respective bank which would have a significant effect on the human environment, unless for at least 120 days before the date of the vote—

"(A) an assessment analyzing the environmental impacts of the proposed action and of alternatives to the proposed action has been completed by the borrowing country or the institution, and been made available to the board of directors of the institution; and

"(B) except as provided in paragraph (2), such assessment or a comprehensive summary of such assessment has been made available to the multilateral development bank, affected groups, and local nongovernmental organizations.

"(2) EXCEPTIONS AND REPORTS.—

"(A) EXCEPTIONS.—The requirement of paragraph (1)(B) shall not apply where the Secretary finds compelling reasons to believe that disclosure in any case described in paragraph (1) would jeopardize the confidential relationship between the borrower country and the respective bank.

"(B) REPORTS BY SECRETARY.—The Secretary shall submit a quarterly report in writing to the Committees specified in subsection (f)(1) of the findings described in subparagraph (A).

"(b) ACCESS TO ASSESSMENTS IN ALL MEMBER COUNTRIES.—The Secretary of the Treasury shall seek the adoption of policies and procedures, through discussions and negotiations with the other member countries of the multilateral development banks and with the management of such banks, which result in access by governmental agencies and interested members of the public of such member countries, to environmental assessments or documentary information containing comprehensive summaries of such assessments which discuss the environmental impact of prospective projects and programs being considered by such banks. Such assessments or summaries should be made available to such governmental agencies and interested members of the public at least 120 days before scheduled board action, and public participation in review of the relevant environmental information should be encouraged.

"(c) CONSIDERATION OF ASSESSMENT.—The Secretary of the Treasury shall—

"(1) ensure that an environmental impact assessment or comprehensive summary of such assessment described in subsection

(a) accompanies loan proposals through the agency review process; and

"(2) take into consideration recommendations from all other interested Federal agencies and interested members of the public.

"(d) DEVELOPMENT OF PROCEDURES FOR SYSTEMATIC ENVIRONMENTAL ASSESSMENT.—The Secretary of the Treasury, in consultation with other Federal agencies, including the Environmental Protection Agency, the Department of State, and the Council on Environmental Quality, shall—

"(1) instruct the United States Executive Director of each multilateral development bank to initiate discussions with the other executive directors of the respective bank and to propose that the respective bank develop and make available to member governments of, and borrowers from, the respective bank, within 18 months after the date of the enactment of this section, a procedure for the systematic environmental assessment of development projects for which the respective bank provides financial assistance, taking into consideration the Guidelines and Principles for Environmental Impact Assessment promulgated by the United Nations Environmental Programme and other bilateral or multilateral assessment procedures; and

"(2) in determining the position of the United States on any action proposed to be taken by a multilateral development bank, develop and prescribe procedures for the consideration of, among other things—

"(A) the environmental impact assessment of the action described in subsection (a);

"(B) interagency and public review of such assessment; and

"(C) other environmental review and consultation of such action that is required by other law.

"(e) USE OF UNITED STATES PERSONNEL.—The Secretary of the Treasury, in consultation with the Secretary of State, the Secretary of the Interior, the Administrator of the Environmental Protection Agency, the Chairman of the Council on Environmental Quality, the Administrator of the Agency for International Development, and the Administrator of the National Oceanic and Atmospheric Administration, shall—

"(1) make available to the multilateral development banks, without charge, appropriate United States Government personnel to assist in—

"(A) training bank staff in environmental impact assessment procedures;

"(B) providing advice on environmental issues;

"(C) preparing environmental studies for projects with potentially significant environmental impacts; and

"(D) preparing documents for public release, and developing procedures to provide for the inclusion of interested nongovernmental organizations in the environmental review process; and

"(2) encourage other member countries of such banks to provide similar assistance.

"(f) REPORTS.—

"(1) IN GENERAL.—The Secretary of the Treasury shall submit to the Committees on Foreign Relations and Environment and

Public Works of the Senate and the Committee on Banking, Finance and Urban Affairs of the House of Representatives—

"(A) not later than the end of the 1-year period beginning on the date of the enactment of this section, a progress report on the efficacy of efforts by the United States to encourage consistent and timely environmental impact assessment of actions proposed to be taken by the multilateral development banks and on the progress made by the multilateral development banks in developing and instituting environmental assessment policies and procedures; and

"(B) not later than January 1, 1993, a detailed report on the matters described in subparagraph (A).

"(2) AVAILABILITY OF REPORTS.—The reports required by paragraph (1) shall be made available to the member governments of, and the borrowers from, the multilateral development banks, and to the public.".

Subtitle D—Debt-for-Development Swaps

SEC. 531. ENCOURAGEMENT OF DEBT-FOR-DEVELOPMENT SWAPS THROUGH LOCAL CURRENCY REPAYMENT.

(a) STATEMENT OF POLICY.—It is the sense of the Congress that—

(1) debt-for-development swaps, where payment is made in local currency at the free market rate, serve a useful purpose by providing banking institutions with constructive opportunities for the reduction of the external debt of highly indebted developing countries in a process that involves the participation of private, nonprofit groups in providing a stimulus to the economic and social development of such developing countries;

(2) debt-for-development swaps provide highly indebted developing countries with a creative method of reducing external debt burdens, while promoting their economic growth and restructuring objectives;

(3) banking institutions should give careful consideration to engaging in such swaps as one means of strengthening overall loan portfolios through the reduction of high external debt burdens while expanding economic opportunities through private sector initiatives; and

(4) in order to avoid any bias against such swaps in the regulatory framework applicable to the financial reporting of banking institutions, where payment is made in local currency at the free market rate, appropriate recognition of the fair market exchange value of the currency so received should be made.

(b) NOTIFICATION RELATING TO LOCAL CURRENCY REPAYMENT THROUGH DEBT-FOR-DEVELOPMENT SWAPS.—Before the end of the 6-month period beginning on the date of the enactment of this section, each appropriate Federal banking agency shall adopt uniform guidelines that will effectuate the policy set forth in subsection (a) concerning the regulatory framework and accounting treatment of debt-for-development swaps involving repayment in local currency at the free market rate. For the purpose of such guidelines, the impact of such swaps on reported loan loss reserves shall be determined by valuing currency received in such swaps at fair market exchange value.

(c) DEFINITIONS.—As used in this section:

(1) APPROPRIATE FEDERAL BANKING AGENCY.—The term "appropriate Federal banking agency" has the meaning given such term in section 903(1) of the International Lending Supervision Act of 1983.

(2) BANKING INSTITUTION.—The term "banking institution" has the meaning given such term in section 903(2) of the International Lending Supervision Act of 1983.

(3) DEBT-FOR-DEVELOPMENT SWAP.—The term "debt-for-development swap" has the meaning given such term in section 1608(b)(2) of the International Financial Institutions Act.

(4) HIGHLY INDEBTED COUNTRY.—The term "highly indebted country" means any country designated as a "Highly Indebted Country" in the annual World Debt Tables most recently published by the International Bank for Reconstruction and Development before the date of the enactment of this section.

Subtitle E—Consolidation of Certain Reporting Requirements

SEC. 541. CONSOLIDATION OF CERTAIN REPORTING REQUIREMENTS.

(a) IN GENERAL.—The International Financial Institutions Act (22 U.S.C. 262c et seq.) is amended by adding at the end the following:

"TITLE XVII—CONSOLIDATED REPORTING REQUIREMENTS

"SEC. 1701. ANNUAL REPORT BY CHAIRMAN OF THE NATIONAL ADVISORY COUNCIL ON INTERNATIONAL MONETARY AND FINANCIAL POLICIES.

"(a) IN GENERAL.—The Chairman shall report annually to the Speaker of the House of Representatives, the President of the Senate, and to the President of the United States on the participation of the United States in the international financial institutions. The Chairman shall present such report to the Speaker of the House of Representatives and the President of the Senate not later than April 1 of each year following the close of the fiscal year covered by such report, except that the report for fiscal year 1989 shall be submitted not later than June 1, 1990.

"(b) CONTENTS OF REPORTS.—Each annual report required by subsection (a) shall contain—

"(1) such data and explanations concerning the effectiveness, operations, and policies of the international financial institutions, such recommendations concerning the international financial institutions, and such other data and material as the Chairman may deem appropriate;

"(2) the reports on each specific issue and topic which is required by any other provision of law to be included in the report of the National Advisory Council on International Monetary and Financial Policies required by section 4(b)(5) of the Bretton Woods Agreements Act, as in effect immediately before the date of the enactment of this section;

"(3) a description of each loan or other form of financial assistance approved by any international financial institution during the fiscal year covered by such report, and a discussion of how such loan or financial assistance will benefit the people, particularly the poor people, of the recipient country;

"(4) a review of the success achieved through the multilateral development banks in reducing or eliminating import restrictions and unfair export subsidies which—

"(A) have been determined to be consistent with international agreements; and

"(B) have a serious adverse impact on the United States;

"(5) a description of the actions taken and the progress made in carrying out subsections (a) and (b) of section 45 of the Bretton Woods Agreements Act;

"(6) the report required by section 2018(c) of the International Narcotics Act of 1986 (title II of Public Law 99–570), discussing the actions taken and progress made in encouraging the multilateral development banks to finance drug eradication and crop substitution programs;

"(7) a description of the progress made by the United States Executive Director of the International Monetary Fund with respect to the goals of section 55 of the Bretton Woods Agreements Act;

"(8) a description of the status of procedures in the multilateral development banks specifically designed to increase the productive role of the poor in the economies of the nations which are borrowers from such banks;

"(9) in consultation with the Secretary of State, a report on the progress toward achieving the goals of title VII (other than section 704), including the information required to be reported pursuant to section 701(c), and, for the fiscal year 1990, the report described in section 1613;

"(10) in consultation with the Secretary of State and the Administrator of the Agency for International Development, an assessment of the progress being made to implement the objectives of title XIII; and

"(11) a report on—

"(A) the progress made in transforming government-owned enterprises into privately owned enterprises as described in section 1612(b);

"(B) the performance of the privately owned enterprises resulting from such transformation; and

"(C) the contributions of development finance companies toward strengthening the private sector in member borrowing countries.

"(c) Definitions.—As used in this title, title XVIII, and title XIX:

"(1) Chairman.—The term 'Chairman' means the Chairman of the National Advisory Council on International Monetary and Financial Policies.

"(2) International financial institutions.—The term 'international financial institutions' means the International Monetary Fund, International Bank for Reconstruction and Development, International Development Association, International Finance Corporation, Multilateral Investment Guarantee Agency, African Development Bank, African Development Fund, Asian Development Bank, Inter-American Development Bank, and Inter-American Investment Corporation.

"(3) Multilateral development institutions.—The term 'multilateral development institutions' means the international financial institutions other than the International Monetary Fund.

"(4) MULTILATERAL DEVELOPMENT BANKS.—The term 'multilateral development banks' means the multilateral development institutions other than the Multilateral Investment Guarantee Agency.

"(d) TESTIMONY REQUIRED.—Upon request of the Committee on Banking, Finance and Urban Affairs of the House of Representatives, the Chairman shall testify before the Committee to support and explain each annual report required by subsection (a). If the President has delegated to a person or persons other than the Chairman the authority to manage United States participation in the international financial institutions which was vested in the President by section 1(b) of the Reorganization Plan No. 4 of 1965, such person or persons shall, upon request of the Committee, accompany the Chairman and testify before the Committee with regard to such report. The Chairman and such other person or persons shall assess, in their testimony, the effectiveness of the international financial institutions, the major issues affecting United States participation, the major developments in the past year, the prospects for the coming year, United States policy goals with respect to the international financial institutions, and any specific issues addressed to them by any member of the Committee.

"SEC. 1702. TRANSMISSION TO THE CONGRESS OF OPERATING SUMMARIES OF THE MULTILATERAL DEVELOPMENT BANKS.

"The Secretary of the Treasury shall transmit to the Congress, on a monthly basis, current copies of the Monthly Operating Summary of the International Bank for Reconstruction and Development, showing the loan proposals or appraisal reports under consideration and the status of those loan proposals or appraisal reports within the Bank. The Secretary of the Treasury shall also transmit to the Congress, at such times as may be appropriate, comparable documents prepared by the other multilateral development banks which show the loans or credits under consideration in the other multilateral development banks.

"SEC. 1703. COMBINED REPORT ON EFFECT OF PENDING MULTILATERAL DEVELOPMENT BANK LOANS ON ENVIRONMENT, NATURAL RESOURCES, PUBLIC HEALTH, AND INDIGENOUS PEOPLES.

"Not later than April 1 and October 1 of each year, the Administrator of the Agency for International Development, in consultation with the Secretary of the Treasury and the Secretary of State, shall submit to the Committee on Appropriations and the Committee on Banking, Finance and Urban Affairs of the House of Representatives, and the Committee on Appropriations and the Committee on Foreign Relations of the Senate, as a combined report, the reports required by section 1303(c) of this Act and by section 537(h)(2) of the Foreign Operations, Export Financing, and Related Programs Appropriations Act, 1988 (sec. 1(e) of Public Law 100–202).

"TITLE XVIII—EXPORT ENHANCEMENT

"SEC. 1802. PROCUREMENT OPPORTUNITIES FOR UNITED STATES FIRMS.

"The Secretary of the Treasury shall instruct the United States Executive Directors of the multilateral development institutions to take all possible steps to ensure that information relating to potential procurement opportunities for United States firms is expeditiously communicated to the Secretary of the Treasury, the Secretary of State, and the Secretary of Commerce, and is disseminated as widely as possible to large and small businesses.

"TITLE XIX—PERSONNEL PRACTICES

"SEC. 1901. PERSONNEL PRACTICES.

"(a) STATEMENT OF POLICY.—It shall be the policy of the United States that no initiatives, discussions, or recommendations concerning the placement or removal of any personnel employed by the international financial institutions shall be based on the political philosophy or activity of the individual under consideration.

"(b) CONSULTATION.—The Secretary of the Treasury shall consult with the Chairman and the ranking minority member of the Committee on Banking, Finance and Urban Affairs of the House of Representatives and the Committee on Foreign Relations of the Senate before any discussion or recommendations by any official of the United States Government concerning the placement or removal of any principal officer of any international financial institutions.".

(b) TRANSFER OF PROVISIONS RELATING TO MULTILATERAL DEVELOPMENT BANK PROCUREMENT.—(1) Section 3202 of the Omnibus Trade and Competitiveness Act of 1988 (22 U.S.C. 262a) is hereby transferred to the International Financial Institutions Act, inserted after the heading of title XVIII (as added by the amendment made by subsection (a) of this section), and redesignated as section 1801.

(2) Section 2302 of the Omnibus Trade and Competitiveness Act of 1988 (15 U.S.C. 4722) is hereby transferred to the International Financial Institutions Act, inserted after section 1802 (as added by the amendment made by subsection (a) of this section), redesignated as section 1803, and amended by striking subsection (c).

(c) CONFORMING AMENDMENT.—Section 701(c) of the International Financial Institutions Act (22 U.S.C. 262d(c)) is amended to read as follows:

"(c)(1) Not later than 30 days after the end of each calendar quarter, the Secretary of the Treasury shall report quarterly on all loans considered by the Boards of Executive Directors of the institutions listed in subsection (a) to the Chairman and ranking minority member of the Committee on Banking, Finance and Urban Affairs of the House of Representatives, or the designees of such Chairman and ranking minority member, and the Chairman and ranking minority member of the Committee on Foreign Relations of the Senate.

"(2) Each report required by paragraph (1) shall—

"(A) include a list of all loans considered by the Board of Executive Directors of the institutions listed in subsection (a) and shall specify with respect to each such loan—

"(i) the institution involved;

"(ii) the date of final action;

"(iii) the borrower;

"(iv) the amount;

"(v) the project or program;

"(vi) the vote of the United States Government;

"(vii) the reason for United States Government opposition, if any;

"(viii) the final disposition of the loan; and

"(ix) if the United States Government opposed the loan, whether the loan meets basic human needs;

"(B) indicate whether the United States has opposed any loan, financial assistance, or technical assistance to a country on human rights grounds;

"(C) indicate whether the United States has voted in favor of a loan, financial assistance, or technical assistance to a country with respect to which the United States had, in the preceding 2 years, opposed a loan, financial assistance, or technical assistance on human rights grounds; and

"(D) in cases where the United States changed its voting position from opposition to support or from support to opposition, on human rights grounds—

"(i) indicate the policy considerations that were taken into account in the development of the United States voting position;

"(ii) describe human rights conditions in the country involved;

"(iii) indicate how the United States voted on all other loans, financial assistance, and technical assistance to such country during the preceding 2 years; and

"(iv) contain information as to how the United States voting position relates to the overall United States Government policy on human rights in such country.".

(d) Repeals.—

Not Reprinted

(e) Other Conforming Amendments.—

Not Reprinted

TITLE VI—MISCELLANEOUS PROVISIONS

SEC. 601. SENSE OF THE CONGRESS THAT THE INTERNATIONAL BANK FOR RECONSTRUCTION AND DEVELOPMENT AND THE INTERNATIONAL MONETARY FUND SHOULD EXPEDITIOUSLY ACT UPON LOAN REQUESTS FROM POLAND.

It is the sense of the Congress that, based on the liberalization of Poland's economic system and the opening of its economic system to market forces, the Secretary of the Treasury should instruct the United States Executive Directors of the International Bank for Reconstruction and Development and of the International Monetary Fund to urge upon their colleagues that their respective institutions move as expeditiously as possible in considering and acting upon loan requests from, and in disbursing approved loans to, Poland.

SEC. 602. SENSE OF THE CONGRESS SUPPORTING ASSISTANCE BY MULTILATERAL LENDING INSTITUTIONS TO ESTABLISH FINANCIAL INSTITUTIONS IN POLAND.

It is the sense of the Congress that the Secretary of the Treasury should instruct the United States Executive Directors of the multilateral development banks (as defined in section 1617 of the International Financial Institutions Act), of the International Finance Corporation, and of the Multilateral Investment Guarantee Agency to enter into discussions with the other executive directors of such institutions and, in such discussions, urge such institutions to consider and act promptly upon (and, in the case of the Multilateral Investment Guarantee Agency, after Poland becomes a member country of such institution) requests by individuals and private businesses in, and the Government of, Poland for financial and technical assistance in the establishment of financial institutions (including institutions such as credit unions, thrift institutions, and commercial banks) and businesses involved in the provision of credit and financial services.

SEC. 603. SENSE OF THE CONGRESS RELATING TO CONDITIONAL FINANCIAL ASSISTANCE BY MULTILATERAL LENDING INSTITUTIONS TO POLAND.

It is the sense of the Congress that the Secretary of the Treasury should instruct the United States Executive Directors of the multilateral development banks (as defined in section 1617 of the International Financial Institutions Act), of the International Monetary Fund, of the International Finance Corporation, and of the Multilateral Investment Guarantee Agency to enter into discussions with the other executive directors of such institutions and propose that such institutions not provide financial assistance or debt forgiveness to Poland until the government of Poland allows and facilitates privately owned entities established in foreign countries to invest in private commercial ventures in Poland.

SEC. 604. SENSE OF THE CONGRESS OPPOSING THE MAKING OF CERTAIN LOANS OR THE EXTENSION OF CERTAIN FINANCIAL AND TECHNICAL ASSISTANCE TO THE PEOPLE'S REPUBLIC OF CHINA.

(a) FINDINGS.—The Congress finds that—

(1) the Government of the People's Republic of China ordered the People's Liberation Army to brutally attack peaceful demonstrators who had assembled in Tiananmen Square;

(2) this attack violated the human rights of the demonstrators;

(3) several thousand innocent and defenseless protesters were killed in the initial assault;

(4) these violations of human rights have evolved into a pattern of continuing repression and reprisals against citizens throughout China as evidenced by the beating of alleged dissidents, the order to the army to shoot "rioters"—the Chinese Government's term for the peaceful demonstrators—on sight, the mass arrest of students and workers, the public declarations by government-controlled media that physicists Fang Lizhi and Li Shuxian (who are being given refuge in the United States Embassy in Beijing) are "guilty" before being afforded due process, and the banning of all independent, unofficial prodemocracy organizations;

(5) the Government of the People's Republic of China is trying to suppress truthful accounts of the actions taken in Beijing and throughout the country, by, among other things, expelling foreign journalists, including the local bureau chief of the Voice of America, from the country;

(6) the People's Republic of China has received almost $8,000,000,000 in development loans from the International Bank for Reconstruction and Development, and increasing amounts of assistance from the Asian Development Bank;

(7) it is morally repugnant that, through such multilateral development banks, United States taxpayer dollars are used to support the present policies of the People's Republic of China;

(8) such development loans cannot be justified on economic grounds because economic development and market reforms cannot be achieved in the environment of repression that now clearly exists there; and

(9) the People's Republic of China is engaging in "a pattern of gross violations of internationally recognized human rights . . .

such as flagrant denial to life, liberty, and the security of person".

(b) STATEMENT OF POLICY.—It is the sense of the Congress that the President should—

(1) instruct the United States Executive Directors of the International Bank for Reconstruction and Development and the Asian Development Bank to use their voices and votes to oppose the making of any loan or the extension of any financial or technical assistance to the People's Republic of China, in accordance with section 701(f) of the International Financial Institutions Act; and

(2) consider the People's Republic of China to be a country described in section 701(a)(1) of such Act until the President determines that the repression and reprisals against persons in connection with the prodemocracy demonstrations have ended.

TITLE VII—MISCELLANEOUS

SEC. 701. SHORT TITLE.

This title may be cited as the "Global Environmental Protection Assistance Act of 1989".

PART A—COMMERCIAL DEBT-FOR-NATURE EXCHANGES

SEC. 711. AMENDMENT TO THE FOREIGN ASSISTANCE ACT.

The Foreign Assistance Act of 1961 is amended by inserting after chapter 6 of part I the following new chapter:

"CHAPTER 7—DEBT-FOR-NATURE EXCHANGES

"SEC. 461. DEFINITION.—For purpose of this chapter, the term 'debt-for-nature exchange' means the cancellation or redemption of the foreign debt of the government of a country in exchange for—

"(1) that government's making available local currencies (including through the issuance of bonds) which are used only for eligible projects involving the conservation or protection of the environment in that country (as described in section 463); or

"(2) that government's financial resource or policy commitment to take certain specified actions to ensure the restoration, protection, or sustainable use of natural resources within that country; or

"(3) a combination of assets and actions under both paragraphs (1) and (2).

"SEC. 462. ASSISTANCE FOR COMMERCIAL DEBT EXCHANGES.—(a) The Administrator of the Agency for International Development is authorized to furnish assistance, in the form of grants on such terms and conditions as may be necessary, to nongovernmental organizations for the purchase on the open market of discounted commercial debt of a foreign government of an eligible country which will be canceled or redeemed under the terms of an agreement with that government as part of a debt-for-nature exchange.

"(b) Notwithstanding any other provision of law, a grantee (or any subgrantee) of the grants referred to in subsection (a) may retain, without deposit in the Treasury of the United States and without further appropriation by Congress, interest earned on the proceeds of any resulting debt-for-nature exchange pending the disbursements of such proceeds and interest for approved program purposes, which may include the establishment of an endowment, the income of which is used for such purposes.

"SEC. 463. ELIGIBLE PROJECTS.—(a) The Administrator of the Agency for International Development shall seek to ensure that debt-for-nature exchanges under this chapter support one or more of the following activities by either the host government, a local private conservation group, or a combination thereof:

"(1) restoration, protection, or sustainable use of the world's oceans and atmosphere;

"(2) restoration, protection, or sustainable use of diverse animal and plant species;

"(3) establishment, restoration, protection, and maintenance of parks and reserves;

"(4) development and implementation of sound systems of natural resource management;

"(5) development and support of local conservation programs;

"(6) training programs to strengthen conservation institutions and increase scientific, technical, and managerial capabilities of individuals and organizations involved in conservation efforts;

"(7) efforts to generate knowledge, increase understanding, and enhance public commitment to conservation;

"(8) design and implementation of sound programs of land and ecosystem management; and

"(9) promotion of regenerative approaches in farming, forestry, fishing, and watershed management.

"(b)(1) In cooperation with nongovernmental organizations, the Administrator of the Agency for International Development shall seek to identify those areas, which because of an imminent threat, are in particular need of immediate attention to prevent the loss of unique biological life or valuable ecosystem.

"(2) The Administrator of the Agency for International Development shall encourage as many eligible countries as possible to propose such exchanges with the purpose of demonstrating to a large number of governments the feasibility and benefits of sustainable development.

"SEC. 464. ELIGIBLE COUNTRIES.—In order for a foreign country to be eligible to participate in a debt-for-nature exchange under this chapter, the Administrator of the Agency for International Development shall determine that—

"(1) the host country is fully committed to the long-term viability of the program or project that is to be undertaken through the debt-for-nature exchange;

"(2) a long-term plan has been prepared by the host country, or private conservation group, which adequately provides for the long-term viability of the program or project that is to be undertaken through the debt-for-nature exchange or that such a plan will be prepared in a timely manner; and

"(3) there is a government agency or a local nongovernmental organization, or combination thereof, in the host country with the capability, commitment, and record of environmental concern to oversee the long-term viability of the program or project that is to be undertaken through the debt-for-nature exchange.

"SEC. 465. TERMS AND CONDITIONS.—(a) The terms and conditions for making grants under this chapter shall be deemed to be fulfilled upon final approval by the Administrator of the Agency for International Development of the debt-for-nature exchange, a certification by the nongovernmental organization that the host government has accepted the terms of the exchange, and that an agreement has been reached to cancel the commercial debt in an agreed upon fashion.

"(b) Grants made under this section are intended to complement, and not substitute for, assistance otherwise available to a foreign country under this Act or any other provision of law.

"(c) The United States Government is prohibited from accepting title or interest in any land in a foreign country as a condition on the debt exchange.

"SEC. 466. PILOT PROGRAM FOR SUB-SAHARAN AFRICA.—(a) The Administrator of the Agency for International Development, in cooperation with nongovernmental conservation organizations, shall invite the government of each country in sub-Saharan Africa to submit a list of those areas of severely degraded national resources which threaten human survival and well-being and the opportunity for future economic growth or those areas of biological or ecological importance within the territory of that country.

"(b) The Administrator of the Agency for International Development shall assess the list submitted by each country under subsection (a) and shall seek to reach agreement with the host country for the restoration and future sustainable use of those areas.

"(c)(1) The Administrator of the Agency for International Development is authorized to make grants, on such terms and conditions as may be necessary, to nongovernmental organizations for the purchase on the open market of discounted commercial debt of a foreign government of an eligible sub-Saharan country in exchange for commitments by that government to restore natural resources identified by the host country under subsection (a) or for commitments to develop plans fcr sustainable use of such resources.

"(2) Notwithstanding any other provision of law, a grantee (or any subgrantee) of the grants referred to in section (a) may retain, without deposit in the Treasury of the United States and without further appropriation by Congress, interest earned on the proceeds of any resulting debt-for-nature exchange pending the disbursements of such proceeds and interest for approved program purposes, which may include the establishment of an endowment, the income of which is used for such purposes.".

PART B—MULTILATERAL FOREIGN ASSISTANCE COORDINATION

SEC. 721. GENERAL POLICY.

It is the sense of the Congress that the Secretary of State should seek to develop an increased consideration of global warming, tropical deforestation, sustainable development, and biological diversity among the highest goals of bilateral foreign assistance programs of all countries.

SEC. 722. POLICY ON NEGOTIATIONS.

(a) IN GENERAL.—The Secretary of State, acting through the United States representative to the Development Assistance Committee of the Organization for Economic Coordination and Development (OECD), should initiate, at the earliest practicable date, negotiations among member countries on a coordinated approach to global warming, tropical deforestation, sustainable development, and biological diversity through bilateral assistance programs that would include—

(1) increased consideration of the impact of developmental projects on global warming, tropical deforestation, and biological diversity;

(2) reduction or elimination of funding for those projects that exacerbate those problems;

(3) coordinated research and development of projects that emphasize sustainable use or protection of tropical forests and support for local conservation efforts;

(4) expanded use of forgiveness of foreign assistance debt in exchange for policy changes or programs that address problems associated with global warming, tropical deforestation, sustainable development, and biological diversity;

(5) increased use of foreign assistance funds and technical assistance in support of local conservation, restoration, or sustainable development efforts and debt-for-nature exchanges;

(6) improved exchange of information on energy efficiency and solar and renewable energy sources, and a greater emphasis on the use of those sources of energy in developmental projects; and

(7) increased use of environmental experts in the field to assess development projects for their impact on global warming, tropical deforestation, and biological diversity.

(b) Implementation of Agreement.—Negotiations described in subsection (a) shall seek to ensure that the recommended changes are implemented as quickly as possible by member countries of the Development Assistance Committee.

TITLE VIII—EFFECTIVE DATE

SEC. 801. EFFECTIVE DATE.

Except as otherwise provided in this Act, this Act and the amendments made by this Act shall take effect on the date of the enactment of this Act.

Approved December 19, 1989.

LEGISLATIVE HISTORY—H.R. 2494:

HOUSE REPORTS: No. 101-271 (Comm. on Banking, Finance and Urban Affairs).
CONGRESSIONAL RECORD, Vol. 135 (1989):
Oct. 18, considered and passed House.
Nov. 21, considered and passed Senate, amended. House concurred in Senate amendments.
WEEKLY COMPILATION OF PRESIDENTIAL DOCUMENTS, Vol. 25 (1989):
Dec. 19, Presidential statement.

URGENT ASSISTANCE FOR DEMOCRACY IN PANAMA ACT OF 1990

An Act to authorize certain United States assistance and trade benefits for Panama, and for other purposes.

Date: February 16, 1990

Bill No.: H.R. 3952

Public Law No.: 101-243

Cite: 104 STAT. 7

Sections reprinted:

TITLE I - PANAMA

- Section 101 - Immediate United States assistance.
  - Subsection (a)(1)(A) - Authority to use funds for economic assistance (in general).
  - Subsection (c) - Brooke-Alexander Amendment.
- Section 102 - Resumption of United States assistance: antinarcotics certification requirements.
- Section 103 - Resumption of trade benefits: antinarcotics certification requirements
- Section 104 - Report on Panamanian bank secrecy laws.

Public Law 101-243
101st Congress

An Act

To authorize certain United States assistance and trade benefits for Panama, and for other purposes.

Be it enacted by the Senate and House of Representatives of the United States of America in Congress assembled,

SECTION 1. SHORT TITLE.

This Act may be cited as the "Urgent Assistance for Democracy in Panama Act of 1990".

TITLE I—PANAMA

SEC. 101. IMMEDIATE UNITED STATES ASSISTANCE.

(a) ECONOMIC ASSISTANCE PROGRAMS.—

(1) AUTHORITY TO USE FUNDS FOR ECONOMIC ASSISTANCE.—

(A) IN GENERAL.—The President may use up to $32,000,000 of funds made available for economic assistance programs in order to provide economic assistance for Panama for fiscal year 1990 notwithstanding the provisions of law specified in subsection (c) of this section.

(c) BROOKE-ALEXANDER AMENDMENT.—The provisions of law referred to in subsections (a)(1), (a)(2), and (b)(2)(A) of this section are section 620(q) of the Foreign Assistance Act of 1961 (22 U.S.C. 2370(q)); and section 518 of the Foreign Operations, Export Financing, and Related Programs Appropriations Act, 1990 (Public Law 101-167), and the corresponding sections of foreign assistance appropriations Acts for prior fiscal years.

SEC. 102. RESUMPTION OF UNITED STATES ASSISTANCE: ANTINARCOTICS CERTIFICATION REQUIREMENTS.

Because the vital national interests of the United States so require and because the Endara Government of Panama has indicated its willingness, and is taking steps, to cooperate fully with the United States to control narcotics production, trafficking, and money laundering, the requirements of paragraphs (1) and (5) of section 481(h) of the Foreign Assistance Act of 1961 (22 U.S.C. 2291(h)) shall cease to apply to Panama as of the date of enactment of this Act to the extent that those requirements became applicable to Panama by reason of the fact that the President did not make a certification with respect to Panama under paragraph (2) of that section at the time the international narcotics control strategy reports for 1988 and 1989 were submitted to the Congress pursuant to section 481(e) of that Act.

SEC. 103. RESUMPTION OF TRADE BENEFITS: ANTINARCOTICS CERTIFICATION REQUIREMENTS.

(a) RESUMPTION UPON DATE OF ENACTMENT.—Because the vital national interests of the United States so require and because the Endara Government of Panama has indicated its willingness, and is taking steps, to cooperate fully with the United States to control narcotics production, trafficking, and money laundering, the conditions specified in section 802(b)(4)(B) of the Narcotics Control Trade Act (19 U.S.C. 2492(b)(4)(B)) shall be deemed to be satisfied as of the date of enactment of this Act with respect to the action taken pursuant to section 802(a) of that Act that is described in subsection (b) of this section.

(b) SPECIFICATION OF BENEFITS.—The action referred to in subsection (a) is the denial to articles imported from Panama of preferential tariff treatment under the Generalized System of Preferences (19 U.S.C. 2461 and following) and the Caribbean Basin Economic Recovery Act (19 U.S.C. 2701 and following) pursuant to Presidential Proclamation 5779 of March 23, 1988.

SEC. 104. REPORT ON PANAMANIAN BANK SECRECY LAWS.

(a) CONGRESSIONAL CONCERNS.—The Congress commends the Endara Government for its cooperation and assistance in freezing Panamanian bank accounts believed to be implicated in narcotics-related and other illegal financial transactions. The Congress remains concerned, however, that the current status of bank secrecy laws in Panama may lend itself to continued criminal abuse of those laws despite the best intentions of the Endara Government.

(b) REPORT.—Therefore, no later than April 15, 1990, the President shall submit a detailed report to the Speaker of the House of Representatives and the Chairman of the Committee on Foreign Relations of the Senate on specific actions being undertaken by the Government of Panama to modify the existing bank secrecy regime in order to facilitate detection and prosecution of criminal activities, including—

(1) the modification of bank secrecy laws by the Government of Panama;

(2) the conclusion of an exchange-of-information agreement between the United States and Panama; and

(3) agreements entered into by the Government of Panama or in the process of negotiation that are designed to deter illegal financial transactions and to facilitate early detection and prosecution of such illegal activities.

LEGISLATIVE HISTORY—H.R. 3952 (S. 2073):

HOUSE REPORTS: No. 101-401, Pt. 1 (Comm. on Foreign Affairs) and Pt. 2 (Comm. on Ways and Means).

CONGRESSIONAL RECORD, Vol. 136 (1990):
Feb. 7, considered and passed House and Senate.

WEEKLY COMPILATION OF PRESIDENTIAL DOCUMENTS, Vol. 26 (1990):
Feb. 14, Presidential remarks and statement.

FOREIGN RELATIONS AUTHORIZATION ACT, FISCAL YEARS 1990 AND 1991

An Act to authorize appropriations for fiscal years 1990 and 1991 for the Department of State, and for other purposes.

Date: February 16, 1990

Bill No.: H.R. 3792

Public Law No.: 101-246

Cite: 104 STAT. 15

Sections reprinted:

TITLE II - UNITED STATES INFORMATIONAL, EDUCATIONAL AND CULTURAL PROGRAMS

Part C - Voice of America

Section 234 - Voice of America broadcasts to Tibet.

Section 235 - Voice of America's Thailand radio facilities.

Section 236 - Voice of America broadcasts to the People's Republic of China.

Part D - Television Broadcasting to Cuba

Section 241 - Short title.

Section 242 - Findings and purposes.

Section 243 - Television broadcasting to Cuba.

Section 244 - Television Marti Service of the United States Information Agency

TITLE IV - INTERNATIONAL ORGANIZATIONS AND COMMISSIONS

Section 405 - Reform in budget decision-making procedures of the United Nations and its specialized agencies.

Section 406 - Annual report to Congress on voting practices at the United Nations.

Section 407 - Denial of visas to certain representatives to the United Nations.

Section 408 - Policy on UNESCO.

Section 411 - Sense of Congress concerning an enhanced role for the International Court of Justice in resolution of international disputes.

Public Law 101-246
101st Congress

An Act

To authorize appropriations for fiscal years 1990 and 1991 for the Department of State, and for other purposes.

SEC. 234. VOICE OF AMERICA BROADCASTS TO TIBET.

(a) ESTABLISHMENT OF SERVICE.—Not later than 90 days after the date of enactment of this Act, the Director of the United States Information Agency shall establish through the Voice of America, a service to provide Voice of America Tibetan language programming to the people of Tibet.

(b) AMOUNT OF PROGRAMMING.—For each of the fiscal years 1990 and 1991, programming broadcasts to the people of Tibet pursuant to this section shall occur for not less than two hours each day.

(c) REPORT.—As soon as possible in the fiscal year 1990, the Director of the United States Information Agency shall submit to the Congress a comprehensive written report detailing the implementation of the programming provided for in this section.

(d) AUTHORIZATION OF APPROPRIATIONS.—In addition to funds otherwise available under subsection (e), there are authorized to be appropriated to the Voice of America for purposes of carrying out this section $1,000,000 for each of the fiscal years 1990 and 1991.

(e) TRANSFER AUTHORITY.—The Director of the United States Information Agency may transfer to Voice of America Tibet Service such amounts appropriated for the "Television and Film Service" for each of the fiscal years 1990 and 1991 as exceed the amounts authorized to be appropriated for each such fiscal year for such Service.

SEC. 235. VOICE OF AMERICA'S THAILAND RADIO FACILITIES.

The Director of the United States Information Agency may enter into a contract for the construction of the Voice of America's Thailand radio facilities for periods not in excess of 5 years or delegate such authority to the Corps of Engineers of the United States Department of the Army if there are sufficient funds to cover at least the Government's liability for payments for the fiscal year in which the contract is awarded plus the full amount of estimated cancellation costs.

SEC. 236. VOICE OF AMERICA BROADCASTS TO THE PEOPLE'S REPUBLIC OF CHINA.

For each of the fiscal years 1990 and 1991, the Voice of America shall provide not less than 12 hours of programming each day for the People's Republic of China.

PART D—TELEVISION BROADCASTING TO CUBA

SEC. 241. SHORT TITLE.

This part may be cited as the "Television Broadcasting to Cuba Act".

SEC. 242. FINDINGS AND PURPOSES.

The Congress finds and declares that—

(1) it is the policy of the United States to support the right of the people of Cuba to seek, receive, and impart information and ideas through any media and regardless of frontiers, in accordance with article 19 of the Universal Declaration of Human Rights;

(2) consonant with this policy, television broadcasting to Cuba may be effective in furthering the open communication of accurate information and ideas to the people of Cuba and, in particular, information about Cuba;

(3) television broadcasting to Cuba, operated in a manner not inconsistent with the broad foreign policy of the United States

and in accordance with high professional standards, would be in the national interest;

(4) facilities broadcasting television programming to Cuba must be operated in a manner consistent with applicable regulations of the Federal Communications Commission, and must not affect the quality of domestic broadcast transmission or reception; and

(5) that the Voice of America already broadcasts to Cuba information that represents America, not any single segment of American society, and includes a balanced and comprehensive projection of significant American thought and institutions, but that there is a need for television broadcasts to Cuba which provide news, commentary, and other information about events in Cuba and elsewhere to promote the cause of freedom in Cuba.

SEC. 243. TELEVISION BROADCASTING TO CUBA.

(a) TELEVISION BROADCASTING TO CUBA.—In order to carry out the purposes set forth in section 242 and notwithstanding the limitation of section 501 of the United States Information and Educational Exchange Act of 1948 (22 U.S.C. 1461) with respect to the dissemination in the United States of information prepared for dissemination abroad to the extent such dissemination is inadvertent, the United States Information Agency (hereafter in this part referred to as the "Agency") shall provide for the open communication of information and ideas through the use of television broadcasting to Cuba. Television broadcasting to Cuba shall serve as a consistently reliable and authoritative source of accurate, objective, and comprehensive news.

(b) VOICE OF AMERICA STANDARDS.—Television broadcasting to Cuba under this part shall be in accordance with all Voice of America standards to ensure the broadcast of programs which are objective, accurate, balanced, and which present a variety of views.

(c) USIA TELEVISION MARTI.—Any program of United States Government television broadcasts to Cuba authorized by this section shall be designated "USIA Television Marti Program".

(d) FREQUENCY ASSIGNMENT.—

(1) Subject to the Communications Act of 1934, the Federal Communications Commission shall assign by order a suitable frequency to further the national interests expressed in this part, except that no such assignment shall result in objectionable interference with the broadcasts of any domestic licensee.

(2) No Federal branch or agency shall compel an incumbent domestic licensee to change its frequency in order to eliminate objectionable interference caused by broadcasting of the Service.

(3) For purposes of section 305 of the Communications Act of 1934, a television broadcast station established for purposes of this part shall be treated as a government station, but the Federal Communications Commission shall exercise the authority of the President under such section to assign a frequency to such station.

(e) INTERFERENCE WITH DOMESTIC BROADCASTING.—

(1) Broadcasting by the Television Marti Service shall be conducted in accordance with such parameters as shall be prescribed by the Federal Communications Commission to preclude objectionable interference with the broadcasts of any domestic licensee. The Television Marti Service shall be governed by the same standards regarding objectionable interference as any domestic licensee. The Federal Communications Commission shall monitor the operations of television broad-

casting to Cuba pursuant to subsection (f). If, on the basis of such monitoring or a complaint from any person, the Federal Communications Commission determines, in its discretion, that broadcasting by the Television Marti Service is causing objectionable interference with the transmission or reception of the broadcasts of a domestic licensee, the Federal Communications Commission shall direct the Television Marti Service to cease broadcasting and to eliminate the objectionable interference. Broadcasts by the Service shall not be resumed until the Federal Communications Commission finds that the objectionable interference has been eliminated and should not recur.

(2) The Federal Communications Commission shall take such actions as are necessary and appropriate to assist domestic licensees in overcoming the adverse effects of objectionable interference caused by broadcasting by the Television Marti Service. Such assistance may include the authorization of non-directional increases in the effective radiated power of a domestic television station so that its coverage is equivalent to the maximum allowable for such facilities, to avoid any adverse effect on such stations of the broadcasts of the Television Marti Service.

(3) If the Federal Communications Commission directs the Television Marti Service to cease broadcasting pursuant to paragraph (1), the Commission shall, as soon as practicable, notify the appropriate committees of Congress of such action and the reasons therefor. The Federal Communications Commission shall continue to notify the appropriate committees of Congress of progress in eliminating the objectionable interference and shall assure that Congress is fully informed about the operation of the Television Marti Service.

(f) Monitoring of Interference.—The Federal Communications Commission shall continually monitor and periodically report to the appropriate committees of the Congress interference to domestic broadcast licensees—

(1) from the operation of Cuban television and radio stations; and

(2) from the operations of the television broadcasting to Cuba.

(g) Task Force.—It is the sense of the Congress that the President should establish a task force to analyze the level of interference from the operation of Cuban television and radio stations experienced by broadcasters in the United States and to seek a practical political and technical solution to this problem.

SEC. 244. TELEVISION MARTI SERVICE OF THE UNITED STATES INFORMATION AGENCY.

(a) Television Marti Service.—The Director of the United States Information Agency shall establish within the Voice of America a Television Marti Service. The Service shall be responsible for all television broadcasts to Cuba authorized by this part. The Director of the United States Information Agency shall appoint a head of the Service who shall report directly to the Director of the Voice of America. The head of the Service shall employ such staff as the head of the Service may need to carry out the duties of the Service.

(b) Use of Existing Facilities of the USIA.—To assure consistency of presentation and efficiency of operations in conducting the activities authorized under this part, the Television Marti Service shall make maximum feasible utilization of Agency facilities and management support, including Voice of America: Cuba Service,

Voice of America, and the United States Information Agency Television Service.

(c) USIA AUTHORITY.—The Agency may carry out the purposes of this part by means of grants, leases, or contracts (subject to the availability of appropriations), or such other means as the Agency determines will be most effective.

SEC. 405. REFORM IN BUDGET DECISION-MAKING PROCEDURES OF THE UNITED NATIONS AND ITS SPECIALIZED AGENCIES.

(a) FINDINGS.—(1) The Congress finds that the United Nations and its specialized agencies have made progress in the formulation and implementation of budget reforms as called for by section 143 of the Foreign Relations Authorization Act, Fiscal Years 1986 and 1987 (Public Law 99-93). Presidential determinations that were required by that and other laws confirm the progress that has been made in this respect.

(2) The Congress remains concerned about the need to make further progress to protect the independence of the international civil service working at the United Nations and urges the President to make vigorous efforts to this end.

(3) The Congress is specifically concerned with the practice of reserving certain professional staff slots in the United Nations Secretariat for nationals of certain member states, and urges the President to pursue vigorously a program of regular rotation in these staff positions among all member states of the United Nations.

(b) FINANCIAL RESPONSIBILITY IN BUDGET PROCEDURES.—To assure financial responsibility in preparation of the assessed budgets of the United Nations and its specialized agencies, it is the sense of the Congress that the President should continue vigorous efforts to ensure continued implementation by the United Nations and its specialized agencies of consensus-based decision-making procedures where applicable on budgetary matters which assure that sufficient attention is paid to the views of the United States and other member states who are major financial contributors to such assessed budgets.

(c) LIMITATION ON ASSESSED CONTRIBUTIONS.—

(1) For assessed contributions authorized to be appropriated by section 102(a)(1) of this Act, the President shall withhold 20 percent of the funds appropriated for the United States assessed contribution to the United Nations or to any of its specialized agencies for any calendar year until the President determines and reports to the Congress that the United Nations or any such agency—

(A) has continued implementation of decision-making procedures on budgetary matters referred to in subsection (b); and

(B) in the case of the United Nations—

(i) is making further progress toward the elimination of the abuse of secondment in the United Nations Secretariat which undermines the independence of the international civil service; and

(ii) is implementing the 15 percent reduction in the staff of the United Nations Secretariat (recommendation 15 of the Group of High Level Intergovernmental Experts to Review the Efficiency of the Administrative and Financial Functioning of the United Nations (Group of 18)) and that such reduction is being equitably applied among the nationals on such staff.

(2) The President shall notify the Congress when each such determination is made. Each such notification shall include

appropriate consultation between the President or his designated representative and the Committee on Foreign Affairs of the House of Representatives and the Committee on Foreign Relations of the Senate.

SEC. 406. ANNUAL REPORT TO CONGRESS ON VOTING PRACTICES AT THE UNITED NATIONS.

(a) IN GENERAL.—Not later than March 31 of each year, the Secretary of State shall transmit to the Speaker of the House of Representatives and the chairman of the Committee on Foreign Relations of the Senate a full and complete annual report which assesses for the preceding calendar year, with respect to each foreign country member of the United Nations, the voting practices of the governments of such countries at the United Nations, and which evaluates General Assembly and Security Council actions and the responsiveness of those governments to United States policy on issues of special importance to the United States.

(b) INFORMATION ON VOTING PRACTICES IN THE UNITED NATIONS.—Such report shall include, with respect to voting practices and plenary actions in the United Nations during the preceding calendar year, information to be compiled and supplied by the Permanent Representative of the United States to the United Nations, consisting of—

(1) an analysis and discussion, prepared in consultation with the Secretary of State, of the extent to which member countries supported United States policy objectives at the United Nations;

(2) an analysis and discussion, prepared in consultation with the Secretary of State, of actions taken by the United Nations by consensus;

(3) with respect to plenary votes of the United Nations General Assembly—

(A) a listing of all such votes on issues which directly affected important United States interests and on which the United States lobbied extensively and a brief description of the issues involved in each such vote;

(B) a listing of the votes described in subparagraph (A) which provides a comparison of the vote cast by each member country with the vote cast by the United States;

(C) a country-by-country listing of votes described in subparagraph (A); and

(D) a listing of votes described in subparagraph (A) displayed in terms of United Nations regional caucus groups;

(4) a listing of all plenary votes cast by member countries of the United Nations in the General Assembly which provides a comparison of the votes cast by each member country with the vote cast by the United States;

(5) an analysis and discussion, prepared in consultation with the Secretary of State, of the extent to which other members supported United States policy objectives in the Security Council and a separate listing of all Security Council votes of each member country in comparison with the United States; and

(6) a side-by-side comparison of agreement on important and overall votes for each member country and the United States.

(c) FORMAT.—Information required pursuant to subsection (b)(3) shall also be submitted, together with an explanation of the statistical methodology, in a format identical to that contained in chapter II of the Report to Congress on Voting Practices in the United Nations, dated March 14, 1988.

(d) STATEMENT BY THE SECRETARY OF STATE.—Each report under subsection (a) shall contain a statement by the Secretary of State discussing the measures which have been taken to inform United States diplomatic missions of United Nations General Assembly and Security Council activities.

(e) TECHNICAL AND CONFORMING AMENDMENTS.—The following provisions of law are repealed:

(1) The second undesignated paragraph of section 101(b)(1) of the Foreign Assistance and Related Programs Appropriations Act, 1984 (Public Law 98-151; 97 Stat. 967).

(2) Section 529 of the Foreign Assistance and Related Programs Appropriations Act, 1986, as enacted by Public Law 99-190 (99 Stat. 1307).

(3) Section 528 of the Foreign Assistance and Related Programs Appropriations Act, 1987, as enacted by Public Law 99-500 (100 Stat. 1783) and Public Law 99-591 (100 Stat. 3341).

(4) Section 528 of the Foreign Operations, Export Financing, and Related Programs Appropriations Act, 1988, as enacted by Public Law 100-202 (101 Stat. 1329).

(5) Section 527 of the Foreign Operations, Export Financing, and Related Programs Appropriations Act, 1989, as enacted by Public Law 100-461.

SEC. 407. DENIAL OF VISAS TO CERTAIN REPRESENTATIVES TO THE UNITED NATIONS.

(a) IN GENERAL.—The President shall use his authority, including the authorities contained in section 6 of the United Nations Headquarters Agreement Act (Public Law 80-357), to deny any individual's admission to the United States as a representative to the United Nations if the President determines that such individual has been found to have been engaged in espionage activities directed against the United States or its allies and may pose a threat to United States national security interests.

(b) WAIVER.—The President may waive the provisions of subsection (a) if the President determines, and so notifies the Congress, that such a waiver is in the national security interests of the United States.

SEC. 408. POLICY ON UNESCO.

(a) CONGRESSIONAL FINDINGS.—The Congress finds that—

(1) the United States withdrew from the United Nations Educational, Scientific, and Cultural Organization (UNESCO) on December 31, 1984, in response to grave and persistent problems in UNESCO under the then-Director General;

(2) chief among these problems was the assault on the free flow of information supported by that Director General and the pervasive ideological conflict fomented by the alliance between totalitarian and developing nations;

(3) UNESCO has since acquired a new Director General, Federico Mayor, who has pledged his support for the free flow of information, the return of UNESCO to the principles enunciated in its Charter, and other needed changes in UNESCO policy;

(4) Soviet Foreign Minister Eduard Shevardnadze stated on October 11, 1988, that the Soviet Union was responsible for "the exaggerated ideological approach [that] undermined tolerance intrinsic to UNESCO," and stated that Soviet policy would improve in this regard;

(5) substantial progress remains to be made in implementing the reforms proposed by the new Director General and in determining the degree to which ideological conflict has actually declined; and

(6) when the United States withdrew from UNESCO, the policy of the United States was that at such time as satisfactory changes were achieved in UNESCO, the United States would act on reentry.

(b) POLICY.—It is the sense of the Congress that the Secretary of State should monitor closely the changes achieved in UNESCO and should work with United States allies and the UNESCO leadership to continue to promote the progress necessary to justify United States consideration of reentry into UNESCO.

(c) REPORT REQUIRED.—Not later than 60 days after the date of the enactment of this Act, the Secretary of State shall prepare and submit to the Congress a report on the activities after December 31, 1984, of the United Nations Educational, Scientific, and Cultural Organization.

SEC. 411. SENSE OF CONGRESS CONCERNING AN ENHANCED ROLE FOR THE INTERNATIONAL COURT OF JUSTICE IN RESOLUTION OF INTERNATIONAL DISPUTES.

(a) FINDINGS.—The Congress makes the following findings:

(1) In 1945, the United States supported the establishment of the International Court of Justice (ICJ) to provide for the orderly resolution of disputes among nations under the rule of law.

(2) The United States, pursuant to Article 93 of the Charter of the United Nations, is also a party to the Statute of the International Court of Justice which provides in Article 36(1) that the International Court of Justice will have jurisdiction over "all cases which the parties refer to it and all matters specially provided for in the Charter of the United Nations or in treaties and conventions in force".

(3) In August 1946, the United States, pursuant to Senate advice and consent (61 Stat. 1218), voluntarily accepted the compulsory jurisdiction of the International Court of Justice in other international disputes under Article 36(2) of the Statute of the International Court of Justice, on certain conditions, and maintained such recognition for four decades from 1946 to 1986 when United States acceptance was terminated.

(4) The United States has utilized the International Court of Justice on numerous occasions to resolve disputes with other nations.

(5) In April 1984, the United States notified the Secretary General of the United Nations that the United States was suspending for two years its acceptance of the compulsory jurisdiction of the International Court of Justice in cases relating to Central America.

(6) In 1985, the United States announced it was terminating, in whole, United States acceptance (effective April 1, 1986) of the compulsory jurisdiction of the International Court of Justice.

(7) The Soviet Union, as a member of the United Nations, is also a party to the Statute of the International Court of Justice and is thus bound by Article 36(1).

(8) The Soviet Union, unlike the United States, has not since the inception of the International Court of Justice voluntarily accepted the compulsory jurisdiction of the ICJ under Article 36(2) or taken any other case voluntarily to the court.

(9) Soviet leader Mikhail Gorbachev, in his address to the United Nations in December of 1988 said: "We believe that the jurisdiction of the International Court of Justice at the Hague as regards the interpretation and implementation of agreements on human rights should be binding on all states.".

(10) The Legal Adviser of the State Department is holding discussions with Soviet officials and representatives of other permanent members of the United Nations Security Council and other states to determine whether and how the International Court of Justice might be used for the peaceful settlement of international disputes through procedures that assure fairness and the protection of legitimate national interests.

(b) SENSE OF CONGRESS.—The Congress commends and strongly supports efforts by the United States to broaden, where appropriate, the compulsory jurisdiction and enhance the effectiveness of the International Court of Justice.

SEC. 413. REVIEW OF MULTILATERAL AND BILATERAL COMMISSIONS.

Not later than 180 days after the date of the enactment of this Act, the Secretary of State shall prepare and submit a report to the Committee on Foreign Affairs of the House of Representatives and the Committee on Foreign Relations of the Senate which provides a review of United States participation in all multilateral and bilateral commissions for which appropriations are authorized to be made under the "International Commissions" account of the Department of State. Together with such comments and recommendations as the Secretary considers appropriate, such report shall include—

(1) a justification for United States participation in each multilateral or bilateral commission;

(2) an assessment of the effectiveness of each multilateral or bilateral commission in which the United States participates; and

(3) information concerning the cost of United States participation in each such commission.

SEC. 414. MEMBERSHIP OF THE PALESTINE LIBERATION ORGANIZATION IN UNITED NATIONS AGENCIES.

(a) PROHIBITION.—No funds authorized to be appropriated by this Act or any other Act shall be available for the United Nations or any specialized agency thereof which accords the Palestine Liberation Organization the same standing as member states.

(b) TRANSFER OR REPROGRAMMING.—Funds subject to the prohibition contained in subsection (a) which would be available for the United Nations or any specialized agency thereof (but for that prohibition) are authorized to remain available until expended and may be reprogrammed or transferred to any other account of the Department of State or the Agency for International Development to carry out the general purposes for which such funds were authorized.

SEC. 415. SENSE OF CONGRESS CONCERNING THE UNITED NATIONS RELIEF AND WORKS AGENCY FOR PALESTINIAN REFUGEES IN THE NEAR EAST (UNRWA).

(a) SENSE OF CONGRESS.—It is the sense of the Congress that—

(1) international burdensharing of the costs of the United Nations Relief and Works Agency for Palestinian Refugees in the Near East (UNRWA) is crucial to the survival of such organization;

(2) the Secretary of State should redouble the efforts of the Department of State to promote international burdensharing of the costs of UNRWA's operations; and

(3) regular and substantial contributions by the Arab states to the budget of the United Nations Relief and Works Agency for Palestinian Refugees in the Near East would reflect the

commitment of Arab states to a peaceful political settlement in the Middle East.

(b) REPORT TO CONGRESS.—The Secretary of State shall prepare and submit a report on progress being made to promote international burdensharing of the costs of the United Nations Relief and Works Agency for Palestinian Refugees in the Near East (UNRWA) to the Committee on Foreign Affairs of the House of Representatives and the Committee on Foreign Relations of the Senate.

SEC. 416. UNITED NATIONS SPONSORSHIP OF A MIDDLE EAST PEACE CONFERENCE.

(a) FINDINGS.—The Congress finds that—

(1) the General Assembly of the United Nations adopted Resolution No. 3379 on November 10, 1975, maintaining that Zionism constituted a form of racism;

(2) most of the proposals for an international peace conference regarding the Middle East have identified the United Nations as the sponsoring organization for such a conference;

(3) all international diplomatic participants in any potential Middle East peace conference must acknowledge the sovereignty of the State of Israel and the right of its citizens to live within secure and permanent boundaries;

(4) United Nations General Assembly Resolution No. 3379 of November 10, 1975, damages the credibility of the General Assembly as a forum for furthering the search for peace in the Middle East; and

(5) the United States does not favor an international conference on the Middle East at this time, and believes that the Israeli proposal for elections that was advanced in May 1989 is the best available vehicle for furthering the Middle East peace process.

(b) POLICY.—The Congress declares, therefore, that—

(1) the United States should use all appropriate means to obtain rescission by the United Nations General Assembly of Resolution No. 3379 and calls upon the General Assembly to do so; and

(2) so long as that resolution remains in effect, the General Assembly and all affiliated agencies of the United Nations constitute an inappropriate forum for the sponsorship of any international conference on the Arab-Israeli conflict.

SEC. 417. CONTRIBUTIONS FOR PEACEKEEPING ACTIVITIES IN SOUTHERN AFRICA.

(a) ASSURANCES THAT ALL CUBAN TROOPS WILL BE WITHDRAWN.—The United States may not, after the date of enactment of this Act, expend any funds authorized to be appropriated by this Act for a contribution or any other assistance with respect to implementation of the Tripartite Agreement until the President certifies to the Congress that—

(1) the United States has received explicit and reliable assurances from each of the parties to the Bilateral Agreement that all Cuban troops will be withdrawn from Angola by July 1, 1991, and that no Cuban troops will remain in Angola after that date; and

(2) the Secretary General of the United Nations has assured the United States that it is his understanding that all Cuban troops will be withdrawn from Angola by July 1, 1991, and that no Cuban troops will remain in Angola after that date.

(b) CONTRIBUTIONS CONDITIONAL ON COMPLIANCE.—The United States may not expend any funds authorized to be appropriated by this Act for a contribution or any other assistance with respect to implementation of the Tripartite Agreement—

(1) if the Government of Cuba fails at any time to comply with any of its obligations under Article 1 of the Bilateral Agreement (relating to the calendar for redeployment and withdrawal of Cuban troops); or

(2) if any Cuban troops remain in Angola after July 1, 1991.

(c) REPORTS TO CONGRESS, COMPLIANCE WITH OBLIGATIONS.—Not more than 15 days after each scheduled phase of the redeployment northward and withdrawal of Cuban troops pursuant to the Bilateral Agreement, the President shall submit to the appropriate congressional committees a report on whether each of the signatories of the Tripartite Agreement is complying with its obligations under the agreement. Whenever he has determined that a material breach of the Tripartite Agreement may have been committed by any of the signatories to that agreement, the President shall so report to the appropriate congressional committees.

(d) DISBURSEMENTS.—Of the amount authorized to be appropriated to be made available for contribution with respect to implementation of the Agreement Among the People's Republic of Angola, the Republic of Cuba, and the Republic of South Africa signed at the United Nations on December 22, 1988 (hereinafter known as the Tripartite Agreement) 50 percent of the annual amount shall be available on October 1, 1989, and the remaining 50 percent on April 1, 1990, only if the President determines and certifies to the appropriate congressional committees as of each date that (1) each of the signatories to the Tripartite Agreement is in compliance with its obligations under the Agreement, (2) the Government of Cuba has complied with its obligations under Article 1 of the Bilateral Agreement (relating to the calendar for redeployment and withdrawal of Cuban troops), (3) the Cubans have not engaged in any offensive military actions against UNITA, including the use of chemical warfare, (4) the United Nations and its affiliated agencies have terminated all funding and other support, in conformity with the United Nations impartiality package, to the South West Africa People's Organization (SWAPO), and (5) the United Nations Angola Verification Mission is demonstrating diligence, impartiality, and professionalism in verifying the departure of Cuban troops and the recording of any troop rotations.

(e) Funding of these activities by the United States may not be construed as constituting recognition of any government in Angola.

(f) For purposes of this section—

(1) the term "Bilateral Agreement" means the Agreement Between the Governments of the People's Republic of Angola and the Republic of Cuba for the Termination of the International Mission of the Cuban Military Contingent, signed at the United Nations on December 22, 1988;

(2) the term "Tripartite Agreement" means the Agreement Among the People's Republic of Angola, the Republic of Cuba, and the Republic of South Africa, signed at the United Nations on December 22, 1988; and

(3) the term "appropriate congressional committees" means the Committees on Appropriations, Foreign Affairs, and Permanent Select Committee on Intelligence of the House of Representatives, and the Committees on Appropriations, Foreign Relations, and the Select Committee on Intelligence of the Senate.

SEC. 704. THE TREATMENT OF THE TURKISH MINORITY BY THE GOVERNMENT OF THE PEOPLE'S REPUBLIC OF BULGARIA AND BULGARIAN REFUGEES IN TURKEY.

(a) FINDINGS.—The Congress finds that—

(1) the Government of the People's Republic of Bulgaria is a signatory to the 1947 Paris Peace Treaty, the Universal Declaration on Human Rights by the United Nations, and the Final Act of the Conference on Security and Cooperation in Europe (also known as the Helsinki Accords);

(2) the Helsinki Accords express the commitment of the participating states to respect the fundamental freedoms of conscience, religion, expression, and emigration, and to guarantee the rights of minorities;

(3) the 1971 Constitution of the People's Republic of Bulgaria declares that fundamental rights will not be restricted because of distinction of national origin, race, or religion, and guarantees minorities the rights to study in their mother tongue and freely practice their religion;

(4) despite its international obligations and constitutional guarantees, the Government of the People's Republic of Bulgaria has taken numerous steps to repress Turkish language and culture, including prohibiting the study of the Turkish language in schools, banning the use of the Turkish language in public, making the receipt and reading of Turkish publications a punishable act, and jamming the reception of Turkish radio and television programs in Bulgaria;

(5) the right of the ethnic Turkish community to freedom of religion has been severely circumscribed by the Government of the People's Republic of Bulgaria, which has closed a number of mosques and barred the importation of copies of the Koran;

(6) emigration by ethnic Turks and others has been banned with only a few exceptions;

(7) beginning in December 1984, the Bulgarian authorities forced the Turkish minority to change their Turkish names to Bulgarian ones, and hundreds of ethnic Turks were killed, injured, or arrested by Bulgarian forces in 1984 and 1985 when they protested this new policy;

(8) the Bulgarian authorities have used both force and coercion to resettle ethnic Turks from their local villages to areas in Bulgaria with small Turkish populations;

(9) in May 1989, Bulgarian troops and police attacked ethnic Turks and others who were peacefully demonstrating against their discriminatory treatment in Bulgaria;

(10) hundreds of demonstrators were killed or wounded in these attacks, and hundreds more were arrested; and

(11) since these demonstrations, the Government of the People's Republic of Bulgaria has forcibly expelled or coerced into emigrating to Turkey thousands of ethnic Turks without either their money or their possessions, often resulting in the separation of families.

(b) POLICY.—It is the sense of the Congress that the Congress—

(1) strongly condemns the brutal treatment of, and blatant discrimination against, the Turkish minority by the Government of the People's Republic of Bulgaria;

(2) calls upon the Bulgarian authorities to immediately cease all discriminatory practices against this community and to release all ethnic Turks and others currently imprisoned because of their participation in nonviolent political acts;

(3) calls upon the Government of Bulgaria to honor its obligations and public statements concerning the right of all Bulgarian citizens to emigrate freely; and

(4) urges the President and Secretary of State to make strong diplomatic representations to Bulgaria protesting its discriminatory treatment of its Turkish minority and to raise this issue in all appropriate international forums, including the Conference on Security and Cooperation in Europe meeting on the environment in Sofia, Bulgaria, this year.

(c) ALLOCATION OF FUNDS FOR ASSISTANCE TO CERTAIN TURKISH REFUGEES.—Of the funds authorized to be appropriated by section 104(a)(1) for the fiscal year 1990, $10,000,000 shall be available only to the Republic of Turkey for assistance for shelter, food, and other basic needs to ethnic Turkish refugees fleeing the People's Republic of Bulgaria and resettling in the sovereign territory of Turkey.

TITLE VIII—PLO COMMITMENTS COMPLIANCE ACT OF 1989

SEC. 801. SHORT TITLE.

This title may be cited as the "PLO Commitments Compliance Act of 1989".

SEC. 802. FINDINGS.

The Congress finds that—

(1) United States policy regarding contacts with the Palestine Liberation Organization (including its Executive Committee, the Palestine National Council, and any constituent groups related thereto (hereafter in this title referred to as the "PLO")) set forth in the Memorandum of Agreement between the United States and Israel, dated September 1, 1975, stated that the United States "will not recognize or negotiate with the Palestine Liberation Organization so long as the PLO does not recognize Israel's right to exist and does not accept United Nations Security Council Resolutions 242 and 338";

(2) section 1302 of the International Security and Development Cooperation Act of 1985 (22 U.S.C. 2151 note; Public Law 99-83), effective October 1, 1985, stated that "no officer or employee of the United States Government and no agent or other individual acting on behalf of the United States Government shall negotiate with the PLO or any representatives thereof (except in emergency or humanitarian situations) unless and until the PLO recognizes Israel's right to exist, accepts United Nations Security Council Resolutions 242 and 338, and renounces the use of terrorism";

(3) the Department of State statement of November 26, 1988, found that "the United States Government has convincing evidence that PLO elements have engaged in terrorism against Americans and others" and that "Mr. [Yasser] Arafat, Chairman of the PLO, knows of, condones, and lends support to such acts; he therefore is an accessory to such terrorism";

(4) Secretary of State Shultz declared on December 14, 1988, that "the [PLO] today issued a statement in which it accepted United Nations Security Council Resolutions 242 and 338, recognized Israel's right to exist in peace and security, and renounced terrorism. As a result, the United States is prepared for a substantive dialogue with PLO representatives";

(5) President Ronald Reagan, subsequent to the decision to open a United States-PLO dialogue, stated that the PLO "must demonstrate that its renunciation of terrorism is pervasive and permanent" and if the PLO reneges on its commitments, the United States "will certainly break off communications";

(6) since the United States agreed to enter into a dialogue with the PLO, there have been several attempted incursions into Israel by the following PLO-affiliated groups: the Popular Struggle Front, the Palestine Liberation Front, the Democratic Front for the Liberation of Palestine, and the Islamic Jihad group;

(7) Yasser Arafat has not renounced any of these incidents, that he has threatened "ten bullets in the chest" to those Palestinians who advocate a cessation of the unrest, and that his principal deputy, Abu Iyad, as well as other senior Al-Fatah figures, have been quoted as saying that the PLO recognition of Israel and renunciation of terrorism is merely tactical and that a Palestinian state is but the first step in the "liberation of Palestine"; and

(8) that the United States should regularly evaluate the PLO's compliance with the commitments made by Yasser Arafat on behalf of the PLO in Geneva on December 14, 1988.

SEC. 803. POLICY.

(a) IN GENERAL.—The Congress reiterates long-standing United States policy that any dialogue with the PLO be contingent upon the PLO's recognition of Israel's right to exist, its acceptance of United Nations Security Council Resolutions 242 and 338, and its abstention from and renunciation of all acts of terrorism.

(b) POLICY TOWARD IMPLEMENTATION OF PLO COMMITMENTS.—It is the sense of the Congress that the United States, in any discussions with the PLO, should seek—

(1) the prevention of terrorism and other violent activity by the PLO or any of its factions; and

(2) the implementation of concrete steps by the PLO consistent with its commitments to recognize Israel and renounce terrorism, including concrete actions that will further the peace process such as—

(A) disbanding units which have been involved in terrorism;

(B) publicly condemning all acts of terrorism;

(C) ceasing the intimidation of Palestinians who advocate a cessation of or who do not support the unrest;

(D) calling on the Arab states to recognize Israel and to end their economic boycott of Israel; and

(E) amending the PLO's Covenant to remove provisions which undermine Israel's legitimacy and which call for Israel's destruction.

(c) POLICY TOWARD RECENT ARMED INCURSIONS INTO ISRAEL BY PLO-AFFILIATED GROUPS.—During the next round of talks with the PLO, should such talks occur after the date of enactment of this Act, the representative of the United States should obtain from the representative of the PLO a full accounting of the following attempted incursions into Israel which occurred after Yasser Arafat's statement of December 14, 1988:

(1) On December 26, 1988, an attempted armed infiltration into Israel by boat by four members of the PLO-affiliated Popular Struggle Front.

(2) On December 28, 1988, an attempted armed infiltration into Israel by three members of the PLO-affiliated Palestine Liberation Front.

(3) On January 24, 1989, an unprovoked attack on an Israeli patrol in Southern Lebanon by the PLO-affiliated Palestine Liberation Front.

(4) On February 5, 1989, an attempted armed infiltration into Israel by nine members of the PLO-affiliated Palestine Liberation Front and Popular Front for the Liberation of Palestine.

(5) On February 23, 1989, an attempted attack on targets in Israel by members of the PLO-affiliated Democratic Front for the Liberation of Palestine.

(6) On February 27, 1989, a PLO-affiliated Popular Front for the Liberation of Palestine ambush of a pro-Israeli Southern Lebanese army vehicle.

(7) On March 2, 1989, an attempted armed infiltration into Israel by four members of the PLO-affiliated Democratic Front for the Liberation of Palestine headed for the civilian town of Zarit.

(8) On March 13, 1989, an attempted armed infiltration into Israel by three members of the PLO-aligned Palestine Liberation Front.

(9) On March 15, 1989, an attempted attack on Israel through Gaza by two members of the Islamic Jihad group.

SEC. 804. REPORTING REQUIREMENT.

(a) REPORT ON ARMED INCURSIONS.—In the event that talks are held with the PLO after the date of enactment of this Act, the Secretary of State, shall, within 30 days after the next round of such talks, report to the Chairman of the Committee on Foreign Affairs of the Senate and the Speaker of the House of Representatives any accounting provided by the representative of the PLO of the incidents described in section 803(c).

(b) REPORT ON COMPLIANCE WITH COMMITMENTS.—Beginning 30 days after the date of enactment of this Act, and every 120 days thereafter in which the dialogue between the United States and the PLO has not been discontinued, the President shall submit to the Speaker of the House of Representatives and the chairman of the Committee on Foreign Relations of the Senate a report, in unclassified form to the maximum extent practicable, regarding progress toward the achievement of the measures described in section 803(b). Such report shall include—

(1) a description of actions or statements by the PLO as an organization, its Chairman, members of its Executive Committee, members of the Palestine National Council, or any constituent groups related thereto, as they relate to the Geneva commitments of December 1988 regarding cessation of terrorism and recognition of Israel's right to exist, including actions or statements that contend that the declared "Palestinian state" encompasses all of Israel;

(2) a description of the steps, if any, taken by the PLO to evict or otherwise discipline individuals or groups taking actions inconsistent with the Geneva commitments;

(3) a statement of whether the PLO, in accordance with procedures in Article 33 of the Palestinian National Covenant, has repealed provisions in that Covenant which call for Israel's destruction;

(4) a statement of whether the PLO has repudiated its "strategy of stages" whereby it seeks to use a Palestinian state in the West Bank and Gaza as the first step in the total elimination of the state of Israel;

(5) a statement of whether the PLO has called on any Arab state to recognize and enter direct negotiations with Israel or to end its economic boycott of Israel;

(6) a statement of whether "Force 17" and the "Hawari Group", units directed by Yasser Arafat that have carried out terrorist attacks, have been disbanded and not reconstituted under different names;

(7) a statement of whether the following PLO constituent groups conduct or participate in terrorist or other violent activities: the Fatah; the Popular Front for the Liberation of Palestine; the Democratic Front for the Liberation of Palestine; the Arab Liberation Front; the Palestine Liberation Front;

(8) a statement of the PLO's position on the unrest in the West Bank and Gaza, and whether the PLO threatens, through violence or other intimidation measures, Palestinians in the West Bank and Gaza who advocate a cessation of or who do not support the unrest, and who might be receptive to taking part in elections there;

(9) a statement of the position of the PLO regarding the prosecution and extradition, if so requested, of known terrorists such as Abu Abbas, who directed the Achille Lauro hijacking during which Leon Klinghoffer was murdered, and Muhammed Rashid, implicated in the 1982 bombing of a PanAm jet and the 1986 bombing of a TWA jet in which four Americans were killed; and

(10) a statement of the position of the PLO on providing compensation to the American victims or the families of American victims of PLO terrorism.

(c) Report on Policies of Arab States.—Not more than 30 days after the date of enactment of this Act, the Secretary of State shall prepare and submit to the Congress a report concerning the policies of Arab states toward the Middle East peace process, including progress toward—

(1) public recognition of Israel's right to exist in peace and security;

(2) ending the Arab economic boycott of Israel; and

(3) ending efforts to expel Israel from international organizations or denying participation in the activities of such organizations.

TITLE IX—PEOPLE'S REPUBLIC OF CHINA

SEC. 901. FINDINGS AND STATEMENTS OF POLICY.

(a) Findings.—The Congress finds that—

(1) on June 4, 1989, the Government of the People's Republic of China ordered an unprovoked, brutal, and indiscriminate assault on thousands of peaceful and unarmed demonstrators and onlookers in and around Tiananmen Square by units of the People's Liberation Army, which resulted in at least 1,000 deaths and several thousand injuries;

(2) the Chinese Government has executed dozens of individuals who participated in prodemocracy demonstrations or who protested the brutal military assault against peaceful demonstrators;

(3) the Government of the People's Republic of China is engaging in widespread mass arrests in the aftermath of the June 4, 1989, military assault in Tiananmen Square, which have resulted in the arrests of thousands of students, workers, and other civilians so far;

(4) independent international human rights organizations, such as Amnesty International and Asia Watch, have documented daily incidences of arbitrary arrests, torture, and beatings by police and military forces in the People's Republic of China;

(5) the Chinese Government has established telephone hotlines and other local communications networks for the express purpose of identifying and imprisoning prodemocracy supporters and political dissidents throughout the country;

(6) officials of the Chinese Government have grossly distorted the Government's actions to suppress the prodemocracy movement, including the clandestine disposal of the bodies of demonstrators without informing their families, and have consistently denied that the massacre in and around Tiananmen Square took place or that abuses of human rights have occurred;

(7) in an effort to conceal the truth about the Chinese Government's brutal suppression of the prodemocracy movement, foreign journalists have been expelled and Voice of America broadcasts are being jammed;

(8) in view of the widespread and continuing repression, noted Chinese intellectuals and advocates of peaceful democratic reform, Fang Lizhi and Li Shuxian, sought refuge at the United States Embassy in Beijing on June 3, 1989, and the United States exercised its prerogatives under longstanding practices of diplomatic missions by granting them refuge; and

(9) the President has condemned the actions of the leaders of the People's Republic of China against participants in the prodemocracy movement in China and has taken several concrete steps to respond to the repression of the movement, including—

(A) suspending all exports of items on the United States Munitions List, including arms and defense related equipment, to the People's Republic of China;

(B) suspending high level government-to-government contact between the United States and the People's Republic of China;

(C) extending the visas of nationals of the People's Republic of China currently in the United States;

(D) offering humanitarian and medical assistance to the injured through the Red Cross;

(E) instructing United States representatives to international financial institutions to seek delay in the consideration of loan requests that are made to those financial institutions and would benefit the People's Republic of China;

(F) suspending action on applications for the issuance by the Overseas Private Investment Corporation of new insurance and financing of investments in the People's Republic of China by United States investors;

(G) opposing the further liberalization of the guidelines of the group known as the Coordinating Committee (COCOM) regarding trade with the People's Republic of China;

(H) taking no further action to implement the agreement for cooperation between the United States and the People's Republic of China relating to the uses of nuclear energy, thereby foreclosing the issuance of new licenses; and

(I) suspending the license for the export of any United States manufactured satellites for launch on launch vehicles owned by the People's Republic of China, including the two Aussat satellites and the Asiasat satellite.

(b) STATEMENTS OF POLICY.—It is the sense of the Congress that—

(1) the President is to be commended for his clear articulation of United States condemnation of the actions of the Government of the People's Republic of China in the killing and persecution of the participants of the prodemocracy movement in the People's Republic of China, and for the responses and measures by the President against the People's Republic of China, which the Congress supports;

(2) the consultative approach that the President has used in coordinating with other countries the United States response to the atrocities committed by the leaders of the People's Republic of China should be supported;

(3) it is essential that the United States speak in a bipartisan and unified voice in response to the events in the People's Republic of China, and that the President be given the necessary flexibility to respond to rapidly changing situations so that the long-term interests of the United States are not damaged;

(4) in this vein, the President should continue to emphasize to the leaders of the Government of the People's Republic of China that resumption of normal diplomatic and military relations between the United States and the People's Republic of China will depend directly on the Chinese Government's halting of executions of prodemocracy movement supporters, releasing those imprisoned for their political beliefs, and increasing respect for internationally recognized human rights;

(5) because human rights violations in a country as populous as the People's Republic of China may have serious implications for the stability of the Asia-Pacific region, the United Nations should, in order to further regional security and peace, condemn the violent repression, mass arrests, abuse of African students, and executions of peaceful demonstrators by the Government of the People's Republic of China and urge the Chinese Government to enter into negotiations with representatives of the prodemocracy movement;

(6) United States policy toward the People's Republic of China should be explicitly linked with the situation in Tibet, specifically as to whether—

(A) martial law is lifted in Lhasa and other parts of Tibet;

(B) Tibet is open to foreigners, including representatives of the international press and of international human rights organizations;

(C) Tibetan political prisoners are released; and

(D) the Government of the People's Republic of China is entering into negotiations with representatives of the Dalai Lama on a settlement of the Tibetan question;

(7) with respect to Hong Kong—

(A) the President should convey to the leaders of the People's Republic of China the importance of living up to its international undertaking with respect to the 1984 Joint Declaration for the future prosperity and stability of Hong Kong; and

(B) the Secretary of State should convey to the Government of the United Kingdom the strong concern of the United States for continued respect for human rights in Hong Kong, and the need to accelerate progress toward representative government through free and fair direct elections;

(8) the United States should offer admission to the United States to any national of the People's Republic of China who is under threat of severe penalty as a result of participating in prodemocracy activities; and

(9) the President should be commended for his courageous and appropriate action, in accordance with the Vienna Convention on Diplomatic Relations and customary international law, in swiftly providing temporary refuge to Fang Lizhi and Li Shuxian at the United States Embassy in Beijing, and the President should continue to provide refuge to those individuals to ensure their personal safety.

(c) ADDITIONAL MEASURES.—It is further the sense of the Congress that, in addition to the measures already taken or required to be taken by this title—

(1) because systematic repression in China continues, the President should urge the Export-Import Bank of the United States to continue to postpone approval of any application for financing United States exports to the People's Republic of China;

(2) under the direction of the Secretary of the Treasury, the United States executive directors of the appropriate international financial institutions should continue to oppose the extension of loans or any other financial assistance by such institutions to the People's Republic of China;

(3) if systematic repression in China deepens, the President should review—

(A) the advisability of continuing to extend most-favored-nation (MFN) trade treatment to Chinese products;

(B) all bilateral trade agreements between the United States and the People's Republic of China;

(C) the bilateral commercial agreements governing Chinese-American cooperation on satellite launches; and

(D) the Chinese-American Agreement for Cooperation on the Peaceful Uses of Atomic Energy, signed at Washington on July 23, 1985;

(4) if systematic repression in China deepens, the President should consult—

(A) with the members of the group known as the Coordinating Committee (COCOM) for the purpose of reviewing the current favorable treatment accorded to high technology exports to the People's Republic of China; and

(B) with the other signatories of the General Agreement on Tariffs and Trade (GATT) for the purpose of reviewing the People's Republic of China's observer status at meetings on GATT and reassessing the People's Republic of China's right to accede to GATT.

SEC. 902. SUSPENSION OF CERTAIN PROGRAMS AND ACTIVITIES.

(a) SUSPENSIONS.—

(1) OVERSEAS PRIVATE INVESTMENT CORPORATION.—The Overseas Private Investment Corporation shall continue to suspend the issuance of any new insurance, reinsurance, guarantees, financing, or other financial support with respect to the Peo-

ple's Republic of China, unless the President makes a report under subsection (b) (1) or (2) of this section.

(2) TRADE AND DEVELOPMENT PROGRAM.—The President shall suspend the obligation of funds under the Foreign Assistance Act of 1961 for any new activities of the Trade and Development Program with respect to the People's Republic of China, unless the President makes a report under subsection (b) (1) or (2) of this section.

(3) MUNITIONS EXPORT LICENSES.—(A) The issuance of licenses under section 38 of the Arms Export Control Act for the export to the People's Republic of China of any defense article on the United States Munitions List, including helicopters and helicopter parts, shall continue to be suspended, subject to subparagraph (B), unless the President makes a report under subsection (b) (1) or (2) of this section.

(B) The suspension set forth in subparagraph (A) shall not apply to systems and components designed specifically for inclusion in civil products and controlled as defense articles only for purposes of export to a controlled country, unless the President determines that the intended recipient of such items is the military or security forces of the People's Republic of China.

(4) CRIME CONTROL AND DETECTION INSTRUMENTS AND EQUIPMENT.—The issuance of any license under section 6(k) of the Export Administration Act of 1979 for the export to the People's Republic of China of any crime control or detection instruments or equipment shall be suspended, unless the President makes a report under subsection (b) (1) or (2) of this section.

(5) EXPORT OF SATELLITES FOR LAUNCH BY THE PEOPLE'S REPUBLIC OF CHINA.—Exports of any satellite of United States origin that is intended for launch from a launch vehicle owned by the People's Republic of China shall remain suspended, unless the President makes a report under subsection (b) (1) or (2) of this section.

(6) NUCLEAR COOPERATION WITH THE PEOPLE'S REPUBLIC OF CHINA.—(A) Any—

(i) application for a license under the Export Administration Act of 1979 for the export to the People's Republic of China for use in a nuclear production or utilization facility of any goods or technology which, as determined under section 309(c) of the Nuclear Non-Proliferation Act of 1978, could be of significance for nuclear explosive purposes, or which, in the judgment of the President, is likely to be diverted for use in such a facility, for any nuclear explosive device, or for research on or development of any nuclear explosive device, shall be suspended,

(ii) application for a license for the export to the People's Republic of China of any nuclear material, facilities, or components subject to the Agreement shall be suspended,

(iii) approval for the transfer or retransfer to the People's Republic of China of any nuclear material, facilities, or components subject to the Agreement shall not be given, and

(iv) specific authorization for assistance in any activities with respect to the People's Republic of China relating to the use of nuclear energy under section 57b.(2) of the Atomic Energy Act of 1954 shall not be given,

until the conditions specified in subparagraph (B) are met.

(B) Subparagraph (A) applies until—

(i) the President certifies to the Congress that the People's Republic of China has provided clear and unequivocal assurances to the United States that it is not assisting and will not assist any nonnuclear-weapon state, either directly or indirectly, in acquiring nuclear explosive devices or the materials and components for such devices;

(ii) the President makes the certifications and submits the report required by Public Law 99-183; and

(iii) the President makes a report under subsection (b) (1) or (2) of this section.

(C) For purposes of this paragraph, the term "Agreement" means the Agreement for Cooperation Between the Government of the United States of America and the Government of the People's Republic of China Concerning Peaceful Uses of Nuclear Energy (done on July 23, 1985).

(7) LIBERALIZATION OF EXPORT CONTROLS.—(A) The President shall negotiate with the governments participating in the group known as the Coordinating Committee (COCOM) to suspend, on a multilateral basis, any liberalization by the Coordinating Committee of controls on exports of goods and technology to the People's Republic of China under section 5 of the Export Administration Act of 1979, including—

(i) the implementation of bulk licenses for exports to the People's Republic of China; and

(ii) the raising of the performance levels of goods or technology below which no authority or permission to export to the People's Republic of China would be required.

(B) The President shall oppose any liberalization by the Coordinating Committee of controls which is described in subparagraph (A)(ii), until the end of the 6-month period beginning on the date of enactment of this Act or until the President makes a report under subsection (b) (1) or (2) of this section, whichever occurs first.

(b) TERMINATION OF SUSPENSIONS.—A report referred to in subsection (a) is a report by the President to the Congress either—

(1) that the Government of the People's Republic of China has made progress on a program of political reform throughout the country, including Tibet, which includes—

(A) lifting of martial law;

(B) halting of executions and other reprisals against individuals for the nonviolent expression of their political beliefs;

(C) release of political prisoners;

(D) increased respect for internationally recognized human rights, including freedom of expression, the press, assembly, and association; and

(E) permitting a freer flow of information, including an end to the jamming of Voice of America and greater access for foreign journalists; or

(2) that it is in the national interest of the United States to terminate a suspension under subsection (a) (1), (2), (3), (4), or (5), to terminate a suspension or disapproval under subsection (a)(6), or to terminate the opposition required by subsection (a)(7), as the case may be.

(c) REPORTING REQUIREMENT.—Sixty days after the date of enactment of this Act, the President shall submit to the Congress a report on—

(1) any steps taken by the Government of China to achieve the objectives described in subsection (b)(1);

(2) the effect of multilateral sanctions on political and economic developments in China and on China's international economic relations;

(3) the impact of the President's actions described in section 901(a)(9) and of the suspensions under subsection (a) of this section on—

(A) political and economic developments in China;

(B) the standard of living of the Chinese people;

(C) relations between the United States and China; and

(D) the actions taken by China to promote a settlement in Cambodia which will ensure Cambodian independence, facilitate an act of self-determination by the Cambodian people, and prevent the Khmer Rouge from returning to exclusive power;

(4) the status of programs and activities suspended under subsection (a); and

(5) the additional measures taken by the President under section 901(c) if repression in China deepens.

SEC. 1005. ASSOCIATION OF DEMOCRATIC NATIONS.

(a) FINDINGS.—The Congress makes the following findings:

(1) It is the policy of the United States to support and promote democratic values and institutions around the world.

(2) Over the last decade, the United States, in concert with other nations, has provided support to those working for democracy in many nations throughout the world.

(3) Such support has advanced the cause of freedom and democracy in those nations by providing international technical expertise on holding free and fair elections, providing international observers to document the conduct of the elections, and in offering economic and humanitarian support to newly established democracies.

(4) On June 8, 1989, at the commencement ceremonies at Harvard University, the newest leader of a democratic nation, Prime Minister Benazir Bhutto of Pakistan, called for the establishment of an Association of Democratic Nations to support the right of peoples everywhere to choose freely their own government.

(5) The goals of the Association would be to promote—

(A) the holding of elections at regular intervals which are open to the participation of all significant political parties, which are fairly administered, and in which the franchise is broad or universal;

(B) respect for fundamental human rights, including freedom of expression, freedom of conscience, and freedom of association;

(C) international recognition of legitimate elections through international election observer missions at all stages of the election, including the campaign, the voting, and the ballot counting;

(D) the mobilization of international opinion and economic measures against the military overthrow of democratic governments; and

(E) the provision of economic assistance to strengthen and support democratic nations.

(b) POLICY.—It is the sense of the Congress that—

(1) the proposal offered by Prime Minister Benazir Bhutto of Pakistan would further the cause of democracy, freedom, and justice and is in the interest of the United States; and

(2) the President of the United States should give serious consideration to the implementation of the proposal, and should provide by December 31, 1989, a report to the Congress assessing the merits of, and estimated annual costs of, establishing such an Association of Democratic Nations.

SEC. 1006. POLICY REGARDING HUMAN RIGHTS ABUSES IN CUBA.

(a) FINDINGS.—The Congress finds that—

(1) the United Nations Commission on Human Rights in 1989 issued its first report on human rights in Cuba, the result of a year-long investigation that concluded on the 30th year of Fidel Castro's rise to power;

(2) that report extensively documented across-the-board human rights abuses, including cases of torture, missing persons, religious persecution, violations of civil and political rights, and violations of economic and social rights;

(3) the United Nations received 137 complaints of "torture, cruel, inhuman or degrading treatment or punishment";

(4) among the abuses reported to the United Nations were sensory deprivation, immersion in a pit latrine, mock executions, overcrowding in special cells, deafening loudspeakers, keeping prisoners naked in front of relatives, and forcing a prisoner about to be executed to carry his own coffin or dig his own grave;

(5) despite the Cuban Government's statements not to harass those who cooperated with the United Nations' investigation, many Cuban citizens who met, or attempted to meet with the United Nations team suffered reprisals;

(6) at least 26 Cuban human rights monitors and independent activists who were arrested in the aftermath of the United Nations investigation are currently serving prison sentences or being held without trial; and

(7) the United Nations Commission on Human Rights approved a resolution on March 9, 1989, calling on the Government of Cuba to cooperate with the Secretary General of the United Nations in settling unresolved questions of human rights.

(b) STATEMENT OF POLICY.—In the interest of promoting respect for internationally recognized human rights in Cuba, the Congress—

(1) calls on the Secretary General of the United Nations to act upon the resolution approved by the Commission on Human Rights March 9, 1989, calling on the Secretary General to take appropriate action to follow up on the Commission's report on human rights in Cuba; and

(2) calls on the Secretary General to specifically urge the Government of Cuba to release at least 26 persons still being held in detention because of their human rights activities.

SEC. 1007. CONCERNING THE SUBMISSION TO THE CONGRESS OF AGREEMENTS PERTAINING TO THE BOUNDARIES OF THE UNITED STATES.

It is the sense of the Congress that all international agreements pertaining to the international boundaries of the United States should be submitted to the Congress for such consideration as is appropriate pursuant to the respective constitutional responsibilities of the Senate and the House of Representatives.

SEC. 1008. REPORT TO CONGRESS CONCERNING OCEANIA.

Not later than 180 days after the date of the enactment of this Act, and one year thereafter, the Secretary of State shall prepare and submit an unclassified report to the Committee on Foreign Affairs of the House of Representatives and the Committee on Foreign Relations of the Senate which—

(1) sets forth in detail the policy of the United States with respect to Oceania, which is comprised of Polynesia, Micronesia, and Melanesia;

(2) examines the nature, extent, and source of political, social, and economic instability affecting states in such region;

(3) assesses the impact and level of communist influence in Oceania;

(4) analyzes projections for the total economic growth of such region, with particular emphasis on the exclusive economic zones (EEZ); and

(5) makes recommendations for specific measures necessary to ensure a strong United States presence in Oceania that contributes to and strengthens democratic institutions and economic growth for the states of the region.

SEC. 1009. REPORT CONCERNING MEXICO.

Not later than 90 days after the date of the enactment of this Act, the Secretary of State shall prepare and submit to the Congress a report concerning the relationship between the United States and Mexico. Such report shall—

(1) analyze potential changes in political, cultural, diplomatic, economic, and other factors as the United States and Mexico move toward greater economic integration and cooperation;

(2) consider the feasibility and effect of a three-way meeting among Canada, Mexico, and the United States to discuss greater economic integration and cooperation;

(3) analyze political, cultural, diplomatic, economic, and other factors related to the development of an economically integrated and cooperative border region between Mexico and the United States; and

(4) evaluate the adequacy of the resources of the Department of State which currently address relations between the United States and Mexico, including a projection of future needs to handle the increasing work load requirements resulting from the growing flow of goods, services, and people across the United States-Mexican border.

BIOLOGICAL WEAPONS ANTI-TERRORISM ACT OF 1989

An Act to implement the Convention on the Prohibition of the Development, Production, and Stockpiling of Bacteriological (Biological) and Toxin Weapons and Their Destruction, by prohibiting certain conduct relating to biological weapons, and for other purposes.

Date: May 22, 1990

Bill No.: S. 993

Public Law No.: 101-298

Cite: 104 STAT. 201

Sections reprinted: All

Public Law 101-298
101st Congress

An Act

To implement the Convention on the Prohibition of the Development, Production, and Stockpiling of Bacteriological (Biological) and Toxin Weapons and Their Destruction, by prohibiting certain conduct relating to biological weapons, and for other purposes.

Be it enacted by the Senate and House of Representatives of the United States of America in Congress assembled,

SECTION 1. SHORT TITLE.

This Act may be cited as the "Biological Weapons Anti-Terrorism Act of 1989".

SEC. 2. PURPOSE AND INTENT.

(a) PURPOSE.—The purpose of this Act is to—

(1) implement the Biological Weapons Convention, an international agreement unanimously ratified by the United States Senate in 1974 and signed by more than 100 other nations, including the Soviet Union; and

(2) protect the United States against the threat of biological terrorism.

(b) INTENT OF ACT.—Nothing in this Act is intended to restrain or restrict peaceful scientific research or development.

SEC. 3. TITLE 18 AMENDMENTS.

(a) IN GENERAL.—Title 18, United States Code, is amended by inserting after chapter 9 the following:

"CHAPTER 10—BIOLOGICAL WEAPONS

"Sec.
"175. Prohibitions with respect to biological weapons.
"176. Seizure, forfeiture, and destruction.
"177. Injunctions.
"178. Definitions.

"§ 175. Prohibitions with respect to biological weapons

"(a) IN GENERAL.—Whoever knowingly develops, produces, stockpiles, transfers, acquires, retains, or possesses any biological agent, toxin, or delivery system for use as a weapon, or knowingly assists a foreign state or any organization to do so, shall be fined under this title or imprisoned for life or any term of years, or both. There is extraterritorial Federal jurisdiction over an offense under this section committed by or against a national of the United States.

"(b) DEFINITION.—For purposes of this section, the term 'for use as a weapon' does not include the development, production, transfer, acquisition, retention, or possession of any biological agent, toxin, or delivery system for prophylactic, protective, or other peaceful purposes.

"§ 176. Seizure, forfeiture, and destruction

"(a) IN GENERAL.—(1) Except as provided in paragraph (2), the Attorney General may request the issuance, in the same manner as provided for a search warrant, of a warrant authorizing the seizure of any biological agent, toxin, or delivery system that—

"(A) exists by reason of conduct prohibited under section 175 of this title; or

"(B) is of a type or in a quantity that under the circumstances has no apparent justification for prophylactic, protective, or other peaceful purposes.

"(2) In exigent circumstances, seizure and destruction of any biological agent, toxin, or delivery system described in subparagraphs (A) and (B) of paragraph (1) may be made upon probable cause without the necessity for a warrant.

"(b) PROCEDURE.—Property seized pursuant to subsection (a) shall be forfeited to the United States after notice to potential claimants and an opportunity for a hearing. At such hearing, the government shall bear the burden of persuasion by a preponderance of the evidence. Except as inconsistent herewith, the same procedures and provisions of law relating to a forfeiture under the customs laws shall extend to a seizure or forfeiture under this section. The Attorney General may provide for the destruction or other appropriate disposition of any biological agent, toxin, or delivery system seized and forfeited pursuant to this section.

"(c) AFFIRMATIVE DEFENSE.—It is an affirmative defense against a forfeiture under subsection (a)(1)(B) of this section that—

"(1) such biological agent, toxin, or delivery system is for a prophylactic, protective, or other peaceful purpose; and

"(2) such biological agent, toxin, or delivery system, is of a type and quantity reasonable for that purpose.

"§ 177. Injunctions

"(a) IN GENERAL.—The United States may obtain in a civil action an injunction against—

"(1) the conduct prohibited under section 175 of this title;

"(2) the preparation, solicitation, attempt, or conspiracy to engage in conduct prohibited under section 175 of this title; or

"(3) the development, production, stockpiling, transferring, acquisition, retention, or possession, or the attempted development, production, stockpiling, transferring, acquisition, retention, or possession of any biological agent, toxin, or delivery system of a type or in a quantity that under the circumstances has no apparent justification for prophylactic, protective, or other peaceful purposes.

"(b) AFFIRMATIVE DEFENSE.—It is an affirmative defense against an injunction under subsection (a)(3) of this section that—

"(1) the conduct sought to be enjoined is for a prophylactic, protective, or other peaceful purpose; and

"(2) such biological agent, toxin, or delivery system is of a type and quantity reasonable for that purpose.

"§ 178. Definitions

"As used in this chapter—

"(1) the term 'biological agent' means any micro-organism, virus, or infectious substance, capable of causing—

"(A) death, disease, or other biological malfunction in a human, an animal, a plant, or another living organism;

"(B) deterioration of food, water, equipment, supplies, or material of any kind; or

"(C) deleterious alteration of the environment;

"(2) the term 'toxin' means, whatever its origin or method of production—

"(A) any poisonous substance produced by a living organism; or

"(B) any poisonous isomer, homolog, or derivative of such a substance;

"(3) the term 'delivery system' means—

"(A) any apparatus, equipment, device, or means of delivery specifically designed to deliver or disseminate a biological agent, toxin, or vector; or

"(B) any vector; and

"(4) the term 'vector' means a living organism capable of carrying a biological agent or toxin to a host.".

(b) WIRE INTERCEPTION.—Section 2516(c) of title 18, United States Code, is amended by adding "section 175 (relating to biological weapons)," after "section 33 (relating to destruction of motor vehicles or motor vehicle facilities),".

(c) CLERICAL AMENDMENT.—The table of chapters for part I of title 18, United States Code, is amended by inserting after the item relating to chapter 9 the following new item:

"10. Biological Weapons .... 175.".

Approved May 22, 1990.

LEGISLATIVE HISTORY—S. 993 (H.R. 237):

HOUSE REPORTS: No. 101-476 accompanying H.R. 237 (Comm. on the Judiciary).
SENATE REPORTS: No. 101-210 (Comm. on the Judiciary).
CONGRESSIONAL RECORD:
Vol. 135 (1989): Nov. 21, considered and passed Senate.
Vol. 136 (1990): May 8, H.R. 237 considered and passed House; proceedings vacated and S. 993 passed in lieu.
WEEKLY COMPILATION OF PRESIDENTIAL DOCUMENTS, Vol. 26 (1990):
May 22, Presidential statement.

JOINT RESOLUTION ON ZIONISM

Joint Resolution calling upon the United Nations to repeal General Assembly Resolution 3379.

Date: June 29, 1990

Bill No.: S.J. Res. 246

Public Law No.: 101-317

Cite: 104 STAT. 285

Sections reprinted: All

Public Law 101-317
101st Congress

Joint Resolution

Calling upon the United Nations to repeal General Assembly Resolution 3379.

Whereas the United Nations will celebrate the forty-fifth anniversary of its charter on June 26, 1990;
Whereas Article I of the United Nations Charter establishes the United Nations as "a center for harmonizing the actions of nations";
Whereas on November 10, 1990, fifteen years will have passed since the adoption of United Nations General Assembly Resolution 3379 which formally declared Zionism to be "a form of racism and racial discrimination";
Whereas Zionism is a national movement of the Jewish people for self-determination, a legitimate and moral aspiration characteristic of many national groups in the modern world;
Whereas United Nations General Assembly Resolution 3379 has had as its overt purpose the delegitimation of the State of Israel;
Whereas United Nations General Assembly Resolution 3379 has impeded the struggle against real forms of racial bigotry and has had the incendiary effect of stimulating and encouraging anti-semitism;
Whereas United Nations General Assembly Resolution 3379 has been used to justify terrorist attacks against innocent people;
Whereas United Nations General Assembly Resolution 3379 is violative of the principles of the United Nations Charter and makes it impossible for the General Assembly to play a credible role in the peaceful resolution of the Arab-Israeli conflict; and
Whereas Public Laws 99-90 (S.J. Res. 98, 1985) and 100-169 (S.J. Res. 205, 1987) and earlier expressions of congressional concern bearing on this subject demonstrate that the United States condemns, denounces, and repudiates United Nations General Assembly Resolution 3379: Now, therefore, be it

Resolved by the Senate and House of Representatives of the United States of America in Congress assembled, That—

(1) the United States calls upon all member states of the United Nations General Assembly to take immediate action to repeal United Nations General Assembly Resolution 3379;

(2) the President shall periodically report to the Congress on progress made toward the repeal of United Nations General Assembly Resolution 3379; and

(3) the Congress commends the President for his commitment to achieving this goal.

Approved June 29, 1990.

LEGISLATIVE HISTORY—S.J. Res. 246:

CONGRESSIONAL RECORD, Vol. 136 (1990):
 May 3, considered and passed Senate.
 June 18, considered and passed House.
WEEKLY COMPILATION OF PRESIDENTIAL DOCUMENTS, Vol. 26 (1990):
 June 29, Presidential statement.

INTER-AMERICAN CONVENTION ON INTERNATIONAL COMMERCIAL ARBITRATION ACT, 1990

An Act to implement the Inter-American Convention on International Commercial Arbitration.

Date: August 15, 1990

Bill No.: H.R. 4314

Public Law No.: 101-369

Cite: 104 STAT. 448

Sections reprinted: All

Public Law 101-369
101st Congress

An Act

To implement the Inter-American Convention on International Commercial Arbitration.

Be it enacted by the Senate and House of Representatives of the United States of America in Congress assembled,

SECTION 1. AMENDMENT TO TITLE 9, UNITED STATES CODE.

Title 9, United States Code, is amended by adding at the end the following:

"CHAPTER 3. INTER-AMERICAN CONVENTION ON INTERNATIONAL COMMERCIAL ARBITRATION

"Sec.

"§ 301. Enforcement of Convention

"The Inter-American Convention on International Commercial Arbitration of January 30, 1975, shall be enforced in United States courts in accordance with this chapter.

"§ 302. Incorporation by reference

"Sections 202, 203, 204, 205, and 207 of this title shall apply to this chapter as if specifically set forth herein, except that for the purposes of this chapter 'the Convention' shall mean the Inter-American Convention.

"§ 303. Order to compel arbitration; appointment of arbitrators; locale

"(a) A court having jurisdiction under this chapter may direct that arbitration be held in accordance with the agreement at any place therein provided for, whether that place is within or without the United States. The court may also appoint arbitrators in accordance with the provisions of the agreement.

"(b) In the event the agreement does not make provision for the place of arbitration or the appointment of arbitrators, the court shall direct that the arbitration shall be held and the arbitrators be appointed in accordance with Article 3 of the Inter-American Convention.

"§ 304. Recognition and enforcement of foreign arbitral decisions and awards; reciprocity

"Arbitral decisions or awards made in the territory of a foreign State shall, on the basis of reciprocity, be recognized and enforced under this chapter only if that State has ratified or acceded to the Inter-American Convention.

"§ 305. Relationship between the Inter-American Convention and the Convention on the Recognition and Enforcement of Foreign Arbitral Awards of June 10, 1958

"When the requirements for application of both the Inter-American Convention and the Convention on the Recognition and Enforcement of Foreign Arbitral Awards of June 10, 1958, are met, determination as to which Convention applies shall, unless otherwise expressly agreed, be made as follows:

"(1) If a majority of the parties to the arbitration agreement are citizens of a State or States that have ratified or acceded to the Inter-American Convention and are member States of the Organization of American States, the Inter-American Convention shall apply.

"(2) In all other cases the Convention on the Recognition and Enforcement of Foreign Arbitral Awards of June 10, 1958, shall apply.

"§ 306. Applicable rules of Inter-American Commercial Arbitration Commission

"(a) For the purposes of this chapter the rules of procedure of the Inter-American Commercial Arbitration Commission referred to in Article 3 of the Inter-American Convention shall, subject to subsection (b) of this section, be those rules as promulgated by the Commission on July 1, 1988.

"(b) In the event the rules of procedure of the Inter-American Commercial Arbitration Commission are modified or amended in accordance with the procedures for amendment of the rules of that Commission, the Secretary of State, by regulation in accordance with section 553 of title 5, consistent with the aims and purposes of this Convention, may prescribe that such modifications or amendments shall be effective for purposes of this chapter.

"§ 307. Chapter 1; residual application

"Chapter 1 applies to actions and proceedings brought under this chapter to the extent chapter 1 is not in conflict with this chapter or the Inter-American Convention as ratified by the United States.".

SEC. 2. CLERICAL AMENDMENT.

The table of chapters at the beginning of title 9, United States Code, is further amended by adding at the end the following new item:

"3. Inter-American Convention on International Commercial Arbitration ..... 301".

SEC. 3. EFFECTIVE DATE.

This Act shall take effect upon the entry into force of the Inter-American Convention on International Commercial Arbitration of January 30, 1975, with respect to the United States.

Approved August 15, 1990.

LEGISLATIVE HISTORY—H.R. 4314 (S. 1941):

HOUSE REPORTS: No. 101-501 (Comm. on the Judiciary).
CONGRESSIONAL RECORD, Vol. 136 (1990):
June 5, considered and passed House.
Aug. 4, considered and passed Senate.

OIL POLLUTION ACT OF 1990

An Act to establish limitations on liability for damages resulting from oil pollution, to establish a fund for the payment of compensation for such damages, and for other purposes.

Date: August 18, 1990

Bill No.: H.R. 1465

Public Law No.: 101-380

Cite: 104 STAT. 484

Sections reprinted:

TITLE I - OIL POLLUTION LIABILITY AND COMPENSATION
- Section 1007 - Recovery by foreign claimants.

TITLE III - INTERNATIONAL OIL POLLUTION PREVENTION AND REMOVAL
- Section 3001 - Sense of Congress regarding participation in international regime.
- Section 3002 - United States-Canada Great Lakes oil spill cooperation.
- Section 3003 - United States-Canada Lake Champlain oil spill cooperation.
- Section 3004 - International inventory of removal equipment and personnel.
- Section 3005 - Negotiations with Canada concerning tug escorts in Puget Sound.

Public Law 101–380
101st Congress

An Act

To establish limitations on liability for damages resulting from oil pollution, to establish a fund for the payment of compensation for such damages, and for other purposes.

SEC. 1007. RECOVERY BY FOREIGN CLAIMANTS.

(a) REQUIRED SHOWING BY FOREIGN CLAIMANTS.—

(1) IN GENERAL.—In addition to satisfying the other requirements of this Act, to recover removal costs or damages resulting from an incident a foreign claimant shall demonstrate that—

(A) the claimant has not been otherwise compensated for the removal costs or damages; and

(B) recovery is authorized by a treaty or executive agreement between the United States and the claimant's country, or the Secretary of State, in consultation with the Attorney General and other appropriate officials, has certified that the claimant's country provides a comparable remedy for United States claimants.

(2) EXCEPTIONS.—Paragraph (1)(B) shall not apply with respect to recovery by a resident of Canada in the case of an incident described in subsection (b)(4).

(b) DISCHARGES IN FOREIGN COUNTRIES.—A foreign claimant may make a claim for removal costs and damages resulting from a discharge, or substantial threat of a discharge, of oil in or on the territorial sea, internal waters, or adjacent shoreline of a foreign country, only if the discharge is from—

(1) an Outer Continental Shelf facility or a deepwater port;

(2) a vessel in the navigable waters;

(3) a vessel carrying oil as cargo between 2 places in the United States; or

(4) a tanker that received the oil at the terminal of the pipeline constructed under the Trans-Alaska Pipeline Authorization Act (43 U.S.C. 1651 et seq.), for transportation to a place in the United States, and the discharge or threat occurs prior to delivery of the oil to that place.

(c) FOREIGN CLAIMANT DEFINED.—In this section, the term "foreign claimant" means—

(1) a person residing in a foreign country;

(2) the government of a foreign country; and

(3) an agency or political subdivision of a foreign country.

TITLE III—INTERNATIONAL OIL POLLUTION PREVENTION AND REMOVAL

SEC. 3001. SENSE OF CONGRESS REGARDING PARTICIPATION IN INTERNATIONAL REGIME.

It is the sense of the Congress that it is in the best interests of the United States to participate in an international oil pollution liability and compensation regime that is at least as effective as Federal and State laws in preventing incidents and in guaranteeing full and prompt compensation for damages resulting from incidents.

SEC. 3002. UNITED STATES-CANADA GREAT LAKES OIL SPILL COOPERATION.

(a) REVIEW.—The Secretary of State shall review relevant international agreements and treaties with the Government of Canada, including the Great Lakes Water Quality Agreement, to determine whether amendments or additional international agreements are necessary to—

(1) prevent discharges of oil on the Great Lakes;

(2) ensure an immediate and effective removal of oil on the Great Lakes; and

(3) fully compensate those who are injured by a discharge of oil on the Great Lakes.

(b) CONSULTATION.—In carrying out this section, the Secretary of State shall consult with the Department of Transportation, the Environmental Protection Agency, the National Oceanic and Atmospheric Administration, the Great Lakes States, the International Joint Commission, and other appropriate agencies.

(c) REPORT.—The Secretary of State shall submit a report to the Congress on the results of the review under this section within 6 months after the date of the enactment of this Act.

SEC. 3003. UNITED STATES-CANADA LAKE CHAMPLAIN OIL SPILL CO-OPERATION.

(a) REVIEW.—The Secretary of State shall review relevant international agreements and treaties with the Government of Canada, to determine whether amendments or additional international agreements are necessary to—

(1) prevent discharges of oil on Lake Champlain;

(2) ensure an immediate and effective removal of oil on Lake Champlain; and

(3) fully compensate those who are injured by a discharge of oil on Lake Champlain.

(b) CONSULTATION.—In carrying out this section, the Secretary of State shall consult with the Department of Transportation, the Environmental Protection Agency, the National Oceanic and Atmospheric Administration, the States of Vermont and New York, the International Joint Commission, and other appropriate agencies.

(c) REPORT.—The Secretary of State shall submit a report to the Congress on the results of the review under this section within 6 months after the date of the enactment of this Act.

SEC. 3004. INTERNATIONAL INVENTORY OF REMOVAL EQUIPMENT AND PERSONNEL.

The President shall encourage appropriate international organizations to establish an international inventory of spill removal equipment and personnel.

SEC. 3005. NEGOTIATIONS WITH CANADA CONCERNING TUG ESCORTS IN PUGET SOUND.

Congress urges the Secretary of State to enter into negotiations with the Government of Canada to ensure that tugboat escorts are required for all tank vessels with a capacity over 40,000 deadweight tons in the Strait of Juan de Fuca and in Haro Strait.

CUSTOMS AND TRADE ACT OF 1990

An Act to make miscellaneous and technical changes to various trade laws.

Date: August 20, 1990

Bill No.: H.R. 1594

Public Law No.: 101-382

Cite: 104 STAT. 629

Sections reprinted:

Public Law 101–382
101st Congress

An Act

To make miscellaneous and technical changes to various trade laws.

TITLE II—CARIBBEAN BASIN ECONOMIC RECOVERY

Subtitle A—Short Title and Findings

SEC. 201. SHORT TITLE.

This title may be cited as the "Caribbean Basin Economic Recovery Expansion Act of 1990".

SEC. 202. CONGRESSIONAL FINDINGS.

The Congress finds that—

(1) a stable political and economic climate in the Caribbean region is necessary for the development of the countries in that region and for the security and economic interests of the United States;

(2) the Caribbean Basin Economic Recovery Act was enacted in 1983 to assist in the achievement of such a climate by stimulating the development of the export potential of the region; and

(3) the commitment of the United States to the successful development of the region, as evidenced by the enactment of the Caribbean Basin Economic Recovery Act, should be reaffirmed, and further strengthened, by amending that Act to improve its operation.

Subtitle D—Miscellaneous Provisions

SEC. 241. TRADE BENEFITS FOR NICARAGUA.

Notwithstanding any other provision of law, the President is authorized to designate Nicaragua as a beneficiary developing country for the purposes of title V of the Trade Act of 1974, as amended, and as a beneficiary country under the Caribbean Basin Economic Recovery Act, and any such designation may remain effective for the duration of the calendar year 1990.

SEC. 242. AGRICULTURAL INFRASTRUCTURE SUPPORT.

It is the sense of Congress that in order to facilitate trade with, and the economic development of, the countries designated as beneficiary countries under the Caribbean Basin Economic Recovery Act, the Secretary of Agriculture should, in consultation with the Agribusiness Promotion Council, coordinate with the Agency for International Development the development of programs to encourage improvements in the transportation and cargo handling infrastructure in these countries for the purpose of improving agricultural trade between these countries and the United States. Such programs should focus on improving distribution of agricultural commodities and products in these countries, and the phytosanitary institutions, quarantine capabilities, and pesticide regulations of these countries regarding agricultural commodities and products.

SEC. 243. EXTENSION OF TRADE BENEFITS TO THE ANDEAN REGION.

(a) FINDINGS.—The Congress finds that:

(1) United States antinarcotics policy places a high priority on assisting the nations of the Andean region of South America, the source of 100 percent of the world's supply of cocaine.

(2) The President and Congress have recognized that United States trade and economic policies play an important role in the

overall United States antidrug strategy in the Andes.

(3) The extension of special trade preferences for articles from the Andean region would help revitalize the national economies of the Andes and further United States antinarcotics policy in the region.

(b) SENSE OF CONGRESS.—The Congress urges the President to—

(1) review the merits of extending the benefits provided under the Caribbean Basin Economic Recovery Act to the Andean region; and

(2) continue to explore additional mechanisms to expand trade opportunities for the Andean region, and report to Congress in a regular and timely fashion on the result of this review.

TITLE IV—EXPORTS OF UNPROCESSED TIMBER

SEC. 487. SHORT TITLE.

This title may be cited as the "Forest Resources Conservation and Shortage Relief Act of 1990".

SEC. 488. FINDINGS AND PURPOSES.

(a) FINDINGS.—The Congress makes the following findings:

(1) Timber is essential to the United States.

(2) Forests, forest resources, and the forest environment are exhaustible natural resources that require efficient and effective conservation efforts.

(3) In the interest of conserving those resources, the United States has set aside millions of acres of otherwise harvestable timberlands in the western United States, representing well over 100,000,000,000 board feet of otherwise harvestable timber.

(4) In recent years, administrative, statutory, or judicial action has been taken to set aside an increased amount of otherwise harvestable timberlands for conservation purposes.

(5) In the next few months and years, additional amounts of otherwise harvestable timberlands may be set aside for conservation purposes, pursuant to the Endangered Species Act of 1973, the National Forest Management Act of 1976, or other expected statutory, administrative, and judicial actions.

(6) There is evidence of a shortfall in the supply of unprocessed timber in the western United States.

(7) There is reason to believe that any shortfall which may already exist may worsen unless action is taken.

(8) In conjunction with the broad conservation actions expected in the next few months and years, conservation action is necessary with respect to exports of unprocessed timber.

(b) PURPOSES.—The purposes of this title are—

(1) to promote the conservation of forest resources in conjunction with State and Federal resources management plans, and other actions or decisions, affecting the use of forest resources;

(2) to take action essential for the acquisition and distribution of forest resources or products in short supply in the western United States;

(3) to take action necessary, to meet the goals of Article XI 2.(a) of the General Agreement on Tariffs and Trade, to ensure sufficient supplies of certain forest resources or products which are essential to the United States;

(4) to continue and refine the existing Federal policy of restricting the export of unprocessed timber harvested from Federal lands in the western United States; and

(5) to effect measures aimed at meeting these objectives in conformity with the obligations of the United States under the General Agreement on Tariffs and Trade.

SEC. 489. RESTRICTIONS ON EXPORTS OF UNPROCESSED TIMBER ORIGINATING FROM FEDERAL LANDS.

(a) PROHIBITION ON EXPORT OF UNPROCESSED TIMBER ORIGINATING FROM FEDERAL LANDS.—No person who acquires unprocessed timber originating from Federal lands west of the 100th meridian in the contiguous 48 States may export such timber from the United States, or sell, trade, exchange, or otherwise convey such timber to any other person for the purpose of exporting such timber from the United States, unless such timber has been determined under subsection (b) to be surplus to the needs of timber manufacturing facilities in the United States.

(b) SURPLUSES.—

(1) DETERMINATIONS BY SECRETARY CONCERNED.—The prohibition contained in subsection (a) shall not apply to specific quantities of grades and species of unprocessed timber originating from Federal lands which the Secretary concerned determines to be surplus to domestic manufacturing needs.

(2) PROCEDURES.—Any determination under paragraph (1) shall be made in regulations issued in accordance with section 553 of title 5, United States Code. Any such determination shall be reviewed at least once in every 3-year period. The Secretary concerned shall publish notice of such review in the Federal Register, and shall give the public an opportunity to comment on such review.

TREASURY, POSTAL SERVICE AND GENERAL GOVERNMENT APPROPRIATIONS ACT, 1991

An Act making appropriations for the Treasury Department, the United States Postal Service, the Executive Office of the President, and certain Independent Agencies, for the fiscal year ending September 30, 1991, and for other purposes.

Date: November 5, 1990

Bill No.: H.R. 5241

Public Law No.: 101-509

Cite: 104 STAT. 1389

Sections reprinted:

Section 630 - Annexation of Kuwait by the Republic of Iraq.
Section 632 - Convention on the Rights of the Child
Section 635 - Taking of civilian hostages by Iraq.

Public Law 101–509
101st Congress

An Act

Making appropriations for the Treasury Department, the United States Postal Service, the Executive Office of the President, and certain Independent Agencies, for the fiscal year ending September 30, 1991, and for other purposes.

SEC. 630. (a) The Senate finds that—

(1) democracy and freedom of the independent Arab nations have been threatened by the invasion and illegal annexation of Kuwait by the Government of the Republic of Iraq;

(2) the safety of American citizens and those of other countries have been directly threatened by the decision of the Government of Iraq to move them and use them as "human shields" at strategic defense and industrial installations;

(3) the stability of world oil production and marketing has been threatened by the illegal Iraqi seizure of Kuwaiti ports and oil production facilities;

(4) the United Nations has condemned Iraq's invasion of Kuwait, has voted to impose an economic embargo on Iraq, and has declared null and void the annexation of Kuwait;

(5) the United Nations Security Council has approved the use of appropriate military force by individual nations to enforce United Nations sanctions;

(6) the President of the United States has taken the lead in unifying world opinion and directing international efforts against the Iraqi aggression and in defense of Saudi Arabia and the other Gulf states;

(7) a majority of Arab nations have condemned Iraq's actions and have supported Arab military and diplomatic efforts to defend the Gulf states and to ensure Iraq's withdrawal from Kuwait;

(8) the United States is deploying tens of thousands of American troops and military hardware to the Persian Gulf in defense of the strategic interests of the United States in the region at costs estimated to be in excess of $40 million a day, during a time of an increasing budget deficit;

(9) a principle position of the United States and its NATO and major non-NATO allies is one of burdensharing in the collective defense of the Western alliance;

(10) the Senate and the American people are deeply concerned about the need for a reduced budget deficit and improved economic growth; and

(11) President George Bush has announced his intention to develop an economic action plan under which nations benefitting from the economic embargo and the military actions in the Persian Gulf assist those nations which are committing their military personnel and materiel to support these United Nations actions.

(b) It is the sense of the Senate that—

(1) the President of the United States should be congratulated for taking the diplomatic initiative to encourage other nations to share the international financial burden of the defense of Saudi Arabia; and

(2) the President of the United States—

(A) in consultation with the allies of the United States in the Persian Gulf defense operation, should—

(i) take steps to ensure that United States allies are sharing an appropriate portion of the collective defense of their interests in the Gulf;

(ii) take steps to ensure that those allies who are precluded from any overt military participation in the Gulf, or who decide against participating in these defensive actions, or who only provide minimal participation are assuming an appropriate financial share of the collective defense commensurate with their national means; and

(iii) take steps to ensure that those oil producing nations which may benefit from increased individual oil production and world oil prices as a result of the embargo of Iraqi and Kuwaiti oil proportionally share the burden of the costs of the embargo, either directly with those nations providing the defense, or by equivalent "inkind" payments, or by assuming some of the other international financial burdens of the major defense-providing nations;

(B) in concert with the Secretary of State, the Secretary of Defense, the Secretary of the Treasury, and the Director of the Office of Management and Budget, shall consult with Congress on the steps the President is taking to meet the goals enumerated in subparagraph (A) and shall provide a report to the Congress no later than November 30, 1990, detailing the progress of such steps to date;

(C) during his consultations with other international leaders, should consider stressing, among other points, that failure by any country to actively contribute in the most appropriate manner for that country could have a detrimental impact on its bilateral relationship with the United States; and

(D) should also inform Congress of any legislative initiatives which need to be taken to meet the goals enumerated in subparagraphs (A) through (C).

SEC. 632. CONVENTION ON THE RIGHTS OF THE CHILD.—(a) FINDINGS.—The Senate finds that—

(1) the future peace and prosperity of all nations depend upon the good health and well-being of the world's children;

(2) the Congress has long recognized the vulnerability of children and has enacted numerous laws that afford them special protections in this country;

(3) similar protections for children are either totally lacking or inadequately enforced in much of the world;

(4) in part as a result of this lack of protection, millions of children are threatened daily by poverty, malnutrition, homelessness, exploitation and abuse, depriving both family and society of their productivity and potential;

(5) the Child Survival and Development Revolution, launched in 1982 to attack the root causes of infant mortality and child ill-health through low-cost means such as universal child immunization and oral rehydration therapy, is saving the lives of more than 3,000,000 children each year and has demonstrated that the number of child deaths can be reduced significantly if available resources are used appropriately;

(6) despite these gains and an emerging international consensus about the importance of protecting children, children both here and abroad will continue to face poverty, sickness, and ill-treatment.

(7) on November 20, 1989, the United States and other members of the United Nations unanimously endorsed the Convention on the Rights of the Child and urged national governments to ratify the Convention and make possible its application as international law;

(8) this Convention, if implemented, will help establish universal legal standards for the care and protection of children against neglect, exploitation, and abuse;

(9) the United States Government, scores of private voluntary organizations, and hundreds of American citizens were actively involved in the drafting of this Convention; and

(10) the United States must continue playing a leading role in the implementation of the Convention to ensure that it becomes a force for improving the lot of children, both in this country and abroad.

(b) SENSE OF THE SENATE.—It is the sense of the Senate that the issue of children's rights and their well-being is important both to the United States and the world at large and that, in consideration thereof, the President should promptly seek the advice and consent of the Senate to the ratification of the Convention on the Rights of the Child, adopted by the United Nations with the support of the United States on November 29, 1989.

SEC. 635. (a) The Congress finds that—

(1) President Saddam Hussein of Iraq has attempted to evade the consequences of his illegal invasion of Kuwait by the taking of civilian hostages;

(2) Saddam Hussein has violated standards of civilized conduct by willfully seeking to endanger the lives of foreign civilians in Kuwait and Iraq;

(3) He has further violated international diplomatic practice by laying siege to Western embassies in Kuwait;

(4) Iraq's conduct both at home and on the battlefield during the recent war with Iran has demonstrated a willingness to use the most barbaric methods of warfare, including the gassing of civilian women and children;

(5) The Nuremberg principles, while denying national guilt for acts of war, do also stipulate that individual leaders may be held responsible for violations of the conventions of war and of civilized behavior;

(6) The taking of hostages, the use of gas, the terrorizing of civilians and diplomats, and other such acts in both peace and war have long been considered crimes against humanity for which prosecution is justifiable.

(b) It is the sense of the Senate that in the event of hostilities between the United States and the government of Iraq it shall be the policy of the United States to pursue Saddam Hussein, other Iraqi leaders, and other such perpetrators as may be determined responsible in order to bring them to justice as war criminals, and to seek their prosecution and punishment under the auspices of an international tribunal with relevant jurisdiction.

NATIONAL DEFENSE AUTHORIZATION ACT FOR FISCAL YEAR 1991

An Act to authorize appropriations for fiscal year 1991 for military activities of the Department of Defense, for military construction, and for defense activities of the Department of Energy, to prescribe personnel strengths for such fiscal year for the Armed Forces, and for other purposes.

Date: November 5, 1990

Bill No.: H.R. 4739

Public Law No.: 101-510

Cite: 104 STAT. 1485

Sections reprinted:

TITLE X - DRUG INTERDICTION AND COUNTER-DRUG ACTIVITIES
- Section 1008 - Study of utility of OH-58D helicopter in detection of cross-border intrusions by drug smugglers.
- Section 1009 - Andean anti-drug efforts.
- Section 1010 - Creation of a multilateral counter-drug strike force.

TITLE XIV - GENERAL PROVISIONS

Part D - Arms Control Matters
- Section 1441 - Sense of Congress on additional nuclear risk reduction measures.
- Section 1442 - START and strategic modernization.
- Section 1443 - Strategic Arms Reduction Talks agreement.

Part E - Matters Relating to Allies and Other Nations
- Section 1454 - Cooperation with Japan on technological research and development.
- Section 1455 - Permanent ceiling on United States Armed Forces in Japan and contributions by Japan to the support of United States forces in Japan.
- Section 1457 - Annual report on United States security arrangements and commitments with other nations.

Public Law 101–510
101st Congress

An Act

To authorize appropriations for fiscal year 1991 for military activities of the Department of Defense, for military construction, and for defense activities of the Department of Energy, to prescribe personnel strengths for such fiscal year for the Armed Forces, and for other purposes.

SEC. 1008. STUDY OF UTILITY OF OH-58D HELICOPTER IN DETECTION OF CROSS-BORDER INTRUSIONS BY DRUG SMUGGLERS

(a) STUDY REQUIRED.—The Secretary of Defense shall conduct a study on the feasibility and effectiveness of using the OH-58D Scout helicopters for detecting, monitoring, and conducting surveillance of the ground movements of drug smugglers along the southwest border of the United States. In carrying out such study, the Secretary shall consider in particular the following matters:

(1) The suitability of the OH-58D helicopter for performing the missions described in the first sentence.

(2) The feasibility of having personnel of the Army National Guard operate and maintain OH-58D helicopters when such personnel are not in Federal service.

(b) INTERAGENCY COORDINATION.—The Secretary shall carry out the study required by subsection (a) in consultation with the Commissioner of the United States Customs Service.

(c) SUBMISSION OF REPORT.—The Secretary shall submit to the Committees on Armed Services of the Senate and the House of Representatives a report containing the results of the study required by subsection (a) not more than 180 days after the date of the enactment of this Act. The Secretary shall include in the report the conclusions of the Secretary based on the study together with such comments and recommendation as the Secretary considers appropriate.

SEC. 1009. ANDEAN ANTI-DRUG EFFORTS

(a) FINDINGS.—Congress makes the following findings:

(1) The support for democratic process and civilian governance in the Andean countries of Peru, Bolivia, and Colombia, the first two of which have only recently emerged from periods of military rule, is a necessary precondition for long-term stability in those countries and for the successful fight against the production and traffic of illegal drugs in those countries.

(2) The separation of military and civilian law enforcement functions has historically been a critical element in democracies around the world, including the United States.

(3) There is a need to determine whether the current policies of the United States unduly emphasize assistance to military entities of those countries rather than civilian law enforcement entities in carrying out anti-drug efforts in those countries and whether such policies might tend to undermine the dual long-term policy goals of the United States of stopping the traffic of drugs at their sources and the preservation of civilian control over the newly established democracies of the Andean countries.

(4) There is a need to assess the impact that United States assistance in the Andean anti-drug effort will have on reducing drug activity and supporting democratic processes in the Andean countries.

(b) REPORT REQUIRED.—(1) Not later than 90 days after the date of the enactment of this Act, the Secretary of State and the Secretary of Defense shall, in consultation with the Director of the Office of National Drug Control Policy, jointly submit to Congress a report detailing current United States policies with respect to the Andean countries in general and with respect to the counter-drug enforcement activities and associated training programs of the United States in such countries in particular.

(2) Such report shall include an analysis of the impact that the involvement of the military forces of the Andean countries in counter-drug enforcement activities has on the democratic institutions of those countries and how the civilian institutions of those countries might be strengthened in order to assure the successful pursuit of a counter-drug strategy.

(3) Such report shall contain specific legislative recommendations for improving the assistance activities of the United States in the Andean countries in order to avoid unnecessary duplications and contradictions in meeting United States policy goals in those countries.

SEC. 1010. CREATION OF A MULTILATERAL COUNTER-DRUG STRIKE FORCE

(a) FINDINGS.—Congress makes the following findings:

(1) Congress has in the past sought approval for a multilateral strike force dedicated to the war on drugs.

(2) The proposal by the Prime Minister of Jamaica for the creation of a multilateral, international counter-drug strike force is the first operative proposal for the use of a multilateral force against the drug cartels in Latin America by a government leader in the Western Hemisphere and should be given serious consideration.

(b) SENSE OF THE CONGRESS.—It is the sense of Congress that—

(1) the Prime Minister of Jamaica is to be commended for his proposal;

(2) the President should call for international negotiations for the purpose of discussing the establishment of an international strike force to counter international drug traffickers; and

(3) the United States should work through the United Nations and other multilateral organizations to determine the feasibility of establishing and using a force and should assist in the establishment of such a force if the President determines the proposal to be feasible.

TITLE XIV—GENERAL PROVISIONS

(1) On June 1, 1990, the President of the United States and the President of the Soviet Union signed a document entitled "Joint Statement on Future Negotiations on Nuclear and Space Arms and Further Enhancing Strategic Stability".

(2) In that document, the two nations pledged to pursue additional confidence-building and predictability measures "that would reduce the possibility of an outbreak of nuclear war as a result of accident, miscalculation, terrorism, or unexpected technological breakthrough, and would prevent possible incidents between them".

(3) As a result of the recent increase in ethnic, national, economic, and political tensions within the Soviet Union, concern has heightened regarding the possible unauthorized or accidental use of Soviet nuclear weapons.

(4) It has been four years since the Department of Defense conducted a comprehensive review of its nuclear control procedures and failsafe mechanisms.

(5) The Joint Chiefs of Staff, in its 1990 Joint Military Net Assessment, concluded that with the recent changes in the global security environment "the risk of nuclear deterrence failing is assessed to be low and at this moment to be decreasing".

(6) While Congress is concerned about continued strategic

offensive and defensive modernization by the Soviet Union and the unpredictable status of the domestic situation in the Soviet Union, at this stage the lessened prospects that nuclear weapons of the United States might have to be employed may afford an opportunity to reconsider past reluctance to use certain positive control measures, such as the installation of permissive action links (PALs) on nuclear weapons deployed at sea by the United States and the installation of post-launch destruct mechanisms on intercontinental ballistic missiles (ICBMs) and submarine launched ballistic missiles (SLBMs) deployed by the United States, as long as appropriate security measures can be developed to protect the integrity of such destruct mechanisms.

(7) On September 15, 1987, the United States and the Soviet Union agreed to establish Nuclear Risk Reduction Centers (NRRCs) in Washington and Moscow.

(8) The NRRCs have made a useful contribution to lowering the risks of accidental or inadvertent nuclear war and are capable of taking on expanded roles.

(b) SENSE OF CONGRESS.—It is the sense of Congress—

(1) that the President of the United States and the President of the Union of Soviet Socialist Republics are to be commended for their June 1, 1990, joint statement to pursue additional nuclear confidence-building measures; and

(2) that, in keeping with that joint statement, the President—

(A) should invite the Soviet Union to join with the United States in conducting separate but parallel, comprehensive reviews of each nation's own nuclear control procedures and failsafe mechanisms; and

(B) should propose to the Soviet Union that representatives of the two nations engage in discussions with the objective of agreeing on additional roles and functions that could be assigned to the Nuclear Risk Reduction Centers to further lessen the risks of the outbreak of nuclear war as the result of misinterpretation, miscalculation, or accident.

(c) REPORT ON ADDITIONAL MEASURES.—Not later than March 1, 1991, the President shall submit to Congress a report (in both classified and unclassified form) assessing additional nuclear risk reduction measures which could be implemented pursuant to the joint statement of June 1, 1990, referred to in subsection (b), including the following:

(1) Assigning to the Nuclear Risk Reduction Centers (NRRCs) such expanded roles as the following:

(A) Serving as a forum for discussions between the two nations on responding to possible nuclear terrorism.

(B) Transmitting notifications that may be required under future arms control treaties.

(C) Transmitting non-urgent notifications and information requests required under Article 5 of the 1971 Agreement on Measures to Reduce the Risk of Outbreak of Nuclear War Between the United States and the Union of Soviet Socialist Republics.

(D) Providing a forum for discussions between the United States and the Soviet Union on restricting nuclear, chemical, and missile proliferation.

(E) Serving as a meeting place for high-level military discussions on nuclear doctrines, forces and activities, and regional security concerns.

(2) Installation of post-launch destruct mechanisms on all intercontinental ballistic missiles (ICBMs) and submarine launched ballistic missiles (SLBMs) deployed by the United States.

(3) Installation by the United States of permissive action links (PALs) on all nuclear weapons at sea.

SEC. 1442. START AND STRATEGIC MODERNIZATION

(a) FINDINGS.—The Congress makes the following findings:

(1) The United States and the Soviet Union are engaged in the Strategic Arms Reduction Talks (START) in Geneva.

(2) In the Joint Statement on the Treaty on Strategic Offensive Arms signed in June 1990, the two sides reaffirmed their determination to have a START agreement completed and ready for signature by the end of 1990.

(3) Under the provisions of a START agreement, both sides will carry out significant reductions in strategic offensive arms.

(4) In the Joint Statement on Future Negotiations on Nuclear and Space Arms and Further Enhancing Strategic Stability, the United States and the Soviet Union agreed to pursue new talks on strategic offensive arms, and on the relationship between strategic offensive and defensive arms.

(5) The objectives of these negotiations will be to reduce further the risk of outbreak of war, particularly nuclear war, and to ensure strategic stability, transparency and predictability through further stabilizing reductions in the strategic arsenals of both countries.

(6) The President's effort to negotiate such agreements is dependent upon the maintenance of a vigorous research and development and modernization program as required for a prudent defense posture.

(7) The Soviet Union has maintained a robust strategic modernization program throughout the course of the START negotiations which continues today.

(b) It is the sense of the Congress that—

(1) the Congress fully supports United States efforts to enhance strategic stability; and

(2) the United States should pursue stabilizing strategic arms reduction agreements while maintaining a vigorous research and development and modernization program for United States strategic forces as required for a prudent defense posture.

SEC. 1443. STRATEGIC ARMS REDUCTION TALKS AGREEMENT

(a) SENSE OF CONGRESS.—It is the sense of the Congress that the President, before concluding an agreement in the Strategic Arms Reduction Talks, should provide to Congress—

(1) a report on whether the SS-23 INF missiles of Soviet manufacture, which the Soviet Union has confirmed have been stationed in the territory of the former German Democratic Republic and in the territories of Czechoslovakia and Bulgaria, constitute a violation of the INF Treaty or constitute deception in the INF negotiations, and whether the United States has reliable assurances that those missiles will be destroyed; and

(2) a report on whether the Krasnoyarsk radar, which the Foreign Minister of the Soviet Union admitted is a clear violation of the 1972 ABM Treaty, has been verifiably dismantled in accordance with United States criteria.

FORM OF REPORTS.—The reports under paragraphs (1) and (2) of subsection (a) should be submitted in both classified and unclassified form.

SEC. 1454. COOPERATION WITH JAPAN ON TECHNOLOGICAL RESEARCH AND DEVELOPMENT

(a) FINDINGS.—Congress makes the following findings:

(1) Japan has developed highly sophisticated research and manufacturing capabilities.

(2) Those capabilities have produced technologies that can be usefully applied to the development and manufacture of both commercial products and defense equipment.

(3) The availability of those technologies to the United States would greatly enhance the development and manufacture of defense equipment for the Armed Forces of the United States.

(4) Since the exchange of notes between the United States and Japan on the transfer of Japanese military technologies in 1983, the level and quality of technological cooperation between the two countries have been unsatisfactory.

(5) Effective cooperation in technology research and development between the United States and Japan would enhance the security of both countries.

(b) SENSE OF CONGRESS.—It is the sense of Congress that—

(1) the United States and Japan should strengthen their cooperation with regard to technology that would contribute to the security of both countries;

(2) technological cooperation between the two countries should be based upon an equitable and mutual sharing of the costs and benefits of that cooperation; and

(3) the Secretary of Defense should improve the staffing, funding, and organization of those activities within the Department of Defense responsible for implementing and overseeing technological cooperation with Japan.

(c) COOPERATION ON RESEARCH AND DEVELOPMENT.—In light of the expressions in subsections (a) and (b), Congress urges and requests the President and directs the Secretary of Defense to pursue vigorously opportunities for the United States and Japan to cooperate in the development of technologies that benefit the security of both countries, particularly those technologies that have both commercial and military applications, commonly referred to as "dual-use" technologies.

(d) COOPERATIVE RESEARCH AND DEVELOPMENT PROJECTS.—(1) Subject to paragraphs (2) and (3), of the funds authorized to be appropriated pursuant to section 201 for basic research, exploratory development, and advanced technology, $10,000,000 shall be available for research and development projects conducted jointly by the United States and Japan, pursuant to a memorandum of understanding or other formal agreement, for the purpose of—

(A) developing new conventional defense equipment; or

(B) modifying existing defense equipment to meet United States defense requirements.

(2)(A) Funds made available for research and development projects under paragraph (1) may be obligated and expended for a particular research project only if the Secretary of Defense determines that—

(i) the particular project will improve, through the application of emerging technology, the conventional defense capabilities of the United States and Japan; and

(ii) the applicable memorandum of understanding or other formal agreement provides for the sharing of costs on an equitable basis.

(B) The Secretary may delegate the performance of the responsibility to make determinations under subparagraph (A) only to the

Deputy Secretary of Defense or the Under Secretary of Defense for Acquisition.

(3) None of the funds made available for research and development projects under paragraph (1) may be used for research and development under the Strategic Defense Initiative.

(e) STAFFING.—The Secretary of Defense is urged to increase the number of personnel assigned to the Office of the Deputy Under Secretary of Defense (International Programs) for the specific purpose of providing oversight of the joint research and development projects of the United States and Japan for which funds are made available under subsection (d).

SEC. 1455. PERMANENT CEILING ON UNITED STATES ARMED FORCES IN JAPAN AND CONTRIBUTIONS BY JAPAN TO THE SUPPORT OF UNITED STATES FORCES IN JAPAN

(a) PURPOSE.—It is the purpose of this section to require Japan to offset the direct costs (other than pay and allowances for United States military and civilian personnel) incurred by the United States related to the presence of United States military personnel in Japan.

(b) PERMANENT CEILING ON UNITED STATES ARMED FORCES IN JAPAN.—Funds appropriated pursuant to an authorization contained in this Act or any subsequent Act may not be used to support an end strength level of all personnel of the Armed Forces of the United States stationed in Japan at any level in excess of 50,000.

(c) SENSE OF CONGRESS ON ALLIED BURDEN SHARING.—(1) Congress recognizes that Japan has made a substantial pledge of financial support to the effort to support the United Nations Security Council resolutions on Iraq.

(2) It is the sense of Congress that—

(A) all countries that share the benefits of international security and stability should, commensurate with their national capabilities, share in the responsibility for maintaining that security and stability; and

(B) given the economic capability of Japan to contribute to international security and stability, Japan should make contributions commensurate with that capability.

(d) NEGOTIATIONS.—At the earliest possible date after the date of the enactment of this Act, the President shall enter into negotiations with Japan for the purpose of achieving an agreement before September 30, 1991, under which Japan offsets all direct costs (other than pay and allowances for United States military and civilian personnel) incurred by the United States related to the presence of all United States military personnel stationed in Japan.

(e) EXCEPTIONS.—(1) This section shall not apply in the event of a declaration of war or an armed attack on Japan.

(2) This section may be waived by the President if the President—

(A) declares an emergency or determines that such a waiver is required by the national security interests of the United States; and

(B) immediately informs the Congress of the waiver and the reasons for the waiver.

SEC. 1457. ANNUAL REPORT ON UNITED STATES SECURITY ARRANGEMENTS AND COMMITMENTS WITH OTHER NATIONS

(a) REPORT REQUIREMENTS.—The President shall submit to the Committees on Armed Services and on Foreign Affairs of the House of Representatives and the Committees on Armed Services and Foreign Relations of the Senate each year a report (in both classified and unclassified form) on United States security arrangements with, and commitments to, other nations.

(b) MATTERS TO BE INCLUDED.—The President shall include in each such report the following:

(1) A description of—

(A) each security arrangement with, or commitment to, other nations, whether based upon (i) a formal document (including a mutual defense treaty, a pre-positioning arrangement or agreement, or an access agreement), or (ii) an expressed policy; and

(B) the historical origins of each such arrangement or commitment.

(2) An evaluation of the ability of the United States to meet its commitments based on the projected reductions in the defense structure of the United States.

(3) A plan for meeting each of those commitments with the force structure projected for the future.

(4) An assessment of the need to continue, modify, or discontinue each of those arrangements and commitments in view of the changing international security situation.

(c) DEADLINE FOR REPORT.—(1) Except as provided in paragraph (2), the President shall submit the report required by subsection (a) not later than February 1 of each year.

(2) In the case of the report required to be submitted in 1991, the evaluation, plan, and assessment referred to in paragraphs (2), (3), and (4) of subsection (b) may be submitted not later than May 1, 1991.

SEC. 1158. ECONOMIC SANCTIONS AGAINST THE REPUBLIC OF IRAQ

If the President considers that the taking of such action would promote the effectiveness of the economic sanctions of the United Nations and the United States imposed with respect to Iraq, and is consistent with the national interest, the President may prohibit, for such a period of time as he considers appropriate, the importation into the United States of any or all products of any foreign country that has not—

(1) prohibited—

(A) the importation of products of Iraq into its customs territory, and

(B) the export of its products to Iraq; or

(2) given assurances satisfactory to the President that such import and export sanctions will be promptly implemented.

SEC. 1159. HUMANITARIAN ASSISTANCE FOR LITHUANIA

(a) SENSE OF CONGRESS.—It is the sense of Congress that the President should provide appropriate forms of humanitarian assistance for Lithuania. Such assistance is necessary as a result of the courageous efforts of the Lithuanian people to rebuild an independent society and state.

(b) AGENCY FOR INTERNATIONAL DEVELOPMENT.—The Administrator of the Agency for International Development should—

(1) furnish such humanitarian assistance through the International Committee of the Red Cross, the Lithuanian Red Cross, CARITAS, and other voluntary relief agencies;

(2) solicit private sector donations of humanitarian assistance for Lithuania;

(3) cooperate with private relief agencies attempting to provide humanitarian assistance to Lithuania; and

(4) make all necessary arrangements to ensure that Lithuanians begin to receive critical humanitarian assistance as soon as possible.

(c) HUMANITARIAN ASSISTANCE FOR LATVIA, ESTONIA, ETC.—Where possible, appropriate humanitarian assistance should also be extended to Latvia and Estonia as well as needy republics of the Soviet Union.

(d) DEFINITION.—As used in this section, the term "humanitarian assistance" includes—

(1) medical supplies;

(2) oil, gas, and fuel for emergency vehicles and medical facilities;

(3) water purification supplies, materials for immunization, and other materials needed to prevent the outbreak of contagious diseases and to safeguard public health;

(4) food and clothing; and

(5) transportation of private donations of humanitarian assistance.

TITLE XVII—MISSILE TECHNOLOGY CONTROLS

SEC. 1701. POLICY

It should be the policy of the United States to take all appropriate measures—

(1) to discourage the proliferation, development, and production of the weapons, material, and technology necessary to produce or acquire missiles that can deliver weapons of mass destruction;

(2) to discourage countries and private persons in other countries from aiding and abetting any states from acquiring such weapons, material, and technology;

(3) to strengthen United States and existing multilateral export controls to prohibit the flow of materials, equipment, and technology that would assist countries in acquiring the ability to produce or acquire missiles that can deliver weapons of mass destruction, including missiles, warheads and weaponization technology, targeting technology, test and evaluation technology, and range and weapons effect measurement technology; and

(4) with respect to the Missile Technology Control Regime ("MTCR") and its participating governments—

(A) to improve enforcement and seek a common and stricter interpretation among MTCR members of MTCR principles;

(B) to increase the number of countries that adhere to the MTCR; and

(C) to increase information sharing among United States agencies and among governments on missile technology transfer, including export licensing, and enforcement activities.

FOREIGN OPERATIONS, EXPORT FINANCING, AND RELATED PROGRAMS APPROPRIATIONS ACT, 1991

An Act making appropriations for foreign operations, export financing, and related programs for the fiscal year ending September 30, 1991, and for other purposes.

Date: November 5, 1990

Bill No.: H.R. 5114

Public Law No.: 101-513

Cite: 104 STAT. 1979

Sections reprinted:

Section 529 - Economic support fund assistance for Israel.
Section 531 - Assistance for El Salvador.
Section 533 (a) - (e) - Environment and global warming.
(Other subsections deal with specific appropriations and are omitted.)
Section 586 - Iraq Sanctions Act of 1990: Short title.
Section 586A - Declarations regarding Iraq's invasion on Kuwait.
Section 586B - Consultations with Congress.
Section 586C - Trade embargo against Iraq.
Section 586D - Compliance with United States sanctions against Iraq.
Section 586E - Penalties for violations of embargo.
Section 586F - Declarations regarding Iraq's long-standing violations of international law.
Section 586G - Sanctions against Iraq.
Section 586H - Waiver authority.
Section 586I - Denial of licenses for certain exports to countries assisting Iraq's rocket or chemical biological, or nuclear weapons capability.
Section 586J - Reports to Congress.
Section 592 - Support for Egyptian military deployments in the Gulf.

Section 595 - Enterprise for the Americas initiative.
Section 599E - International Criminal Court.
Section 599G - Poland: Economy
Section 599H - Precursor chemicals.
Section 599I - Vietnam travel.
Section 601 - International Forestry Cooperation Act of 1990: Short title.
Section 602 - Forestry and related natural resource assistance.
Section 603 - Tropical deforestation assessment and assistance.
Section 604 - Institute of Tropical Forestry.

Public Law 101–513
101st Congress

An Act

Making appropriations for foreign operations, export financing, and related programs for the fiscal year ending September 30, 1991, and for other purposes.

section 1302 of the International Security and Development Cooperation Act of 1985 (Public Law 99-83), no employee of or individual acting on behalf of the United States Government shall recognize or negotiate with the Palestine Liberation Organization or representatives thereof, so long as the Palestine Liberation Organization does not recognize Israel's right to exist, does not accept Security Council Resolutions 242 and 338, and does not renounce the use of terrorism.

ECONOMIC SUPPORT FUND ASSISTANCE FOR ISRAEL

SEC. 529. The Congress finds that progress on the peace process in the Middle East is vitally important to United States security interests in the region. The Congress recognizes that, in fulfilling its obligations under the Treaty of Peace Between the Arab Republic of Egypt and the State of Israel, done at Washington on March 26, 1979, Israel incurred severe economic burdens. Furthermore, the Congress recognizes that an economically and militarily secure Israel serves the security interests of the United States, for a secure Israel is an Israel which has the incentive and confidence to continue pursuing the peace process. Therefore, the Congress declares that it is the policy and the intention of the United States that the funds provided in annual appropriations for the Economic Support Fund which are allocated to Israel shall not be less than the annual debt repayment (interest and principal) from Israel to the United States Government in recognition that such a principle serves United States interests in the region.

ASSISTANCE FOR EL SALVADOR

SEC. 531. (a) STATEMENT OF POLICY.—United States military assistance to the Government of El Salvador shall seek three principal foreign policy objectives, as follows: (1) to promote a permanent settlement and cease-fire to the conflict in El Salvador, with the Secretary General of the United Nations serving as an active mediator between the opposing parties; (2) to foster greater respect for basic human rights, and the rule of law; and (3) to advance political accommodation and national reconciliation.

(b) MAXIMUM LEVEL OF MILITARY ASSISTANCE.—Of the funds available for United States military assistance for fiscal year 1991, not more than $85,000,000 shall be made available for El Salvador.

(c) PROHIBITION OF MILITARY ASSISTANCE.—(1) PROHIBITION.—Subject to paragraph (2), no United States military assistance may be furnished to the Government of El Salvador if the President determines and reports in writing to the Congress that—

(A) after he has consulted with the Secretary General of the United Nations, the Government of El Salvador has declined to participate in good faith in negotiations for a permanent settlement and cease-fire to the armed conflict of El Salvador;

(B) the Government of El Salvador has rejected or otherwise failed to support an active role for the Secretary General of the United Nations in mediating that settlement;

(C) the Government of El Salvador has rejected a plan for the settlement of the conflict which—

(i) has been put forward by the Secretary General of the United Nations in accordance with the terms and procedures in the April 4, 1990 Geneva Communique and the May 21, 1990 Caracas Accord between the Government of El Salvador and the FMLN;

(ii) includes a proposal for an internationally monitored cease-fire; and

(iii) has been accepted, within 15 days from its announcement, by the FMLN and is being complied with by the FMLN;

(D) the Government of El Salvador has failed to conduct a thorough and professional investigation into, and prosecution of those responsible for the eight murders at the University of Central America on November 16, 1989; or

(E) the military and security forces of El Salvador are assassinating or abducting civilian noncombatants, are engaging in other acts of violence directed at civilian targets, or are failing to control such activities by elements subject to the control of those forces; or

(F) the Government of El Salvador has failed to actively seek and encourage a law enforcement service from outside El Salvador, such as Scotland Yard or INTERPOL, to accompany and monitor investigators of the Government of El Salvador in their investigation into the eight murders at the University of Central America on November 16, 1989.

(2) REQUIREMENT FOR RESUMPTION OF ASSISTANCE.—Assistance prohibited under paragraph (1) may only be resumed pursuant to a law subsequently enacted by the Congress.

(d) WITHHOLDING OF MILITARY ASSISTANCE.—(1) IN GENERAL.—Fifty per centum of the total United States military assistance allocated for El Salvador for fiscal year 1991 shall be withheld from obligation or expenditure (as the case may be) except as provided in paragraphs (2) and (3).

(2) RELEASE OF ASSISTANCE.—The United States military assistance withheld pursuant to paragraph (1) may be obligated and expended only if the President determines and reports in writing to the Congress that—

(A) after he has consulted with the Secretary General of the United Nations, the representatives of the FMLN—

(i) have declined to participate in good faith in negotiations for a permanent settlement and cease-fire to the armed conflict in El Salvador, or

(ii) have rejected or otherwise failed to support an active role for the Secretary General of the United Nations in mediating that settlement;

(B) the FMLN has rejected a plan for the settlement of the conflict which—

(i) has been put forward by the Secretary General of the United Nations in accordance with the terms and procedures in the April 4, 1990 Geneva Communique and the May 21, 1990 Caracas Accord between the Government of El Salvador and the FMLN;

(ii) includes a proposal for an internationally monitored cease-fire; and

(iii) has been accepted, within 15 days from its announcement, by the Government of El Salvador and is being complied with by the Government of El Salvador;

(C) the survival of the constitutional Government of El Salvador is being jeopardized by substantial and sustained offensive military actions or operations by the FMLN;

(D) proof exists that the FMLN is continuing to acquire or receive significant shipments of lethal military assistance from outside El Salvador, and this proof has been shared with the Congress; or

(E) the FMLN is assassinating or abducting civilian non-combatants, is engaging in other acts of violence directed at civilian targets, or is failing to control such activities by elements subject to FMLN control.

(3) EXCEPTION.—Notwithstanding any other provision of law, funds withheld pursuant to paragraph (1) of this subsection may be disbursed to pay the cost of any contract penalties which may be incurred as a result of such withholding of funds under this subsection.

(e) CONDITION FOR TERMINATION OF ALL UNITED STATES ASSISTANCE.—(1) PROHIBITION.—Subject to paragraph (2), no United States assistance may be furnished to El Salvador if the duly-elected head of Government of El Salvador is deposed by military coup or decree.

(2) REQUIREMENT FOR RESUMPTION OF ASSISTANCE.—Assistance prohibited under paragraph (1) may only be resumed pursuant to a law subsequently enacted by the Congress.

(f) ESTABLISHMENT OF A FUND FOR CEASE-FIRE MONITORING, DEMOBILIZATION, AND TRANSITION TO PEACE.—(1) ESTABLISHMENT OF FUND.—There is hereby established in the Treasury of the United States a fund to assist with the costs of monitoring a permanent settlement of the conflict, including a cease-fire, and the demobilization of combatants in the conflict in El Salvador, and their transition to peaceful pursuits, which shall be known as the "Demobilization and Transition Fund" (hereafter in this section referred to as the "Fund"). Amounts in this Fund shall be available for obligation and expenditure only upon notification by the President to the Congress that the Government of El Salvador and representatives of the FMLN have reached a permanent settlement of the conflict, including a final agreement on a cease-fire.

(2) TRANSFER OF CERTAIN MILITARY ASSISTANCE FUNDS.—Upon notification of the Congress of a permanent settlement of the conflict, including an agreement on a cease-fire, or on September 30, 1991, if no such notification has occurred prior to that date, the President shall transfer to the Fund any United States military assistance funds withheld pursuant to subsection (d) of this section.

(3) USE OF THE FUND.—Notwithstanding any other provision of law, amounts in the Fund shall be available for El Salvador solely to support costs of demobilization, retraining, relocation, and re-employment in civilian pursuits of former combatants in the conflict in El Salvador, and of the monitoring of the permanent settlement and cease-fire.

(4) DURATION OF AVAILABILITY OF FUNDS.—Notwithstanding any other provision of law, amounts transferred to the Fund shall remain available until expended.

(g) STRENGTHENING CIVILIAN CONTROL OVER THE MILITARY.—In order to strengthen the control of the democratically-elected civilian Government of El Salvador over the armed forces of that country, United States military assistance for any fiscal year may be delivered to the armed forces of El Salvador only with the prior approval of the duly elected President of El Salvador.

(h) SUPPORT FOR DEMOCRACY.—(1) ESTABLISHING A PROGRAM.—The Secretary of State, through agreement with the National Endowment for Democracy or other qualified organizations, shall establish and carry out a program of education, training, and dialogue for the purpose of strengthening democratic political and legal institutions in El Salvador.

(2) ELECTION MONITORING.—Of the amounts made available to carry out this subsection, up to $2,000,000 may be used for support for monitoring the 1991 municipal and National Assembly elections in El Salvador, and for monitoring the registration and campaign

processes leading up to those elections, by appropriate organizations such as the United Nations, the Organization of American States, the Carter Center, the National Democratic Institute for International Affairs, the National Republican Institute for International Affairs, and the Center for Electoral Assistance and Promotion (CAPEL) of San Jose, Costa Rica.

(3) ASSISTANCE.—Up to $10,000,000 of funds appropriated under the heading "Economic Support Fund" for fiscal year 1991 may be used to carry out this subsection.

(i) REPORTING REQUIREMENTS.—Sixty days after the date of enactment of this Act and every 180 days thereafter, the President shall submit to the Congress a report describing—

(1) the willingness or unwillingness of the Government of El Salvador and the FMLN to negotiate seriously and in good faith for the purpose of achieving a permanent settlement to the conflict in El Salvador, including a cease-fire, and providing appropriate information regarding criteria described in subsections (c) and (d)(2); and

(2) the status of investigations into the politically motivated murders listed in section 538 of this Act.

(j) DEFINITIONS.—For purposes of this section—

(1) the term "United States assistance" has the same meaning as is given to such term by section 481(i)(4) of the Foreign Assistance Act of 1961 (22 U.S.C. 2291(i)(4)) and includes United States military assistance as defined in paragraph (2); and

(2) the term "United States military assistance" means—

(A) assistance to carry out chapter 2 (relating to grant military assistance) or chapter 5 (relating to international military education and training) of part II of the Foreign Assistance Act of 1961; and

(B) assistance to carry out section 23 of the Arms Export Control Act.

ENVIRONMENT AND GLOBAL WARMING

SEC. 533. (a) It is the policy of the United States that sustainable economic growth must be predicated on the sustainable management of natural resources. The Secretary of the Treasury shall instruct the United States Executive Director of each multilateral development bank (MDB) to promote vigorously within each MDB the expansion of programs in areas which address the problems of global climate change through requirements to—

(1) expand programs in energy conservation, end use energy efficiency, and renewable energy and promotion by—

(A) continuing to augment and expand professional staffs with expertise in these areas;

(B) giving priority to these areas in the "least cost" energy sector investment plans;

(C) encouraging and promoting these areas in policy-based energy sector lending;

(D) developing loans for these purposes; and

(E) convening seminars for MDB staff and board members on these areas and alternative energy investment opportunities;

(2) provide analysis for each proposed loan to support additional power generating capacity comparing demand reduction costs to proposal costs;

(3) continue to assure that environmental impact assessments (EIA) of proposed energy projects are conducted early in the project cycle, include consideration of alternatives to the proposed project, and encourage public participation in the EIA process;

(4) continue to include the environmental costs of proposed projects with significant environmental impacts in economic assessments; and

(5) continue to provide technical assistance as a component of energy sector lending.

(b) The Secretary of the Treasury shall, not later than March 1, 1991, submit an annual report to the Congress which shall include—

(1) a detailed description of how the natural resource management initiatives mandated by this section have been incorporated in the Administration's efforts to address Third World Debt (the Brady Plan);

(2) a detailed description of progress made by each of the MDBs in adopting and implementing programs meeting the standards set out in subsection (a) including, in particular, efforts by the Department of the Treasury to assure implementation of this section, progress made by each MDB in subsection (a)(1)(B), and the amounts and proportion of lending in the energy sector for projects or programs in subsection (a)(1);

(3) the progress the Inter-American Development Bank has made in implementing environmental reforms;

(4) an updated analysis of each MDB's forestry sector loans, and a current analysis of each MDB's energy sector loans, and their impact on emissions of CO_2 and the status of proposals for specific forestry and energy sector activities to reduce CO_2 emissions; and

(5) the progress the International Bank for Reconstruction and Development has made in implementing the recommendations set forth in the April 1, 1988, report on "Debt-for-Nature Swaps" by the World Bank.

(c)(1) The Administrator of the Agency for International Development shall update and issue guidance to all Agency missions and bureaus detailing the elements of the "Global Warming Initiative", which will continue to emphasize the need to reduce emissions of greenhouse gases, especially CO_2 and CFCs, through strategies consistent with continued economic development. This initiative shall continue to emphasize the need to accelerate sustainable development strategies in areas such as reforestation, biodiversity, end-use energy efficiency, least-cost energy planning, and renewable energy, and shall encourage mission directors to incorporate the elements of this initiative in developing their country programs.

(2) The Administrator shall pursue this initiative by, among other things—

(A) increasing the number and expertise of personnel devoted to this initiative in all bureaus and missions;

(B) devoting increased resources to technical training of mission directors;

(C) accelerating the activities of the Multi-Agency Working Group on Power Sector Innovation;

(D) focusing tropical forestry assistance programs on the key middle- and low-income developing countries (hereinafter "key countries") which are projected to contribute large amounts of greenhouse gases to the global environment;

(E) assisting countries in developing a systematic analysis of the appropriate use of their total tropical forest resources, with the goal of developing a national program for sustainable forestry;

(F) focusing energy assistance activities on the key countries, where assistance would have the greatest impact on reducing emissions from greenhouse gases; and

(G) continuing to follow the directives with respect to key countries and countries that receive large Economic Support

Fund assistance contained in section 534(b)(3) of Public Law 101-167.

(3) None of the funds appropriated in this Act shall be available for any program, project or activity which would—

(A) result in any significant loss of tropical forests; or

(B) involve industrial timber extraction in primary tropical forest areas.

(4) Funds appropriated to carry out the provisions of sections 103 and 106 of the Foreign Assistance Act of 1961, as amended, may be used by the Agency for International Development, notwithstanding any other provision of law, for the purpose of supporting tropical forestry and energy programs aimed at reducing emissions of greenhouse gases with regard to the key countries in which deforestation and energy policy would make a significant contribution to global warming, except that such assistance shall be subject to sections 116, 502B, and 620A of the Foreign Assistance Act of 1961.

(5) Funds appropriated by this Act to carry out the provisions of sections 103 and 106 of the Foreign Assistance Act of 1961 may be used for expenses (including related support costs) relating to the environment and energy sectors, of employees or individuals detailed to or employed by the Agency for International Development, particularly those involved with the "Global Warming Initiative" described in this subsection.

IRAQ SANCTIONS ACT OF 1990

SEC. 586. SHORT TITLE.

Sections 586 through 586J of this Act may be cited as the "Iraq Sanctions Act of 1990".

SEC. 586A. DECLARATIONS REGARDING IRAQ'S INVASION OF KUWAIT.

The Congress—

(1) condemns Iraq's invasion of Kuwait on August 2, 1990;

(2) supports the actions that have been taken by the President in response to that invasion;

(3) calls for the immediate and unconditional withdrawal of Iraqi forces from Kuwait;

(4) supports the efforts of the United Nations Security Council to end this violation of international law and threat to international peace;

(5) supports the imposition and enforcement of multilateral sanctions against Iraq;

(6) calls on United States allies and other countries to support fully the efforts of the United Nations Security Council, and to take other appropriate actions, to bring about an end to Iraq's occupation of Kuwait; and

(7) condemns the brutal occupation of Kuwait by Iraq and its gross violations of internationally recognized human rights in Kuwait, including widespread arrests, torture, summary executions, and mass extrajudicial killings.

SEC. 586B. CONSULTATIONS WITH CONGRESS.

The President shall keep the Congress fully informed, and shall consult with the Congress, with respect to current and anticipated events regarding the international crisis caused by Iraq's invasion of Kuwait, including with respect to United States actions.

SEC. 586C. TRADE EMBARGO AGAINST IRAQ.

(a) Continuation of Embargo.—Except as otherwise provided in this section, the President shall continue to impose the trade embargo and other economic sanctions with respect to Iraq and Kuwait that the United States is imposing, in response to Iraq's invasion of Kuwait, pursuant to Executive Orders Numbered 12724 and 12725 (August 9, 1990) and, to the extent they are still in effect, Executive Orders Numbered 12722 and 12723 (August 2, 1990). Notwithstanding any other provision of law, no funds, credits, guarantees, or insurance appropriated or otherwise made available by this or any other Act for fiscal year 1991 or any fiscal year thereafter shall be used to support or administer any financial or commercial operation of any United States Government department, agency, or other entity, or of any person subject to the jurisdiction of the United States, for the benefit of the Government of Iraq, its agencies or instrumentalities, or any person working on behalf of the Government of Iraq, contrary to the trade embargo and other economic sanctions imposed in accordance with this section.

(b) HUMANITARIAN ASSISTANCE.—To the extent that transactions involving foodstuffs or payments for foodstuffs are exempted "in humanitarian circumstances" from the prohibitions established by the United States pursuant to United Nations Security Council Resolution 661 (1990), those exemptions shall be limited to foodstuffs that are to be provided consistent with United Nations Security Council Resolution 666 (1990) and other relevant Security Council resolutions.

(c) NOTICE TO CONGRESS OF EXCEPTIONS TO AND TERMINATION OF SANCTIONS.—

(1) NOTICE OF REGULATIONS.—Any regulations issued after the date of enactment of this Act with respect to the economic sanctions imposed with respect to Iraq and Kuwait by the United States under Executive Orders Numbered 12722 and 12723 (August 2, 1990) and Executive Orders Numbered 12724 and 12725 (August 9, 1990) shall be submitted to the Congress before those regulations take effect.

(2) NOTICE OF TERMINATION OF SANCTIONS.—The President shall notify the Congress at least 15 days before the termination, in whole or in part, of any sanction imposed with respect to Iraq or Kuwait pursuant to those Executive orders.

(d) RELATION TO OTHER LAWS.—

(1) SANCTIONS LEGISLATION.—The sanctions that are described in subsection (a) are in addition to, and not in lieu of the sanctions provided for in section 586G of this Act or any other provision of law.

(2) NATIONAL EMERGENCIES AND UNITED NATIONS LEGISLATION.—Nothing in this section supersedes any provision of the National Emergencies Act or any authority of the President under the International Emergency Economic Powers Act or section 5(a) of the United Nations Participation Act of 1945.

SEC. 586D. COMPLIANCE WITH UNITED NATIONS SANCTIONS AGAINST IRAQ.

(a) DENIAL OF ASSISTANCE.—None of the funds appropriated or otherwise made available pursuant to this Act to carry out the Foreign Assistance Act of 1961 (including title IV of chapter 2 of part I, relating to the Overseas Private Investment Corporation) or the Arms Export Control Act may be used to provide assistance to any country that is not in compliance with the United Nations Security Council sanctions against Iraq unless the President determines and so certifies to the Congress that—

(1) such assistance is in the national interest of the United States;

(2) such assistance will directly benefit the needy people in that country; or

(3) the assistance to be provided will be humanitarian assistance for foreign nationals who have fled Iraq and Kuwait.

(b) IMPORT SANCTIONS.—If the President considers that the taking of such action would promote the effectiveness of the economic sanctions of the United Nations and the United States imposed with respect to Iraq, and is consistent with the national interest, the President may prohibit, for such a period of time as he considers appropriate, the importation into the United States of any or all products of any foreign country that has not prohibited—

(1) the importation of products of Iraq into its customs territory, and

(2) the export of its products to Iraq.

SEC. 586E. PENALTIES FOR VIOLATIONS OF EMBARGO.

Notwithstanding section 206 of the International Emergency Economic Powers Act (50 U.S.C. 1705) and section 5(b) of the United Nations Participation Act of 1945 (22 U.S.C. 287c(b))—

(1) a civil penalty of not to exceed $250,000 may be imposed on any person who, after the date of enactment of this Act, violates or evades or attempts to violate or evade Executive Order Numbered 12722, 12723, 12724, or 12725 or any license, order, or regulation issued under any such Executive order; and

(2) whoever, after the date of enactment of this Act, willfully violates or evades or attempts to violate or evade Executive Order Numbered 12722, 12723, 12724, or 12725 or any license, order, or regulation issued under any such Executive order—

(A) shall, upon conviction, be fined not more than $1,000,000, if a person other than a natural person; or

(B) if a natural person, shall, upon conviction, be fined not more than $1,000,000, be imprisoned for not more than 12 years, or both.

Any officer, director, or agent of any corporation who knowingly participates in a violation, evasion, or attempt described in paragraph (2) may be punished by imposition of the fine or imprisonment (or both) specified in subparagraph (B) of that paragraph.

SEC. 586F. DECLARATIONS REGARDING IRAQ'S LONG-STANDING VIOLATIONS OF INTERNATIONAL LAW.

(a) IRAQ'S VIOLATIONS OF INTERNATIONAL LAW.—The Congress determines that—

(1) the Government of Iraq has demonstrated repeated and blatant disregard for its obligations under international law by violating the Charter of the United Nations, the Protocol for the Prohibition of the Use in War of Asphyxiating, Poisonous or Other Gases, and of Bacteriological Methods of Warfare (done at Geneva, June 17, 1925), as well as other international treaties;

(2) the Government of Iraq is a party to the International Covenant on Civil and Political Rights and the International Covenant on Economic, Social, and Cultural Rights and is obligated under the Covenants, as well as the Universal Declaration of Human Rights, to respect internationally recognized human rights;

(3) the State Department's Country Reports on Human Rights Practices for 1989 again characterizes Iraq's human rights record as "abysmal";

(4) Amnesty International, Middle East Watch, and other independent human rights organizations have documented extensive, systematic, and continuing human rights abuses by the Government of Iraq, including summary executions, mass

political killings, disappearances, widespread use of torture, arbitrary arrests and prolonged detention without trial of thousands of political opponents, forced relocation and deportation, denial of nearly all civil and political rights such as freedom of association, assembly, speech, and the press, and the imprisonment, torture, and execution of children;

(5) since 1987, the Government of Iraq has intensified its severe repression of the Kurdish minority of Iraq, deliberately destroyed more than 3,000 villages and towns in the Kurdish regions, and forcibly expelled more than 500,000 people, thus effectively depopulating the rural areas of Iraqi Kurdistan;

(6) Iraq has blatantly violated international law by initiating use of chemical weapons in the Iran-Iraq war;

(7) Iraq has also violated international law by using chemical weapons against its own Kurdish citizens, resulting in tens of thousands of deaths and more than 65,000 refugees;

(8) Iraq continues to expand its chemical weapons capability, and President Saddam Hussein has threatened to use chemical weapons against other nations;

(9) persuasive evidence exists that Iraq is developing biological weapons in violation of international law;

(10) there are strong indications that Iraq has taken steps to produce nuclear weapons and has attempted to smuggle from the United States, in violation of United States law, components for triggering devices used in nuclear warheads whose manufacture would contravene the Treaty on the Non-Proliferation of Nuclear Weapons, to which Iraq is a party; and

(11) Iraqi President Saddam Hussein has threatened to use terrorism against other nations in violation of international law and has increased Iraq's support for the Palestine Liberation Organization and other Palestinian groups that have conducted terrorist acts.

(b) HUMAN RIGHTS VIOLATIONS.—The Congress determines that the Government of Iraq is engaged in a consistent pattern of gross violations of internationally recognized human rights. All provisions of law that impose sanctions against a country whose government is engaged in a consistent pattern of gross violations of internationally recognized human rights shall be fully enforced against Iraq.

(c) SUPPORT FOR INTERNATIONAL TERRORISM.—(1) The Congress determines that Iraq is a country which has repeatedly provided support for acts of international terrorism, a country which grants sanctuary from prosecution to individuals or groups which have committed an act of international terrorism, and a country which otherwise supports international terrorism. The provisions of law specified in paragraph (2) and all other provisions of law that impose sanctions against a country which has repeatedly provided support for acts of international terrorism, which grants sanctuary from prosecution to an individual or group which has committed an act of international terrorism, or which otherwise supports international terrorism shall be fully enforced against Iraq.

(2) The provisions of law referred to in paragraph (1) are—

(A) section 40 of the Arms Export Control Act;

(B) section 620A of the Foreign Assistance Act of 1961;

(C) sections 555 and 556 of this Act (and the corresponding sections of predecessor foreign operations appropriations Acts); and

(D) section 555 of the International Security and Development Cooperation Act of 1985.

(d) MULTILATERAL COOPERATION.—The Congress calls on the President to seek multilateral cooperation—

(1) to deny dangerous technologies to Iraq;

(2) to induce Iraq to respect internationally recognized human rights; and

(3) to induce Iraq to allow appropriate international humanitarian and human rights organizations to have access to Iraq and Kuwait, including the areas in northern Iraq traditionally inhabited by Kurds.

SEC. 586G. SANCTIONS AGAINST IRAQ.

(a) IMPOSITION.—Except as provided in section 586H, the following sanctions shall apply with respect to Iraq:

(1) FMS SALES.—The United States Government shall not enter into any sale with Iraq under the Arms Export Control Act.

(2) COMMERCIAL ARMS SALES.—Licenses shall not be issued for the export to Iraq of any item on the United States Munitions List.

(3) EXPORTS OF CERTAIN GOODS AND TECHNOLOGY.—The authorities of section 6 of the Export Administration Act of 1979 (50 U.S.C. App. 2405) shall be used to prohibit the export to Iraq of any goods or technology listed pursuant to that section or section 5(c)(1) of that Act (50 U.S.C. App. 2404(c)(1)) on the control list provided for in section 4(b) of that Act (50 U.S.C. App. 2403(b)).

(4) NUCLEAR EQUIPMENT, MATERIALS, AND TECHNOLOGY.—

(A) NRC LICENSES.—The Nuclear Regulatory Commission shall not issue any license or other authorization under the Atomic Energy Act of 1954 (42 U.S.C. 2011 and following) for the export to Iraq of any source or special nuclear material, any production or utilization facility, any sensitive nuclear technology, any component, item, or substance determined to have significance for nuclear explosive purposes pursuant to section 109b. of the Atomic Energy Act of 1954 (42 U.S.C. 2139(b)), or any other material or technology requiring such a license or authorization.

(B) DISTRIBUTION OF NUCLEAR MATERIALS.—The authority of the Atomic Energy Act of 1954 shall not be used to distribute any special nuclear material, source material, or byproduct material to Iraq.

(C) DOE AUTHORIZATIONS.—The Secretary of Energy shall not provide a specific authorization under section 57b. (2) of the Atomic Energy Act of 1954 (42 U.S.C. 2077(b)(2)) for any activity that would constitute directly or indirectly engaging in Iraq in activities that require a specific authorization under that section.

(5) ASSISTANCE FROM INTERNATIONAL FINANCIAL INSTITUTIONS.—The United States shall oppose any loan or financial or technical assistance to Iraq by international financial institutions in accordance with section 701 of the International Financial Institutions Act (22 U.S.C. 262d).

(6) ASSISTANCE THROUGH THE EXPORT-IMPORT BANK.—Credits and credit guarantees through the Export-Import Bank of the United States shall be denied to Iraq.

(7) ASSISTANCE THROUGH THE COMMODITY CREDIT CORPORATION.—Credit, credit guarantees, and other assistance through the Commodity Credit Corporation shall be denied to Iraq.

(8) FOREIGN ASSISTANCE.—All forms of assistance under the Foreign Assistance Act of 1961 (22 U.S.C. 2151 and following) other than emergency assistance for medical supplies and other forms of emergency humanitarian assistance, and under the

(2) the Government of Iraq is in substantial compliance with its obligations under international law, including—

(A) the Charter of the United Nations;

(B) the International Covenant on Civil and Political Rights (done at New York, December 16, 1966) and the International Covenant on Economic, Social, and Cultural Rights (done at New York, December 16, 1966);

(C) the Convention on the Prevention and Punishment of the Crime of Genocide (done at Paris, December 9, 1948);

(D) the Protocol for the Prohibition of the Use in War of Asphyxiating, Poisonous or Other Gases, and of Bacteriological Methods of Warfare (done at Geneva, June 17, 1925);

(E) the Treaty on the Non-Proliferation of Nuclear Weapons (done at Washington, London, and Moscow, July 1, 1968); and

(F) the Convention on the Prohibition of the Development, Production and Stockpiling of Bacteriological (Biological) and Toxin Weapons and on Their Destruction (done at Washington, London, and Moscow, April 10, 1972); and

(3) the President has determined that it is essential to the national interests of the United States to exercise the authority of subsection (a).

(c) CERTIFICATION OF FUNDAMENTAL CHANGES IN IRAQI LEADERSHIP AND POLICIES.—The authority of subsection (a) may be exercised 30 days after the President certifies to the Congress that—

(1) there has been a fundamental change in the leadership of the Government of Iraq; and

(2) the new Government of Iraq has provided reliable and credible assurance that—

(A) it respects internationally recognized human rights and it will demonstrate such respect through its conduct;

(B) it is not acquiring, developing, or manufacturing and it will not acquire, develop, or manufacture (i) ballistic missiles, (ii) chemical, biological, or nuclear weapons, or (iii) components for such weapons; has forsworn the first use of such weapons; and is taking substantial and verifiable steps to destroy or otherwise dispose of any such missiles and weapons it possesses;

(C) it is not and will not provide support for international terrorism; and

(D) it is and will continue to be in substantial compliance with its obligations under international law, including all the treaties specified in subparagraphs (A) through (F) of subsection (b)(2).

(d) INFORMATION TO BE INCLUDED IN CERTIFICATIONS.—Any certification under subsection (b) or (c) shall include the justification for each determination required by that subsection. The certification shall also specify which paragraphs of section 586G(a) the President will waive pursuant to that certification.

SEC. 586I. DENIAL OF LICENSES FOR CERTAIN EXPORTS TO COUNTRIES ASSISTING IRAQ'S ROCKET OR CHEMICAL, BIOLOGICAL, OR NUCLEAR WEAPONS CAPABILITY.

(a) RESTRICTION ON EXPORT LICENSES.—None of the funds appropriated by this or any other Act may be used to approve the licensing for export of any supercomputer to any country whose government the President determines is assisting, or whose govern-

Arms Export Control Act (22 U.S.C. 2751 and following) shall be denied to Iraq.

(b) CONTRACT SANCTITY.—For purposes of the export controls imposed pursuant to subsection (a)(3), the date described in subsection (m)(1) of section 6 of the Export Administration Act of 1979 (50 U.S.C. App. 2405) shall be deemed to be August 1, 1990.

SEC. 586H. WAIVER AUTHORITY.

(a) IN GENERAL.—The President may waive the requirements of any paragraph of section 586G(a) if the President makes a certification under subsection (b) or subsection (c).

(b) CERTIFICATION OF FUNDAMENTAL CHANGES IN IRAQI POLICIES AND ACTIONS.—The authority of subsection (a) may be exercised 60 days after the President certifies to the Congress that—

(1) the Government of Iraq—

(A) has demonstrated, through a pattern of conduct, substantial improvement in its respect for internationally recognized human rights;

(B) is not acquiring, developing, or manufacturing (i) ballistic missiles, (ii) chemical, biological, or nuclear weapons, or (iii) components for such weapons; has forsworn the first use of such weapons; and is taking substantial and verifiable steps to destroy or otherwise dispose of any such missiles and weapons it possesses; and

(C) does not provide support for international terrorism;

ment officials the President determines are assisting, Iraq to improve its rocket technology or chemical, biological, or nuclear weapons capability.

(b) NEGOTIATIONS.—The President is directed to begin immediate negotiations with those governments with which the United States has bilateral supercomputer agreements, including the Government of the United Kingdom and the Government of Japan, on conditions restricting the transfer to Iraq of supercomputer or associated technology.

SEC. 586J. REPORTS TO CONGRESS.

(a) STUDY AND REPORT ON THE INTERNATIONAL EXPORT TO IRAQ OF NUCLEAR, BIOLOGICAL, CHEMICAL, AND BALLISTIC MISSILE TECHNOLOGY.—(1) The President shall conduct a study on the sale, export, and third party transfer or development of nuclear, biological, chemical, and ballistic missile technology to or with Iraq including—

(A) an identification of specific countries, as well as companies and individuals, both foreign and domestic, engaged in such sale or export of, nuclear, biological, chemical, and ballistic missile technology;

(B) a detailed description and analysis of the international supply, information, support, and coproduction network, individual, corporate, and state, responsible for Iraq's current capability in the area of nuclear, biological, chemical, and ballistic missile technology; and

(C) a recommendation of standards and procedures against which to measure and verify a decision of the Government of Iraq to terminate the development, production, coproduction, and deployment of nuclear, biological, chemical, and offensive ballistic missile technology as well as the destruction of all existing facilities associated with such technologies.

(2) The President shall include in the study required by paragraph (1) specific recommendations on new mechanisms, to include, but not be limited to, legal, political, economic and regulatory, whereby the United States might contribute, in conjunction with its friends, allies, and the international community, to the management, control, or elimination of the threat of nuclear, biological, chemical, and ballistic missile proliferation.

(3) Not later than March 30, 1991, the President shall submit to the Committee on Appropriations and the Committee on Foreign Relations of the Senate and the Committee on Appropriations and the Committee on Foreign Affairs of the House of Representatives, a report, in both classified and unclassified form, setting forth the findings of the study required by paragraph (1) of this subsection.

(b) STUDY AND REPORT ON IRAQ'S OFFENSIVE MILITARY CAPABILITY.—(1) The President shall conduct a study on Iraq's offensive military capability and its effect on the Middle East balance of power including an assessment of Iraq's power projection capability, the prospects for another sustained conflict with Iran, joint Iraqi-Jordanian military cooperation, the threat Iraq's arms transfer activities pose to United States allies in the Middle East, and the extension of Iraq's political-military influence into Africa and Latin America.

(2) Not later than March 30, 1991, the President shall submit to the Committee on Appropriations and the Committee on Foreign Relations of the Senate and the Committee on Appropriations and the Committee on Foreign Affairs of the House of Representatives, a report, in both classified and unclassified form, setting forth the findings of the study required by paragraph (1).

(c) REPORT ON SANCTIONS TAKEN BY OTHER NATIONS AGAINST IRAQ.—(1) The President shall prepare a report on the steps taken by other nations, both before and after the August 2, 1990, invasion of Kuwait, to curtail the export of goods, services, and technologies to Iraq which might contribute to, or enhance, Iraq's nuclear, biological, chemical, and ballistic missile capability.

(2) The President shall provide a complete accounting of international compliance with each of the sanctions resolutions adopted by the United Nations Security Council against Iraq since August 2, 1990, and shall list, by name, each country which to his knowledge, has provided any assistance to Iraq and the amount and type of that assistance in violation of each United Nations resolution.

(3) The President shall make every effort to encourage other nations, in whatever forum or context, to adopt sanctions toward Iraq similar to those contained in this section.

(4) Not later than every 6 months after the date of enactment of this Act, the President shall submit to the Committee on Appropriations and the Committee on Foreign Relations of the Senate and the Committee on Appropriations and the Committee on Foreign Affairs of the House of Representatives, a report in both classified and unclassified form, setting forth the findings of the study required by paragraph (1) of this subsection.

SUPPORT FOR EGYPTIAN MILITARY DEPLOYMENTS IN THE GULF

SEC. 592. MULTILATERAL DEBT NEGOTIATIONS.—The Congress finds that Egypt has official debt obligations that far exceed the amounts owed to the United States. The Congress further finds that Egypt's debt situation can be addressed effectively only in a multilateral context involving its major creditor governments and addressing both military and economic debt.

Therefore, before the authority contained in subsection (b) is exercised, the President shall seek to convene a multilateral conference of the major official creditors of the Government of Egypt for the purpose of adjusting Egypt's official debt in a manner which reflects the real collectability of that debt.

The President in such negotiations shall explicitly and strongly encourage other governments holding major amounts of Egyptian military debt to give that debt the same treatment that it is being accorded by the United States.

(a) DEBT MORATORIUM.—(1) There shall be a moratorium on the payment obligation by Egypt beginning on October 1, 1990, and ending on March 31, 1991, with respect to the notes described in paragraph (2).

(2) The notes with respect to which this moratorium shall apply are all notes made by Egypt evidencing amounts owed by Egypt to the United States (or any agency of the United States) as a result of loans made before October 1, 1990, by the United States (or any of its agencies) to Egypt under the Arms Export Control Act (all such loans being hereinafter collectively referred to as the "AECA Loans").

(3) Section 518 of this Act, section 620(q) of the Foreign Assistance Act of 1961, and any other provision that similarly restricts the furnishing of assistance to countries in default on payment to the United States of principal or interest shall not apply during the moratorium described in paragraph (1) with respect to amounts owed by Egypt under the AECA Loans.

(4) Nothing in this subsection shall interfere with, or otherwise diminish, the obligation of the Secretary of Defense as guarantor with respect to the AECA Loans.

(b) DEBT CONSOLIDATION IN THE DEPARTMENT OF DEFENSE.—As soon as feasible after the enactment of this Act, the Secretary of Defense shall—

(1) issue to the Secretary of the Treasury sufficient notes or other obligations to purchase all notes made by Egypt evidencing amounts owed by Egypt to the United States (or any agency of the United States), other than amounts already owed to the Secretary of Defense, as a result of AECA Loans; and

(2) purchase all such notes made by Egypt, such purchase being considered to discharge the responsibilities of the Secretary of Defense as guarantor of such notes.

(c) PRESIDENTIAL REPORT ON THE REAL VALUE OF EGYPTIAN DEBT OWED TO THE UNITED STATES AND PRESIDENTIAL MILITARY DEBT REDUCTION AUTHORITY.—After the Department of Defense has taken the actions described in subsection (b)—

(1) the President shall submit a report to Congress in which he determines the value of the AECA Loans and all other loans owed by Egypt to the United States based on realistic payment expectations as of October 1, 1990, and an explanation of the factors considered by the President in determining the value; and

(2) after the President has submitted the report to Congress provided for in paragraph (1), the President may—

(A) reduce the amount owed by Egypt to the Secretary of Defense to an amount that equals the value of the AECA Loans as determined by the President in the report described in paragraph (1);

(B) direct the Secretary of Defense to amend, modify or otherwise alter the notes described in subsection (a)(2) so that the amended, modified or altered notes (the "amended notes") evidence a principal amount owed by Egypt to the Secretary of Defense equal to the value of the AECA Loans as determined under paragraph (1), and contain such terms and conditions as the President may determine consistent with the purposes of this section, provided that such terms and conditions shall not—

(i) reflect any interest accrued in respect of the period between October 1, 1990, and March 31, 1991; and

(ii) require Egypt to make any payment before March 31, 1991; and

(C) reduce the amount owed by the Secretary of Defense under all notes or other obligations issued by the Secretary of Defense to the Secretary of the Treasury that are related to any guarantees of any AECA Loans (including all notes or other obligations issued under subsection (b)) by multiplying it by a fraction, the numerator of which shall equal the value of the AECA Loans as determined under paragraph (1), and the denominator of which shall equal the sum of (i) the amount owed by the Secretary of Defense under notes issued to the Secretary of the Treasury pursuant to subsection (b)(1), plus (ii) the amount owed by Egypt as a result of the AECA Loans to the Secretary of Defense as of October 1, 1990, plus (iii) the amount that Egypt would have owed as a result of the AECA Loans to the Secretary of Defense in respect of the period beginning October 1, 1990, and ending immediately before the President makes the reduction described in subsection (c)(2)(A).

The military debt reduction authority provided by this subsection shall be limited such that no reduction shall result in a decrease in the principal value of the AECA Loans below the discounted net present value which would result from a restructuring of the AECA Loans according to the terms and conditions which apply to the loans of the International Development Association (principal shall be repayable over 40 years and shall bear no interest, and there shall be a 10 year grace period after which period 2 per centum of the loan shall be repaid annually for a period of 10 years, and 4 per centum of the loan shall be repaid annually during the remaining years).

(d) Debt cancellation authority.—(1) The President, notwithstanding any other provision of law, in the context of the multilateral debt negotiations provided for in this section may reduce to zero the amended notes (in the manner specified in subsection (e)(2) (A) and (B)) only if other major holders of Egyptian military debt agree to equal or comparable reductions. If such other creditors do not agree to comparable reductions in their Egyptian military debt the President shall so report to Congress.

(2) If the President reports to Congress under paragraph (1) then he may further determine that it is essential to the national security interests of the United States to unilaterally cancel the requirement of Egypt to repay the United States for such Egyptian military debt.

(e) Considerations.—(1) In making this determination under subsection (d)(2), the President may consider—

(A) the unique nature of Egypt's contribution to Desert Shield, and its leadership role in supporting international efforts in the face of Iraqi aggression in the Arabian Peninsula;

(B) the impact on the Egyptian economy of the events surrounding the Iraqi aggression;

(C) the long-term prospects for economic growth and stability in Egypt, and the effect on those prospects of such a determination;

(D) the role that Egypt's assumption of FMS debt played in furtherance of the common security interests of Egypt

ENTERPRISE FOR THE AMERICAS INITIATIVE

SEC. 595. (a) It is the sense of the Congress that the President's Enterprise for the Americas Initiative could encourage and support market-oriented reform and economic growth in Latin America and the Caribbean through interrelated actions to promote investment reforms, debt reduction and environmental protection.

(b) It is further the sense of the Congress that the President's proposal for the Enterprise for the Americas Initiative should be given prompt consideration.

and the United States, and the role if any that such debt was expected to have relative to other forms of official debt in generating income and promoting growth in the Egyptian economy;

(E) the willingness of other countries to participate in efforts to address the issue of official Egyptian military debt on a multilateral basis; and

(F) any other national security interests of the United States.

(2) If the President determines in the report provided for in subsection (d) that doing so is essential to the success of Desert Shield, or to enhance peace and stability in the Middle East, then he is hereby authorized to reduce to zero—

(A) the amount owed by Egypt to the Secretary of Defense under the amended notes; and

(B) the amount owed by the Secretary of Defense under all notes or other obligations issued by the Secretary of Defense to the Secretary of the Treasury that are related to any guarantees of any AECA Loans, including all notes or other obligations issued under subsection (b)(1).

(f) The President may carry out the purposes of this section notwithstanding any other provision of law.

INTERNATIONAL CRIMINAL COURT

SEC. 599E. (a) The Congress finds that—

(1) the international community has defined as criminal conduct in various international conventions, certain acts such as war crimes, crimes against humanity, torture, piracy and crimes on board commercial vessels, aircraft hijacking and sabotage of aircraft, crimes against diplomats and other internationally protected persons, hostage-taking, and illicit drug cultivation and trafficking;

(2) in spite of these international conventions, the effective prosecution of those who commit criminal acts has been seriously obstructed in certain cases because of problems of extradition and differences between the legal and judicial systems of individual nations;

(3) the jurisdiction of the International Court of Justice extends only to cases involving governments, and not to individual criminal cases;

(4) the concept of an international criminal court has been under consideration in the United Nations and other international fora for many years, including proposals and reviews undertaken in 1990 by the United Nations General Assembly, the International Law Commission, and the Eighth United Nations Congress on the Prevention of Crime and the Treatment of Offenders;

(5) the international military tribunals established in Nuremburg, Germany, and Tokyo, Japan, following World War

II also establish a precedent for international criminal tribunals; and

(6) there is growing movement among nations of the world to formulate their economic, political and legal systems on a multilateral basis.

(b) It is the sense of Congress that—

(1) the United States should explore the need for the establishment of an International Criminal Court on a universal or regional basis to assist the international community in dealing more effectively with criminal acts defined in international conventions; and

(2) the establishment of such a court or courts for the more effective prosecution of international criminals should not derogate from established standards of due process, the rights of the accused to a fair trial and the sovereignty of individual nations.

(c) The President shall report to the Congress by October 1, 1991, the results of his efforts in regard to the establishment of an International Criminal Court to deal with criminal acts defined in international conventions.

(d) The Judicial Conference of the United States shall report to the Congress by October 1, 1991, on the feasibility of, and the relationship to, the Federal judiciary of an International Criminal Court.

POLAND

SEC. 599G. (a)(1) The freely-elected Government of Poland has reshaped the country's economic policies with great courage and consistency in a manner that will foster the establishment of a functioning market economy in the near future;

(2) the Government of Poland and people alike have proven their willingness to endure economic hardships, such as a marked drop in the standard of living, in employment levels, and in the nation's industrial output, in order to create the necessary conditions for a comprehensive economic reform;

(3) the economic program is based on the recognition of the Polish authorities that a stable and easily convertible currency is paramount to the economic transformation of Poland;

(4) inflation in Poland has actually declined and the budget deficit been reduced as a consequence of the determination of Poland's policy makers;

(5) private ownership of the means of production has been achieved on a broad basis;

(6) the continued success of economic reform hinges upon tangible improvements in the economic conditions for each and every citizen;

(7) private sector companies from the United States and elsewhere have responded very favorably to the Government of Poland's determination to bring about meaningful reform;

(8) the greatest challenge for the new government is to service the staggering debt run up by the previous communist regime; and

(9) the servicing of this debt out of current revenues endangers a successful completion of the reform process because it consumes a large part of the resources needed for economic expansion: Now, therefore, be it

(b) The sense of the Congress that—

(1) Poland's debt service should be reduced in the appropriate manner to safeguard the promising reform concept;

(2) any solution of this problem should entail a broad range of approaches, such as outright debt reduction, debt service reduction, and lengthening of maturities, as well as an infusion of new capital;

(3) the Western governments, which are Poland's major creditors, should take speedy action in this area and private banks should also be prepared to contribute their share to this effort of reducing Poland's debt in order to allow the newly democratized country to bring its market reform program to a successful conclusion; and

(4) the President should undertake the appropriate measures on the part of the United States to bring the deliberations in the Paris Club to a favorable decision on the issue of reducing Poland's debt.

PRECURSOR CHEMICALS

SEC. 599H. (a) NEGOTIATIONS.—(1) The Attorney General shall enter into negotiations with the appropriate law enforcement and judicial agencies and any other officials of any foreign country with jurisdiction over companies who manufacture, market, sell or purchase certain precursor and/or essential chemicals used in the production of illicit narcotics. The priority of negotiations should be determined based on an assessment by the Attorney General which countries have jurisdiction over companies that may be knowingly or unknowingly supplying chemicals for the illicit manufacture of controlled substances.

(2) The purposes of the negotiations shall be to (a) establish a list of precursor and essential chemicals contributing to the illicit manufacture of controlled substances, as defined in section 102 of the Controlled Substances Act (21 USC 802); (b) reach one or more international agreements on a method for maintaining records of transactions of these listed chemicals; (c) establish a procedure by which such records may be made available to (and kept confidential as necessary by) United States law enforcement authorities for the exclusive purpose of conducting an investigation relative to precursor chemicals, essential chemicals and/or controlled substances contributing to the manufacture of illicit narcotics; and (d) encourage chemical source countries to enact national chemical control legislation which would (i) impose specific record keeping and reporting requirements for domestic transactions involving listed chemicals; (ii) establish a system of permits or declarations for imports and exports of listed chemicals; and (iii) authorize government officials to seize or suspend shipments of listed chemicals based on evidence that they may be destined for the illicit manufacture of controlled substances.

(b) REPORTS.—Not later than one year after the date of enactment of this Act, the Attorney General shall submit an interim report to the Judiciary Committee and the Foreign Relations Committee of the Senate on progress in the negotiations. Not later than eighteen months from the date of enactment, the Attorney General shall submit a final report to the aforementioned Senate Committees on the result of negotiations identifying countries with which agreements have not been reached and which have jurisdiction over companies believed to be engaged in the manufacture, marketing, sale or purchase of precursor and/or essential chemicals used in illicit manufacture of controlled substances.

(c) PENALTIES.—After consulting with the Attorney General and the Director of the Office of National Drug Control Policy, the President shall impose penalties or sanctions including temporarily or permanently prohibiting any corporation, partnership, individual or business association (i) refusing to maintain records for the purpose of monitoring and regulating transactions of listed precursor chemicals, or (ii) refusing to make such records available to United States law enforcement authorities for investigative purposes (in coordination with the local law enforcement agency in which such corporation, partnership, individual, or business association resides, is created or has its principal place of business) from engaging in any or all transactions, in goods or services, within the commerce of the United States.

(d) DEFINITIONS.—A record under subsection (a) shall be retrievable and include the date of the transaction, the identity of each party to the transaction, including the ultimate consignee, and accounting of the quantity and form of listed chemical(s) and a description of the method of transfer.

(e) This section shall not apply to the manufacture, distribution, sale, import or export of any drug which may, under the Federal Food, Drug and Cosmetic Act be lawfully sold over-the-counter without prescription.

VIETNAM TRAVEL

SEC. 599I. (a) The Senate hereby finds—

(1) the Government of the United States has maintained economic sanctions against the government of the Socialist Republic of Vietnam since April 30, 1975 under the auspices of the Trading with the Enemy Act, and as regulated by the Office of Foreign Assets Control of the United States Department of Treasury,

(2) individual citizens of the United States are authorized to travel in Vietnam but are limited in monetary expenditures to $100 per day, to be used only for personal travel related expenses, and are prohibited from conducting business dealings with Vietnam or citizens of Vietnam,

(3) the international community, exclusive of the United States, has significantly increased its commercial contacts within Vietnam, and that foreign investment in Vietnam doubled from January 1989 to January 1990,

(4) the government of the Socialist Republic of Vietnam has been cooperative in working with the United States and other nations toward a settlement of the Cambodian political situation,

(5) by the end of 1989, the government of Vietnam had completed a withdrawal of its combat troops from the territory of Cambodia, and

(6) pending a final Cambodian settlement, the remaining questions regarding United States POWs and MIAs are the most important factor in determining the future course of United States-Vietnamese relations.

(b) It is the sense of the Senate, that in recognition of the fact that the government of Vietnam has been cooperative in working toward a resolution of longstanding issues of conflict with the United

States, that the $100.00 per day limit on personal expenses of United States citizens travelling in Vietnam should be raised to an appropriate level.

TITLE VI—INTERNATIONAL FORESTRY COOPERATION

SEC. 601. SHORT TITLE.

This title may be cited as the "International Forestry Cooperation Act of 1990".

SEC. 602. FORESTRY AND RELATED NATURAL RESOURCE ASSISTANCE.

(a) FOCUS OF ACTIVITIES.—To achieve the maximum impact from activities undertaken under the authority of this title, the Secretary shall focus such activities on the key countries which could have a substantial impact on emissions of greenhouse gases related to global warming.

(b) AUTHORITY FOR INTERNATIONAL FORESTRY ACTIVITIES.—In support of forestry and related natural resource activities outside of the United States and its territories and possessions, the Secretary of Agriculture (hereinafter referred to in this title as the Secretary) may—

(1) provide assistance that promotes sustainable development and global environmental stability, including assistance for—

(A) conservation and sustainable management of forest land;

(B) forest plantation technology and tree improvement;

(C) rehabilitation of cutover lands, eroded watersheds, and areas damaged by wildfires or other natural disasters;

(D) prevention and control of insects, diseases, and other damaging agents;

(E) preparedness planning, training, and operational assistance to combat natural disasters;

(F) more complete utilization of forest products leading to resource conservation;

(G) range protection and enhancement; and

(H) wildlife and fisheries habitat protection and improvement;

(2) share technical, managerial, extension, and administrative skills related to public and private natural resource administration;

(3) provide education and training opportunities to promote the transfer and utilization of scientific information and technologies;

(4) engage in scientific exchange and cooperative research with foreign governmental, educational, technical and research institutions; and

(5) cooperate with domestic and international organizations that further international programs for the management and protection of forests, rangelands, wildlife and fisheries, and related natural resource activities.

(c) ELIGIBLE COUNTRIES.—The Secretary shall undertake the activities described in subsection (b), in countries that receive assistance from the Agency for International Development only at the request, or with the concurrence, of the Administrator of the Agency for International Development.

SEC. 603. TROPICAL DEFORESTATION ASSESSMENT AND ASSISTANCE.

In support of the Tropical Forestry Action Plan and to specifically address tropical deforestation and degradation, the Secretary may—

(1) support and actively participate in global and regional meetings that seek to reform such Plan;

(2) together with the United States Agency for International Development, and other Federal agencies, provide technical assistance to tropical countries for the formulation of national forestry sector development strategies; and

(3) cooperate with tropical countries on research, training, and technical programs aimed at implementing national forestry sector development strategies.

SEC. 604. INSTITUTE OF TROPICAL FORESTRY.

(a) EXPANSION.—The Secretary shall expand the capabilities of and construct additional facilities at the Caribbean National Forest and Institute of Tropical Forestry in Puerto Rico, as the Secretary determines necessary to support the purpose of this title, and as funds are appropriated for such expansion and construction.

(b) TROPICAL FORESTRY PLANS.—Not later than 1 year after the date of enactment of this Act, the Secretary shall prepare and submit to the Committee on Agriculture, Nutrition, and Forestry of the Senate, the Committee on Agriculture of the House of Representatives, and to the Committees on Appropriations of the Senate and House of Representatives, a tropical forestry plan for the expansion and construction of additional facilities under subsection (a). Such plan shall include provisions for—

(1) the construction or acquisition of a major center for education, interpretation, and appreciation of the benefits and methods of the intelligent management of tropical forests;

(2) the acquisition or construction of facilities for housing and classroom instruction near the Caribbean National Forest/Luguillo Experimental Forest; and

(3) the acquisition or construction of facilities for the study and recovery of endangered tropical wildlife, fish and plant species.

MILITARY CONSTRUCTION APPROPRIATIONS ACT, 1991

An Act making appropriations for military construction for the Department of Defense for the fiscal year ending September 30, 1991, and for other purposes.

Date: Nov. 5, 1990

Bill No.: H.R. 5313

Public Law No.: 101-519

Cite: 104 STAT. 2240

Sections reprinted:

Section 132 - Antiterrorism Act of 1990.

Public Law 101-519
101st Congress

An Act

Making appropriations for military construction for the Department of Defense for the fiscal year ending September 30, 1991, and for other purposes.

ANTITERRORISM ACT OF 1990

SEC. 132. (a) SHORT TITLE.—This section may be cited as the "Antiterrorism Act of 1990".

(b) TERRORISM.—Chapter 113A of title 18, United States Code, is amended—

(1) in section 2331 by striking subsection (d) and redesignating subsection (e) as subsection (d);

(2) by redesignating section 2331 as 2332 and striking the caption for section 2331 and inserting the following:

"§ 2332. Criminal penalties";

(3) by inserting before section 2332 as redesignated the following:

"§ 2331. Definitions

"As used in this chapter—

"(1) the term 'international terrorism' means activities that—

"(A) involve violent acts or acts dangerous to human life that are a violation of the criminal laws of the United States or of any State, or that would be a criminal violation if committed within the jurisdiction of the United States or of any State;

"(B) appear to be intended—

"(i) to intimidate or coerce a civilian population;

"(ii) to influence the policy of a government by intimidation or coercion; or

"(iii) to affect the conduct of a government by assassination or kidnapping; and

"(C) occur primarily outside the territorial jurisdiction of the United States, or transcend national boundaries in terms of the means by which they are accomplished, the persons they appear intended to intimidate or coerce, or the locale in which their perpetrators operate or seek asylum;

"(2) the term 'national of the United States' has the meaning given such term in section 101(a)(22) of the Immigration and Nationality Act;

"(3) the term 'person' means any individual or entity capable of holding a legal or beneficial interest in property; and

"(4) the term 'act of war' means any act occurring in the course of—

"(A) declared war;

"(B) armed conflict, whether or not war has been declared, between two or more nations; or

"(C) armed conflict between military forces of any origin.";

(4) by adding immediately after section 2332 as redesignated the following new sections:

"§ 2333. Civil remedies

"(a) ACTION AND JURISDICTION.—Any national of the United States injured in his person, property, or business by reason of an act of international terrorism, or his estate, survivors, or heirs, may sue therefor in any appropriate district court of the United States and shall recover threefold the damages he sustains and the cost of the suit, including attorney's fees.

"(b) ESTOPPED UNDER UNITED STATES LAW.—A final judgment or decree rendered in favor of the United States in any criminal proceeding under section 1116, 1201, 1203, or 2332 of this title or section 1472 (i), (k), (l), (n), or (r) of title 49 App. shall estop the defendant from denying the essential allegations of the criminal offense in any subsequent civil proceeding under this section.

"(c) ESTOPPED UNDER FOREIGN LAW.—A final judgment or decree rendered in favor of any foreign state in any criminal proceeding shall, to the extent that such judgment or decree may be accorded full faith and credit under the law of the United States, estop the defendant from denying the essential allegations of the criminal offense in any subsequent civil proceeding under this section.

"§ 2334. Jurisdiction and venue

"(a) GENERAL VENUE.—Any civil action under section 2333 of this title against any person may be instituted in the district court of the United States for any district where any plaintiff resides or where any defendant resides or is served, or has an agent. Process in such a civil action may be served in any district where the defendant resides, is found, or has an agent.

"(b) SPECIAL MARITIME OR TERRITORIAL JURISDICTION.—If the actions giving rise to the claim occurred within the special maritime and territorial jurisdiction of the United States, as defined in section 7 of this title, then any civil action under section 2333 of this title against any person may be instituted in the district court of the United States for any district in which any plaintiff resides or the defendant resides, is served, or has an agent.

"(c) SERVICE ON WITNESSES.—A witness in a civil action brought under section 2333 of this title may be served in any district where the witness resides, is found, or has an agent.

"(d) CONVENIENCE OF THE FORUM.—The district court shall not dismiss any action brought under section 2333 of this title on the grounds of the inconvenience or inappropriateness of the forum chosen, unless—

"(1) the action may be maintained in a foreign court that has jurisdiction over the subject matter and over all the defendants;

"(2) that foreign court is significantly more convenient and appropriate; and

"(3) that foreign court offers a remedy which is substantially the same as the one available in the courts of the United States.

"§ 2335. Limitation of actions

"(a) IN GENERAL.—Subject to subsection (b), a suit for recovery of damages under section 2333 of this title shall not be maintained unless commenced within 3 years from the date the cause of action accrued.

"(b) CALCULATION OF PERIOD.—The time of the absence of the defendant from the United States or from any jurisdiction in which the same or a similar action arising from the same facts may be maintained by the plaintiff, or any concealment of his whereabouts, shall not be reckoned within this period of limitation.

"§ 2336. Other limitations

"No action shall be maintained under section 2333 of this title for injury or loss by reason of an act of war.

"§ 2337. Suits against government officials

"No action shall be maintained under section 2333 of this title against—

"(1) the United States, an agency of the United States, or an officer or employee of the United States or any agency thereof acting within his official capacity or under color of legal authority; or

"(2) a foreign state, an agency of a foreign state, or an officer or employee of a foreign state or an agency thereof acting within his official capacity or under color of legal authority.

"§ 2338. Exclusive Federal jurisdiction

"The district courts of the United States shall have exclusive jurisdiction over an action brought under this chapter."; and

(5) by amending the table of sections to read as follows:

"CHAPTER 113A—TERRORISM

"Sec.
"2331. Definitions.
"2332. Criminal penalties.
"2333. Civil remedies.
"2334. Jurisdiction and venue.
"2335. Limitation of actions.
"2336. Other limitations.
"2337. Suits against government officials.
"2338. Exclusive Federal jurisdiction.".

(c) TABLE OF CONTENTS.—The table of contents of part 1, title 18, United States Code, is amended by striking:

"113A. Extraterritorial jurisdiction over terrorist acts abroad against United States nationals .... 2331."

and inserting in lieu thereof:

"113A. Terrorism .... 2331.".

FOREIGN DIRECT INVESTMENT AND INTERNATIONAL FINANCIAL DATA IMPROVEMENTS ACT OF 1990

An Act to augment and improve the quality of international data compiled by the Bureau of Economic Analysis under the International Investment and Trade in Services Survey Act by allowing that agency to share statistical establishment list information compiled by the Bureau of the Census, and for other purposes.

Date: November 7, 1990

Bill No.: S.2516

Public Law No.: 101-533

Cite: 104 STAT. 2344

Sections reprinted: All.

Public Law 101–533
101st Congress

An Act

To augment and improve the quality of international data compiled by the Bureau of Economic Analysis under the International Investment and Trade in Services Survey Act by allowing that agency to share statistical establishment list information compiled by the Bureau of the Census, and for other purposes.

Be it enacted by the Senate and House of Representatives of the United States of America in Congress assembled,

SECTION 1. SHORT TITLE.

This Act may be cited as the "Foreign Direct Investment and International Financial Data Improvements Act of 1990".

SEC. 2. FINDINGS.

The Congress makes the following findings:

(1) The United States Government collects substantial amounts of information from foreign owned or controlled business enterprises or affiliates operating in the United States.

(2) Additional analysis and presentation of this information is desirable to assist the public debate on the issue of foreign direct investments in the United States.

(3) Information collected from foreign owned or controlled firms by the Bureau of Economic Analysis has serious analytical limitations because it is largely collected on an "enterprise" basis that does not permit an adequate analysis by industry groupings.

(4) Statistical and analytic comparisons of the performance of foreign owned or controlled businesses operating within the United States with other business enterprises operating within the same industry can be accomplished under sections 2(b) and 5(c) of the International Investment and Trade in Services Survey Act, and under Executive Order Numbered 11961, without the need to collect additional information, by sharing with other authorized Government agencies the employer identification numbers maintained by the Bureau of Economic Analysis.

(5) Public disclosures of confidential business information collected by the United States Government relating to international direct investment flows could cause serious damage to the accuracy of the statistical data base.

(6) The General Accounting Office may have limited access to Government data on foreign direct investment.

SEC. 3. REPORT BY SECRETARY OF COMMERCE.

(a) ANNUAL REPORT ON FOREIGN DIRECT INVESTMENT IN THE UNITED STATES.—Not later than 6 months after the date of the enactment of this Act, and not later than the end of each 1-year period occurring thereafter, the Secretary of Commerce shall submit to the Committee on Energy and Commerce, the Committee on Ways and Means, and the Committee on Foreign Affairs of the House of Representatives, to the Committee on Commerce, Science, and Transportation of the Senate, and to the Joint Economic Committee of the Congress a report on the role and significance of foreign direct investment in the United States. Such report shall address the history, scope, trends, market concentrations, and effects on the United States economy of such investment. In addition, the Secretary of Commerce shall, if requested by any such committee, appear before that committee to provide testimony with respect to any report under this subsection.

(b) SOURCES OF DATA.—In preparing each report under subsection (a), the Secretary of Commerce, or the Secretary's designees, shall consider information collected by—

(1) the Bureau of Economic Analysis under the International Investment and Trade in Services Survey Act (22 U.S.C. 3101 and following);

(2) the Bureau of the Census on industry, manufacturing, research and development, and trade, under title 13, United States Code;

(3) the Bureau of Labor Statistics pertaining to information collected under the International Investment and Trade in Services Survey Act, but only to the extent that such information is in a form that cannot be associated with, or otherwise identify, directly or indirectly, a person, including any enterprise or establishment;

(4) the Secretary of Commerce or the Secretary's designee pursuant to section 2 of Executive Order 11858 of May 7, 1975;

(5) the United States Department of Agriculture under the Agricultural Foreign Investment Disclosure Act of 1978 (7 U.S.C. 3501 and following);

(6) the Department of the Treasury under section 6039C of the Internal Revenue Code of 1986 (26 U.S.C. 6039C), but only to the extent that such information is in a form that cannot be associated with, or otherwise identify, directly or indirectly, a person, including any enterprise or establishment;

(7) the Department of Energy under section 657(8) of the Department of Energy Organization Act (42 U.S.C. 7267(8)), but only to the extent that such information is in a form that cannot be associated with, or otherwise identify, directly or indirectly, a person, including any enterprise or establishment;

(8) other Federal agencies not referred to in paragraphs (1) through (7), but only to the extent that such information is in a form that cannot be associated with, or otherwise identify, directly or indirectly, a person, including any enterprise or establishment;

(9) foreign governments and agencies thereof; and

(10) private sector sources.

(c) ANALYSES.—(1) The analysis in each report prepared under subsection (a) shall, to the extent of available data, compare business enterprises controlled by foreign persons with other business enterprises in the United States with respect to employment, market share, value added, productivity, research and development, exports, imports, profitability, taxes paid, and investment incentives and services provided by State and local governments (including quasi-governmental entities).

(2) Each such analysis shall be done by significant industry sectors and geographical regions, except that information shall not be presented in a way in which any person, including any business enterprise or establishment, can be identified. The restriction con-

tained in the preceding sentence on presentation of information does not apply to information that is obtained from foreign governments or agencies thereof and that has been published pursuant to the lawful disclosure of the information. To the extent that data are available, each such analysis shall include an analysis, together with current levels and trends, of the number and market share of business enterprises at least 10 percent of the voting securities or other evidences of ownership of which are owned or controlled by a foreign person, and of the number and market share of the establishments of such business enterprises, that are engaged substantially in the production or coproduction of any critical technologies included in the most recent plan submitted to the Congress under section 2368 of title 10, United States Code, or included in the most recent report submitted to the President under section 603 of the National Science and Technology Policy, Organization, and Priorities Act of 1976.

SEC. 4. REPORTS BY GENERAL ACCOUNTING OFFICE.

(a) IN GENERAL.—The Comptroller General, to the extent permitted by law, including section 8 of this Act, is authorized to review the information described in section 3(b) for purposes of preparing the report required under subsection (b) of this section. Nothing in this section authorizes disclosure of any individually identifiable data or information in any form that can be associated with or otherwise identify, directly or indirectly, any person, including any enterprise or establishment.

(b) REPORT.—Not later than 5 months after each report issued by the Secretary of Commerce under section 3, the Comptroller General of the United States shall submit to the Committee on Energy and Commerce, the Committee on Ways and Means, and the Committee on Foreign Affairs of the House of Representatives, to the Committee on Commerce, Science, and Transportation of the Senate, and to the Joint Economic Committee of the Congress, a report—

(1) analyzing the report of the Secretary of Commerce;

(2) making recommendations for changes in the analysis done in the report due the following year under section 3;

(3) making recommendations for improving the collection by respective Federal agencies of data on foreign direct investment in the United States, including use of private sector data, and improving survey questionnaires to obtain useful and consistent information that avoids unnecessary redundancy among Federal agencies;

(4) reviewing the status and processes for reconciliation of data exchanged as required by this Act and the amendments made by this Act, and making any recommendations for improving and augmenting international financial data;

(5) making recommendations for possible additional policy coordination within the executive branch affecting foreign direct investment in the United States; and

(6) making recommendations for improvement of the coverage, industry classification, and consistency among Federal agencies of their respective surveys.

Reports under this subsection shall be issued only with respect to the first 3 reports issued by the Secretary of Commerce under section 3.

(c) OTHER REVIEWS AND REPORTS.—(1) The Comptroller General may, to the extent permitted by law, including section 5(c) of the International Investment and Trade in Services Survey Act (22 U.S.C. 3104(c)) and section 8 of this Act, also review data and information at the Bureau of the Census, the Bureau of Labor Statistics, and the Bureau of Economic Analysis and from time to time report to the Committee on Energy and Commerce, the Committee on Ways and Means, and the Committee on Foreign Affairs of the House of Representatives, the Committee on Commerce, Science, and Transportation of the Senate, and to the Joint Economic Committee of the Congress.

(2) The Comptroller General shall, in carrying out paragraph (1), comply with procedures relating to access to and disclosure of data and information established within the Federal statistical agencies referred to in paragraph (1), and maintain any and all individually identifiable data and information at the statistical agency where the information is reviewed.

(d) CONFIDENTIALITY; REVIEW BY OTHER AGENCIES.—In preparing any report under this section, the Comptroller General shall not—

(1) disclose any confidential business information or present any information in a way in which any person, including a business enterprise or establishment, can be identified; or

(2) combine, match, or use in any other way individually identifiable data or information maintained by any of the Federal statistical agencies referred to in subsection (c) with any other individually identifiable confidential data or information that is not collected by such statistical agencies.

Before issuing any such report, the Comptroller General shall in each instance submit the report to the head or heads of the agency or agencies from which confidential or identifiable information described in the preceding sentence was obtained. The agency or agencies concerned shall promptly review the report for the purpose of assuring that the confidentiality of such information and identity is maintained, and for any other purpose, and shall provide the Comptroller General with appropriate comments or other suggestions within 10 working days after receiving the report.

(e) RIGHT OF ACCESS.—The access by the Comptroller General to information under this Act shall be in conformity with section 716 of title 31, United States Code.

SEC. 5. ACCESS TO CENSUS DATA BY BUREAU OF ECONOMIC ANALYSIS.

(a) ACCESS TO DATA.—Title 13, United States Code, is amended by adding at the end the following:

"CHAPTER 10—EXCHANGE OF CENSUS INFORMATION

"Sec.

"401. Exchange of census information with Bureau of Economic Analysis.

"§ 401. Exchange of census information with Bureau of Economic Analysis.

"(a) EXCHANGE OF INFORMATION.—The Bureau of the Census shall exchange with the Bureau of Economic Analysis of the Department of Commerce information collected under this title, and under the International Investment and Trade in Services Survey Act, that pertains to any business enterprise that is operating in the United

States, if the Secretary of Commerce determines such information is appropriate to augment and improve the quality of data collected under the International Investment and Trade in Services Survey Act. Information provided to the Bureau of Economic Analysis by the Bureau of the Census shall be only those data collected directly from respondents by the Bureau of the Census.

"(b) REQUESTS FOR INFORMATION.—The Director of the Bureau requesting information under this section shall make the request in writing and shall certify that the information will be used only for statistical activities performed to improve the quality of data collected under the authority of title 13, United States Code, and the International Investment and Trade in Services Survey Act.

"(c) DEFINITION.—As used in subsection (a), the terms 'business enterprise' and 'United States' have the meanings given those terms in section 3 of the International Investment and Trade in Services Survey Act.".

(b) CONFORMING AMENDMENTS.—(1) The table of chapters at the beginning of title 13, United States Code, is amended by adding at the end the following:

"10. Exchange of census information .... 401".

(2) Section 9(a) of title 13, United States Code, is amended by inserting after "section 8" the following: "or chapter 10".

SEC. 6. AMENDMENTS TO THE INTERNATIONAL INVESTMENT AND TRADE IN SERVICES SURVEY ACT.

(A) PURPOSE.—Section 2(b) of the International Investment and Trade in Services Survey Act (22 U.S.C. 3101(b)) is amended by inserting after "the impact of such investment and trade," in the first sentence the following: "to authorize the collection and use of information on direct investments owned or controlled directly or indirectly by foreign governments or persons,".

(b) REPORTING REQUIREMENT.—Section 4(a)(5) of the International Investment and Trade in Services Survey Act (22 U.S.C. 3103(a)(5)) is amended by inserting before the period the following: ", including, with respect to foreign direct investment in the United States, information on ownership by foreign governments of United States affiliates by country, and tables, on an aggregated basis, of business enterprises the ownership or control of which by foreign persons is more than 50 percent of the voting securities or other evidences of ownership of such enterprises, and business enterprises the ownership or control of which by foreign persons is 50 percent or less of the voting securities or other evidences of ownership of such enterprises".

(c) BUREAU OF ECONOMIC ANALYSIS REPORT.—Section 4 of the International Investment and Trade in Services Survey Act (22 U.S.C. 3103) is amended by adding at the end the following new subsection:

"(h)(1) The President, or the designee of the President responsible for monitoring the impact of foreign investment in the United States, coordinating implementation of United States policy on investment, and investigating foreign acquisitions under section 721 of the Defense Production Act of 1950 (50 App. U.S.C. 2170), may request a report from the Bureau of Economic Analysis of the Department of Commerce. When such request is made in connection with an investigation under such section 721, the report shall be provided within 14 days after the request is made. When such request is not made in connection with an investigation under such section 721, the report shall be provided within 60 days after the request.

"(2) A report requested under paragraph (1) shall contain the best available information on the extent of foreign direct investment in a given industry, including a breakdown of total investment in the industry, and any foreign government investment in the industry, by country of the foreign owner, and any other information that the Bureau of Economic Analysis or such designee of the President considers relevant. The industry information provided shall be at the most detailed level available of Standard Industrial Classification, subject to the requirements of section 5.".

(d) ACCESS TO INFORMATION.—Section 5 of the International Investment and Trade in Services Survey Act (22 U.S.C. 3104) is amended—

(1) by redesignating subsection (d) as subsection (e); and

(2) by inserting after subsection (c) the following:

"(d) The Bureau of the Census of the Department of Commerce is authorized, for purposes of augmenting and improving the quality of data collected by the Bureau of the Census, to have, upon written request, access to data relating to business enterprises that is collected directly by the Bureau of Economic Analysis for purposes of this Act. The Bureau of Labor Statistics of the Department of Labor is authorized, for purposes of augmenting and improving the data collected by the Bureau of Labor Statistics, to have access, upon written request, to selected identification information on business enterprises and data on international services transactions, that is collected directly by the Bureau of Economic Analysis for purposes of this Act. Officers and employees of the Bureau of the Census and the Bureau of Labor Statistics shall, for purposes of subsection (c), be deemed to be officials or employees designated to perform functions under this Act.".

(e) CONFORMING AMENDMENTS.—Section 5 of the International Investment and Trade in Services Survey Act is amended—

(1) in subsection (c)(2) by striking "(d)" and inserting "(e)"; and

(2) in subsection (e), as redesignated by subsection (d)(1) of this section, by inserting "or (d)" after "(c)".

SEC. 7. ACCOUNTABILITY FOR TIMELY REPORTING.

(a) AFFIRMATION BY A RESPONSIBLE OFFICER.—Section 5(b) of the International Investment and Trade in Services Survey Act (22 U.S.C. 3104(b)) is amended by adding at the end the following: "When a report under paragraph (2) is furnished under oath, such oath shall be by the officer of such person who is directly responsible for the maintenance and compilation of such information, and shall certify that the report was prepared in accordance with this Act, is complete, and is to such officer's best knowledge and belief, substantially accurate, except in a case in which, in accordance with rules and regulations issued under this Act, estimates have been provided because data are not available from customary accounting records or precise data could not be obtained without undue burden, and the data subject to such estimates has been noted in the report.".

(b) CIVIL PENALTIES.—Section 6(a) of the International Investment and Trade in Services Survey Act (22 U.S.C. 3105(a)) is amended by striking "may be subject to a civil penalty not exceeding $10,000" and inserting "shall be subject to a civil penalty of not less than $2,500, and not more than $25,000,".

SEC. 8. ACCESS TO INFORMATION; CONFIDENTIALITY.

(a) CONFIDENTIALITY.—(1) Those officers and employees who have access to information under this Act to which the provisions of section 9 of title 13, United States Code, apply must have been sworn, as provided for in section 23(c) of such title, to observe the limitations imposed by section 9(a) of such title and to be subject to the provisions of section 214 of such title to the same extent as such section applies to officers or employees of the Bureau of the Census.

(2) Only those officers and employees who have sworn to observe the provisions of section 5(c) of the International Investment and Trade in Services Survey Act (22 U.S.C. 3104(c)) may have access under this Act to information to which such provisions apply, and such officers and employees are subject to the penalties for improper disclosure of such information provided in section 5(e) of that Act to the same extent as such section applies to officers or employees designated to perform functions under that Act.

(3) Those officers and employees referred to in paragraphs (1) and (2) of this section shall be subject to any other restriction or penalty imposed by law with respect to disclosure of information to which such officers or employees have access under this Act.

(b) VIOLATIONS AND PENALTIES.—Whoever is in possession of information made available to any department or agency by virtue of this Act or the amendments made by this Act and discloses the information in any form which can be associated with, or otherwise identify, any person, including any business enterprise or establishment, shall be fined not less than $2,500 nor more than $25,000 or imprisoned not more than 5 years, or both.

(c) UNLAWFUL ACCESS.—Whoever procures, by fraud, misrepresentation, or other unlawful act, access to information made available to any department or agency by virtue of this Act or the amendments made by this Act shall be fined not less than $2,500 nor more than $25,000 or imprisoned not more than 5 years, or both.

(d) INFORMATION IMMUNE FROM PROCESS.—Information obtained under this Act shall be immune from legal process and shall not be used as evidence or for any purpose in any Federal, State, or local government action, suit, or other administrative or judicial proceeding except as necessary to enforce requirements imposed by law on the collection of information, to enforce the provisions of subsections (b) and (c).

(e) IMPLEMENTATION.—(1) The Secretary of Commerce shall be responsible for the implementation of the exchange of information under this Act between the Bureau of the Census and the Bureau of Economic Analysis, and shall resolve any questions on access to information, data, or methodology that may arise between the Bureau of the Census and the Bureau of Economic Analysis, except that the Secretary shall not construe this section in a manner which would prevent the augmentation and improvement of the quality of international data collected under the International Investment and Trade in Services Survey Act. The Bureau of Economic Analysis and the Bureau of the Census shall agree in writing to the data to be shared under this Act.

(2) The Director of the Office of Management and Budget shall be responsible for the implementation of the exchange of information under this Act between the Bureau of Economic Analysis and the Bureau of Labor Statistics, and shall resolve any questions on access to information, data, or methodology that may arise between the

Bureau of Economic Analysis and the Bureau of Labor Statistics, except that the Director shall not construe this section in a manner which would prevent the augmentation and improvement of the quality of international data collected under the International Investment and Trade in Services Survey Act.

SEC. 9. CONSTRUCTION OF THE ACT.

(a) IN GENERAL.—Nothing in this Act or the amendments made by this Act shall be construed to require any business enterprise or any of its officers, directors, shareholders, or employees, or any other person, to provide information beyond that which is required before the enactment of this Act.

(b) IMPLEMENTATION.—All departments and agencies implementing this Act and the amendments made by this Act shall, with respect to surveys or questionnaires used in such implementation—

(1) eliminate questions that are no longer necessary,

(2) cooperate with one another in order to ensure that questions asked are consistent among the departments and agencies, and

(3) develop new questions in order to obtain more refined statistics and analyses,

consistent with the purposes of the provisions of law amended by this Act and the Paperwork Reduction Act of 1980.

SEC. 10. DEFINITIONS.

For purposes of this Act—

(1) the terms "foreign", "direct investment", "international investment", "United States", "business enterprise", "foreign person", and "United States person" have the meanings given those terms in section 3 of the International Investment and Trade in Services Survey Act (22 U.S.C. 3102); and

(2) the term "foreign direct investment in the United States" means direct investment by foreign persons in any business enterprise that is a United States person.

Approved November 7, 1990.

LEGISLATIVE HISTORY—S. 2516 (H.R. 4520):

HOUSE REPORTS: No. 101-855, Pt. 1 (Comm. on Foreign Affairs) and Pt. 2 (Comm. on Energy and Commerce), both accompanying H.R. 4520.
SENATE REPORTS: No. 101-443 (Comm. on Commerce, Science, and Transportation).
CONGRESSIONAL RECORD, Vol. 136 (1990):
Oct. 18, considered and passed Senate.
Oct. 23, considered and passed House.
WEEKLY COMPILATION OF PRESIDENTIAL DOCUMENTS, Vol. 26 (1990):
Nov. 7, Presidential statement.

CZECHOSLOVAKIA NONDISCRIMINATORY TREATMENT JOINT RESOLUTION, 1990.

Joint Resolution approving the extension of nondiscriminatory treatment (most favored nation treatment) to the products of Czechoslovakia.

Date: November 8, 1990

Bill No.: H.J. Res. 649

Public Law No.: 101-541

Cite: 104 STAT. 2380

Sections reprinted: All

Public Law 101-541
101st Congress

Joint Resolution

Approving the extension of nondiscriminatory treatment (most favored nation treatment) to the products of Czechoslovakia.

Resolved by the Senate and House of Representatives of the United States of America in Congress assembled, That the Congress approves the extension of nondiscriminatory treatment with respect to the products of Czechoslovakia transmitted by the President to the Congress on September 6, 1990.

Approved November 8, 1990.

LEGISLATIVE HISTORY—H.J. Res. 649 (S.J. Res. 361):

HOUSE REPORTS: No. 101-773 (Comm. on Ways and Means).
SENATE REPORTS: No. 101-537 accompanying S.J. Res. 361 (Comm. on Finance).
CONGRESSIONAL RECORD, Vol. 136 (1990):
Oct. 17, considered and passed House.
Oct. 24, considered and passed Senate.
WEEKLY COMPILATION OF PRESIDENTIAL DOCUMENTS, Vol. 26 (1990):
Nov. 8, Presidential statement.

SECURITIES ACTS AMENDMENTS OF 1990

An Act to amend the Federal securities laws in order to facilitate cooperation between the United States and foreign countries in securities law enforcement.

Date: November 15, 1990

Bill No.: H.R. 1396

Public Law No.: 101-550

Cite: 104 STAT. 2713

Sections reprinted:

Section 101 - Short title.

TITLE II - INTERNATIONAL SECURITIES LAW ENFORCEMENT

Section 201 - Short title: International Securities Enforcement Cooperation Act of 1990.

Section 202 - Release of records by the commission.

Section 203 - Sanctions against broker or dealer, associated persons, or persons seeking association.

Section 204 - Definition of foreign financial regulatory authority.

Section 205 - Sanctions against investment advisers or persons associated or seeking association with a registered investment adviser or investment company.

Section 206 - Definition of foreign securities authority and foreign financial regulatory authority.

Section 207 - Reimbursement of expenses incurred in providing assistance to a foreign securities authority.

Public Law 101-550
101st Congress

An Act

To amend the Federal securities laws in order to facilitate cooperation between the United States and foreign countries in securities law enforcement.

Be it enacted by the Senate and House of Representatives of the United States of America in Congress assembled,

SECTION 1. SHORT TITLE.

This Act may be cited as the "Securities Acts Amendments of 1990".

TITLE II—INTERNATIONAL SECURITIES LAW ENFORCEMENT

SEC. 201. SHORT TITLE.

This title may be cited as the "International Securities Enforcement Cooperation Act of 1990".

SEC. 202. RELEASE OF RECORDS BY THE COMMISSION.

(a) IN GENERAL.—Section 24 of the Securities Exchange Act of 1934 (15 U.S.C. 78x) is amended—

(1) in subsection (b), by striking "Nothing in this subsection shall authorize the Commission to withhold information from the Congress."; and

(2) by adding at the end thereof the following new subsections:

"(c) CONFIDENTIAL DISCLOSURES.—The Commission may, in its discretion and upon a showing that such information is needed, provide all 'records' (as defined in subsection (a)) and other information in its possession to such persons, both domestic and foreign, as the Commission by rule deems appropriate if the person receiving such records or information provides such assurances of confidentiality as the Commission deems appropriate.

"(d) RECORDS OBTAINED FROM FOREIGN SECURITIES AUTHORITIES.—Except as provided in subsection (e), the Commission shall not be compelled to disclose records obtained from a foreign securities authority if (1) the foreign securities authority has in good faith determined and represented to the Commission that public disclosure of such records would violate the laws applicable to that foreign securities authority, and (2) the Commission obtains such records pursuant to (A) such procedure as the Commission may authorize for use in connection with the administration or enforcement of the securities laws, or (B) a memorandum of understanding. For purposes of section 552 of title 5, United States Code, this subsection shall be considered a statute described in subsection (b)(3)(B) of such section 552.

"(e) SAVINGS PROVISIONS.—Nothing in this section shall—

"(1) alter the Commission's responsibilities under the Right to Financial Privacy Act (12 U.S.C. 3401 et seq.), as limited by section 21(h) of this Act, with respect to transfers of records covered by such statutes, or

"(2) authorize the Commission to withhold information from the Congress or prevent the Commission from complying with an order of a court of the United States in an action commenced by the United States or the Commission.".

(b) CONFORMING AMENDMENTS.—

(1) INVESTMENT COMPANY ACT OF 1940.—Section 45(a) of the Investment Company Act of 1940 (15 U.S.C. 80a-44) is amended by striking "It shall be unlawful" and inserting "Except as provided in section 24(c) of the Securities Exchange Act of 1934, it shall be unlawful".

(2) INVESTMENT ADVISERS ACT OF 1940.—Section 210(b) of the Investment Advisers Act of 1940 (15 U.S.C. 80b-10(b)) is amended by striking "subsections (c) and (e) of section 209" and inserting "subsections (c) and (d) of section 209 of this title and section 24(c) of the Securities Exchange Act of 1934".

SEC. 203. SANCTIONS AGAINST BROKER OR DEALER, ASSOCIATED PERSONS, OR PERSONS SEEKING ASSOCIATION.

(a) AUTHORITY OF THE COMMISSION TO SANCTION BROKERS AND DEALERS FOR FOREIGN VIOLATIONS.—Section 15(b) (15 U.S.C. 78o(b)) of the Securities Exchange Act of 1934 is amended—

(1) in paragraph (4)(B), by inserting after "misdemeanor" the following: "or of a substantially equivalent crime by a foreign court of competent jurisdiction";

(2) in paragraph (4)(B)(i), by inserting after "burglary," the following: "any substantially equivalent activity however denominated by the laws of the relevant foreign government,";

(3) in paragraph (4)(B)(ii)—

(A) by inserting after "transfer agent," the following: "foreign person performing a function substantially equivalent to any of the above,";

(B) by inserting after "(7 U.S.C. 1 et seq.)" the following: "or any substantially equivalent foreign statute or regulation";

(4) in paragraph (4)(B)(iii), by inserting after "securities" the following: ", or substantially equivalent activity however denominated by the laws of the relevant foreign government";

(5) in paragraph (4)(B)(iv), by inserting after "United States Code" the following: ", or a violation of a substantially equivalent foreign statute";

(6) in paragraph (4)(C)—

(A) by inserting after "transfer agent," the following: "foreign person performing a function substantially equivalent to any of the above,";

(B) by inserting after "Commodity Exchange Act" each time it appears the following: "or any substantially equivalent foreign statute or regulation"; and

(C) by inserting after "insurance company," the following: "foreign entity substantially equivalent to any of the above,"; and

(7) by inserting after subparagraph (F) of paragraph (4) the following:

"(G) has been found by a foreign financial regulatory authority to have—

"(i) made or caused to be made in any application for registration or report required to be filed with a foreign financial regulatory authority, or in any proceeding before a foreign financial regulatory authority with respect to registration, any statement that was at the time and in the light of the circumstances under which it was made false or misleading with respect to any material fact, or has omitted to state in any application or report to the foreign financial regulatory authority any material fact that is required to be stated therein;

"(ii) violated any foreign statute or regulation regarding transactions in securities, or contracts of sale of a commodity for future delivery, traded on or subject to the rules of a contract market or any board of trade;

"(iii) aided, abetted, counseled, commanded, induced, or procured the violation by any person of any provision of any statutory provisions enacted by a foreign government, or rules or regulations thereunder, empowering a foreign financial regulatory authority regarding transactions in securities, or contracts of sale of a commodity for future delivery, traded on or subject to the rules of a contract market or any board of trade, or has been found, by a foreign financial regulatory authority, to have failed reasonably to supervise, with a view to preventing violations of such statutory provisions, rules, and regulations, another person who commits such a violation, if such other person is subject to his supervision.".

(b) EXTENSION OF DEFINITION OF STATUTORY DISQUALIFICATION TO INCLUDE FOREIGN VIOLATIONS.—Section 3(a)(39) of such Act (15 U.S.C. 78c(a)(39)) is amended—

(1) in subparagraph (A)—

(A) by inserting after "self-regulatory organization," the following: "foreign equivalent of a self-regulatory organization, foreign or international securities exchange,";

(B) by inserting after both "(7 U.S.C. 7)," and "(7 U.S.C. 21),", the following: "or any substantially equivalent foreign statute or regulation,"; and

(C) by inserting after "contract market", the following: "or foreign equivalent";

(2) by striking subparagraph (B) and inserting the following:

"(B) is subject to—

"(i) an order to the Commission, other appropriate regulatory agency, or foreign financial regulatory authority—

"(I) denying, suspending for a period not exceeding 12 months, or revoking his registration as a broker, dealer, municipal securities dealer, government securities broker, or government securities dealer or limiting his activities as a foreign person performing a function substantially equivalent to any of the above; or

"(II) barring or suspending for a period not exceeding 12 months his being associated with a broker, dealer, municipal securities dealer, government securities broker, government securities dealer, or foreign person performing a function substantially equivalent to any of the above;

"(ii) an order of the Commodity Futures Trading Commission denying, suspending, or revoking his registration under the Commodity Exchange Act (7 U.S.C. 1 et seq.); or

"(iii) an order by a foreign financial regulatory authority denying, suspending, or revoking the person's authority to engage in transactions in contracts of sale of a commodity for future delivery or other instruments traded on or subject to the rules of a contract market, board of trade, or foreign equivalent thereof;";

(3) by redesignating subparagraphs (D) and (E) as subparagraphs (E) and (F), respectively;

(4) by inserting after subparagraph (C) the following:

"(D) by his conduct while associated with any broker, dealer, municipal securities dealer, government securities broker, government securities dealer, or any other entity engaged in transactions in securities, or while associated with an entity engaged in transactions in contracts of sale of a commodity for future delivery or other instruments traded on or subject to the rules of a contract market, board of trade, or foreign equivalent thereof, has been found to be a cause of any effective suspension, expulsion, or order by a foreign or international securities exchange or foreign financial regulatory authority empowered by a foreign government to administer or enforce its laws relating to financial transactions as described in subparagraph (A) or (B) of this paragraph;";

(5) in subparagraph (E) (as redesignated by paragraph (3) of this subsection) by striking "(A), (B), or (C)" and inserting "(A), (B), (C), or (D)"; and

(6) in subparagraph (F) (as redesignated) by striking "(D) or (E)" and inserting "(D), (E), or (G)" and by inserting after "such paragraph (4)" the first place it appears the following: "or any other felony".

(c) CONFORMING AMENDMENTS.—The Securities Exchange Act of 1944 (15 U.S.C. 78a et seq.) is amended—

(1) in sections 15(b)(6), 15B(c)(2), 15B(c)(4), 15C(c)(1)(A), 15C(c)(1)(C), 17A(c)(3)(A), and 17A(c)(4)(C), by striking "(A), (D), or (E)" and inserting "(A), (D), (E), or (G)"; and

(2) in section 15C(f)(2), by striking "or the rules or regulations under any such other provision" and inserting "the rules or regulations under any such other provision, or investigations pursuant to section 21(a)(2) of this title to assist a foreign securities authority".

SEC. 204. DEFINITION OF FOREIGN FINANCIAL REGULATORY AUTHORITY.

Section 3(a) of the Securities Exchange Act of 1934 (15 U.S.C. 78c(a)) is amended by adding at the end thereof the following new paragraph:

"(51) The term 'foreign financial regulatory authority' means any (A) foreign securities authority, (B) other governmental body or foreign equivalent of a self-regulatory organization empowered by a foreign government to administer or enforce its laws relating to the regulation of fiduciaries, trusts, commercial lending, insurance, trading in contracts of sale of a commodity for future delivery, or other instruments traded on or subject to the rules of a contract market, board of trade, or foreign equivalent, or other financial activities, or (C) membership organization a function of which is to regulate participation of its members in activities listed above.".

SEC. 205. SANCTIONS AGAINST INVESTMENT ADVISERS OR PERSONS ASSOCIATED OR SEEKING ASSOCIATION WITH A REGISTERED INVESTMENT ADVISER OR INVESTMENT COMPANY.

(a) INVESTMENT COMPANY ACT OF 1940.—Section 9(b) of the Investment Company Act of 1940 (15 U.S.C. 80a-9(b)) is amended—

(1) by striking "or" at the end of paragraphs (1) and (2);

(2) by striking the period at the end of paragraph (3) and inserting a semicolon; and

(3) by inserting after paragraph (3) the following:

"(4) has been found by a foreign financial regulatory authority to have—

"(A) made or caused to be made in any application for registration or report required to be filed with a foreign securities authority, or in any proceeding before a foreign securities authority with respect to registration, any statement that was at the time and in light of the circumstances under which it was made false or misleading with respect to any material fact, or has omitted to state in any application or report to a foreign securities authority any material fact that is required to be stated therein;

"(B) violated any foreign statute or regulation regarding transactions in securities or contracts of sale of a commodity for future delivery traded on or subject to the rules of a contract market or any board of trade;

"(C) aided, abetted, counseled, commanded, induced, or procured the violation by any other person of any foreign statute or regulation regarding transactions in securities or contracts of sale of a commodity for future delivery traded on or subject to the rules of a contract market or any board of trade;

"(5) within 10 years has been convicted by a foreign court of competent jurisdiction of a crime, however denominated by the laws of the relevant foreign government, that is substantially equivalent to an offense set forth in paragraph (1) of subsection (a); or

"(6) by reason of any misconduct, is temporarily or permanently enjoined by any foreign court of competent jurisdiction from acting in any of the capacities, set forth in paragraph (2) of subsection (a), or a substantially equivalent foreign capacity, or from engaging in or continuing any conduct or practice in connection with any such activity or in connection with the purchase or sale of any security.".

(b) INVESTMENT ADVISERS ACT OF 1940.—Section 203(e) of the Investment Advisers Act of 1940 (15 U.S.C. 80b-3(e)) is amended—

(1) in paragraph (2) by inserting after "misdemeanor" the following: "or of a substantially equivalent crime by a foreign court of competent jurisdiction";

(2) in paragraph (2)(A), by inserting after "burglary," the following: "any substantially equivalent activity however denominated by the laws of the relevant foreign government,";

(3) in paragraphs (2)(B) and (3)—

(A) by inserting after "transfer agent," the following: "foreign person performing a function substantially equivalent to any of the above,"; and

(B) after "Commodity Exchange Act" each place it appears, the following: "or any substantially equivalent statute or regulation";

(4) in paragraph (2)(C), by inserting after "securities" the following: "or substantially equivalent activity however denominated by the laws of the relevant foreign government";

(5) in paragraph (2)(D) by inserting after "United States Code" the following: ", or a violation of substantially equivalent foreign statute";

(6) in paragraph (3)—

(A) by inserting after "court of competent jurisdiction" the following: ", including any foreign court of competent jurisdiction,"; and

(B) by inserting after "insurance company," the following: "foreign entity substantially equivalent to any of the above,";

(7) in paragraph (5), by inserting after "this title," the following: "the Commodity Exchange Act,"; and

(8) by inserting after paragraph (6) the following new paragraph:

"(7) has been found by a foreign financial regulatory authority to have—

"(A) made or caused to be made in any application for registration or report required to be filed with a foreign securities authority, or in any proceeding before a foreign securities authority with respect to registration, any statement that was at the time and in light of the circumstances under which it was made false or misleading with respect to any material fact, or has omitted to state in any application or report to a foreign securities authority any material fact that is required to be stated therein;

"(B) violated any foreign statute or regulation regarding transactions in securities or contracts of sale of a commodity for future delivery traded on or subject to the rules of a contract market or any board of trade;

"(C) aided, abetted, counseled, commanded, induced, or procured the violation by any other person of any foreign statute or regulation regarding transactions in securities or contracts of sale of a commodity for future delivery traded on or subject to the rules of a contract market or any board of trade, or has been found, by the foreign finanical regulatory authority, to have failed reasonably to supervise, with a view to preventing violations of statutory provisions, and rules and regulations promulgated thereunder, another person who commits such a violation, if such other person is subject to his supervision.".

(c) CONFORMING AMENDMENT.—Section 203(f) of the Investment Advisers Act of 1940 (15 U.S.C. 80b-3(f)) is amended by striking "paragraph (1), (4), or (5)" and inserting "paragraph (1), (4), (5), or (7)".

SEC. 206. DEFINITION OF FOREIGN SECURITIES AUTHORITY AND FOREIGN FINANCIAL REGULATORY AUTHORITY.

(a) INVESTMENT COMPANY ACT OF 1940.—Section 2(a) of the Investment Company Act of 1940 (15 U.S.C. 80a-2(a)) is amended by inserting after paragraph (48) the following:

"(49) 'Foreign securities authority' means any foreign government or any governmental body or regulatory organization empowered by a foreign government to administer or enforce its laws as they relate to securities matters.

"(50) 'Foreign financial regulatory authority' means any (A) foreign securities authority, (B) other governmental body or foreign equivalent of a self-regulatory organization empowered by a foreign government to administer or enforce its laws relating to the regulation of fiduciaries, trusts, commercial lending, insurance, trading in contracts of sale of a commodity for future delivery, or other instruments traded on or subject to the rules of a contract market, board of trade or foreign equivalent, or other financial activities, or (C) membership organization a function of which is to regulate the participation of its members in activities listed above.".

(b) INVESTMENT ADVISERS ACT OF 1940.—Section 202(a) of the Investment Advisers Act of 1940 (15 U.S.C. 80B-2(a)) is amended by inserting after paragraph (22) the following:

"(23) 'Foreign securities authority' means any foreign government, or any governmental body or regulatory organization empowered by a foreign government to administer or enforce its laws as they relate to securities matters.

"(24) 'Foreign financial regulatory authority' means any (A) foreign securities authority, (B) other governmental body or foreign equivalent of a self-regulatory organization empowered by a foreign government to administer or enforce its laws relating to the regulation of fiduciaries, trusts, commercial lending, insurance, trading in contracts of sale of a commodity for future delivery, or other instruments traded on or subject to the rules of a contract market, board of trade or foreign equivalent, or other financial activities, or (C) membership organization a function of which is to regulate the participation of its members in activities listed above.".

SEC. 207. REIMBURSEMENT OF EXPENSES INCURRED IN PROVIDING ASSISTANCE TO A FOREIGN SECURITIES AUTHORITY.

Section 4 of the Securities Exchange Act of 1934 (15 U.S.C. 78d) is amended by adding at the end thereof the following new subsection:

"(f) REIMBURSEMENT OF EXPENSES FOR ASSISTING FOREIGN SECURITIES AUTHORITIES.—Notwithstanding any other provision of law, the Commission may accept payment and reimbursement, in cash or in kind, from a foreign securities authority, or made on behalf of such authority, for necessary expenses incurred by the Commission, its members, and employees in carrying out any investigation pursuant to section 21(a)(2) of this title or in providing any other assistance to a foreign securities authority. Any payment or reimbursement accepted shall be considered a reimbursement to the appropriated funds of the Commission.".

USE OF INVENTIONS IN OUTER SPACE ACT, 1990

An Act to amend title 35, United States Code, with respect to the use of inventions in outer space.

Date: November 15, 1990

Bill No.: S.459

Public Law No.: 101-580

Cite: 104 STAT. 2863

Sections reprinted: All

Public Law 101–580
101st Congress
An Act

To amend title 35, United States Code, with respect to the use of inventions in outer space.

Be it enacted by the Senate and House of Representatives of the United States of America in Congress assembled,

SECTION 1. INVENTIONS IN OUTER SPACE.

(a) IN GENERAL.—Chapter 10 of title 35, United States Code, is amended by adding at the end the following:

"§ 105. Inventions in outer space

"(a) Any invention made, used or sold in outer space on a space object or component thereof under the jurisdiction or control of the United States shall be considered to be made, used or sold within the United States for the purposes of this title, except with respect to any space object or component thereof that is specifically identified and otherwise provided for by an international agreement to which the United States is a party, or with respect to any space object or component thereof that is carried on the registry of a foreign state in accordance with the Convention on Registration of Objects Launched into Outer Space.

"(b) Any invention made, used or sold in outer space on a space object or component thereof that is carried on the registry of a foreign state in accordance with the Convention on Registration of Objects Launched into Outer Space, shall be considered to be made, used or sold within the United States for the purposes of this title if specifically so agreed in an international agreement between the United States and the state of registry.".

(b) TABLE OF CONTENTS.—The table of sections of chapter 10 of title 35, United States Code, is amended by adding at the end the following:

"105. Inventions in outer space.".

SEC. 2. SPECIAL RULES.

(a) EFFECTIVE DATE.—Subject to subsections (b), (c), and (d) of this section, the amendments made by the first section of this Act shall apply to all United States patents granted before, on, or after the date of enactment of this Act, and to all applications for United States patents pending on or filed on or after such date of enactment.

(b) FINAL DECISIONS.—The amendments made by the first section of this Act shall not affect any final decision made by a court or the Patent and Trademark Office before the date of enactment of this Act with respect to a patent or an application for a patent, if no appeal from such decision is pending and the time for filing an appeal has expired.

(c) PENDING CASES.—The amendments made by the first section of this Act shall not affect the right of any party in any case pending in a court on the date of enactment of this Act to have the party's rights determined on the basis of the substantive law in effect before such date of enactment.

(d) NON-APPLICABILITY.—The amendments made by the first section of this Act shall not apply to any process, machine, article of manufacture, or composition of matter, an embodiment of which was launched prior to the date of enactment of this Act.

Approved November 15, 1990.

LEGISLATIVE HISTORY—S. 459 (H.R. 2946):

SENATE REPORTS: No. 101-266 (Comm. on the Judiciary).
CONGRESSIONAL RECORD, Vol. 136 (1990):
May 1, considered and passed Senate.
Oct. 26, H.R. 2946 considered and passed House; proceedings vacated and S. 459 passed in lieu.
WEEKLY COMPILATION OF PRESIDENTIAL DOCUMENTS, Vol. 26 (1990):
Nov. 15, Presidential statement.

FASTENER QUALITY ACT

An Act to require that certain fasteners sold in commerce conform to the specifications to which they are represented to be manufactured, to provide for accreditation of laboratories engaged in fastener testing, to require inspection, testing, and certification, in accordance with standardized methods, of fasteners used in critical applications to increase fastener quality and reduce the danger of fastener failure, and for other purposes.

Date: November 16, 1990

Bill No.: H.R. 3000

Public Law No.: 101-592

Cite: 104 STAT. 2943

Sections reprinted: All.

Public Law 101-592
101st Congress
An Act

To require that certain fasteners sold in commerce conform to the specifications to which they are represented to be manufactured, to provide for accreditation of laboratories engaged in fastener testing, to require inspection, testing, and certification, in accordance with standardized methods, of fasteners used in critical applications to increase fastener quality and reduce the danger of fastener failure, and for other purposes.

Be it enacted by the Senate and House of Representatives of the United States of America in Congress assembled,

SECTION 1. SHORT TITLE.

This Act may be cited as the "Fastener Quality Act".

SEC. 2. FINDINGS AND PURPOSE.

(a) FINDINGS.—The Congress finds that—

(1) the American economy uses billions of fasteners each year;

(2) millions of mismarked, substandard, counterfeit, and other nonconforming fasteners have been sold in commerce to end-users in the United States, and their use has dramatically increased the risk of equipment and infrastructure failures;

(3) both the military and civilian sectors of the economy have encountered unnecessary, unwarranted, and dangerous equipment and construction failures, as well as extraordinary expenses, as a result of the use of nonconforming fasteners;

(4) the sale in commerce of nonconforming fasteners and the use of nonconforming fasteners in numerous critical applications have reduced the combat readiness of the Nation's military forces, endangered the safety of other Federal projects and activities, and cost both the public and private sectors large sums in connection with the retesting and purging of fastener inventories;

(5) the purchase and use of nonconforming fasteners stem from material misrepresentations about such fasteners made by certain manufacturers, importers, and distributors engaged in commerce;

(6) current fastener standards of measurement evaluate bolts and other fasteners according to multiple criteria, including strength, hardness, and composition, and provide grade identification markings on fasteners to make the characteristics of individual fasteners clear to purchasers and users;

(7) current tests required by consensus standards, designed to ensure that fasteners are of standard measure, are adequate and appropriate for use as standards in a program of high-strength fastener testing;

(8) the lack of traceability by lot number of fasteners sold in commerce is a serious impediment to effective quality control efforts; and

(9) the health and safety of Americans is threatened by the widespread sale in commerce of mismarked, substandard, and

counterfeit fasteners, a practice which also harms American manufacturers, importers, and distributors of safe and conforming fasteners, and workers in the American fastener industry.

(b) PURPOSE.—In order to protect public safety, to deter the introduction of nonconforming fasteners into commerce, to improve the traceability of fasteners used in critical applications, and generally to provide commercial and governmental customers with greater assurance that fasteners meet stated specifications, it is the purpose of this Act to create procedures for the testing, certification, and distribution of certain fasteners used in commerce within the United States.

SEC. 3. DEFINITIONS.

As used in this Act, the term—

(1) "alter" means to alter—

(A) by through-hardening,

(B) by electroplating of fasteners having a minimum tensile strength of 150,000 pounds per square inch, or

(C) by machining;

(2) "consensus standards organization" means the American Society for Testing and Materials, American National Standards Institute, American Society of Mechanical Engineers, Society of Automotive Engineers, or any other standard-setting organization determined by the Secretary to have comparable knowledge, expertise, and concern for health and safety in the field for which such organization purports to set standards;

(3) "container" means any package of fasteners traded in commerce;

(4) "Director" means the Director of the National Institute of Standards and Technology;

(5) "fastener" means—

(A) a—

(i) screw, nut, bolt, or stud having internal or external threads, or

(ii) a load-indicating washer,

with a nominal diameter of 5 millimeters or greater, in the case of such items described in metric terms, or ¼ inch or greater, in the case of such items described in terms of the English system of measurement, which contains any quantity of metal and is held out as meeting a standard or specification which requires through-hardening,

(B) a screw, nut, bolt, or stud having internal or external threads which bears a grade identification marking required by a standard or specification,

(C) a washer to the extent that it is subject to a standard or specification applicable to a screw, nut, bolt, or stud described in subparagraph (B), or

(D) any item within a category added by the Secretary in accordance with section 4(b),

except that such term does not include any screw, nut, bolt, or stud that is produced and marked as ASTM A 307 Grade A;

(6) "grade identification marking" means any symbol appearing on a fastener purporting to indicate that the fastener's base material, strength properties, or performance capabilities conform to a specific standard of a consensus standards organization or other person;

(7) "importer" means a person located within the United States who contracts for the initial purchase of fasteners manufactured outside the United States for resale or such person's use within the United States;

(8) "Institute" means the National Institute of Standard and Technology;

(9) "lot" means a quantity of fasteners of one part number fabricated by the same production process from the same coil or heat number of metal as provided by the metal manufacturer and submitted for inspection and testing at one time;

(10) "manufacturer" means a person who fabricates fasteners, or who alters any item so that it becomes a fastener;

(11) "original equipment manufacturer" means a person who uses fasteners in the manufacture or assembly of its products and sells fasteners to authorized dealers as replacement or service parts for its products;

(12) "private label distributor" means a person who contracts with a manufacturer for the fabrication of fasteners bearing the distributor's distinguishing insignia;

(13) "Secretary" means the Secretary of Commerce;

(14) "standards and specifications" means the provisions of a document published by a consensus standards organization, a government agency, or a major end-user of fasteners which defines or describes dimensional characteristics, limits of size, acceptable materials, processing, functional behavior, plating, baking, inspecting, testing, packaging, and required markings of any fastener; and

(15) "through-harden" means heating above the transformation temperature followed by quenching and tempering.

SEC. 4. SPECIAL RULES FOR FASTENERS.

(a) WAIVER REQUIREMENT.—If the Secretary determines that any category of fastener is not used in critical applications, the Secretary shall waive the requirements of this Act with respect to such category.

(b) ADDITIONAL ITEMS.—If the Secretary determines that—

(1) a category of screw, nut, bolt, or stud which is not described in section 3(5)(A)(i) or (B),

(2) a category of item which is associated with a fastener described in section 3(5)(A), (B), or (C), or

(3) a category of item which serves a function comparable to that served by a fastener so described

is used in critical applications, the Secretary may include such category under section 3(5)(D) and therefore within the definition of fasteners under this Act.

(c) NOTICE AND OPPORTUNITY FOR COMMENTS.—The Secretary shall provide advance notice and the opportunity for public comments prior to making any determination under subsections (a) and (b) and shall act through the Director in making any such determination.

SEC. 5. TESTING AND CERTIFICATION OF FASTENERS.

(a) REQUIREMENT.—(1) No fastener shall be offered for sale or sold in commerce unless it is part of a lot which—

(A) conforms to the standards and specifications to which the manufacturer represents it has been manufactured; and

(B) has been inspected, tested, and certified as provided in subsections (b) and (c) of this section.

(2)(A) Paragraph (1)(B) of this subsection shall not apply to fasteners which are part of a lot of 50 fasteners or less if, within 10 working days after the delivery of such fasteners, or as soon as practicable thereafter—

(i) inspection, testing, and certification as provided in subsections (b) and (c) is carried out; and

(ii) written notice detailing the results of such inspection, testing, and certification is sent (I) to all purchasers of such fasteners, except retail sellers and retail consumers, and (II) to any retail seller or retail consumer who, prior to delivery, requests such written notice.

(B) If a fastener is sold under this paragraph, each purchaser of such fastener, except for retail sellers and retail consumers unless such retail sellers and retail consumers request such notice in advance, shall be provided, contemporaneously with each sale and delivery, written notice stating that such fastener has not yet been inspected, tested, and certified as required by this Act.

(b) Inspection and Testing.—(1) The manufacturer of a lot of fasteners shall cause to be inspected and tested a representative sample, as provided in paragraph (2) of this subsection, of the fasteners in such lot to determine whether the lot conforms to the standards and specifications to which the manufacturer represents it has been manufactured. Such inspection and testing shall be performed by a laboratory accredited in accordance with the procedures and conditions specified by the Secretary under section 6. The standards and specifications to which the manufacturer represents such lot has been manufactured shall be disclosed by the manufacturer to the laboratory at the time the lot is submitted for inspection and testing under this paragraph. The manufacturer of a lot may perform the inspection and testing required by this paragraph in a laboratory which it owns or with which it is otherwise affiliated, if such laboratory is accredited in accordance with the procedures and conditions specified by the Secretary under section 6; unless the Secretary finds that, as to a specific type of fastener and as to a specific type of inspection or testing, a ban on manufacturer ownership or affiliation with the accredited laboratory would increase the protection of health and safety of the public or industrial workers.

(2) The size, selection, and integrity of the sample to be inspected and tested under paragraph (1) shall be governed—

(A) by the standards and specifications to which the manufacturer represents the fasteners in the sample have been manufactured; or

(B) if such standards and specifications do not provide for the size, selection, or integrity of the sample, by sampling procedures prescribed by the Secretary, who shall to the extent practicable use consensus testing standards and related materials.

Nothing in this paragraph shall prohibit a purchaser from requiring the inspection and testing of a greater number of fasteners from a lot than is specified in the applicable standards and specifications or in the applicable sampling procedures prescribed by the Secretary.

(c) Laboratory Report of Testing.—If a laboratory performing the inspection and testing under subsection (b)(1) determines, as to the characteristics selected under the sampling procedures prescribed by the Secretary and based on the sample examined, that a lot conforms to the standards and specifications to which the manufacturer represents it has been manufactured, the laboratory shall provide to the manufacturer a written inspection and testing report with respect to such lot. The report, which shall be in a form prescribed by the Secretary by regulation, shall—

(1) state the manufacturer's name, the part description, and the lot number and note the grade identification mark and insignia found on the fastener;

(2) reference the standards and specifications disclosed by the manufacturer with respect to such lot under subsection (b)(1) or, where applicable, certified by the manufacturer under section 7(c)(1);

(3) list the markings and characteristics selected under the Secretary's procedures for testing, such as the chemical, dimensional, physical, mechanical, and any other significant characteristics required by the standards and specifications described in paragraph (2) and specify the results of the inspection and testing under subsection (b)(1);

(4) state whether, based on the samples provided as representative of the lot, such lot has been found after such inspection and testing to conform to such standards and specifications; and

(5) bear the original signature of a laboratory employee or officer determined by the Secretary to be responsible for the accuracy of the report and of the inspection and testing to which it relates.

SEC. 6. LABORATORY ACCREDITATION.

(a) ESTABLISHMENT OF ACCREDITATION PROGRAM.—(1) Within 180 days after the date of enactment of this Act, the Secretary, acting through the Director, shall issue regulations which shall include—

(A) procedures and conditions, including sampling procedures referred to in section 5, for the accreditation by the Institute of laboratories engaged in the inspection and testing of fasteners under section 5;

(B) procedures and conditions (which shall be consistent with the procedures and conditions established under subparagraph (A)), using to the extent practicable the requirements of national or international consensus documents intended to govern the operation of accreditation bodies, under which private entities may apply for approval by the Secretary to engage directly in the accreditation of laboratories in accordance with the requirements of this Act; and

(C) conditions (which shall be consistent with the procedures and conditions established under subparagraph (A)), under which the accreditation of foreign laboratories by their governments or organizations recognized by the Director shall be deemed to satisfy the laboratory accreditation requirements of this section.

(2) Upon establishing a laboratory accreditation program under paragraph (1), the Secretary shall publish a notice in the Federal Register stating that the Secretary is prepared to accept applications for accreditation of such laboratories.

(3) No accreditation provided under the terms of this subsection shall be effective for a period of greater than 3 years.

(b) LABORATORY ACCREDITATION PROCEDURES.—Existing Institute accreditation procedures stated in part 7 of title 15, Code of Federal Regulations, as in effect on the date of enactment of this Act, supplemented as the Secretary considers necessary, shall be used to accredit laboratories under the accreditation program established under subsection (a).

(c) ENSURING COMPLIANCE.—(1) The Secretary shall ensure that—

(A) private entities accrediting laboratories under procedures and conditions established under subsection (a)(1)(B) comply with such procedures and conditions, and

(B) laboratories accredited by such private entities, or by foreign governments pursuant to subsection (a)(1)(C), comply with the requirements for such accreditation.

(2) The Secretary may require any such private entity or laboratory to provide all records and materials that may be necessary to allow the Secretary to carry out this subsection.

(d) OPERATION OF LABORATORY ACCREDITATION PROGRAM.—(1) The Director may hire such contractors as are necessary to carry out the accreditation program established under subsection (a).

(2) Costs to the Institute and to the Secretary for the establishment and operation of the accreditation program under this section shall be fully reimbursable to the Institute or to the Secretary, as appropriate, through fees or other charges for accreditation services under such program.

(e) RECOMMENDATIONS TO CONSENSUS STANDARDS ORGANIZATIONS.—The Director shall periodically transmit to appropriate consensus standards organizations any information or recommendations that may be useful in the establishment or application by such organizations of standards and specifications for fasteners.

SEC. 7. SALE OF FASTENERS SUBSEQUENT TO MANUFACTURE.

(a) DOMESTICALLY PRODUCED FASTENERS.—It shall be unlawful for a manufacturer to sell any shipment of fasteners (except fasteners for which the Secretary has waived the requirements of this Act pursuant to section 4) which are manufactured in the United States unless the fasteners are accompanied, at the time of delivery, by a written certificate by the manufacturer certifying that—

(1) the fasteners have been manufactured according to the requirements of the applicable standards and specifications and have been inspected and tested by a laboratory accredited in accordance with the procedures and conditions specified by the Secretary under section 6; and

(2) an original laboratory testing report described in section 5(c) is on file with the manufacturer, or under such custody as may be prescribed by the Secretary, and available for inspection.

(b) FASTENERS OF FOREIGN ORIGIN.—(1) Except as provided in paragraph (2) of this subsection, it shall be unlawful—

(A) for any person to sell to any importer, and

(B) for any importer to purchase,

any shipment of fasteners which are manufactured outside the United States unless delivery of such shipment to such importer is accompanied by a manufacturer's certificate as described in subsection (a), an original laboratory testing report described in section 5(c), with respect to each lot from which such fasteners were taken, and any other relevant lot identification information.

(2) The requirement under paragraph (1) of this subsection that the delivery of such a shipment to such importer be accompanied by an original laboratory testing report shall not apply in the case of fasteners imported into the United States—

(A) as products manufactured within a nation which is party to a congressionally-approved free trade agreement with the United States that is in effect, so long as the Secretary certifies that satisfactory arrangements have been reached by which purchasers within the United States can readily gain access to an original laboratory testing report for such fasteners; or

(B) as Canadian-origin products under the United States-Canada Automobile Pact for use as original equipment in the manufacture of motor vehicles.

(c) OPTION FOR IMPORTERS AND PRIVATE LABEL DISTRIBUTORS.—(1) Notwithstanding section 5(a) and subsections (a) and (b) of this section, delivery of a lot, or portion of a lot, of fasteners may be made to an importer or private label distributor without the required original copy of the laboratory testing report if—

(A) the manufacturer provides to the importer or private label distributor a manufacturer's certificate certifying that the fasteners have been manufactured according to the requirements of the applicable standards and specifications; and

(B) the importer or private label distributor assumes responsibility in writing for the inspection and testing of such lot or portion by a laboratory accredited in accordance with the procedures and conditions specified by the Secretary under section 6.

(2) If the importer or private distributor assumes the responsibility in writing for the inspection and testing of such lot or portion, the provisions of section 5(a) and subsections (a) and (b) of this section shall apply to the importer or private label distributor in the same manner and extent as to a manufacturer; except that the importer or private label distributor shall provide to the testing laboratory the manufacturer's certificate described under paragraph (1) of this subsection.

(d) ALTERATIONS SUBSEQUENT TO MANUFACTURE.—(1) Any person who significantly alters a fastener so that such fastener no longer conforms to the description in the relevant certificate issued under section 5(c), and who thereafter offers for sale or sells such altered fastener, shall be treated as a manufacturer for purposes of this Act and shall cause such altered fastener to be inspected and tested under section 5 or this section as though it were newly manufactured, unless delivery of such fastener to the purchaser is accompanied by a written statement noting the original lot number, disclosing the subsequent alteration, and warning that such alteration may affect the dimensional or physical characteristics of the fastener.

(2) Any person who knowingly sells an altered fastener and who did not alter such fastener shall provide to the purchaser a copy of the statement required by paragraph (1).

(e) COMMINGLING.—(1) Subject to paragraph (2), it shall be unlawful for any manufacturer or any person who purchases any quantity of fasteners for resale at wholesale to commingle like fasteners from different lots in the same container; except that such manufacturer or such person may commingle like fasteners of the same type, grade, and dimension from not more than two tested and certified lots in the same container during repackaging and plating operations: *Provided,* That any container which contains like fasteners from two lots shall be conspicuously marked with the lot identification numbers of both lots.

(2) Paragraph (1) does not apply to sales by original equipment manufacturers to their authorized dealers for use in assembling or

servicing products produced by the original equipment manufacturers.

(f) SUBSEQUENT PURCHASER.—(1) It shall be unlawful for any person to sell fasteners, of any quantity, to any person who purchases such fasteners—

(A) for sale at wholesale, or

(B) for assembling components of a product or structure for sale,

unless the container of fasteners sold is conspicously marked with the number of the lot from which such fasteners were taken, except that this requirement shall not apply to sales by original equipment manufacturers to their authorized dealers for use in assembling or servicing products produced by the original equipment manufacturer.

(2) If a person who purchases fasteners for purposes other than those described in paragraph (1) (A) and (B) so requests either prior to the sale or at the time of sale, the seller shall conspicuously mark the container of fasteners with the lot number from which such fasteners were taken.

(g) REGULATIONS.—The Secretary may issue such regulations as may be necessary to ensure compliance with the provisions of this section.

SEC. 8. MANUFACTURERS' INSIGNIAS.

(a) GENERAL RULE.—No fastener which is required by the standards and specifications to which it was manufactured to bear a raised or depressed insignia identifying its manufacturer or private label distributor shall be offered for sale or sold in commerce unless the manufacturer or private label distributor of such fastener has complied with the requirements prescribed by the Secretary in connection with the program established under subsection (b) of this section.

(b) RECORDATION.—The Secretary shall establish, by regulation, a program to provide for the recordation of the insignias of manufacturers and private label distributors described in subsection (a), to ensure the traceability of a fastener to its manufacturer or private label distributor.

SEC. 9. REMEDIES AND PENALTIES.

(a) CIVIL REMEDIES.—(1) The Attorney General may bring an action in an appropriate United States district court for appropriate declaratory and injunctive relief against any person who violates this Act or any regulation under this Act.

(2) An action under paragraph (1) may not be brought more than 10 years after the date on which the cause of action accrues.

(b) CIVIL PENALTIES.—(1) Any person who is determined by the Secretary, after notice and an opportunity for a hearing, to have violated this Act or any regulation under this Act shall be liable to the United States for a civil penalty of not more than $25,000 for each violation.

(2) The amount of the penalty shall be assessed by the Secretary by written notice. In determining the amount of the penalty, the Secretary shall consider the nature, circumstances, and gravity of the violation and, with respect to the person found to have committed the violation, the degree of culpability, any history of prior violations, the effect on ability to continue to do business, any good

faith attempt to achieve compliance, ability to pay the penalty, and such other matters as justice may require.

(3) Any person against whom a civil penalty is assessed under paragraph (2) of this section may obtain review thereof in the appropriate court of the United States by filing a notice of appeal in such court within 30 days from the date of such order and by simultaneously sending a copy of such notice by certified mail to the Secretary. The findings and order of the Secretary shall be set aside by such court if they are found to be unsupported by substantial evidence, as provided in section 706(2) of title 5, United States Code.

(4) The Secretary may compromise, modify, or remit, with or without conditions, any civil penalty which is subject to imposition or which has been imposed under this section prior to referral to the Attorney General under paragraph (5).

(5) A civil penalty assessed under this subsection may be recovered in an action brought by the Attorney General on behalf of the United States in the appropriate district court of the United States. In such action, the validity and appropriateness of the final order imposing the civil penalty shall not be subject to review.

(6) For the purpose of conducting any hearing under this section, the Secretary may issue subpoenas for the attendance and testimony of witnesses and the production of relevant papers, books, and documents, and may administer oaths. Witnesses summoned shall be paid the same fees and mileage that are paid to witnesses in the courts of the United States. In case of contempt or refusal to obey a subpoena served upon any person pursuant to this paragraph, the district court of the United States for any district in which such person is found, resides, or transacts business, upon application by the United States and after notice to such person, shall have jurisdiction to issue an order requiring such person to appear and give testimony before the Secretary or to appear and produce documents before the Secretary, or both, and any failure to obey such order of the court may be punished by such court as a contempt thereof.

(c) CRIMINAL PENALTIES.—(1) Whoever knowingly certifies, marks, offers for sale, or sells a fastener in violation of this Act or a regulation under this Act shall be fined under title 18, United States Code, or imprisoned not more than 5 years, or both.

(2) Whoever intentionally fails to maintain records relating to a fastener in violation of this Act or a regulation under this Act shall be fined under title 18, United States Code, or imprisoned not more than 5 years, or both.

(3) Whoever negligently fails to maintain records relating to a fastener in violation of this Act or a regulation under this Act shall be fined under title 18, United States Code, or imprisoned not more than 2 years, or both.

SEC. 10. RECORDKEEPING REQUIREMENTS.

(a) LABORATORIES.—Laboratories which perform inspections and testing under section 5(b) shall retain for 10 years all records concerning the inspection and testing, and certification, of fasteners under section 5.

(b) MANUFACTURERS, IMPORTERS, PRIVATE LABEL DISTRIBUTORS, AND PERSONS WHO MAKE SIGNIFICANT ALTERATIONS.—Manufacturers, importers, private label distributors, and persons who make significant alterations shall retain for 10 years all records concerning the inspection and testing, and certification, of fasteners under section 5, and shall provide copies of any applicable laboratory testing report or manufacturer's certificate upon request to any subsequent purchaser of fasteners taken from the lot to which such testing report or manufacturer's certificate relates.

SEC. 11. RELATIONSHIP TO STATE LAWS.

Nothing in this Act shall be construed to preempt any rights or causes of action that any buyer may have with respect to any seller of fasteners under the law of any State, except to the extent that the provisions of this Act are in conflict with such State law.

SEC. 12. CONSTRUCTION.

Nothing in this Act shall be construed to limit or otherwise affect the authority of any consensus standards organization to establish, modify, or withdraw any standards and specifications under any other law or authority in effect on the date of enactment of this Act.

SEC. 13. REGULATIONS.

The Secretary shall within 180 days after the date of enactment of this Act issue such regulations as may be necessary to implement this Act.

SEC. 14. ADVISORY COMMITTEE.

Within 90 days after the date of enactment of this Act, the Secretary shall appoint an advisory committee consisting of representatives of fastener manufacturers, importers, distributors, end-users, independent laboratories, and standards organizations. The Secretary and Director shall consult with the advisory committee—

(1) prior to promulgating any regulations under this Act; and

(2) in such other matters related to fasteners as the Secretary may determine.

SEC. 15. APPLICABILITY.

The requirements of this Act shall be applicable only to fasteners fabricated 180 days or more after the Secretary issues final regulations required under sections 5, 6, and 8, except that the Secretary may extend such time period if the Secretary determines that an insufficient number of laboratories have been accredited to perform the volume of inspection and testing required. Upon any such extension, and every 6 months thereafter during such extension, the Secretary shall submit a report to the Congress explaining the reasons for such extension and the steps being taken to ensure the accreditation of a sufficient number of laboratories.

Approved November 16, 1990.

LEGISLATIVE HISTORY—H.R. 3000:

HOUSE REPORTS: No. 101-211, Pt. 1 (Comm. on Science, Space, and Technology) and Pt. 2 (Comm. on Energy and Commerce).
SENATE REPORTS: No. 101-388 (Comm. on Commerce, Science, and Transportation).
CONGRESSIONAL RECORD:
Vol. 135 (1989): Sept. 19, considered and passed House.
Vol. 136 (1990): Oct. 26, considered and passed Senate, amended. House concurred in Senate amendment.

ANTARCTIC PROTECTION ACT OF 1990

An Act to protect and conserve the continent of Antarctica, and for other purposes.

Date: November 16, 1990

Bill No.: H.R. 3977

Public Law No.: 101-594

Cite: 104 STAT. 2975

Sections reprinted: All.

Public Law 101-594
101st Congress

An Act

To protect and conserve the continent of Antarctica, and for other purposes.

Be it enacted by the Senate and the House of Representatives of the United States of America in Congress assembled,

SECTION 1. SHORT TITLE.

This Act may be cited as the "Antarctic Protection Act of 1990".

SEC. 2. FINDINGS AND PURPOSE.

(a) FINDINGS.—Congress finds that—

(1) the Antarctic continent with its associated and dependent ecosystems is a distinctive environment providing a habitat for many unique species and offering a natural laboratory from which to monitor critical aspects of stratospheric ozone depletion and global climate change;

(2) Antarctica is protected by a series of international agreements, including the Antarctic Treaty and associated recommendations, the Convention on the Conservation of Antarctic Seals, and the Convention on the Conservation of Antarctic Marine Living Resources, which are intended to conserve the renewable natural resources of Antarctica and to recognize the importance of Antarctica for the conduct of scientific research;

(3) recurring and recent developments in Antarctica, including increased siting of scientific stations, poor waste disposal practices, oil spills, increased tourism, and the over-exploitation of marine living resources, have raised serious questions about the adequacy and implementation of existing agreements and domestic law to protect the Antarctic environment and its living marine resources;

(4) the parties to the Antarctic Treaty have negotiated a Convention on the Regulation of Antarctic Mineral Resources Activities which the United States has signed but not yet ratified;

(5) the Convention on the Regulation of Antarctic Mineral Resources Activities does not guarantee the preservation of the fragile environment of Antarctica and could actually stimulate movement toward Antarctic mineral resource activity;

(6) the exploitation of mineral resources in Antarctica could lead to additional degradation of the Antarctic environment, including increased risk of oil spills;

(7) the Antarctic Treaty Consultative Parties have agreed to a voluntary ban on Antarctic mineral resource activities which needs to be made legally binding;

(8) the level of scientific study, including necessary support facilities, has increased to the point that some scientific programs may be degrading the Antarctic environment; and

(9) the planned special consultative meeting of parties to the Antarctic Treaty and the imminence of the thirtieth anniver-

sary of the Antarctic Treaty provide opportunities for the United States to exercise leadership toward protection and sound management of Antarctica.

(b) PURPOSE.—The purpose of this Act is to—

(1) strengthen substantially overall environmental protection of Antarctica;

(2) prohibit prospecting, exploration, and development of Antarctic mineral resources by United States citizens and other persons subject to the jurisdiction of the United States;

(3) urge other nations to join the United States in immediately negotiating one or more new agreements to provide an indefinite ban on all Antarctic mineral resource activities and comprehensive protection for Antarctica and its associated and dependent ecosystems; and

(4) urge all nations to consider a permanent ban on Antarctic mineral resource activities.

SEC. 3. DEFINITIONS.

For the purposes of this Act:

(1) The term "Antarctica" means the area south of the Antarctic Convergence as defined in section 303(1) of the Antarctic Marine Living Resources Convention Act of 1984 (16 U.S.C. 2432).

(2) The term "Antarctic mineral resource activity" means prospecting, exploration, or development in Antarctica of mineral resources, but does not include scientific research within the meaning of article III of the Antarctic Treaty, done at Washington on December 1, 1959.

(3) The term "development" means any activity, including logistic support, which takes place following exploration, the purpose of which is the exploitation of specific mineral resource deposits, including processing, storage, and transport activities.

(4) The term "exploration" means any activity, including logistic support, the purpose of which is the identification or evaluation of specific mineral resource deposits. The term includes exploratory drilling, dredging, and other surface or subsurface excavations required to determine the nature and size of mineral resource deposits and the feasibility of their development.

(5) The term "mineral resources" means all nonliving natural nonrenewable resources, including fossil fuels, minerals, whether metallic or nonmetallic, but does not include ice, water, or snow.

(6) The term "person" means any individual, corporation, partnership, trust, association, or any other entity existing or organized under the laws of the United States, or any officer, employee, agent, department, or other instrumentality of the Federal Government or of any State or political subdivision thereof.

(7) The term "prospecting" means any activity, including logistic support, the purpose of which is the identification of mineral resource potential for possible exploration and development.

(8) The term "Under Secretary" means the Under Secretary of Commerce for Oceans and Atmosphere.

SEC. 4. PROHIBITION OF ANTARCTIC MINERAL RESOURCE ACTIVITIES.

Pending a new agreement among the Antarctic Treaty Consultative Parties in force for the United States, to which the Senate has given advice and consent or which is authorized by further legislation by the Congress, which provides an indefinite ban on Antarctic mineral resource activities, it is unlawful for any person to engage in, finance, or otherwise knowingly provide assistance to any Antarctic mineral resource activity.

SEC. 5. INTERNATIONAL AGREEMENT.

(a) It is the sense of Congress that the Secretary of State should enter into negotiations with the Antarctic Treaty Consultative Parties to conclude one or more new international agreements to—

(1) conserve and protect permanently the natural environment of Antarctica and its associated and dependent ecosystems;

(2) prohibit or ban indefinitely Antarctic mineral resource activities by all parties to the Antarctic Treaty;

(3) grant Antarctica special protective status as a land of science dedicated to wilderness protection, international cooperation, and scientific research;

(4) ensure that the results of all scientific investigations relating to geological processes and structures be made openly available to the international scientific community, as required by the Antarctic Treaty; and

(5) include other comprehensive measures for the protection of the Antarctic environment.

(b) It is the sense of Congress that any treaty or other international agreement submitted by the President to the Senate for its advice and consent to ratification relating to mineral resources or activities in Antarctica should be consistent with the purpose and provisions of this Act.

SEC. 6. ENFORCEMENT.

(a) IN GENERAL.—A violation of this Act or any regulation promulgated under this Act is deemed to be a violation of the Antarctic Marine Living Resources Convention Act (16 U.S.C. 2431-2444) and shall be enforced under that Act by the Under Secretary or another Federal official to whom the Under Secretary has delegated this responsibility.

(b) PENALTY.—If the Under Secretary determines that a person has violated section 4—

(1) that person shall be ineligible to locate a mining claim under the mining laws of the United States; and

(2) the Secretary of the Interior shall refuse to issue a patent under the mining laws of the United States, or a lease under the laws of the United States related to mineral or geothermal leasing, to any such person who attempts to perfect such patent or lease application after the Under Secretary has made such determination.

SEC. 7. AUTHORIZATION OF APPROPRIATIONS.

There are authorized to be appropriated—

(1) to the Under Secretary not more than $1,000,000 for each of fiscal years 1991 and 1992 to carry out the purposes of this Act; and

(2) to the Secretary of State not more than $500,000 for each of fiscal years 1991 and 1992 to carry out section 5 of this Act.

Approved November 16, 1990.

LEGISLATIVE HISTORY—H.R. 3977 (S. 2575):

HOUSE REPORTS: No. 101-692, Pt. 1 (Comm. on Merchant Marine and Fisheries).
CONGRESSIONAL RECORD, Vol. 136 (1990):
Oct. 15, considered and passed House.
Oct. 16, S. 2575 considered and passed Senate.
Oct. 24, H.R. 3977 considered and passed Senate, amended.
Oct. 26, House concurred in Senate amendment.
WEEKLY COMPILATION OF PRESIDENTIAL DOCUMENTS, Vol. 26 (1990):
Nov. 16, Presidential remarks.

AVIATION SECURITY IMPROVEMENT ACT OF 1990

An Act to promote and strengthen aviation security, and for other purposes.

Date: November 16, 1990

Bill No.: H.R. 5732

Public Law No.: 101-604

Cite: 104 STAT. 3066

Sections reprinted:

Section 1 - Short title; Table of contents
Section 2 - Findings.

TITLE II - UNITED STATES RESPONSE TO TERRORISM AFFECTING AMERICANS ABROAD

Section 201 - International negotiations concerning aviation security.
Section 202 - Coordinator for counterterrorism.
Section 203 - Passenger manifest.
Section 204 - Department of State notification of families of victims.
Section 205 - Designation of State Department-family liaison and toll-free family communications system.
Section 206 - Disaster training for State Department personnel.
Section 207 - Department of State responsibilities and procedures at international disaster site.
Section 208 - Recovery and disposition of remains and personal effects.
Section 209 - Assessment of Lockerbie experience.
Section 210 - Official Department of State recognition.
Section 211 - United States Government compensation for victim of terrorism.
Section 212 - Overseas security electronic bulletin board.

Public Law 101-604
101st Congress

An Act

To promote and strengthen aviation security, and for other purposes.

Be it enacted by the Senate and House of Representatives of the United States of America in Congress assembled,

SECTION 1. SHORT TITLE; TABLE OF CONTENTS.

(a) SHORT TITLE.—This Act may be cited as the "Aviation Security Improvement Act of 1990".

(b) TABLE OF CONTENTS.—

SEC. 2. FINDINGS.

Congress finds that—

(1) the safety and security of passengers of United States air carriers against terrorist threats should be given the highest priority by the United States Government;

(2) the report of the President's Commission on Aviation Security and Terrorism, dated May 15, 1990, found that current aviation security systems are inadequate to provide such protection;

(3) the United States Government should immediately take steps to ensure fuller compliance with existing laws and regulations relating to aviation security;

(4) the United States Government should work through the International Civil Aviation Organization and directly with foreign governments to enhance aviation security of foreign carriers and at foreign airports;

(5) the United States Government should ensure that enhanced security measures are fully implemented by both United States and foreign air carriers;

(6) all nations belonging to the Summit Seven should promptly amend the Bonn Declaration to extend sanctions for all terrorist acts, including attacks against airports and air carrier ticket offices;

(7) the United States Government, in bilateral negotiations with foreign governments, should emphasize upgrading international aviation security objectives;

(8) the United States Government should have in place a mechanism by which the Government notifies the public, on a case-by-case basis and through the application of a uniform national standard, of certain credible threats to civil aviation security;

(9) the United States Government has a special obligation to United States victims of acts of terrorism directed against this Nation and should provide prompt assistance to the families of such victims and assure that fair and prompt compensation is provided to such victims and their families;

(10) the United States should work with other nations to treat as outlaws state sponsors of terrorism, isolating such sponsors politically, economically, and militarily;

(11) the United States must develop a clear understanding that state-sponsored terrorism threatens United States values and interests, and that active measures are needed to counter more effectively the terrorist threat; and

(12) the United States must have the national will to take every feasible action to prevent, counter, and respond to terrorist activities.

TITLE II—UNITED STATES RESPONSE TO TERRORISM AFFECTING AMERICANS ABROAD

SEC. 201. INTERNATIONAL NEGOTIATIONS CONCERNING AVIATION SECURITY.

(a) UNITED STATES POLICY.—It is the policy of the United States—

(1) to seek bilateral agreements to achieve United States aviation security objectives with foreign governments;

(2) to continue to press vigorously for security improvements through the Foreign Airport Security Act and the foreign airport assessment program; and

(3) to continue to work through the International Civil Aviation Organization to improve aviation security internationally.

(b) NEGOTIATIONS FOR AVIATION SECURITY.—(1) The Department of State, in consultation with the Department of Transportation, shall be responsible for negotiating requisite aviation security agreements with foreign governments concerning the implementation of United States rules and regulations which affect the foreign operations of United States air carriers, foreign air carriers, and foreign international airports. The Secretary of State is directed to enter, expeditiously, into negotiations for bilateral and multilateral agreements—

(A) for enhanced aviation security objectives;

(B) to implement the Foreign Airport Security Act and the foreign airport assessment program to the fullest extent practicable; and

(C) to achieve improved availability of passenger manifest information.

(2) A principal objective of bilateral and multilateral negotiations with foreign governments and the International Civil Aviation Organization shall be improved availability of passenger manifest information.

SEC. 202. COORDINATOR FOR COUNTERTERRORISM.

The Coordinator for Counterterrorism shall be responsible for the coordination of international aviation security for the Department of State.

SEC. 203. PASSENGER MANIFEST.

(a) MANDATORY AVAILABILITY OF PASSENGER MANIFEST.—Section 410 of the Federal Aviation Act of 1958 (49 U.S.C. App. 1380) is amended to read as follows:

"SEC. 410. PASSENGER MANIFEST.

"(a) REQUIREMENT.—Not later than 120 days after the date of the enactment of this section, the Secretary of Transportation shall require all United States air carriers to provide a passenger manifest for any flight to appropriate representatives of the United States Department of State—

"(1) not later than 1 hour after any such carrier is notified of an aviation disaster outside the United States which involves such flight; or

"(2) if it is not technologically feasible or reasonable to fulfill the requirement of this subsection within 1 hour, then as expeditiously as possible, but not later than 3 hours after such notification.

"(b) CONTENTS.—For purposes of this section, a passenger manifest should include the following information:

"(1) The full name of each passenger.

"(2) The passport number of each passenger, if required for travel.

"(3) The name and telephone number of a contact for each passenger.".

(b) IMPLEMENTATION.—In implementing the requirement pursuant to the amendment made by subsection (a) of this section, the Secretary of Transportation shall consider the necessity and feasibility of requiring United States carriers to collect passenger manifest information as a condition for passenger boarding of any flight subject to such requirement.

(c) FOREIGN AIR CARRIERS.—The Secretary of Transportation shall consider a requirement for foreign air carriers comparable to that imposed pursuant to the amendment made by subsection (a).

(d) INFORMATION FROM UNITED STATES PASSPORTS.—Notwithstanding any other provision of law, to the extent provided in appropriation Acts, for each fiscal year not more than $5,000,000 in passport fees collected by the Department of State may be credited to a Department of State account. Amounts credited to such account shall be available only for the costs associated with the acquisition and production of machine-readable United States passports and visas and compatible reading equipment. Amounts credited to such account are authorized to remain available until expended.

(e) CONFORMING AMENDMENT TO TABLE OF CONTENTS.—The table of contents contained in the first section of the Federal Aviation Act of 1958 is amended by striking the item relating to section 410 and inserting the following:

"Sec. 410. Passenger manifest.".

SEC. 204. DEPARTMENT OF STATE NOTIFICATION OF FAMILIES OF VICTIMS.

(a) DEPARTMENT OF STATE POLICY.—It is the policy of the Department of State pursuant to section 43 of the State Department Basic Authorities Act to directly and promptly notify the families of victims of aviation disasters abroad concerning citizens of the United States directly affected by such a disaster, including timely written notice. The Secretary of State shall ensure that such notification by the Department of State is carried out notwithstanding notification by any other person.

(b) DEPARTMENT OF STATE GUIDELINES.—Not later than 60 days after the date of the enactment of this Act, the Secretary of State shall issue such regulations, guidelines, and circulars as are necessary to ensure that the policy under subsection (a) is fully implemented.

SEC. 205. DESIGNATION OF STATE DEPARTMENT-FAMILY LIAISON AND TOLL-FREE FAMILY COMMUNICATIONS SYSTEM.

(a) DESIGNATION OF STATE DEPARTMENT-FAMILY LIAISON.—Not later than 60 days after the date of the enactment of this Act, the Secretary of State shall issue such rules and guidelines as are necessary to provide that in the event of an aviation disaster directly involving United States citizens abroad, if possible, the Department of State will assign a specific individual, and an alternate, as the Department of State liaison for the family of each such citizen.

(b) TOLL-FREE COMMUNICATIONS SYSTEM.—In the establishment of the Department of State toll-free communications system to facilitate inquiries concerning the affect of any disaster abroad on United States citizens residing or traveling abroad, the Secretary of State shall ensure that a toll-free telephone number is reserved for the exclusive use of the families of citizens who have been determined to be directly involved in any such disaster.

SEC. 206. DISASTER TRAINING FOR STATE DEPARTMENT PERSONNEL.

(a) ADDITIONAL TRAINING.—The Secretary of State shall institute a supplemental program of training in disaster management for all consular officers.

(b) TRAINING IMPROVEMENTS.—

(1) In expanding the training program under subsection (a), the Secretary of State shall consult with death and bereavement counselors concerning the particular demands posed by aviation tragedies and terrorist activities.

(2) In providing such additional training under subsection (a) the Secretary of State shall consider supplementing the current training program through—

(A) providing specialized training to create a team of "disaster specialists" to deploy immediately in a crisis; or

(B) securing outside experts to be brought in during the initial phases to assist consular personnel.

SEC. 207. DEPARTMENT OF STATE RESPONSIBILITIES AND PROCEDURES AT INTERNATIONAL DISASTER SITE.

(a) DISPATCH OF SENIOR STATE DEPARTMENT OFFICIAL TO SITE.—Not later than 60 days after the date of the enactment of this Act, the Secretary of State shall issue such rules and guidelines as are necessary to provide that in the event of an international disaster, particularly an aviation tragedy, directly involving significant numbers of United States citizens abroad not less than one senior officer from the Bureau of Consular Affairs of the Department of State shall be dispatched to the site of such disaster.

(b) CRITERIA FOR DEPARTMENT OF STATE STAFFING AT DISASTER SITE.—Not later than 60 days after the date of the enactment of this Act, the Secretary of State shall promulgate criteria for Department of State staffing of disaster sites abroad. Such criteria shall define responsibility for staffing decisions and shall consider the deployment of crisis teams under subsection (d). The Secretary of State shall promptly issue such rules and guidelines as are necessary to implement criteria developed pursuant to this subsection.

(c) STATE DEPARTMENT OMBUDSMAN.—Not later than 60 days after the date of the enactment of this Act, the Secretary of State shall issue such rules and guidelines as are necessary to provide that in the event of an international aviation disaster involving significant numbers of United States citizens abroad not less than one officer or employee of the Department of State shall be dispatched to the disaster site to provide on-site assistance to families who may visit the site and to act as an ombudsman in matters involving the foreign local government authorities and social service agencies.

(d) CRISIS TEAMS.—Not later than 60 days after the date of the enactment of this Act, the Secretary of State shall promulgate procedures for the deployment of a "crisis team", which may include public affairs, forensic, and bereavement experts, to the site of any international disaster involving United States citizens abroad to augment in-country Embassy and consulate staff. The Secretary of State shall promptly issue such rules and guidelines as are necessary to implement procedures developed pursuant to this subsection.

SEC. 208. RECOVERY AND DISPOSITION OF REMAINS AND PERSONAL EFFECTS.

It is the policy of the Department of State (pursuant to section 43 of the State Department Basic Authorities Act) to provide liaison with foreign governments and persons and with United States air carriers concerning arrangements for the preparation and transport to the United States of the remains of citizens who die abroad, as well as the disposition of personal effects. The Secretary of State shall ensure that regulations and guidelines of the Department of State reflect such policy and that such assistance is rendered to the families of United States citizens who are killed in terrorist incidents and disasters abroad.

SEC. 209. ASSESSMENT OF LOCKERBIE EXPERIENCE.

(a) ASSESSMENT.—The Secretary of State shall compile an assessment of the Department of State response to the Pan American Airways Flight 103 aviation disaster over Lockerbie, Scotland, on December 21, 1988.

(b) GUIDELINES.—The Secretary of State shall establish, based on the assessment compiled under subsection (a) and other relevant factors, guidelines for future Department of State responses to comparable disasters and shall distribute such guidelines to all United States diplomatic and consular posts abroad.

SEC. 210. OFFICIAL DEPARTMENT OF STATE RECOGNITION.

Not later than 60 days after the date of the enactment of this Act, the Secretary of State shall promulgate guidelines for appropriate ceremonies or other official expressions of respect and support for the families of United States citizens who are killed through acts of terrorism abroad.

SEC. 211. UNITED STATES GOVERNMENT COMPENSATION FOR VICTIMS OF TERRORISM.

(a) COMPENSATION.—The President shall submit to the Congress, not later than one year after the date of the enactment of this Act, recommendations on whether or not legislation should be enacted to authorize the United States to provide monetary and tax relief as compensation to United States citizens who are victims of terrorism.

(b) BOARD.—The President may establish a board to develop criteria for compensation and to recommend changes to existing laws to establish a single comprehensive approach to victim compensation for terrorist acts.

(c) INCOME TAX BENEFIT FOR VICTIMS OF LOCKERBIE TERRORISM.—

(1) IN GENERAL.—Subject to paragraph (2), in the case of any individual whose death was a direct result of the Pan American Airways Flight 103 terrorist disaster over Lockerbie, Scotland, on December 21, 1988, any tax imposed by subtitle A of the Internal Revenue Code of 1986 shall not apply—

(A) with respect to the taxable year which includes December 21, 1988, and

(B) with respect to the prior taxable year.

(2) LIMITATION.—In no case may the tax benefit pursuant to paragraph (1) for any taxable year, for any individual, exceed an amount equal to 28 percent of the annual rate of basic pay at Level V of the Executive Schedule of the United States as of December 21, 1988.

SEC. 212. OVERSEAS SECURITY ELECTRONIC BULLETIN BOARD.

Not later than 60 days after the date of the enactment of this Act, the Secretary of State shall issue such rules and regulations as may be necessary to establish, under the Bureau of Consular Affairs, an electronic bulletin board accessible to the general public. Such bulletin board shall contain all information, updated daily, which is available on the Overseas Security Electronic Bulletin Board of the Bureau of Diplomatic Security.

SEC. 213. ANTITERRORISM ASSISTANCE.

(a) AVIATION SECURITY.—In addition to amounts otherwise authorized to be appropriated, there are authorized to be appropriated $7,000,000 for fiscal year 1991 for aviation security assistance under chapter 8 of part II of the Foreign Assistance Act of 1961 (22 U.S.C. 2349aa et seq.), relating to antiterrorism assistance.

(b) TRAINING SERVICES.—Section 573 of the Foreign Assistance Act of 1961 (22 U.S.C. 2349aa2) is amended in subsection (d) by striking out paragraphs (1), (2), and (3) and inserting in lieu thereof the following new paragraphs:

"(1) Training services (including short term refresher training) provided pursuant to this chapter may be conducted outside the United States only if—

"(A) the training to be conducted outside the United States will be provided during a period of not more than 30 days;

"(B) such training relates to—

"(i) aviation security;

"(ii) crisis management;

"(iii) document screening techniques;

"(iv) facility security;

"(v) maritime security;

"(vi) VIP protection; or

"(vii) the handling of detector dogs, except that only short term refresher training may be provided under this clause; and

"(C) at least 15 days before such training is to begin, the Committee on Foreign Affairs of the House of Representatives and the Committee on Foreign Relations of the Senate are notified in accordance with the procedures applicable to reprogramming notifications.

"(2) Personnel of the United States Government authorized to advise eligible foreign countries on antiterrorism matters shall carry out their responsibilities, to the maximum extent possible, within the United States. Such personnel may provide advice outside the United States on antiterrorism matters to eligible foreign countries for periods not to exceed 30 consecutive calendar days.

"(3)(A) Except as provided in subparagraph (B), employees of the Department of State shall not engage in the training of law enforcement personnel or the provision of services under this chapter.

"(B) Subparagraph (A) does not apply to training (including short term refresher training) or services provided to law enforcement personnel by employees of the Bureau of Diplomatic Security with regard to crisis management, facility security, or VIP protection.".

SEC. 211. ANTITERRORISM MEASURES.

(a) GUIDELINES FOR INTERNATIONAL AVIATION TRAVELERS.—For the purpose of notifying the public, the Secretary of State, in consultation with the Secretary of Transportation, shall develop and publish guidelines for thwarting efforts by international terrorists to enlist the unwitting assistance of international aviation travelers in terrorist activities. Notices concerning such guidelines shall be posted and prominently displayed domestically and abroad in international airports.

(b) DEVELOPMENT OF INTERNATIONAL STANDARDS.—The Secretary of State and the Secretary of Transportation in all appropriate fora, particularly talks and meetings related to international civil aviation, shall enter into negotiations with other nations for the establishment of international standards regarding guidelines for thwarting efforts by international terrorists to enlist the unwitting assistance of international aviation travelers in terrorist activities.

(c) PUBLICATION OF REWARDS FOR TERRORISM-RELATED INFORMATION.—For the purpose of notifying the public, the Secretary of State shall publish the availability of United States Government rewards for information on international terrorist-related activities, including rewards available under section 36(a) of the State Department Basic Authorities Act of 1956 (22 U.S.C. 2708(a)) and chapter 204 of title 18, United States Code. To the extent appropriate and feasible, notices making such publication shall be posted and prominently displayed domestically and abroad in international airports.

(d) SENSE OF CONGRESS.—It is the sense of Congress that the Secretary of Transportation should take appropriate measures to utilize and train properly the officers and employees of other United

States Government agencies who have functions at international airports in the United States and abroad in the detection of explosives and firearms which could be a threat to international civil aviation.

SEC. 215. PROPOSAL FOR CONSIDERATION BY THE INTERNATIONAL CIVIL AVIATION ORGANIZATION.

Not later than 60 days after the date of the enactment of this Act, the Secretary of State, in consultation with the Secretary of Transportation, shall propose to the International Civil Aviation Organization the establishment of a comprehensive aviation security program which shall include (1) training for airport security personnel, (2) grants for security equipment acquisition for certain nations, and (3) expansion of the appropriate utilization of canine teams in the detection of explosive devices in all airport areas, including use in passenger screening areas and nonpublic baggage assembly and processing areas.

Approved November 16, 1990.

LEGISLATIVE HISTORY—H.R. 5732:

CONGRESSIONAL RECORD, Vol. 136 (1990):
- Oct. 1, considered and passed House.
- Oct. 23, considered and passed Senate, amended.
- Oct. 24, House concurred in Senate amendment.

WEEKLY COMPILATION OF PRESIDENTIAL DOCUMENTS, Vol. 26 (1990):
- Nov. 16, Presidential statement.

O

GLOBAL CHANGE RESEARCH ACT OF 1990

An Act to require the establishment of a United States Global Change Research Program aimed at understanding and responding to global change, including the cumulative effects of human activities and natural processes on the environment, to promote discussions toward international protocols in global change research, and for other purposes.

Date: November 16, 1990

Bill No.: S. 169

Public Law No.: 101-606

Cite: 104 STAT. 3096

Sections reprinted:

Section 1 - Short title.
Section 2 - Definitions.
TITLE II - INTERNATIONAL COOPERATION IN GLOBAL CHANGE RESEARCH
Section 201 - Short title.
Section 202 - Findings and purposes.
Section 203 - International discussions.
Section 204 - Global Change Research Information Office.

Public Law 101-606
101st Congress

An Act

To require the establishment of a United States Global Change Research Program aimed at understanding and responding to global change, including the cumulative effects of human activities and natural processes on the environment, to promote discussions toward international protocols in global change research, and for other purposes.

Be it enacted by the Senate and House of Representatives of the United States of America in Congress assembled,

SECTION 1. SHORT TITLE.

This Act may be cited as the "Global Change Research Act of 1990".

SEC. 2. DEFINITIONS.

As used in this Act, the term—

(1) "Committee" means the Committee on Earth and Environmental Sciences established under section 102;

(2) "Council" means the Federal Coordinating Council on Science, Engineering, and Technology;

(3) "global change" means changes in the global environment (including alterations in climate, land productivity, oceans or other water resources, atmospheric chemistry, and ecological systems) that may alter the capacity of the Earth to sustain life;

(4) "global change research" means study, monitoring, assessment, prediction, and information management activities to describe and understand—

(A) the interactive physical, chemical, and biological processes that regulate the total Earth system;

(B) the unique environment that the Earth provides for life;

(C) changes that are occurring in the Earth system; and

(D) the manner in which such system, environment, and changes are influenced by human actions;

(5) "Plan" means the National Global Change Research Plan developed under section 104, or any revision thereof; and

(6) "Program" means the United States Global Change Research Program established under section 103.

TITLE II—INTERNATIONAL COOPERATION IN GLOBAL CHANGE RESEARCH

SEC. 201. SHORT TITLE.

This title may be cited as the "International Cooperation in Global Change Research Act of 1990".

SEC. 202. FINDINGS AND PURPOSES.

(a) FINDINGS.—The Congress makes the following findings:

(1) Pooling of international resources and scientific capabilities will be essential to a successful international global change program.

(2) While international scientific planning is already underway, there is currently no comprehensive intergovernmental mechanism for planning, coordinating, or implementing research to understand global change and to mitigate possible adverse effects.

(3) An international global change research program will be

important in building future consensus on methods for reducing global environmental degradation.

(4) The United States, as a world leader in environmental and Earth sciences, should help provide leadership in developing and implementing an international global change research program.

(b) PURPOSES.—The purposes of this title are to—

(1) promote international, intergovernmental cooperation on global change research;

(2) involve scientists and policymakers from developing nations in such cooperative global change research programs; and

(3) promote international efforts to provide technical and other assistance to developing nations which will facilitate improvements in their domestic standard of living while minimizing damage to the global or regional environment.

SEC. 203. INTERNATIONAL DISCUSSIONS.

(a) GLOBAL CHANGE RESEARCH.—The President should direct the Secretary of State, in cooperation with the Committee, to initiate discussions with other nations leading toward international protocols and other agreements to coordinate global change research activities. Such discussions should include the following issues:

(1) Allocation of costs in global change research programs, especially with respect to major capital projects.

(2) Coordination of global change research plans with those developed by international organizations such as the International Council on Scientific Unions, the World Meteorological Organization, and the United Nations Environment Program.

(3) Establishment of global change research centers and training programs for scientists, especially those from developing nations.

(4) Development of innovative methods for management of international global change research, including—

(A) use of new or existing intergovernmental organizations for the coordination or funding of global change research; and

(B) creation of a limited foundation for global change research.

(5) The prompt establishment of international projects to—

(A) create globally accessible formats for data collected by various international sources; and

(B) combine and interpret data from various sources to produce information readily usable by policymakers attempting to formulate effective strategies for preventing, mitigating, and adapting to possible adverse effects of global change.

(6) Establishment of international offices to disseminate information useful in identifying, preventing, mitigating, or adapting to the possible effects of global change.

(b) ENERGY RESEARCH.—The President should direct the Secretary of State (in cooperation with the Secretary of Energy, the Secretary of Commerce, the United States Trade Representative, and other appropriate members of the Committee) to initiate discussions with other nations leading toward an international research protocol for cooperation on the development of energy technologies which have minimally adverse effects on the environment. Such discussions should include, but not be limited to, the following issues:

(1) Creation of an international cooperative program to fund research related to energy efficiency, solar and other renewable

energy sources, and passively safe and diversion-resistant nuclear reactors.

(2) Creation of an international cooperative program to develop low cost energy technologies which are appropriate to the environmental, economic, and social needs of developing nations.

(3) Exchange of information concerning environmentally safe energy technologies and practices, including those described in paragraphs (1) and (2).

SEC. 204. GLOBAL CHANGE RESEARCH INFORMATION OFFICE.

Not more than 180 days after the date of enactment of this Act, the President shall, in consultation with the Committee and all relevant Federal agencies, establish an Office of Global Change Research Information. The purpose of the Office shall be to disseminate to foreign governments, businesses, and institutions, as well as the citizens of foreign countries, scientific research information available in the United States which would be useful in preventing, mitigating, or adapting to the effects of global change. Such information shall include, but need not be limited to, results of scientific research and development on technologies useful for—

(1) reducing energy consumption through conservation and energy efficiency;

(2) promoting the use of solar and renewable energy sources which reduce the amount of greenhouse gases released into the atmosphere;

(3) developing replacements for chlorofluorocarbons, halons, and other ozone-depleting substances which exhibit a significantly reduced potential for depleting stratospheric ozone;

(4) promoting the conservation of forest resources which help reduce the amount of carbon dioxide in the atmosphere;

(5) assisting developing countries in ecological pest management practices and in the proper use of agricultural, and industrial chemicals; and

(6) promoting recycling and source reduction of pollutants in order to reduce the volume of waste which must be disposed of, thus decreasing energy use and greenhouse gas emissions.

LEGISLATIVE HISTORY—S. 169:

SENATE REPORTS: No. 101-40 (Comm. on Commerce, Science, and Transportation).
CONGRESSIONAL RECORD, Vol. 136 (1990):
Feb. 6, considered and passed Senate.
Oct. 26, considered and passed House, amended.
Oct. 27, Senate concurred in House amendments.
WEEKLY COMPILATION OF PRESIDENTIAL DOCUMENTS, Vol. 26 (1990):
Nov. 16, Presidential remarks.

O

NATIONAL AERONAUTICS AND SPACE ADMINISTRATION AUTHORIZATION ACT, FISCAL YEAR 1991

An Act to authorize appropriations for the National Aeronautics and Space Administration for research and development, space flight, control and data communications, construction of facilities, and research and program management, and for other purposes.

Date: November 16, 1990

Bill No.: S. 2287

Public Law No.: 101-611

Cite: 104 STAT. 3188

Sections reprinted:

Section 1 - Short title.

TITLE I - NATIONAL AERONAUTICS AND SPACE ADMINISTRATION AUTHORIZATIONS.

Section 101 - Findings.

Section 102 - Policy

Section 112 - Space shuttle use policy.

Section 113 - Life sciences strategic plan.

Section 114 - Study on international cooperation in planetary exploration.

TITLE II - LAUNCH SERVICES PURCHASE.

Section 201 - Short title.

Section 202 - Findings.

Section 203 - Definitions.

Section 204 - Requirement to procure commercial launch services.

Section 205 - Purchase of launch services.

Section 206 - Other activities of the National Aeronautics and Space Administration.

Public Law 101-611
101st Congress

An Act

To authorize appropriations to the National Aeronautics and Space Administration for research and development, space flight, control and data communications, construction of facilities, and research and program management, and for other purposes.

Be it enacted by the Senate and House of Representatives of the United States of America in Congress assembled,

SECTION 1. SHORT TITLE.

This Act may be cited as the "National Aeronautics and Space Administration Authorization Act, Fiscal Year 1991".

TITLE I—NATIONAL AERONAUTICS AND SPACE ADMINISTRATION AUTHORIZATIONS

SEC. 101. FINDINGS.

The Congress finds that—

(1) over the next decade, the United States aeronautics and space program will be directed toward major national priorities of understanding, preserving, and enhancing our global environment, hypersonic transportation, human exploration, and emerging technology commercialization;

(2) the United States aeronautics and space program is supported by an overwhelming majority of the American people;

(3) the United States aeronautics and space program genuinely reflects our Nation's pioneer heritage and demonstrates our quest for leadership, economic growth, and human understanding;

(4) the United States space program is based on a solid record of achievement and continues to promote the objective of international cooperation in the exploration of the planets and the universe;

(5) the United States aeronautics and space program generates critical technology breakthroughs that benefit our economy through new products and processes that significantly improve our standard of living;

(6) the United States aeronautics and space program excites the imagination of every generation and can stimulate the youth of our Nation toward the pursuit of excellence in the fields of science, engineering, and mathematics;

(7) the United States aeronautics and space program contributes to the Nation's technological competitive advantage;

(8) the United States aeronautics and space program requires a sustained commitment of financial and human resources as a share of the Nation's Gross National Product;

(9) the United States space transportation system will depend upon a robust fleet of space shuttle orbiters and expendable and reusable launch vehicles and services;

(10) the United States space program will be advanced with an assured funding stream for the development of a permanently manned space station with research, experimentation, observation, servicing, manufacturing, and staging capabilities for lunar and Mars missions;

(11) the United States aeronautics program has been a key factor in maintaining preeminence in aviation over many decades;

(12) the United States needs to maintain a strong program with respect to transatmospheric research and technology by developing and demonstrating National Aero-Space Plane technology by a mid-decade date certain;

(13) the National Aeronautics and Space Administration is primarily responsible for formulating and implementing policy that supports and encourages civil aeronautics and space activities in the United States; and

(14) commercial activities of the private sector will substantially and increasingly contribute to the strength of both the United States space program and the national economy.

SEC. 102. POLICY.

It is declared to be national policy that the United States should—

(1) rededicate itself to the goal of leadership in critical areas of space science, space exploration, and space commercialization;

(2) increase its commitment of budgetary resources for the space program to reverse the dramatic decline in real spending for such program since the achievements of the Apollo moon program;

(3) ensure that the long-range environmental impact of all activities carried out under this title are fully understood and considered;

(4) promote and support efforts to advance scientific understanding by conducting or otherwise providing for research on environmental problems, including global change, ozone depletion, acid precipitation, deforestation, and smog;

(5) forge a robust national space program that maintains a healthy balance between manned and unmanned space activities and recognizes the mutually reinforcing benefits of both;

(6) maintain an active fleet of space shuttle orbiters, including an adequate provision of structural spare parts, and evolve the orbiter design to improve safety and performance, and reduce operational costs;

(7) sustain a mixed fleet by utilizing commercial expendable launch vehicle services to the fullest extent practicable;

(8) support an aggressive program of research and development designed to enhance the United States preeminence in launch vehicles;

(9) continue and complete on schedule the development and deployment of a permanently manned, fully capable, space station;

(10) develop an advanced, high pressure space suit to support extravehicular activity that will be required for Space Station Freedom when Assembly Complete is reached;

(11) establish a dual capability for logistics and resupply of the space station utilizing the space shuttle and expendable launch vehicles, including commercial services if available;

(12) continue to seek opportunities for international cooperation in space and fully support international cooperative agreements;

(13) maintain an aggressive program of aeronautical research and technology development designed to enhance the United States preeminence in civil and military aviation and improve the safety and efficiency of the United States air transportation system;

(14) conduct a program of technology maturation, including flight demonstration in 1997, to prove the feasibility of an air-breathing, hypersonic aerospace plane capable of single-stage-to-orbit operation and hypersonic cruise in the atmosphere;

(15) seek innovative technologies that will make possible advanced human exploration initiatives, such as the establishment of a lunar base and the succeeding mission to Mars, and provide high yield technology advancements for the national economy; and

(16) enhance the human resources of the Nation and the quality of education.

SEC. 112. SPACE SHUTTLE USE POLICY.

(a)(1) It shall be the policy of the United States to use the Space Shuttle for purposes that (i) require the presence of man, (ii) require the unique capabilities of the Space Shuttle or (iii) when other compelling circumstances exist.

(2) The term "compelling circumstances" includes, but is not limited to, occasions when the Administrator determines, in consultation with the Secretary of Defense and the Secretary of State, that important national security or foreign policy interests would be served by a Shuttle launch.

(3) The policy stated in subsection (a)(1) shall not preclude the use of available cargo space, on a Space Shuttle mission otherwise consistent with the policy described under subsection (a)(1), for the purpose of carrying secondary payloads (as defined by the Administrator) that do not require the presence of man if such payloads are consistent with the requirements of research, development, demonstration, scientific, commercial, and educational programs authorized by the Administrator.

(b) The Administrator shall, within six months after the date of enactment of this Act, submit a report to the Congress setting forth a plan for the implementation of the policy described in subsection (a)(1). Such plan shall include—

(1) details of the implementation plan;

(2) a list of purposes that meet such policy;

(3) a proposed schedule for the implementation of such policy;

(4) an estimate of the costs to the United States of implementing such policy; and

(5) a process for informing the Congress in a timely and regular manner of how the plan is being implemented.

(c) At least annually, the Administrator shall submit to the Congress a report certifying that the payloads scheduled to be launched on the space shuttle for the next four years are consistent with the policy set forth in subsection (a)(1). For each payload scheduled to be launched from the space shuttle, which do not require the presence of man, the Administrator shall, in the certified report to Congress, state the specific circumstances which justified the use of the space shuttle. If, during the period between scheduled reports to the Congress, any additions are made to the list of certified payloads intended to be launched from the Shuttle, the

Administrator shall inform the Congress of the additions and the reasons therefor within 45 days of the change.

(d) The report described in subsection (c) shall also include those National Aeronautics and Space Administration payloads designed solely to fly on the space shuttle which have begun the phase C/D of its development cycle.

SEC. 113. LIFE SCIENCES STRATEGIC PLAN.

(a) FINDINGS.—The Congress finds that—

(1) the current knowledge base in life sciences is not compatible with the National Aeronautics and Space Administration's current objectives in space, and the National Aeronautics and Space Administration lacks an adequate strategic plan to acquire a knowledge base;

(2) it is critical to the success of manned missions in space, be they commercial operations of microgravity laboratories or manned missions to Mars, that a realistic appraisal of the influences of the space environment on biological systems is completed and appropriate protective countermeasures developed;

(3) the space station is rapidly approaching design maturity without a corresponding development of the physiological and other human factors knowledge base necessary for long-term manned operations in space; and

(4) space station laboratory hardware specifications are being fixed before fully establishing the objectives and requirements for life sciences research.

(b) STRATEGIC PLAN.—The Administration shall—

(1) review currently proposed manned space flight missions in order to—

(A) identify the physiological and other human factors knowledge base necessary to determine the human capacity to adapt to and perform effectively in the space environment according to mission requirements, including identifying which life sciences parameters must be measured and which technologies, processes, and procedures must be developed; and

(B) develop a schedule indicating when specific components of information, technologies, processes, or procedures identified under subparagraph (A) will need to be acquired or developed in order to verify that human adaptability requirements of manned space flight missions can be achieved;

(2) develop a strategy plan for life sciences research and technology development sufficient to accomplish the life sciences knowledge base acquisition schedule developed under paragraph (1)(B), including—

(A) a crew certification plan setting acceptable crew conditioning standards for Extended Duration Orbiter operations and verifying countermeasures sufficient to meet those standards before actual Extended Duration Orbiter operations; and

(B) a life sciences implementation plan for the design and development of the space station, to be provided as part of the Preliminary Design Review for the space station, and to include crew adaptability standards; and

(3) verify the physiological and technical feasibility of the life sciences implementation plan developed under paragraph (2)(B), as part of the Critical Design Review for the space station.

SEC. 114. STUDY ON INTERNATIONAL COOPERATION IN PLANETARY EXPLORATION.

(a) FINDINGS.—The Congress finds that—

(1) the President on July 20, 1989, established the long-range goal of establishing a lunar base, followed by manned exploration of Mars in the early twenty-first century;

(2) the United States and the Soviet Union, in cooperation with other countries, are currently planning further unmanned missions to the Moon and to Mars with the possible goal of landing a human on Mars;

(3) a series of international missions to expand human presence beyond Earth orbit would further a spirit of, and follow through on the commitment made in, the 1987 agreement between the Soviet Union and the United States for space cooperation, as well as the successful cooperative agreements the United States has pursued with over one hundred countries since its inception, including the agreement with Japan, Canada, and the European countries for Space Station Freedom;

(4) international manned missions beyond Earth orbit could further encourage a cooperative approach in world affairs unrelated to activities in space;

(5) international manned missions beyond Earth orbit could save the individual nations involved tens of billions of dollars over national missions; and

(6) a multilateral effort for manned missions to establish a lunar colony, a Mars mission, and any other missions that have the goal of establishing human presence beyond Earth's orbit and possibly landing a human on Mars would lead to greater understanding of our universe and greater sensitivity to our own planet.

(b) STUDY.—The National Space Council shall conduct a study on International Cooperation in Planetary Exploration (hereafter in this section referred to as the "study").

(c) PURPOSE OF STUDY.—The purpose of the study is—

(1) to develop an inventory of technologies and intentions of all national space agencies with regard to lunar and planetary exploration, both manned and unmanned;

(2) to seek ways, through direct communication with appropriate officials of other nations or otherwise, to enhance the planning and exchange of information and data among the United States, the Soviet Union, European countries, Canada, Japan, and other interested countries with respect to unmanned projects beyond Earth orbit, in anticipation of later international manned missions to the Moon and to other bodies, including the possible goal of an international manned mission to Mars;

(3) to prepare a detailed proposal that most efficiently uses the resources of the national space agencies in cooperative endeavors to establish human presence beyond Earth orbit;

(4) to develop priority goals that accomplish unmet needs that could not be achieved by any individual country;

(5) to explore the possibilities of international unmanned probes to the Moon and Mars, and the possibilities for international manned missions beyond Earth's orbit; and

(6) to devise strategies for such cooperation that would prevent the unwanted transfer of technology.

In developing the inventory under paragraph (1), and in preparing the detailed proposal under paragraph (3), consideration shall be given to the potential contributions of commercial providers of space goods and services.

(d) REPORT.—The National Space Council shall, within one year after the date of the enactment of this Act, prepare and submit to Congress a report—

(1) outlining a preliminary strategy for cooperation among the United States, the Soviet Union, European countries, Canada, Japan, and other interested countries, based on their respective national strengths, with respect to unmanned projects beyond Earth orbit, in anticipation of later international manned missions to the Moon and to other bodies, including the possible goal of an international manned mission to Mars;

(2) including a conceptual design of a possible international manned mission, in coordination with the preliminary strategy referred to in paragraph (1), with target dates and a breakdown of responsibilities by nation;

(3) containing an inventory of planned and anticipated missions, manned and unmanned, that are being considered by national space agencies and commercial providers of space goods and services; and

(4) containing an inventory of space exploration technologies that either—

(A) are not immediately available in the United States but are available from other nations; or

(B) are available in the United States but are available from other nations in equal or superior form.

TITLE II—LAUNCH SERVICES PURCHASE

SEC. 201. SHORT TITLE.

This title may be cited as the "Launch Services Purchase Act of 1990".

SEC. 202. FINDINGS.

The Congress finds that—

(1) the United States commercial launch industry is technically capable of providing reliable and cost efficient access to space and is an essential component of national efforts to assure access to space for Government and commercial users;

(2) the Federal Government should encourage, facilitate, and promote the United States commercial launch industry, including the development and enhancement of commercial launch facilities, in order to ensure United States economic preeminence in space;

(3) the interests of the United States will be served if the commercial launch industry is competitive in the international marketplace;

(4) commercial vehicles are effective means to challenge foreign competition;

(5) the use by the Federal Government of performance specifically in lieu of detailed specifications relating to vehicle design, construction, and operation will facilitate the efficient operation of the United States commercial launch industry;

(6) the procurement of commercial launch services in a commercially reasonable manner permits a reduced level of Federal Government regulation and oversight and economies of scale which may result in significant cost savings to the commercial launch industry and to the United States.

(7) it is the general policy of the Federal Government to purchase needed goods and services, including launch services, from the private sector to the fullest extent feasible; and

(8) predictable access to National Aeronautics and Space Administration launch markets would encourage continuing United States private sector investment in space and related activities.

SEC. 203. DEFINITIONS.

For the purposes of this title—

(1) the term "commercial provider" means any person providing launch services, but does not include the Federal Government;

(2) the term "launch services" means activities involved in the preparation of a launch vehicle and its payload for space transport and the conduct of transporting a payload;

(3) the term "launch vehicle" means any vehicle constructed for the purpose of operating in, or placing a payload in, outer space; and

(4) the term "payload" means an object which a person undertakes to place in outer space by means of a launch vehicle, and includes subcomponents of the launch vehicle specifically designed or adapted for that object.

SEC. 204. REQUIREMENT TO PROCURE COMMERCIAL LAUNCH SERVICES.

(a) In General.—Except as otherwise provided in this section, the National Aeronautics and Space Administration shall purchase launch services for its primary payloads from commercial providers whenever such services are required in the course of its activities.

(b) Exceptions.—The National Aeronautics and Space Administration shall not be required to purchase launch services as provided in subsection (a) if, on a case by case basis the Administrator of the National Aeronautics and Space Administration determines that—

(1) the payload requires the unique capabilities of the space shuttle;

(2) cost effective commercial launch services to meet specific mission requirements are not reasonably available and would not be available when required;

(3) the use of commercial launch services poses an unacceptable risk of loss of a unique scientific opportunity; or

(4) the payload serves national security or foreign policy purposes.

Upon any such determination, the Administrator shall, within 30 days, notify in writing the Committee on Science, Space, and Technology of the House of Representatives and the Committee on Commerce, Science, and Transportation of the Senate of the determination and its rationale.

(c) National Aeronautics and Space Administration Launch Vehicles.—Launch vehicles shall be acquired or owned by the National Aeronautics and Space Administration only—

(1) as required under circumstances described in subsection (b); or

(2) by the National Aeronautics and Space Administration for conducting research and development on, and testing of, launch technology.

(d) Phase-In Period.—Subsections (a) and (c) shall not apply to launch services and launch vehicles purchased by the National Aeronautics and Space Administration before the date of enactment of this Act.

(e) Historical Purposes.—This title shall not be interpreted to prohibit the National Aeronautics and Space Administration from acquiring, owning, or maintaining launch vehicles solely for historical display purposes.

SEC. 205. PURCHASE OF LAUNCH SERVICES.

(a) Full and Open Competition.—(1) Contracts to provide launch services to the National Aeronautics and Space Administration under section 204 shall be awarded on the basis of full, fair, and open competition, consistent with section 2304 of title 10, United States Code, and section 311 of the National Aeronautics and Space Act of 1958.

(2) The National Aeronautics and Space Administration shall limit its requirements for submission of cost or pricing data in support of a bid or proposal to that data which is reasonably required to protect the interests of the United States.

(b) Specification Systems.—Reasonable performance specifications, not detailed Government design or construction specifications, shall be used to the maximum extent feasible to define requirements for a commercial provider bidding to provide launch services. This subsection shall not preclude the National Aeronautics and Space Administration from requiring compliance with applicable safety standards.

SEC. 206. OTHER ACTIVITIES OF THE NATIONAL AERONAUTICS AND SPACE ADMINISTRATION.

(a) Commercial Payloads on the Space Shuttle.—Commercial payloads may not be accepted for launch as primary payloads on the space shuttle unless the Administrator of the National Aeronautics and Space Administration determines that—

(1) the payload requires the unique capabilities of the space shuttle; or

(2) launching of the payload on the space shuttle is important for either national security or foreign policy purposes.

(b) Report.—By March 15, 1991, the Administrator, in consultation with the Office of Federal Procurement Policy, shall submit to the Committee on Science, Space, and Technology of the House of Representatives and the Committee on Commerce, Science, and Transportation of the Senate a report outlining the minimal requirements for documentation and other administrative data needed to procure launch services in a commercially reasonable manner, including—

(1) the need for data to integrate a payload with a launch vehicle;

(2) the need for data to carry out mission-specific modifications to the launch vehicle;

(3) the need for notification to the National Aeronautics and Space Administration of changes, delays, or difficulties in the construction or preparation of a launch vehicle that may affect the delivery of its payload to its destination at the time and under the conditions provided for under the contract between the United States and its contractors;

(4) the need for data to protect public health and safety; and

(5) the need for cost or pricing data for the fulfillment of a contract.

Approved November 16, 1990.

LEGISLATIVE HISTORY—S. 2287:

SENATE REPORTS: No. 101-455 (Comm. on Commerce, Science, and Transportation).
CONGRESSIONAL RECORD, Vol. 136 (1990):
Oct. 24, considered and passed Senate.
Oct. 25, considered and passed House.

NEW ANTARCTIC PROTECTION TREATY JOINT RESOLUTION, 1990

Joint Resolution calls for the United States to encourage immediate negotiations toward a new agreement among Antarctic Treaty Consultative Parties, for the full protection of Antarctica as a global ecological commons.

Date: November 16, 1990

Bill No.: S.J. Res. 206

Public Law No.: 101-620

Cite: 104 STAT. 3340.

Sections reprinted: All.

Public Law 101-620
101st Congress
Joint Resolution

Calling for the United States to encourage immediate negotiations toward a new agreement among Antarctic Treaty Consultative Parties, for the full protection of Antarctica as a global ecological commons.

Whereas Antarctica, like the great oceans and the atmosphere, is a part of the global commons;

Whereas the Antarctic region, including the continent and the Southern Ocean, is a fragile ecosystem that supports an amazing abundance of life, and is, in turn, crucial to other life on Earth;

Whereas Antarctica is a critical area in the study and documentation of global change;

Whereas negotations of the Antarctic Treaty Consultative Parties have resulted in the Convention on the Regulation of Antarctic Mineral Resource Activities;

Whereas the Convention on the Regulation of Antarctic Mineral Resource Activities, while requiring consideration of environmental impacts prior to allowing minerals development in Antarctica, does not guarantee preservation of the Antarctic environment; and

Whereas the challenge to humankind is to ensure that Antarctica is stewarded in a manner that conserves its unique environment and preserves its value for scientific research: Now, therefore, be it

Resolved by the Senate and House of Representatives of the United States of America in Congress assembled, That—

(1) Antarctica is a global ecological commons, and should, therefore, be subject to a new agreement or protocol which supplement the Antarctic Treaty of 1959, providing for comprehensive environmental protection of Antarctica, and which should for an indefinite period establish Antarctica as a region closed to commercial minerals development and related activities;

(2) under such new agreements, information about mineral or other resources in Antarctica should be obtained under strictly controlled arrangements and should be openly shared in the international scientific community;

(3) the Convention on the Regulation of Antarctic Mineral Resource Activities, though a considerable step forward, does not guarantee protection of the fragile environment of Antarctica and could actually stimulate movement toward commercial exploitation;

(4) pending the negotiation and entry into force of the new agreements referred to in paragraph (1) the Convention on the Regulation of Antarctic Mineral Resource Activities should not be presented to the Senate for advice and consent to ratification;

(5) until such new agreements enter into force, the United States should support the interim restraint measures currently in effect among the Consultative Parties to the Antarctic Treaty; and

(6) the negotiation of a new agreements referred to in paragraph (1) should be fully supported by the United States at the November 1990 meeting of the Antarctic Treaty Consultative Parties in Santiago, Chile.

Approved November 16, 1990.

LEGISLATIVE HISTORY—S.J. Res. 206 (H.J. Res. 418):

CONGRESSIONAL RECORD, Vol. 136 (1990):
Oct. 1, H.J. Res. 418 considered and passed House.
Oct. 4, S.J. Res. 206 considered and passed Senate.
Oct. 23, considered and passed House, amended.
Oct. 24, Senate concurred in House amendment.

O

INTERNATIONAL NARCOTICS CONTROL ACT OF 1990

An Act to authorize international narcotics control activities for fiscal year 1991, and for other purposes.

Date: November 21, 1990

Bill No.: H.R. 5567

Public Law No.: 101-623

Cite: 104 STAT. 3350

Sections reprinted:

Section 1 - Short title and table of contents.
Section 4 - General provisions relating to assistance for Andean countries.
Section 8 - Number of members of United States Armed Forces in Andean countries.
Section 11 - Extradition of United States citizens.
Section 12 - Congressional review of narcotics-related assistance for Afghanistan.
Section 13 - Training of host country pilots.
Section 17 - Debt-for-drugs exchanges.

Public Law 101-623
101st Congress

An Act

To authorize international narcotics control activities for fiscal year 1991, and for other purposes.

Be it enacted by the Senate and House of Representatives of the United States of America in Congress assembled,

SECTION 1. SHORT TITLE AND TABLE OF CONTENTS.

(a) SHORT TITLE.—This Act may be cited as the "International Narcotics Control Act of 1990".

(b) TABLE OF CONTENTS.—The table of contents for this Act is as follows:

SEC. 4. GENERAL PROVISIONS RELATING TO ASSISTANCE FOR ANDEAN COUNTRIES.

(a) PRESIDENTIAL DETERMINATION REQUIRED.—Assistance may be provided for an Andean country pursuant to the authorizations of appropriations provided in section 2(a) and section 3(a), and excess defense articles may be transferred to Bolivia, Colombia, or Peru in fiscal year 1991 pursuant to section 517 of the Foreign Assistance Act of 1961 (22 U.S.C. 2321k), only if the President determines that—

(1) that country is implementing programs to reduce the flow of cocaine to the United States in accordance with a bilateral or multilateral agreement, to which the United States is a party, that contains specific, quantitative and qualitative, performance criteria with respect to those programs;

(2) the armed forces and law enforcement agencies of that country are not engaged in a consistent pattern of gross violations of internationally recognized human rights, and the government of that country has made significant progress in protecting internationally recognized human rights, particularly in—

(A) ensuring that torture, cruel, inhuman, or degrading treatment or punishment, incommunicado detention or detention without charges and trial, disappearances, and other flagrant denials of the right to life, liberty, or security of the person, are not practiced; and

(B) permitting an unimpeded investigation of alleged violations of internationally recognized human rights, including providing access to places of detention, by appropriate international organizations (including nongovernmental organizations such as the International Committee of the Red Cross) or groups acting under the authority of the United Nations or the Organization of American States; and

(3) the government of that country has effective control over police and military operations related to counternarcotics and counterinsurgency activities.

(b) NOTIFICATIONS TO CONGRESS.—Not less than 15 days before funds are obligated pursuant to section 2(a) or section 3(a), the President shall transmit to the congressional committees specified in section 634A(a) of the Foreign Assistance Act of 1961 (22 U.S.C. 2394-1) a written notification in accordance with the procedures applicable to reprogrammings under that section. Such notification shall specify—

(1) the country to which the assistance is to be provided;

(2) the type and value of the assistance to be provided;

(3) in the case of assistance provided pursuant to section 3(a), the law enforcement or other units that will receive the assistance; and

(4) an explanation of how the proposed assistance will further—

(A) the objectives specified in subsection (a) of this section, and

(B) in the case of assistance under section 3(a), the purposes specified in section 3(b).

(c) COORDINATION WITH INTERNATIONAL NARCOTICS CONTROL ASSISTANCE PROGRAM.—Assistance authorized by section 2(a) and section 3(a) shall be coordinated with assistance provided under chapter 8 of part I of the Foreign Assistance Act of 1961 (22 U.S.C. 2291 and following; relating to international narcotics control assistance).

(d) CONDITIONAL WAIVER OF BROOKE-ALEXANDER AMENDMENT.—For fiscal year 1991, section 620(q) of the Foreign Assistance Act of 1961 (22 U.S.C. 2370(q)) and section 518 of the Foreign Operations, Export Financing, and Related Programs Appropriations Act, 1991, shall not apply with respect to narcotics-related assistance for an Andean country, provided the President has made the determination described in subsection (a) of this section.

(e) AUTHORITY TO WAIVER REQUIREMENT TO WITHHOLD 50 PERCENT OF ASSISTANCE PENDING CERTIFICATION.—Section 481(h)(1)(A) of the Foreign Assistance Act of 1961 (22 U.S.C. 2291(h)(1)(A)) shall not apply with respect to Bolivia, Colombia, and Peru for fiscal year 1991 if the President—

(1) determines that its application would be contrary to the national interest; and

(2) transmits written notification of that determination to the congressional committees specified in section 634A(a) of the Foreign Assistance Act of 1961 (22 U.S.C. 2394-1) in accordance with the procedures applicable to reprogrammings under that section.

SEC. 8. NUMBER OF MEMBERS OF UNITED STATES ARMED FORCES IN ANDEAN COUNTRIES.

MONTHLY REPORTS.—Within 15 days after the end of each month, the President shall submit to the Congress a report listing the number of members of the United States Armed Forces who were assigned or detailed to, or otherwise performed functions in, each Andean country at any time during that month.

SEC. 11. EXTRADITION OF UNITED STATES CITIZENS.

(a) IN GENERAL.—Chapter 209 of title 18, United States Code, is amended by adding at the end the following new section:

"§ 3196. Extradition of United States citizens

"If the applicable treaty or convention does not obligate the United States to extradite its citizens to a foreign country, the Secretary of State may, nevertheless, order the surrender to that country of a United States citizen whose extradition has been requested by that country if the other requirements of that treaty or convention are met.".

(b) SECTION ANALYSIS.—The section analysis for chapter 209 of title 18, United States Code, is amended by adding at the end the following:

"3196. Extradition of United States citizens.".

SEC. 12. CONGRESSIONAL REVIEW OF NARCOTICS-RELATED ASSISTANCE FOR AFGHANISTAN.

Not less than 15 days before obligating funds made available for any fiscal year to carry out the Foreign Assistance Act of 1961 or the Arms Export Control Act for any assistance for Afghanistan that has narcotics control as one of its purposes, the President shall notify the congressional committees specified in section 634A(a) of the Foreign Assistance Act of 1961 (22 U.S.C. 2394-1) in accordance with the procedures applicable to reprogramming notifications under that section.

SEC. 13. TRAINING OF HOST COUNTRY PILOTS.

(a) INSTRUCTION PROGRAM.—Not less than 90 days after the date of enactment of this Act, the President shall implement, under chapter 8 of part I of the Foreign Assistance Act of 1961 (22 U.S.C. 2291 and following; relating to international narcotics control assistance), a detailed program of instruction to train host country pilots, and other flight crew members, to fly host country aircraft involved in counternarcotics efforts in Andean countries. Such program shall be designed to eliminate direct participation of the United States Government (including participation through the use of either direct hire or contract personnel) in the operation of such aircraft.

(b) REQUIREMENT FOR REPLACEMENT OF UNITED STATES GOVERNMENT PILOTS BY HOST COUNTRY PILOTS.—The President shall ensure that, within 18 months after the date of enactment of this Act, flight crews composed of host country personnel replace all United States Government pilots and other flight crew members (including both direct hire or contract personnel) for host country aircraft involved in airborne counternarcotics operations in the Andean countries.

(c) AIRCRAFT SUBJECT TO REQUIREMENTS.—As used in this section, the term "host country aircraft" means any aircraft made available to an Andean country by the United States Government under chapter 8 of part I of the Foreign Assistance Act of 1961, or any other provision of law, for use by that country for narcotics-related purposes.

SEC. 17. DEBT-FOR-DRUGS EXCHANGES.

(a) FINDINGS.—The Congress finds that—

(1) section 10 of the International Narcotics Control Act of 1989 gives the President the authority to provide relief with respect to certain debt owed to the United States Government by the Government of Bolivia, the Government of Colombia, or the Government of Peru if the President determines that that

country is implementing programs to reduce the flow of cocaine to the United States;

(2) President Bush has endorsed the concept of debt relief with respect to debt owed by Latin American governments to the United States Government in his "Enterprise for Americans Initiative", announced June 27, 1990; and

(3) President Bush has proposed forgiveness of foreign military sales debt owed by the Government of Egypt to the United States Government.

(b) USE OF DEBT-FOR-DRUGS AUTHORITY.—The Congress urges the President to use the authority provided in section 10 of the International Narcotics Control Act of 1989 to forgive debt owed to the United States Government by the Government of Bolivia, the Government of Colombia, and the Government of Peru.

Approved November 21, 1990.

LEGISLATIVE HISTORY—H.R. 5567:

CONGRESSIONAL RECORD, Vol. 136 (1990):
- Oct. 22, considered and passed House.
- Oct. 26, considered and passed Senate, amended.
- Oct. 27, House concurred in Senate amendment.

WEEKLY COMPILATION OF PRESIDENTIAL DOCUMENTS, Vol. 26 (1990):
- Nov. 21, Presidential statement.

FISHERY CONSERVATION AMENDMENTS OF 1990

An Act to authorize appropriations to carry out the Magnuson Fishery Conservation and Management Act through fiscal year 1993, and for other purposes.

Date: November 28, 1990

Bill No.: H.R. 2061

Public Law No.: 101-627

Cite: 104 STAT. 4436

Sections reprinted:

Section 1 - Short title; table of contents.

TITLE I - AMENDMENTS TO MAGNUSON FISHERY CONSERVATION AND MANAGEMENT ACT.

Section 101 - Findings, purposes, and policy.

Section 102 - Definitions.

Section 103 - Authority with respect to highly migratory species.

Section 104 - Foreign fishing.

Section 105 - International fishery agreements.

Section 106 - Permits for foreign fishing.

Section 107 - Driftnet fishing.

TITLE IX - DOLPHIN PROTECTION CONSUMER INFORMATION.

Section 901 - Dolphin protection.

Public Law 101-627
101st Congress

An Act

To authorize appropriations to carry out the Magnuson Fishery Conservation and Management Act through fiscal year 1993, and for other purposes.

Be it enacted by the Senate and House of Representatives of the United States of America in Congress assembled,

SHORT TITLE; TABLE OF CONTENTS

SECTION 1. (a) SHORT TITLE.—The Act may be cited as the "Fishery Conservation Amendments of 1990".
(b) TABLE OF CONTENTS.—

TITLE I—AMENDMENTS TO MAGNUSON FISHERY CONSERVATION AND MANAGEMENT ACT

FINDINGS, PURPOSES, AND POLICY

SEC. 101. (a) FINDINGS.—Section 2(a) of the Magnuson Fishery Conservation and Management Act (16 U.S.C. 1801(a)) is amended by adding at the end the following new paragraph:

"(8) The collection of reliable data is essential to the effective conservation, management, and scientific understanding of the fishery resources of the United States.".

(b) PURPOSES.—(1) Section 2(b)(1) of the Magnuson Fishery Conservation and Management Act (16 U.S.C. 1801(b)(1)) is amended by striking "except highly migratory species".

(2) Section 2(b)(5) of the Magnuson Fishery Conservation and Management Act (16 U.S.C. 1801(b)(5)) is amended by striking "prepare, monitor, and revise" and inserting in lieu thereof "exercise sound judgment in the stewardship of fishery resources through the preparation, monitoring, and revision of".

(c) POLICY.—Section 2(c) of the Magnuson Fishery Conservation and Management Act (16 U.S.C. 1801(c)) is amended—

(1) in paragraph (3) by inserting "considers the effects of fishing on immature fish and encourages development of practical measures that avoid unnecessary waste of fish;" immediately after "and enforcement;"

(2) by striking "and" at the end of paragraph (4); and

(3) by striking the period at the end of paragraph (5) and inserting in lieu thereof ", and to secure agreements to regulate fishing by vessels or persons beyond the exclusive economic zones of any nation; and"; and

(4) by adding at the end the following new paragraph:

"(6) to foster and maintain the diversity of fisheries in the United States.".

DEFINITIONS

SEC. 102. (a) GENERAL.—Section 3 of the Magnuson Fishery Conservation and Management Act (16 U.S.C. 1802) is amended—

(1) by redesignating paragraph (16) as paragraph (17), by redesignating paragraph (17) as paragraph (19), by redesignating paragraphs (18) through (23) as paragraphs (21) through (26), respectively, and by redesignating paragraphs (24) through (27) as paragraphs (28) through (31), respectively;

(2) in paragraph (7), by striking ", birds, and highly migratory species" and inserting in lieu thereof "and birds";

(3) by amending paragraph (14) to read as follows:

"(14) The term 'highly migratory species' means tuna species, marlin (Tetrapturus spp. and Makaira spp.), oceanic sharks, sailfishes (Istiophorus spp.), and swordfish (Xiphias gladius).";

(4) by inserting immediately after paragraph (15) the following new paragraph:

"(16) The term 'large-scale driftnet fishing' means a method of fishing in which a gillnet composed of a panel or panels of webbing, or a series of such gillnets, with a total length of one and one-half miles or more is placed in the water and allowed to drift with the currents and winds for the purpose of entangling fish in the webbing.";

(5) by inserting immediately after paragraph (17), as so redesignated, the following new paragraph:

"(18) The term 'migratory range' means the maximum area at a given time of the year within which fish of an anadromous species or stock thereof can be expected to be found, as determined on the basis of scale pattern analysis, tagging studies, or other reliable scientific information, except that the term does not include any part of such area which is in the waters of a foreign nation.";

(6) by inserting immediately after paragraph (19), as so redesignated, the following new paragraph:

"(20) The term 'observer' means any person required or authorized to be carried on a vessel for conservation and management purposes by regulations or permits under this Act.";

(7) by inserting immediately after paragraph (26), as so redesignated, the following new paragraph:

"(27) The term 'tuna species' means the following:

"Albacore Tuna—Thunnus alalunga;
"Bigeye Tuna—Thunnus obesus;
"Bluefin Tuna—Thunnus thynnus;
"Skipjack Tuna—Katsuwonus pelamis; and
"Yellowfin Tuna—Thunnus albacares."; and

(8) by adding at the end the following new paragraph:

"(32) The term 'waters of a foreign nation' means any part of the territorial sea or exclusive economic zone (or the equivalent) of a foreign nation, to the extent such territorial sea or exclusive economic zone is recognized by the United States.".

(b) CONFORMING AMENDMENT.—Section 101(b)(1) of the Magnuson Fishery Conservation and Management Act (16 U.S.C. 1811(b)(1)) is amended by striking "any foreign nation's" and all that follows and inserting in lieu thereof "any waters of a foreign nation.".

AUTHORITY WITH RESPECT TO HIGHLY MIGRATORY SPECIES

SEC. 103. (a) GENERAL.—Section 102 of the Magnuson Fishery Conservation and Management Act (16 U.S.C. 1812) is amended to read as follows:

"SEC. 102. HIGHLY MIGRATORY SPECIES.

"The United States shall cooperate directly or through appropriate international organizations with those nations involved in fisheries for highly migratory species with a view to ensuring conservation and promoting the objective of optimum utilization of such species throughout their range, both within and beyond the exclusive economic zone.".

(b) CONFORMING AMENDMENT.—The entry for section 102 in the table of contents in the first section of the Magnuson Fishery Conservation and Management Act is amended to read as follows:

"Sec. 102. Highly migratory species.".

(c) EFFECTIVE DATE.—The amendments made by this section shall take effect on January 1, 1992.

FOREIGN FISHING

SEC. 104. Subsection (d) of section 201 of the Magnuson Fishery Conservation and Management Act (16 U.S.C. 1821) is amended to read as follows:

"(d) TOTAL ALLOWABLE LEVEL OF FOREIGN FISHING.—The total allowable level of foreign fishing, if any, with respect to any fishery subject to the exclusive fishery management authority of the United States, shall be that portion of the optimum yield of such fishery which will not be harvested by vessels of the United States, as determined in accordance with this Act.".

INTERNATIONAL FISHERY AGREEMENTS

SEC. 105. (a) HIGHLY MIGRATORY SPECIES AGREEMENTS.—Section 202 of the Magnuson Fishery Conservation and Management Act (16 U.S.C. 1822) is amended by redesignating subsection (e) as subsection (f) and by inserting immediately after subsection (d) the following new subsection:

"(e) HIGHLY MIGRATORY SPECIES AGREEMENTS.—

"(1) EVALUATION.—The Secretary of State, in cooperation with the Secretary, shall evaluate the effectiveness of each existing international fishery agreement which pertains to fishing for highly migratory species. Such evaluation shall consider whether the agreement provides for—

"(A) the collection and analysis of necessary information for effectively managing the fishery, including but not limited to information about the number of vessels involved, the type and quantity of fishing gear used, the species of fish involved and their location, the catch and bycatch levels in the fishery, and the present and probable future condition of any stock of fish involved;

"(B) the establishment of measures applicable to the fishery which are necessary and appropriate for the conservation and management of the fishery resource involved;

"(C) equitable arrangements which provide fishing vessels of the United States with (i) access to the highly migratory species that are the subject of the agreement and (ii) a portion of the allowable catch that reflects the traditional participation by such vessels in the fishery;

"(D) effective enforcement of conservation and management measures and access arrangements throughout the area of jurisdiction; and

"(E) sufficient and dependable funding to implement the provisions of the agreement, based on reasonable assessments of the benefits derived by participating nations.

"(2) ACCESS NEGOTIATIONS.—The Secretary of State, in cooperation with the Secretary, shall initiate negotiations with respect to obtaining access for vessels of the United States fishing for tuna species within the exclusive economic zones of other nations on reasonable terms and conditions.

"(3) REPORTS.—The Secretary of State shall report to the Congress—

"(A) within 12 months after the date of enactment of this subsection, on the results of the evaluation required under paragraph (1), together with recommendations for addressing any inadequacies identified; and

"(B) within six months after such date of enactment, on the results of the access negotiations required under paragraph (2).

"(4) NEGOTIATION.—The Secretary of State, in consultation with the Secretary, shall undertake such negotiations with respect to international fishery agreements on highly migratory species as are necessary to correct inadequacies identified as a result of the evaluation conducted under paragraph (1).

"(5) SOUTH PACIFIC TUNA TREATY.—It is the sense of the Congress that the United States Government shall, at the earliest opportunity, begin negotiations for the purpose of extending the Treaty on Fisheries Between the Governments of Certain Pacific Island States and the Government of the United States of America, signed at Port Moresby, Papua New Guinea, April 2, 1987, and it Annexes, Schedules, and implementing agreements for an additional term of 10 years on terms and conditions at least as favorable to vessels of the United States and the United States Government.".

(b) DETERMINATIONS OF SECRETARY OF STATE.—(1) Section 205(a) of the Magnuson Fishery Conservation and Management Act (16 U.S.C. 1825(a)) is amended—

(A) in paragraph (1) by striking "traditional" and by inserting "including fisheries for tuna species," immediately after "authority,"; and

(B) in paragraph (2) by striking "highly migratory" and inserting in lieu thereof "tuna".

(2) The amendments made by this subsection shall take effect on January 1, 1992.

PERMITS FOR FOREIGN FISHING

SEC. 106. (a) FEES.—Section 204(b)(10) of the Magnuson Fishery Conservation and Management Act (16 U.S.C. 1824(b)(10)) is amended to read as follows:

"(10) FEES.—

"(A) Fees shall be paid to the Secretary by the owner or operator of any foreign fishing vessel for which a permit has been issued pursuant to this section. The Secretary, in consultation with the Secretary of State, shall establish a schedule of reasonable fees that shall apply nondiscriminatorily to each foreign nation.

"(B) Amounts collected by the Secretary under this paragraph shall be deposited in the general fund of the Treasury.".

(b) SANCTIONS.—Section 204(b)(12) of the Magnuson Fishery Conservation and Management Act (16 U.S.C. 1824(b)(12)) is repealed.

DRIFTNET FISHING

SEC 107. (a) GENERAL.—Section 206 of the Magnuson Fishery Conservation and Management Act (16 U.S.C. 1826) is amended to read as follows:

"SEC. 206. LARGE-SCALE DRIFTNET FISHING.

"(a) SHORT TITLE.—This section incorporates and expands upon provisions of the Driftnet Impact Monitoring, Assessment, and Control Act of 1987 and may be cited as the 'Driftnet Act Amendments of 1990'.

"(b) FINDINGS.—The Congress finds that—

"(1) the continued widespread use of large-scale driftnets beyond the exclusive economic zone of any nation is a destructive fishing practice that poses a threat to living marine resources of the world's oceans, including but not limited to the North and South Pacific Ocean and the Bering Sea;

"(2) the use of large-scale driftnets is expanding into new regions of the world's oceans, including the Atlantic Ocean and Caribbean Sea;

"(3) there is a pressing need for detailed and reliable information on the number of seabirds, sea turtles, nontarget fish, and marine mammals that become entangled and die in actively fished large-scale driftnets and in large-scale driftnets that are lost, abandoned, or discarded;

"(4) increased efforts, including reliable observer data and enforcement mechanisms, are needed to monitor, assess, control, and reduce the adverse impact of large-scale driftnet fishing on living marine resources;

"(5) the nations of the world have agreed in the United Nations, through General Assembly Resolution Numbered 44-225, approved December 22, 1989, by the General Assembly, that a moratorium should be imposed by June 30, 1992, on the use of large-scale driftnets beyond the exclusive economic zone of any nation;

"(6) the nations of the South Pacific have agreed to a moratorium on the use of large-scale driftnets in the South Pacific through the Convention for the Prohibition of Fishing with Long Driftnets in the South Pacific, which was agreed to in Wellington, New Zealand, on November 29, 1989; and

"(7) increasing population pressures and new knowledge of the importance of living marine resources to the health of the global ecosystem demand that greater responsibility be exercised by persons fishing or developing new fisheries beyond the exclusive economic zone of any nation.

"(c) POLICY.—It is declared to be the policy of the Congress in this section that the United States should—

"(1) implement the moratorium called for by the United Nations General Assembly in Resolution Numbered 44-225;

"(2) support the Tarawa Declaration and the Wellington Convention for the Prohibition of Fishing with Long Driftnets in the South Pacific; and

"(3) secure a permanent ban on the use of destructive fishing practices, and in particular large-scale driftnets, by persons or vessels fishing beyond the exclusive economic zone of any nation.

"(d) INTERNATIONAL AGREEMENTS.—The Secretary, through the Secretary of State and the Secretary of the department in which the Coast Guard is operating, shall seek to secure international agreements to implement immediately the findings, policy, and provisions of this section, and in particular an international ban on large-scale driftnet fishing. The Secretary, through the Secretary of State, shall include, in any agreement which addresses the taking of living marine resources of the United States, provisions to ensure that—

"(1) each large-scale driftnet fishing vessel of a foreign nation that is party to the agreement, including vessels that may operate independently to develop new fishing areas, which operate beyond the exclusive economic zone of any nation, is included in such agreement;

"(2) each large-scale driftnet fishing vessel of a foreign nation that is party to the agreement, which operates beyond the exclusive economic zone of any nation, is equipped with satellite transmitters which provide real-time position information accessible to the United States;

"(3) statistically reliable monitoring by the United States is carried out, through the use of on-board observers or through dedicated platforms provided by foreign nations that are parties to the agreement, of all target and nontarget fish species, marine mammals, sea turtles, and sea birds entangled or killed by large-scale driftnets used by fishing vessels of foreign nations that are parties to the agreement;

"(4) officials of the United States have the right to board and inspect for violations of the agreement any large-scale driftnet fishing vessels operating under the flag of a foreign nation that is party to the agreement at any time while such vessel is operating in designated areas beyond the exclusive economic zone of any nation;

"(5) all catch landed or transshipped at sea by large-scale driftnet fishing vessels of a foreign nation that is a party to the agreement, and which are operated beyond the exclusive economic zone of any nation, is reliably monitored and documented;

"(6) time and area restrictions are imposed on the use of large-scale driftnets in order to prevent interception of anadromous species;

"(7) all large-scale driftnets used are constructed, insofar as feasible, with biodegradable materials which break into segments that do not represent a threat to living marine resources;

"(8) all large-scale driftnets are marked at appropriate intervals in a manner that conclusively identifies the vessel and flag nation responsible for each such driftnet;

"(9) the taking of nontarget fish species, marine mammals, sea turtles, seabirds, and endangered species or other species protected by international agreements to which the United

States is a party is minimized and does not pose a threat to existing fisheries or the long-term health of living marine resources; and

"(10) definitive steps are agreed upon to ensure that parties to the agreement comply with the spirit of other international agreements and resolutions concerning the use of large-scale driftnets beyond the exclusive economic zone of any nation.

"(e) REPORT.—Not later than January 1, 1991, and every year thereafter until the purposes of this section are met, the Secretary, after consultation with the Secretary of State and the Secretary of the department in which the Coast Guard is operating, shall submit to the Committee on Commerce, Science, and Transportation of the Senate and the Committee on Merchant Marine and Fisheries of the House of Representatives a report—

"(1) describing the steps taken to carry out the provisions of this section, particularly subsection (c);

"(2) evaluating the progress of those efforts, the impacts on living marine resources, including available observer data, and specifying plans for further action;

"(3) identifying and evaluating the effectiveness of unilateral measures and multilateral measures, including sanctions, that are available to encourage nations to agree to and comply with this section, and recommendations for legislation to authorize any additional measures that are needed if those are considered ineffective;

"(4) identifying, evaluating, and making any recommendations considered necessary to improve the effectiveness of the law, policy, and procedures governing enforcement of the exclusive management authority of the United States over anadromous species against fishing vessels engaged in fishing beyond the exclusive economic zone of any nation;

"(5) containing a list and description of any new fisheries developed by nations that conduct, or authorize their nationals to conduct, large-scale driftnet fishing beyond the exclusive economic zone of any nation; and

"(6) containing a list of the nations that conduct, or authorize their nationals to conduct, large-scale driftnet fishing beyond the exclusive economic zone of any nation in a manner that diminishes the effectiveness of or is inconsistent with any international agreement governing large-scale driftnet fishing to which the United States is a party or otherwise subscribes.

"(f) CERTIFICATION.—If at any time the Secretary, in consultation with the Secretary of State and the Secretary of the department in which the Coast Guard is operating, identifies any nation that warrants inclusion in the list described under subsection (e)(6), the Secretary shall certify that fact to the President. Such certification shall be deemed to be a certification for the purposes of section 8(a) of the Fishermen's Protective Act of 1967 (22 U.S.C. 1978(a)).

"(g) EFFECT ON SOVEREIGN RIGHTS.—This section shall not serve or be construed to expand or diminish the sovereign rights of the United States, as stated by Presidential Proclamation Numbered 5030, dated March 10, 1983, and reflected in this Act or other existing law.

"(h) DEFINITION.—As used in this section, the term 'living marine resources' includes fish, marine mammals, sea turtles, and seabirds and other waterfowl.".

(b) CONFORMING AMENDMENT.—The entry for section 206 in the table of contents in the first section of the Magnuson Fishery Conservation and Management Act is amended to read as follows:

"Sec. 206. Large-scale driftnet fishing.".

TITLE IX—DOLPHIN PROTECTION CONSUMER INFORMATION

DOLPHIN PROTECTION

SEC. 901. (a) SHORT TITLE.—This section may be cited as the "Dolphin Protection Consumer Information Act".

(b) FINDINGS.—The Congress finds that—

(1) dolphins and other marine mammals are frequently killed in the course of tuna fishing operations in the eastern tropical Pacific Ocean and high seas driftnet fishing in other parts of the world;

(2) it is the policy of the United States to support a worldwide ban on high seas driftnet fishing, in part because of the harmful effects that such driftnets have on marine mammals, including dolphins; and

(3) consumers would like to know if the tuna they purchase is falsely labeled as to the effect of the harvesting of the tuna on dolphins.

(c) DEFINITIONS.—For purposes of this section—

(1) the terms "driftnet" and "driftnet fishing" have the meanings given those terms in section 4003 of the Driftnet Impact Monitoring, Assessment, and Control Act of 1987 (16 U.S.C. 1822 note);

(2) the term "eastern tropical Pacific Ocean" means the area of the Pacific Ocean bounded by 40 degrees north latitude, 40 degrees south latitude, 160 degrees west longitude, and the western coastlines of North, Central, and South America;

(3) the term "label" means a display of written, printed, or graphic matter on or affixed to the immediate container of any article;

(4) the term "Secretary" means the Secretary of Commerce; and

(5) the term "tuna product" means a food item which contains tuna and which has been processed for retail sale, except perishable sandwiches, salads, or other products with a shelf life of less than 3 days.

(d) LABELING STANDARD.—(1) It is a violation of section 5 of the Federal Trade Commission Act for any producer, importer, exporter, distributor, or seller of any tuna product that is exported from or offered for sale in the United States to include on the label of that product the term "Dolphin Safe" or any other term or symbol that falsely claims or suggests that the tuna contained in the product was harvested using a method of fishing that is not harmful to dolphins if the product contains—

(A) tuna harvested on the high seas by a vessel engaged in driftnet fishing; or

(B) tuna harvested in the eastern tropical Pacific Ocean by a vessel using purse seine nets which do not meet the requirements for being considered dolphin safe under paragraph (2).

(2) For purposes of paragraph (1)(B), a tuna product that contains tuna harvested in the eastern tropical Pacific Ocean by a fishing vessel using purse seine nets is dolphin safe if—

(A) the vessel is of a type and size that the Secretary has determined is not capable of deploying its purse seine nets on or to encircle dolphin; or

(B)(i) the product is accompanied by a written statement executed by the captain of the vessel which harvested the tuna certifying that no tuna were caught on the trip in which such tuna were harvested using a purse seine net intentionally deployed on or to encircle dolphin;

(ii) the product is accompanied by a written statement executed by—

(I) the Secretary or the Secretary's designee, or

(II) a representative of the Inter-American Tropical Tuna Commission,

which states that there was an approved observer on board the vessel during the entire trip and that purse seine nets were not intentionally deployed during the trip on or to encircle dolphin; and

(iii) the statements referred to in clauses (i) and (ii) are endorsed in writing by each exporter, importer, and processor of the product.

(e) ENFORCEMENT.—Any person who knowingly and willfully makes a statement or endorsement described in subsection (d)(2)(B) that is false is liable for a civil penalty of not to exceed $100,000 assessed in an action brought in any appropriate district court of the United States on behalf of the Secretary.

(f) REGULATIONS.—The Secretary, in consultation with the Secretary of the Treasury, shall issue regulations to implement this section not later than 6 months after the date of the enactment of this Act, including regulations establishing procedures and requirements for ensuring that tuna products are labeled in accordance with subsection (d).

(g) TREATMENT OF FISH CAUGHT WITH DRIFTNETS.—Section 101(a)(2) of the Marine Mammal Protection Act of 1972 (16 U.S.C. 1371(a)(2)) is amended—

(1) in subparagraph (C) by striking "and" after the semicolon at the end;

(2) in subparagraph (D) by striking the period at the end and inserting "; and"; and

(3) by adding at the end the following:

"(E)(i) except as provided in clause (ii), in the case of fish or products containing fish harvested by a nation whose fishing vessels engage in high seas driftnet fishing, shall require that the government of the exporting nation provide documentary evidence that the fish or fish product was not harvested with a large-scale driftnet in the South Pacific Ocean after July 1, 1991, or in any other water of the high seas after July 1, 1992, and

"(ii) in the case of tuna or a product containing tuna harvested by a nation whose fishing vessels engage in high seas driftnet fishing, shall require that the government of the exporting nation provide documentary evidence that the tuna or tuna product was not harvested with a large-scale driftnet anywhere on the high seas after July 1, 1991.

For purposes of subparagraph (E), the term "driftnet" has the meaning given such term in section 4003 of the Driftnet Impact Monitoring, Assessment, and Control Act of 1987 (16 U.S.C. 1822 note).".

(h) NEGOTIATIONS.—The Secretary of State shall immediately seek, through negotiations and discussions with appropriate foreign governments, to reduce and, as soon as possible, eliminate the practice of harvesting tuna through the use of purse seine nets intentionally deployed to encircle dolphins.

(i) EFFECTIVE DATE.—Subsections (d) and (e) shall take effect 6 months after the date of the enactment of this Act.

CRIME CONTROL ACT OF 1990

An Act to control crime.

Date: November 29, 1990

Bill No.: S. 3266

Public Law No.: 101-647

Cite: 104 STAT. 4789

Sections reprinted:

Public Law 101-647
101st Congress

An Act

To control crime.

Be it enacted by the Senate and House of Representatives of the United States of America in Congress assembled,

SECTION 1. SHORT TITLE.

This Act may be cited as the "Crime Control Act of 1990".

TITLE I—INTERNATIONAL MONEY LAUNDERING

SEC. 101. REPORTS ON USES MADE OF CURRENCY TRANSACTION REPORTS.

Not later than 180 days after the effective date of this section, and every 2 years for 4 years, the Secretary of the Treasury shall report to the Congress the following:

(1) the number of each type of report filed pursuant to subchapter II of chapter 53 of title 31, United States Code (or regulations promulgated thereunder) in the previous fiscal year;

(2) the number of reports filed pursuant to section 6050I of the Internal Revenue Code of 1986 (regarding transactions involving currency) in the previous fiscal year;

(3) an estimate of the rate of compliance with the reporting requirements by persons required to file the reports referred to in paragraphs (1) and (2);

(4) the manner in which the Department of the Treasury and other agencies of the United States collect, organize, analyze and use the reports referred to in paragraphs (1) and (2) to support investigations and prosecutions of (A) violations of the criminal laws of the United States, (B) violations of the laws of foreign countries, and (C) civil enforcement of the laws of the United States including the provisions regarding asset forfeiture;

(5) a summary of sanctions imposed in the previous fiscal year against persons who failed to comply with the reporting requirements referred to in paragraphs (1) and (2), and other steps taken to ensure maximum compliance;

(6) a summary of criminal indictments filed in the previous fiscal year which resulted, in large part, from investigations initiated by analysis of the reports referred to in paragraphs (1) and (2); and

(7) a summary of criminal indictments filed in the previous fiscal year which resulted, in large part, from investigations initiated by information regarding suspicious financial transactions provided voluntarily by financial institutions.

SUBJECT INDEX

A

E

F

G

H

O

P

Q

R

Z